Correspondence

Correspondence

1904–1938

Sigmund Freud and Anna Freud

Edited by
Ingeborg Meyer-Palmedo

Translated by
Nick Somers

polity

GOETHE-INSTITUT

The translation of this work was supported by a grant from the Goethe-Institut which is funded by the German Ministry of Foreign Affairs.

Polity Press
65 Bridge Street
Cambridge CB2 1UR, UK

Polity Press
350 Main Street
Malden, MA 02148, USA

ISBN-13: 978-0-7456-4149-2

A catalogue record for this book is available from the British Library.

Typeset in 10 on 11 pt Times New Roman MT by
Servis Filmsetting Ltd, Stockport, Cheshire
Printed and bound in Great Britain by Edwards Brothers Malloy, USA

Contents

Illustrations and Facsimiles

Illustrations

Facsimiles

Preface to this Edition

The transcription of this correspondence was based on the collection of photocopies made available to me. Unclear passages were later checked by me against the originals in the Library of Congress in Washington, DC; reference is made in the notes to those passages that are still defective or unclear. The verification also showed that some letters were not in the right place chronologically or were missing altogether; some of the letters described in the footnotes as 'missing' could be among the few items that are currently still locked up and thus inaccessible to me.

The letters, postcards, telegrams and memos are numbered sequentially in chronological order – as in other published collections of Freud's correspondence – with initials to indicate the author; postscripts or additions that were evidently sent together with the relevant letter are not numbered separately.

As envelopes are not available except in rare instances, addresses can be given only for postcards. The start and end of the letter (place, date and salutation, closing and signature) are shown as originally written [translator's note: for the sake of clarity the months are written out in full] with occasional editorial additions in square brackets by way of explanation and further elaboration in the notes if needed. Freud used different-sized paper with a preprinted letterhead, over which he wrote the date by hand (see facsimile, p. 315). To avoid tedious repetition, this is commented on only when it first occurs or in special cases. Anna usually wrote the letterheads by hand; exceptions are noted.

Idiosyncratic spelling or grammar peculiarities are noted, particularly when it is uncertain whether the form was the correspondents' customary way of speaking or a mistake. Telegrams are reproduced in their original form, including transmission errors or garbled messages, with omissions once again being shown in square brackets. Abbreviations (except for commonly known ones like e.g. or i.e.) are usually completed. Slips of the pen are always noted if referred to by the correspondents, but also where they might be of interest. All editorial comments in the text are in square brackets. Underlining is replaced by italics. Titles of books, magazines, essays, etc., appear in the letters as in the original, but are written out in the notes as they appear in the Bibliography. Patients' names are revealed in cases where they have already been identified in the literature.

Persons, places, institutions and so on are generally commented on where they occur for the first time in the letters; in only a few instances was it more practical or sensible to deviate from this principle.

All quotations, dates and other information are referenced in angled brackets. The abbreviations refer to the four bibliographies; 'Freud' without initials refers to Sigmund Freud; 'Freud to', 'Anna to', and similar formulations without further source information, refer to the list of unpublished material. The notes often contain several literature sources, which deal with the same information in different contexts, shed light on it from another angle or provide an alternate interpretation, and in some cases also with reference to further reading. The numerous cross-references within the correspondence are designed to enable the context to be more easily understood if it is not evident from the sequence of letters.

Some of the bibliographical explanations might appear superfluous to initiates, but I believe that they will be useful to interested readers who are not as familiar with psychoanalysis and its representatives, and for whom the relevant literature is not easily accessible, to give them an idea of the significance of the persons to psychoanalysis and to the correspondents, and to enable them to conduct further research if they so desire. The same applies to some historical or geographical information and other specificities.

Translator's Note

The page references in the footnotes and text relate, where possible, to the original English versions or published English translations of the works concerned (see Bibliography). If the reference or quotation does not occur in these works, the page reference relates to the German version and is indicated as such.

Acknowledgements

Freud once said that not only psychoanalysis but also the research into its history is a highly convivial undertaking. This became evident to me in my efforts to draw up a list of people who helped me to compile this book. I should like to thank all of these 'water bearers'. First, however, I should like to express my particular gratitude to a few individuals.

Gerhard Fichtner shared his wealth of knowledge with me and willingly offered his expertise and extensive scientific background; he was not only untiring in the provision of information and assistance – including the often difficult deciphering of Freud's handwriting – but during the entire preparation he was also an indefatigable interlocutor, patient teacher and dear friend on whom I could rely at all times.

Albrecht Hirschmüller provided all possible assistance in scientific and practical matters. He also gave me an early insight into his work on an edition of the correspondence between Freud and Minna Bernays, which in several instances overlapped with the Freud–Anna correspondence.

Andreas Hamburger was the first person to read my manuscript and thereafter showed critical and compassionate understanding and provided indispensable advice; he encouraged me untiringly when I was faced by difficulties and helped me over many a crisis on the way.

I was exhilarated in many ways by the encounter with Günter Gödde, who always had an open ear for me in our invigorating and often long conversations. He also shepherded me carefully from my solitary writing desk to a small group of other researchers on the history of psychoanalysis, from whom I received additional feedback and encouragement.

Christfried Tögel received me with open arms whenever I asked him for information or help and also navigated a number of obstacles in the creation of the book. At the same time he provided me with a place to stay and accompanied me in London, introducing me to the Freud Museum. There, Michael Molnar offered me unhindered access to all parts of his archive and also provided competent assistance.

Through Inge Weber and Daria Rothe, the editors of Anna Freud's correspondence with Lou Andreas-Salomé, I obtained the most fruitful inspiration in a mutually refreshing exchange of impressions and results;

my frank and honest conversations with them gave rise to many invigorating ideas and offered confirmation of a number of facts. Dorothee Pfeiffer unhesitatingly allowed me to quote from unpublished parts of Lou Andreas-Salomé's letters to Sigmund Freud.

Tom Roberts gave me permission to quote from his manuscript *Vienna and Manchester – the Correspondence between Sigmund Freud and Sam Freud 1911–1938*, with the authentic original wording of the correspondence; these letters have been published to date only in translations – without mention of his name as editor.

A give-and-take relationship developed with Ernst Falzeder during the collaboration on the Freud/Ferenczi correspondence, which was of benefit in many ways to my work. Michael Schröter, editor of the recently published Freud–Eitingon correspondence, showed great interest on several occasions and also generously and trustingly let me see his manuscript before it was printed.

Regine Lockot found the opportunity after the manuscript had been completed to add valuable details to the notes, which I was allowed to include.

Among the large number of people who supported me with general information, maps, indications and encouragement, I should like to mention in particular Peter Lambda (Tibberton, Gloucestershire), Ernst Federn (Vienna), Victor Ross (Great Chart, Kent), Gertraud Sperka (Fellbach), Ursula Köhler (Frankfurt), Karin A. Dittrich (Munich), Herbert Will (Munich) and Karl Förster (Polling).

As I made use of the various libraries and other institutions – whose existence and services I gratefully availed myself of – I realized that it is not the institutions themselves but again and again the people in them who offered me their friendly cooperation, interest and ideas and professional expertise, giving me valuable information and often good tips. In this regard, I should specifically like to mention Herbert Bareuther (library of the Sigmund Freud Institute, Frankfurt), Dagmar Möller and Klaus von Bomhardt (Psychoanalytische Arbeitsgemeinschaft, Institut der DPV, Munich), Elfried Hermann (secretariat of the Department of the History of Medicine, University of Tübingen), Inge Späth (library of the Department of the History of Medicine, University of Tübingen), Angela Glantz and Martina Stuprich (Murnau community library), Mathhew von Unwerth (Abraham A. Brill Library of the New York Psychoanalytic Institute), Patrick T. Lawlor (Rare Book and Manuscript Library, Columbia University, New York), Fred Bauman, Bruce Kirby, Ahmed Johnson, Pat Kerwin, Margaret McAleer (Library of Congress, Manuscript Division, Washington, DC), Manfred Skopec (Department of the History of Medicine, University of Vienna), Kurt Mühlberger (archive of the University of Vienna), Herbert Tschulk (Municipal Department 8, Vienna, City Archives), Ferdinand Gutschi (archive of the Academy of Fine Arts in Vienna), Walburg Gáspár-Ruppert (Department of Sociology and Social and Economic Sciences, University of Vienna),

Elisabeth Groschopf (Institute of Austrian Dialect and Name Lexica of the Austrian Academy of Sciences, Vienna), staff of the International Youth Library (Munich), Kai Sammet (Department of the History of Medicine, Hamburg-Eppendorf University Clinic), Ina S. Lorenz (Institute for the History of German Jews, Hamburg), Christiane Adam (library of the Ärtzl. Verein der Ärztekammer Hamburg), Dagmar Bickelmann (State Archive of the Free and Hanseatic City of Hamburg), Angelika Voss (Research Unit for Contemporary History, Hamburg).

I obtained important local information and support during my on-the-spot research: on the Ritten from Annemarie and Theo Senn (Klobenstein), the officials of the Klobenstein municipal authority – Ruth Ploner, Nikolaus Ramoser (demographic departments) and Siegfried Treibenreif (building department), Peter Righi, director of Ritten tourist association (Klobenstein), the inhabitants of Klobenstein, particularly Marie-Therese von Braitenberg, Rosa Schnitzler, Christoph Pan, and of Soprabolzano, particularly Gretel Unterhofer, Karl Ramoser and family, Josef Frötscher; and Francesco Marchioro, Bolzano. In Bad Reichenhall/Thumsee/Bayerisch Gmain from Johannes Lang (town archivist, Bad Reichenhall), in Bad Gastein from Laurenz Krisch.

Apart from all the persons mentioned by name, I should also like to thank all those indicated in the notes, including unnamed members of offices and authorities.

Mark Paterson, Tom Roberts and, with particular enthusiasm and conscientiousness, Stephanie Ebdon, Sigmund Freud Copyrights Inc. (London), encouraged the project in many ways, amongst other things by granting me permission to conduct research in the Library of Congress and the Otto Rank archive and to copy and quote from unpublished material.

Within the publishing company I benefited from the assistance above all of Ilse Grubrich-Simitis – who also originally suggested the publication of this correspondence – as well as Monika Schoeller and Peter Sillem, who helped in the completion of the book. An old colleague, Wolfgang Kloft, selflessly brought his proofreading experience and competence to bear in a careful and dependable contribution, and Peter W. Schmidt allowed me to profit from his production expertise. I take sole responsibility, of course, for the nature of the extensive notes.

Last but not least I am profoundly grateful to Marion Palmedo, New York. She provided me with countless information, addresses, telephone calls, accommodation and a thousand other details abroad. Above all, she offered her sisterly love and affection from the start to the end of the process, accepting me and consistently lifting me up along the way.

Abbreviations

Collected Papers	Sigmund Freud, *Collected Papers* (5 vols)
DBA N. F.	Deutsches Biographisches Archiv, Neue Folge
FM	Freud Museum
Grinstein	Alexander Grinstein, *The Index of Psychoanalytic Writings* (preface by Ernest Jones, vols 1–14)
G. W.	Sigmund Freud, *Gesammelte Werke* (18 volumes and an unnumbered Supplement)
IJ	*The International Journal of Psychoanalysis*
Imago	*Imago, Zeitschrift für Anwendung der Psychoanalyse auf die Geiseswissenschaften*
IZ	*Internationale Zeitschrift für ärztliche Psychoanalyse*
Jb	*Jahrbuch für psychoanalytische und psychopathologische Forschungen*
Jb. Psychoanal.	*Jahrbuch der Psychoanalyse, Beitrage zur Theorie, Praxis und Geschichte*
Journal	See *IJ*
Kürschner	*Kürschners deutscher Gelehrtenkalender*
LoC AF	The Library of Congress, The Papers of Anna Freud
LoC SF	The Library of Congress, The Papers of Sigmund Freud
ORC	Special Collections: The Papers of Otto Rank
'Press'	The Psychoanalytical Press
Ψ	Psycho-
ΨA	Psychoanalysis
ψα	psychoanalytical
Review	*The Psychoanalytical Review, A Journal Devoted to an Understanding of Human Conduct*
S. E.	*The Standard Edition of the Complete Psychological Works of Sigmund Freud* (24 vols)
Standard Edition	See *S. E.*
Verlag	Internationaler Psychoanalytischer Verlag
Zeitschrift	See *IZ*

Introduction

This book contains the first published correspondence between Freud and one of his six children, the youngest daughter, Anna. Both correspondents are well known, with biographical details previously published by other competent authors, so it is not necessary to repeat these details here. Many of those publications cite fragments of letters from Freud and Anna, generally as illustrations to serve the authors' purposes. So a reading of the correspondence in its entirety gives unexpected insights into aspects that – even if they have been touched on elsewhere – assume their full significance only in the context of the texts. To avoid spoiling the reader's enjoyment of discovery, only a few of these aspects will be mentioned in this introduction.

One significant finding is the importance of 'nature' – not only in Freud's life but also for the other members of the family whose 'hunger for air and light'[1] drove them out into the country from the confines of the gloomy sea of houses in the city, allowing them to enjoy the 'delightful quiet', 'magnificent pine forest', 'surprising walks' and 'well-being composed of all those things'.[2] Suitable places to spend the summer holidays were thus also chosen months in advance:[3] 'You know that what we both need is varied forest landscape with the odd mushroom . . .'.[4] Even the clothing was chosen to fit the holiday mood. Anna associated nature with a yearning for the 'simple life',[5] the uninhibited feeling of freedom while carrying out physical work in the country[6] being symbolic of movement, 'excess energy', 'experiencing life'.[7] The 'dream of a house' with a garden and gardening work – being close to the earth – is also part of this context.[8] At the same time, nature was a refuge and retreat to rest and recover in solitude and to carry out intellectual work undisturbed – the unity of the physical and cognitive self. Holidays in 'natural surroundings' were always a welcome opportunity as well for family get-togethers and for seeing friends and visitors.[9]

Martin, Freud's eldest son, described many of these natural encounters in his book *Sigmund Freud – Man and Father*, memories written long after the events had taken place. In the correspondence here they were written down as they happened, spontaneous and unadorned first-hand records, and are all the more vivid as a result. As most of the letters were written from holiday locations or in connection with them, this love of nature is all the more intense. Freud and Anna repeatedly describe their impressions, be it in long descriptions, as asides or cursorily in telegrams. As we discover these places ourselves in this way in the letters or notes[10] and put ourselves in the correspondents' situation, the deep significance of the 'intimate contact with nature'[11] becomes understandable; we realize that – if not completely free of the tourist fashion of the time of 'conquering nature'[12] – it was by no means just an external ingredient, in the sense of the 'aestheticization of nature', but an indispensable element of their lives that fed their creative energies.

Throughout the letters we also learn of the relations between family members, friends, acquaintances, colleagues, students and patients; we obtain an insight into the overlaps and interactions that connected them in so many ways and that have already been studied variously and in other contexts in the literature.[13] Overlaps of this type are typical of a social life in which career, study and private life naturally affect one another, embedded in the specific sociocultural context. In the case of psychoanalysis and the requirement today that professional and personal considerations be kept strictly separate, we might find it slightly odd that this distinction was so casually neglected. We should bear in mind, however, that in its early days analysis was not anything like as well known as it is today, and that until the end of the First World War patients usually entered analysis through recommendation from friends or acquaintances who had heard of it or undergone it themselves. And these circles were the same ones in which the analysts moved privately.[14] Furthermore, it might be argued that with its inherent associative method, psychoanalysis is a natural vehicle for encouraging connections – of whatever type – since its analysing-comprehending approach makes it extremely receptive and sensitive. Nor should we forget that the introduction of psychoanalysis was followed by a painful empirical process, lasting years or even decades, before the force of transference and its effects were gradually recognized in their entirety, theoretically conceptualized and taken appropriately into account in the treatment.[15]

Another unexpected and astonishing aspect in this context is the willingness with which Freud and Anna were able to accept people for what they were – even when they had conflicting views. Freud was known, not without reason, for his brusqueness and coldness, and for the unusual brutality with which he rebuffed people if he did not like them, even turning away in disappointment from close friends if he did not agree with their ideas or feared they might lose sight of the essence of psychoanalysis.[16] Even Anna has been reproached on occasion for disdainfully rejecting others. This correspondence contains numerous examples to disprove this assertion: in fact both correspondents tended to understand, acknowledge and even appreciate the peculiarities of others. Disparaging remarks – whether regarding friends and acquaintances or their own relatives – are infrequent and quite moderate.[17]

This is particularly striking when looking for signs of the precarious relationship between Anna and her mother that is so frequently described in the literature.[18] Anna corresponded regularly with Martha Freud, spent holidays with her, accompanied her on journeys, looked after her and dutifully reported to her father on her condition.[19] Whatever the reason – whether she was merely following the family's unspoken rules for dealing tactfully with one another or whether she was showing respect for the real solidarity of the couple and was trying to spare her beloved father – these letters give no indication of unusual tension between mother and daughter, unless this is to be inferred solely from Anna's excessive emphasis on her love for her father.

Anna lived without interruption from birth in her parents' house and therefore outside the correspondence was able to speak directly to her father, and this is clearly reflected in the language of the letters. In some places they read as if there were some kind of conspiracy between them, a type of intimacy, sprinkled with a distinctive fine and gentle humour.[20] There is, of course, a lot unspoken between the lines and understood without even the need for allusion. It can merely be sensed from the tone: open, free, unencumbered, without reserve, with an honesty that in Freud's letters occasionally borders on the brusque; Anna does not react hurt, however, but rather takes up such remarks and asks for clarification, demonstrating an admirable ability to stand up for herself without causing offence.[21]

The volume of correspondence was determined by the family situation; they wrote to each other only when at least one of the correspondents was away from home – travelling, on holiday, in hospital, at conferences or for other reasons – with large gaps between. In view of the intermittent nature of the correspondence, one would not expect a coherent impression of the father–daughter relationship, so it is all the more surprising to find recurrent themes emerging. There are three directions that illustrate this: the strands 'Freud' and 'Anna' combine with 'psychoanalysis' to form a kind of triple helix. They merge, branch out, drift apart and come together again, ultimately bonding indissolubly with one another. Freud himself makes this connection in a letter congratulating Anna on her birthday: 'I can see from you how old I am, because you are as old as psychoanalysis. Both have caused me concerns but I basically expect more enjoyment from you than from it.'[22] He describes here a unique relationship, whose development and evolution can be traced in the letters.

At the start of the correspondence Freud was forty-eight years old. The passion of his earlier years had subsided to a more moderate level. One has the sense that he has now more or less found his place in the world and basically settled on a way of approaching things. He is well established professionally, sounds serene, balanced and calm. At first glance he gives the impression of a figure standing on a solid foundation, somehow unmovable.

Anna is quite the opposite: at the age of eight and a half she was already literate but otherwise an 'untamed' and developing child personality; she writes with youthful enthusiasm of her dramatic, crisis-ridden development, her unhappiness, rebellion and demands, alternately struggling with doubt, searching and experimenting. We can accompany her for a while on this path and then experience how she gradually and gingerly enters the world of psychoanalysis, how she ventures, hesitantly at first and yet thirsting for knowledge, by trial and error, ultimately finding her feet as she slowly becomes acquainted with the various aspects to become an 'experienced, patient and sympathetic analyst'.[23]

At first it is only the voice of the older generation that speaks: Papa, Mama, Aunt. The father mentions Anna's letters from 1904 to 1909 but appears not to have kept them – perhaps because they were too child-like? Anna's first surviving letter (6 AF), written when she was fourteen and a half, however, surprises us: it is not at all innocent, but full of problems and worries which have apparently tormented her for some time,[24] and which, as can be seen, continue to do so for years before she is finally able to look back at this time with a smile and self-deprecating allusions.[25]

The appendix operation she underwent in March 1908 and her slow recovery from it might be seen as an organic aspect or expression of this difficulty.[26] But this is not the main focus of her letter; at the forefront – as in practically every letter – is her great attachment to her father and her concern for his well-being, with a specific interest from the outset in his work and his colleagues. In this letter she not only seeks her father's love, but also fights for an equal place amongst her brothers and sisters. As the youngest of six children, unable initially to compete with the others, she felt excluded and burdensome to the older ones, and the resultant sense of boredom and abandonment[27] led her to seek attention through audacity, boldness and 'being different'. Even years later, during a visit to England, she still doubted her position in the family, feeling her presence or absence would be unnoticed by her brothers and sisters: 'I think only I would feel the difference.'[28]

Her desire to do things with the others is summed up in the words: '*I should also like* very much to travel alone with you once as Ernst and Oli are doing now',[29] and stresses the strength of her desire shortly afterwards with four exclamation marks, in which her entire childish misery is reflected.[30] In a letter to Ernest Jones decades later, Anna commented: 'I remember that he [Freud] sent me a picture postcard from Athens [in 1904] which I still see most vividly although to my regret I cannot find it now. [It still hasn't surfaced today.] It showed a little girl in a bathing suit pushing a toy sailboat in blue waters and he had written underneath "Möcht' auch nach Athen!" ["Wish also for Athens!"], an allusion to my very many wishes at the time.'[31] Even earlier she described to Max Eitingon this 'me too' as an unspecified desire '*also* to have something' or 'to have something at all', a 'wanting-to-have-something' that she classified as 'dependence'.[32]

With this 'möcht' auch' [me too] formulation, Anna plunges directly into a theme complex that dominated the following letters (up to 32

AF): her strong wishes are linked with feelings of unhappiness and inadequacy;[33] she writes that in her condition – referred to merely as 'it' – she has inexplicable worries, is listless, dissatisfied, has severe backache and is 'tired', 'stupid', in short 'not sensible' – she finds herself trapped in a web of interactions. Freud describes her as 'a bit odd'.[34] Because of her 'passionate overzealousness' in all activities she found herself unable to experience pleasure or enjoyment, and her excessive ambition had caused her to alienate herself from her own natural instincts.[35] Anna was thus all the more desperate to do something about her 'condition' and to be or become healthy and 'sensible'. On several occasions she asked her father for help.[36]

Freud reacted ambivalently. On the one hand he loved Anna's intellectual vitality, her rebelliousness, her 'being different'. 'Being well behaved is dull from the outset,' he concluded,[37] and illustrated it further with the nickname 'black devil', with which he showed Anna his approval.[38] On the other hand he could see how she suffered from her diffuse lethargy, how she lost weight and was ruining her health. He hoped that a long stay in Italy (which then had to be relocated to Merano) would bring an improvement.[39] Anna should become accustomed to 'idleness' and 'take each day as it comes' to 'take a cooler approach' to her plans.[40]

She did indeed recover 'excellently' and was developing 'gratifyingly'[41] – after father and daughter, on conclusion of the cure in Merano, had taken an Easter trip of several days together to Verona and Venice (for which Freud even cancelled a planned visit to his now married daughter Sophie),[42] and she spent some weeks in Marienbad the following year with Mama and Aunt.[43] A somewhat lighter tone can be felt in her letters after the second half of 1913. Having working hard for months, Anna, a lively, intelligent young girl with diverse interests, could now enjoy her holiday experiences with girlfriends or family. Although some of the problems persisted, she experienced greater clarity and was less dominated by them. The visit to England in 1914, Anna's war work in a day nursery and in the American Joint Distribution Committee,[44] and finally the demands of teaching also contributed to Anna's recovery. After spending a summer in the country doing all the things she enjoyed, she reported in 1918: 'I now have to be serious for many days; a quite unaccustomed feeling.' And in summer 1919 she finally learnt in Bayerisch Gmain how to be idle.[45]

But there was more. What exactly had Freud expected of his daughter after her return from Merano? 'We will recognize a change if you no longer ascetically shun the distractions of your age but enjoy doing what other girls take pleasure in.'[46] In other words, he wished for her to conform to the prevailing image of girls or women, as her sisters already did.[47]

He therefore suggested that she should stop being concerned about her career and postpone her teaching plans for a while.[48] He would have preferred her to be dismissed ('on account of a deficient singing voice'), he once confided in Sándor Ferenczi;[49] and when a few years later Anna considered giving up teaching, he was willing to support her.[50] However, he did send her a congratulation card for passing her teacher's examination[51] and admitted to her: 'You have turned out a little different than Math and Soph; you have more intellectual interests and will probably not be as happy with a purely female activity. Your inclinations are also likely to find expression in your choice of husband.' At the same time, he pointed out that 'by and large you can still look forward to the discovery that your sisters chose the right path'.[52]

More insistent efforts by Freud to suggest marriage and a family for Anna are only hinted at in the correspondence, for example, in a letter to Hamburg, where Anna was keeping house temporarily for her brother-in-law Max Halberstadt after the death of her sister Sophie, demonstrating maternal instincts as she looked after her two small orphaned nephews:[53] 'I hope that you settle into this phase of your life as well as in the previous one' [i.e., psychoanalysis, which was occupying her increasingly].[54] And yet, at the same time, he warned her against potential suitors, e.g., Jones and Lampl.[55] He complained about his dilemma to Lou Andreas-Salomé, who enjoyed his most intimate confidence: 'Sometimes I urgently wish her a good man, sometimes I shrink from the loss.'[56] This wavering is reflected on an envelope that probably contained a birthday gift. Written on it are the words 'Contribution to marriage fund or to independence.'[57]

Meanwhile Anna stubbornly sought to find her own 'other' way. She decided initially to become a teacher after all;[58] she clearly found recognition there and was very popular with her pupils. She was certainly helped here by her talent, capabilities and ability to empathize with children, but it was also hard and sometimes frightening physical work; in spite of impressive success, she did not feel really gratified by this work.[59]

Should she try writing? Pencil and pen had always enthralled her; she talked of her efforts at writing on several occasions in her letters, experimented with prose[60] and poetry, which an acting student friend rehearsed 'so as to be able to recite it'.[61] A year later she reported from Berlin that she had started a new story that had been worrying her the entire summer: 'It will be a little different than all the earlier ones; also more detailed. I'd like to finish it before coming to Vienna.'[62] Freud did not encourage her; at all events he never mentioned it in his replies and appears rather to have been dismissive. Anna wrote to Lou Andreas-Salomé: 'For the first time I had a daydream or story in my head with a female main figure (it was even a love story). I wanted to start writing it down immediately but Papa thought that I should leave it and think about my paper. And now it's gone . . .'[63]

At the same time, Anna's interest in psychoanalysis was steadily growing. While she had earlier translated texts from English under Freud's supervision, then read proofs, listened to Freud's lectures and attended the International Psychoanalytic Congress in Budapest as a guest,[64] Freud now involved her more in the setting up of the *Verlag* and its English affiliate, the 'Press', which also necessitated translations from German into English.[65] In this way he gained an enthusiastic assistant and also satisfied one of Anna's needs: 'You will have a hard time of it at first . . . but I think it will work and then it will be exactly what you wanted. . . . Then you would be in the thick of it.'[66]

She was also 'in the thick of it' because after the Budapest Congress she had started an analysis with her father – mentioned only once by Anna in the correspondence[67] – during which she also attempted some interpretations of her own dreams.[68] Four years later she said of this start: 'If I had not been more distant from him at the time, I could not have done it with Papa at all.' And later: 'There is no contradiction in your undergoing analysis in a place that you would prefer to come to for love's sake alone. I did the same thing, and perhaps because of it, the two things became inextricably bound together for me.'[69] As we shall see later, p. 12, Lou Andreas-Salomé also explained Anna's 'rare form of happiness' through the 'welding' of her link to her father with her own ambitious ego.

From this point – after summer 1919 and then again after the departure of the sons from Berggasse and Sophie's untimely death (1920)[70] – the quantity, volume and frequency of the correspondence increased strikingly; apart from the usual 'family reports', the letters on both sides discussed Freud's scientific work and organizational business matters in greater detail, the interchange became more concentrated and intensive in general and there was an unending succession of topics. With Anna's deeper penetration into psychoanalysis, her future problems once again became more pressing. Pulled to and fro between her various 'parts' – teacher, translator, writer and, of course, private person – she found it 'very difficult to manage'.[71] When she finally decided after long hesitation to quit teaching in 1920[72] in expectation of an increase in 'excess energy', she was still overcome by doubts: in the relaxed holiday atmosphere of Altaussee in August she did not regret for a minute having given up school,[73] but two months later – in her brother-in-law's house in Hamburg – she suffered from exhaustion, with physical and emotional discomfiture, and admitted: 'I feel so out of everything now without having been able to find a replacement that does me good.'[74]

She had by now intensified her psychoanalytical studies and extended her knowledge – in exchanges with her father and his colleagues, through attentive attendance at the meetings of the Vienna group, direct involvement in Freud's scientific works and his practice and, not least, through her detailed secretarial, translation and editing work for the *Verlag*'s books and magazines.[75] She later described the training of the time in her 'Curriculum vitae of a lay analyst': 'I also have in common with the few remaining analysts of my generation the circumstance that our analytic training took place at a period before the official psychoanalytic training institutes came into being. We were trained by our personal analysts, by extensive reading, by our own, unsupervised efforts with our first patients, and by lively interchange of ideas and discussion of problems with our elders and contemporaries.'[76] In September 1920, Anna once more took part in a Psychoanalytic Congress, still as a guest.[77] But with the long pause in her active contact with psychoanalysis through visits to

Hamburg and Berlin until the end of the year, she once again hesitated; she still did not feel confident about her practical psychoanalytical capabilities, emphasized her flawed interpretations[78] and concluded: 'You see, everyone can do much more than me.'[79] Freud comforted her, telling her to wait until she came back, when she would be 'at the source' again and would be able to find out all about the state of the *Verlag*, the negotiations with Jones and whatever else she wished to know. He also promised her the prospect of translations.[80] And six months later he assured her: 'I successfully asserted your claims with the *Verlag*.'[81]

Anna's development nevertheless continued to worry him. He followed it with ambivalent feelings. He did not apparently give serious consideration at first to a career as a practising analyst but rather saw her as a collaborator in the cause of psychoanalysis;[82] he still thought that marriage would be the best path for Anna: 'My Anna,' he admitted to Lou Andreas-Salomé, 'who is unreasonable enough to cling to her old father. The child gives me enough worries: how will she bear the lonely life and whether I can drive her libido from the hiding place into which it has crawled.'[83] And elsewhere he wrote that 'the whole trend of her life did not please' him. But his efforts to enable them to part from one another were in vain: 'I cannot free her from me, and nobody is helping me with it.'[84] He ultimately turned directly to Lou for advice: he sent Anna to her[85] in the hope that Lou would be a 'durable' and 'splendid' friend.[86] His wish was fulfilled. 'I cannot express how pleased I am that you take so affectionate an interest in her. She had wished for years to make your acquaintance. . . . If she is to amount to something – I hope she has some good aptitudes to start with – she needs influence and associations that will satisfy high demands. Inhibited through me on the male side, she has so far had a good deal of bad luck with her women friends. She has developed slowly, is younger than her years not only in looks.'[87] And Lou promised him: 'From meeting to meeting things will get better and better, and the more grimly the world threatens to plunge to its doom, the merrier we shall be!'[88]

This friendship gave Anna an unprecedented boost, which is also echoed in her letters from Göttingen. She felt so well there that she would like to have given up one of the initiation rings given to her by her father,[89] writing how she was overwhelmed by the strength and extent of this turnabout, which had enabled her to 'realize for the first time all that there is in the world.'[90] Inspired by this new vital impetus, Anna became more self-confident. Under Lou's wing she wrote her first paper, through which she became an official member of the Vienna Psychoanalytic Society,[91] and was able to report afterwards: 'I now suddenly have the confidence to talk analytically and fear that I will soon even be joining in the discussion.'[92] 'Since I visited you,' she wrote a year later, 'everything here is again indescribably more beautiful, easier, more enjoyable and self-evident, as if all of the colours had been refreshed with something.'[93] And in the same letter she was able to write about experiences with her first patients, who had come to her in the new year.[94]

It was at this time that Anna found reinforcement – as a result of Freud's critical illness[95] – for her wish to remain permanently in her parents' house, a desire that she expressed in a letter to Lou: 'I am sure you know what is the dearest and most important thought amongst all the things you have said to me. At every birthday I recall that without you I might not have found it out but rather that I would have been unsettled by those who wished to send me away from here out of fear for my future. And yet, even without any future, I still have as much here and more than others manage to achieve in a whole lifetime.'[96] Now the decision as to her existence was also *made possible* – paradoxically? – by this fateful necessity. In this phase her patients were 'the fixed point to which everything else is attached.' 'My patients are the only immutable thing.'[97] Thus she decided to become a psychoanalyst and also to be her father's main carer.[98] At first Freud was opposed to the idea as he didn't want to see her prematurely in the sad role of carer for old, sick parents.[99] He could no longer prevent this, but beforehand he was able to fulfil a long-standing childhood wish for her (and himself) that had once before been considered,[100] of travelling together to Rome.[101]

The correspondence continues to provide information on their progress, not least through the gaps between the letters; after the interruption caused by Freud's cancer operation, Anna did not leave her father for a long time.[102] Instead, she not only took on increasing household duties[103] in the following years but also acquired her own circle within the new setting.

In addition to her continued training in psychiatry, special education, juvenile criminality and related subjects,[104] she extended her activities in all areas of the psychoanalytical movement – intellectual, institutional, personal and practical – to achieve prominent positions, including at the international level. In this way she took the strain off Freud both in family matters and in organizational and public commitments, from which he increasingly withdrew, 'spoiled' by Anna's help, to 'leave the burden' to her.[105] This was also beneficial for the 'psychoanalysis strand': Anna was not only her father's confidante, scout, defender and propagator of his theory, but also had her own psychoanalytical achievements – with further developments in research, practice, teaching, establishment of new institutions and magazines – which were equal to those of Freud and continued after his death until the end of her own life. Freud was able to witness the early stages of this evolution.[106]

In addition, Anna became more 'sociable', forming new friendships,[107] which gave her precious energy for her varied undertakings, reshaping her 'scope for action' in this way. She soon forged 'the most pleasant and unclouded relationship'[108] with her contemporary Dorothy Burlingham, which developed into a lifelong partnership. The 'symbiosis'[109] between Freud's household and that of Dorothy and her children gave her family security and enjoyment as well as the possibility for close professional collaboration. Anna also allowed herself two longer breaks (1927 and 1930) with Dorothy, leaving her father with the rest of the family.

On both occasions the correspondence was revived, albeit with a different tone and structure. Telegrams became the regular form of contact and letters were far less frequent.[110] Anna's letters revealed a much brighter underlying mood: she was calmer, more relaxed and, in spite of the enormous strain, more unconcerned than before (see, e.g., ill. 17). Her daily reports of hiking tours – often in telegram style or even as telegrams – were full of the joys of travel and adventure. And as far as can be judged from the letters, she refrained from mentioning the worries and concerns caused by her father's illness.[111]

This was not just because of the agreement that the two had made.[112] Anna was *internally* more relaxed and free; so free that she was readily able to admit her bond with her father. In a letter to Paul Federn (about another matter) she says of it: 'It is not dependence on *others*, as you perhaps fear. I believe I am dependent only on my father (and so completely that that's enough!)'[113] As this relationship gradually became reversed, with Freud more dependent on Anna due to his increasing disability,[114] her restraint and tact in dealing with his reliance on her ensured that he lost nothing of his independence and authority.

She was also candid in her criticism of her father. As the letters show, she learnt to transform her early childhood rebellion into constructive activity. She defended her objections in a positive manner, criticizing constructively without causing unnecessary hurt or annoyance. At the same time she stood up purposefully and coherently for her deviating opinions or wishes. She did not try to persuade her father;[115] she gained his ear with objective and reasoned arguments and could, if necessary, back down without losing face, able to accept compromises or wait for the right moment.[116]

One example illustrates how considerate Anna was in formulating criticisms.[117] As mentioned earlier, Freud never encouraged Anna's writing efforts, although 'writing' was an existential problem for her.[118] She did not reproach him for it in the letters. But when she gave him her book, *The Ego and Mechanisms of Defence*, for his eightieth birthday, she added a dedication: 'Writing books as the supreme defence mechanism against all dangers from within and without.' Gerhard Fichtner, who made this phrase known in a lecture,[119] saw it as a 'premonition of what was to come'; I should like to add that the formulation *also* contains an affectionate and respectful reference to the earlier disregard for her writing efforts.

In this gentle manner, she managed to integrate two apparently irreconcilable conditions:[120] she could accept her father's undisputed authority yet take independent initiatives in accordance with her aptitudes and inclinations, while professionally introducing innovations based on psychoanalytical principles. And her special talents were well suited to the field of child therapy, one hardly investigated by Freud but with which she was familiar from her teaching and personal experience of small nephews and nieces. In this way she accommodated her father and made it easy for him to accept criticism and acknowledge her independence; she remained the loyal daughter without betraying her integrity – and thus established her emancipation.

This conciliatory trait also no doubt made Anna particularly suited for work as a mediator, frequently needed by Freud regarding differences with others or difficult theoretical discussions.[121] She was just as deliberate, for example, in her argumentation with regard to the ideas of Melanie Klein, by whom she was fiercely attacked on account of her different theoretical and methodological approach. Through her restrained and objective attitude she managed to prevent a threatened schism within psychoanalysis and the continent, although Jones – who, along with other British analysts, supported Klein's position – had taken the opportunity to criticize Anna's own analysis by her father.[122]

As the letters show, this ability was not a finished skill that could be simply carried around and brought out when needed. It had to be reformulated every time in a lifelong process, according to the circumstances.[123] This attitude is consistent with Anna's credo, derived from her observation of children on which her practical work is based: every child (person) is different; within their uniqueness they are ruled by personal and singular aptitudes and fates. They should therefore be dealt with in a manner that takes account of this situation, following their personal rhythm and in a way appropriate to their individual nature. There are no generally valid rigid rules; guidelines have to be found and reinvented in each case, and continuously developed. Thus, there is no *single* way, but an inexhaustible variety of possibilities that can be used or tried out to deal with the demands of life. As an illustration of these possibilities, 'Aunt Anna' once showed her nephew Ernstl, as he wrote in his memoirs, that plasticine could be reshaped in countless ways. 'With her mischievous humour,' she communicated to him 'that it is sometimes even possible to do the same with real people'.[124]

Freud's fear, which he once expressed to Lou Andreas-Salomé, that Anna 'has an extraordinary gift for being unhappy and yet probably not enough talent to let herself be stimulated to triumphant production by such unhappiness',[125] was allayed by Anna, who did the opposite. This very talent, and the way in which she applied it to her life,[126] enhanced her ability to empathize with children and achieve exemplary results. Freud finally revised his opinion: 'She has grown into a capable independent person who has been blessed with insight into matters that merely confuse others.'[127] And with her success, 'the child' experienced professional satisfaction and personal fulfilment: 'Anna is splendid, in spirits, achievement and in all human relationships. It is amazing how clear and independent her scientific work has become.'[128]

I cannot agree with the reproach often made of Freud that through Anna's bond with him he inhibited her and deprived her of irretrievable experiences – quite apart from the fact that it is impossible to have two conflicting experiences at the same time (at the best staggered). It is true that Anna failed to detach from her father through marriage, but this does not necessarily mean that he deprived her of the possibility of married life, which was the female ideal at the time – and what this would have brought her is in any case a matter for speculation. Her own desires, which she pursued with stubborn determination and ultimately achieved, can be summed up in a letter to Lou Andreas-Salomé: 'I am glad that it's not me who is getting married today. I still like it very much the way I am now.'[129] And a year later she repeated: 'I am not cut out for marriage . . . no more than a table or a sofa or my own rocking chair.'[130]

Lou, who herself had had a particularly strong relationship with her father, discussed this problem in a letter to Freud of 3 August 1924, in connection with Anna's analysis by her father:

> Sometimes I wonder heretically whether analysis could not also become a great loss for her, since a libido that is out of the ordinary can also produce a very rare form of happiness – as in Anna's case. Is it really likely that she would find it within the normal bounds? In the short time during which a female being owns her father, she can experience far greater happiness than a husband and child would provide. Obviously, Anna has a talent for unhappiness, as you say – but perhaps mainly because she cannot allow herself what she has without concern.[131]

And almost a year later:

> Regarding the rest of what you write: Anna and her analysis. You sound a little annoyed, saying that no one is helping you to detach Anna from you and also know in fact how little I would be willing intentionally to do so. But if I may do so clearly, I would like to share a thought on this matter: apart from the paternal bond – which everyone has to a greater or lesser extent – there has always been another decisive feature of Anna for me, which comes from an ambitious ego and is firmly welded to the former; as if full libidinal enjoyment came for her only through the combination of the two, which in her case is so successful that libido, ego assertion and the father's admired and identified superego form an otherwise barely conceivable harmonious whole. You say in your letter that the suppressed genitality could cause her problems in life, but we should also consider that in this person, in whom the libido is so strongly linked to the raised glance and value identification, the pure genital experience takes second place to another one: a completely unhysterical if slightly inhibited way, typified usually by breadth and richness, instead of the more pointed release in a sexually more needful individual love. If that is so . . . it would be a crime to take away even the smallest point from the crown that is offered to Anna through the special position she was born into. And even if that means a struggle because it will make her life less simple and smooth, it is still worthwhile! Who else can offer this?[132]

The letters published here illustrate just how much effort it took Freud to overcome his original conception of femininity. They show how changes took place in Freud as Anna developed, even if their subtle nature render them less obvious and so not immediately recognizable at first glance.[133] The initial impression that Freud's personality was static and unchanging does not hold up – just as Freud's theories also evolved and did not remain static. It took years of inner struggle for him to accept that his ideal of the 'female calling', which had still applied to Mathilde and Sophie, could be abandoned without loss in the case of his youngest daughter. We see how he repeatedly clung to this ideal, expressing concern with his opposition to her search for a career, her 'work zeal'.[134] He required a long transformation period before he could fully accept Anna's 'differentness' – not least under Anna's own dogged influence – and see both modes of existence as equally viable, allowing Anna to be more than merely her 'father's daughter'.

Then, however, he did everything possible to clear the path that Anna had chosen for herself, to encourage and support her, showing consideration for her and her work.[135] This also allowed her the possibility of creating a distance from him *in a way appropriate to her*. And as he noted how Anna formed her own extended family with Dorothy, the children and her nephew Ernstl (including her own school and the realization of her 'dream of a house'), as well as developing a large circle of friends – a community into which she incorporated Freud and psychoanalysis as an overriding model for them all – and how she found and took advantage of opportunities for enjoyment, developing inner strength, he was able to accept Anna's life plan rather than to perceive it as a vital and tension-filled difference. 'Very pleased to hear how your trip is going. . . . Apparently not the most conventional . . . but a selection according to individual taste.'[136] By allowing this coexistence without 'victim roles', he was then himself able to share her personal happiness and professional success with pride and satisfaction of his own. 'Her development seems so gratifying to me that every reverberation *also does me* very much good.'[137] And six years later he wrote to Stefan Zweig how 'exceptionally happy' he was in his home 'with my wife and children and in particular with one daughter who to a rare extent satisfies all the expectations of a father.'[138] This in turn contributed to Anna's undiminished fulfilment – successful reciprocity.

In this way the strands of the triple helix remained permanently intertwined until Freud's death and possibly beyond: 'It is curious,' wrote Anna to Stefan Zweig, 'but I cannot mourn him properly as one otherwise does . . . . Mourning is somehow no adequate feeling for the fact that he has died. Perhaps my bond with him was more serious than the separation from him. At any rate, what one has received from him is always much more than what other people even possess.'[139] 'But as far as my feelings are concerned, it seems to me as if this whole separation were something temporary, something transient . . . something like in earlier years when my father was away on journeys.'[140]

The letters from these 'earlier years' can be read in two ways: on the one hand as a moving documentation that, fragmentarily but full of life, provides an insight into the growth and development of a very special form of father–daughter relationship; on the other hand as a precious gift, the full value of which is revealed (as the many references in the notes indicate) only when these letters are viewed as fragments in a more comprehensive mosaic of the other written testimonies of both correspondents – Sigmund Freud and Anna.

Ingeborg Meyer-Palmedo

Notes

1 Mathilde Freud, 11 March 1907, quoted in Gödde [2003], p. 88.
2 Freud, 2002*b*, p. 128.
3 For example, 3 SF and notes 2, 4, 5; 6 AF and note 2; 48 SF, note 2; 71 AF and note 7; 76 SF, note 1; 80 SF, note 2; 256 SF and note 3; 266 SF, note 2; 271 and note 2; 277 SF, note 6.
4 55 SF.
5 6 AF, note 9; 14 AF; 173 AF, note 2; 270 AF, note 3; 69 AF and note 6.
6 77 AF, 79 AF and note 6; 101 AF; 108 AF.
7 141 AF and note 2.
8 36 AF and note 6; 287 SF and note 20.
9 251 SF and note 3. See also Gödde [2003], pp. 176f. When travelling to the country became too difficult in Freud's later years, the family spent the summer months in natural surroundings on the outskirts of Vienna (126 SF and notes 13–15).
10 Which for that reason are often quite detailed.
11 Freud/Andreas-Salomé, 27 July 1916, pp. 50f.
12 Kos (ed.) [1992], pp. 21, 25.
13 Links to further reading are indicated in the relevant places.
14 The importance of 'socializing' for Freud, as well as for his family and the development of psychoanalysis, can be clearly seen in many places in this correspondence.
15 See, e.g., Grubrich-Simitis [1995b], pp. 11, 18, 24f.; ibid. [1986], pp. 272–4 and note 33; ibid. [2005], pp. 273ff. See also Anna's own comments about analysis with her father, here p. 7 and note 69.
16 In this correspondence only the split from Rank and Sándor Ferenczi is discussed (287 SF).
17 See 42 SF and note 5, 108 AF, 156 AF, 158 AF, 159 SF, 161 SF–169 SF, 185 AF–188 AF (Loe Kann); 108 AF, 156 AF, 162 AF, 163 AF (Herbert Jones); 42 SF–44 SF, 100 SF, 257 SF (Ernest Jones); 174 AF (Max Eitingon); 131 AF (Hanns Sachs); 42 SF, 43 SF, 45 AF (Emanuel Freud); 144 AF, 150 AF, 160 AF, 162 AF (Max Halberstadt); 129 AF, 139 AF, 140 SF, 147 SF, 162 AF (Ernst Halberstadt). Examples of disparaging comments are much fewer: 183 AF (millionairesses); 187 SF (Paul Federn); 82 AF, 163 SF (Rószi von Freund); 159 SF and note 6, 161 SF–163 SF, 166 SF, 175 SF, 181 SF (Ditha Bernays); 159 SF, 196 SF (Esti Freud).
18 See, e.g., Young-Bruehl, pp. 27, 28, 54.
19 'I will certainly look after Mama as well as I can and keep you informed' (144 AF). A few further examples from the large number of references:

17 AF–19 AF, 74 AF–79 AF, 180 AF–183 AF, 211 SF (correspondence); 6 AF, 33 AF and note 5–37 AF, 60 AF, 122 AF/MF, 144 AF– 47 AF, 170 AF, 174 AF (health); 116 AF, 120 AF, 170 AF–177 AF, 183 AF, 185 AF, 188 AF (travel, holidays).

20 This is difficult to illustrate with brief quotations, but is revealed more in the overall context of the remarks and replies; see also note 17.

21 147 AF as one such example.

22 137 SF.

23 Freud to Lou Andreas-Salomé, 10 May 1925, quoted in Gay, p. 441.

24 See 5 MF/SF and notes 1, 10.

25 See, e.g., 132 AF, 135 AF, 158 AF, 221 AF, 225 AF.

26 5 MF/SF, note 1. On the subject of appendicitis and the appendix operation and their sequels, see Gödde [2003], pp. 129–31; see also 98 AF (descending pains), 127 AF (abdominal pains).

27 Anna to Muriel Gardiner, p. 64; see 295 AF, note 3; also Freud, M. [1999], p. 55. For her wish to be older than she actually was, see 200 SF, note 4, and 295 SF.

28 45 AF.

29 6 AF (my emphasis).

30 7 AF and note 3.

31 27 February 1954; quoted in Young-Bruehl, p. 39.

32 Anna to Max Eitingon, 19 February 1926, LoC AF, Cont. 24. See also Young-Bruehl, p. 186.

33 For the link between Anna's feeling of inadequacy and her 'wanting to have' (= 'possession'), see her letter (66) to Lou Andreas-Salomé (Anna/Lou), 16 December 1922, pp. 119–21.

34 25 SF.

35 28 SF.

36 For example, 26 AF. See also Young-Bruehl, p. 156.

37 161 SF.

38 14 AF. See also 102 SF.

39 19 AF and note 1; 22 SF.

40 20 SF, 22 SF. Similar advice recurs repeatedly in later periods.

41 25 SF, note 4; 28 SF, note 6.

42 See Freud to Oskar Pfister: 'Apart from that, I am looking forward to Easter, which I am going to spend in Venice with my small and now only daughter' ⟨1963*a*, 11 March 1913, p. 61). See 28 SF and note 5, and 185 SF/MF, note 5.

43 31 SF, 32 AF; 25 SF, 28 SF and note 5; 33 AF, note 2.

44 47 SF, note 6.

45 84 AF. See also 244 AF and 96 AF, 103 AF, e.g., and also 132 AF.

46 28 SF.

47 43 SF.

48 22 SF.

49 Freud/Ferenczi II. 542 F, 8 April 1915, p. 56. For Freud's view of female tasks and vocation, see, e.g., his letter to his daughter Mathilde ⟨26 March 1908, in 1960*a* [dated 19 March 1908 in the English translation]; also the 'courting letters' in ibid., 1882–6; Jones I, p. 180⟩.

50 128 SF.

51 48 SF.

52 43 SF.

53 Eitingon, whom Anna visited afterwards, had the impression 'that the atmosphere of the children in H[amburg] had suited her very well' ⟨Freud/Eitingon, 189 E, 11 November 1920, p. 220⟩. See also Anna's reports from Hamburg in 1920 (127 AF, 129 AF) and in 1922 (156 AF, 158 AF, 160 AF, 162 AF).
54 157 SF.
55 42 SF; 151 AF and note 3. For Freud's 'marriage policy' for his three daughters, see Gödde [2003], pp. 155–61.
56 Freud to Lou Andreas-Salomé, 3 July 1922, quoted in Gay, p. 438.
57 154 SF and note 3.
58 39 AF and note 2.
59 53 AF; 84 AF, note 7; 86 AF; 96 AF; 101 AF; 141 AF, note 2.
60 105 AF; 101 AF and note 1.
61 114 AF.
62 132 AF.
63 Anna/Lou, letter 22, 18 May 1922, p. 47. More about Anna's continued writing efforts and Lou Andreas-Salomé's encouragement in Anna/Lou, e.g., letters 50, 51, 53, 161, and elsewhere. See also Molnar [2005].
64 49 AF, 60 AF, 69 AF, 74 AF, 86 AF, 89 SF, 100 SF, 101 AF, 114 AF, 118 AF.
65 98 AF, 100 SF and note 6.
66 100 SF.
67 96 AF; see also 132 AF, note 5.
68 For example, 96 AF, 101 AF, 103 AF, 114 AF, 147 AF.
69 Anna/Lou, letter 59, 24 November 1922, p. 105; Anna/Eva, letter 8, 22 March 1929, p. 112.
70 Text after 106 SF.
71 101 AF.
72 141 AF and note 2.
73 120 AF.
74 127 AF.
75 To mention just a few references: 95 SF, 108 AF and note 8, 112 SF, 125 SF, 126 SF, 157 SF, 159 SF, 181 SF; and an example from Anna's many comments: 'I am reading your new work here with great pleasure. I really like the idea of the ego ideal' (132 AF). The correspondence does not contain any theoretical discussion, however, and was carried out face-to-face ⟨see, for example, Anna/Lou, letters 37, 47, 49, 52, 54, 56, 59, 61, 70, 75, 77, 78⟩.
76 Anna Freud (1967 [1964]), in *Writings*, vol. V, p. 511.
77 123 AF/SF.
78 108 AF.
79 131 AF.
80 130 SF.
81 138 SF.
82 See 168 AF, note 6.
83 Freud to Lou Andreas-Salomé, 3 July 1922, quoted in Gay, pp. 440f.
84 Ibid., 10 May 1925, quoted in Gay, p. 441. For Freud's emotional attachment to his three daughters, see also Gödde [2003], pp. 161–5.
85 153 AF.
86 166 SF.
87 Freud/Andreas-Salomé, 3 July 1922, p. 117.
88 Freud/Andreas-Salomé, 5 August 1922, p. 117.
89 174 AF.

90 169 AF. The full extent of this friendship can only be seen in Anna's correspondence with Lou Andreas-Salomé (Anna/Lou).
91 168 AF and note 6.
92 Anna/Lou, letter 27, 6 June 1922, p. 55.
93 Ibid., letter 91, 6 April 1923, p. 169.
94 Ibid., letters 22, 27, 82, 84, 85, 103.
95 197 SF, note 3.
96 Anna/Lou, letter 204, 4 December 1924, pp. 384f.
97 Anna/Lou, letter 93, pp. 172f.; 98, p. 180.
98 198 SF, note 5; text after 201 SF/AF.
99 198 SF.
100 35 SF.
101 201 SF/AF and Appendixes 1 and 2; text after 201 SF/AF.
102 203 SF and note 3.
103 Anna now 'by nature dominates it [the house] more and more' ⟨Freud/Ferenczi III, 899 F, 30 March 1922, p. 78⟩. This 'domestic domination' continued to grow in the future.
104 See *Writings*, vol. 5, pp. 511–13; 170 AF, note 8; also Gay, pp. 435–7.
105 Freud/Ferenczi III, 1001 F, p. 203 ⟨also ibid., 942 F⟩; 1085 F, p. 289. See also 270 AF, note 4; many other references, e.g., in Freud/Ferenczi III, 1140 F, 1148 F, 1160 Fer, 1202 Fer–1205 Fer, 1214 Fer, 1218 Fer, PS to 1223 Fer, 1225 F, 1226 Fer.
106 Many references in this correspondence from 1923 onwards.
107 Eva Rosenfeld, Jeanne Lampl-De Groot, Ruth Mack-Brunswick and Marie Bonaparte are but a few of those mentioned in the letters.
108 244 AF.
109 Freud, see 212 SF, note 4.
110 After 1930 the correspondence was even more sparing; up to Freud's death only twelve items, all from Freud, survive.
111 See also 'Epilogue', p. 407.
112 198 SF.
113 27 September 1933; LoC, The Papers of Paul Federn, folder 'Anna Freud'.
114 'Anna is becoming increasingly indispensable to me . . . [she] is excellent as ever and without her I would be quite lost' ⟨Freud to Alexander Freud, 24 September 1938; in the same tone also ibid., 4 and 28 September 1928, LoC SF, Cont. 1⟩. See also Freud/Andreas-Salomé, 16 May 1935; Gay, p. 440–3; Molnar [1996], p. 255; also 270 SF, note 4, 298 SF, note 22.
115 23 AF, 108 AF, 111 AF, 168 AF, 185 AF.
116 23 AF, 147 AF, 160 AF, 244 AF.
117 In a similar humorous admonishing and gentle manner, e.g., also in 49 AF; 62 AF; 108 AF. This is usually embedded in an overall context, with the sentence structure, order and subtle nuances in the tone and reactions creating 'le ton qui fait la musique'. See note 20.
118 See, for example, Anna/Lou, letters 50, 51 (p. 93); Molnar [2004], pp. 163–6.
119 Fichtner [2003], unpublished manuscript, p. 13.
120 In a similar way, Anna also demanded from child analysts that they deal with opposites at the same time; from a specific constitution of the child, the 'fact that the child's superego is weak' and the child's incapability to control 'the instincts that have been freed', she inferred the need for an educational approach: 'The analyst accordingly combines in his own person two difficult

and diametrically opposed functions: he has to analyse and educate, that is to say, in the same breath he must allow and forbid, loosen and bind again' ⟨*Writings I*, p. 65; also ibid., p. 61⟩.

121 287 SF and note 15; 291 SF; 251 SF, note 2. See also, for example, Freud/Ferenczi III, 986 F (p. 185), 1175 F (p. 178), 1176 Fer, 1177 F, 1184 Fer, PS to 1237 Fer, 1239 Fer; *Rundbrief*, Budapest, 16 May 1925.

122 Freud/Jones, letters 502, 503; see also Freud/Eitingon, 422 E and notes 1 and 2; 209 SF, note 2 and 216 AF, note 2. Jones III, p. 318, describes another situation 'rescued' by Anna's intervention (see 251 SF, note 2).

123 Norbert Elias has a comprehensive and convincing description in his theories of these transformation processes, which are not linear, but with irregular advances and setbacks.

124 Freud, W. E. [1987], p. 206.

125 13 May 1924, quoted in Gay, p. 441.

126 See Anna/Lou, letter 305.

127 Freud to Arnold Zweig, 2 April 1937, in 1968*a*, p. 140.

128 Freud to Ernst Freud, 17 January 1938, in 1960*a*, p. 436.

129 Anna/Lou, letter 78, 4 February 1923, p. 148.

130 Ibid., letter 148, 3 January 1924, p. 266.

131 LoC SF, Cont. 16. This passage is absent from Freud/Andreas-Salomé. The following year Lou quoted to Anna a saying by Goethe: 'Voluntary dependence is the most beautiful state' ⟨Anna/Lou, letter 239, 28 June 1924, p. 456⟩.

132 LoC Cont. 16 (passage omitted in Freud/Andreas-Salomé). See also Gay, p. 437–42; in this volume, p. 7.

133 The age difference should be taken into account: when Freud died Anna was not yet as old as he had been at the start of the correspondence.

134 See also Gödde [2003], pp. 233–7.

135 See Gay, p. 441; Freud/Eitingon, 748 F, 4 December 1932.

136 228 SF.

137 Freud/Ferenczi III, 1185, 30 March 1930, p. 391 (my emphasis).

138 Freud 1960*a*, 18 May 1936, p. 425.

139 28 October 1939, quoted in Molnar [1996], p. 264. (See Lucie Freud in 'Epilogue' after 298 SF.)

140 Anna Freud to Stefan Zweig, 13 February 1940, quoted in Molnar [1996], p. 264.

Part I

Correspondence

1904

1 SF[1]

PROF. DR. FREUD

4 July 1904
[Vienna], IX. Berggasse 19[2]

My dear Anna,
It is very nice of you to have written to me for once,[3] so I will also write back properly. I think you made a mistake in your letter and meant to write that you had put on 1 kilo; if it is correct that you have lost weight, however, Aunt[4] should feed you char[5] until you put it back on again. At your age you should put on weight without fear of getting fat.[6] Mama[7] already has her sleeper ticket for Thursday evening [7 July], then you will all be there except the last remaining person, who is already looking forward very much to coming later.[8] Your old
Papa

1 Before this first letter in the transcribed correspondence was a vaccination certificate, included here as Appendix 4 (see 256 SF, note 1).
2 Letter card with preprinted letterhead.
3 Anna's letter appears to be missing. 'The family spent their summer holidays in Bavaria in the first years of the century; . . . in 1902, 1903 and 1904 in the Villa Sonnenfels, near Berchtesgaden ⟨Jones II, p. 16; see also Freud, M. [1999], chs IV–VI, VIII–X, XIII–XIX⟩.
4 'Aunt' without a name usually refers to Minna Bernays (1865–1941), Martha Freud's sister, who lived in the Freud household temporarily from November 1895 and permanently after summer 1896 ⟨Introduction by Albrecht Hirschmüller to Freud/Bernays, p. 9⟩. (See also ill. 2.) She had travelled ahead with the children on holiday. 'The family would move out of Vienna in June when the hot weather began and he usually joined them in the middle of July for a month or longer' ⟨Jones II, p. 16⟩.
5 Freshwater salmonid fish, genus *Salvelinus*, a popular fish endemic to southern Germany, particularly in Alpine regions, e.g., in the depths of Alpine lakes.
6 See Freud's letter to Anna in 5 MF/SF, also 6 AF and note 4, 15 AF, 19 AF,

21 AF, 22 SF, 26 AF, 30 SF. The topic of putting on weight was to recur with Freud's grandson Ernstl, see e.g., 129 AF, 140 AF, 141 AF.

7 Martha Freud (1861–1951), daughter of Berman and Emmeline Bernays; married to Sigmund Freud since 14 September 1886 ⟨Stammbaum Lange: Bernays Family, 'Genealogical Tree IIa', p. 6; Freud 1960*a*, letter recipients Bernays, Martha, and Freud, Martha⟩ (see ill. 2). For details of her family of origin, see the Annex by Albrecht Hirschmüller in Freud/Bernays.

8 On 12 July 1904; the holiday on Königsee Lake ended for Freud on 28 August ⟨Tögel [1989], p. 153⟩. The following day he travelled with his brother to Greece, returning to Vienna on 10 September ⟨Tögel [2002], pp. 175–7; Freud 2002*b*, pp. 178–93⟩. Freud sent Anna a postcard from Athens, which appears to have been lost (see Introduction, p. 4 and note 31).

1905

2 SF[1]

Frl Anna Freud
Alt-Aussee[2]
N 32
Styria

[Bolzano], 4 September 1905[3]

Aunt and Papa,[4] who are sitting here in the sun and can see the Rose Garden,[5] hope that you[6] are having some good weather.[7]

1 Picture postcard (written in pencil): 'The Rose Garden near Bolzano'.
2 Written 'Altaussee' today; popular summer holiday resort on Altaussee Lake in the Salzkammergut in Styria. The Ausseerland is one of the most beautiful regions in Austria. Aristocrats and dignitaries went there to relax, while intellectuals, literati, musicians and other artists took inspiration from it ⟨Schauer; Stephan⟩. The Freud family had already spent their holidays there on several occasions ⟨Freud, 1985*c*, *passim*; Freud, M. [1999], pp. 51f., 60–3; Freud, 2002b, 12 and 13 September 1905; Tögel [1989], pp. 151, 152, 154⟩. The house belonging to Karl Köberl, no. 32, 'still exists today, a beautiful old farmhouse in Salzberggasse – the house is called Pressl – was rented in its entirety to guests in the summer while the farmer's family moved to the ancillary buildings as was customary at the time' ⟨thanks to Johann Linortner for the oral information, Altaussee, 1 May 2002⟩. In his memoirs ([1999], pp. 51, 54f.), Martin Freud describes the friendly relations between the locals and the visitors, who often maintained contacts and developed work relationships beyond the summer holidays. See 125 SF and note 15, and 116 SF, note 2.
3 The date is on the lower edge of the picture side of the card.
4 The two had left the rest of the family in Altaussee on 3 September and set off on a trip through northern Italy and Switzerland, returning to Vienna on 23 September ⟨Jones II, p. 27f.; Tögel [2002], p. 95f.; Freud, 2002*b*, pp. 197–207⟩. See 226 AF, 235 AF, note 6.
5 The Rose Garden, a massif in the western Dolomites notable for its variety of forms, is a landmark in the Bolzano region and is particularly renowned for the evening glow on the steep rock formations at sunset ⟨Delago, p. 121f.⟩.

6 Martha and the children.
7 For the rainy climate in Altaussee, see, e.g., 122 AF/MF and note 1.

1908

3 SF

PROF. DR. FREUD

7 July 1908
[Vienna], IX. Berggasse 19[1]

My dear Anna,
Really, if I weren't already very impatient to get to Dietfeldhof,[2] your letter[3] would make me so. I also liked it very much when I was there for the first time in April, when white snow still lay between the clumps of yellow primroses. Strawberries and mushrooms are a very welcome prospect; we are bound to discover some lovely walks in no time.[4] Perhaps we can rent the Aschauer pond[5] for ourselves alone, so that there will be room for us all to bathe.

Your brother Martin is very proud of having passed his exam so well[6] and will soon appear in your midst with a new travelling bag and velour hat. Lampl[7] will be coming with him but they will soon be setting off on their great holiday trip with which they intend to inaugurate their independence.[8] As for us, we will alternate between reading and writing and taking walks in the woods; if only the Almighty doesn't spoil the summer for us by making it rain all the time, it could be very beautiful.

My greetings to all your brothers and sisters;[9] before you have re-read this letter a few times we will be there, too – on the morning of 16 July.

Affectionately,
Papa

1 Preprinted letterhead. (See 'Preface to this Edition'; cf. facsimile on p. 315.)
2 '. . . a beautiful isolated house', outside and to the west of Berchtesgaden ⟨Freud/Ferenczi I, 10 F, 10 May 1908, p. 11⟩. Freud had selected it in April during 'half a day of solitude' before the Salzburg Congress ⟨Freud/Jung, 82 F, p. 137⟩ and had special letterheads printed for the stay (see, e.g., Freud/Ferenczi I, 17 F). He spent his holidays there that year from 16 July to 31 August 1908, and the family was joined for some of the time by Ferenczi, who still enthused about it years later: 'The unforgettably beautiful days of Dietfeldhof . . . belong to the most

beautiful recollections of my life' ⟨Freud/Ferenczi III, 907 Fer, 16 July 1922, pp. 82–3; I, 9 Fer–17 F⟩.

3 Missing.

4 Walks while looking for berries and mushrooms together were among Freud's favourite holiday pastimes. 'Our expeditions had the warmth of a delightful story which is well constructed and never lacking a good climax. They . . . always had a particular purpose; it might be searching for or collecting something, or it might be exploring some particular place' ⟨Freud M. [1999], pp. 57f.⟩.

5 On the way to Bischofswiesen near Dietfeldhof. A lake to swim in or better still a 'private pond' would have been a welcome holiday addition for the Freud family (see 256 SF, note 4, and 257 SF and note 20). Today there is a large concrete public bathing lake on the site that gives little indication of the 'idyllic pond' of that time.

6 Jean Martin (1889–1967), the eldest of the three sons ⟨Stammbaum Lange: Freud Family, 'Genealogical Tree', p. I⟩. He passed his *Reifeprüfung* (school-leaving examination) with 'distinction' ⟨Reifezeugnis, FM London; Freud M. [1999], pp. 102, 144⟩.

7 Hans Lampl (1889–1958), a school friend of Martin and close friend of the family. Later doctor of medicine and analyst (see correspondence, *passim*) ⟨Mühlleitner, pp. 199–201⟩.

8 'I had now, in a sense, become of age with the right to go where I pleased for my holidays' (Freud M. [1999], p. 144).

9 Mathilde ('Math'; 1887–1978); Oliver ('Oli'; 1891–1969); Ernst L.[udwig] (1892–1970); Sophie ('Soph'; 1893–1920) ⟨Stammbaum Lange: Freud Family, 'Genealogical Tree', pp. I, II⟩ (see ill. 2).

4 SF[1]

Miss Anna Freud
Berchtesgaden
Baiern Germany
Dietfeldhof

[Blackpool,[2]] Friday, 4 September 1908

Dear Anna,
Please send my greetings to all, large and small,[3] in Dietfeldhof. Perhaps I can take you to a beach like this some time.[4]
Papa
[In their own handwriting]:
Greetings to everyone from Uncle Emanuel.[5]
[in English] Hearty greetings from Bertha.[6]

1 Booklet of pictures entitled *Blackpool Pictorial Letters*. The cover also served as envelope; apart from empty sheets for writing on, it contained six colour or black-and-white pictures of Blackpool, the popular seaside resort in Lancashire on the Irish Sea coast.

2 'On September 1, I have to go to England, where my brother's family awaits me,' Freud wrote to Ferenczi, who had wanted to travel with him to the

Netherlands ⟨Freud/Ferenczi I, 17 F, 4 August 1908, p. 17; see also Freud/Jung, 101 F, p. 161⟩. In *The Psychopathology of Everyday Life*, Freud mentions an error during a trip to England as an example of 'how a wish that has been reluctantly suppressed can be satisfied by means of an "error"' ⟨1901*b*, ch. X, 'Errors', example 16 added in 1910, the quote from example 14⟩.

3 Martha, her sister Minna and the children. The other news from Southport, St Anne's and London had been sent to Mathilde and the whole family ⟨Freud, 2002*b*, pp. 239–61, which also includes the manuscript on pp. 250–5, 'Bermerkungen über Gesichter und Männer, National Portrait Gallery' ('Notes on Faces and Men, National Portrait Gallery') (2002*c*), with detailed comments by Michael Molnar [2002]⟩.

4 For comments on Freud's wish to visit England again, see the introduction to Tögel [2002], p. 237f. Freud left England on 15 September and travelled after a short stay in Berlin with his sister Marie Freud to Zurich on 17 September to visit C. G. Jung ⟨Freud/Jung, 107 J–109 F with intermediate text pp. 169–72). He spent the rest of the holidays with Minna on a trip through northern Italy ⟨Tögel [2002], p. 262f.; Freud 2002*b*, pp. 264–71⟩.

5 Emanuel Freud (1833–1914) ⟨Stammbaum Lange: Freud Family, 'Genealogical Tree', p. I⟩ (see also 24 SF and note 3). Freud's elder half-brother from Jakob Freud's first marriage; he had already emigrated to England with his family in 1899 ⟨Freud M. [1999], pp. 10, 12f.; Jones I, p. 15⟩.

6 Bertha Freud (1859–1940), third of seven children of Emanuel and Marie Freud (see 42 SF, note 12) ⟨Stammbaum Lange, ibid.⟩.

1910

5 MF/SF

[to Mathilde and Anna[1] in Semmering[2]]
[Vienna] Sunday [2 January 1910]

My dear good children,
We received a card and letter from you today[3] and send you sincere greetings. We are delighted to hear that it is doing Robert[4] so much good. It will have been good for everyone in the end. I'm not sure whether I will come up there or not – if it is all so costly that 200 kr. is not enough for a week. I think that is what you are suggesting, isn't it? I would prefer it if Robert were to leave you out there with the child at least over the holiday, i.e. Thursday,[5] then no one would have to pay again for two carriages, travel money, and tips, don't you think? Not to mention another pair of galoshes and gaiters. Please let me know immediately, dear child – I mean Mathildchen – whether you think I'm right. I would have sincerely liked for Annerl to spend a little more time outside tobogganing, but I hadn't thought it would be so expensive.[6] We spent the holidays very quietly and alone, went to bed earlier than usual on New Year's Eve and waited yesterday in vain until 1.30 a.m. for Ernstl,[7] who was in Lilienfeld[8] and simply stayed away overnight and all of today. That's how I spent the holiday.

Greetings and kisses to all of my three dear *lovely* children.
Mama

[On his own notepaper]

PROF. DR. FREUD
2 January 1910
[Vienna], IX. Berggasse 19

Dear Mathilde,
I only want to add to Mama's letter that I don't want to spoil *your* holiday up there for reasons of thrift. As far as I am concerned you can stay as long as you want. But I don't think it's worth the expense for Mama to take

over, if you take the equipment, lack of activity except for tobogganing, the poor food and Frau W.[9] into account. Come back with Annerl and let me know how I can send you the missing money and how much you need. You can say at all events that I will pay by postal order.

I hope it wasn't too much of a sacrifice for you, particularly as Robert has had such a good time in the last few days. I don't know whether he will still be with you when you receive this letter.

Sincerely,
Papa

Dear Anna,
Provided you don't ask whether you can toboggan here in the rooms,[10] for the money saved I will find all kinds of things for you to enjoy when you get home. You don't need to go to school until you have put on some weight again. Perhaps you can take a couple of private lessons in the meantime.[11] During this quiet time we have had only two children[12] at home.

Affectionately,
Papa

1 Mathilde and Anna had been spending their winter holidays in Semmering since 27 December 1909; 'both are doing not badly, but also not very well' ⟨Freud/Ferenczi I, 96 F, 1 January 1910, p. 118⟩. Mathilde was suffering from the after-effects of a near-fatal appendix operation in 1905 (at the time Freud performed a 'sacrificial act', which he describes in *Everyday Life* [1901*b*, p. 169]) ⟨Freud/Ferenczi I, e.g., 52 F, 75 F; Freud/Jung 64 F and elsewhere; Young-Bruehl, p. 45⟩. Anna had also lost weight as a result of an appendix operation (in March 1908) and been off school for a lengthy period ⟨Freud/Binswanger, 63 F; Young-Bruehl, pp. 54, 55, 59⟩. Although she had recovered physically, she often felt tired afterwards, 'stupid' and not 'sensible', as she herself described it; see Introduction and, e.g., 8 AF, 19 AF, note 1, 23 AF–27 AF, also 244 AF and note 7.

2 A pass at an altitude of 981 metres on the border of Lower Austria and Styria, popular mountain spa resort ⟨Kos [1984], [1992]; Freud/Ferenczi I, 93 F⟩. Freud knew and appreciated the area from earlier visits ⟨Freud 1985c, e.g., letters 10, 25–8, 48–50; Tögel [1989], p. 150f.; Kos [1984], p. 122⟩. Later (1924–8) he rented a house with the family in Semmering for the entire summer; see 203 SF, 244 AF, note 2, 250 SF, note 3.

3 Missing.

4 Robert Hollitscher (1875–1959), Viennese businessman married to Mathilde since 7 February 1909 ⟨Freud/Ferenczi I, 20 F, 37 F with marriage announcement⟩ (see ill. 3). For details of Robert Hollitscher and his family, see Gödde [2003].

5 6 January, Epiphany. Although Martha grew up in an orthodox Jewish family and remained a devout Jew, the Freud family observed the Christian holidays in Austria ⟨Freud M, [1999], p. 81; Gay, pp. 38, 54, 600f.⟩.

6 In his memoirs (1999, p. 44), Martin talks of his mother's thriftiness. See also 149 SF and note 3.

7 Ernst Freud, the youngest of the three sons.

8 Locality south-west of Vienna, on the Traisen approx. 30 km south of St Pölten ⟨Kleindel, p. 297⟩. 'Ernst dances incessantly from one house ball to another,' wrote Mathilde on 19 January 1910 to her youthful friend of the time ⟨Gödde [2003], p. 347⟩.
9 Unknown.
10 For Anna's sometimes unusual wishes, see 7 AF and note 3, also 10 SF and 13 SF.
11 See 11 AF/EF and note 3. For Anna Freud's school years, see Peters, pp. 10ff.; Young-Bruehl, pp. 47–55.
12 Sophie and Ernest ⟨Freud/Binswanger, 20 F, 31 December 1909, pp. 27f.⟩.

6 AF

Bistrai,[1] 13 July 1910

Dear Papa,
Now the sad fact that we won't be seeing each other until 1 August is certain,[2] we should at least correspond by letter. I am fine here and I like Dr Jekels[3] a lot. I am doing my best to get as well by autumn as the short time will allow. I am also putting on weight and am already quite plump and fat,[4] but am not being paid anything for it. Dr Jekels is very nice to us and talks a lot about you. He won't lend me *Gradiva*,[5] however, without your explicit permission. Have you finished being treated by Dr Zweig?[6] And won't you upset your stomach again in The Hague?[7] The boys should watch out for you properly. I should also like very much to travel alone with you once[8] as Ernst and Oli are doing now. We only go out on rides here with Dr Jekels; I always sit in the box seat, but without a fishing rod and with my shoes on.[9] I am sure you are looking forward to closing the office completely tomorrow. Dr Jekels keeps on telling us how he dreads seeing his patients[10] and I can imagine how much more unpleasant it must be for you, since you have even more. Most of the people in the establishment are very disagreeable and always stare at us because they can't imagine what we are doing here; very few of them can speak German either. Aunt is very glad that we are not in the Black Forest, because it's snowing there. I don't think it's right that Mama is still in the apartment; she won't eat properly and will ruin herself completely. I would like very much to visit Grandma[11] in Hamburg; do you think we will do it?[12] I am looking forward very much to Holland and everything there. Then we will finally all be together again.[13]

I hope you have a good journey and enjoy yourself in The Hague.
With a kiss,
Anna

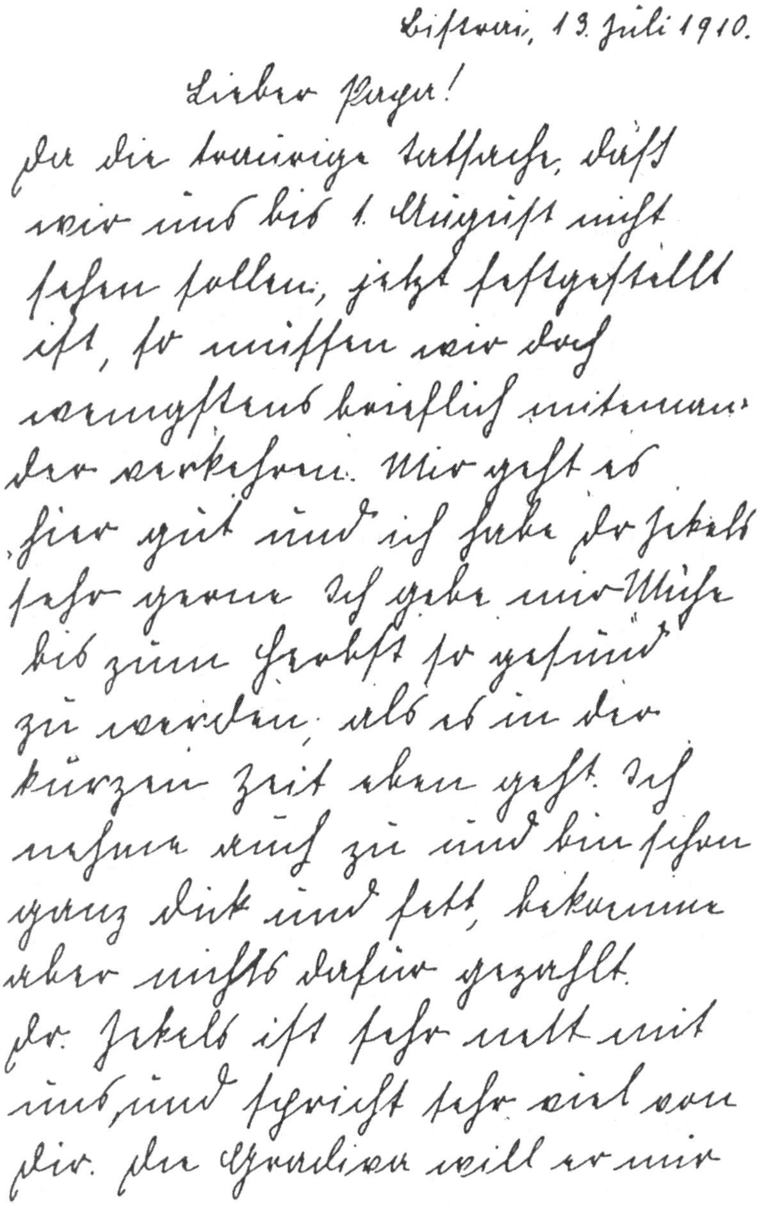

Bistrai, 13. Juli 1910.
Lieber Papa!
Da die traurige Tatsache, daß
wir uns bis 1. August nicht
sehen sollen, jetzt festgestellt
ist, so müssen wir doch
wenigstens brieflich miteinan-
der verkehren. Mir geht es
hier gut und ich habe Dr. Jekels
sehr gerne. Ich gebe mir Mühe
bis zum Herbst so gesund
zu werden, als es in der
kurzen Zeit eben geht. Ich
nehme auch zu und bin schon
ganz dick und fett, bekomme
aber nichts dafür gezahlt.
Dr. Jekels ist sehr nett mit
uns, und spricht sehr viel von
Dir. Die Gradiva will er mir

I Anna's letter of 13 July 1910; page 1 of Anna's first surviving correspondence to her father

1 In former Austria-Silesia, now Poland (near Bielitz [Bielsko], on the border with Galicia), where Jekels (see note 3) had owned and directed a sanatorium since 1897; 'it was once customary to spend vacations in the private sanatoriums of physician friends' ⟨Peters, p. 12; see also Freud/Bernays, letters 146 Mi–152 Mi⟩.

2 'We sent an advanced guard, consisting of an aunt and two trifles [Sophie and Anna], to Dr Jekels in Bistrai [on 1 July] and the two elders then [on 14 July] wanted to follow by 1 August and send the boys off to adventures in the meantime. But we found out that Bistrai doesn't have enough room, and it's not suitable in any other way either. The boys, except for Martin, were unable to find lodging and so I called it off with Jekels and am at a loss as to what to do' ⟨Freud/Ferenczi I, 144 F, 3 July 1910, p. 184; also Freud/Jung, 194 F, 26 May 1910, p. 322 and note 4 (in this somewhat discrepant description)⟩. Young-Bruehl (p. 55), by contrast, suggests that the constant tensions between Sophie and Anna were the reason why the family did not take their holidays together that year. Minna remained in Bistrai with the two girls until 28 July and then travelled with them to Hamburg, where they arrived on Friday 29 July, and replaced Martha, who was looking after her sick mother ⟨Freud/Bernays, letters 150 Mi–161 Mi⟩. Martha continued with the children to Noordwijk. Freud had spent the first two weeks of the holiday in the Netherlands with the two younger boys: 'My address from the 17th until the end of July is Hotel Wittelbrug, The Hague. I am going with Oli and Ernst, my wife will stay here [in Vienna] then go to Hamburg. On August 1 there will be a big reunion in Hamburg' ⟨Freud/Ferenczi I, 146 F, 10 July 1910, p. 188⟩. For Martha's mother's condition, see 8 AF, note 2; also Freud/Jung, 190 F, 2 May 1910, p. 315.

3 Ludwig Jekels (1867–1954), doctor of medicine, neurologist and psychiatrist. He had attended the Salzburg Congress in 1908 as a guest and had then sat in at several meetings of the Vienna Wednesday Society since November 1909, becoming a member of the Society in April 1910. 'It is principally due to L. Jekels that psychoanalysis has been introduced to Polish scientific and literary circles' ⟨Freud 1914*d*, p. 33⟩. After the First World War he settled in Vienna and was highly regarded in the Society. He started working at the Psychoanalytic Training Institute in 1923; later he helped for a time in Stockholm to introduce psychoanalysis to Sweden. He remained friendly with Freud and his family throughout his life. 'Without doubt Dr Jekels is of particular merit, and what he has done for the children and for myself cannot be compensated with money' ⟨Minna to Freud in: Freud/Bernays, letter 154 Mi⟩. See also the copy of a letter of thanks in 1920 from Freud and Martha to Jekels, 'one of Freud's oldest students' ⟨*Sigmund Freud-Haus*, p. 44, exhibit 223⟩. In later years Jekels was also one of Freud's tarock partners ⟨Jones III, p. 185⟩. In 1938 he emigrated via Australia to the USA, where he had a psychiatric practice in New York ⟨*Minutes II*, pp. 498f. and elsewhere; Sterba, p. 137f.; Mühlleitner, p. 170f.⟩.

4 'Anna has put on 80 dg again in the last week, which doesn't stop her being a little meshuggene. The doctor adores her and thinks that she shouldn't be sent back to Vienna and the school but doesn't have any sensible advice to give' ⟨Minna to Freud in: Freud/Bernays, letter 147 Mi⟩ (see also Introduction, p. 4). In the autumn Anna went back to school after all (see 11 AF/EF and 12 AF).

5 *Delusions and Dreams in Jensen's Gradiva* (Freud 1907*a*).
6 Walter Zweig (1872–1953), doctor of medicine, Privatdozent (lecturer) in gastrointestinal diseases in Vienna; from 1932, extraordinary professor ⟨Fischer I. [1932–3]; Engelhardt [2002]⟩. In a letter to Abraham on 13 May 1914, Freud described him jokingly as his 'personal physician' Freud/Abraham, p. 238 and note⟩. Freud suffered repeatedly from gastrointestinal complaints (see this correspondence) ⟨e.g., Freud/Ferenczi III, 1187 F; Jones III, p. 172f.⟩.
7 Gay (p. 430) incorrectly reads this as 'Harz'.
8 This wish was fulfilled three years later; see 32 AF, also note 3 in the following letter.
9 'The doctor is untiringly charming and attentive and spoils the children terribly. Anna has fulfilled at least one of her dreams today: she walks barefoot, always sits in the box seat when we travel and rolls hoops along the road – in other words, back to nature!' ⟨Minna to Freud in: Freud/Bernays, letter 146 Mi⟩. Anna later recalls this 'barefoot, unconstrained childhood self' in a poem called *Dreams*, extracts of which are quoted by Young-Bruehl (p. 82f., 95). See also 173 AF, note 2.
10 '. . . the nervous ones . . . who are incidentally no more abhorrent to anyone than to the doctor himself; he curses every arrival' ⟨Minna to Freud, ibid.⟩.
11 Emmeline [Elga] Bernays, née Philipp (1830–1910); she died the same year on 27 October ⟨Stammbaum Lange: Bernays Family, 'Genealogical Tree IIa', p. 6⟩. See details in Appendix by Albrecht Hirschmüller in Freud/Bernays.
12 Yes; cf. note 2: 'The little ones . . . thrived so well in Bistrai but the days here have made them quite miserable' ⟨Minna to Freud in: Freud/Bernays, letter 153 Mi⟩.
13 'I am writing to you . . . after we three had drawn the other members of the family to us' ⟨Freud/Ferenczi I, 153 F, 2 August 1910, p. 195⟩. For details of the visit and events in the Netherlands, see Freud/Ferenczi I, 157 F–167 Fer, and Freud 2002*b*, pp. 321–32.

7 AF[1]

[Bistrai, 25 July 1910][2]

I also want[3] to go riding!!!![4]
and play tarock![5]
Anna

1 This and the next letter were not in the correspondence package. I should like to thank Marion Palmedo, New York, for finding them in the LoC SF in the correspondence between Freud and Minna Bernays. I thank Albrecht Hirschmüller, publisher of this correspondence, for providing copies of the texts.
2 This is not a separate letter by Anna but an addition to a letter from Minna Bernays to Freud ⟨Freud/Bernays, letter 149 Mi⟩. It is included here because it relates closely to other items in this correspondence.
3 This phrase ('möchte auch') appears to be a family idiom (see 221 AF). Anna's sister Sophie quotes it, for example, with meaningful exclamation marks on a

slip of paper (undated) to Freud: 'Dear Papa, I also want to go riding! (and swim).' (See also Introduction, p. 4.) In her book *The Ego and the Mechanisms of Defence*, Anna describes a case study and the various wishes of the patient, saying: 'Her everlasting cry of "Me too!" was a nuisance to her elders' ⟨1936, in *Writings II*, p. 124⟩.

4 For comments about riding, see 8 AF, 10 SF, 12 AF, also 79 AF. See also note 4 to Minna's letter to Freud (149 Mi) in Freud/Bernays.

5 Tarock is a skat-like card game that Freud played regularly with friends on Saturday evenings: 'He was playing this in the nineties, and probably earlier; later on it became an institution. . . . The initiator was Professor Königstein . . . and many years later Freud's own children replaced his friends' ⟨Jones I, p. 362⟩. See also, e.g., 11 AF/EF, 15 AF, also 85 SF and note 4. 'It is interesting to note that Freud's tarock partners were not psychoanalysts; evidently this was one domain in which he temporarily separated himself from "the Cause"' ⟨Haynal, p. xxi⟩. See also note 4 to Minna's letter to Freud (149 Mi) in Freud/Bernays.

8 AF[1]

Hotel-Pension 'Noordzee'
W. Van Beelen
Noordwijk aan Zee[2]

Professor
Dr Sigm. Freud
ferma imposta
Roma[3]

4 September1910
[Post stamp: 'Noord 5.9.10']
[Receipt stamp: 'Roma (Centro) 8.9.10']

Dear Papa! Mama is not writing today because she's packing.[4] There is nothing special to report. I have been riding twice and find it much nicer than swimming and shovelling combined. Math wrote to ask for your address. Ernst and I are travelling the day after tomorrow in the evening. The sea today is quite rough, just a few metres from the dunes. It's a pity you can't see it. We couldn't go out on to the terrace at all today. There's a terrible storm. I am now fairly sensible.

Greetings to you and Dr Ferenczi.[5]
Anna
[In Martha's handwriting]
10,000 greetings from Mama
It's wild! The sea, I mean.

1 See 7 AF, note 1; postcard with printed sender.

2 The family had been spending part of their summer holidays here since 1 August (see 6 AF, note 2) ⟨Freud/Ferenczi I, 153 F⟩. Originally they had wanted to stay

in Klobenstein [Collalbo] (Freud/Ferenczi I, 67 F), but the situation changed in May: 'The poor health of our grandmother (aged 80) makes it necessary to reduce the distance between her and us, so we have decided in favour of a beach resort in Holland within a day's journey of Hamburg' ⟨Freud/Jung, 190 F, 2 May 1910, p. 315; Freud/Ferenczi I, 132 F⟩.

3 Freud had travelled in the meantime to Italy with Ferenczi. After several attempts to find a reasonably priced ship passage, they ultimately took the train via Paris and Rome to Sicily. ⟨For further details of the planning, see Freud/Ferenczi I, 147 Fer–167 Fer; also Jones II, p. 91; Tögel [2002], pp. 333–5; Freud 2002*b*, pp. 336–62.⟩

4 The family returned again until 13 September to Hotel Wittebrug in The Hague; however, Ernst and Anna travelled on to Vienna (see 9 EF/AF, 11 AF/EF; also Jones II, p. 90).

5 Sándor Ferenczi (1873–1933), doctor of medicine, Hungarian neurologist, psychiatrist and psychoanalyst with a practice as a general practitioner and neuropsychiatrist, and expert for the court in Budapest. Apart from his medical activities, Ferenczi had a wide variety of cultural interests and personal contacts with Budapest intellectuals. He had an extremely close but also conflictual relationship with Freud, which is reflected in their copious correspondence. Freud himself described it as a 'an intimate community of life, feeling and interest' ⟨Freud/Ferenczi III, 1241 F, 11 January 1933, p. 446⟩. Ferenczi was co-founder (and president in 1918) of the International Psychoanalytical Association and presented the draft statutes at the second IPA meeting on 30–31 March 1910 in Nuremberg ⟨Ferenczi [1910], see Freud/Ferenczi I, 114 Fer, 16 February 1910, p. 141; Rank [1910–11], p. 741f, [1911], p. 131; Jones II, p. 76f.⟩. He created the Hungarian Psychiatric Society in 1913 ⟨*IZ*, vol. 1 [1913], p. 617⟩. He was also one of the initiators of the 'Secret Committee'. See also Freud's congratulations to Ferenczi on his fiftieth birthday (1923i), his obituary (1933c), Federn P. [1933] and Barlint [1970]; also this correspondence, particularly 287 SF.

9 EF/AF[1]

Professor
Sigmund Freud
Palermo
ferma in posta

[Post stamp: Berlin-Oesterr. [rest illegible] Bahnpost
Train 3. 7 September 1910]

[Printed: Greetings from the dining car]

Where we are sitting comfortably and eating.
Ernst & Anna

1 Colour picture postcard: 'Greetings from the dining car'; on the top right is a picture of a dining car, entitled 'Deutscher Eisenbahn-Speisewagen-Betrieb G. Kromrey & Söhne', left of the picture 'Wien, Hof-Museum'. Apart from Anna's signature, everything is written in Ernst Freud's handwriting (in pencil).

10 SF[1]

Frl Anna Freud
c/o Hollitscher[2]
Vienna
IX Türkenstrasse 29
Austria

Palermo, 10 September 1910

Dear Anna,
Here is a sample of our surroundings. I'll look for a horse[3] for you.
Affectionately,
Papa

1 Colour picture postcard: 'Palermo – Monte Pellegrino'.
2 See 5 MF/SF, note 4. As the following letters show, Anna stayed frequently with Mathilde until the return of the rest of the family on 16 September: 'Annerl has been with us for two days. I find her quite pretty; she looks well and has the best intentions – she is a poor thing and torments herself terribly with everything' ⟨Mathilde to Freud, 9 September 1910, LoC SF, Cont. 11⟩. At the start of the year, Mathilde had reported to her adolescent friend: 'Annerl is still a little anaemic and out of sorts but will soon turn out to be a big girl' ⟨Gödde [2003], p. 347⟩.
3 See 7 AF and note 4.

11 AF/EF

Vienna, 11 September 1910

Dear Papa,
I hope you receive this letter, but I have no idea where you will be later and can therefore only write to Palermo.

Ernst and I arrived safely in Vienna. The journey was very pleasant. We took a sleeping car and were frequently in the dining car and spent a lot of money. Ernst had a temperature before we left and is still not quite well here. (None of us has cholera yet.[1]) Lampl met us at the station. We are now leading a bohemian life; I usually eat at Mathilde's, Ernst also quite often at the Wintersteins.[2] I have already been back to school; I have a small examination in October because I don't have my grades.[3] It starts properly the day after tomorrow. I think I have been quite sensible, at least I am trying to be. The weather is incredibly bad and it has been raining continuously since yesterday; I hope not where you are. I spend almost the entire day at Mathilde's; it's very lonely in the apartment. I don't yet know when Mama will be coming.[4] Aunt Pauli[5] is already in Vienna, Grandma[6] not yet. Rosi[7] continues to outgrow me.

I played tarock yesterday evening with Ernst and Robert and did not return until after the gate had been locked. Robert had just lost the lock-out money[8] for both of us. Math tells lots of amusing stories about Lavarone. It must have been really nice.[9] At the moment, however, it is hard to imagine in Vienna that the sun exists. By the time you receive this letter, Papa, I will already be in school and hope that everything will be all right.

Greetings and a kiss,
Anna

[On the back of the last sheet in Ernst's handwriting]

Dear Papa,
Here I am back in Vienna; it's raining, I eat at other people's and go to school, where practically all of my old teachers have been struck down, which is really quite sad. I am also beginning to recover from the summer and am already looking forward to the next sunnier one.

Greetings, also to Dr Ferenzy,[10]
Ernst

1 'Seven cases of cholera were reported in Vienna from 23 August to 17 September, of which two were fatal' ⟨*Münchener medizinische Wochenschrift*, vol. 57/2 (Jul–Dec) 1910, p. 2167⟩. The cholera pandemic, which broke out after the turn of the century (1902–23), reached Europe from Asia in 1910. The first occurrence in Vienna was reported in August. 'There is considerable agitation within the authorities (but fortunately not in the public) as a result of these incidents. A major conference took place in the city hall attended by delegates from the Ministry of the Interior, the Lower Austrian governor's office, the police, municipal health department, etc. All of the imperial police district health officers have been summoned for consultation ⟨ibid., p. 1864⟩. See also 12 AF and note 1, 13 SF and notes 4 and 5.

2 It is unlikely that the family of Baron Alfred von Winterstein, who joined the Vienna Psychoanalytic Society on 26 October 1910, is meant here. At all events, there is no indication in his memoirs that there was such a close family relationship with the Freuds ⟨Winterstein, unpublished⟩.

3 Probably because of the absence from school during the winter spa cure in 1909–10; see 5 MF/SF and note 1; also 6 AF, note 4.

4 Martha remained with Oliver and Sophie in The Hague until 13 September ⟨Martha's PS to a letter from Oliver, 10 September, to Freud in Palermo; LoC SF, Cont. 11⟩. They were expected back after a stopover in Berlin on 16 September (Freud 1960*a*, p. 290).

5 Freud's sister Pauline ('Pauli/Paula') Regine (1864–*c.* 1942). After the death of her husband, Valentin Winternitz (1859–1900), with whom she had lived in New York, she returned to Europe on 1 July 1900 with her daughter Rose, who was four and a half at the time ⟨Freud 1985*c*, pp. 410, 414, 417, 421; Stammbaum Lange: Freud Family, 'Genealogical Tree', p. IV; for the year of death, see Tögel [1990] and [2004*b*], pp. 42–5 and notes 18–24⟩.

6 Freud's mother, Amalie Freud, née Nathansohn (1835–1930) ⟨Stammbaum Lange: Freud Family, 'Genealogical Tree', p. II⟩; she frequently spent the summer months in Bad Ischl (see this correspondence). After the war, she

also often spent the winter there ⟨Freud/Sam, 27 October, 24 November 1910; 22 July, 15 October 1920⟩.

7 Rose ('Rosi') Beatrice Winternitz (1896–1969), daughter of Freud's sister Pauline ⟨Stammbaum Lange: Freud Family, 'Genealogical Tree', p. IV⟩.

8 'Sperrgeld': money paid to the porter for opening the street door after it had been locked. ⟨Thanks to Ernst Federn, Vienna, for this information.⟩

9 Mathilde had been recovering in the summer from a further abdominal operation in Lavarone in the south of Tyrol ⟨Gödde, [2003], p. 139f., with extracts from hitherto unpublished letters from Mathilde to her father, 15–16 July and 22 September 1910⟩. The Freuds had often spent their holidays there in the past (1900, 1906, 1907) and had particularly enjoyed the region ⟨Freud 1985*c*, letter 253; 2002*b*, pp. 126–8; Freud/Jung, 201 F; Freud M. [1999], pp. 111–35⟩. See also 200 SF, note 4.

10 Written that way. The sons, particularly Martin, had made friends with Ferenczi (Freud M. [1999], p. 109), fulfilling Freud's wish: 'Now and then you will take a meal with us or climb a mountain with my boys' ⟨Freud/Ferenczi I, 10 F (Dietfeldhof), 10 May 1908, p. 11; see also ibid., 12 F and 13 Fer⟩.

12 AF

Vienna, [Tuesday] 13 September 1910

Dear Papa,

My school started today. But we just filled out attendance forms and received the timetable, and it's only from tomorrow that I will have four hours of classes. I am leading a bohemian existence at the moment. I usually eat at Mathilde's; today I was at Aunt Pauli's and have been invited tomorrow to the Wintersteins; I am going this evening with Ernst to Lampl's. Sometimes I am at home in between, where I have eight or nine rooms at my disposal. I get on very well with Ernst; we only see each other occasionally. I have had news several times from Mama; everyone should be returning at the end of the week. There is already a huge pile of mail for you; I don't know how you'll get around to reading it all. Lots of acquaintances are also asking after you, and everyone is surprised that you are suddenly in Palermo. Have you read that the cholera has already reached Naples? Will you be giving it a wide berth?[1] I have completely given up riding and swimming here and go, like other normal people, on foot. I like going to Mathilde's; she doesn't go out very much and it is hugely comfortable. I can talk to her in a way that I can't with anyone else.[2] The apartment is fine and is beginning to turn itself the right way round again. We are getting a very nice bathroom with a gas stove, and the kitchen has been enlarged.[3] I haven't seen Uncle Alexander or Sopherl at all.[4] Grandma is still in Ischl.[5] She is apparently very well. I hope that Dr Ferenczi is taking sufficient care of you and that you haven't upset your stomach.[6] Tomorrow is your wedding anniversary;[7] isn't that a good excuse to send you an extra-large number of greetings and kisses?[8] I do so and remain as always,

Your Anna

And will you please write to me?

1 'We won't be affected by the cholera either here or elsewhere later,' wrote Freud to Martha from Florence on 4 September; two days after Anna's letter he wrote from Palermo: 'We read here for the first time about rumours of cholera in Naples. . . . In Sicily there has been no sign to date, in other words less than in Vienna or in Budapest' ⟨2002*b*, pp. 337, 353⟩. (See also Mathilde's letter to her father of 22 September 1910, quoted in Gödde [2003], p. 140.) Since the occurrence of the disease in Europe, the specialist journals reported regularly and in detail about its progress. In particular, the *Münchener medizinische Wochenschrift* ran a column entitled 'Daily Notes' in which it provided meticulous reports from all regions, states and cities with precise figures and sometimes even individual cases.

2 'Mathilde today still remains the good, wise elder daughter, always ready to help,' is how Lou Andreas-Salomé characterized Freud's eldest daughter, recalling a visit to the Freuds ⟨journal entry by Lou Andreas-Salomé, quoted by Ernst Pfeiffer, note 142 in: Freud/Andreas-Salomé, p. 230⟩ (see ill. 4). See also 26 AF and note 4.

3 'In 1917, 92 per cent of the apartments in Vienna still had no WC of their own and 95 per cent had no running water' ⟨Weissensteiner, p. 121⟩. See also 132 AF. The bathroom was to return later as a metaphor: 'I discover with amazement that I also have something akin to narcissism . . . I don't remember it from earlier. I think it needs a bathroom of its own to survive' ⟨Anna/Eva, spring [summer?] 1925, letter 1, p. 109⟩.

4 Freud's brother Alexander [Gottfried Ephraim] (1866–1943), specialist and senior court expert of the Austrian monarchy for freight, transport and tariff matters, extraordinary professor at the Export Academy in Vienna, since 1904 sole proprietor of the Allgemeiner Tarif-Anzeiger publishing company, which issued a journal of the same name. Through his teaching and publications on his specialization (today it would be called logistics), and the corresponding in-depth geographical, linguistic, product and legal knowledge, he was highly appreciated and in great demand in European specialist circles. He received several honours including the title in 1902 of 'Kaiserlicher Rat' (imperial councillor). He married Sophie Sabine, née Schreiber (1878–1970), on 7 February 1909, and they had one son, Harry (see 119 SF and note 4) ⟨Stammbaum Lange: Freud Family, 'Genealogical Tree', p. IV; Kursidem, unpublished; letterhead Allgemeiner Tarif-Anzeiger, Vienna I, Handelskammer-Palais, Biberstr. 16 (FM London); Leupold-Löwenthal [1988]⟩. See also Freud 1985*c*, letter 195 and note 1. For details of Alexander's professorship, see Example 2 of Misreadings in Freud's *The Psychopathology of Everyday Life* (1901*b*, pp. 108f.).

5 Bad Ischl, the cultural and geographical centre of the Salzkammergut. Emperor Franz Josef visited it regularly from 1849, and after 1875 the imperial couple resided there for many years in summer, attracting 'many celebrities, aristocrats, statesmen and artists'. Ischl was designated a spa resort in 1920 ⟨'Kleine Historiche Städte', 'Bad Ischl', p. 8⟩.

6 'The food since Genoa magnificent, my stomach very grateful for it. My intestines are not getting better' ⟨Freud to Martha, 4 September 1910, 2002*b*, p. 338⟩.

7 14 September 1886, Hamburg.

8 Full stop rather than question mark in the original.

13 SF

Syracuse, 18 September 1910

My dear Anna,
Thank you most sincerely for your dear letter, which arrived today, from the time of your solitude, which by today is already over.

It is hardly worth replying now that everything has changed so radically but I reproach myself nevertheless for not having written a longer letter to you. But the travel, the many new things and difficulties should be sufficient excuse. Perhaps I had a bad conscience as well for having been unable to keep my rash promise of bringing you something special. You yourself, with all your skill at surprising us with your wishes,[1] would find it difficult – not even[2] in the city of Palermo – to find something to bring back. The products of Sicily that would be of interest to us are sulphur, papyrus and antiques. I possess samples of all three but unfortunately, as you see, you cannot have any of them.[3] I will make it up to you in Vienna. After I have indulged myself so much I would also like to give you a treat.

Sicily was and is wonderful, but the sirocco has been blowing here for the last two days and is hard to put up with. It spoils one's enjoyment and shatters the illusion of being in a special kind of paradise. News of the cholera in Naples is also contradictory; no one knows what kind of travel problems it will cause[4] and so it is possible that this lovely trip will end earlier than we intended.[5]

I am pleased to hear that you can talk with Mathilde; she is really the right person for you and is also very fond of you. You should also be magnanimous and try to get on better with your other sister,[6] otherwise you will end up like two of your aunts,[7] who could never get along as children either and as a punishment have not been apart from one another for many long years, since love and hate are not so different from one another.

I am also very curious to see how the changes at home are getting on. Tell Mama that if the cloth on my desk is too dirty, she should have Spitz replace it quickly *before* my arrival[8] and see that the desk itself is in order. Karlsbader[9] should also be ready so that I can continue the suspended cure.

As you can see, my thoughts are more towards home than with Archimedes, who has a monument to him below my window next to Arethusa.[10]

Greetings to you and all of the others.
Affectionately,
Papa

1 See 5 MF/SF and note 10.
2 As written – possibly 'even' is meant.
3 'Shopping is the only thing that is very difficult. There is not much that is different from anywhere else and is asking to be taken home – pack me now [in English] – as a souvenir,' wrote Freud to Martha on 15 September. 'Robert is

the only one who will get the sulphur he asked for – his wish is practical and appropriate to the place' ⟨2002*b*, p. 352f.⟩.

4 The Austrian Ministry of the Interior sent a decree to all provincial political authorities regarding 'precautions to prevent the infiltration of cholera from Italy' ⟨*Wiener medizinische Wochenschrift*, vol. 60 (1910), col. 2183⟩.

5 'I returned rather hurriedly yesterday from Syracuse–Palermo–Rome to avoid the cholera in Naples, hence the delay; normally I answer your letters more promptly' ⟨Freud to Oskar Pfister, 27 September 1910, 1963*a*, p. 44⟩.

6 'For Anna Freud, Sophie was the most difficult sibling, the focus of her jealousy – and Sophie awarded this honour to her little sister too. . . . The two youngest Freuds developed their version of a common sisterly division of territories: "beauty" and "brains". . . . Elsa Reiss . . . was engaged as a private tutor . . . But this plan, though it provided a supplement to the boring schooling, also aggravated the younger Freud sisters' rivalry, for Sophie was included in the tutoring arrangement. Anna chafed at the slow pace of the lessons Fräulein Reiss designed for them both, and Sophie resented yielding to her sister any share of the tutor's attention' ⟨Young-Bruehl, pp. 45f., 48, further details pp. 42–4, 46⟩. While Young-Bruehl emphasizes the rivalry between the two girls, Peters highlights another aspect of their relationship; see 25 SF and note 4.

7 The two sisters of Freud being referred cannot be identified; Tögel ([2002], p. 359, note 39) suspects Anna, married name Bernays, and Paula Winternitz.

8 Presumably Freud's joiner; see, e.g., Freud to Martha, 23 September 1908; to the family 24 September 1909 ⟨2002*b*, pp. 267, 315⟩.

9 Karlsbader mineral water with Glauber's salt. Freud continued to drink it in later years for his gastrointestinal problems; see, e.g., 126 SF, 184 SF ⟨also Lampl to Ernst Freud, 18 January 1921, FM London, Box 31 B⟩.

10 Freud and Ferenczi lived in the old town (on the island Ortygia): 'One should live . . . in the city centre, if possible not too far from Arethusa's spring on the waterside promenade with a view of the port'; the 'source of the nymph Arethusa, which rises on the west bank of the city close to the sea surrounded by a semicircular wall' ⟨Peterich [1963], p. 668⟩. See also Freud to the family, 18 September (2002b, p. 356). Archimedes (c.285–212 BC), the most important Greek mathematician and physicist, engineer and inventor, who was killed when the Romans conquered Syracuse. See Tögel [2002], p. 359, note 41, on the same letter.

1911

14 AF

A. F.[1]

[Oberbozen?,[2]] 15 July 1911

Dear Papa,
I don't know if you will still recognize me when you come to us because I have got very tanned, and yesterday an old gentleman asked Mama why I came to the countryside at all when I already looked so good. I do a lot of walking here, in contrast to Vienna, and go on very long walks alone[3] or with Mama. In general Mama and I, the two healthy ones, like it a lot here, Aunt and Sophie less so.[4] We went yesterday to two wonderful viewpoints from where we could see down as far as Gries.[5] Sophie found the first cep, which we will eat today for lunch.[6] I think you will like it here a lot, because you don't have to go very far to find delightful spots; just around the house it's not very pretty,[7] which doesn't please Aunt. I look forward to your arrival, and I plan to take you to all the nice places, because I know my way around a little now. I think you will also have much more peace and quiet to write here than in Karlsbad;[8] the train[9] runs only once an hour and there are no carriages or automobiles.[10]

Oli sent us a telegram today saying that he will be coming tomorrow. We have received a letter and card from Ernst[11] and Martin.[12] Ernst appears to have employed Willi[13] as his personal private secretary. We received your letter of today and found the matter of the suit quite astonishing.[14] We are always very happy to receive your letters. Just think, yesterday night I had a frightful dream about the first day of school in the autumn. I hope that it doesn't come true for a long time, because I like it enormously here and don't want to leave for a long time yet.

Dear Papa, no one has called me 'Black Devil' for so long and I miss it. I look forward to your arrival.

Anna

1 Preprinted initials.

2 It is not possible to determine whether this and the next letter were written in Oberbozen [Soprabolzano] or in Klobenstein [Collalbo]. Both are on the Ritten [Renon], a porphyry high plateau (approx. 1,000–1,300 metres) north of Bolzano, known as a summer holiday resort with delightful views of the Alps. Originally rooms were rented in Oberbozen at Gasthof Hofer (now Hotel Post Victoria), but it was necessary to move afterwards to Klobenstein for lack of space ⟨Freud/Ferenczi I, 235 F, 237 F; Freud/Jung, 266 F⟩. Anna's description of her activities and the general situation and location of the house would suggest that both letters were written in Oberbozen (see explanations in notes on this and the next letter); a picture postcard from Freud to Sophie on 18 July 1911 was also addressed to Gasthof Hofer. ⟨I should like to thank the inhabitants and the individuals mentioned in the Acknowledgements for personal information in my research on the Ritten.⟩

3 See 15 AF and note 9.

4 Minna Bernays was often poorly (see, e.g., 28 SF, 42 SF and note 14, 95 SF and note 5, 294 SF and note 2, text after 295 SF, 297 SF and note 19). ⟨Details of Minna's illnesses can be found in the introduction by Albrecht Hirschmüller to Freud/Bernays, p. 20.⟩ Sophie was also frequently sick and for that reason spent several weeks in April and May with her mother in Karlsbad [Karlovy Vary] ⟨Freud/Ferenczi I, 211 F, 221 F; Freud/Jung, 255 F; Peters, p. 16; Young-Bruehl, p. 42⟩. (The statement in Jones II, p. 101, that Freud 'had the company of his daughter Sophie' in Karlsbad in *July* is incorrect. ⟨Freud to Sophie, 18 July 1911⟩.)

5 A community on the northern outskirts of Bolzano, which was independent at the time. One of the viewpoints from where it is still possible today to see Gries was almost certainly Merltennen, which can be reached in fifteen minutes on foot from the small village of Maria Himmelfahrt [Maria Assunta] (approx. 1.5 km north-west of Soprabolzano). The second point could have been the Maria Himmelfahrt Church or the small gloriette on the southern outskirts of the village belonging to the Bolzano family Menz (now very overgrown), or perhaps – above the Menz memorial – the 'linden-lined ramp . . . from where one can look down, as if from a cockpit, into Eisacktal [Valle Isarco] and the jagged peaks' of the Dolomites ⟨Hosp, p. 41⟩.

6 '. . . once we had 82 ceps; we ate some of them and some will be dried for Vienna' ⟨Anna/Lou, letter 37, 12 August 1922, p. 65⟩.

7 The neighbouring Hofer farm, which belonged to the guesthouse at the time, had just been taken over and was in a dilapidated state; the barn, cattle trough and ancillary buildings were being renovated, which might have detracted from the 'beauty' of the surrounding area. ⟨I should like in particular to thank Karl Ramoser, son of Josef Ramoser, Soprabolzano, who owned the farm at the time, for his detailed description and insight into his *Chronik Hofer Hof* [*c.* 1946].⟩

8 'Karlsbad, the largest and oldest of the three [the two other spas in Egerland (Chebsko) being Franzensbad (Františkovy Lázně) and Marienbad (Mariánské Lázně)], has developed into a spa specializing in gallbladder, gastrointestinal and metabolic diseases. Its outstanding success in these areas is world-renowned and it was one of the leading spas.' Many of the cures involved drinking the waters ⟨Zörkendörfer, p. 162⟩. (For the transformation of the Bohemian spas and the planning and conservation problems of today, see Joas.) Freud stayed there at Haus Columbus from 9 to 30 July for treatment of the 'colitis earned in New York' ⟨Freud/Jones, letter 64, 9 August 1911, p. 113; Freud/Jung, 255 F; Freud/Ferenczi I, 232 F⟩. 'Dr van Emden . . . and his wife

are going to Karlsbad, where I will dedicate an hour to him on an afternoon walk' ⟨Freud/Ferenczi, ibid., p. 294⟩. See 18 SF/MF and note 6.

9 The Rittener Bahn, which ran from 1907 on from Bozen via Maria Himmelfahrt and Oberbozen to Klobenstein ⟨*Ritten*, pp. 21–3; Armbruster, pp. 106–10⟩. In Soprabolzano, the track runs right next to the wall of the guesthouse and stops a few metres further on. In Klobenstein, the tracks and station are so far from the hotel that they are not a nuisance.

10 Since 1959–71, a wide road has wound its way up from Bolzano valley; the cog railway from Bolzano to Soprabolzano was replaced in 1966 by an aerial cableway; on the plateau, however, the narrow-gauge railway still runs from Maria Assunto to Collalbo. 'A ride in the wooden carriages takes passengers back to the "good old days" and is an experience in itself, which no tourist should miss' ⟨*Ritten*, p. 8f.⟩.

11 After completing his *Matura* (school-leaving examination), Ernst had been on a rest cure at the Cottage Sanatorium because of an ulcer or gastroduodenal fissure ⟨Freud/Ferenczi I, 216 F, 239 F; Freud/Jung, 255 F⟩. He was admitted to hospital again in August 1917 for a duodenal ulcer ⟨Freud/Ferenczi II, 699 F⟩. See 76 SF and note 12, also 87 SF and notes 6 and 7.

12 Martin was performing military service in Millstadt; he had had a serious skiing accident at the beginning of the year and had been convalescing ever since ⟨Freud M. [1999], pp. 175–7; Freud/Ferenczi I, 195 F, 199 F, 204 F, 207 F, 239 F; Freud/Jones, letter 49; Freud/Jung, 236 F⟩.

13 Possibly Willi Bardas, son of family friends, who is mentioned several times in Freud's 'Reisebriefe' (2002*b*, pp. 41, 46–8, 382; see also Freud's letter to Martha on 13 July 1911). He published in *Imago* and played a Beethoven piano sonata at the opening of the Berlin Psychoanalytic Institute ⟨thanks to Regine Lockot⟩. Ernst Freud wrote to his father from Berlin on 6 December 1924: 'I enclose an article about Willi Bardas, which I am sure will interest you. I see his wife quite often' ⟨FM London, Box 22; thanks to Gerhard Fichtner for verification of the name⟩.

14 'Ida sent my silk coat after the cleaners had got mixed up and I have sent the wrong one to Vienna' ⟨Freud to Martha, 13 July 1911⟩.

15 AF

A. F.[1]

[Oberbozen?,[2]] 19 July 1911

Dear Papa,
Thank you for your card,[3] which I received today. I continue to be very well and even went on a three-hour excursion the day before yesterday with Oli. We were also on the Mitterstillerwand,[4] which offers a wonderful view of the Dolomites; you must go there when you come. I'm a good walker and have the biggest appetite in the hotel, because I'm hungry at all times of the day. Ida[5] arrived here safely this morning. She is not staying at our hotel because there are no rooms vacant, but in the tourist residence just behind it.[6] She says that Ernst is in very good spirits and well looked after in the sanatorium. Frau Lampl,[7] who visited him, wrote the same thing to Mama. I recently went to see the earth pyramids[8] with Oli and

they are really splendid. Unfortunately, you can't get up close to them because they are on a steep slope on the other side of a gorge. Now that Oli is here I no longer need to go on walks on my own, and that is much more agreeable, although it is no problem here as the people are all very good-natured.[9] We have bought a map which shows all of the possible walks. I prefer, however, to walk first and then find out afterwards where we have been. We brought the chess set and tarock cards with us from Vienna. You will play tarock again with us this year, won't you? Otherwise I'll forget how to play, and that would be dangerous, because I was never very good in the first place. I am now reading a lot and trying occasionally to revise chemistry, but summer doesn't seem the right time to do it.

If you really want to bring me something from Karlsbad, Papa, I would prefer a little bowl for my desk rather than a piece of jewellery.[10] That would give me more pleasure because I sit at my desk more often than I put on jewellery. Besides, you can't see something on your own neck without making a considerable effort.

Kessler[11] must know you very well by now. For him you are probably what hotels call a regular. Mama wanted to write to him that he shouldn't sell you anything else, but I am very much against that idea.

I'm sorry to hear that you are not feeling well in Karlsbad. And how can that be right in a place that is meant to make you very healthy?[12] I have decided that I will never go to a spa and will achieve this by remaining healthy. Hopefully you will also be finished with Karlsbad very soon and will then come to us. When do you think that will be?[13] I am looking forward to seeing you again on the Ritten.[14]

Anna

1 Preprinted initials.

2 No place is indicated in this letter either. It is possible that the 'small move' that Freud mentions in his letter of 20 July 1911 to Ferenczi had taken place by this time ⟨Freud/Ferenczi I, 235 F, p. 296⟩. It is more likely, however, that the move did not take place until shortly before Freud's arrival on the Ritten, since Freud's letter of 25 July 1911 to Martha is still addressed to the 'Hoferhaus' and has no forwarding indication. It is also likely that Anna would have mentioned the move in one of her letters. Unfortunately, the successor hotel to Gasthof Hof no longer has any of the old records, and the entries in the Posthotel in Klobenstein at this time are incomplete; of Freud's friends and family members only Ferenczi (20 August–8 September), Martin (1–15 September), Ernst (8–15 September) and Mathilde (8–15 September) are mentioned. ⟨I would like to thank Anne-Marie and Theo Senn for allowing me to examine the guest books and Francesco Marchioro, Bolzano, who arranged access and helped me in my research.⟩

3 Missing.

4 Written thus in German. There is no official location with this name, but it can only be the steep cliff on the south side of the Mitterstiel Lake (approx. 1.5 km south of the Wolfsgruben [Costalavora] Lake), which offers a magnificent panorama.

5 Probably a servant; see 14 AF, note 14 ⟨Freud to Martha, 13 July, 23 July 1911⟩.
6 No information could be obtained about a 'tourist residence' in either Soprabolzano or Collalbo.
7 Hans Lampl's mother.
8 Columns of earth formed from glacial moraine with porphyry or granite 'hats'; they can be found at several sites on the Renon Mountain, the most well-known being Finsterbach Valley between Longomoso and Maria Assunta and in the Katzenbach Valley below Soprabolzano ⟨*Ritten*, pp. 16–18⟩.
9 'Don't let a child go into the forest alone,' wrote Freud to Martha in a letter of 13 July.
10 See 16 AF/OF.
11 An antique dealer in Karlsbad ⟨oral information from the Karlovy Vary city authorities⟩.
12 Anna is no doubt referring to letters to Martha in which he complains of 'a mixture of ill temper, fatigue and local discomfort': 'Irritability that is quite alien to me is appearing, inability to bear the small unpleasantnesses, complete absentmindedness; the emptiness associated with a life for the sake of a full stomach is becoming intolerable for me' ⟨12 July, 13 July 1911; Jones quotes slightly differently – perhaps retranslated – in vol. II, p. 101⟩. On 20 July, Freud wrote to Ferenczi: 'The first thing I am experiencing here – as in a cure – is the emergence of my bodily ailments and along with them a deep malaise with interesting symptoms that give me something to think about but don't reveal any solution' ⟨Freud/Ferenczi I, 235 F, p. 296⟩. These symptoms recurred in 1913 (see 60 AF, note 1). Ferenczi urged Freud several times to give up the Karlsbad cure ⟨ibid., 417 Fer and elsewhere⟩. Freud trusted the doctor's opinion, however, that Karlsbad is very suited for 'an old intestinal catarrh with working parts' ⟨Freud to Martha, 9 July 1911, FM London, and 12 July 1911, LoC SF⟩. He remained convinced even years later: 'The baths are announcing their effect by reviving the complaints against which they are taken, which is as it should be' ⟨Freud to Oscar Rie from Bad Gastein, 4 August 1921, in 1960*a*, p. 340⟩.
13 On 31 July 1911; beforehand the family had moved from Oberbozen to Hotel Post in Klobenstein ⟨Freud/Ferenczi I, 237 F; Freud/Jung, 266 F, 268 F⟩.
14 'Here on the Ritten it is divinely beautiful and comfortable. I have discovered in myself an inexhaustible desire to do nothing, except for the hour or two that I spend reading new things' ⟨Freud/Jung, 270 F, 1 September 1911, p. 442⟩. The 'new things' refer to his thoughts on religious psychology which he had already mentioned to Ferenczi: 'Perhaps the woods of Klobenstein will also see things come into being which I – or perhaps you – will later be able to present to the world'; and then a week later, 'I am totally totem and taboo' ⟨Freud/Ferenczi I, 239 F, 4 August 1911, 240 F, 11 August 1911, p. 300⟩. See also the editorial note regarding *The 'Uncanny'* (1919*h*) in note 7 to letter 54 F to Ludwig Binswanger on 2 May 1911 ⟨Freud/Binswanger, pp. 67f.⟩.

Silver Wedding Anniversary (1911)

On 14 September 1911 the entire family congregated at Hotel Post in Klobenstein to celebrate the silver wedding anniversary of Martha and Freud. A photograph shows them all at the table (Martha on Freud's left,

Anna on his right) ⟨*Freud-Bildbiographie*, p. 193, fig. 207⟩. A plaque on the outside wall of the house recalls the family event; in 2001 a second plaque was added by Francesco Marchioro, director of the Italian institute Imago – Research in Applied Psychoanalysis, Bolzano, who in 1993 established the 1st International Congress "Totem and Taboo" in commemoration of the scientific event and has since then organized further congresses in Collalbo and Bolzano as well as the Freud Weeks, biennial symposiums on the Ritten under the auspices of the Sigmund Freud Society in Vienna ⟨personal information⟩.

On 15 September the family departed; in Innsbruck Freud left the rest of the family and travelled alone to Zurich; see 16 AF/OF and note 2.

16 AF/OF

A. F.[1]

[Vienna] 18 September 1911

Dear Papa,
I hope that you have been well since we left you in Innsbruck[2] and that you are now comfortably installed in Zurich. Everything has gone well with us. We continued from Linz in first class, once again only because we were nice to the conductor. It was therefore very pleasant and Math was able to lie down full length for practically the whole journey.[3] We have made our apartment here very comfortable,[4] and the maids say that a lot of patients have already called for you. At the moment I am the housekeeper, more or less, but there are only three of us at table,[5] the paltry remnants of a once large family. Dr Rie[6] has already visited us today and took me with him in his car to the Cottage,[7] where I visited Aunt Rosa.[8] He said that all three children are going to school this year and that they are doing well. Aunt Rosa asks whether you will be visiting Hermann while you are in Switzerland. He writes that he is very happy and likes living there.[9] I visited my school today [Monday]; it starts properly on Wednesday, and practically everyone I know is already in Vienna. I am also beginning to get used to being back and everything is fine again. The agate bowl you bought for me is already on my desk.
Greetings and a kiss,
Anna

[Written by Oliver Freud on the back of the last sheet]:

Dear Papa,
There hasn't really been much happening here, and Anna has already told you most of it, so there is very little for me to add. There was apparently trouble yesterday at the demonstrations because of the price increases,[10] particularly in Ottakring,[11] where the army had to intervene. We were unaffected by it here.

We all think that it is good that you don't have to go to England;[12] the long journey would hardly be worth it for the few days.[13] Just in case, I am sending you details of the only decent train to Hanover[14] that I could find in the timetable.

With affectionate greetings,
Your son Oliver

1 Preprinted initials.
2 On the return journey from Klobenstein on 15 September Freud travelled from Innsbruck to Zurich and Küsnacht, where he visited Jung from 16 to 19 September 1911. He then continued to Weimar for the 3rd International Psychoanalytic Congress (21–22 September 1911) ⟨Freud/Jung, intermediate text, p. 443⟩. Martha 'stayed on in the mountains' (probably with Minna and Sophie, see note 5) ⟨Jones II, p. 102⟩.
3 Because of her frequently recurring discomfort following a botched appendectomy in 1905 (see 5 MF/SF and note 1).
4 During the absence of the Freud family in the summer the apartment usually underwent a thorough cleaning ⟨Freud to the family, 3 September 1912 [not in 2003*e*]⟩; see 171 AF.
5 Anna, Oliver and probably Ernst, who had spent a few days at Aussee with Mathilde after staying in the sanatorium and then travelled with her to Klobenstein, only then returning home together with the others (see 15 AF, note 2); Martin was back in Millstadt ⟨Freud/Ferenczi I, 239 F, 4 August 1911⟩.
6 Oscar (also 'Oskar') Rie (1863–1931), doctor of medicine, Viennese paediatrician, Freud family doctor and close friend of Freud, formerly Freud's assistant at the Kassowitz Institute; he wrote with Freud *Klinische Studie über die halbseitige Cerebrallähmung der Kinder* (Clinical Study of Infantile Cerebral Paralysis) (1891*a*). Rie was also one of his tarock partners ⟨1960*a*, p. 341⟩. He became a member of the Vienna Wednesday Society on 7 October 1908 (*Minutes II*). His wife Melanie, née Bondy, a sister of Ida Fleiss, was a painter and friend of Martha Freud ⟨Young-Bruehl, p. 479, note 17⟩. She had two daughters, Margarete and Marianne, who were friends with Anna, and a son, Norbert. 'Forty-five years ago, when as a newly married man (1886) I announced the opening of my office for the treatment of the nervous disorders of children, he [Oscar Rie] came to me first as an intern and then as an assistant. Afterwards he became the physician of our children and our friend, with whom we shared everything for a generation and a half. One of his daughters, Marianne [Kris], became an analyst, as you know; the other married the analyst [Dr Hermann] Nunberg, so that the ties became possibly even closer,' wrote Freud on 18 September 1931, the day after Rie's death, to Marie Bonaparte ⟨quoted in Schur, p. 430⟩. See, for example, Freud to Wilhelm Fliess (7August 1901, in 1985*c*, p. 446), and to Rie (4 August 1921, in 1960*a*, pp. 340–1).
7 A villa district (18th district) on the outskirts of Vienna between the future districts of Währing and Döbling with lush parks and green spaces. It was established in the second half of the nineteenth century, according to suggestions by the Viennese architect Heinrich Ferstel, by the Wiener Cottage-Verein für Schichten des gehobenen Bürgertums [Vienna Cottage Association for

the Higher Bourgeoisie] ⟨Czeike [1984], ill. 342 and caption⟩. See 126 SF and note 15.

8 Freud's sister Regina Debora ('Rosa') (1860–*c.*1943), widowed Graf, whom Freud had earlier been particularly fond of ⟨Freud 1895*c*, letter 240; 2003*l*; Fichtner [2003]; Jones I, p. 11, 369; Jones II, p. 215; for year of death, see Tögel [1990], which differs from Stammbaum Lange, Freud Family, 'Genealogical Tree', p. IV, and Tögel [2004*b*], note 18⟩. After the death of her husband, the lawyer Heinrich Graf (1852–1908), Rosa and her mother lived at Karl-Ludwig-Strasse 40 in the Cottage district ⟨Stammbaum Lange, Freud Family, 'Genealogical Tree', p. IV; Jones II, p. 57; Freud/Andreas-Salomé, 12 January 1922, p. 111 and note 144, p. 231; picture postcard from the Freud family to Rosa, 14 September 1911, LoC SF, Cont. II⟩. See also Anna/Lou, letter 56, p. 99f.

9 Hermann Graf (1897–1917), son of Rosa and Heinrich Graf. He suffered particularly at the death of his father and his mother's resultant pain. Thanks to Freud's intervention (1977*j*) he had lived since summer 1911 in Switzerland in the family of Paul Häberlin, philosopher and teacher, who had an educational institute ⟨Freud/Abraham, 9 March 1909, p. 86; see also Tögel [1990], p. 1021⟩. Hermann is the nephew whose dream Freud cites in *The Interpretation of Dreams* as an example of a certain type of children's dream (1900*a*, pp. 130f.).

10 Bad harvests in the summer because of drought had led to increases in the price of food throughout Austria, which gave rise to unrest: '17 September – demonstrations at the price increases in front of Vienna city hall and subsequent clashes between demonstrators and the police and cavalry units in Bellariastrasse. It was only when the Deutschmeister arrived that order was restored. [. . .] In the afternoon there were serious clashes in front of the workers' home in Ottakring. One worker was killed with a bayonet and many were injured' ⟨Kleindel, p. 302⟩.

11 Former suburb, later 16th district, known as a workers' district ⟨Czeike [1984], caption to ill. 368⟩.

12 Grammar mistake in German.

13 Philipp, the younger of Freud's half-brothers (born 1834; for discussion of his precise birth date, see comments by Krüll, p. 91 and note 20, p. 213 and note 22), had died on 29 August; Emanuel informed Freud of this 'with the very understandable hope that he would see me again this autumn. And so I have decided to go on to England, Holland, Belgium or wherever he would like to meet me' ⟨Freud/Binswanger, 59 F, 10 September 1911, p. 73 and note 4⟩, and then suggested that they meet in Hanover after the Weimar Congress, which he described as 'surprisingly comfortable' ⟨Freud to the family, 17 September 1911⟩.

14 Oliver, who had already shown a particular interest as a child in 'routes, distances, names of places and mountains' and was noted for his precision, was the family specialist – along with Freud's brother Alexander – in transport connections; see 167 AF ⟨Freud 1985*c*, p. 364, also p. 195; Jones II, pp. 90, 439; Freud M. [1999], p. 55⟩.

17 AF

A. F.[1]

[Vienna] 21 September 1911

Dear Papa,
I have to tell you our news again, although we still haven't heard anything from you.[2] But you probably have less time and are busier than we are here. I now go to school regularly and properly and have quickly got used to it and find it quite nice. I visited Dr Teich[3] with Oli yesterday about being excused from drawing and we also met his wife; we both liked her very much. The boys are behaving themselves and Oli in particular is very cooperative when I have to be accompanied[4] or have to do an errand. He has even invited me this evening to the Grabenkino cinema. I write daily to Mama and also receive [a] letter practically every day; I don't yet know when Mama will be coming. I would also like to hear something from you; how the Congress went, how you are, where we should now send our letters and lots more.[5] I even dreamt about you last night, but it wasn't nice at all. Where will you meet Uncle Emanuel[6] and when do you expect to be there?[7] Your apartment already looks nice and tidy. I have been over there a lot recently to choose some things from among the Kipling things.[8] I couldn't find the 'Soldatenlieder'.[9] I am looking forward a lot to your return and send my regards to Dr Ferenczi and Dr Jung.[10] Do you remember that Dr Jung had dinner with us once[11] when I was the only woman in the house, like now.

I send you a kiss and lots of greetings.
Anna

1 Preprinted initials.
2 Freud was at the Congress in Weimar; see 16 AF/OF, note 2 ⟨Jones II, pp. 95–7, 100; *Zentralblatt für Psychoanalyse* II, year 1912 (1911–12), vol. 2 (1911), pp. 100–5⟩.
3 Unidentified.
4 For details of the conventions about going out and propriety in the behaviour of young women in general, and the basically traditional concept of women in the education of Freud's daughters, see, for example, Mathilde's letters to her youthful friend Eugen Pachmayr of 9 and 30 October 1903, in Gödde [2003], pp. 289 and 295, and the associated editorial comments, ibid., pp. 67–70, 73, 230 ff.
5 Grammar mistake in German.
6 See 16 AF/OF, note 13. After the Congress, Freud remained in Weimar for a short while for discussions with Abraham ⟨Freud/Abraham, letter 115A, note 1⟩.
7 Freud wrote to Jones on 9 August 1911 that he didn't have to be in Vienna before 30 September ⟨Freud/Jones, letter 64, p. 113⟩.
8 Rudyard Kipling (1865–1936), English writer, Nobel Prize for Literature in 1907. Freud included *The Jungle Book* in a series of 'ten good books' that the

publisher Hugo Heller had asked ten outstanding personalities to name ⟨Freud 1906*f*⟩. Young-Bruehl (p. 70) states that Freud had sent Anna three books by Kipling as a 'summer-vacation present' in 1911. There is no mention of this in these letters. She refers to a letter from Anna of 21 September 1914 (which I have not been able to find to date); perhaps there is a confusion with the date or with the books sent to Merano for Anna's birthday (see 20 SF and 21 AF)?

9 Hans Sachs translated Kipling's *Barrack-Room Ballads and Other Verses* (1892/6) into German in 1910 as *Soldaten-Lieder und andere Gedichte* [*Soldiers' Songs and Other Poems*] ⟨Freud/Jones, letter 64, 9 August 1911, p. 113⟩.

10 Carl Gustav Jung (1875–1961), Swiss psychologist and psychiatrist, from 1900 to 1909 assistant, later senior physician and private lecturer with Eugen Bleuler at the 'Burghölzi', the Psychiatric University Clinic in Zurich (where he met Karl Abraham, Max Eitingon, Abraham A. Brill and others). He corresponded with Freud from 1906; in spring 1907, he visited him in person with Ludwig Binswanger ⟨Fichtner [1992], pp. XV–XVIII; Freud/Binswanger, pp. xxxi–xxxiii⟩. He became Freud's student and colleague; Freud saw him as his 'successor and crown prince' ⟨Freud/Jung, 139 F, 16 April 1909, p. 218⟩. From 1910 to 1914, he was the first president of the International Psychoanalytical Association ⟨*Jb*, vol. 2 (1910), p. 742; Freud/Jung, intermediate text, p. 304⟩. From 1912 onwards, Jung began to move away from Freud, developing his Analytical Psychology ⟨Freud/Jung; McGuire, pp. xiv–xix; Jung [1962], pp. 113–15 and ch. 'Psychiatric Activities'⟩. See also 297 SF.

11 Probably during Jung's second visit to Freud in late March 1909 ⟨Freud/Jung, intermediate text, p. 215⟩.

1912

18 SF/MF[1]

Frl Anna Freud
Lovrana[2]
c/o Abbazia
Pension Schattenfroh[3]
Beauregard

[Karlsbad], Freundschaft[s]saal[4]
21 July 1912

Dear single[5] daughter,
I get so hungry from drinking, bathing and waiting that I have to write. That is our situation at the moment. Apart from that, the rest of the day is very amusing, usually in the company of Emden.[6]

Think about what you would like me to bring you from Karlsbad.

Affectionately,

Papa

[On the address side of the card, in Martha Freud's handwriting]:
My dear Anna, I have to thank you for two lovely letters and I am always infinitely pleased to receive news from you. Is the bathroom really so nice? We are beginning to feel better. We were quite miserable for the first few days. We are also getting to like our rooms better. The Emdens are very nice. Thousand greetings to you all.[7]

Mama

1 Postcard.
2 In Istria; at the time administered by the Austrian Empire as the 'Austrian-Illyrian Littoral' on the Adriatic. Minna spent a holiday here with Sophie ⟨Freud to Max Halberstadt, 24 July 1912, in: 1960*a*, p. 298, note 3⟩. Evidently Anna was also there.
3 This line is in Martha Freud's handwriting.
4 Freud and Martha were on a cure in Karlsbad from 15 July to 14 August

1912. 'We are living here in the *Goldener Schlüssel*. "Freundschaftssaal" is our breakfast room' ⟨Freud/Ferenczi I, 313 F, 20 July 1912, p. 395, also 311 F (this picture postcard shows the 'Etbl. Freundschaftssaal'), 318 F; Freud to Max Halberstadt, 7 July 1912, in: 1960*a*, p. 297; Jones II, pp. 104f.⟩.

5 In early July, Sophie had unexpectedly become engaged to Max Halberstadt while visiting her relatives in Hamburg for a few weeks (see 23 AF, note 3) ⟨Freud to Max Halberstadt, 7 July 1912, ibid.⟩. He had just visited his future parents-in-law in Karlsbad (on 17 July) ⟨Freud/Ferenczi I, 311 F, 316 F; Freud to Max Halberstadt, 24 July 1912, in: 1960*a*⟩. They now had the prospect of the couple's wedding, so that Anna was the last of the three daughters to be left at home. See the recurrent formulation 'single'; Freud used it in other letters (e.g., to Pfister, 11 March 1913, 1963*a*, p. 60; Freud/Abraham, 27 March 1913, p. 180). Anna did not in fact become the only child left at home until Martin's marriage in late 1919, when all three brothers had moved out (see text following 106 SF) ⟨Freud/Sam, 17 December 1919⟩. Then she no longer had to 'make up for three' (see 23 AF and note 5, 24 SF) but 'for six brothers and sisters' (see 58 AF, note 9; Anna/Lou, 27 July 1915, letter 323).

6 Jan E. G. Emden (1868–1950), doctor of medicine; since 1911 member of the Vienna Psychoanalytic Society, until the Dutch group was founded in 1917, whose president he was in 1919 and 1920 ⟨*IZ*, vol. 6 (1920), p. 376⟩. The Emdens had already been with them in Karlsbad the previous year (see 14 AF, note 8). 'I have here a very intelligent man from Leyden, Dr. *van Emden*, who is teaching himself ψA and will then practise it on patients' ⟨Freud/Ferenczi I, 223 F, 28 May 1911, p. 286; see also Freud/Jung, 255 F and elsewhere⟩. A year later van Emden spent a few weeks in Vienna while his wife furnished a house in The Hague 'to which he is moving to practise ψA' ⟨Freud/Jung, 311 F, 21 April 1912, p. 499⟩. The same year he translated Freud's American lectures into Dutch. The couple soon became personal friends of the Freud family. During Anna's visit to England in 1914 he frequently acted as an intermediary in her correspondence with Vienna after the outbreak of war; see, for example, 47 SF, also 117 SF, 152 SF ⟨see also Freud/Jones, letter 218, 15 January 1917, p. 321⟩.

7 Minna and the two girls.

Summer Holidays (1912)

The continuation of the summer holidays for the family, from 15 to 30 August, began in Hotel Latemar on Lago de Carezza, where Max Halberstadt also spent a few days ⟨Freud to Max Halberstadt, 24 July 1912, in: 1960*a*⟩. Ferenczi joined them during a short stay subsequently in Bolzano, from 31 August to 1 September; it was planned that he would spend a week with them all in San Cristoforo (near Trento) until he and Freud set off for England to visit Jones ⟨Freud/Ferenczi I, 320 F–323 Fer⟩.

In Bolzano, however, the news reached them that Mathilde needed surgery again – this time with the sad result that her pregnancy was terminated, making it impossible for her to have children ⟨Freud/Jones, letter 87; for details of Mathilde's various diseases, see Gödde [2003], pp. 46–8, 78–84, 98–100, 129–31, 139–44⟩. Freud left the others and travelled immediately on 2 September with Ferenczi to Vienna ⟨Freud to the family,

3 September 1912, extract in 2003*e*, p. 141f.⟩. Four days later they joined the family in San Cristoforo, where they all remained until 14 September ⟨Freud/Jones, letter 90, 7 September 1912; picture postcard from Freud and family, 14 September 1912, from San Cristoforo to Marie Freud, who had discovered the 'beautiful spot' for herself, LoC SF, Cont. 1 (now Freud 2004*d*)⟩.

The excitement had weakened Freud to such an extent, however, that he no longer felt up to travelling to England and abandoned the idea. Instead he allowed himself a few days of relaxation in Rome, again with Ferenczi. They left on 15 September and set off home on 27 September. The family had already returned to Vienna ⟨Freud/Jones, letter 92; Freud to Martha from Rome, 20 and 25 September 1912, in: 1960*a*; Freud/Ferenczi I, 324 Fer; Jones II, pp. 107ff.⟩.

19 AF

[Merano,][1] 26 November 1912

Dear Papa,
I must write to you once so that you don't forget me while I'm away. I can announce the first piece of news right away because I weighed myself again yesterday and have already put on half a kilogram. I think that is quite a lot for the short time. I always eat as much as I can[2] and I am quite sensible. I think about you a lot and look forward to receiving a letter from you, if you have time to write. I have heard that your library is now back in order[3] and that your last lecture[4] in the small lecture theatre was particularly good; otherwise I don't know anything about what you are doing. Was the trip to Munich[5] very tiring? I always try to work out where you are at a given moment. You really should come and visit me for a few days at Christmas. It is wonderful here; there are magnificent walks, including ones, if you want, where you don't meet a soul. Only there are no mushrooms at this time of year. I feel as if I have been away from home for a long time,[6] but I have settled down well. It is very pleasant to live here, and I don't feel like doing anything else because I am never bored. Some days I feel very well, but on other days I still have severe back pain and am then very tired.[7] I am very spoiled here,[8] much more than at home, and it's just fortunate that I am too old for it to harm me. I get on extremely well with Edith.[9] She copies everything I do and I feel very grown up compared with her. In fact I am already quite old. Is it really as quiet at home as Mama writes in every letter?[10] I can't imagine it.

I send you my greetings and a kiss.
Anna

1 Renowned spa resort in South Tyrol at the foot of the Küchelberg; it is particularly appreciated on account of its mild climate even in winter. Anna spent the winter months here at the guesthouse of her sister-in-law, Marie Rischawy.

She had originally intended to embark on an eight-month trip to Italy, accompanied by Aunt Minna, to strengthen her physical and mental health and think about her future plans (see 22 SF and note 2). In a letter to Max Eitingon of 26 November 1925, Anna recalled: 'I should go back to Taormina for a winter. It's fourteen years since I was there.' Because of Sophie's engagement and forthcoming marriage, these plans had to be changed, since Minna was required to run the household so that Martha and Sophie could set up the future apartment in Hamburg 〈Freud/Jones, letter 83; see also Jones II, p. 105; Peters, p. 14; Young-Bruehl, pp. 56–7〉. (For details of the Halberstadts' living arrangements in Hamburg, see Weinke, p. 111f).

2 Young-Bruehl (p. 59) mentions a 'mild eating disturbance' about which there is 'no further contemporary information', however.

3 During the summer months Freud's study – initially except for his books – was completely refurbished: 'According to Alex it is impossible to clean the library with a vacuum cleaner, but further inquiries should be made' 〈Freud to family, 3 September 1912 [not in 2003*e*]〉.

4 The university lectures that Freud had given while researching and teaching at the University of Vienna since the winter semester 1886–7 were originally devoted to neuropathology, major neuroses and psychotherapy; after the winter semester of 1909–10, they mainly involved a presentation of the basic principles of psychoanalysis and research findings. In the early years they took place in various institutes, and from 1903–4 onwards regularly on Saturdays from 7 to 9 p.m. in the lecture theatre of the Psychiatric Clinic of the General Hospital 〈Gicklhorn, pp. 149–56 and 191〉. See also 27 AF, 72 SF and note 5.

5 A conference of the directors of the psychoanalytic associations took place in Munich on 23 November 1912 〈Freud/Ferenczi I, 349 F; Jones II, pp. 155, 164f.; Freud/Jung, pp. 521f.〉.

6 I was unable to find out the precise date; Peters (p. 14) speaks of a five-month stay (see ill. 5 and 6: Freud and Anna at around this time).

7 Anna cites these and other symptoms in describing her health at the time – which she simply refers to as 'it' – in several of the letters in this correspondence. See 26 AF; see also 5 MF/SF, note 1, and 6 AF, note 4. Young-Bruehl (p. 46) attributes the back pain to Anna's posture (see 22 SF, note 1).

8 With Marie Rischawy (1874–1936), a widowed sister of Robert Hollitscher 〈Gödde [2003], p. 144; Steiermärkisches Landesarchiv, Graz, Dept. 1D, 23 August 2002; for the date of death (29 September 1936): inheritance certificate of 22 April 1937, 8A 966/36 22T.Z413/37, Josefstadt-Vienna local court〉. Mathilde had also spent some time in the same house to 'recuperate' 〈Freud to Mathilde, 19 March 1908, in 1960*a*, p. 280〉. It is here that she met her husband, Robert Hollitscher 〈Young-Bruehl, p. 45 with the spelling 'Rischavy' compared with 'Rischawy' in the documents such as Perfahl, p. 42〉. Further details about the pensione in Merano could not be obtained 〈Merano municipal archive, 10 June 2002〉. From 1916 at the latest, Marie Rischawy ran a guesthouse in Altaussee; see 71 AF, note 1, 72 SF and note 2.

9 Marie Rischawy's daughter (Freud 1960*a*, p. 303, note 5). Anna remained in permanent contact with her until her death of sepsis in 1931 〈Anna/Lou, 11 June 1931 and *passim*; see also Young-Bruehl, p. 193f.; Molnar [1996], p. 99〉.

10 Full stop rather than a question mark in the original.

20 SF

PROF. DR. FREUD

28 November 2010
Vienna, IX. Berggasse 19

My dear Anna,
I haven't been able to write to you before because since your departure, which already seems ages ago, life here has been hectic; and the Sunday in Munich – with the night journey before and after, discussion in between lasting from 9 a.m. till 11.40 p.m. – wasn't exactly a rest cure. In any case, I know the ladies of the house keep you regularly informed about anything worth knowing.[1] Today's letter, however, is meant as a birthday congratulation. As you know, I am always premature on such happy occasions. Today I gave an order to Heller,[2] which I trust will arrive in time and be what you want. Your monthly allowance will reach you in your new home via the post office savings bank.

I have no doubt that you will put on more weight and feel better once you have grown accustomed to the idleness[3] and the sunshine. You might as well abandon the embroidery[4] until after the wedding;[5] it probably isn't very good for your back just now. Otherwise keep well and enjoy all that is offered you by the winter in Merano and the care of your sister-in-law, Frau Marie.

I don't think I shall be going away for Christmas; as a matter of fact, I am expecting Dr Abraham[6] to visit me here. As you know, I am no longer master of my free time, a condition however that I quite enjoy.

I don't think you have seen my room since it was redecorated, or have you? It has turned out very well. Before you return for good we will do your room too; writing table and carpet are in any case assured.

I send you fond greetings and wish you all the best for your seventeenth (hard to believe that I too was once so young!) and please give my kind regards to Frau Marie and Edith.

Your Papa

1 Grammar mistake in the original.

2 Hugo Heller (1870–1923), book and art dealer, Freud's publisher in Vienna until the founding of the *Verlag*; since 1902 member of the Vienna Psychoanalytic Association ⟨see *Minutes II*, p. 117; Mühlleitner, p. 14f.⟩. He was a Social Democrat and a friend of Karl Kautsky and Victor Adler. As publisher of *Neue Blätter für Literatur und Kunst* he organized a survey of readers in 1906, called *Vom Lesen und von guten Büchern* [*About Readers and Good Books*], in which Freud also participated (1906*f*). His rooms were a meeting place for the artists and intellectuals of the time in Vienna: 'For the last three years in winter I have organized a few intimate literary evenings for invited guests in my art salon. Rilke, Hofmannsthal, Wassermann, Thomas Mann, Stehr, Ginzkey, Heinrich Mann, Hermann Bang, Hesse and others have given me the honour of accepting my invitation and reading out some of their writing in my small, intimate room' ⟨Hugo Heller to Anna Bahr-Mildenburg, 1 August 1910, quoted in Worbs, p. 145⟩. For

details of Hugo Heller's significance 'as a link between the literary and psychoanalytic scene in Vienna' and in Viennese culture at the turn of the century as a whole, see Worbs, pp. 143–8. Freud himself gave a talk on 6 December 1907 in front of ninety people in Heller's salon, entitled 'Creative Writers and Day-Dreaming' (1908*e*); he reported on it to Jung: 'It must have been heavy fare for all the writers and their wives. . . . If nothing else, it was an incursion into territory that we have barely touched upon so far, but where I might easily settle down' ⟨Freud/Jung, 55 F, 8 December 1907, p. 103; also Jones II, p. 385 (with a different letter date)⟩.

3 Spelling mistake in the original ⟨cf. Jones III, p. 149⟩.

4 'Sticken' (embroidery) in Freud and Anna's handwriting and not 'Stricken' (knitting) as incorrectly transcribed in many publications ⟨e.g., also Young-Bruehl, p. 46⟩. See also 21 AF, 25 SF, 26 AF, 74 AF.

5 Of Sophie, who secretly became engaged to Max Halberstadt in Hamburg during the summer: 'Sophie's engagement has been concluded in the meantime, is already in the Hamburg papers, and is supposed to be made public today in Vienna. He is a particularly fine and serious person. We easily recognized that much in him in Karlsbad. I think she will have it very good with him' ⟨Freud/Ferenczi I, 316 F, 28 July 1912, p. 398; see also Freud to Max Halberstadt, 7 July 1912, in 1960*a*⟩. The marriage took place at Berggasse 19, Vienna, on 26 January 1913 ⟨Stammbaum Lange: Freud Family, 'Genealogical Tree', p. II. (Jones II, p. 111, and Peters, p. 14, give the wedding day as 14 January, but see 28 SF)⟩. (See ill. 7 and 8.)

6 Karl Abraham (1877–1925), doctor of medicine, neurologist and psychiatrist, with his own practice in Berlin since 1907; the first psychoanalyst in Germany; he was one of Freud's most important students and colleagues. After establishing an informal psychoanalytic group in 1908, he transformed it in 1910 into the Berlin Psychoanalytic Society, which he presided over until his death. He was joined in 1909 by Max Eitingon. Abraham was a member of the 'Secret Committee'. Not least because of his outstanding character, he managed 'to make Berlin in many respects the centre of the entire international psychoanalytic movement' ⟨Jones [1926], p. 179⟩. Apart from important theoretical and clinical work, he built up a solid training structure through events, seminars and teaching analyses, which was continued after 1920 through the establishment of the Berlin Psychoanalytic Institute with polyclinic and teaching academy. At the same time, he was actively involved in writing and organization within the psychoanalytic movement. In 1924, he became president of the International Association (a position he had already held provisionally until the end of the First World War after Jung's resignation) and remained in office until his death ⟨Cremerius, 1969 [1971]; Abraham, H. [1971, 1976]; Freud/Abraham; Jones [1926]⟩. For details of the Christmas visit, see Freud/Abraham, 13 October, 12 December, 27 December 1912.

21 AF

A. F.[1]

[Merano] 9 December 1912

Dear Papa,
I have to write to you again to tell you that I have put on more weight. I weighed myself today and have put on a whole kilogram in the last

fourteen days, making 1½ kg since my arrival. That's quite a lot, don't you think? At least this time you can see my good intentions. Thank you for your letter, which I was very pleased to receive. Is it *completely* certain that Dr Abraham is coming? I'm really happy about the books; it's exactly what I wanted, as you know. I will soon have a large library and will no longer have to be so concerned that Sophie is taking so many things to Hamburg. My birthday was wonderful. Unfortunately, I have not yet seen the library next to your desk but I can imagine that it must be very nice. I sometimes hear about you but only very rarely, and I hope that you don't have too much to do. I feel like I have been away from home and not seen you for an eternity. Will you write to me again? I would like that a lot. I really have given up the embroidery completely and am enjoying Merano, as you wrote in your last letter. I am very happy to hear that I will be getting a new desk and carpet.

I send you greetings and a kiss from the one who is very soon to be your only daughter.

Anna

1 Preprinted initials.

22 SF

PROF. DR. FREUD

13 December 1912
Vienna, IX. Berggasse 19

My dear little Anna,
I hear that you are already worrying again about your immediate future. So it seems that putting on 1½ kg still hasn't changed you much. I now want to set your mind at rest by reminding you that the original plan was to send you to Italy for eight months in the hope that you would return straight and plump[1] and at the same time quite worldly and sensible.[2] Actually, we hadn't dared to hope that a few weeks in Merano would achieve this transformation, and so had already prepared ourselves at your departure for not seeing you at the wedding[3] or so soon afterwards in Vienna. I think you should now slowly accustom yourself to this terrible prospect. The ceremony can be performed quite well without you, for that matter also without guests, company, etc., which you don't care for anyhow.[4] Your plans for school[5] can easily wait till you have learned to take a cooler approach to them.[6] They won't run away from you. It can only do you good to take each day as it comes and enjoy having such lovely sun in the middle of winter.

So now, if you are reassured that your stay in Merano won't be disturbed in the immediate future, I can tell you that we all enjoy your letters very much but we also *won't be worried* if you feel too lazy to write every day. The time for toiling away will come for you too, but you are still quite young.

Give my kind regards to Frau Doctor[7] and Edith and feel as well and happy as your father would like you to be.

1 Young-Bruehl associates Anna's postural problems with the rivalry with her sister: 'She also developed a slightly hunched forward posture – one that hours of sitting over knitting [sic] aggravated – of the sort adolescents use for hiding' ⟨Young-Bruehl, p. 46⟩. See also 79 AF and note 5; also Peters who remarked on Freud's concern about Anna's 'slightly bent back': 'Freud's concerns proved to be groundless. Anna Freud was always very slender, and even if she never "straightened" her back, [. . .] she remained in excellent health into advanced age' ⟨Peters, p. 14⟩.
2 See 19 AF, note 1. In a letter to Jones, Freud had emphasized the need for Anna to have 'some nice sights in young years' and compensation for the effort in the last school year ⟨Freud/Jones, letter 83, 11 August 1912, p. 151⟩. She took her school-leaving examination at the Cottage-Lyzeum in early summer 1912 (not 1911, as Peters, p. 12, states). In her observations on regression in chapter 3, section III, of her book *Normality and Pathology in Childhood* (p. 102), she recalls 'being myself a member of a class of sixth formers who were overstrained due to a timetable which arranged for a series of difficult subjects in succession without sufficient intervening breaks'.
3 See 20 AF, note 5.
4 See 28 SF and note 2.
5 To become a teacher; see 23 AF, 39 AF and notes 1 and 2.
6 See 28 SF, 2nd paragraph.
7 Marie Rischawy: 'Frau Rischawy was [. . .] known as "Fr Dr" as was customary in Austria! [. . .] Yes, I also called her Frau Doctor, like everyone else' ⟨for this information, I thank Frau Pepi Pucher, Altaussee, 8 July 2002⟩. 'A Dr Benj. Rischawy, spa doctor, lived at Habsburgstr. 44 in Merano from 1904 to 1909.' He might have been the deceased husband of Marie Rischawy, but it cannot be determined for certain ⟨Merano municipal archive, Bolzano province, 10 June 2002⟩.

23 AF

A. F.[1]

[Merano,] 16 December 1912

Dear Papa,
I received your letter this morning and was very surprised by the contents; I also have to write you a long letter today and hope that you have time to read it, because very often I feel I shouldn't bother you with letters. First of all, I should like to report that today was my weighing day again and this week I have put on another 1 kg. That is really a lot and so you can see that I am really making every effort with eating and the rest and that it is also doing some good. I have also become far more sensible since I have been here. You would be surprised how much, but it is not possible for you to notice it from so far away. But it is much too difficult to be as sensible as you would like, and I don't know whether I will ever be able to learn

now.[2] But I am not concerned any more and am just waiting to see how everything turns out. I am enjoying myself very much here and am particularly fond of Frau Doctor, but I found it very strange of you to write that I shouldn't come home for the wedding but only later. I don't quite know what to say: I am very pleased to be able to stay here quietly without a fixed date for my departure, but on the other hand I am very sorry that I won't see Sophie again before she leaves, or Max.[3] I feel as if I haven't seen you for a terribly long time, because even though you don't have much time in Vienna, it's still different and I can at least come over to you for a while in the evenings. And you are not opposed to school in general, are you? If I wait until I can do it without too much effort,[4] that will also be all right with you, won't it? I won't think about it any more for now. It is really so nice and pleasant here and it's a great shame that you can't come to visit me, because after Christmas there won't be an opportunity for a long time. Did you really know even before I left that I would be away for so long? I really thought that I would be home for Christmas. Do you miss me sometimes as well? Is it not a great expense for you if I stay here for so long when you now have Sophie's wedding as well and everyone is saying how bad the times are? I have been feeling much better the last few weeks and [I] will be very happy if I can come home strong and healthy and can do everything. Then you will finally have a daughter in full health; I will have in any case to make up for three.[5] For now I just send you very many greetings and promise to be sensible, and hope that perhaps I will hear from you again soon. Lots of kisses,

Your little Anna

1 Preprinted initials.
2 See 5 MF/SF, note 1.
3 Max Halberstadt (1882–1940), Sophie's fiancé. He was a portrait photographer, renowned in German and foreign specialist circles, and had won several prizes for his artistic portraits. He had had his own studio in Hamburg since 1907, which soon became 'one of the leading establishments of this type'. As a gifted and versatile artist he extended his repertoire from portraits, particularly photographs of children, towards the end of the 1920s, to include photo montages, publicity photography, architecture and interior design pictures and landscapes. He was co-founder of the Society of German Photographers and, until the Nazis came to power, was a member of the examination board of the photographers' guild. In 1920, the magazine *Photofreund* devoted a special issue to him with many illustrations ⟨Weinke, pp. 110–75, including illustrations pp. 119–75; quotation p. 111⟩.
4 See Freud's comments on Anna's 'passionate excess' in 28 SF (and Anna's mention of 'surplus energy' in 141 AF); Freud was to complain again later about Anna's overzealousness, e.g., 209 SF, note 6. See also Young-Bruehl, p. 49.
5 See 18 SF/MF, end of note 5.

1913

24 SF

PROF. DR. FREUD

1 January 1913
Vienna, IX. Berggasse 19

My dear Anna,
Today I finally have time to send you New Year's greetings. I am very pleased to hear that you are making yourself healthy and strong for your serious duties as a single[1] daughter while your predecessor plays out her last roles. It is good that you have managed to accept this necessary renunciation so easily. You won't regret it.

We have had a lot of indirect news about you, all good, but the impression remains that the later weeks are always more valuable than the earlier ones, and for that reason we don't yet want to talk about your coming home.

The months since your departure have been particularly busy for me. The holiday period, which ends today or at least on 6 [January],[2] has therefore been very welcome. My cold has unfortunately not gone away or is starting up again. A trip to Merano would have been very useful, but then I would have had to reproach myself for not travelling to Southport for Uncle Emanuel's eightieth birthday.[3] So I prefer to stay nicely at home.

I was at the opera yesterday and the day before. The first time I didn't get there until the third act, but the other time I only missed one scene. Rare events nevertheless, particularly with such frequency.

I therefore think that you should continue to enjoy your stay and send us nice letters about your progress.

My regards to Frau Doctor and affectionate greetings from
Your father

1 See 18 SF/MF and note 5.
2 Epiphany; see 5 MF/SF, note 5.
3 See 4 SF, note 4. (For confusion about Emanuel's date of birth, see explanations and references in Krüll, p. 213.)

25 SF

PROF. DR. FREUD 5 January 1913
Vienna, IX. Berggasse 19

My dear Anna,
I was very sorry to hear[1] that you are not feeling well again. But at least now I am sure, my child, that there is nothing physically the matter with you. I have an old suspicion about the reason for your condition, which seems to me to be more and more probable and I would like to tell you about it so that you will not need to torment yourself unnecessarily.

You know, of course, that you are a bit odd. I have been observing you long enough and have always hoped that you would be insightful enough to overcome it. I had no doubt that you got backache directly while embroidering[2] because you had mixed feelings about finally[3] finishing the wedding present for Sophie. Now you have suddenly become unwell again and I suspect it has to do with Max's presence in Vienna and with the promised (or cancelled?) visit to you during the honeymoon.

The age-old jealousy of Sophie, for which, as I realize, you are not to blame but rather her,[4] seems to have been transferred to Max and to torment you. You are concealing something from us and perhaps from yourself as well.

Take some advice, don't have secrets and don't be bashful. You shouldn't remain a child for ever but gain the courage to boldly face up to life and what it has to offer.

I send you my affectionate greetings and look forward to frank words from you,

Your father

1 No doubt via the 'indirect news' from Merano, mentioned by Freud in his previous letter.
2 'Sticken' (embroidering), not 'Stricken' (knitting); see 20 AF, note 4.
3 This word was inserted subsequently between the lines by Freud.
4 See 13 SF and notes 6 and 7. In a letter to Sophie three months later, Freud wrote: 'I do not wish to fulfil your other wish to have Anna with you during the time in Marienbad. Nor have I said anything to her about your invitation, nice though it is. The child is now recovering excellently and should not be thrown out of balance again. We chose Marienbad instead of Karlsbad so that we can be with her together with Aunt. Are you already starting to react to the puerile jealousy I predicted?' ⟨Freud to Sophie, 21 April March 1913⟩. Instead Sophie and Max came to Marienbad from Hamburg to visit the Freuds ⟨Freud/Binswanger, letter 92F, 27 July 1913, p. 119 and note 2⟩. (For details of Marienbad, see 33 AF, note 2.) The relationship between the two young girls is described by Peters (pp. 18–19) as follows: 'Sophie stirred boundless admiration in Anna with [. . .] her beauty and femininity. [. . .] The relationship between the two sisters will remind those familiar with Anna Freud's writings of the motif of "altruistic surrender", which she described much later as a form of ego defense whose roots obviously lie partly in self-observation' (see also Anna Freud [1936], ch. 10, in *Writings II*, pp. 122–34).

26 AF

A. F.[1]

[Merano] 7 January 1913[2]

Dear Papa,
I received your letter today and wanted to write to you anyway to thank you for your last letter, which made me very happy. I am now quite well again and I hope that whatever I had will not recur. I wondered a great deal what it was, because I am not really sick. It comes over me somehow and then I am very tired and feel obliged to worry about all kinds of things that are otherwise quite natural, about my being here and about my doing nothing all day long[3] when I am not sick, and things like that. I am no longer embroidering Sophie's cover and I always feel a little bad when I think that I would like to have finished it. Naturally I think very often about Sophie's wedding but I am actually indifferent about Max because he is a complete stranger to me; I don't really like him but I am certainly not jealous of him. It's not nice to say so, but I am glad that Sophie is getting married because the constant arguments between us were so terrible; she didn't mind because she didn't care for me, but I liked her a lot and always admired her a little. I cannot, however, understand why she is marrying Max because she also hardly knows him. But I cannot imagine that his presence in Vienna and all that has anything to do with how I am, and I really don't know why I sometimes feel so well and sometimes not, and want to know so that I can do something about it. I would like so much to be sensible like Mathilde,[4] and I don't know why everything takes so long with me. I am really very well and I enjoy it here a lot, and when I come to Vienna I will also be able to start doing all the things I like again, but when I have a stupid day everything looks wrong to me. Today, for example, I cannot understand how it can be so stupid sometimes. I don't want to go through this again because I want to be or at least become a sensible person but I can't always help myself alone; whenever I had something like this in Vienna, I would always talk to Trude[5] about it, and then everything was all right again.

Please understand that I would not have written all this to you because I don't like to worry you, but I did so merely because of what you wrote to me. Now I am fine and when I return home you will see that I have become strong and healthy because I absolutely want it and so it will happen. I weighed myself today and have put on another ½ kg, and I deliberately went on quite a long walk, which did not tire me as before. The weather and sun are becoming increasingly nice and warm and I am looking forward to the time when everything starts blooming, which won't be long here. It is naturally much nicer to go for walks here than it is in Vienna, and you would have enjoyed it immensely if you had come, which would have been lovely.

I send you many, many greetings and a kiss. Please write to me again soon if you can, then I will also become sensible if you help me a little.
Anna
I have not been able to write anything more because I don't know more myself, but I certainly don't keep any secrets from you.

1 Preprinted initials.
2 Mistakenly '1912' in the original.
3 Anna was also concerned by such doubts later in her life; for example, she asked Lou Andreas-Salomé in 1923: 'Don't you find it terrible that I am living here half-idle, learning nothing new, earning no money and simply taking everything as it comes?' ⟨Anna/Lou, letter 73 p. 133⟩. See also her otherwise obvious need 'to be a useful member of human society' (132 AF) and an almost identical formulation by Mathilde in 1907 in one of her youthful letters ⟨in Gödde [2003], p. 331⟩.
4 See 12 AF and note 3.
5 Gertrud Baderle, a fellow pupil and close school friend of Anna; her married name was Hollstein ⟨Young-Bruehl, p. 50; Peters, pp. 11, 17f.⟩. Anna met her again in 1922 while visiting August Aichhorn in his 'home for neglected children' in St Andrä, which 'belonged to the city of Vienna and takes the place of a correctional institute'; Trude worked there as a 'matron and nurse' ⟨Anna to Kata, 21 December 1921, 12 January 1922⟩. See also 170 AF and note 9.

27 AF

[Merano] 31 January 1913

Dear Papa,
I haven't heard from you for a frightfully long time and wanted to write to you again to tell you that I am very well. I go for very long walks without getting really tired and in general am living like a completely healthy person without getting tired or stupid things like that. Frau Gebert from Berlin[1] is now here with us and is very nice. I always go on walks with her and I like her very much. It would be wonderful if Mathilde were to come here as she plans to do. Try hard to persuade her if you can; I would be terribly pleased. Then I would have someone to travel back with; in any case I don't like travelling alone. I'm glad that the wedding is over. I was a little annoyed not to be there – that's only natural – but I've already received a lot of reports about it. In all the letters I receive, you are the only one that no one writes anything much about – how you are, what you are doing, if you are very busy – and I would therefore be very pleased if you would write to me again yourself. Lampl writes to me sometimes about your lectures,[2] which must be very good this year. I have also read some of your books here. You shouldn't be upset: I'm big now and it is not therefore surprising that they interest me. Could you not send me the latest issue of *Imago*,[3] which I missed in Vienna? It must feel quite strange for you at home without any daughters, and I suppose you travel alone in the car as well. Do you always have flowers on your desk? But you don't need me for that any more because other people have always brought you some, and

much nicer ones at that. I hope that you don't forget me, however, before I come back in person; it won't be much longer now. In the meantime I send you my sincere greetings and a kiss.
Anna

1 Helene Gebert, another sister of Robert Hollitscher, who was married to Dr Gebert, Berlin. In the correspondence between Alix and James Strachey, Alix mentions her during a long visit to Berlin in 1924–5 as her 'unwanted intimate' ⟨*Bloomsbury* [1995], p. 75 and note 3⟩. See also 28 SF and 29 SF, note 2.
2 See 19 AF and note 5. The lectures in the winter semester of 1912–13 were entitled 'Einzelne Kapitel aus der Lehre von der Psychoanalyse' ('Selected Chapters from the Theory of Psychoanalysis') ⟨Gicklhorn, p. 155⟩. Lampl had attended Freud's lectures regularly since 1912 and in the winter semesters of 1915–17, he attended them with Anna ⟨Gicklhorn, p. 171, no. 143, incorrectly there as 'Lampe'⟩. See 72 SF, note 5.
3 *Imago, Zeitschrift für Anwendung der Psychoanalyse auf die Geisteswissenschaften.* The first volume was published in 1912 by Hugo Heller & Cie., Leipzig and Vienna. It contained the introductory passages (1912*i*) and the first two chapters of Freud's *Totem and Taboo* (1912–13*a*). The name *Imago* was suggested by Hanns Sachs in reference to the novel (1906) by the Swiss author Carl Spitteler (1845–1924) 'in which the tricks and masks of the unconscious, its inroads into consciousness, and its stimulation of the creative powers are presented with consummate mastership' ⟨Sachs [1950], p. 63⟩. The magazine was originally going to be called 'Eros und Psyche' ⟨Freud/Jones, letter 64, 9 August 1911, p. 113⟩. For details of the changes in title and publication forms, see the list of abbreviations.

28 SF

PROF. DR. FREUD

2 February 1913
Vienna, IX. Berggasse 19

My dear single daughter,
Your letter arrived just at the right time. I wanted to write to you today, the first Sunday since the wedding. You know how glad we were to hear that you are very well. I hope as well that you are still enjoying yourself there, even if Math doesn't come and you realize that Helene Gebert is sick.[1] I think you will be able to stand it for another month.

When you are here we shall have to see whether you can avoid the fervent overzealousness in your activities that has been your downfall to date. You are now demanding the rights of a grown-up girl and I am glad to accord them to you. You will then have understood, however, from the books you have read that you were so overzealous, restless and unsatisfied because, like a child, you ran away from many things that a grown-up girl should not be afraid of. We will recognize the change when you no longer ascetically shun the distractions of your age but enjoy doing what other girls take pleasure in.[2] There is enough room[3] for serious interests. If one is too ambitious, too sensitive and wants to remain remote from a part of one's life and one's own nature, the things one actually does wish to undertake will also be affected. You will have free access to all educational aids here if you wish to use them for the right purpose.

We are quite well on the whole. If the little ones continue to leave like this to find their own way, we will be tempted to exchange Vienna for a quieter place where we can still work; for Salzburg, let's say.[4] But that won't come into consideration for another four to five years and by then we will be quite old.

I am still well supplied with flowers and work. Nor do you need to worry about how much your stay is costing. As it turns out, you are replacing Aunt, who otherwise used to spend these months in the more pleasant South. It will have done you a lot of good and no harm to any of us.

Your sister is now in her own house. We hope that this will be the start of a happy life with her husband, a very dependable man whom she chose herself. I am wondering whether to visit her at Easter.[5] I can hardly postpone visiting Uncle Emanuel, who is now eighty, and I can then return via Hamburg. Otherwise Mama will no doubt be the first person to visit her.

I will send you a spare copy of *Imago* if I can find one. You mustn't leave it in Merano, however, because it was actually for Mathilde. I have just revised the first issue of the second volume.[6]

I send you my affectionate greetings and hope that your paths are good and agreeable in every sense.

Your father

Send my regards to Robert's two sisters[7] and the naughty Edith.[8]

1 See 29 SF and note 2.
2 Anna herself called the efforts to comply with this wish her 'attempts at socializing'; see 114 AF. In a letter to Lou Andreas-Salomé, she later stated that she had fallen back into her 'hermit existence' ⟨Anna/Lou, letter 7, 18 January 1922, p. 18; see also Young-Bruehl, p. 95f.⟩.
3 Young-Bruehl (p. 59) misreads this as 'hardly'. Her translation of the letter is abbreviated and reformulated, no doubt to avoid the contradiction caused by the misreading.
4 'Salzburg is delightful again; it would have been nice if I could already have looked at apartments for us,' wrote Minna on this subject to Freud a few months later ⟨Freud/Bernays, letter 166 Mi, 12 July 1913⟩. See also 71 AF, end of note 7.
5 Freud went to collect Anna from Merano instead; see 30 SF and 31 SF. The visit to Sophie was postponed until Christmas 1913 ⟨Freud/Ferenczi I, 442 F⟩. See 58 AF, note 9.
6 The third issue of this year contains Freud's essay 'The Theme of the Three Caskets' (1913*f*); Freud wrote of it to Ferenczi on 9 July 1913: 'My next company will be my little daughter, who is now developing so gratifyingly (you have surely long ago guessed this subjective condition of the "choice of caskets")' ⟨Freud/Ferenczi I, 409 F, p. 499⟩. The idea had already occurred to him, however, in June 1912: 'A single thought that will amuse you was that the introductory scene in Lear must mean the same as the selection scene in the Merchant of Venice. Three caskets are the same as three women, three sisters. The third is always the correct choice' ⟨ibid., 307 F, 23 June 1912, p. 387⟩. At the time Anna had just finished her *Matura* at the Lyzeum. See 22 SF, note 2.

7 Marie Rischawy and Helen Gebert.
8 'Fesch', in the sense of 'cheeky'. See, e.g., 155 SF and note 10.

29 SF

PROF. DR. FREUD

16 February 1913
Vienna, IX. Berggasse 19

Dear Child,
For some time we have been given to understand from letters from Frau Marie to Mathilde that you no longer get on as well with her as at the beginning, while you have been discreetly silent about it. Now you yourself say[1] that Helene's illness is making itself felt,[2] and it is therefore about time that we asked what is going on with you two, a lot, a little, and why you thought it necessary to leave us to rely completely on reports from other sources. That is certainly more worrying for us than if we heard from you what the differences are about. If it has become awkward for you, we certainly won't force you to stay longer but will have you return as soon as you want. Put your discretion aside and tell us about it. You can rest assured that we believe everything you write. I look forward to an answer without delay. I send you my affectionate greetings and am very pleased to hear your other good news.
Your father

1 Not in the present correspondence.
2 Helene Gebert is to be handled with care, reported Lou Andreas-Salomé to Anna some years later, 'because it is evident that she is overwrought inside' ⟨Anna/Lou, letter 67, 19 December 1992, p. 122⟩. Alix Strachey also described Helene as 'tiresome' and 'a hysterical character'; 'she talks in a continuous violent stream, attends to nothing I say, & expects to be listened to with intense concentration' ⟨*Bloomsbury*, 7 November 1924, 31 January 1925, 1995, pp. 110, 192⟩.

30 SF

PROF. DR. FREUD

19 February 1913
Vienna, IX. Berggasse 19

Dear Child,
I was very pleased to receive your letter[1] and am satisfied that it is nothing else. In these circumstances, I would make the following suggestion to you. Stay there until Easter and I will come to collect you on Saturday, 22 March. We will stay for a few days at the hotel in Bolzano, since Tuesday is also a holiday and we don't have to be back in Vienna until Wednesday morning. In the meantime you can use the time to put on some more weight. Just let me know if you cannot move freely or travel on these days.

Obviously you will have to allow me the option of changing the plan

if something turns up, but I don't see any obstacles at the moment and I think it will be all right.
With affectionate greetings,
Your father

1 Apparently missing.

31 SF

PROF. DR. FREUD

10 March 1913
Vienna, IX. Berggasse 19

Dear Child,
Here are the final details about our trip at Easter.

As spring in Bolzano will still not have properly arrived in twelve days' time and a stay in Merano offers nothing new for you and no rest for me, I have put the following together: I will leave on the evening of Thursday the 20th and will arrive in *Bolzano at 11.45 a.m. on Good Friday*,[1] where I will meet you with Frau Doctor or Edith. We will have a relaxed lunch, discuss everything that has been going on and then travel on to Verona at 2.30 p.m. with the N[orth]S.[outh] Express, arriving at around 5 p.m. We will stay some of Saturday in Verona and will make the two-hour journey on the same day to Venice, where we will spend our Easter holidays.[2] I presume you will already have sent most of your baggage from Merano to Vienna by then. Mama will send you one of our leather bags in good time for the five days of the Ital.[ian] trip. You don't need to learn Italian by then.[3] Everything else will work out; it will be a lovely end to your long holiday.

Greet Frau Doctor sincerely; you should really invite her to come to Bolzano. Write soon to let us know if you are in agreement.
Affectionately,
Father

1 Spelling mistake in German.
2 In Hotel Britannia; see 247 AF.
3 But see Young-Bruehl, p. 51 (without citation of source): 'On the family's visits to the Dolomites and during a stay she made on her own in 1912 in Merano, she learned enough Italian to read newspapers and simple novels and to discover that she could not read Dante [. . .].' This statement is not quite compatible with Anna's utterance to Lou Andreas-Salomé: 'I would really like to learn Italian, for Papa's and my trip to Rome' ⟨Anna/Lou, letter 61, 3 December 1922⟩.

32 AF

[Merano] 13 March 1913

Dear Papa,
The plans sound better with every letter from you and this time I go a city further south with every line I read. So something is to come of the Italian trip after all,[1] and to be with you is much nicer than it would otherwise

have been. I am looking forward terribly to Venice, Papa; I really didn't think that I would be going there so soon.[2] Until now I was afraid that something would come between you and the trip, but now that you have even booked the sleeping car, it looks as if everything is certain.[3] Frau Doctor would be pleased to come with me to Bolzano and probably Edith as well, as she would like to meet you after I have spoken so much about you. I will, of course, organize the baggage as you ask in your letter. Fortunately, I can now do my hair myself. I learned it specially for our trip and I can already do it very well.[4] I want to look respectable when I am with you. I am already terribly impatient and can hardly wait for Friday. I haven't seen you for such a long time and I am looking forward so much to Venice, especially the gondolas and the canals, which I have always imagined to be so beautiful.[5] I have already seen so many pictures of them.

I send you lots and lots of greetings, Papa, and a kiss, and thank you for having had such a good idea and for going on such a nice journey with me. Today I can already say 'See you soon'. With lots of greeting,

Anna

1 See 19 AF, note 1, 22 SF and note 2.
2 See 247 AF.
3 'This evening I am going to Bolzano to pick up Anna. I want to spend the holidays with her in Verona and Venice' ⟨Freud/Ferenczi I, 385 F, 20 March 1913, p. 475⟩. They returned to Vienna on 26 March ⟨Freud/Abraham, 27 March 1913⟩.
4 For Anna's hairstyle at the time, see, for example, ill. 6; see also the Freuds' picture postcard from Brioni, 40 SF and note 3.
5 On 26 March 1913, Freud wrote to his daughter Sophie: 'Our Easter trip was very nice. I met Anna in Bolzano with Uncle [Alexander] and his Sophie [. . .]. On Saturday evening I was alone with Anna in Venice and enjoyed her surprise at the incredible magnificence of this old enchantress.' They returned via Trieste, where Freud had carried out histological research at a zoological test laboratory as a student in 1875–6, which gave rise to his first scientific publications (1877*a* and *b*, 1878*a*) ⟨Jones II, p. 111⟩.

33 AF

J. Bemelmans
Grand Hotel des Alpes
San Martino di Catrozza
Tyrol[1]

7 September 1913

Dear Papa,

We are still[2] in San Martino because Hartungen[3] didn't want Mama to travel today, and we couldn't get reservations for tomorrow. We hope to be in Klobenstein finally on Tuesday [9 September]. Mama was really wretched for the first two days and yesterday also went to lie down after lunch until the evening.[4] I always have my meal sent up and we have tried to make it as comfortable as possible.[5] Today Mama got up completely, but she is still not very lively. I think that Klobenstein will do her good as well. The weather remains fine apart from the occasional rain in the afternoons. The Hammerschlags were here yesterday and will probably be coming again today.[6] Hartungen has been looking after Mama very well. We have heard from Martin that he is staying in Riva until the 8th or 9th.[7] There was also a letter yesterday from Sophie, saying that she is now fine and feels very well. The rest of our mail is probably taking the sun in beautiful Klobenstein. We are really well here, however, and lack for nothing. I even managed to get the 'Neue Freie Presse' again. It is still delivered for Herr Graetz[8] although he left a long time ago, and every day when I collect the mail I take it with me, as if it were ours. We were really lucky with this subscription by proxy. At the bazaar I bought a Tauchnitz[9] book on Friday and a Reclam on Saturday; so I did quite well. The former was a Kipling that I hadn't heard of before. I have eaten some of the cheese that Abraham and Ferenczi[10] sent you and it was really very good. I can now operate the lift very well and almost always get it to stop properly because I have had plenty of opportunity to practise when I order food or talk to the concierge about leaving and on other similar occasions. I hope everything is fine in Munich[11] and that you are taking good care of yourself. Please give my regards to the entire Congress. I hope you were able to understand my telegrams;[12] Mama didn't want me to go into more detail. Please write to me soon. I send you a kiss and remain your

Anna

1 Letterhead with vignette.
2 Since 11 August; prior to that, from 13 July to 10 August, Freud, Martha, Anna and Aunt Minna (from 15 July) had been taking a cure in Marienbad (see 59 SF, note 2) ⟨Freud/Ferenczi I, 409 F; Freud/Bernays, letter 166 Mi; Jones II, pp. 112f⟩. Freud left San Martino for Munich on 5 September (see notes 10 and 11).
3 Christoph (V) Hartung von Hartungen (1882–1967), double doctor of medicine (Austria 1906, Italy 1914), then spa doctor in San Martino; after the First World War general practitioner and internationally acclaimed homeopath working independently in Vienna, Merano, Como and Sies am Schlern [Siusi allo Sciliar], 1929–31 lecturer in psychology at the Hochschule für Welthandel in Vienna [now Vienna University of Economics and Business]. He came from a well-known Austrian medical family. He was a cosmopolitan polymath with wide-ranging interests in biology, ethnology, psychology, religion and ethics, music, literature and art, with family connections and close acquaintanceship with representatives of these disciplines. His brother, Erhard Hartung v. Hartungen, also a doctor in their father's sanatorium in Riva, mentions the acquaintanceship with Freud in his memoirs (and elsewhere). I thank Klaus Hartung v. Hartungen, Klausdorf bei Kiel, for all family information, including note 4. See also 'Dr. Ch. E. von Hartungen (Riva)', reporter on Italian literature in *Zentralblatt für Psychoanalyse*, vol. I (1911), p. 125, and *Minutes III*, p. 320, note 5.
4 'The little doctor sent up a whole arsenal of medicaments again this evening [. . .] Basically he is the right doctor, something we have never had before,'

wrote an impressed Martha to Freud on 6 September 1913. In the estate of the v. Hartungen family is a visiting card from Freud of 5 September 1913 (1995*n*) in which he expresses thanks 'for the excellent assistance'. It was not possible to determine whether this card was enclosed with the money mentioned in 34 AF.

5 'The little one has looked after me devotedly and has not left my side' ⟨Martha to Freud, 6 September 1913⟩.

6 Leontine (née Bardach) and Albert Hammerschlag (1863–1935), doctor of medicine, former assistant at Nothnagel Clinic, specialist in internal medicine and since 1893 Privatdozent (lecturer). He was a son of Freud's revered religious teacher, Samuel Hammerschlag (see Freud's obituary 1904*e*) ⟨Fischer I, 1932–3; confirmation these 'Hammerschlags' are being referred to in a letter from Martha to Freud, 6 September 1913⟩.

7 Martin was studying law and would complete his doctorate towards the end of the year; see 37 AF, note 2 ⟨Freud M. [1999], p. 178⟩.

8 Unknown; probably another holiday guest at the hotel.

9 A Leipzig publishing bookshop and printers, known amongst other things for its 'Collection of British and American Authors', started in 1841. In 1886, it introduced 'Students' Tauchnitz Editions', a set of English and American works with German introductions and commentaries ⟨*Meyers Grosses Konversations-Lexikon* (Bibliographisches Institut: Leipzig-Vienna, 1909⟩. The publishers existed until 1970. ⟨I thank Karl H. Pressler, antique dealer in Munich, for his friendly assistance.⟩

10 Both were in San Martino for a time: 'Ferenczi joined the family there on August 15 – Abraham was also there for a few days – and he travelled with Freud together to the Munich Congress' ⟨Jones II, p. 113; Freud/Ferenczi I, 409 F, p. 499⟩.

11 At the 'Fourth Private Psychoanalytical Association' Congress on 7 and 8 September 1913 in Hotel Bayerischer Hof. Here the final break with Jung became apparent; at the time, however, Anna would not have known about the tension between the Swiss and the Austrian groups ⟨Jones II, pp. 114–16; Freud/Jung, pp. 549f., 576⟩. The Congress report was published late and in a deliberately factual and terse style ⟨*IZ*, vol. 2, 1914, p. 406f.⟩; the official reasons were explained by Abraham ⟨ibid., p. 297 and p. 405f.; Andreas-Salomé ([1958], pp. 190ff. also describes what occurred at the congress⟩.

12 Missing. Martha mentions a telegram in her letter to Freud of 6 September 1913.

34 AF

[Klobenstein] 11 September 1913

Dear Papa,
Mama and I have just moved from the annexe, which smelled very bad, to a delightful room with loggia in the new building.[1] The weather is also surprisingly fine, snow on the mountains and the most beautiful sunshine here. Mama, whom I had difficulty initially in persuading not to leave for home right away, has already admitted that this morning on the Eisackeck[2] alone was worth the trip up.[3] We are really very happy and hope that you are too.[4] Yesterday we received a letter from Dr Hartungen in San Martino, addressed to Mama, in which he thanked us for the money. So he accepted it after all, which Mama is very glad about. Mama is now fully fit

and shows no ill effects. We go on very nice walks together. The blackberries this year are unfortunately not yet ripe, although I have sought out the best places, but the hazelnuts are already quite good. Yesterday afternoon we visited my Adam's woman;[5] she recognized us immediately and asked after everybody. She doesn't have Adam any more but another delightful child in his place, who still plays with the woolly cat I gave Adam two years ago. There are two new benches on the way there, but otherwise everything is just the same. I don't know, but I find Klobenstein almost prettier than any of the other places we have been, even San Martino. As in all places, however, there is something horrible: in this case Herr Bresch![6] He would be all right in small doses, but he always comes for a long rather than a short time. On the first day we were not very skilful, but now we have had practice and usually disappear when he comes along. Otherwise there are no familiar faces here. There were a lot of people from last time, Bolfras,[7] Kassowitz,[8] etc., but they have already left. We will probably stay until Monday because there are no sleeping berths to Vienna available before then. It was nevertheless a very good idea to travel up here.

I send you affectionate greetings and a kiss,
Anna
Sincere greetings to Aunt.
Greetings from Mama[9]

1 In the Posthotel, purchased by Johann Bemelmans in 1907 and renovated in subsequent years (see 15 AF, note 13); the annexe is now a respectable apartment and office building (opposite the town offices). The 'smell' could have come from an adjacent barn, which was replaced later by an apartment building; at the time of my research (2000 and 2001) it was being demolished to make way for a new building. The former hotel has seen numerous alterations and additions and is now an expansive complex known as 'Bemelmans Post'.

2 There is no place with this official name on the Ritten, but rather a viewpoint that the Freuds might have given this name among themselves, because it is the only place from where some of the Eisack [Isarco] can be seen. It is known as Atzwanger Aussicht, to the east of Klobenstein, and offers an extensive view not only into the Eisack Valley but also of the imposing Schlern, Rosengarten and Latemar chain and other parts of the Dolomites. ⟨I should like to thank Hannsjörg Hager, Alpine Auskunft, Bolzano, for this friendly information.⟩

3 Martha liked it so much that she even decided 'to spend at least some of next summer up here again' ⟨Martha to Freud, 12 September 1913⟩.

4 Freud was travelling with Minna Bernays to Rome ⟨Freud/Bernays, letter 169 Mi–173 Mi⟩. They had met in Bologna on 9 September right after the Congress in Munich, arriving in Rome on 11 September, where they stayed at the Eden Hotel (see 35 SF and note 1). They returned to Vienna on 29 September ⟨Jones II, p. 116; Freud/Ferenczi I, 415 F; Tögel [2002], p. 371f.; Freud 2002*b*, pp. 373–6⟩.

5 Unidentified despite local research.

6 Probably another holiday guest; although the name doesn't appear in the incomplete guest list for 1913, it was listed the previous year: 'Hermann Bresch, independent gentleman, Vienna, accompanied by Frau Bresch'.

7 'Last time', of course, refers to 1911 (see 14 AF–16 AF/OF). In that year several members of this family are entered in the guest list: Vilma von Schlick, née Baroness Bolfras, Vienna, with child and nanny (19 August–8 September) – Ecx. [sic] Baron Arthur von Bolfras, k.u.k. G.d.I. etc., Vienna, with spouse (22 August–7 September) – Baron Egon Bolfras, Zagreb (23 August–7 September).

8 No entry for this name in the guest list in 1911 or 1913. Possibly Karl Kassowitz, son of Dr Max Kassowitz (1842–23 June 1913), a Viennese paediatrics professor with whom Freud used to go hiking in the mountains ⟨Jones I, p. 365⟩. As director of the Erstes Öffentliches Kinder-Krankeninstitut [First Public Children's Hospital], Max Kassowitz had set up a neurology department for Freud in 1886, which Freud headed until 1897 ⟨Kris, p. 532 and note 24⟩. While at school the children of the two families played together ⟨Freud 1985*c*, letters 199 and 200; Young-Bruehl, p. 47⟩. Freud published important essays (1891*a* and 1893*b*) in the compendium *Beiträge zur Kinderheilkunde* published by Kassowitz 'with which he is regarded today as the founder of the currently evolving discipline of neuropaediatrics' ⟨Grubrich-Simitis [1978], vol. 2, p. 547; see also Freud 1893*j*⟩.

9 The following day Martha wrote to Freud and Minna; Anna added a PS to this letter: 'Dear Papa, It occurs to me that Rome is the capital of Italy and that nevertheless I only put two 5-mark stamps on the letter to you [i.e., this letter 34 AF]. So there will be more from me soon. Anna' ⟨Martha to Freud, 12 September 1913⟩.

35 SF[1]

Frl Anna Freud
Klobenstein a/Ritten
Posthotel
Austria, Tyrol

[Rome] 13 September 1913[2]

Papa to his future travel companion[3]

1 Colour picture postcard with a painting by Ernesto Richter, Rome: 'No. 9 – Rome – Castello S. Angelo et Cupola di San Pietro' with stamp 'Eden Hotel – Roma'. The picture also shows the Tiber Bridge and a large stretch of the river with fishing boats on it.

2 Date and text are on the picture side (in the water, so to speak) (perhaps because on the other side was printed: 'N. B. Sul lato anteriore della presente si scrive soltanto l'indirizzo' ['Only the address to be written on the front of this card'].

3 See 37 AF and note 4, 38 SF and note 2.

36 AF

[Klobenstein] 14 September 1913

Dear Papa,
Yesterday we received Aunt's letter and your telegram,[1] but the advice in the telegram to remain here came too late. We have already booked our

sleeping-car berths for tomorrow and don't really regret it, although it is very nice here. Mama doesn't want to leave the boys to manage on their own any longer and we also want to see Hella[2] and Martha[3] for a few days. And now Mama is completely rested, almost better than before. Yesterday the weather wasn't so nice, but we still went on an excursion and stopped to eat in the delightful new little Alpenheim guesthouse above Rappersbichl.[4] We are really well and are leading a lazy life, getting up late, not dressing up and going early to bed. Yesterday I sought out our old rocky site on the Föhnhügel[5] and it is almost more beautiful than it was two years ago. The path up to it is almost completely overgrown. There is a cigar butt under the pine needles and I really think that it is one of yours; at least it looks like it. I would love to buy the Föhnhügel and build my house on the meadow[6] between the two wooded sections. I was not able to visit our mushroom sites because Mama doesn't like to go there and it is too far for me on my own. Besides, looking for mushrooms is not as much fun when you're not there. We don't see so much of Herr Bresch any more. Mama has trained him to bring us his newspaper punctually every day, and he does that now.[7] He only ever goes walking on the Föhnpromen.[ade] so we avoid that. Tomorrow we will pack and then travel down at 12.37 p.m. because we still have a couple of errands to do in Bolzano if we can cope with the heat. I am looking forward a little to Vienna again and particularly to my desk. Did you really meet the poet Rilke[8] in Munich? How? And what is he like?

I send you a kiss and lots of greetings,
Anna

1 Freud's letters and telegrams to Martha from his trip to Rome have not survived ⟨Tögel [2002], p. 372⟩.
2 Hella Felicitas Bernays (1893–1994), fourth child of Freud's sister Anna and Eli Bernays, who had emigrated to New York in 1894 ⟨Stammbaum Lange: Freud Family, 'Genealogical Tree', p. III; Tögel [2002], p. 207⟩.
3 Hella's sister Martha Bernays (1894–1979), the fifth child of Anna and Eli Bernays. The sisters were visiting Europe for the summer with their mother and were alone at the time in Vienna after having previously spent an extended time in Goisern (see 58 AF and note 1) ⟨Freud-Bernays, A., pp. 149–52⟩.
4 Today 'Rappersbühel'; Pension Alpenheim has become Residence Kristall. ⟨I thank Josef Frötscher, Soprabolzano, for his friendly information.⟩
5 Today usually 'Fenn' rather than 'Föhn', i.e., Fennhügel, Fennpromenade.
6 This site is used today for events. Anna harboured the dream of her own house for many years before she was finally able to fulfil it. It 'was once an old daydream of mine. I had a large ancient castle in a very beautiful park in which lots of one- and two-room houses were dispersed. All of my visitors had one of these little houses and were their own lords of the manor' ⟨Anna/Lou, letter 236, 1 June 1925, p. 450; see also Freud/Jones, PS to letter 220, p. 323⟩. See end of 98 AF, 101 AF, 135 AF. For mention of later weekend houses, see 287 SF and note 20. Guests played an important role in this regard (see 257 SF, note 13; but also 28 SF, note 2).

7 Martha also mentions him in her letter to Freud of 12 September 1913.
8 Rainer Maria Rilke (1875–1926). Lou Andreas-Salomé made the introduction during the Congress in Munich: 'I was pleased to be able to introduce Rainer to Freud. They got on well and we stayed together in the evening and late into the night' ⟨Andreas-Salomé [1958], p. 191⟩. Two years later, Anna was to meet Rilke herself when he visited the Freuds in Vienna while performing military service and attended Oliver's first wedding ⟨Freud/Ferenczi II, 585 F⟩. On that occasion he wrote a dedication to Anna in his *Buch der Bilder* [*The Book of Images*], of which she owned a copy published by Insel (see facsimiles pp. 76f.). The friendship was kept up. When Ernst later lived in Munich (see 96 AF and note 1) he met Rilke on several occasions ⟨e.g., Freud/Andreas-Salomé, 1 April 1915 (p. 28), 21 March 1916 (p. 39), 4 August 1916, 15 June 1919; Rilke to Freud, 17 February 1916, LoC SF, Cont. 40⟩. See also 168 AF and note 9.

37 AF

[Vienna] 16 September 1913

Dear Papa,
We are now back in Vienna. The journey went well and we had pleasant fellow passengers and arrived not at all tired to very good weather. I slept from Lienz to Gloggnitz. I am very happy to be back in Vienna and in particular I find my room nice and large. I have already finished unpacking and putting things away, everything placed on the desk where it belongs, and the display cabinet has also been arranged. The snakes look very good.[1] Mama has not yet finished and hasn't therefore been able to get round to writing. Hella and Martha were here this morning; I don't feel particularly attracted to them at present. Martin is studying hard again[2] when he is not with them.[3] Mathilde was here all morning; she was very nice and looks very well. She gave me a miniature picture of herself in a beautiful frame and I put it out right away. We received your last letter before leaving Klobenstein. I was very pleased with the card and particularly what was written on it.[4] We didn't change our plans, partly because the weather there had not been very good recently. It was really a good way to end the summer. All of my vases arrived intact and Math was amazed that I had 'added' so much this summer (by that I mean things, of course). There are flowers everywhere from the maids, and the apartment looks very nice in general. I am glad to hear that you are having such a good time in Rome and that you are well. I send my affectionate regards to Aunt and a kiss to you.

Anna

II Name and dedication in Anna Freud's copy of *Das Buch der Bilder* by Rainer Maria Rilke, Insel-Verlag (Leipzig, 1913) (see 36 SF, note 8). (My thanks to Christfried Tögel and Gerhard Fichtner for the indication and copy.) © Freud Museum, London

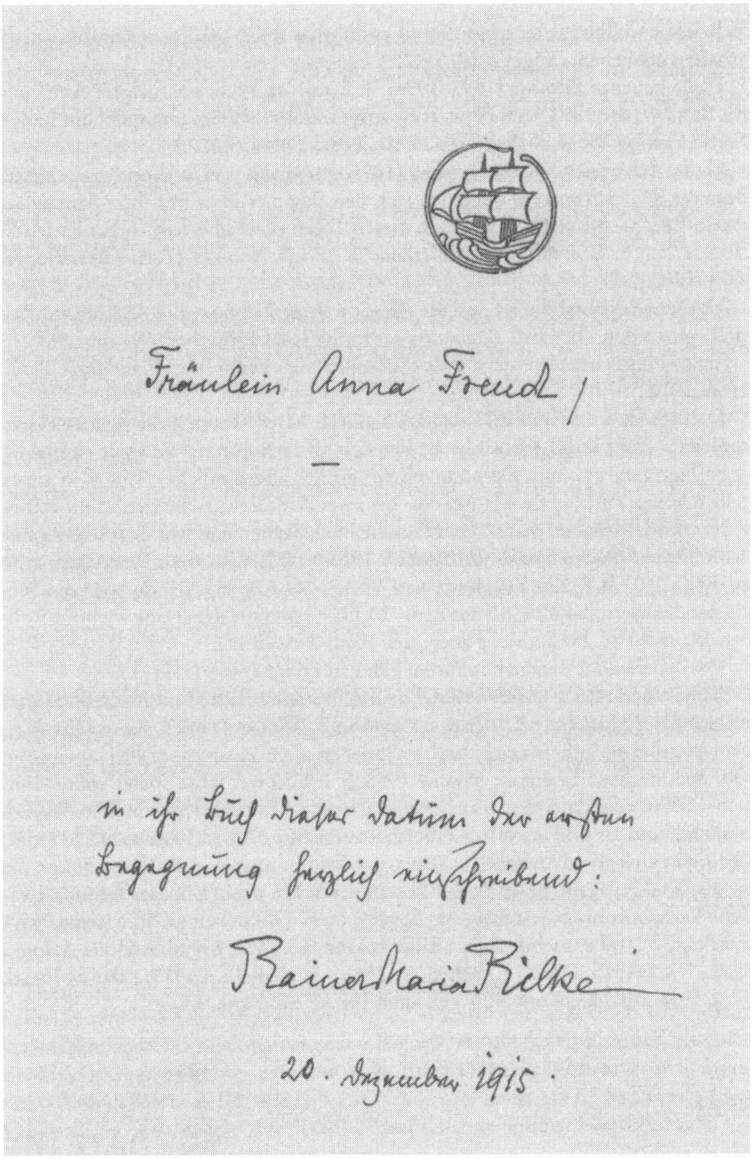

'Fräulein Anna Freud / cordially recording the date of the first meeting in her book: Rainer Maria Rilke, 20 December 1915'

1 This sentence was added between the lines afterwards.
2 'Martin has now successfully passed his third state examination with the corresponding oral examination and now has only a small oral examination before him and will be able to graduate at the end of October–November' ⟨Freud/Ferenczi I, 409 F, 9 July 1913, p. 500, also 419 F⟩. Martin still lived in Berggasse while studying economics and law ⟨Freud M. [1999], pp. 156, 160f.⟩.
3 'Hella . . . was really more a sister than a cousin to me . . . and . . . a charming girl' ⟨Freud M. [1999], pp. 56f.⟩.
4 See 35 SF, 201 SF/AF.

38 SF[1]

Austria
Frl Anna Freud
Vienna
IX Berggasse 19

[Rome] 22 September 1913

Dear Anna,
You should really take a look at this for yourself.[2]
Papa

1 Colour picture postcard: 'Tivoli – Le Cascatelle', with stamp 'Eden Hotel – Roma'.
2 Ten years later Anna was to stay at the same hotel with her father; see text after 201 SF/AF.

39 AF

[Vienna] 24 September 1913

Dear Papa,
I received your nice card today and fear that if you have views like that every day you will no longer be able to get used to our Berggasse again, although it is also very nice here. I am looking forward very much to having something to do again soon. In the next few days I also have a meeting with Frl. Reiss[1] and two young women teachers about preparing for my teaching examination.[2] As for everything else, I shall wait for your return. The weather is very bad and going out is therefore no pleasure; we only managed one very nice excursion on Sunday to Hermannskogl.[3] Hella and Martha are leaving today. Martin and Ernst are a bit sad, not because they are leaving but because they wasted all their money on them.[4] When are you coming back to Vienna?[5] We are all looking forward very much to your return. I am very curious to hear what Aunt Minna will have to say. Lots of people are asking after you and one even wanted an appointment on 1 October, but I didn't give him one. I'm sure that Aunt will be interested to know that Else Leitner[6] gave birth to a son yesterday.

Dr Lustgarten's wife[7] was also here to visit Mama. Otherwise there is nothing special to report.

Once more I send you lots of sincere greetings and a kiss.

Anna

1 Elsa Reiss, headmistress of the primary school that Anna had attended, had prepared her for entrance to the Cottage-Lyzeum; see 13 SF, note 6.

2 'Anna is insatiable with her education plans' ⟨Freud/Ferenczi I, 419 F, 1 October 1913, p. 510⟩. The 'teaching examination' refers to the acceptance for training; see 22 SF and notes 2 and 5, 48 SF and note 3.

3 The highest point in the city of Vienna (543 m) with the Habsburgwarte viewing platform ⟨Baedeker 1926, p. 144⟩.

4 See 37 AF and note 3.

5 Freud left Rome on 27 September and arrived in Vienna on 29 September ⟨Freud/Jones, letter 142; Freud/Ferenczi I, 418 F⟩.

6 Unknown.

7 Presumably the wife of one of Freud's fellow students, the chemist Dr Sigmund Lustgarten, whom Martha Freud also knew well; at the time he was an assistant in Prof. Ludwig's Chemistry Institute, then assistant to the dermatologist Prof. Kaposi in Vienna General Hospital, and later emigrated to New York ⟨see multiple references in Freud 1960*a*; also in Jones I, e.g., pp. 65, 82, 179f., 369⟩.

1914

40 SF[1]

Frl Anna Freud
Vienna
IX Berggasse 19

[Brioni[2]] 12 April 1914

Miss a very intelligent female ape[3] doing her toilet.
Pa

1 Picture postcard; written in pencil.
2 The largest of the Brijuni [Brionian] islands off the Adriatic coast. Freud spent Easter there with Ferenczi and Rank. Anna was originally meant to come with them. 'Are you in the mood to undertake something this Easter [12 April]? . . . Would you like to take the little one along? She is amusing; you know her from the Pordoijoch, of course' ⟨Freud/Ferenczi I, 456 F, 15 February 1914, p. 540⟩. Anna got whooping cough, however, 'and naturally can't come; she has been very good and herself proposed that I take someone else along in her place. Rank has accepted . . .' ⟨ibid., 468 F, 5 April 1914, p. 548⟩. Young-Bruehl's claim (p. 65) that Ferenczi replaced Anna is not correct.
3 Written thus. The picture shows a clothed chimpanzee in a room decorated with tree trunks; it is combing itself in front of the clothes stand, with articles of clothing draped on it, an umbrella and a mirror, with a washstand next to it with bowl and candle. It appears to be a photograph of a real animal posed for the postcard. See 32 AF, in which Anna talks about her hairdressing.

41 AF[1]

Freud
Villa Fasolt
Karlsbad 1[2]

Southampton,[3] 16 July [1914]

Wonderful[4] journey
met[5] by doctor Jones[6]
[unsigned]

1 Telegram; noted by hand.

2 Freud had been taking a cure here with Martha since 13 July 1914 ⟨Freud/Ferenczi I, 483 F; II, 487 F, 489 F; Freud/Jones, letter 198⟩. 'Freud's summer plans had been to go to Karlsbad for intestinal treatment on July 12, from there to Seis in the Southern Dolomites for his holiday proper, then to the Psycho-Analytical Congress Abraham was arranging in Dresden on September 20, and after that to Holland to deliver a lecture at the University of Leyden on September 24. His daughter would join him there on her return from England and he would escort her home' ⟨Jones II, pp. 193f.; Freud/Jones, letter 192; Freud/Ferenczi I, 472 F, 475 F, 480 F; Freud/Abraham, 13 May 1914⟩. Because of the outbreak of war he could complete only the first part of this plan; on 4 August, Martha and he had to return to Vienna 'with the last evening train that was even permitted to run' ⟨Freud to Sophie and Max Halberstadt, 6 August 1914; Freud/Ferenczi II, 496 F⟩.

3 Anna had already planned to visit England at the beginning of the year; 'Even my little daughter wants to go to England by herself this year' ⟨Freud/Abraham, 15 February 1914, p. 218⟩. Young-Bruehl's claim (p. 65) that Anna wanted to reward herself after her teacher's examination is perhaps based on the incorrect dating of this examination (see 48 SF, note 3). 'My daughter will leave the 7th of this month, pass over to England the 15th and no doubt you will have opportunity to see her in August or before' ⟨Freud/Jones, letter 195, 7 July 1914, p. 289⟩. Jones believes that Freud had allowed himself to be deceived by the initial quiet after the excitement over the assassination of the Austrian crown prince and his wife in Sarajevo on 28 June 1914, 'otherwise he would hardly have allowed his youngest daughter to leave for Hamburg on July 7 and certainly not to continue her journey to England, where she proposed to spend a couple of months, on July 18' ⟨Jones II, p. 190⟩.

4 German 'herrlich', corrected from 'herzlich' [sincere].

5 In 1979, Anna Freud recalled her arrival in England: 'Then, at age eighteen, I spent my first holiday in England, partly with friends near Arundel, partly in a girls' boarding school on the south coast. When my boat from the continent docked, there was Ernest Jones on the landing stage, with a bouquet of flowers in his hands to welcome me. I was flattered and impressed, though not without a lurking suspicion that his interest was directed more to my father than to myself, a circumstance to which I had become used' ⟨*Writings VIII*, p. 347⟩. Jones accompanied Anna and her friend on the difficult onward journey to the house of the Pring family in Arundel (see 42 SF, note 9; see also 45 AF and notes 5 and 6) ⟨Freud/Jones, letter 199⟩. For details of Anna's trip to England, see also Young-Bruehl, pp. 65–70.

6 Ernest Jones (1879–1958), doctor of medicine, English neurologist and psychoanalyst; he was the first person to practise analysis in England. In 1908, he attended the Salzburg Congress and then a meeting of the Wednesday Society in Vienna. From 1908 to 1912, he taught at the university in Toronto, Canada; in 1911, he founded the American Psychoanalytic Society in Washington with James J. Putnam, which he transformed in 1919 into the British Psychoanalytical Society and chaired from 1920 to 1940. He was one of the initiators of the 'Secret Committee' and in 1924 founded the London Clinic of Psychoanalysis. From 1920 to 1924, and 1929 to 1949, he was president of the International Psychoanalytical Association, which subsequently appointed him honorary president for life. His three-volume biography of Freud (Jones I, II and III)

remains a standard work today ⟨Jones [1959], pp. 140–65, 219ff., 225f., 229f., 248–54; *Minutes I*, pp. 389–91, Freud 1929*a*; Freud/Jones, letter 148 and note 2; Brome; Winnicott⟩.

42 SF

Karlsbad

PROF. DR. FREUD Vienna, IX. Berggasse 19

16 July 1914

My dear Anna,
I have followed the news of your small world trip with great interest. The telegram saying you have landed in England has just arrived, and the addition 'met by Dr Jones' prompted me to indicate something to you now that I would otherwise have kept until later.

I know from the most reliable sources[1] that Dr Jones has serious intentions of wooing you. It is probably the first time in your young life, and I wouldn't dream of depriving you of the freedom that your two elder sisters enjoyed. But it happens that you have lived more intimately with us, and I cherish the hope that it will be more difficult for you than for them to make a decision about your life without seeking our (in this case my) consent beforehand.[2]

As you know, Dr Jones is a friend and very valuable colleague of mine. That could be one further temptation for you. I therefore cannot but draw your attention to the fact that there are two types of reasons that speak against him, some that apply just to you and some that also apply to us. Ultimately, however, they both converge.

As far as we are concerned, our wish is that you should not commit yourself or marry at such a young age before you have seen, learned and experienced a bit more and know more about people. I suppress the regret I would feel for having you so far away from me; that would be easily sacrificed to other advantages. From our own experience we would also like to spare you a long engagement.[3] In that regard Dr Jones, who must be nearly thirty-five and will soon need a wife, is also very unsuitable.

You will no doubt attach greater value to the other reservations that only concern you and are not as obvious as the first ones. Jones is no doubt a tender and good man who will love his wife dearly and be very grateful for her love. But I know from his first wife,[4] whom you certainly know and appreciate with her remarkable abnormalities and splendid character traits,[5] that he is not the right man for a more refined feminine person. He had to work his way up from a very small family and a difficult situation,[6] devoted his interest primarily to scientific matters and failed to acquire the tact and finer consideration that a spoiled and also very young and somewhat fragile girl will expect from her husband. In order to appreciate him and to forgive him for all sorts of things you would need to be a good five years older, and then he would be too old for you. It was no doubt these more intimate things that prompted Loe to warn you of his advances before I knew anything of the matter. In the end, however, I could only agree with her.

Moreover, Jones is in reality much less independent and more in need of support than he appears. He requires an experienced and perhaps even an older woman. When left to himself – and that is the worst I can say about him – he shows a tendency to move[7] into precarious situations and then to gamble everything, which for me would not guarantee your security.

Perhaps you find this entire warning superfluous and will assure me that you have never considered him seriously. But you must then know what his intentions are, which you will no doubt handle with tact and gracious prudence. I would advise you not to avoid communicating with him, but at all events to try not to find yourself alone with him. Ferenczi, who will be spending August in London,[8] our relations, or Miss Pring[9] herself could easily act as cover for you if you wish to remain firm. I believe that you should and that you should not allow it to come to a declaration. Postpone your visits to London until you have company and do not allow yourself to be picked up by him alone. You also owe it to the man. Please write to me about it.

Sam[10] (61 Bloom St, Manchester) expressed his willingness today to provide you with money and already has my first transfer.[11] Obviously, you should also visit Uncle Emanuel, Marie and the old cousins[12] and be very friendly to them, even if you cannot spend as long with them as they will demand. I also received word today that the other Joneses[13] have left.

We have good accommodation here and spent three days in dreadful heat before enjoying a rainy day today. We are now finally in direct communication with everyone. Aunt really appears to have pleurisy so that she will no doubt have to prolong her stay indefinitely at the sanatorium.[14] She doesn't have fever, however.

I send you affectionate greetings and wish you all the luck you need to make this trip a pleasant memory.

Father

1 From Loe Kann (see note 4).

2 'Annerl sent a telegram yesterday, to the effect that she has arrived safely in Southampton and was met by Ernest Jones. I took the opportunity to make clear to her my position on the matter right away, for the whole thing really doesn't suit me, and I don't want to lose the dear child to a clear act of revenge [see note 13], irrespective of everything that speaks rationally against it. I think Loe will also keep watch like a dragon' ⟨Freud/Ferenczi II, 488 F, 17 July 1914, p. 2⟩. See 43 AF–45 AF; also 257 AF and note 11. For Jones's later reaction to Freud's opinions, see Young-Bruehl, pp. 67f.

3 Freud and Martha suffered considerably from the separation during their long engagement. See 'courtship letters' 1882 to 1886 in Freud 1960*a*.

4 Louise ('Loe') Dorothea Kann (?–1945), who lived with Jones for seven years and assumed his name during this time. During summer 1913 she left Jones but they remained friends. Because of the medication for a severe kidney ailment, Loe became addicted to morphine and at Jones's request went to Freud for

analysis from October 1912 to summer 1914 ⟨Brome, p. 82f.; Jones [1959], pp. 129f., 187; Freud/Jones, 1912ff., *passim*⟩. Freud found Loe 'extraordinarily dear' and described her as 'an extremely intelligent, deeply neurotic Jewess' and 'actually a jewel' ⟨Freud/Ferenczi I, 307 F, 23 June 1912, p. 387; 409 F, 9 July 1913, p. 499; 395 F, 13 May 1913, p. 486⟩.

5 See 161 SF–163 SF. In his letters to Freud, Jones mentions her neurotic excess, particularly her manifest capacity for suffering and an indomitable thoroughness in all things, e.g., 'I must tell you the latest story of Loe. She replaced Trottie [Loe's dog] by a more obvious symbol, a cock, who always slept in her bedroom. A time came when she had to go away for a while, so that it had to take its place with the hens in the fowl-coop. Lest, however, it should suffer from fear or loneliness in this unaccustomed environment she had her bed moved there also and slept there with it for the first two nights until it no longer found it strange' ⟨Freud/Jones, letter 328, 30 November 1912, pp. 444f.⟩. See also Appignanesi and Forrester, pp. 226–39.

6 See Jones [1959], p. 15f.

7 Possibly a slip of the pen: 'begeben' [put himself] rather than 'bewegen' [move].

8 See Freud/Ferenczi I, 482 Fer; II, 492 Fer. Ferenczi had to abandon his plans on 27 July, however, because of the outbreak of war ⟨Freud/Ferenczi I, 493 Fer⟩. Anna had by then become well acquainted with Ferenczi (see 40 SF, note 2; see also the repeated greetings to him in these letters, and Freud/Ferenczi *passim*).

9 Mabel Pring, the friend in whose family Anna was staying in Arundel. 'The family in Arundel is an excellent one, and she [Anna] could not be in better hands' ⟨Jones to Freud, 27 July 1914, in Freud/Jones, letter 201, p. 296; also letter 210 and Anna's PS to letter 220, p. 323⟩.

10 Soloman ('Sam') Freud (1860–1945), son of Freud's half-brother, Emanuel ⟨Stammbaum Lange: Freud Family, 'Genealogical Tree', p. I – although 'Sam' is not short for 'Samuel'⟩. See also Freud/Sam correspondence.

11 Freud/Sam, 13 July 1914.

12 Marie, née Rockach/Rokach, wife of Emanuel (*c.* 1835/6–1923). Seven children resulted from the marriage (perhaps eight): Johann ('John', born 1855 in Freiburg; 'disappeared from Manchester after 1875'); Pauline ('Pauli', 1856–1944); Bertha (1859–1940); Sam (1860–1945); Mathilda (1862–8); Harriet Emily (1865–8); and Henrietta (1866), who died after just nineteen days. ⟨Stammbaum Lange: Freud Family, 'Genealogical Tree', p. I; also Krüll, p. 313 and note 9, p. 358, note 23 (without the associated reference in the summary on p. 313).

13 Loe Kann Jones and Herbert Jones (known as 'Davy'), a wealthy American ⟨Freud/Jones, letter 115 and note 2⟩. They had married in Budapest at the end of May ⟨Freud/Ferenczi I, telegram 476 F, 24 May 1914⟩. Rank and Freud had been witnesses. 'I have come back yesterday at night from Budapest where we – Rank and I and Ferenczi as an interpreter – have helped Loe to become Mrs Herbert Jones. I am sure it must be hard for you, and so it is for me when I remember the series of events from the evening in the Weimar coffeehouse when you offered me her treatment to the moments when I assisted to her wedding with another. It is a most remarkable chain of changes between persons and feelings of such and the most striking points seem to me, that our relations have not been spoiled and that I have learned even to like the other man' ⟨Freud/Jones, letter 192, 2 June 1914, p. 285; in general letters 191–7⟩. See also Young-Bruehl, p. 65, albeit with a different month for the wedding.

14 Minna was being treated at Cottage-Sanatorium ⟨Freud/Jones, letter 197⟩. See also 43 AF (4th paragraph), 46 SF and note 4.

43 SF

PROF. DR. FREUD Karlsbad, 22 July 1914
Vienna, IX. Berggasse 19

My dear Anna,
On the contrary, I am very happy with your letter[1] and would have had nothing more to write to you about it if it weren't to advise you against withdrawing too much at the moment. I mean you should not avoid him but can quite easily accept guidance and suggestions; you should be as natural as possible and establish a basis of friendship and equality, which works well particularly in England, and just avoid being alone with him where he could make a definite approach. I am sure you have the talent to do that – after all you are a woman. When Ferenczi is there you can join all of the excursions. If a more intimate conversation should occur, say something about your plans for the future, which could serve Dr Jones as a warning and above all appear confident rather than coy. On the whole, as long as I can be reassured about where you stand, I am actually not displeased that your stay in England is also offering you this experience. These are things that you have to learn and cannot avoid. Dr Jones needs a wife to protect him from the temptations that a doctor is exposed to. Do you think it is absurd to divert his interest to Mabel's sister,[2] whom you like so much?

I am glad that you are feeling so at home in your new surroundings, but I think it is only right and proper that you should contact Uncle at 61 Bloom St, Manchester, *as soon as possible*, after which it will be up to him when he visits or invites you. Uncle is very sensitive, as you know, very stubborn and strange, but is full of gentleness. Your visit on the whole will be too short for all your plans and demands. You have turned out a little different from Math and Soph; you have more intellectual interests and will probably not be as happy with a purely female activity. Your inclinations are also likely to find expression in your choice of husband, but by and large you can still look forward to the discovery that your sisters chose the right path.

According to the latest news, Loe and Herbert Jones spent some time in The Hague. I don't yet know whether they have crossed the Channel and smuggled in Trottie.[3] You should write to her soon in London; I think she is expecting it.

It is really beautiful here, a little too warm, and we are trying this time to make it as comfortable as possible and to behave like rich people. Mama got a string of pearls for her birthday,[4] nothing compared with what every American woman wears around her neck, but still a piece of jewellery, the acquisition of which is giving her plenty to think about. Aunt wants to go to Semmering until we meet in Seis.[5] The catarrh is healing, but she feels very weak. Your brothers are all asking for your address, a sign of your esteem in the family. Rosi[6] asked for and received a contribution for a trip to Munich. I take it you know when Grandma will be seventy-nine years old.[7]

I can even work a little here because no one is forcing me to. A manuscript[8] has already been sent to Rank.[9] It's a pity that today the stay is already half over.

You can tell Dr Jones that a whole book on psychoanalysis has been published by the two Frenchmen, Régis and Hesnard (Bordeaux)[10] (by F. Alcan, Paris), a highly systematic summary with a lot of insight.[11]

I greet you affectionately and will write to you again soon. Please let me know everything that goes on with and around you.

Your father

1 Not present in the collection made available to me. See Freud's letter of the same day to Ferenczi: 'Anna writes from England that Jones is behaving very nicely toward her and the family whose guest she is; he was there the first Sunday and has promised to come back on the next one. I won't do anything to disturb their relations. The little one should only learn how to assert herself, and she will probably be adroit enough to get out of the way of a declaration that can only lead to disappointment. She feels quite sure of herself' ⟨Freud/Ferenczi II, 491 F, 22 July 1914, p. 7⟩.

2 Perhaps Connie, whom Jones mentioned in a later letter to Freud ⟨Freud/Jones, letter 210, 17 June 1915⟩. For Jones's marriage, see 126 SF, note 3.

3 Loe's dog: 'On Wednesday she [Loe] returns to Holland to fetch Trottie' ⟨Jones to Freud, in Freud/Jones, letter 201, 27 July 1914, p. 296⟩.

4 On 26 July.

5 But see 41 AF, note 2.

6 See 45 AF and note 8.

7 On 18 August.

8 1914*g*; the third technical work in this series, 1915*a*, followed shortly afterwards ⟨Freud/Jones, letter 200, Freud/Abraham, 27 July 1914⟩.

9 Otto Rank (formerly Rosenfeld) (1884–1939), D.Phil. Coming from a poor background, he was unable to study originally but was able to do so later, encouraged and supported financially by Freud. Prior to that he had already acquired on his own a good level of literary, philosophical and also psychoanalytical knowledge. In 1905 he met Freud and his circle and soon became his 'zealous and dependable secretary' ⟨Freud 1914*d*, p. 25; also Freud/Jones, letter 248, 28 July 1919, p. 353; see also Jones II, pp. 180f.⟩. Rank was secretary of the Vienna Psychoanalytic Society (1906–15), one of the founder members of the 'Secret Committee' and also an untiring editor of *Imago* and *Zeitschrift* ⟨Mühlleitner, pp. 250–3; List; Taft; Lieberman; Zottl⟩. In 1924 Freud was thinking of him for president of the Vienna Group ⟨Freud/Jones, letter 421, p. 540; Freud/Ferenczi III, 952 F, p. 137⟩. Nothing came of it, however, because Rank, who had meanwhile begun to investigate his own theoretical and therapy concepts, had distanced himself from Freud on his return from a visit of several months to the USA. See 287 SF and note 11.

10 Emmanuel Régis (1855–1918), doctor of medicine, professor of psychiatry in Bordeaux since 1905, and his assistant Angelo-Louis-Marie Hesnard, *La psychoanalyse des névroses et des psychoses*, 1914. The two had already been in contact with Freud some time earlier ⟨Freud/Abraham, 2 January 1912, p. 145; Freud/Jones, letter 70; Régis and Hesnard, 1913⟩.

11 On 17 May 1914, Freud mentioned to Jones the preparations with F. Alcan for French translations ⟨Freud/Jones, PS to letter 189, p. 280⟩. Although nothing came of it, the book was a further step in the spread of psychoanalysis in France that had started in 1911 ⟨Freud/Jung, 223 F, 255 F; Morichau-Beauchant, 1911, 1912; Freud 1914*d*, p. 32⟩. On the reception of psychoanalysis generally in France, see also Scheidhauer, Roudinesco, Goldschmidt (p. 11; also Bolzinger, who focuses, however, on Freud's neuropathological works). ⟨For the last reference, I thank Georges-Arthur Goldschmidt, Paris, 6 September and 6 October 1999.⟩ See also 125 SF and note 19.

44 SF

PROF. DR. FREUD [Karlsbad] 22 July 1914
Vienna, IX. Berggasse 19

My dear Anna,
I recently had the opportunity to write Dr Jones a few lines advising him, without being rude, not to make advances towards you.[1] Perhaps he will allow himself to be told, and you will have no more difficulties with him. Enjoy yourself in every way and don't take it so tragically. Please let me know as well if you think it necessary for us to give Mabel a formal invitation to London.

Affectionately,
Papa

1 'I thank you very much for your kindness with my little daughter. Perhaps you know her not enough. She is the most gifted and accomplished of my children and a valuable character besides. Full of interest and learning, se[e]ing sights and getting to understand the world. She does not claim to be treated as a woman, being still far away from sexual longings and rather refusing man. There is an outspoken understanding between me and her that she should not consider marriage or the preliminaries before she gets 2 or 3 years older. I don't think she will break the treaty' ⟨Freud/Jones, letter 200, 22 July 1914, p. 294⟩. Jones answered on 27 July 1914: 'I had already fully appreciated what you write about her. She has a beautiful character and will surely be a remarkable woman later on, provided that her sexual repression does not injure her. She is of course tremendously bound to you, and it is one of those rare cases where the actual father corresponds to the father-imago. [para] I am glad to give you good reports of her, for her health is excellent and she seems to be having a happy time, reacting bravely to her new surroundings' ⟨ibid., letter 201, pp. 295f⟩.

45 AF

[Arundel,[1]] 26 July 1914

Dear Papa,
I thank you very much for your letter and was particularly relieved that it came so soon and gave me such good advice. It brought me back down to earth and put right the confusion that your first letter had caused. I wrote and sent off a letter to Uncle Emanuel the same day. If they should invite me to Manchester I will do my best to be nice and pleasant to everyone. I am much better at that now and it is also easier when there is no one present who knows how I am otherwise.[2] Today I also wrote to Mrs Jones in London, since I have heard that she is already there. I dream terribly often of her, last night too. I have also heard that she had a bad crossing and is not very well.[3] I was very sorry about that because you know that I am extraordinarily fond of her.[4]

My life here has been the same the whole time. I get on extremely well with everyone in the house and am teased terribly by the brothers.[5] I feel very much at home, not at all like a guest, and am no longer bored as I was on the first two days. We are always doing something, even if it is difficult to say exactly what. But that's how holidays should be. I am now really good friends with Mabel and at home she has changed very much for the better.[6] We have talked about going to St Leonards[7] on Saturday. Unfortunately, she will only be staying with me there for three or four days, because she doesn't have more time. But I am sure I shall settle in there very quickly and I am sure it is very pretty. I am also *very*[8] pleased that Rosi is travelling to Munich.

Yesterday was a very exciting day; I was out from nine in the morning until midnight, and that is also why I haven't answered your letter until today. Dr Jones picked Mabel and me up in an automobile with a friend – Mr Martin, whom you might know from Frau Jones[9] – and we had a splendid excursion. We went first to Henley and then down the Thames on a motorboat and a different route back home. We saw a frightful amount of things in this way and I hadn't imagined that England was so beautiful. Have you seen all the houses and palaces on the Thames? Each one is more beautiful than the last and unlike anything we have in Austria. It was really a wonderful day and Mabel in particular was so completely happy with everything that it was worth it for that alone. We are both still hot and burnt from the wind and sun, and the whites of my eyes look as funny as they do on negroes. I would not have agreed to go, however, if you had not written that I could. We want to go on even more excursions when Dr Ferenczi is here. Can I not say that I want to pay for myself? I believe that Dr Ferenczi is quite sensible about such things. And I have so much money. But yesterday was really nice.[10]

Now, Sunday morning, everyone has gone to church and I have lots of time and quiet to write. I am very curious to hear about Mama's birthday. Had you already given her the pearl necklace, or did you only do so today?

You will just have to see that Mama wears it. I am sure that it is very nice. I am very pleased to hear that you are making your life so comfortable in Karlsbad and that you also find time to write because I think that[11] is the best combination for you. And it must be very nice to write something.[12]

I heard something yesterday from Dr Jones that[13] did not please me greatly; it was the news that Dr Abraham wants to visit you in Seis.[14] I know that you like him a lot, but it would be nicer if you could be left completely in peace for the summer. Do you still send the *Wiener Klinische Z.*[15] to Lampl? You probably know already that he is very unhappy in Reichenau[16] and will probably leave.[17] I feel very sorry for him. I haven't yet heard anything from my brothers and sisters but would be very pleased to have news from them. What you wrote about my esteem in the family sounds very nice, but I can't quite believe that it is true. I don't think it would make a great difference at home, for example, if I were no longer there. I think only I would feel the difference.

I must stop now and go downstairs. I'll leave everything else I have to write for the next letter. I am glad to know that you will write again soon. I greet and kiss you lots and hope that you continue to enjoy yourself.

Anna

1 A small town in Sussex near the south-east coast of England.
2 See 28 SF and note 2.
3 Probably from Jones ⟨Freud/Jones, letter 201, 27 July 1914, p. 296⟩.
4 See 108 AF and note 2.
5 Jones mentions three of these brothers in a later letter to Freud ⟨Freud/Jones, letter 210, 17 June 1915, p. 311⟩.
6 Anna apparently met Mabel in Vienna. It is impossible to say from the sources available to me whether she accompanied Anna on the journey or just met her in Southampton ⟨Freud/Jones, letter 199, p. 293⟩.
7 St Leonard's, a girls' boarding school on the south-east coast of England.
8 Doubly underlined in the handwritten letter. Young-Bruehl's claim (p. 69) that Anna's cousin Rosi Winternitz accompanied her to St Leonard's conflicts with this description; see 43 SF and note 6; nor does Freud mention Rosi in his letter to Sam announcing Anna's visit ⟨Freud/Sam, 7 July 1914⟩.
9 Probably Louis Charles Martin, 'Professor of English at Liverpool, who left first for the Sorbonne and then Sweden', a friend of Jones from his time in Canada ⟨Jones [1959], p. 186⟩. On 3 October 1914, he passed on to Jones the news from Freud that Anna had arrived back safely in Vienna ⟨editorial note in: Freud/Jones, after letter 203, p. 299⟩. See also Martin L. C., 1920.
10 See Freud/Jones, letter 201, p. 296.
11 Grammar mistake in German.
12 See 101 AF and note 1; see also Introduction, p. 10 and p. 6.
13 Grammar mistake in German.
14 Since May, Freud and Abraham had been writing about spending 'the whole summer together' and then travelling together to the Psychoanalytical Congress (see 41 AF, note 2) ⟨Freud/Abraham, 13 May, 15 May, 18 July (quotation p. 261), 23 July, 27 July 1914⟩.
15 Either *Wiener klinische Wochenschrift* or *Wiener klinische Rundschau.*

16 Perhaps Reichenau an der Rax, a tourist community in the valley of the Schwarza in the south of Lower Austria where the Freuds had earlier frequently spent their holidays ⟨Tögel [1989], p. 150f.; Freud 1985*c*; Freud/Bernays, letter 145 S/Mi.⟩.

17 Hans Lampl obtained his doctorate on 23 January 1914 and then worked at Vienna General Hospital before doing military service until 15 June. From 11 August 1914, he was 'aspirant and stand–in secondary doctor in the dissection department of Wilheminen-Spital in Vienna', where he carried out serological research into 'problems of immunology' in close collaboration with department head Karl Landsteiner, the discoverer of blood groups. He remained there as an assistant – interrupted by periods of military service – until 1 May 1921 ⟨Speiser and Smekal, pp. 61, 111f., 142; Lampl; Landsteiner and Lampl 1915–18; Lampl and Landsteiner; the information by Young-Bruehl (p. 96) is not completely correct⟩. There are no details in his curriculum vitae about the time from 15 June to 11 August 1914 or his activity in Reichenau. See 125 SF, note 12.

46 SF

PROF. DR. FREUD — Karlsbad, 28 July 1914
Vienna, IX. Berggasse 19

My dear Anna,

Your letter and experiences are very pleasing. You are right: when Ferenczi is there you can *insist* on paying your way. You have enough money, £20 with Sam, and he will send you more if you need it.[1] But now we are the more interesting ones. You cannot imagine how the sudden outbreak of war[2] has changed everything, and you are missing out to a certain extent by not being in your fatherland at this time. At the moment it is impossible to determine anything. The trains will be stopped tonight because of the mobilization; we are thus trapped here and hope, but don't know for sure, that we can depart on the 3rd for Munich.[3] Aunt, who apparently is not at all herself, complains a lot about being on her own and refuses to make the journey alone to Tyrol.[4] Fortunately, the mail is still working in all directions, but you need prior legitimation to send a telegram. Also, non-urgent telegrams take longer to arrive than letters. I would like to write more, but even several sheets would not be enough. It is a strange, interesting but uneasy time.[5]

Mama's birthday was, of course, quite disrupted by the excitement of these days. The nicest thing that the post brought were your photographs; Max has done a really good job with the profile in particular.[6] She received the string of pearls a week ago but is wearing it as if she was born with it!

Martin's address is Salzburg, Makartplatz 6; Oli: Millstatt am See, Forellenheim; Ernst's address you already have: [Munich] Augustenstr. 15.

I have not yet heard anything from Loe Jones but will inquire soon. You don't write whether Trottie is still alive.[7] I am still waiting to hear lots from you and expect amongst other things a reply to my last letter.

I greet you affectionately and am pleased for everything you find to admire, most of which is unfamiliar to me.

Your father

1 See Freud/Sam, 7 July 1914.
2 Freud's letter is dated on the day of Austria-Hungary's declaration of war on Serbia ⟨Ploetz [1980], p. 34⟩.
3 See 41 AF, note 2.
4 See 42 SF and note 15. 'We returned here from Karlsbad on 5 August. My sister-in-law, who is at last recovering, was back before us, as her sanatoria had closed' ⟨Freud/Abraham, 25 August 1914, p. 271⟩.
5 For Freud's reaction to the outbreak of war and his changing attitude to the war, see Jones II, pp. 192f.; Freud/Ferenczi, 498 F.
6 Max had apparently taken photos of Anna when she visited the Halberstadts in Hamburg before continuing to England (see 41 AF, end of note 3).
7 Jones reported on 3 August: 'Loe has safely smuggled Trottie over, but after unheard-of difficulties and fatigues' ⟨Freud/Jones, letter 202, p. 297⟩.

47 SF[1]

Miss Anne[2] Freud
c/o Dr Jan van Emden
The Hague
Jan van Nassaustr. 84
Holland[3]

[Vienna] 22 August 1914

Dear Child,
I'm pleased to see your handwriting again[4] and to hear that you are well and being brave.[5] Don't attempt to travel alone, but join Jones if relations with America should cause you to move to The Hague.[6] We are all well here together; Aunt is finally recovering, Martin is a volunteer in Salzburg. You still have money with Sam. We know nothing about your relations with Uncle Em[anuel][7] and family. Keep well and write as often as possible via Emden.

Your Papa

1 Postcard.
2 Written thus.
3 The address is crossed out and replaced in another handwriting by 'Berggasse 19, Vienna, Austria'. The postcard was thus returned with the stamp 'The Hague 16 September 1914'.
4 'On her first excursion into the world our little Annerl has run into turmoil. We have been cut off from her completely since 29 July,' wrote Freud on 6 August 1914 to Sophie and Max Halberstadt.
5 A card from Anna is missing; Freud reported on 23 August 1914 to Ferenczi: 'Yesterday I finally got a card from Annerl which had been rerouted through The Hague, which says that she was in London for a day with Loe and Davy

Jones and that thereupon she returned to St Leonards. She writes that *Trottie* was very glad to see her again! . . . Davy Jones adds the following words: Your daughter is frightfully brave, if you could see her, you would be extremely proud of her behaviour' ⟨Freud/Ferenczi II, 498 F, p. 13⟩. See also the impressive study by Molnar [2005].

6 Anna was already on her way home; Loe and Herbert Jones organized her return journey ⟨Freud's letter of thanks to Herbert and Loe (undated) in 1960*a*, p. 311; Jones II, p. 194⟩. 'The great news of the day is that Annerl arrived here surprisingly after ten days' journey via Gibraltar, Genoa, Pontebba, travelling with the Austrian Ambassador,' wrote Freud to Martin in Salzburg shortly afterwards ⟨Freud, M. [1999], 26 August 1914, p. 180⟩. Anna had to leave most of her luggage behind, however. Jones brought some of it with him in March 1919 when he travelled to meet Rank and others in Switzerland (see 162 AF and note 2). 'Rank has taken over a suitcase with Anna's things and has brought it here safely. Great jubilation with the accompaniment of chocolate-tangerines-Havanas' ⟨Freud/Ferenczi II, 805 F, 12 April 1919, pp. 345f.; also Freud/Jones, letters 224, 233, 244⟩. The rest arrived later: 'To my great pleasure my jewellery from England and my beautiful handbag have now finally arrived' ⟨Anna to Kata, 7 October 1919⟩. Back in Vienna, Anna devoted herself again to her teacher training: 'Annerl is, as always, industrious and gratifying' ⟨Freud/Ferenczi II, 513 F, 9 November 1914, p. 24⟩. At the same time she worked in a day nursery for workers' children and, towards the end of the war, voluntarily for the American Joint Distribution Committee, which provided accommodation for homeless war children ⟨Freud/Jones, p. 306; Young–Bruehl, pp. 99f.⟩. (See also Introduction p. 44 and note 5; also Anna's experiences in the Second World War in *Heimatlose Kinder*, Anna Freud, 1971.)

7 Just a few weeks later, on 17 October, Emanuel had a fatal accident: 'Yesterday I received news of the death of my eldest brother . . . the information says: railway accident. I think he couldn't bear the war' ⟨Freud/Ferenczi II, 515 F, 11 November 1914⟩.

1915

48 SF[1]

Frl Anna Freud
Vienna
IX Berggasse 19

[Königssee][2] 28 June 1915

Good luck with the exam![3]
Papa and
[in her own handwriting] Tante Minna

1 Picture postcard; 'Hotel Schiffmeister, Königssee'.
2 Freud travelled to Berchtesgaden on Saturday 26 June to look with Minna, who was in Bad Reichenhall at the time, for summer holiday accommodation on the Salzberg (see also 174 AF, note 10) ⟨Freud/Ferenczi II, 548 F⟩. For the selected accommodation, see 50 SF and note 1.
3 Anna's first teacher's examination: 'Anna is . . . studying for her teaching examination and will, one hopes, be dismissed on account of a deficient singing voice. She is, incidentally, developing charmingly, more gratifyingly than any other of the six children' ⟨Freud/Ferenczi II, 542 F, 8 April 1915, p. 56⟩. See also 49 AF, note 1, 53 AF and note 6. Young-Bruehl (p. 64) incorrectly dates the examination as 'June 1914', as does Peters (p. 22). For the second teacher's examination, see 84 AF, note 7. Young-Bruehl (p. 72, without source citation) also claims that Anna overcame the problem of the 'lack of a singing voice' with the aid of private tuition from concert singer Hedwig Schick (wife of fellow-analyst Eduard Hitschmann). Peters (p. 36) also mentions this, referring to a personal statement by Anna. See 162 AF, note 6, however.

49 AF

[Bad Ischl][1] 12 July 1915

Dear Papa,
I am beginning to think that I will have to travel to England again and have all kinds of strange experiences so that you will write me another

long letter. Anyway, I am sitting quietly in Ischl, surrounded by cousins[2] and aunts,[3] but I want to hear from you. Whether you are writing a lot, whether you are looking forward to Karlsbad and whether it is very quiet, at least. You will already have heard that I am having a very good time here: life is all very comfortable and easy. And Mausi[4] is not at all as bad as I thought. I found a rather shabby cep yesterday, but also picked cauliflower mushrooms, which you would surely have disdained. Those are the big events here. I have started again[5] on the Putnam[6] translation and am enjoying my box of books. Every night I dream about the exam again and now feel well and truly tested. But I haven't ever failed.

I think a lot about you and Mama and wonder how you are. I have only had one piece of news. The clock lights up powerfully every night and keeps perfect time.

Write a long letter to me soon. I send you a long kiss and remain,

Your Anna

1 'Anna, after taking her examination to be an elementary school teacher and signing a contract which makes her an instructor at her own school (Frl Goldmann) has gone to Ischl to her grandmother and aunts' ⟨Freud/Ferenczi II, 550 F, 10 July 1915, p. 64⟩. See also 84 AF, note 7, and 86 AF, note 5.

2 Rosi and Mausi (see note 4). The relationship among the cousins was alternately tense and close; see Young-Bruehl, pp. 73–5, 93, 96–8.

3 Aunt Paula and Aunt Dolfi (see 57 SF and note 2); perhaps also Aunt Rosa some of the time (see 67 AF) ⟨Young-Bruehl, pp. 73–5⟩.

4 Cäcilie ('Mausi') Graf (1898–1918), daughter of Freud's sister, Rosa, and Heinrich Graf ⟨Freud 1985*c*, p. 332; Stammbaum Lange: Freud Family, 'Genealogical Tree', p. IV (with 1899 erroneously as year of birth)⟩. See also 53 AF and note 2.

5 Anna translated a lecture by Putnam to the Association of American Physicians (1913), entitled 'On Certain of the Broader Issues of the Psychoanalytical Movement'; see 60 AF and note 7, and 69 AF and note 8. Freud himself translated an article by Putnam anonymously for the *Zentralblatt für Psychoanalyse* with an added footnote (1911*j*). He paid tribute to Putnam's work in greater detail in the preface (1921*a*) to Putnam's *Addresses on Psychoanalysis*.

6 Dr James Jackson Putnam (1846–1918), professor of neurology at Harvard Medical School, Cambridge, MA; he 'is not only one of the most eminent neurologists in America but also a man everywhere greatly respected for his unimpeachable character and high moral standards'. Since 1911 he had 'taken his place without any doubt in the forefront of the pioneers of psychoanalysis' (Freud 1911*j*, p. 766). He founded the American Psychoanalytic Association in 1911 with Jones and was its first president. He established the Boston Psychoanalytic Society in 1914, the 'activities' of which were 'to be the various medical and cultural aspects of psychoanalysis' ⟨*Journal of Abnormal Psychology*, vol. IX, no. 1, April–May 1914, p. 71; obituaries: Freud 1919*b*, Jones 1920*b*⟩. See also Freud 1971*a*.

50 SF

PROF. DR. FREUD

14 July 1915
Vienna, IX. Berggasse 19

My dear Anna,
We will be leaving finally on Saturday evening at 10.15.[1] The evenings until then are taken. Today Rank was here out of uniform;[2] also Ernst, who had had himself assigned some official tasks so that he would have time to take his leave properly.[3] Tomorrow, Prof. Loewy,[4] who already visited us one lunchtime, is coming. He left Rome a week before the declaration of war, which was expected daily at the time.[5] On Friday Uncle Alex is to share the wartime evening meal with us. During the day there is the usual last-minute business. I started clearing up the antiques today.[6] The son of the Egyptian king is still standing alone on the desk, abandoned by all the gods and with only the Nubian head and the long Neith from Sais to keep him company. Altogether very little is being destroyed; only the contents of the small glass case have to be removed. If the Russians come to Vienna unexpectedly in the meantime, they will notice the empty space immediately.

Last night it was terribly hot and humid and impossible to sleep; today, finally, it's a bit cooler. You appear to have much more welcome rain than us. We are very curious and very uncertain as to how the summer will turn out.

Rank brought the Greek grammar, but it is so well-thumbed and marked up that I will buy a new one after all.[7] I have arranged with Aunt Pauli to send her 100 K every ten days (from 7 July), of which 20 are an allowance for you and Rosi for your additional activities while you are there. I hope in this way that you will not want for anything. It's a good thing that there is no fee to pay for your repeat exams, otherwise it wouldn't be enough. We are glad to hear that you have managed so far to make your stay comfortable and hope that it will remain so until we see each other again.

Send my regards to everyone and keep the best greeting for yourself.

Your Father

1 For the first part of the holidays to Karlsbad, where Freud and Martha remained from 18 July to 12 August ⟨Freud/Ferenczi II, 550 F, 553 F, 560 F⟩. For the second half of the holidays in Berchtesgaden, from 13 August. See 66 SF and note 1, and 68 SF/MF.

2 Rank had originally attempted to avoid being conscripted ⟨Freud/Ferenczi II, 521 F⟩, but was ultimately called up in June 1915; he remained provisionally in Vienna and continued his editing work during this time ⟨ibid., 554 F⟩. This did not last, however: in January 1916, he was posted as an editor to the official Austrian army publication *Krakauer Zeitung* (see 74 AF, note 13) ⟨ibid., 573 F, 585 F, 589 F, 594 F, 780 F⟩.

3 'Ernst was already here a few times from Wiener Neustadt and is always splendid' ⟨Freud/Ferenczi II, 548 F, 21 June 1915, p. 62⟩.

4 Emanuel Löwy (1857–1938), renowned Austrian archaeologist, one of Freud's few *Du* friends (from his student days), since 1889 in Rome, after 1918 in Vienna: 'Recently I was treated to a stimulating evening by my friend Emanuel Lowy, who is professor of archaeology in Rome. He is a scholar as solid as he is honest and a decent human being, who pays me a visit every year and usually keeps me up until three in the morning. He is spending his fall vacation here where his family lives' ⟨Freud to Wilhelm Fliess, 5 November 1897, 1985*c*, pp. 177f.; see also Freud's youthful letters to Eduard Silberstein, 1989*a*, pp. 71 and note 5, 86, 172⟩.

5 Following a secret agreement with the Entente, which promised to grant Italy South Tyrol as far as the Brenner and Istria and Dalmatia, Italy declared war on Austria-Hungary on 23 May 1915 ⟨Ploetz [1980], p. 839; Kleindel, p. 308⟩.

6 The collection of antiquities was 'a source of extraordinary invigoration' for Freud. 'These things put me in a good mood and speak of distant times and countries' ⟨Freud to Wilhelm Fliess, 1985*c*, 6 December 1896, p. 214, 6 August 1899, p. 366. See also Gay, p. 171⟩.

7 See 52 SF and note 3, 58 AF and note 11.

51 SF[1]

Frl Anna Freud
Bad Ischl
Lärchenwald 12

Karlsbad, 18 July 1915

Dear Anna,
Write to us at 'Rudolfshof', which we have just moved into. Don't go swimming for *too* long, too often or when it is cold. It will make you very anaemic. Enjoy yourself otherwise.

Affectionate greetings,
Papa

1 Postcard.

52 SF

PROF. DR. FREUD

[Rudolfshof] Karlsbad, 18 July 1915
Vienna, IX. Berggasse 19

My dear Anna,
You are the recipient of the first letter from our new quarters. Mama is resting in the next room and I have to be at the doctor at 4 o'clock. It is 3.30, cold and overcast, which we are interpreting for the time being as a restful change. The journey was tiresome at the end because from Marienbad[1] we had to change from an express to a local train, which took two hours instead of one. Villa Fasolt, where we were so worried about you last year,[2] is not even open this year. We had to drive around for two hours before we

found this very pleasant house, which we knew from Emden. We have two rooms, intended as a bedroom and a living room, but we have changed them around a bit so that they match their occupiers' requirements rather than their original intended purpose. Mama's room has the famous balcony and mine has a delightful writing niche, which I am inaugurating with this letter. I hope I can write a lot as I brought only two books, an exercise book and a grammar, both in the same (neutral) foreign language.[3] The rooms have high ceilings and are airy, light, elegant. Apparently they cost almost twice as much last year. We were very hungry at lunchtime and ate extremely well, possibly too much. It was not that cheap, although not as expensive as in our beloved Vienna. There is a pastry that is almost light grey and tastes very good. We already tried out ham rolls in Marienbad. The peace here is very marked. The war elsewhere has been transformed into peace.

On the train we met an acquaintance, Herr Kaufmann, brother of the doctor.[4] Asked whether he was an optimist or a pessimist, he answered cleverly that he was a sophist. You can only understand that if you know that 'soff' in Hebrew means 'end'. He assured us that peace with Russia was very close. May God in his almightiness prove him right.

We hope that there will be something from you poste restante. Now I have to rouse the doctor.[5]

Affectionate regards,
Papa

1 See 59 SF, note 2.
2 When Anna found herself in England at the outbreak of war.
3 Presumably the books for Anna, who wanted to learn Greek (see 50 SF and note 7, 58 AF). 'Neutral' could refer to the fact that at the start of the war Greece was still neutral ⟨suggestion kindly provided by Andreas Hamburger⟩. It was not until 2 July 1917 that it declared war on the Central Powers (Austria-Hungary, Germany, Turkey, Bulgaria) ⟨Ploetz [1940], pp. 460f., 542; Ploetz [1980], pp. 839, 843; Kleindel, pp. 306, 313⟩.
4 Rudolf Kaufmann (1871–1927), doctor of medicine, Viennese specialist in internal medicine and cardiovascular diseases, whom Freud held in high esteem on account of his 'outstanding achievement with Sophie' ⟨Freud/Ferenczi I, 409 F, 9 July 1913, p. 499⟩. In a letter to Wilhelm Fliess of 4 March 1895, Freud noted the wish-fulfilling tendency of dreams, citing a dream by this doctor (in other words a normal, non-psychotic person) ⟨1985*c*, p. 114⟩. The brother is presumably the Viennese businessman Josef Kaufmann (1868–1922) ⟨indication from Wolfgang Kloft⟩.
5 Probably Dr Kolisch (see 61 SF and note 1).

53 AF

[Bad Ischl] 19 July 1915

Dear Papa,
I was delighted to receive your letter [50 SF] and the postcard today with your address on it. I am glad to know once again where I can write to you

because one feels quite excluded and in the midst of war when one doesn't know where the other party is. I was very sorry not to have been able to witness the removal of your gods; I hope you did it all properly so that we don't have any unpleasant surprises when we unpack in the autumn. In the short time since my last letter little or nothing has changed. Since you noted that there are no fees to pay, my exam dreams have lost all of their attraction and have withdrawn for the time being. I am not short of ideas, however, and every night I dream instead of Frau Jones,[1] and today that I had become blind. It was terrible and it is something that I have dreamt quite often. You shouldn't think that I have changed my opinion, which we have already talked about, just because I am getting on with Maus here. About that I am right. Besides she has a kind of pitying contempt for me, which is difficult to explain.[2] We are all very grateful to you for the 20 K as it gives us much more freedom of movement. We used it to eat our first snack at 'Nockentoni' behind Pfandl.[3] Our excursions are gradually getting longer, but the idea of being a strong person takes some getting used to, so we are only going out for half-days at the moment. Sitting around, reading and studying are also very pleasant, and the hammock in particular is a great temptation for me. I am in any case being very sensible about bathing.

I think you should write a few words to Grandma. We couldn't tell her that you had written to Aunt P[auli] as she would be very jealous; also if I tell her that you have written to me. I am sure she will be delighted at your arrival,[4] and you are also sure to like it a lot. Ischl is quiet this year and the woods are magnificent; you should come for a couple of days.[5]

I'm beginning to feel apprehensive about teaching in the autumn;[6] perhaps it will be much more difficult than I think. It was quite irresponsible of Frl Dr[7] to hire me so trustingly. I hope the summer will last a long time (perhaps I can learn something as well).

Rosi is developing a number of agreeable characteristics; she sends her regards, as does Aunt P[auli], who will no doubt reply to your letter and who is enjoying her role as landlady.

I will say goodnight for now before going on an evening stroll with Rosi to the post office. I send you and Mama a kiss. Write again *soon*.

Your Anna

1 Loe Kann Jones.
2 There could be a letter from Freud to Anna missing here. At all events there is no indication in the available documentation that Freud 'seized upon this little opportunity to try negotiating a rapport', as Young-Bruehl states (p. 73). For further details of the relationship between Anna and her cousin Maus, see the correspondence Anna/Lou ⟨1921–3 *passim*⟩.
3 The restaurant Nockentoni and the Poststüberl Pfandl both still exist today ⟨Wolfgangsee, p. 76⟩.
4 But see 68 SF/MF.
5 See the following letters up to 68 SF/MF.

6 This would be Anna's first year as a trainee teacher (see 48 SF and note 3).
7 Dr Salome (Salka) Goldman(n) (1870–after June 1942), headmistress of Cottage-Lyzeum, which Anna had herself attended ⟨Peters, pp. 10ff.⟩.

54 SF

PROF. DR. FREUD Kbd Rudolfshof, 21 July 1915
Vienna, IX. Berggasse 19

My dear Anna,
The postman brought five letters apart from yours today and thus re-established our contact with the world. All kinds of interesting things. Martin wrote on 11 July that he received a grazing wound in the right arm during an encounter with an enemy patrol but is already recovering. As he wrote himself and his handwriting was normal it cannot have been anything really serious. But it's still the first case in our house. He describes himself as being very tired but in the best of spirits. Sophie writes that Ernstl[1] can already take several steps and has discovered that she is his mammi. Since then he has been very affectionate with her but at the same time is ruining all the furniture he can reach. Dr Sachs[2] says that they are doing without his involvement in the European war until 16 August. He is back in Vienna.[3]

Your own letter was no less interesting. The fact that you now find teaching so difficult is no doubt merely your way of reproaching yourself for having such a good time, and is therefore groundless. Carry on as you are doing. We also sometimes feel uneasy about the comfortable life that we have made for ourselves here. I try to attenuate it[4] by continuing all the writing I started in Vienna.[5] My room and writing niche are very elegant. Spa life is in full flow; Mama already looks better and is enjoying it a lot. On the social front there is nothing to report yet.

I thank Rosi very much for her greetings and good qualities. Hopefully the money will be sufficient for all your undertakings, otherwise some more can be sent.

Hoping that you continue to enjoy your stay during the day and will slowly abandon any nightlife, I send you my affectionate regards,

Your father

1 Wolfgang Ernst ('Ernstl/Ernsti', born 11 March 1914), the first son of Sophie and Max Halberstadt ⟨Stammbaum Lange: Freud Family, 'Genealogical Tree', p. II⟩. He took his mother's maiden name after his father's death ⟨Freud, W. E. [1987], p. 200⟩. See 146 SF, note 4.
2 Hanns Sachs (1881–1947), doctor of law, imperial and court attorney; until 1918 he worked as a jurist in Vienna before moving temporarily to Zurich, where he opened a psychoanalytical practice. From 1910 to 1920 he was a member of the Vienna Psychoanalytic Society (thereafter the Berlin group), and from 1912 to 1927 he belonged to the 'Secret Committee'. He organized the publication of the magazine *Imago* in 1912 with Rank. In 1920 he moved to Berlin where he taught

analysis at the Psychoanalytical Institute. In 1932 he emigrated to the USA and was one of the few lay analysts in Boston, MA ⟨Mühlleitner, pp. 279–81; Sachs, e.g. p. 62f.⟩.

3 He was then conscripted but released after twelve weeks of training ⟨Jones II, p. 203⟩.

4 The German 'sie' is written over 'es'. See also Freud/Andreas-Salomé (30 July 1915, p. 32): 'I am writing to you from an idyll, which we, my wife and I, have defiantly and stubbornly created for ourselves [. . .]'.

5 A collection of twelve essays in which Freud pursues his intention of placing psychoanalysis on a solid basis and which he wanted to publish as a book entitled *Zur Vorbereitung einer Metapsychologie (Preliminaries to a Metapsychology)*. See the section 'Papers on Metapsychology', in Freud, *S. E.*, vol. XIV, in particular 'Editor's Introduction', pp. 105–7. Five of these essays were published: 1915*c*, 1915*d*, 1915*e*, 1916–17*f*, 1916–17*g*; the twelfth essay, entitled 'Overview of the Transference Neuroses', appeared posthumously after its rediscovery in 1983 ⟨Grubrich-Simitis [1985]⟩.

55 SF

PROF. DR. FREUD [Karlsbad] Rudolfshof, 22 July 1915
Vienna, IX. Berggasse 19

My dear Anna,
There's not much to report from here. We are living very comfortably. Mama no longer has any signs of rheumatism. I write when I feel like it. It would all be very nice if we could be sure about the future, but we can't.

I have a serious request for you today. Mama cannot make her mind up to cross the border after Karlsbad[1] and I have also become apprehensive because of the increasing restrictions. Now we have read the warning in the German newspapers not to conceal documents at the border and at the same time the indication that their verification could take some time. That means that I cannot take the manuscript I am working on at the moment to Berchtesgaden[2] without being exposed to all kinds of uncertainties.

Under these circumstances, Mama thought that Marie Valerie-Bad, which is in fact just a hotel, in Goisern[3] would be a good place for the three of us to stay. It has the advantage that it can be checked out. I would therefore ask you to go by train some time next week with Rosi to Goisern, and look at the house and the rooms, try out the food, inquire about the prices and pass everything in critical review. There won't be any shortage of flat walks but you know that what we both need is varied forest landscape with the odd mushroom, so that we don't have to take the train if we feel like one. You should also find out whether there will be three rooms available on 8–9 August. We would then be near Ischl but not in Ischl itself, which has certain advantages. The costs of the expedition for two people should be calculated separately. If you like it, you can even reserve by telephone after hearing from us.

I hope you continue to enjoy good weather and the good life and remain,
Affectionately,
Your Papa

1 After finishing the spa cure in Karlsbad.
2 This was the next planned holiday destination; see 50 SF, note 1.
3 Today Bad Goisern, approx. 10 km south of Bad Ischl in the 'wide and appealing Goiserertal' on the path of the historical brine pipeline; it was 'once described as the "most beautiful village in the monarchy"' ⟨Verein Regionalentwicklung, p. 4⟩.

56 AF

[Bad Ischl] 23 July 1915

My dear Papa,
I was pleased to read in your two letters that you have found a comfortable war-less existence and that you are still getting the extra editions from Vienna. I think one can get used quite easily to the pleasant taste.[1] I was concerned at first about Martin's graze, but from what you write it sounds as if it wasn't too bad. And perhaps it will protect him from worse. I would like to have known whether he stayed with his company or was sent to the hospital. I hope we will hear more soon.

My nightlife, if often uncomfortable, is nevertheless very interesting sometimes. It recently brought me a meeting between you and Dr Putnam to discuss the translation of an English word.[2] That's something that I can't have so easily during the day. I have written a letter to Frau Jones but not yet posted it. It's difficult to write when you haven't seen the other person for such a long time and have thought about them so much. Should I send regards from you next time I write?

Our successful excursion made us want to go for another walk and we have therefore arranged a splendid tour for tomorrow. I had better not write anything more because otherwise it's bound to rain. The postman here knows me now, and I'm sure that after the five letters you received at once your postman also knows who you are. And yet apart from the letters from you and Mama, I don't get any proper mail, only picture postcards. Lampl has also failed to write this year as he usually does.[3]

You don't mention whether the shops are open in Karlsbad. There is a mineral shop here but not up to the nephrite standard.[4] Rosi and I are really interested only in the cake shops, particularly after we return from swimming. Do the Emdens know that you are in Karlsbad? I still believe that they will come. Write to me again soon and tell me what you have been up to.

What do you think about visiting little Ernst in the autumn? By then he should be able to say 'aunt' and would be pleased to see us.[5]

I will end now with a goodnight kiss, so that I am well rested for the excursion.

Your Anna

1 'We like to quote an advertisement that is very common here: "It is easy to get used to the pleasant taste"' ⟨Freud/Abraham, 4 May 1915, pp. 309f.⟩; see also 221 AF, 239 AF.
2 See 49 AF and note 6.
3 See 27 AF and note 2.
4 Nephrite (jade) is a hard grey-green material that is often made into jewellery ⟨kind addition by Wolfgang Kloft⟩.
5 The visit to the Halberstadts in Hamburg did indeed take place in the second half of September, but Freud went on his own (see 67 AF, note 4); Anna went at Christmas (see 69 AF, note 6).

57 SF

PROF. DR. FREUD

[Karlsbad] 26 July 1915
Vienna, IX. Berggasse 19

My dear Anna,
We are looking forward to your report on the reconnaissance trip to Goisern and thank you in the meantime for your amusing and regular letters. I'd like to tell you today how Mama's birthday went – or is going, because it is only 4 p.m. Apart from the usual birthday money, I gave her a barometer which has already proved its worth. (I gave it to her a few days ago.) It drops suddenly and refuses stubbornly to rise again. In Karlsbad the weather changes on average three to five times a day. Today we have already had seven shifts from hot sunshine to gloomy rain. We cannot therefore make the planned excursion to Hans Heiling.[1]

Apart from that we have a resplendent bouquet of roses in the room to make up for all the gifts of flowers that cannot come in these uncertain times, and we intend today to send a 100 K donation by mail for two charities that Mama has chosen. The most delightful present, however, is a new photo of Ernstl standing up and reaching for a sausage attached to the wall. I've no doubt that it captures him brilliantly but we can't make him out well because the photo is taken from behind. We were very pleased to receive this interesting picture.

Letters and telegrams have arrived from all concerned, obviously with the exception of Martin, whom we last heard from on the 15th of this month. I suppose he can't calculate when his congratulations might arrive and is therefore excused.

I have sent Aunt Pauli the second instalment with the same amount for you and an additional 50 K for Aunt Dolfi.[2] The time passes quickly and the money as well. Today it is already the start of our second week in Karlsbad. I hope we will see each other soon, refreshed and with no more worries than are unavoidable in these times.

With affectionate greetings,
Your Papa

1 Hans Heiling, character in a German-Bohemian folk legend, an earth and mountain spirit whose loved one chooses another bridegroom. During the wedding ceremony Heiling turns the couple and the wedding guests into stone. (In Heinrich Marschner's opera Heiling does not carry out this vengeful act.) Another version of the legend has Heiling as a Faustian character who acquires knowledge by promising to be faithful to a water fairy. When he breaks his promise she turns him and his guests into stone ⟨e.g., Karell, pp. 141f.⟩. There is a rock formation on the banks of the Ohře between Karlsbad and Loket, which is said to resemble the petrified guests. It remains a popular excursion destination to this day.

2 Freud's sister, Esther Adolphine ('Dolfi') Freud (1862–1942). She remained unmarried and lived with their mother whom she selflessly looked after. Freud often expressed the family's gratitude to her and sent 'pocket money' (e.g., 22 July 1930, in 1960*a*, p. 396). After their mother's death on 12 September 1930, he invited her to recover at his summer residence in Grundlsee ⟨Freud/Eitigon, 610 F; Freud 1992*i*, 17 September 1930, p. 82⟩. See 277 SF, note 4.

58 AF

[Bad Ischl] 27 July 1915

My dear Papa,
I have some very sad news: apart from two rooms that are not suitable for us, there is nothing free now or for the next month in Goisern. Otherwise everything was exactly as we would have wished it to be and the hotel owner, who naturally remembered Aunt Anna,[1] was very friendly. He said he knew the professor, the man with blond hair and a beard, who was always there. That must have been Lampl, as we explained to him. But otherwise it wasn't much fun because I was quite annoyed that[2] there were no prospects for us or Rosi. The man said we should have booked in June. Because we were so annoyed we turned the unsuccessful trip into a wonderful excursion. We walked to Goisern, of course, and had planned to try out the food and then return. Instead we continued on foot to Steeg,[3] went by rowing boat to Hallstatt,[4] and came back the same way.[5] We have just arrived back at the house after being away for thirteen hours: eight hours of walking, three hours rowing, two hours rest. Fortunately, there was a good evening meal waiting for us because, as there were three of us, on a meatless day we couldn't get enough to eat anywhere. I am not the least tired, just burnt and full of blisters from rowing. It was wonderful. But what are we going to do now for the summer? I don't know of anywhere else around here because Strobl[6] would not be suitable for us. If you have any ideas, I would, of course, be glad to travel there. I have heard confirmation of the border difficulties with Germany from a number of people and imagine it's not something you want to subject yourselves to. If only we could find something nice!

Thank you for your two letters and your description of Mama's birthday. I was particularly pleased to hear about the barometer, which we could also use here. At present we can control the weather only with our raincoats. We both had one today in our rucksacks and also a woollen jacket. So, of course, the sun shone brightly all day. As all this carrying around is also of benefit to the entire population of Ischl, however, we don't mind doing it. I would love to have seen the picture of Ernstl.

I was particularly pleased to hear about Martin's citation and the possibility of an award.[7] He does us proud. I dreamt recently that I had to defend a dairy farm belonging to us from the enemy. My sabre was broken, however, and I felt ashamed in front of the enemy when I drew it out. When I woke up I was lying at attention in the bed with my hands down the seams of my nightdress. I have not been able to find out whether Oli took the position[8] or whether I will see him still this summer. How am I supposed to make up for six brothers and sisters next winter?[9] I received a very nice letter from Math today, which sounds, however, as if she is anything but happy. Berchtesgaden was apparently not right for her after all.[10] I feel sorry for her, because it is so nice when there's plenty to do. I have read Cicero's First Oration Against Catilina, partly with Maus and partly on my own. I liked it a lot and didn't find it so difficult. I am looking forward to learning Greek.[11] Please put down any mistakes in this letter to the thirteen-hour excursion. It is now the fourteenth hour and I will go quickly to post it so that you get the news about Goisern as soon as possible. It's such a pity.

Write again soon. Lots of kisses from your

Anna

[Written upside down at the end of the last sheet]:

As you can't really call the excursion a trip to Goisern, it would not be right for me to mention expenses.

1 Freud's sister, Anna, married name Bernays (1858–1955), spent part of her holidays in Europe in 1913, in Goisern with her three daughters and two grandchildren. On 18 August, she organized a large birthday celebration in the hotel dining room for her mother: 'Our small guesthouse supplied the fresh trout, chickens and cakes' ⟨Freud-Bernays, A., pp. 151f.⟩.

2 Grammar mistake in the German.

3 On Lake Hallstatt.

4 Written 'Hallstaat'.

5 Young-Bruehl (p. 74) writes that the 'rowing episode' resulted in an argument with her aunts, leading to Anna's departure to spend part of her holidays with the Rie family. It is not clear whether this occurred in 1915 or 1916. In neither instance is there any reference in the correspondence to a change of holiday plans. Rowing remained one of Anna's favourite pastimes throughout her life ⟨e.g., Anna/Eva, letters 16, 17⟩.

6 On Lake Wolfgang.

7 Martin obtained the 'citation' after his graze wound; the award came somewhat later: 'On Wednesday the 13th I was roused from sleep by a dark figure, . . . my son Martin. He . . . wore the big medal for bravery on his muddy uniform' ⟨Freud/Ferenczi II, 571 F, 17 October 1915, p. 82; Freud/Abraham, 1 August 1915⟩.

8 'Oli . . . for the time being is helping out at his uncle's office [Alexander], but is negotiating with his previous firm for a position at a railway construction site in the Steiermark and could go there at the end of the month. So, the lot of old age, loneliness, is clearly in the offing' ⟨Freud/Ferenczi II, 550 F, 10 July 1915, p. 64⟩. Oliver had studied in Berlin and passed his engineering examination on the same day that Anna passed her teaching exam (see 48 SF). See also 59 SF and note 7.

9 Anna had already done so temporarily when Freud was in Berlin and Hamburg at Christmas 1913: 'It will be very quiet at home, three lonesome womenfolk [Martha, Minna and Anna]' ⟨Freud/Ferenczi I, 21 December 1913, p. 528⟩. See also 18 SF/MF, note 5.

10 But see 68 SF/MF.

11 See 50 SF and 52 SF.

59 SF

PROF. DR. FREUD [Karlsbad] 29 July 1915
Vienna, IX. Berggasse 19

My dear Anna,

Thank you very much for your news. I am sorry to hear how it ended up, because now we don't know anything. Aunt herself advises against Berchtesgaden,[1] and everyone else against the guesthouses in the Salzkammergut after the cure in Karlsbad. We are thinking of taking another cure in Marienbad,[2] provided that the weather is warm and dry.[3] It would have several disadvantages and I don't like it very much. You might then perhaps prefer to stay in Ischl as well. Or else we can go from here to Salzburg and look for something nearby, so that you can come too.

We recently received welcome letters from Martin with a photograph of a horse and a pencil sketch of him done by an officer. He looks like a Cossack, but the horse looks very thin. We heard today that Walter Pick[4] has been wounded, fortunately only slightly; perhaps he will get leave. We have had bad weather here with bright periods yesterday for the first time. I have a temporary upset stomach and Martha has the start of a periosteal infection, hopefully also passing. It is difficult to find real comfort this summer.

I have received the card from both of you.[5] I don't think you should go on such long walks. Four to five hours is really enough. The landlady[6] should keep a closer watch on you.

Oli took the position but it is not sure when he will start, perhaps not until early September, and he has not yet signed the contract.[7]

I send you my affectionate regards and will tell you about everything that happens.

Papa

1 Minna Bernays, who had been staying in Bad Reichenhall, was then at Villa Hofreit near Berchtesgaden before Freud; see 48 SF, note 2, and 66 SF.

2 Marienbad (Mariánské Lázně), the 'international spa belonging to Tepl Abbey', the third of the three large spas in the Cheb region ⟨Reininger, p. 201; also Zörkendörfer, pp. 148–64⟩. The Fourteenth International Psychoanalytic Congress took place there in 1936 ⟨*IZ*, vol. 23 (1937), pp. 164–203 and 331ff.⟩.
3 Freud, Martha, Minna and Anna had been there together in 1913 for a cure (33 AF, note 2) but had a very negative impression; see 60 AF and note 1.
4 A friend of Freud's children; they remained in contact later on as well ⟨picture postcard from Hotel Tauernpasshöhe, Post Rastadt, of 29 December 1931, from Martin and son Walter Freud to Ernst Freud, with signed greetings by Walter Pick and others; FM London, Box 31A⟩. Pick's mother, who was in Marienbad at the time, reported the news of his wounding ⟨Freud to Sophie and Max Halberstadt, 29 July 1915⟩. See also 166 SF.
5 Not contained in this package.
6 Paula Winternitz, see 53 AF.
7 On 7 September 1915, Oliver then became 'an engineer with a permanent position' ⟨Freud/Ferenczi II, 566 F, p. 79⟩.

60 AF

[Bad Ischl] 30 July 1915

My dear Papa,

The letter I have just received doesn't sound anything like as happy as your previous ones. I don't know whether it is because of the upset stomach, the periosteal infection or the summer plans, but I don't like any of it. I can't do anything about the first two, but I can say something about the third. I find Marienbad anything but a good idea and I am actually quite appalled by it. You didn't like it there and I certainly didn't either.[1] I am still counting on spending the second half of the summer with you and Mama, however. In any case, I couldn't extend my stay here very much even if I wanted to, because Dora Steiner[2] has already booked and there's not enough room for both of us at the same time. I don't want to stay here anyway; however pleasant it has been, I have always regarded the stay as a transition. On the other hand, the Salzburg idea is not at all bad and it is something that I have already considered. I hope that's what you decide to do. If not, I would, of course, come to Marienbad. There can't be that big a difference in the cost, because I need enough money here, as I have discovered. What about travelling to Grandma's birthday, though?[3]

Our walks might seem very long, but we don't notice it. If you want to take a good look at the countryside half a day is not enough, especially as we take lots of rests in the hot weather and only walk when it's cool. Eating outdoors is also fun.[4] I find walking quite easy this year and don't get tired at all. We will have to take a rest now in any case, however, because the weather has turned bad again. I just want to make the most of the summer and am so happy that I can walk well, which has never been the case before. I've also abandoned swimming as a result.

Today was a sad day because the maid broke the bowl that Mama recently brought to me from Sophie. I'm just glad that it wasn't the nephrite bowl. I declared my desk taboo on the very first day, but unfortunately the bowl was somewhere else. I was most annoyed.

Otherwise everything is unchanged and in good order. I have now started the book about Egypt.[5] Aunt Dolfi thanks you sincerely. She has not written because she has been very poorly during the last few days. She seems to have permanent ups and downs and her voice[6] is different every day.

In the translation[7] I don't quite know what 'Übertragung' means? Is it the transference of ideas from the doctor to the patient?[8] I am not sure and cannot therefore use it properly.

I am very curious to find out in your next letter whether you have come to a firm decision. I hope it's not Marienbad. But you won't get rid of me so easily! I trust that by the time you receive this letter you and Mama will both have recovered. I truly hope so and remain with a kiss,

Your Anna

Unfortunately I don't dream at all any more.

1 Anna said later to Jones that 'it was the only time she ever remembers her father being depressed' ⟨Jones II, p. 112⟩. Freud himself wrote to Jones from Marienbad on 10 August 1913: 'We had a bad time here, it was too cold and wet. I can scarcely write from rheumatism in my right arm' ⟨Freud/Jones, letter 134, p. 217⟩. He wrote to Ferenczi on 5 August 1913 that he was 'moody, irritable, tired. . . . Always ruminating over the same dark thoughts, taking little things hard, aversion to food [. . .]' ⟨Freud/Ferenczi I, 414, pp. 504f.⟩. See also 15 AF, note 12.

2 Unknown.

3 Her eightieth birthday on 18 August.

4 Rosi recalled these excursions in a letter to Anna many years later: 'On one, we walked to Lake Wolfgang and camped on the left shore, near the forest. We had a camp stove and prepared our meals. . . . The other excursion was to Hallstatt. . . . A thunderstorm approached, and we were very frightened that we might not reach the shore. We rowed with all our strength, though, and made it' ⟨8 April 1948, quoted in Young-Bruehl, p. 74⟩.

5 Written thus ('Egypten' instead of 'Ägypten'). Perhaps Anna was reading *History of Egypt* by the American Egyptologist Breasted, which Freud owned ⟨Fichtner, unpublished manuscript [2003], p. 9⟩. But Freud also used this spelling (see 50 SF), which appears not to have been unusual at the time ⟨see, e.g., *Freudiana*, facsimile, p. 31; also in other documents (thanks to Gerhard Fichtner)⟩.

6 It is possible that her health affected her voice. In a letter to his brother Alexander on 18 August 1916 Freud also mentioned that 'Dolfi's voice is not good'.

7 Apart from the lecture by J. J. Putnam (see 49 AF and note 6), Anna Freud also translated an essay by Ernest Jones in summer 1915, entitled 'Professor Janet über Psychoanalyse. Eine Erwiderung'. Both translations appeared in *IZ*, vol. 4 (1916/17), pp. 1–20 and 34–43, with the translator indicated not by name but as 'Translated by **'. In some later translations (see, e.g., 96 AF and note 9) Anna is mentioned by name. See also 125 SF, note 7, and 144 AF, note 6.

8 See Freud's answer in the following letter. Anna's question probably refers

to a point in Putnam's talk in which he says: 'Any intelligent, careful person may . . . through prudence and caution, avoid exciting in the patient, in any serious degree, the sense of dependence on the physician ("Übertragung") [German in the original] which has often proved a formidable objection to every kind of mental therapy.' Anna used the same word, which Putnam saw as synonymous with 'dependence', adding the descriptive 'geistig' [mental] in the latter case (p. 5): 'Jeder Arzt, der einigermaßen intelligent und gewissenhaft ist, kann . . . durch Behutsamkeit und Vorsicht vermeiden, daß in dem Patienten ein ernsterer Grad von Übertragung entstehe, von jener geistigen Abhängigkeit, die jeder Art psychischer Therapie so oft zum Vorwurf gemacht worden ist.' In his article, Jones used only 'transference', the English term for 'Übertragung' (p. 406); in the German translation, it then reads: 'Übrigens verwechselt Professor Janet . . . die "Verschiebung" ["displacement"] mit dem davon ganz verschiedenen Vorgang der "Übertragung" ["transference"].'

61 SF

PROF. DR. FREUD

Kbd., 1 August 1915
Vienna, IX. Berggasse 19

My dear Anna,
I would like to answer quickly to your letter of today to put your mind at rest. We are both well again and have abandoned Marienbad, but not you. We are now thinking, as Dr Kolisch[1] advises, of extending our stay here until the 15th and then coming to a hotel in Ischl to celebrate the birthday, and spending the rest of the summer either in Ischl or Aussee, wherever we can find something. I am sure you will be happy with that.

The accident with your desk is not the only one. The hardworking and strong girl here also threw your picture on the floor in the first few days and broke the glass. Unfortunately, that didn't serve as enough of a lesson for me. A few days later she knocked over and broke an ashtray; I'm sure she regretted that it was only the porphyry one and not the nephrite bowl I left at home. That gave me back my energy, and after some discussion I showed her a large piece of paper which I had tacked with drawing pins over the desk, on which is written:

Do not touch the desk!
On pain of punishment!

That seems to have done the trick.

I have also had the chance to do some other creative writing here. In front of the 'Hall of Friendship', where we have breakfast, is a man with a weighing station, which for years he has invited guests to use with the following atrocious four-liner:

So wahr daß Gottes Augenlicht
Hat jeder Kurgast sein Gewicht
Darum soll er es nicht unterlassen,

im Freundschaftssaal sich wägen lassen.
[As true as the light of God's own eyes
Every spa guest has his weight and size
So he should not let his chances slip
Of getting weighed in the Hall of Friendship]

I finally took the liberty of asking the man where he got the verse from, to which he replied that it was his own work and that he knew that it was not free of errors. Touched by his modesty, I decided to find a replacement for this absurdity and the next day, taking his own ideas, offered him the following verse:

So wie ein Herz und Angesicht
Hat jeder Kurgast ein Gewicht
Damit ihm das nicht werd' zur Qual,
Wag' er sich oft beim Freundschaftssaal
[As head and heart are given by fate
So every spa guest has his weight
That this should not torment him at all
Let him weigh himself oft in the Friendship Hall][2]

He was highly complimentary and promised to display it next season.

I am sure I have already written that Ernst is meant to have departed yesterday.[3] I received a card yesterday from Martin in which he mentions[4] a fourteen-day leave.[5]

There was a tarock game here for the first time a few days ago with the Brothers.[6]

'Übertragung' is a technical term signifying the transference of the patient's latent tender or hostile feelings to the doctor.

In spite of the difficult times – one can get used to anything – we have taken up contact with Frau Schapira[7] again. After much urging, Mama has finally had her pearls restrung and can now enjoy them for the first time. An ostentatious old brooch has been purchased for Grandma, for you a little opaline thing is being made, and I am bargaining for a nephrite bowl that is marvellously beautiful, but strangely with an old German coin cemented in the middle. We haven't yet agreed on a price for it.

Affectionate greetings,
Your Papa

1 The spa doctor in Karlsbad ⟨editorial note on the copy of this letter in the German version of Freud 1960*a*, p. 513⟩.
2 Translation by Michael Molnar in *American Imago*, vol. 53 no. 3 (autumn 1996), pp. 201–4.
3 Ernst was posted for duty on the Dniester in eastern Galicia ⟨Freud/Ferenczi II, 559 F, 560 F⟩.

4 Martin had been 'out since January 20' ⟨ibid., 559 F, 31 July 1915, p. 74⟩.
5 Grammar mistake in German.
6 The Brothers, members of the Israelitischer Humanitäts-Verein 'Wien' B'nai B'rith VII no. 449, which Freud joined in 1897 ⟨Knöpfmacher, W., p. 5; Knoepfmacher, H. [1979], p. 65⟩. He took an active part in the life of the association from 1897 to 1917, with discussions, committee work and a total of thirteen lectures ⟨Knöpfmacher, W., pp. 25, 30, 35, 38, 41, 45, 49, 50, 52, 59, 67, 68, 71; see also ibid., pp. 97, 98, 121; Knoepfmacher, H. [1979], pp. 63–72⟩. See also Freud 1985*c*, letter 150, Freud's lecture to members of the association (1926*j*, and 1915*i*, 1926*k*, *1935e*, 1965*g* and 1979*d*).
7 Possibly a shopkeeper in Karlsbad.

62 AF

[Bad Ischl] 3 August 1915

Dear Papa,
Just imagine, from Friday to today, Tuesday, I was without any signs of life from you, probably because of the post office here, which is really behaving most shabbily. I was all the more pleased to receive Mama's card[1] and your letter, because I was getting quite worried. As you can imagine, I am completely in agreement with the plans as they now stand. I'm sure we will be able to find something from here. At all events, I am happy now. It was not a good idea for you to separate yourselves completely from me.

You hadn't written anything to me about Ernstl's departure, so I was very surprised. I would very much like to know his exact Feldpost [army post office] address, also whether he is already an officer cadet, and how he is being employed. And whether he has taken his dog with him. I would be very pleased if Martin's leave enabled him to visit you here. I don't want to miss him, because I am sure he has an enormous amount to tell us.

I am sorry about your bowl. My nephrite bowl has taken refuge in the desk drawer, where it feels very safe. This is not a good place for it. By contrast, the negotiations with Frau Schapira are very much to my taste. I am in favour of your deciding to be rich and taking the bowl, because I would like to see it. Is it New Zealand or real green?

You don't need to worry about my walks. They don't tire me, because we always walk on the flat, something that Rosi and Maus are already not too happy about.[2] But I am too lazy for a real climb. In any case, we were condemned to inactivity for the whole of last week because Rosi was out of action. That was very good for my translation and also the book about Egypt. All that is missing from it are instructions on how to read hieroglyphics.[3] It is extremely interesting and yet easy to read. Is the story you wrote about the weigher man really true? The verse is very good and has the right number of feet; but it sounds so improbable to me. The card from Traunkirchen should have arrived by now.[4] I am still fascinated by the daggers and will have to look to see if the junk dealers here have any.

My former knife collection was not what I wanted and I have therefore stopped it. Now I will have to start a new one.

My dreams are becoming terribly shabby. I recently dreamt of a large mug of coffee with whipped cream. That's practically a reversion to 'strawberries, wild strawberries, etc.'[5] Fortunately, this drop in the intellectual level has not harmed the rest of my well-being.

Affectionate regards to you and Mama.

With a kiss,

Your Anna

1 Not in this collection of letters; perhaps it is the communication of 31 July mentioned in 63 SF.
2 More than thirty years later Rosi wrote to Anna: 'I got angry at you because you always wanted to walk on flat paths, instead of in the mountains' ⟨8 April 1948, quoted in Young-Bruehl, p. 74⟩.
3 Jean-François Champollion, the founder of Egyptology, managed to decipher hieroglyphics in 1822. Freud once compared himself with Champollion in a memo (1993*h*).
4 Missing here; see 63 SF.
5 Reference to a childhood dream of Anna's, which Freud used in *The Interpretation of Dreams*: 'My youngest daughter, then nineteen months old, had had an attack of vomiting one morning and had been consequently kept without food all day. During the night after this day of starvation she was heard calling out excitedly in her sleep: "Anna Fweud, stwawbewwies, wild stwawbewwies, omblet, pudden!"' ⟨1900*a*, p. 130⟩.

63 SF[1]

Frl Anna Freud
c/o Winternitz
Bad Ischl
Lärchenwald 12

Kbd., 4 August 1915

My dear Anna,

Your card[2] of 2 August received today complains of the absence of news from us. We wrote to you on 31 July and 1 August.[3] I hope you have now received those letters. We are fine. We have informed you of our plans, and there has been no change since then.

Best regards, Papa

1 Postcard sent back and forth several times, with several stamps: in Karlsbad on 4 August (date of dispatch); in Bad Ischl on 5 August 1915 (marked 'unknown'); again in Bad Ischl on 6 August 1915 (receipt).
2 Presumably the card from Traunkirchen mentioned in 62 AF.
3 The communication of 31 July is missing from this collection. It is presumably 'Mama's card', mentioned by Anna in 62 AF.

64 SF

PROF. DR. FREUD [Karlsbad] 5 August 1915
Vienna, IX. Berggasse 19

My dear Anna,
Received your long-awaited letter today. Don't worry, the bowl is Chinese nephrite and is standing on the taboo desk with another exotic item next to it. Today we can give you precise information and tasks.

We will be leaving here in the evening of the 14th and expect to arrive in Ischl at midday (11.51) on Sunday, 15 August. Mama asks you to make sure that she is not met by the family and invited to lunch. She expects to feel miserable and will wish to rest for a couple of hours. The best thing would be if you were at the station alone. By then you should have organized for us *one* large, airy room in the Kreuz or Stern[1] or anywhere else that looks good to you and where we can stay until the morning of the 19th. In that time we hope to have found something for ourselves, or else will give in to the idea of Math and Aunt and move to Hofreit, Königssee, which we are unwilling to do because of the post.[2]

No news yet from Ernst, so no Feldpost number. In Martin's last three cards (up to 25 July) he has made no further mention of leave. Oli should be able to come to Ischl for the 18th. If you find out anything yourself about staying in the Salzkammergut, please go ahead and organize it.

The story of the weigher man is completely true. We are both very well. I will close now because it's time for my bath.[3]

Affectionate regards,
Papa

P. S. Money sent today.

1 Both of these houses still exist today; they are no longer hotels, but rather apartment buildings ⟨kind thanks to Elisabeth Riener, Kurdirektion Bad Ischl, for this information, 24 July 2002⟩.
2 See 66 SF and note 4, and 68 SF/MF.
3 Spelling mistake in German.

65 AF

[Bad Ischl] 6 August 1915

Dear Papa,
Aunt Dolfi has asked around in a few hotels and discovered that it is terribly full everywhere. There's nothing at all at Bauer and Hotel Elisabeth[1] only with difficulty. A two-bed room there costs 24 K per night, by the way. It would be good if you could write to me exactly when you are coming, whether I should book something, and how much it should cost. Then at least you won't have to travel around and search. Does it have to be a very elegant hotel? There is quite a nice one nearby, but everything is

incredibly expensive where the food is halfway decent; and that is the most important thing for you at the moment. Perhaps we can find something for later on between Ischl and Goisern. There are a couple of nice places there, such as St Agatha. Ischl itself has become terribly crowded in the last week.

I now have four days of Ischl rain behind me, during which even a non-rheumatic person would be certain to get stiff and cold. By way of compensation, it is blazing hot today and everything is gradually thawing again. There is no flour for the people of Ischl and the baker advised us against buying bread today because it is too bad. The bread for patients has also got worse. It shouldn't last for too long, however.

Yesterday Alma Rosenthal[2] visited me and we accompanied her back as far as Mitterweissenbach, with several showers on the way. As consolation, the news from Warsaw and Ivangorod was awaiting us and there was a lot of cheering, and flags.[3] So the midday papers were right after all. I hope you celebrated with the purchase of the nephrite bowl.

I'm in a very bad mood today and don't know why.[4] Perhaps the rain has got to me.

Write again soon; I haven't heard anything from you for a while.

With a kiss,

Your Anna

Recently I dreamed that you were a king and I was a princess, and that someone wanted to separate us through political intrigues. It was not at all nice but quite thrilling.

1 Bauer no longer exists; Hotel Elisabeth only as an apartment building (as 64 SF, note 1); see 69 AF, note 2.
2 Unknown.
3 The battles of Warsaw and Ivangorod: in October 1914 the Russians had taken both of these strongholds on the Vistula; Ivangorod was retaken by Austro-Hungarian troops on 4 August 1915, and Warsaw by the army of Prince Leopold of Bavaria on 5 August ⟨Ploetz [1940], pp. 497f., 514; Kleindel, p. 309⟩. See 67 AF and note 6.
4 See Freud's comments in *The Psychopathology of Everyday Life*: 'When a member of my family complains to me of having bitten his tongue, pinched a finger, or the like, he does not get the sympathy he hopes for, but instead the question: "Why did you do that?"' ⟨1901*b*, p. 180 (the paragraph was added in 1907); see also the following paragraph⟩. See 74 AF and note 11, and the PS to 98 AF.

66 SF

PROF. DR. FREUD [Karlsbad] 7 August 1915
Vienna, IX. Berggasse 19

My dear Anna,

The plot to keep us separated has certainly failed. You might be a princess who has to tend geese, as in the fairy tale, but I am now clearly a king without a realm. If Ischl is so expensive, so full and so badly provided for, then we shall not hold our court there. We are hesitating now about going there at all and are just waiting for your next letter before we make our decision. If we don't go to Ischl, we shall travel directly to Berchtesgaden and Hofreit, where Aunt, Math and Robert are now. We will send you a telegram so we can meet in Salzburg or you can travel directly. In that case we would not be obliged to stay here until the 14th but could leave earlier, on Wednesday or Thursday.[1] We will decide on all these things in the next few days.

As you know, *Mama* is greatly opposed to travelling, and after Karlsbad I am now afraid of bad bread.

Warsaw and Ivangorod also did us a lot of good here. Yesterday evening a rumour spread that Görz had been abandoned to the Italians,[2] but it appears not to be true and would not in any case be decisive. I would prefer the taking of Riga.[3]

We have heard nothing from Martin since the 25th; and from Ernst, who departed eight days ago, we have absolutely no news and don't even know his Feldpost number. It can't be much worse in Germany after all.[4]

The weather that you write as being so bad is also changeable here, but we shouldn't complain. It has not ruined a full day and in fact it's a blessing that it is never very hot.

If you are still trying to find a room, the maximum we can pay is 12 K (for both beds). You can also send us a telegram if you think it necessary. If I cannot send you any more money and pay for the rest of your lodging from here, you can overdraw for the journey; it will be made good by the bank.

I look forward to hearing from you and seeing you again soon.

Your Papa

1 That is what happened: 'On August 12 we are going from here [. . .]' ⟨Freud/Ferenczi II, 560 F, 9 August 1915; 562 F, 14 August 1915, p. 76⟩. See also 68 SF/MF.

2 This report might refer to Freud's 'war misreadings', which he added as one of several examples to the 5th edition of his *Psychopathology of Everyday Life* ⟨1901*b*, p. 113⟩. Gorizia [German: Görz] remained in the hands of the Austro-Hungarian troops in the heavy fighting during the battles of Isonzo in 1915–16, before being occupied on 9 August 1916 by Italian units after bloody combat ⟨Ploetz [1940], p. 530⟩.

3 Riga was attacked in August 1915 by the German navy during the conquest of the Russian fortress belt in northern Courland, but was not taken by German troops until 3 September 1917 after a long period of attritional warfare ⟨ibid., pp. 516, 526⟩.

4 The poor Feldpost communication was the main reason why soldiers preferred to take their leave in Austria rather than in Germany. See 64 SF and 68 SF/MF.

67 AF[1]

Dr S. Freud
Karlsbad
Rudolfshof
Bohemia

[Bad Ischl] 7 August 1915

Dear Papa,
It's a great pity that our letters keep crossing. The letter I received from you yesterday answered all the questions that I asked in the letter I sent to you yesterday and it was thus quite superfluous. I went with Rosi straightaway to the village and made inquiries. Now that I don't have to bother with the best hotels it is much easier.[2] You can have a nice room in the Kreuz, Stern or Post. Which of them will be decided on the 12th, when I can see the rooms. But it is quite certain and you can depend on it. Rosi also advised me against giving the precise arrival time. So you are also covered in this regard as well. I am really looking forward to seeing you and Mama and believe that the rest of the summer will be really nice. As soon as it stops raining (which doesn't look likely at the moment) I would like to take a walk with Rosi to St Agatha and look at the possibilities there. I am really happy that Oli will be coming.

Hermann[3] is presently in Salzburg again, where Aunt Rosa will probably visit him. We don't know what will be happening to him afterwards. You never write anything about Sophie.[4] Do you have any news?

I weighed myself again and the result was not very upsetting. Rosi and I have therefore decided quite literally to eat up the 20 K that will be coming now. It is not possible to go on excursions in this weather anyway. We are getting on very well again; with Maus most of the time but not always.[5]

Yesterday there was a torch-lit procession and we marched and sang along. It was very solemn.[6] Are you receiving my letters regularly? I write to you every day and post the letters straightaway. Your letters sometimes take one day, sometimes three. I remain with a kiss,

Your Anna

1 Folded letter with sheet pasted inside.
2 Replaces the deleted word 'simpler'.
3 Hermann Graf reported as a 'seventeen-year-old volunteer' in 1914 (see 69 AF) and was later posted to Italy ⟨Freud-Bernays, A., p. 173⟩. He was seriously wounded there on 18 June 1917 and died three days later in hospital ⟨Freud to Martin, 26 June 1917; Freud/Abraham, 13 July 1917⟩.
4 Freud visited her after these summer holidays in the second half of September ⟨Tögel [1989], p. 156: 16–27 September; Jones II, p. 204: from 13 September for two weeks⟩. 'Then I am going to Hamburg, as far as Berlin with my sister-in-law, and will probably return a few days before the end of the month' ⟨Freud/Ferenczi II, 566 F, 7 September 1915, p. 78⟩. Freud used the last days of September to visit Ferenczi, who was stationed in Pápa ⟨ibid., 569 F⟩.

5 See 53 AF and note 2.
6 The *Ischler Wochenblatt* of 8 August 1915 had a long report entitled 'Victory Celebration at the Fall of Warsaw and Ivangorod', which in effusive tones described details of the 'patriotic enthusiasm' of the population and the declarations of loyalty to the 'beloved emperor'. 'At 8 o'clock in the evening a solemn *torch-lit procession* set off from the Kurpark, headed by the k. k. Salinenkapelle and with lively participation by the honourable spa guests and the local inhabitants, through the town' ⟨with grateful thanks to Wolfgang Degeneve, president of the Ischler Heimatverein⟩.

68 SF/MF

PROF. DR. FREUD — Kbd., 9 August 1915
Vienna, IX. Berggasse 19

My dear Anna,
It's decided. We are leaving in the morning of Thursday [12 August] for Munich, where we will spend the night, and expect to be in Berchtesgaden at Friday noon.

I am sending you 120 K by money order so that you can pay for the rest of your lodging and your journey. Make sure that you don't arrive in Villa Hofreit after us. If you send a telegram with your arrival time, we will meet you at the station. You can also arrive sooner if you want. I imagine you would prefer to. You could also stay for the time being in Ischl and travel back with me on the 19th as I will most probably travel during the day[1] to Ischl. But then I think why should you spend almost a week less with us.

This decision was prompted by Mama's unwillingness to make an extra journey and to spend a week in temporary accommodation. But your reports on the crowding and bad bread in Ischl also played a role. We can also imagine what it would all have cost. My gastrointestinal problems have become so much worse on account of the cure that I need to remain careful.[2] It can't be so bad in Hofreit if Math has gone there again[3] and Aunt as well. The cheapness is also an argument. The main objection to Germany[4] is no longer applicable now that we see that we cannot expect any Feldpost in the fatherland either. There has been no news from Martin since 25 July. Yesterday we finally received a card from Ernst dated 2 August, but from Marmoros Sziget[5] and still without a Feldpost number.

I look forward to seeing you again soon. Mama also wants to add something.

Affectionately,
Papa

[In Martha's handwriting on the second page of the letter]

My dear[est] Annerl, I am sure you are surprised at the change in our plans, but after what you wrote we weren't really keen on going there, and both Aunt and Math have been very persuasive about our coming to Berchtesgaden. I expect that you will also leave on Thursday or Friday and come over. From Salzburg to Berchtesgaden; a local train goes just from there to Königssee.[6] You can inquire with Math or Aunt so that someone meets you at Berchtesgaden. Robert is also there already. Please tell Aunt Dolfi that a box with clean shirts for Papa will be arriving from Löhl at her address.[7] She should leave it unopened until Papa comes. Look after yourself, my dear, I look forward to seeing you. Mama

1 18 August, Amalie Freud's birthday.
2 In June, Freud had written that 'with respect to that I am better than since 1909' ⟨Freud/Ferenczi II, 548 F, 21 June 1915, p. 62⟩.
3 See 58 AF and note 10.
4 Bad post communication; see 64 SF and 66 SF.
5 Written thus: 'Ernst went away on July 30, up to now a card from him from Máramaros-Sziget, a station on the way to East Galicia' ⟨Freud/Ferenczi II, 560 F, 9 August 1915, p. 75⟩.
6 'The Königsseebahn from Berchtesgaden to Königssee was decided by the law of 16 August 1908, and this electrified route started operation on 29 May 1909.' It was shut down in 1965–6; today it is replaced by increasing car and bus traffic on a new highway ⟨*Königssee*, pp. 33, 45f.⟩.
7 Illegible; it could be Löbl.

69 AF

[Bad Ischl] 10 August 1915

Dear Papa,
I am waiting for your reply telegram and am very interested to read the final decision. The post is so slow and I would really like to know what is going to happen. It would be very nice if you came and for a couple of days I'm sure it wouldn't be so unpleasant. I wouldn't advise you to stay for a long time, however. Grandma is already terribly looking forward to seeing you, and the weather is nice at the moment. You can get very good things for Karlsbad stomach at Zauner,[1] and the food at Elisabeth[2] is supposed to be good. Besides, I have promised Rosi that we will go with you once to Zauner and try out every item there. We've been wanting to do that the whole time as we are unfortunately very greedy. At all events, I am very curious to receive your reply.[3]

Hopefully, you have already had word from the boys. Please write to me straightaway if you do hear from them.[4] I am always afraid for Ernst because he is sure to want to do something special. Rosi is already back from Salzburg,[5] and Hermann is apparently very well. He said of Martin that he is very hardworking and that everyone has great respect for him.

Rosi and I have hatched a great plan for Christmas, Easter or the next summer holidays. We want to take a trip to Germany with our own money (which has, of course, first to be earned). Simple, of course, just with a rucksack as luggage, that kind of thing. I'm sure it will be very nice.[6]

This afternoon Rosi and I are going with Frau Sidonie Schwarz,[7] whom we both like very much, to Goisern. The rain is already waiting for us in the bad-weather zone up there.

I had a very dear letter from Math. She writes that she has heard about different plans from you but that the only certainty is that you will be coming to Ischl. Whether it is indeed certain is precisely what I would like to know.

I have a couple of questions from the translation[8] for you, but I will keep them until we meet.[9]

Affectionate regards and a kiss,
Your Anna

1 Zauner confectionery 'has existed since 1832 and is managed by the Zauner family. Specialities such as "Zaunerstollen" are shipped worldwide and the confectionery is an attraction for international guests and celebrities' (as 64 SF, note 1).
2 See 65 AF.
3 The postcard 70 SF came instead of a telegram.
4 It was not until 1 September 1915 that Freud could write 'Good news from both warriors' ⟨Freud/Ferenczi II, 564 F, p. 77⟩.
5 She had presumably accompanied Aunt Rosa there; see 67 AF.
6 Nothing came of this trip at Christmas: 'Annerl has said that she is spending her vacation in Hamburg, where my son-in-law has just left his house to go on a training exercise' ⟨Freud/Ferenczi II, 583 F, 17 December 1915, p. 97; also 585 F⟩. It is possible that the plan came to fruition in 1916: 'Anna will go on a hiking tour over Easter [. . .]' ⟨ibid., 601 F, 12 March 1916, p. 119⟩. Years later she took (another) rucksack trip; see 270 AF–286 AF.
7 Unknown in Bad Ischl (Bad Ischl registration office, 2004). It cannot be determined whether it was the same person as the 'Frau Sidonie Schwarz, Vienna' lodging at Villa Zäzilie in Bad Gastein on 19 July 1919 ⟨*Badgastein. Liste*, 1919; I thank Laurenz Krisch, Bad Gastein, for allowing me to examine the guest lists⟩.
8 Spelling mistake in German. Presumably Anna is referring to the translation of the essay by J. J. Putnam (see 49 AF and note 6). In 1915 Anna also worked on the translation of an article by Ernest Jones, however (see 60 AF and note 7).
9 This occurred on 13 August in Schönau am Königssee, where the Freuds spent the rest of their holiday until 11–13 September in Villa Hofreit ⟨Freud/Ferenczi II, 560 F, 562 F, 566 F⟩. Anna travelled back to Vienna with Mathilde earlier: 'Today I accompanied my two daughters to Salzburg on their way home and was indeed quite surprised to notice the decline in my mood after the goodbyes, how much my libido had been satisfied by them. But the little one is also a particularly sweet and interesting creature' ⟨Freud/Ferenczi II, 566 F, 7 September 1915, p. 78⟩.

70 SF

Frl Anna Freud
c/o Winternitz
Bad Ischl
Lärchenwald 12[1]

Kbd 10 August 1915

My dear Anna,
Your telegram has just arrived.[2] We have already decided, however, and hope that you will also be happy. A card today from Martin that he was able to equip himself in a 'conquered town' with underwear and other things for 100 K. Weather here heavy and rainy. Take care.
Affectionate greetings Papa
[In the margin]
Martin is Batt *9* Feldpost *64*

1 The address side of this postcard is quite interesting: 'Winternitz' and 'Bad Ischl' are crossed out and replaced by 'Lerchenwald Strasse 12'; this and the detail '*Not Dr Herber*' are also crossed out; in between is the comment 'left for *Königssee Upper Bavaria!!!!!*' with the place and province heavily underlined and emphasized with the same coloured pencil with five exclamation marks. The card was franked in Karlsbad on 10 August and three times in Bad Ischl on 12, 13 and 14 August 1915.
2 Missing.

1916

71 SF

[Altaussee][1] 23 August 1916

Dear Papa,
After five days of rain the sun has finally come back today; probably for lack of water. This morning Robert and I visited the Ries,[2] but only found Marianne.[3] We had to dry our coats on the stove. In the afternoon, the weather turned fine, however, and we went to the Blaa Alm, where we found and ate masses of raspberries. It would be nice if the weather were to remain fine. Then I could still make something of the fourteen days.

I overslept yesterday morning and didn't wake up until Aunt Lichtheim[4] knocked on my door at 9.45 a.m. She wanted to invite me to elevenses but didn't dare to enter the room because my walking shoes were in front of the door. They are so big that she said to the housekeeper that there must be a man staying there. In the afternoon I had a very nice tea with her with Gertie Rie.[5] I have been invited to Käthe H.[6] tomorrow afternoon. Everyone is very nice.

I am not at all happy about the news from Gastein. I was really expecting a letter from you or Mama today. I would love to know if you are happy and whether your second impression of Gastein is better than your first.[7] What news do you have of Oli[8] and the other two?[9] The Fürths[10] told me that they had spoken to you and that Aunt was going to Gastein as well. Was it very difficult to take leave of the Bristol?[11]

There are two very nice girls here in the guesthouse, whom I will certainly look up back in Vienna. There are also some very strange people, whom I can describe better orally. Everybody eats and laughs a frightful amount. I'm not quite able to keep up in either of those two departments.

I am not studying here at all and I am being quite lazy. But I[12] It's also quite agreeable like that.

I hope that you will write to me very soon.

Greetings to you, Mama and Aunt

Your Anna

1 Since 14 August Anna had been spending some of her holidays here with her sister-in-law Marie Rischawy, who had transferred her guesthouse from Merano to Altaussee; see 72 SF and note 2. Ernst, who was on leave, accompanied Anna on the journey; see note 9 ⟨*Kalender*, unpublished, 14 August 1916⟩. Mathilde and Robert Hollitscher also spent some time at the guesthouse. Robert returned earlier, but Anna and Mathilde remained until around 10 September (see 74 AF, 75 SF).

2 The Rie family and the other friends mentioned in this letter were also on holiday in Altaussee.

3 Marianne Rie (1900–80), the third child of Oscar and Melanie Rie. She later studied medicine, obtained her doctorate in 1925 and trained as a psychoanalyst, playing an important role until her death in particular as a child analyst. In 1927 she married the art historian and analyst Ernst Kris ⟨Mühlleitner, pp. 190f.⟩.

4 Anna's godmother, after whom she was named. Anna Lichtheim (1861–1938) was the daughter of Freud's religion teacher Samuel Hammerschlag. She was a teacher, widowed in 1885 after a brief marriage ⟨Freud 1992*i*, p. 63; Jones I, p. 179⟩. Her husband, Rudolf Lichtheim, was the brother of neurologist Professor Ludwig Lichtheim (1845–1928) from Königsberg [now Kaliningrad] ⟨Fichtner [2008*a*], p. 71⟩, whose aphasia theory was studied in detail by Freud in *On Aphasia (A Critical Study)*, 1891*b*. Anna Lichtheim was 'a favourite patient of Freud's' ⟨Jones I, p. 245 and note 3⟩. She was the 'Irma' in Freud's dream about Irma's injection ⟨Hirschmüller [1989], p. 129 and note 7; *The Interpretation of Dreams* [1900*a*], pp. 122–33⟩. On 7 July 1914 she had accompanied Anna on her trip to Hamburg (before her journey to England, see 41 AF) ⟨Young-Bruehl, p. 28⟩.

5 Possibly Gertie Rie (1899–?), a daughter of Alfred Rie.

6 Probably Kata Hammerschlag, daughter of Leontine and Albert Hammerschlag, 'student of chemistry', whose sudden death is mentioned in letters by Freud and Anna to Ernst Freud ⟨Freud to Ernst, 26 June 1919; Anna to Ernst, 18 July 1919⟩.

7 Freud had originally wanted to go to Bad Gastein for a cure with Martha (and possibly Anna, see 73 SF and note 1) on 15 July. On 16 July they met up with Minna and Anna in Salzburg, who had spent a few days in Weissenbach on Lake Attersee ⟨Freud/Ferenczi II, 611 F, 614 F⟩. From Salzburg, Freud went on a reconnoitre to Bad Gastein on 18 July ⟨*Kalender*, unpublished, 18 July 1916⟩, after which he changed his plans: 'Having been frightened away from Gastein after a short visit, we (four of us) have taken up residence for a longer time in the Hotel Bristol, where the first Congress [the first meeting of psychoanalysts on 26–7 April 1908] was, and are at least well fed and welcome. Living in the country is too difficult right now' ⟨Freud/Ferenczi II, 615 F, 22 July 1916, p. 135⟩. 'The attractions and comforts of this beautiful city [see 28 SF and note 4], the good postal connections and food supply have caused us to give up that intimate contact with nature which usually means so much to us' ⟨Freud/Andreas-Salomé, 27 July 1916, pp. 50f.⟩. Freud, Martha and Minna ultimately travelled to Gastein on 20 August; see the next postcard. They returned to Vienna, again via Salzburg, on 15 September; see 75 SF and note 7 ⟨*Kalender*, unpublished, 20 August, 15 September 1916⟩.

8 Oliver was working as an engineer in railway, tunnel and barrack construction, initially as a civilian and from 1 December 1916 in the military; see 74 AF, note

12. He had married the medical student Ella Haim in December 1915 but the marriage lasted only a few months ⟨Freud/Ferenczi II, 566 F, 575 F, 581 F, 589 F⟩. At Easter 1916 Freud visited his son where he was stationed to 'make him aware of what he is still unconvinced of, that he has to view his imminent divorce as a piece of luck' ⟨ibid., 605 F, 13 April 1916, p. 124 and note 2⟩. The marriage was officially dissolved on 10 September 1916 ⟨*Kalender*, unpublished⟩.

9 Martin and Ernst had been involved since 15 May in the 'big offensive' by the Austro-Hungarian troops in South Tyrol and had been promoted to lieutenant ⟨Freud/Ferenczi II, 611 F, 589 F; *Kalender*, unpublished, 1 January/1 August 1916⟩. They arrived on leave in Vienna on 6 and 7 August, respectively ⟨*Kalender*, unpublished⟩. Freud wrote to Ferenczi on 16 November, 'There is good news from the boys', and on 22 December, 'Martin is here with the cadre, and a frequent guest' ⟨Freud/Ferenczi II, 629 F, p. 153; 634 F, p.166; *Kalender*, unpublished, 10 December 1916⟩.

10 Probably the family of Dr. med. Julius Fürth (1859–1923), doctor in Vienna, whom Freud had known since the start of his medical career and who came to Freud's lectures at the university ⟨Gicklhorn, p. 170; see 120 S, note 4, in Freud/Bernays⟩. In 1895 he founded Sanatorium Fürth ⟨Thonke; thanks to the Department of History of Medicine, Vienna⟩. Martin had been treated there after his skiing accident in 1914 (see 14 AF, note 12) ⟨Freud/Ferenczi I, 195 F⟩. Mathilde had also been admitted there for her operation in 1912 (see text after 18 SF/MF) ⟨Freud to family, 3 September 1912, extract in 2003*e*⟩.

11 See note 7.

12 These two words are crossed out.

72 SF[1]

Frl Anna Freud
c/o Frau Rischawy
Alt-Aussee
Starlvilla [Puchen 52][2]

[Sender (handwritten):] V. [Villa Dr.] Wassing[3]

Badgastein,[4] 24 August 1916

My dear Anna,
Gastein is wonderful, just a little cold, sometimes very cold. It's also raining quite a lot but not as ferociously as where you are. It has been dry here for the last two days. The air and water are first-rate, also the food. There could be a shortage of white bread, however. I have found nice forests with promising soil and both yesterday and today a large fresh mushroom. I hope for more after 1 September. I am bargaining for a Chinese animal. Lectures not coming on well.[5] Affectionate greetings, Papa

1 Postcard.

2 Marie Rischawy initially rented this house, which still exists today, for her guesthouse; in 1918 she bought it from the descendants of the former owner, Ignaz Starl. After her own death in 1936 it was transferred to Robert

Hollitscher, a niece Helene Hollitscher, and the nephews Dr Karl and Dr Fritz Gebert ⟨Häuser-Verzeichnis des Gerichtsbezirk Aussee, 1900 edition – thanks to Johannes Linortner, Altaussee⟩; entries in the land registry ⟨according to letter of 23 August 2002; thanks to Steierisches Landesarchiv, dept. 1D, Graz⟩; inheritance certificate T. Z. 413/37 ⟨thanks to Bezirksgericht Irdning⟩. See also 111 AF and note 5.

3 Dr Anton Wassing (originally Wassertrilling; 1860–1941) ⟨Schnitzler [1985], p. 143; [1981], also p. 841, note 8⟩. Wassing had been the community doctor and head of the local hospital in Bad Gastein, but since 1904 had had a practice in Vienna in winter and worked as spa doctor in his villa on Kaiserpromenade in Gastein in the summer. He received various awards and titles for his services to the community. He was forced to 'sell' his property in 1940 because he was Jewish, and died in 1941 in hospital in Vienna. In 1949 the property was restituted to his descendants and 'until recently' was run by nuns under the name Kurhaus Goldeck ⟨I thank Laurenz Krisch, Bad Gastein, for this information⟩. When I visited in 2002, the house was closed and abandoned. A new owner is now apparently refurbishing it for reopening as Hotel Excelsior ⟨telephonic information from Laurenz Krisch, 8 June 2004⟩.

4 Now written Bad Gastein (approx. 990–1,050 m), 75 km south of Salzburg, world-renowned spa resort frequented by guests of the highest calibre; 'in a picturesque setting on an escarpment [Hohe Tauern] between the upper and lower valley floors on either side of the Achse, which rushes down through the gorge in the centre of the town in two magnificent waterfalls of 63 and 85 m in height [see end of 110 SF]'. Its worldwide reputation is due to its thermal springs, which contain radon ⟨Baedeker, 1923, p. 422⟩.

5 Part III of *Introductory Lectures on Psychoanalysis* (1916–1917*a*), entitled 'General Theory of the Neuroses', which Freud was preparing for the coming winter semester and which he had started to draft in Salzburg: 'I have already written three lectures, which weren't getting at all easy for me' ⟨Freud/Ferenczi II, 618 F, 2 August 1916, p. 137; also Freud/Andreas-Salomé, 27 July 1916⟩. By September he had completed a further six of the thirteen chapters (see 75 SF and note 5) ⟨Jones II, p. 245, cites as a source a letter by Freud to Ferenczi of 20 September 1916, which is apparently missing (it is not in Freud/Ferenczi II)⟩. In his Preface to the *New Introductory Lectures on Psychoanalysis* (1933*a*), Freud describes how they came about: 'My *Introductory Lectures on Psychoanalysis* were delivered during the two Winter Terms of 1915–16 and 1916–17 in a lecture room of Vienna Psychiatric Clinic before an audience gathered from all the Faculties of the University. The first half of the lectures were improvised, and written out immediately afterwards; drafts of the second half were made during the intervening summer vacation at Salzburg, and delivered word for word in the following winter.' Among the listeners in 1915–16 were Anna, Mathilde, Ella Haim and Lampl ⟨Freud/Ferenczi II, 573 F; Jones II, pp. 245–52; Gay, p. 325⟩.

73 SF

Badgastein, 26 August 1916

My dear Anna,
Thank you for your letter, which overlapped with my card. It's clear that where you are is better for you than our old company.[1] The rain

must have been magnificent; now I am sure that it is getting brighter, however, because we also have fine weather. Yesterday was a quite singular day.

We are fine. Mama and Aunt are quite blissful about the mixture of elegance and informality, good food, splendid air, superb water, fairytale views, comfortable accommodation,[2] etc., and therefore say nothing about all the countless acquaintances, or even about the fact that there has been no white bread for two days and that one has to present oneself in person complete with pearl necklaces at the baker, who lives up to his name Schurk [scoundrel], for a packet of miserable rusks. The black bread is uneatable.

In the mornings I have been exploring the forest but have not found anything else and am looking forward eagerly to 1 September, when the guests will be leaving and the mushrooms arriving. Work is going better again, albeit slowly. The printing of 'Dream' has started in earnest.[3] The baths are wonderfully pleasant but make one really tired, probably like any hot bath where there is no shower. I am still awaiting the rejuvenating effect.[4] Aunt bathes every other day; we take a break every three days.

The Chinese porcelain dog now watches me as I write. If you like it, it will find a spot on your desk. I am buying another one for Uncle [Alexander], who also likes these beasts a lot.

I had to do a consultancy on the second day here, and the fine for doing so will be used for this.

I send you my affectionate greetings and my regards to Math, and trust that you will make great progress in socializing.[5]

Papa

1 In July there had been some discussion that Anna might also go to Bad Gastein; see 71 AF, note 7 ⟨Freud/Ferenczi II, 614 F⟩. Anna's wish in this regard was not fulfilled in 1921 either (see 139 AF and note 4). It was not until 1923 that she discovered the place for herself, which she found 'quite superb' ⟨Anna/Lou, letter 114, 11 July 1923, p. 202⟩. See 196 SF, note 3.

2 They liked it so much at Dr Wassing's house that they always rented there on subsequent stays in Bad Gastein and soon felt quite at home (see, e.g., 93–5 SF, 106 SF, 109 SF, 110 SF, 142 SF).

3 'The Dream' is the title of Part II of the *Lectures* (1916–1917*a*). Because of the war, typesetting and printing took months; it was not until 18 December 1916 that Freud announced to Andreas-Salomé: 'I sent off the second part of the *Lectures* to you today' ⟨Freud/Andreas-Salomé (German version), p. 61; see Freud/Ferenczi II, 598 F, 601 F, 609 F, 614 F⟩.

4 The rejuvenating effects of the baths were (and still are) claimed in the advertising for the spa.

5 See 28 SF and note 2.

74 AF

Alt-Aussee, 28 August 1916

Dear Papa,
I must start with the end of your letter: I have really made great progress in socializing. After I was at tea with Gerti Rie the day before yesterday, Aunt Lichtheim picked me up today and we visited the Karpluses,[1] because they wanted to see us. Tomorrow I am invited to Margaretl Rie[2] for tea and am also meant to go some time soon to the other Hammerschlags.[3]

I think Aunt Lichtheim has decided to show me everywhere; it seems quite strange to me. But she is immensely nice and dear and I see her practically every day. And at least you don't have to change to go and visit.[4]

Robert unfortunately left today and just learnt about the declaration of war on Romania at the station.[5] It caused a great furore here and people are in a very bad mood as a result. Some left straightaway for Vienna.

I was very pleased to receive your letter. I hadn't thought that you would like Gastein so much. You wouldn't have to queue for rusks here; we have snow-white milk bread for breakfast (one piece per person) and real black bread, which is also very good, and another lighter loaf without corn. Instead we eat our corn sometimes in the form of kukuruz, and that is naturally much better.

I am very curious to see the porcelain animal or beast. I have heard incidentally that Kessler[6] is also in Gastein. Robert gave Math a very nice lapis lazuli brooch; there is a stone shop down at the market. Robert was very nice this time and quite different from how he was in Vienna;[7] we got on splendidly.

Could you send me the magazine containing my translations?[8] Math wanted to see it; but only if you don't need it, of course. It's not important. I am looking forward to hearing the new lectures this winter. Do you have corrections of 'Dream' that I could read?[9] I have huge amounts of time. There are lots of books here, because others, like me, have brought lots with them and we exchange them. Strangely, I don't feel like reading at the moment, however; perhaps because I don't have a light next to the bed. At all events, I fall asleep immediately and hardly dream. Math says I am recovering so well because I read so little. Instead I am embroidering a lot,[10] and my yellow cover is famous in Aussee. That's not so difficult here. I wanted today to climb through a window (that's the custom here) and almost broke my neck. It was a bad chair, which fell over with me, and I have a large bruise and will probably be quite stiff tomorrow. Why I did it I do not know.[11]

Rosi and Dora Steiner arrived here early yesterday and stayed until this afternoon. I didn't have such a good time with them, however.

This is my fourteenth day here, over the halfway mark.

I hope to receive a letter from you very soon. We have no news whatsoever of Sophie, Martin and Ernst. Only Oli[12] has sent a card with Rank.[13]

I send you a kiss.

Your Anna

Mama should also write again soon.

1 Valerie and Johann Paul Karplus. Dr med. Karplus (1866–1936) was an assistant at the Krafft-Ebings Psychiatric and Neurological Clinic from 1894 to 1900, and at the Physiological Institute from 1903 to 1917, and professor of psychiatry in Vienna from 1914. In 1917, he became head of the Neurology Department of the Polyclinic ⟨Fischer, I. [1932–3]; thanks to Albrecht Hirschmüller for the year of death⟩. In the chapter entitled 'Theoretical' of *Studies on Hysteria* (1895*d*) co-written with Freud, Josef Breuer mentions Karplus's example of overdetermination (p. 213, note 1). His wife, Valerie, was the daughter of one of Freud's earlier patients, Anna von Lieben (1847–1900), whom Freud (under the pseudonym 'Cäcilie M.') described as his 'teacher' for the development of psychoanalysis ⟨1985*c*, 8 February 1897, p. 229, and editorial note to letter of 29 August 1888, p. 26; 1895*d*, pp. 69 note, 76–8; Fichtner and Hirschmüller; Winter, pp. 80, 103; Tögel [1994], pp. 129–32; Swales, p. 11 and elsewhere; Appignanesi and Forrester, p. 91⟩. As close relatives of the Auspitz family, the Karpluses were able to stay in their summer villa in Altaussee (see 116 AF and notes 2 and 3).

2 Margarete Rie (1899–1986), the elder of the two daughters of Melanie and Oscar Rie; she later became an actress and married the psychoanalyst Hermann Nunberg in 1929. In 1932 the family emigrated to the USA ⟨Mühlleitner, p. 237; thanks to Henry Nunberg, New York, for the year of death⟩. The two friends spent holidays together in Bayerisch Gmain in 1919 and 1920 (see 93 SF and ff.), and in Altaussee (see 107 SF and ff.).

3 This could be Dr. jur. Paul Hammerschlag (1860–1933), director of the Credit-Anstalt in Vienna, brother of Anna Lichtheim and Albert Hammerschlag, and his wife, Bertha, née Breuer (1870–1962) ⟨Hirschmüller [1978], p. 48 and note 191; Wiener Heimatrolle (Wiener Stadt- und Landesarchiv); Freud 1992*i*, p. 153⟩. In 1927, a Bertha Hammerschlag bought house no. 118 in Altaussee ⟨land registry entry; thanks to Johannes Linortner, Altaussee⟩.

4 But see 116 AF, 3rd paragraph.

5 On 27 August 1916, Romania declared war on Austria-Hungary and invaded Transylvania. The First Romanian Army was subsequently defeated at the Battle of Hermannstadt [now Sibiu] (26–9 September) and the Second Army at Kronstadt [Brasov] (7–9 October). On 6 December 1916, Bucharest was captured by the allied troops. In the Treaty of Bucharest between Romania and the Central Powers of 7 May 1918, the division of territories in Romania was negotiated ⟨Kleindel, pp. 306, 310, 315⟩.

6 See 15 AF and note 11. Not listed in the Gastein guest list for 1916 (see 69 AF, note 7).

7 'In the family, Robert Hollitscher was notorious for his gloomy outlook' ⟨Molnar [1996], p. 167 and note 3; e.g., Freud/Bernays, letter 167 Mi⟩. But see 84 AF and note 11.

8 The two translations both appeared in *IZ*, vol. 4, no. 1 (1916–17); see 60 AF, note 7.

9 Full stop rather than question mark in the handwritten letter.

10 See 20 SF and note 4.

11 See 65 AF and note 4. It is perhaps no coincidence that Anna reports her near-accident directly after mentioning embroidery, the activity that caused her so much pain in Merano.

12 Oliver was apparently trying to change jobs; he left the tunnel construction company in November. 'Oli released from tunnel' and 'Oli arrived in Krakow', noted Freud ⟨*Kalender*, unpublished, 20 and 29 November 1916⟩. On 2 December he enlisted 'for military training in Cracow' ⟨Freud/Andreas-Salomé, 3 December 1916, p. 54; *Kalender*, unpublished, 2 December⟩. 'Oli's reports from Cracow sound very gratifying' ⟨Freud/Ferenczi II, 634 F, p. 166, 629 F, 631 F⟩. In July 1917 he had 'officer's exam' ⟨*Kalender*, unpublished, 14 July⟩.

13 Rank was stationed at the time in Krakow (see 50 SF, note 2), where he remained until the end of 1918 ⟨Freud/Ferenczi II, 769 F⟩. He suffered severe depression there in the winter of 1916–17, and again at the end of 1917 ⟨ibid., 629 F, 651 Fer, 720 F, III, 837 F, 1001 F, 1009 Fer; Freud/Abraham, 26 December 1917⟩. In Krakow he met his future wife, psychology student Beata (Tola) Mincer (1896–1967). They married on 7 November 1918 and moved to Vienna ⟨Freud/Ferenczi II, 780 F, 1 January 1919, p. 321⟩. Beata became an analyst herself and a member of the Vienna Psychoanalytic Society in 1923 ⟨Mühlleitner, pp. 248f.; Lieberman, pp. 220f.; Freud/Ferenczi II, 774 Fer and note 5, 775 F; Roazen [1993], p. 24⟩.

75 SF

Badgastein, 5 September 1916

My dear Anna,

You are right[1] that I haven't written to you for a long time. I am pressed for time a bit since I started playing cards every afternoon with Rolf's father[2] and have to listen to stories in the evening until 10 o'clock with him and various professors, privy councillors[3] and even a Berlin excellency (Waldeyer[4]) in the salon at Straubinger.[5] I am writing at the same time and have successfully completed the eighth lecture. I don't think the ninth will be finished before I return.[6] We are thinking of leaving on the 10th or 11th and arriving back home on the 14th or 15th after a stop in Salzburg.[7]

No decisive news from outside. You will no doubt have heard about Ernst and Martin from Mama; they appear to be having a quieter time of it now. Sophie still doesn't know what she will do because Max's fate is uncertain.[8]

Please tell Math that I am jealous of her luck with mushrooms. Since the first two large ones, I have not found any more and have given up looking. I haven't bought anything either, partly because there is nothing tempting and partly because there is no money here.

So basically you have learnt nothing new.

Affectionate greetings and look forward to seeing you soon,

Papa

1 A letter from Anna appears to be missing.

2 Presumably Alfred Francis Pribram, whose fourth son (born 1909) was called Rolf ⟨Zouzelka, p. 36⟩. Pribram had been staying since 24 August 1916 at Haus Gruber ⟨*Badgastein. Liste* 1916, no. 83, serial no. 3480⟩. A letter of 25 August 1917 from Freud to Pribram strengthens my suspicion: Freud expresses thanks

for Pribram's 'card from Gastein, the place where we renewed our old acquaintanceship' ⟨LoC SF, Cont. 38⟩.

3 In the spa guest lists for this time, apart from other 'professors, privy councillors' and 'excellencies', there are also various entries, for example, 'Julius Wagner-Jauregg', 'Friedrich Wenckebach' and 'Josef Halban'.

4 Heinrich Wilhelm Gottfried von Waldeyer-Hartz (1836–1921), doctor of medicine and professor of pathological anatomy, since 1883 employed in Berlin. He worked among other things on the histology of the nervous system and the development of reproductive organs – areas in which Freud had also worked at the start of his career. He quotes him, for example, in his description of the fibrillar structure of nerve fibres ⟨1882*a*, p. 13; see also 1877*a* and *b*, 1878*a*, 1881*a*, 1884*b*, *d* and *f*, 1885*d*, 1886*b* and *c*, 1887*f*, 1891*a*,1893*b* and *d*, 1893–4*a*, 1897*a*⟩. Waldeyer coined the words 'chromosome' and 'neuron'. 'In retrospect [Freud] may be regarded as one of the precursors of the neuron theory elaborated by Waldeyer in 1891' ⟨Anzieu II, p. 541⟩.

5 Renowned centrally located hotel, family-owned without interruption since 1603, and the site of a historical Prussian-Austrian event, when Bismarck negotiated the terms of the Gastein Convention in 1865 ⟨Zimburg, p. 359; Hinterseer and Kritsch, pp. 43f.; Holzner; Ploetz [1980], pp. 753f.⟩. At the time of Freud's stay, the owner, Karl Straubinger, was mayor and chairman of the spa committee ⟨*Badgastein. Liste* 1916, Introduction⟩. Today (May 2002) the building complex stands empty.

6 See 72 SF, note 5.

7 Freud's entry in the *Kalender* unpublished, 1916: 12.9 'In Salzburg', 15.9 'In Vienna'.

8 Sophie had wanted to travel to Vienna in April: 'Sophie and the child are coming already before Easter in order to stay here until fall' ⟨Freud/Ferenczi II, 603 F, 24 March 1916, p. 122⟩. She postponed the journey, however, when her husband, who was lying wounded in hospital in France, was released and sent home ⟨ibid., 605 F⟩. Max subsequently resumed his profession, working as a civilian in the air force: 'Max aircraft photographer Hanover' ⟨*Kalender*, unpublished, 28 October 1916⟩. It was not until 17 November that Sophie returned to her parents' home, where she remained until May 1917 ⟨Freud/Ferenczi II, 631 F, 668 F, 674 F; *Kalender*, unpublished, 14 May 1917⟩.

1917

76 SF

PROF. DR. FREUD

Csorbató,[1] 22 August 1917
Vienna, IX. Berggasse 19

My dear Anna,
Your first letter[2] spoke of all kinds of good things and gave reason to hope that the situation would remain so. Just imagine the anticipation with which we await your letters. You had gone missing for us for two days because your telegram[3] naturally did not arrive until late yesterday evening.

Fairy-tale weather here since your departure, such that we don't like to think of having to leave soon. Our move[4] was completed quickly with the aid of Grete Ilm.[5] The small terrace on which the desk is positioned so that it can be reached from outside[6] is much more comfortable than the upper one. We were afraid at first of burglars but they appear to be as unknown here as in Switzerland in William Tell's time,[7] and several ladies form a security guard in front of the house, Mama reckons.

A new member of the society (Mory Society[8]) has arrived, Dr Steiner,[9] a colleague of Martin, very ugly, but polite and clever, who is staying with us for now, but is planning the longest mountain tours. The Kolmers[10] are also becoming closer; they are leaving on Saturday, however.

I received no reply to my telegram to Lampl. I decided three days later to send a telegram to Urbantschitsch[11] to ask whether he could do something for him,[12] but U. is not in Vienna either, as all I received was a formal piece of useless information from his assistant. I finally received a letter this morning from Ernst in Graz, saying that Lampl had managed to get him admitted to the hospital in the Stift Barracks and that he hoped to arrive the following day (20th) in Vienna. When we are in Vienna we will see what happens.[13]

We get up early and have discovered that morning is really the best time of the day. Today Mama finally visited the waterfall[14] with Grete I.[lm] and Dr Steiner and was very proud of it; I travelled at 7.42 a.m. to Felsö-Nagyi but it was disappointing. Not a single mushroom there, whereas I found at least one a day here. It is too dry; I need a proper day's rain.

Right: on Monday evening a large basket of fresh eggs arrived from Eitingon.[15] They have not yet been counted,[16] like prisoners after a battle. We still haven't run out of visitors either. Today we missed Dr Garai,[17] who wanted to bring greetings from Ernst.

[In the margin]

Enjoy yourself and send my regards to the lady of the house and the other Ferenczis.[18]

Affectionately,

Papa

1 Ferenczi, who was quite familiar with the High Tatra, had with great difficulty found two rooms for Freud, Martha and Anna for the summer, in Villa Theresia near Lake Csorba ('Csorbató'). It was here that they spent the first part of the holidays together from 1 July to 19 August ⟨Freud/Ferenczi II, 658, 667 Fer–688 Fer, *passim*⟩.

2 Missing.

3 Missing, but mentioned in Freud's letter of 21 August 1917 to Gizella Pálos ⟨Freud/Ferenczi II, 702 F⟩. Anna had been invited to stay in the country by Ferenczi's sister Ilona (married name Zoltán) ⟨ibid., 696 Fer, 697 F, 699 F⟩. On the way she visited Max Eitigon in Miskolcz (see note 15) ⟨Freud/Eitigon, 110 E, 111 F, 112 E⟩.

4 By switching rooms in the guesthouse it had been possible to extend the holidays until the end of August ⟨Freud/Ferenczi II, 697 F, 699 F⟩.

5 A friend of Hanns Sachs, who was staying at Hotel Mory. She had attended a meeting of the Vienna Psychoanalytic Society in June of that year and was to do so again in December ⟨Freud/Ferenczi II, 683 Fer, 685 Fer, 697 F; *Protokolle IV*, pp. 301, 306⟩. Jones wrote: 'A sister of my wife's, Grete Ilm, a well-known actress, was also of the party and she cherished many memories of the interesting time there' ⟨Jones II, p. 217⟩.

6 'We . . . moved into a room with veranda on the ground floor in the same house, where I am now writing to you, amid a swarm of insects, halfway on to the street. Nevertheless it is very beautiful' ⟨Freud/Ferenczi II, 701 F, 20 August 1917, p. 235⟩.

7 Reference to Schiller's play *William Tell*: 'Suspicion lurks, With darkling treachery in every nook./Even to our inmost rooms they force their way,/These myrmidons of power; and soon we'll need/To fasten bolts and bars upon our doors.'

8 In 'Hotel Móry not far from Csorbató' further acquaintances of Ferenczi spent their summer holidays, and he himself also stayed there ⟨Freud/Ferenczi II, 685 Fer, 690 F; Freud/Abrahams, 13 July 1917⟩.

9 Unknown.

10 Unknown.

11 Rudolf von Urbantschitsch (1879–1964), doctor of medicine, from 1908 to 1914 member of the Vienna Psychoanalytic Society ⟨*Minutes I*, pp. 204, 276⟩. He came from an aristocratic family from the Habsburg monarchy and had connections to influential Viennese circles, with whose support, amongst other things, he established the Cottage-Sanatorium in 1908 (see 219 SF and note 3).

During the war part of it was reserved as a hospital for officers. It was sold in 1922. In 1923–4 Urbantschitsch pursued his plan of setting up a psychoanalytical sanatorium and asked Freud and Martha for their assistance; the project failed, however ⟨Freud/Ferenczi III, 939 Fer, 958 Fer, 960 F, 961 Fer, 965 Fer; Jones III, pp. 109f.; Mühlleitner, p. 349, describes the situation somewhat differently; Urbantschitsch himself appears to have given differing information about it; see also Urban [1958], pp. 193–9⟩. In 1936 he emigrated to the USA and was naturalized there in 1943 as Dr Rudolf von Urban ⟨Mühlleitner, pp. 348f.; Plankers and Federn, pp. 125f.⟩.

12 Meaning Ernst: 'Ernst is in the hospital in Agram [Zagreb] with a diagnosis of ulcer [duodenal], so on the way to the hinterland with the aid of Dr Garai' ⟨Freud/Ferenczi II, 699 F, 16 August 1917, p. 233⟩.

13 See 79 AF and note 7.

14 Ferenczi had obtained a travel guide for the Tatra and proposed some tours: 'I recommend . . . the outing . . . to the "Five Lakes" . . . From Tátrafüred by cable car . . . from there further on foot in the Kohlbach Valley (Tarpatak) with a pretty waterfall' ⟨Freud/Ferenczi II, 699 F, 16 August 1917, p. 221⟩.

15 Max Eitingon (1881–1943), doctor of medicine, psychiatrist, neurologist and psychoanalyst in Berlin. In 1907, as the 'first emissary', he sought out Freud from Zurich. 'He was to become in later years one of Freud's best friends' ⟨Jones II, p. 35⟩. He also repeatedly provided financial support for Freud and psychoanalysis in difficult situations ⟨e.g., Freud/Eitingon, 154 F⟩. See also 100 SF and notes 9 and 11, and 117 SF, end of note 7. He was stationed in Miskolez from August 1916 ⟨Freud/Eitingon, 89 E–131 E, *passim*, with numerous editorial notes; overall Schröter [2004]⟩.

16 'The last today was a basket with approximately forty to fifty eggs from Eitingon' ⟨Freud/Ferenczi II, 701 F, 20 August 1917, p. 235; Freud/Eitingon, 110 E, 112 F and note 2⟩. See also 78 SF and note 4.

17 Perhaps the husband of the dentist Dr Garai, 'the lady who made herself known as your instrument in all these room reservations' ⟨Freud/Ferenczi II, 690F, 6 July 1917, p. 226, 691 Fer⟩.

18 Other relatives of Ferenczi were visiting Kótaj; see 77 AF.

77 AF

[to Martha Freud]

Kotaj,[1] 24 August 1917

Dear Mama,
I have now been away for six days and have still received no news from you, although every day I go out to meet our Russian postman, one of the few people here who can speak German. Rosi asked in the letter you forwarded to me whether we would be in Vienna at the end of August[2] and whether she could live with us then. She asked Uncle if she could extend her holiday, but doesn't know exactly when she has to be in Vienna. Could you perhaps write her a card about staying? I think it would be quite easy to arrange.

Yesterday I rode with the old Frau Ferenczi[3] to Sósto, but I didn't drive the carriage myself, because she is too old to be thrown about by me.

Today, however, I rode to the river again, went swimming, lay in the sun and picked up Berti Zoltan[4] from the station. In doing so, I taught myself to hold both reins in the left hand and the whip in the right hand; our old coachman is quite pleased with me. I can now converse with him quite well in Hungarian about the weather and swimming. It is very hot, and bathing in the lukewarm river is very refreshing as a result. I have hardly seen a cloud here and the star-filled sky at night is one of the most beautiful imaginable.

Frau Zoltán's daughter[5] and small child are supposed to be coming here, but we are waiting for them in vain at the moment. I have forgotten to tell you before that a telegram *always* takes more than a day to get here, so please let me know in good time when you are leaving.

I have been told that some of the fields are already being ploughed. Perhaps I can also try it tomorrow,[6] like Emperor Joseph.[7] I watched the milking and the farmer asked me if I wanted to try it out, but I didn't want to inflict myself on the cow. We have seventeen cows and a large number of calves. Yesterday I also encountered a herd of around a hundred pigs; you can't give them a wide and respectful enough berth.

I wrote to the Eitingons after my arrival here, also Robert, Rosi and Frl Dr.[8]

With greetings to everyone.

Your Anna

1 A small village around 75 km east of Miskolcz, the provincial town in which Ferenczi was born.

2 The Freuds did not travel 'from Csorbató to Vienna' ⟨*Kalender*, unpublished, 1917⟩ until 1 September.

3 Sándor Ferenczi's mother Rosa, née Eibenschütz (1840–1921), who lived in Miskolcz and was apparently visiting her daughter ⟨Freud/Ferenczi I, 45 Fer, note 1; also 184 Fer, p. 238⟩.

4 Bertalan Zoltán, one of the two sons of Ilona and Joseph Zoltán ⟨Freud/Ferenczi II, 747 Fer and note 2⟩.

5 Margit; she arrived the following day (see 79 AF).

6 According to the 'tradition' [see note 7] Anna is referring to, Emperor Joseph II was travelling with his retinue in 1769 on the imperial road from Brünn [Brno] to Olmütz [Olomouc]. 'During the journey he saw . . . a peasant ploughing with two horses. As the emperor sympathized with the fate (serfdom) of the peasants, he had the carriage stop. He went up to the peasant and asked him personally about his concerns and needs. The emperor then guided the plough for a bit to find out for himself about the arduous work of the peasants' ⟨Legner, pp. 9f.; I thank Gertrud Sperka and Anton Schuster, Loket, Czech Republic, for the indication⟩. This event is captured in a painting by Emil Perchan in the Technical Museum in Vienna. It used to be printed in farmers' calendars and was therefore well known.

7 Emperor Joseph II (1741–90), eldest son of Maria Theresa and Emperor Franz I. He was an enlightened absolutist, abolishing serfdom and establishing several welfare institutions (e.g., the first public children's hospital in Vienna in 1787, where a Department for Nervous Diseases was opened a hundred

years later, which Freud directed until 1897; he also ordered that all Jews in Austria were to have surnames ⟨Aron, p. 291; but see also the description of his ambivalent attitude to the Jews in Austria in: Krüll, pp. 75ff.⟩. Because of his social attitude, Joseph II lived on in many true and reconstructed anecdotes as a favourite of the people of German Austria. The monument in his honour in the Hofburg in Vienna has the inscription 'Saluti publicae vixit / non diu sed totus' [For the well-being of his country he lived not long but wholly], which featured in Freud's dream 'non vixit' (in 1900*a*). Freud mentions Joseph II in his essays 'Lines of Advance in Psychoanalytic Therapy' (1919*a*) and 'On Beginning the Treatment' (1913*c*), and 'our local tradition' in connection with the problem of unpaid treatment.

8 Dr Salka Goldman[n], director of the Cottage-Lyzeum, where Anna taught.

78 SF[1]

Csorbató, 25 August 1917

My dear Anna,
Once again, of course, nothing today from you. It might not be your fault. I won't wait any longer and am forwarding the letters for you that have arrived here.

Continued fine weather, no rain at all.[2] We have decided to stay until Saturday, the 1st.[3] You will receive further details, possibly by telegram. I go often into the forest. Mushrooms are appearing again. Supply of eggs, cheese, butter, etc., gradually running out, as planned.[4]

Affectionate greetings,
Papa

1 Letter card.

2 At the start of the holiday it had been bitterly cold: 'I am stuck here in the Tatra, shivering. If there were such a thing as a cold paradise, it might well be here'; '[. . .] it would be ideal if [. . .] the Tatra could be heated, as Anna says' ⟨Freud/Andreas-Salomé, 13 July 1917, p. 61; Freud/Ferenczi II, 6 July 1917, 690 F, p. 225⟩.

3 On 20 August, Freud wrote in a letter to Ferenczi: 'We plan to leave on the 30th or 31st, probably by way of Pressburg [Bratislava] and with Grete Ilm, with whom we are on very good terms' ⟨Freud/Ferenczi II, 701 F, p. 235⟩. The detour via Budapest mentioned by Tögel [1989], p. 157, appears to have been cancelled (see the *Kalender* entry cited in 77 AF, note 2). On the return train journey Freud wrote his essay 'A Childhood Recollection from *Dichtung und Wahrheit*' (1917*b*). (Editorial preface to this work in *S. E.*, vol. XVII, p. 146.)

4 In a letter to Abraham, Freud described the generosity of friends and supporters: 'friendship and loyalty are taking the form of generosity, with the result that we are able to wallow in the abundance of bread, butter, sausages, eggs and cigars, rather like the chief of a primitive tribe' ⟨Freud/Abraham, 21 August 1917, p. 355. See also, e.g., Freud/Ferenczi II, 667 Fer, 670 Fer, 674 F, 675 Fer, 677 Fer, 681 Fer, etc.⟩. See also 84 AF, note 6; 162 AF, note 1.

79 AF

Kótaj, 26 August 1917

Dear Mama and Papa,
Dr Ferenczi sent me a telegram yesterday[1] that he was expecting me in Budapest for two or three days. He said that accommodation was available. I sent you a telegram; perhaps I will go after all and arrive back in Vienna three days later. I would like to know, however, when you are finally leaving, and I am very sorry not to have received a single line from you, although I have already been here a week. If you wire back in the affirmative to my telegram today[2] I *won't* meet you in Pressburg, as I don't want to cut short my stay here. Once I have received your telegram reply, I will wire my decision so that Dr Sachs doesn't expect me in vain in Pressburg.

Margit, Frau Zoltán's daughter, arrived here yesterday with her two-year-old little girl. Margit is very pretty and nice and she is very easy to get on with. It has become much cosier here as a result and I am reluctant to leave.

Today I had my first riding lesson.[3] It was wonderful and I wasn't afraid at all, although at the end it got faster. My horse was a young, very tall, beautiful golden chestnut who behaved extraordinarily well. It worked quite well with dirndl and black trousers and I also had high riding boots.[4] I even sat straight.[5]

In the afternoon I had less luck with milking. In spite of pressing and pulling, no milk would come out, and I had to make do with drinking the milk from another freshly milked cow. It tastes so good that I will do it every day. Ploughing is much easier; I recently ploughed quite a long furrow.[6]

I would really like to know whether Ernst[7] is already in Vienna and if Martin[8] is still in Linz. Also what you have been doing lately in Csorbató.

I won't write another letter now because I don't think you will get it in time. Please send me a telegram with your departure date.

With lots of greetings and kisses,
Your Anna

1 'I telegraphed Frl Anna that she should stay in Budapest for at least two to three days. Good lodgings have been taken care of. I hear she feels well in Kótaj' ⟨Freud/Ferenczi II, 703 Fer, 27 August 1917, p. 236⟩.
2 Anna's telegram and the reply are both missing.
3 See 7 AF and note 4.
4 Not as Young-Bruehl (p. 79) states '. . . riding horseback in dirndl and black stockings – for lack of a proper habit.' Moreover, the claim that Anna went ahead of her parents to Hungary is not confirmed here.
5 See 22 AF and note 1.
6 Country life always gave Anna 'a feeling of strength, health and freedom' ⟨Anna/Lou, letter 118, 5 August 1923, p. 211⟩. See also 101 AF and note 8, and 141 AF and note 2.

7 See 76 SF and note 12. Freud's *Kalender* entry next to the dates from approx. 23 to 29 August 1917 (written diagonally across all the days) says: 'Ernst to Vienna suffering' ⟨*Kalender*, unpublished⟩. On 10 September Freud wrote: 'Ernst is here in the hospital with a diagnosis of ulcus duodeni and comes home often. He doesn't look particularly well, is trying to get a longer leave' ⟨Freud/Ferenczi II, 704 F, p. 237⟩. He was granted this leave, which he spent at home ⟨ibid., 708 F⟩. He was transferred to Vienna towards the end of the year: 'He is now comfortably here and is living as though in a separate peace' ⟨ibid., 717 F, 16 December 1917, p. 251⟩.

8 'Martin [is] presently the problem child as an observer at the Isonzo (Wippach)' ⟨Freud/Ferenczi II, 708 F, 24 September 1917, p. 241; also 704, 10 September⟩. From there he took part from 23 September in the Isonzo offensive, which lasted until early December. On 1 March of the following year he was promoted to Oberleutnant (first lieutenant) ⟨ibid., 713 F, 715 F, 733⟩.

1918

80 SF[1]

Csorbato[2] [2 August 1918] 9h[3]

Ann Fried at
freund[4]burg.brau bp X

journey interesting[5] Willi[6] delightful[7]
beautiful weather[8] on mama's arrival
fresh[9] and happy[10] luggage
just arrived[11] greetings and thanks
to all friends[12] papa

1 This telegram was not in the transcriptions of the correspondence or in the LoC. The original was kindly given to me by Peter Lambda (see note 6), Tibberton, Gloucester (England). It is now in the possession of the Archiv zur Geschichte der Psychoanalyse e. V., Berlin.

2 Freud had already started making arrangements for the summer holidays at the beginning of the year: 'Ferenczi is taking a great deal of trouble to fix us up again [as in 1917] in the Tatras, where he can spend the holidays with us.' ⟨Freud/Abraham, 29 May 1918, p. 378; Freud/Ferenczi II, pp. 260–92 *passim*⟩. As the rooms in Csorbató were not available until 1 August, the Freuds decided after some hesitation to accept the invitation of Dr Anton von Freund (see note 4) to spend the first part of their holidays at his house in Steinbruch (Köbánya, 10th district of Budapest) ⟨Freud/Ferenczi II, 743 Fer, 744 F, 750 Fer, 751 F, 753 F⟩. 'I set out in a few days with my little (twenty-two-year-old) daughter for Budapest, where a friend and newfound patron of psychoanalysis has offered us accommodation in his villa, until I get permission to go to the Tatra on 1 August in the company of Ferenczi' ⟨Freud/Andreas-Salomé, 1 July 1918, p. 82⟩. Anna and Freud travelled by ship to Budapest on 8 July ⟨*Kalender*, unpublished, 8 July 1918: 'To Köbanya'; see also Freud 1960*a*, p. 328 (the indication 'August' there must be a writing or printing error; also the date '5 July' in Jones II, p. 222⟩. Von Freund had already offered his villa for the holiday in Balatonföldvár on Lake Balaton in 1917 ⟨Freud/Ferenczi II, 675 Fer⟩. At that time Freud declined the invitation as he was able to change rooms and stay in Csorbató (see 76 AF and notes 1 and 4).

3 Receipt stamp: Budapest, 3 Aug 1918, 10h ⟨I thank Bence Laszló Thorday, Budapest/Murnau, for the kind translation of the Hungarian symbols on the telegram form⟩.

4 Anton (Antál) von Freund (1880–1920), D.Phil., owner and director of Steinbrucher Bürgerliche Brauerei AG, Budapest ⟨Anton v. Freund to Freud, letterhead 4 November 1918, FM London⟩. 'He was the most powerful promoter' of psychoanalysis, 'possessing every gift which can charm and captivate' ⟨Freud 1920*c*, p. 267⟩. 'The man [. . .] is not merely a wealthy man, but a man of sterling worth and high intellectual gifts, who is greatly interested in analysis. He is the sort of person one would have to invent if he did not already exist' ⟨Freud/Abraham, 27 August 1918, p. 381⟩. On 5 and 12 June 1918 v. Freund was a guest listener at the meetings of the Vienna Psychoanalytic Society, and on 19 November he was accepted as a member ⟨*Protokolle IV*, pp. 313–15⟩. See also 89 SF, note 1.

5 Anna remained initially in Steinbruch when Freud set off for Csorbató on 1 August with Ferenczi; she followed on 11 August ⟨*Kalender*⟩.

6 Willi (Vili; 1911–95), son of Kata and Lajos Lévy. Freud had met him the previous year together with his mother in the Tatra ⟨Freud/Ferenczi II, 697 F; Lévy, pp. 2f.⟩. Freud and Ferenczi took the seven-year-old, accompanied by his nanny, Annie, from Budapest to his aunt (Regine Vidor), who was spending the summer with her family in Lomnicz near Csorbató in their own bungalow ⟨ibid., pp. 7f.⟩. As an adult, Willi Lévy changed his name to Peter Lambda (after the Greek letter λ with which his father used to sign his newspaper articles). He initially studied medicine in Vienna but stopped in 1934 and went back to Budapest, where he became a sculptor and writer. He emigrated in 1938 to England, where he made a bust of Freud, the three casts of which are to be found at the Freud Museum in London, Anna Freud's later established children's clinic in Hampstead and in the Menninger Institute in Topeka, Kansas, USA ⟨personal information from Peter Lambda; Lambda, 'Recollections', unpublished; see also Freud to Willi⟩.

7 Written 'reisend' [travelling] instead of 'reizend'.

8 Written 'Wittez' instead of 'Wetter'.

9 Written 'errisch' instead of 'frisch'.

10 Martha Freud had spent the holidays until then with Sophie. 'I am going with Anna . . . to Steinbruch as a guest of Freund, that is to say, his sister Levy; in the meantime my wife is going to Schwerin, where Sophie urgently wishes her presence' ⟨Freud/Ferenczi II, 751 F, 18 June 1918, p. 289, also p. 292⟩. The year before the Halberstadts had already spent some time in Schwerin: 'Sophie went to Schwerin with her husband after a week of torment. Let us hope they will stay there together and will be able to nourish themselves' ⟨ibid., 674 F, 22 May 1917, p. 207⟩. At the end of 1918 they returned to Hamburg ⟨ibid., 780 F⟩.

11 Written 'aurogefolgt' instead of 'ausgefolgt'.

12 Reference in particular to Dr v. Freund and Dr Lévy and their families, also Ferenczi and his friends, who often visited ⟨Lévy, pp. 5f.; Ferenczi to v. Freund, 26 July 1918⟩.

81 SF

PROF. DR. FREUD

Csorbató, 2 August 1918
Vienna, IX. Berggasse 19
1 p.m.

My dear Anna,
The first letter from here. The others are at lunch, which I declined on account of a condition that I know only too well,[1] which arose yesterday. I hope I will be well tomorrow. I have decided to blame the accidents on my incredible sensitivity to rancid butter, which is certainly the case, but which has to be kept in strict secrecy from Frau Kara.[2]

We found Mama unexpectedly well and fresh still in Csorba, where she had waited two hours for our train. This morning we made ourselves at home somewhat. My writing niche is the most delightful I have ever had. It is now certain that you can stay alone in the smaller room. I am not going to give up the space here. Incidentally, we have given up your room for eight to ten days and have been able to save a lot that way, on the condition that it will be vacated for you as soon as you arrive.

The weather today is beautiful. I don't have enough superlatives to describe it. A remarkably good year for mushrooms; I will have a lot to do. The coffee house is finished and the entire establishment should be much more respectable and trim.[3]

Mama's news from Berlin and Hamburg is not very good.

Max and Soph are staying in Schwerin and are giving up their apartment in Hamburg, and have rented a very nice four-room apartment in Schwerin in its place. I am therefore unlikely to go there in September.[4] I could tell you a lot more, but time is pressing and it is also too nice to write; I have all kinds of other things to do. So I won't say anything about what is going on around you in Budapest, and hope that you will be comfortable there until you come to us.

Greetings to everyone from me and Mama, particularly to Kata and Antál, and write to us before you get off the train here.

Papa

1 No doubt an 'acute stomach upset' as the previous year in Csorbató ⟨Freud/Ferenczi II, 697 F, 8 August 1917, p. 231⟩.

2 Kata F. Lévy (1883–1969), a sister of Anton v. Freund, married to Dr Lajos Lévy. During the absence of the v. Freunds she kept house for them in Steinbruch; Freud had already met her the previous year in Csorbató. She was a certified primary school teacher, later psychoanalyst, member first of the Hungarian and then of the British Psychoanalytic Society. In 1954 the couple emigrated to England, where she was in close contact with Anna Freud ⟨Lévy; preface and pp. 3–7; Anna to Kata and Freud to Kata, *passim*⟩.

3 Than the previous year; see 76 SF.

4 Freud had already wanted to visit Sophie in Schwerin early in the year: 'If travelling were not now forbidden and subject to all sorts of penalties, I should very

much like to go to see my daughter and grandson at Easter [. . .] but it cannot be done' ⟨Freud/Abraham, 22 March 1918, p. 374⟩. The postponement this time was for other reasons; see 82 AF, note 2.

82 AF

Budapest, 5 August 1918
10 p.m.

My dear Papa,
Someone just brought me your letter as I was preparing to go to bed and I was so happy to receive it that I wanted to reply to it straightaway. I blame myself for the butter; I always thought that you shouldn't eat it. I hope you are well again now; Mama should look after you better than I have done. You don't say anything about what Mama thinks of my not being there;[1] I am pleased to read about the solution with the room; both solutions. But what difference does it make to your trip to Sophie if she stays in Schwerin?[2] I am sure she will find it difficult to give up the apartment. I have received another two letters here from Mama from Schwerin.

Now let me tell you what is going on here. We moved[3] today to Szalay utco 3,[4] where it is extremely comfortable. I am in Willi's room and am writing at his desk. I am regarded as a kind of substitute for him and am being treated extremely well. Dr Lévy[5] is starting to be incredibly nice; he always picks out the best things for me to eat, offers me all his books and even gave me a delightful photo of Willi today. I get on very well with Frau Kata.[6] She missed you a lot on the first day[7] but then she was very busy and that helped her to get over it. I think it did the start of our friendship good that I stayed here. The last few days in Steinbruch were less agreeable but all the more interesting. As you know, I rarely use Jewish proverbs but this time there was one that I just couldn't get out of my head: 'As man sagt meschugge, sollst Du glauben' ['Now there's someone who is *really* meshugge!']. I am referring to Frau Ro[z]si, who has terrible moods and makes her life and that of her husband a misery. You are probably in the best position to know how much.[8] For a long time I didn't think it was that bad. I also feel sorry for the child.[9] I have become good friends with Vera. How the two babies[10] nevertheless turned out so delightfully is a mystery to me. Frl Kokoschka[11] is not doing very well. In the old villa we had a very nice farewell evening, but our nice supper spot in the new villa has been ruined for Frau Kata and myself.

Unfortunately, our trip together will not be possible.[12] The old lady[13] is not well and the two sisters-in-law make it impossible for Frau Kata to travel. It will be hard for her to stay here, but I think personally that she would otherwise make too much trouble for herself in the family. She will follow on at all events. I could travel on Saturday with Dr Freund and Vera. I will be travelling via Csorba and will send a telegram beforehand, but if it coincides with supper there is of course no need for anyone to pick me up.

It will not be difficult for me to be nice here and I am glad to be able to live as a respectable person in spite of the many strange things that you now know of. I also had a dream, but I prefer to keep it to myself and to tell you about it when I see you. I am looking forward very much to seeing you and Mama again, but I would also like to stay a few more days here.

Lots of kisses for you and Mama.

Your Anna

[In Kata's handwriting]

Unfortunately, it will not be possible to follow your advice – but I think that you would agree with me now. My brother will be travelling in my place. I am glad to hear that you are so happy.

[Diagonally in the margin]

Many sincere regards, also to Frau Professor.[14]

Kata[15]

1 See 80 SF, note 5.

2 'My trip to Schwerin planned for mid-September has had to be called off because Sophie will be in Hamburg at the time to give up the apartment' ⟨Freud to Martin, 5 August 1918⟩.

3 Spelling mistake in German.

4 From the house of Dr v. Freund in Steinbruch to Kata and Dr Lajos Lévy in Budapest (see 83 SF). There is no indication either from the telegram (80 SF) or from the subsequent letters that Anna worked 'for several weeks' as a teacher in a school near Budapest trying out the project method used later in the private school in Hietzing ⟨Young-Bruehl, p. 79, without citing a source⟩. Ross, who also mentions this teaching assignment in Hungary, states that he does not know this story at first hand but rather from hearsay ⟨Ross [1994], pp. 23–48; thanks for oral information (6 June 2004)⟩. It could therefore have been in the time between 9 and 31 July (see 80 SF, note 2).

5 Lajos [Ludwig] Lévy (1875–1961), doctor of medicine, specialist in internal medicine. He was a long-time friend of Ferenczi, whose doctor he also was ⟨Freud/Ferenczi, *passim*⟩. He was editor, amongst other things, of the magazine *Gyóyászat* (Medicine), founder member of the Hungarian Psychoanalytic Society (1913) and director from 1918 of the Jewish Hospital in Budapest. Between 1923 and 1928 he visited Freud frequently (also later occasionally) in Vienna and also provided medical consultation ⟨Freud/Ferenczi I, p. 112, note 2; Freud to Lajos Lévy, LoC SF, Cont. 36; Schur, p. 358, note 4; Young-Bruehl, p. 79; Molnar [1996], p. 63; see also *Protokolle IV*, p. 297, note 3 (although the identity there is doubtful)⟩.

6 See Anna to Kata, between 1917 and 1968.

7 She had started analysis with Freud in Budapest ⟨Lévy, pp. 2, 4⟩. See 87 SF.

8 Rózsi v. Freund, née Bródy (1887–?), Anton v. Freund's second wife. She had been analysed by Freud in 1916 and the results were described in 'The Taboo of Virginity' (1918*a*) ⟨Freud/Ferenczi II, 608 Fer, 611 F, 627 Fer, 676 F, 708 F; Lévy, p. 5; Freud to Kata, *passim*; Anton v. Freund to Freud, 4 January, 26 April, 27 June 1916 (FM London); see also, e.g., Freud/Ferenczi III, 834 Fer⟩.

9 Vera (1912–91), v. Freund's daughter from the first marriage ⟨Freud/Ferenczi II, 730 Fer, note 3⟩.
10 Presumably the two children from the second marriage: Erzsébet, married name Berki (1916–89), and Antal (born 6 February 1918, later Dr Anthony Toszeghi in London) ⟨Freud/Ferenczi II, 627 Fer, note 1, 730 Fer, note 2⟩.
11 Possibly the cook in the v. Freund household: 'My sister-in-law left us the cook and maid from her household and while the maid Mariska proved irreplaceable, the cook, who was a new and untried acquisition, did not turn out to be a success' ⟨Lévy, pp. 4f.⟩. She had travelled with Freud and Anna on the ship from Vienna to Budapest ⟨Anton v. Freund to Freud, 1 July 1918, FM London⟩.
12 Freud had invited Kata to go to the Tatra ⟨Freud to Kata, 5 August 1918⟩.
13 Kata Lévy's mother-in-law ⟨Lévy, p. 8⟩.
14 The last four words were squeezed in afterwards.
15 Only after Dr Lévy's mother had died a few days later was Kata Lévy able to travel to the Tatra and spend a few weeks there with the Freuds, initially in Csorbató, where she shared Anna's room, and then in Lomnicz ⟨Freud to Kata, 12 August 1918; Anna to Kata, 10 September 1918⟩.

83 SF[1]

Frl Anna Freud
c/o Dr Levy
Budapest V
Szálay ut 3

Csorbató, 5 August 1918

Dear Anna,
We are well except that there is a little too much rain. The Vidors[2] visited yesterday with Willi, very enjoyable. Have Dr Schachter[3] prescribe mag. bismuthi[4] to bring with you; it does me a lot of good. Lots of mushrooms, lots of changes of clothing.[5] Looking forward, of course, to news from you. Affectionate regards to F[reund]s and L.[évy]s from your
Papa

1 Postcard.
2 Emil and Regine Vidor, a sister of Anton v. Freund and Kata Lévy.
3 The last letter of the name has been corrected and is thus difficult to read; it could also be an 'l' or a 't'. It probably refers to the 'young Schächter', mentioned by Ferenczi in a letter to Freud of 18 July 1920; he was the son of his late close friend, Dr Miksa (Max) Schächter ⟨Freud/Ferenczi III, 849 Fer, p. 31; I, 111 Fer and note 2; II, 651 Fer and note 1⟩.
4 Magma bismuthi, lac bismuthi, milk of bismuth ⟨Hunnius [1998]⟩.
5 'I remember a morning full of rain, which stopped after lunch. [. . .] It began to pour again while we were under way and my rucksack was heavy not only with mushrooms but also from the rain. [. . .] When we finally arrived back in an indescribable state, to the consternation of Frau Professor, the water was streaming off our clothes' ⟨Lévy, pp. 8f.⟩; see also 95 AF and note 10.

84 AF

[Vienna][1] Friday, 13 September 1918

Dear Papa,
I have asked Dr Sachs, who is delivering this letter,[2] to pass on the message that I should be sent an urgent telegram tomorrow at all costs. I don't know at all whether to expect you or not.[3] I was very surprised about the Congress being moved[4] and find it a shame because the internationality will probably be reduced as a result to a minimum. But I can't really judge from here. I am curious to hear whether you spent a few more days in Lomnitz;[5] I'm sure that would be the best thing. Take your time in Budapest as well. Here you won't get anything decent to eat in any case. I am still living off the Budapest bread, eggs and confectioneries, although I have invited people to share on several occasions. You must tell Dr Levy again how well his gifts[57]are lasting. I am very well and everyone says I look splendid. I am making myself comfortable here as well, and don't worry too much about school. Teaching doesn't start until tomorrow week.[7]

I have just received an invitation to the Congress from Dr v. Freund saying that accommodation for me has been taken care of. But I can't really come. I would have to absent myself from school on Saturday and Monday and I can't do that at the beginning. I'm sure you would not be in favour either. Otherwise I would like very much to come.

Math arrives today. I am looking forward very much to seeing her. Martin left yesterday with a heavy heart. In the matter of Esti D.[8] Martin behaved very correctly and was very nice in general.[9]

I send you and Mama lots of greetings. I now have to be serious for many days; a quite inhabitual feeling.

Your Anna

Your patients telephone without interruption.

[In Hollitscher's handwriting]

It is hereby certified that Fräulein Anna Freud is in the best of health, very pretty, eating well and is thus in splendid spirits. Thanks to her pleasant and endearing character, the said person has otherwise gained my approval to such a degree that I can heartily recommend her to any one (any *man*).

Robert Hollitscher[10]

1 Anna had had to finish her holidays early because of the start of school (see note 7) ⟨Lévy, p. 8⟩. She interrupted her journey home in Budapest so as to spend a short time again in Dr Lévy's apartment ⟨Anna to Kata, 10 September 1918⟩.

2 Hanns Sachs was about to depart for Budapest to help with the preparations for the 5th International Psychoanalytical Congress; Ferenczi was expecting him the following day ⟨Freud/Ferenczi II, 757 Fer⟩.

3 The Freuds had wanted to return home again before the start of the Congress, but as the next letters show, they changed these plans, to Anna's approval: 'Persuade Mama and Papa . . . to stay until the Congress. . . . I am fine' ⟨Anna to Kata, 13 September 1918⟩.

4 The Congress was originally to have been held in Breslau [Wroclaw] on 21 and 22 September 1918 ⟨Freud/Abraham, pp. 381, 382⟩, but the Ministry of War made difficulties and questioned whether the Congress should be held at all, as Ferenczi reported: 'When I made the suggestion of holding it in Budapest it turned out that I have only put into words the secret wish of Rank and Dr Freund. . . . We had Frl Annerl informed of this turn of events by telegram' ⟨Freud/Ferenczi II, 754 Fer, 10 September 1918, p. 292; also 756 Fer⟩.

5 They did, continuously putting off their departure ⟨Freud/Ferenczi II, 755 F, 756 Fer, 758 F⟩.

6 The word 'supplies' is deleted before this word. Freud had already written to Abraham about this phenomenon: 'A remarkable feature of these times which I have not yet mentioned to you is the way in which we have been victualled for one year or so by patients and friendly followers. Actually we live on gifts, like a doctor's family in the old days. Our Hungarians, with Ferenczi and Eitingon at their head, as well as some Budapest families who stick to ψα, keep us supplied with cigars, flour, lard, bacon, etc., either free of charge or at incredibly low prices, and I have also found other such quartermasters here in Vienna.' And Abraham confirmed: 'What you write about the return to the system of payment in kind in your practice is quite familiar to me. These are strange times' ⟨Freud/Abraham, 29 May, 21 June 1918, pp. 378, 380⟩. See 78 SF and note 4.

7 In 1917 Anna had already become a class teacher at the Cottage-Lyzeum after the first two probationary years (1915–16 and 1916–17): 'Anna with fiery zeal in her work, she earns contractually 2,000 crowns a year' ⟨Freud/Ferenczi II, 708 F, 24 September 1917, p. 241⟩. On 15 April 1918 (and not 1917 as Peters, p. 23, says), she sat her Second Teaching Examination 'with nice success' ⟨Freud/Ferenczi II, 740 F, 21 April 1918, p. 279; also 737 F; also Freud/Andreas-Salomé, 21 April 1918⟩. See 49 AF, note 1, and 86 AF, note 5.

8 Ernestine ('Esti') Drucker. A year later (on 28 September 1919, soon after Martin's return from war captivity) they became engaged, and married on 7 December 1919; see 104 SF, note 2.

9 'This time he was much more brotherly towards me than usual' ⟨Anna to Kata, 13 September 1918⟩. Previously Martin had spent some of his leave in the Tatra ⟨Lévy, p. 9⟩.

10 'I always invite Robert for tea and supper and we get on very well as always whenever we are alone' ⟨Anna to Kata, 10 September 1918⟩. See 74 AF and note 7.

85 SF

PROF. DR. FREUD — Lomnicz,[1] 13 September 1918
Vienna, IX. Berggasse 19

Dear Anna,

As you know everything has suddenly changed. Besides, Willi was sent home today with Frl.[2] Great anticipation whether the gentle father, who really didn't want this, will come to L.[omnicz] or not.[3] Kata is turning it into a test. She is very contented but otherwise a foot-scratcher ['Kratzerfuss' = hen], hopelessly untalented and no replacement[4] for you. The company with Emil[,][5] Géza Mendel,[6] and Heidi D.[7] from Palota[8] all get on well without any dissonance. The weather is grimly cold and wet, no compensation at all for the poor August.

We want to stay for about another week and to be in Budapest on the 18th to 20th. We will send a telegram. I hope you are not too lonely and won't hold it against us. We originally intended to stick to the plan and leave today but there was such an uproar. In fact you could now take part in the Congress on the 28th/29th in Budapest. I look forward to news and letters from you and send you affectionate greetings.

Papa

1 Because the rooms in Csorbató could only be rented until the end of August, Kata's sister, Frau Vidor, offered the Freuds her cottage in the slightly lower Lomnicz, as she herself was returning home with her family on 1 September. The two localities were connected by a narrow-gauge railway via Tátrafüred ⟨Lévy, pp. 7, 10⟩.
2 Fräulein Anni (also Annie or Anny), Willi Lévy's nanny.
3 He came on 15 September; see 87 SF ⟨Freud/Ferenczi II, 757 F⟩.
4 This could refer to the following recollection by Kata: 'After lunch the Professor played cards (Franzefuss) with his daughter Anna. When she left I was meant to take her place but I had no talent for cards and made atrocious mistakes which dearly tried the Professor's patience and which I am still ashamed of now' ⟨Lévy, p. 9⟩.
5 Perhaps Emil v. Freund, brother of Kata Lévy and Anton v. Freund. He managed the brewery in Steinbruch together with Anton v. Freund and lived there in his father's 'old villa'. He spent some of the summer in the Tatra; see, e.g., 87 SF. Or Kata's brother-in-law Emil Vidor ⟨Lévy, preface and p. 2⟩.
6 Unknown; perhaps 'relatives in Palota' (87 SF).
7 Unknown; as note 6.
8 There are two places that could be referred to, one in Kom. Maros-Torda in northern Transylvania, which belonged at the time to Hungary, approx. 50 km south-east of Besztercze ⟨*Atlas*, 136 E 3⟩; the other Casanád-Palota, a good 200 km south of Miskolcz, halfway between Szegedin and Arad ⟨*Atlas*, 79/80 G 5⟩.

86 AF

[Vienna] 17 September 1918

Dear Papa,

Thank you for your letter from Lomnic,[1] which I have just received. The weather is now so magnificent that it must be fine where you are too. I wonder whether I should really send the mail to Budapest or whether you will stay longer in Lomnic after all.

Of course I would like to attend the Congress.[2] I will ask at school tomorrow if they can find a replacement for Saturday. But I would have to be back for Monday, so would have to leave Sunday evening.[3] We can discuss all that directly.

There is now a lot to do in school.[4] Everything is going very well and Frl Dr[5] says that both Frl Dellisch[6] and I already know our way around splendidly, but it's very tiring. Also the food is terrible. For lunch and dinner I have beans and potatoes and they both already fill me with horror. They simply take your appetite away. Just imagine, for supper I sometimes drink Steinbruch beer. You will also find it difficult to get used to, but it's the same for everyone.

On Sunday I had a very nice outing for the day with Math and Robert. Edith[7] arrived there yesterday.

Enjoy yourselves in Hungary and bring plenty of food with you. I will stop writing now because we will be talking to each other soon. Or will you stay in Budapest until the Congress? Just don't come on Friday as I have a meeting in the evening.

Best regards,
Your Anna

1 Written that way.
2 See 89 SF, note 1.
3 This was easy to arrange because Freud also wanted to return on Sunday 29 September; see 89 SF.
4 'This year all of the administrative work is being done just by Frau Dr G., Frl Dellisch and myself. There was a lot to do, but it went very well and we all enjoyed ourselves' ⟨Anna to Kata, 22 September 1918⟩.
5 'Dr Salka Goldman [sic] . . . praised her apprentice performance with third, fourth, and fifth graders during the 1915–16 and 1916–17 school years and her first venture as *Klassenlehrerin* (head teacher) for the second grade during 1917–18' (see 84 AF, note 7), particularly her 'great zeal' and 'conscientious preparations' and her 'gift for teaching'. 'Dr Goldman also hired Anna Freud on a part-time basis as her secretary and assistant.' For her students, Anna created 'an oasis of warmth and enthusiasm' and at the same time she managed to achieve 'excellent discipline' in her classrooms ⟨Young-Bruehl, pp. 76f.⟩ (see ill. 12). For Anna's dedication and sensitivity, see also Peters, pp. 23–5.
6 Josephine Dellisch. 'She is a grammar school teacher of French and German, a few years older than me, very intelligent and educated, a complete lady and has a very strong educational influence on adolescent children' ⟨Anna to Ernst Freud, 11 February 1920, FM London⟩. She later worked for some years as a teacher in the progressive Wickersheim country boarding school near Saalfeld, Thuringia ⟨*Bloomsbury* [1995], pp. 5, 82 and note 6, 94, 96; there also, see further details of her relationship to Alix and James Strachey⟩. After the war she lived and worked in the Odenwaldschule on the Bergstrasse ⟨Josephine Dellisch to Anna, 26 October 1946, LoC AF, Cont. 17⟩. See also 127 SF and note 1.
7 Edith Rischawy, Robert's niece.

87 SF

PROF. DR. FREUD T.[atra] Lomnic[1], 17 September 1918
Vienna, IX. Berggasse 19

My dear Anna,
Mail delivery is miserable. I hope to have given you the most important news from Budapest. We are gradually winding down here. The weather has become splendidly fine. Dr Levy arrived Sunday lunchtime. We have decided that we will be home Sunday evening, the 22nd. You can meet us. We don't yet know what time we will be leaving here for Budapest and how long we will spend there, because we have not yet managed the sleeping arrangements. Before I finish this letter I should be able to give you more definite information. We are leaving before the Levys.

I presume that the proofs from Prochaska[2] have been sent to Vienna and that you have forwarded them to me here by express mail. Perhaps they will arrive this afternoon. In spite of the luxurious life here, I cannot suppress a certain longing for an orderly relationship to my surroundings. The desire to work is unmistakably calling.

Kata's treatment[3] has progressed as far as it can on an irregular ambulatory basis and is now faltering. Continuation in Vienna. The committee in Budapest appears to want to make the Congress very pompous and authentically Hungarian. I will try to put a damper on it as far as I can from here.[4]

Ernst is back from Kassa,[5] with 'Kanzleibefund' [fit for clerical work][6] as he puts it; he is staying here until the 24th[7] and is then also travelling via Budapest.[8] He is going with Emil Fr.[eund] to Kesmark,[9] where we went on an excursion on Saturday, some of the way on foot. The company of the relatives in Palota, Emil, Géza and Frl Heddy,[10] is very agreeable.

Evening: I still cannot tell you when we will be leaving here. But you can take it as certain that we will be arriving on *Sunday* evening and you should contact Herr Weiss from the brewery in good time to arrange for us to be picked up.

Affectionately,
Papa

1 Written that way.
2 The (then still 'k. k. Hof-') Buchdruckerei Karl Prochaska in Teschen [Český Těšín], north Moravia. At the time Freud was preparing the fourth volume of his *Sammlung kleiner Schriften zur Neurosenlehre* (Vienna: Heller, 1918) and was awaiting galley proofs of 'Further Recommendations in the Technique of Psychoanalysis' (1913*c*, 1914*g*, 1915*a*), 'The Theme of the Three Caskets' (1913*f*) and 'The Taboo of Virginity' (1918*a*) ⟨Lévy, p. 14; *Kalender* unpublished, 17 April, 5 December 1918⟩.
3 The analysis commenced in Steinbruch; see 82 AF, note 6.
4 'The hints that you want to develop the Congress in a ceremonial-official direc-

tion have less of my sympathy. . . . I also ask that you exert an influence on Dr Freund such that he reins in his inclinations towards generous hospitality' ⟨Freud/Ferenczi II, 758 F, 17 September 1918, p. 295⟩.

5 Kosice, approx. 50 km north-north-east of Miskolcz, now part of Slovakia.

6 In March, Ernst 'has succeeded in putting through a preliminary peace for himself, in a recent determination he received a "C" classification and hopes to stay at the "B" classification at the now expected superarbitrium' ⟨Freud/Ferenczi II, 735 F, 17 March 1918, p. 273; also 737 F⟩.

7 'Two of my sons [Martin and Ernst] are near us here in the Tatras' ⟨Freud/Abraham, 27 August 1918, p. 382⟩. On 10 September Ferenczi reported that he had met Ernst in Széplak ⟨Freud/Ferenczi II, 754 F, p. 293⟩. And Kata Lévy recalls: 'One day Ernst came on leave from the army. He had been in a military convalescence home close to Csorbato in the Tatra' ⟨Lévy, p. 6⟩. Since August 1917 Ernst had had several lengthy periods of sick leave and hospitalization, most recently for tuberculosis ⟨Freud/Ferenczi II, 699 F, 704 F, 708 F, 709 F, 713 F, 715 F, 717 F, 733 F, 737 F, 740 F, 742 F, 751 F; see also Jones II, pp. 229f.⟩. He later stayed in Arosa for that reason; see 133 SF and note 12.

8 He attended the Congress there as a guest; see 90 AF, note 1.

9 Késmark, a small village nearby, below the Lomnicz peak. Food was also bought there occasionally ⟨Lévy, p. 10⟩.

10 See 85 SF and notes 6 and 7.

88 SF

PROF. DR. FREUD　　Lomnic,[1] 19 September 1918
Vienna, IX. Berggasse 19

My dear Anna,
They have managed to persuade us to stay until the Congress: all possible influences and the enchantingly beautiful weather. Mama gave in before me; I just went along with it. Look out for yourself as best you can and do not stint yourself.

Dr Levy will be in Vienna on Tuesday and will contact you and also bring my black suit. Please tell the patients that I will be back on 30 September and will start on 1 October.

I am sorely missing a set of proofs from Prochaska. I hope you have already forwarded them to Budapest, otherwise send them as quickly as possible here or to the Freunds.[2] We will be leaving for Budapest on the 25th. If you see Sachs, remind him that he should bring my fountain pen with him. My good one is broken; I can hardly write.

I presume you are getting money; enjoy yourself. I am surprised myself at the change.

Papa

1 Written that way.

2 Freud later gave the sorely missed proofs to Kata as a souvenir of their time together in the Tatra ⟨Lévy, p. 14⟩.

89 SF

PROF. DR. FREUD T.[atra] L.[omnicz], 21 September 1918
Vienna, IX. Berggasse 19

My dear Anna,
I am taking the opportunity to send you a few more lines via Dr Levy. I hope you have received our letters and now know everything, including the mail and the matter of the missing proofs from Prochaska.

We have had the best week of our stay so far; but I already have the reservation for a half-compartment for Wednesday morning to Budapest.[2]

If you can come to the Congress,[2] you are welcome. We will be returning to Vienna on Sunday night.

Many affectionate greetings,
Papa

1 For the 5th International Psychoanalytic Congress. It took place under the chairmanship of Karl Abraham on 28 and 29 September 1918 in the Hungarian Academy of Sciences. Freud read his essay 'Lines of Advance in Psychoanalytic Therapy' (1919*a*), which he had written while staying in Steinbruch at the house of Anton v. Freund. Ferenczi was elected president of the International Psychoanalytical Association and Anton v. Freund secretary general ⟨*IZ*, vol. 5 (1919), pp. 52–7⟩. (See also Jones II, pp. 221–4, and Freud/Andreas-Salomé, 4 October 1918, p. 83; Freud 1923*i*.) Shortly after the end of the war on 7 November 1918 Ferenczi sent the Congress report with the following comments to Freud: 'A few changes have been made for the purpose of expunging the warlike character of our Congress' ⟨Freud/Ferenczi II, 770 Fer, p. 309⟩.

2 At this Congress the generous donation by an 'unnamed member' of the Budapest Psychoanalytic Society – it was Anton v. Freund – was announced; it was designed to enable Freud, apart from other things, to set up a publishing company devoted exclusively to psychoanalytical literature 'to promote scientific publications, particularly for the efficient design of the Society's magazines' that would be a 'non-profit business' and could thus take better account of the authors' interests than 'tended to be the case with book dealer publishers' ⟨Freud 1919*c*, pp. 267, 269; *IZ*, vol. 5 [1919], pp. 55f.; *Rundbriefe 1*, pp. 40–4⟩. After numerous transactions, the Internationaler Psychoanalytischer Verlag was founded in Vienna in January 1919. It was a GmbH (limited company) with v. Freund, Freud, Ferenczi and Rank as partners, the latter also being managing director. He was assisted by his wife, Beata, and Anna Freud and Theodor Reik. Jones later replaced v. Freund, who was terminally ill (see 95 AF, note 14, 96 AF, note 6). In February 1921, A. J. Storfer replaced Reik as assistant when Reik moved temporarily to Berlin; the same year Eitingon joined the management unofficially and raised considerable sums of money. In 1925, Anna herself became a member of the GmbH (see 100 SF, notes 4 and 5) ⟨Freud 1919*c*, 1920*c*, p. 268; Freud/Ferenczi II, 737 F (7 April 1918) to 782 F (6 January 1919), *passim*, III 1027 Fer, and elsewhere; Freud/Jones, letter 275, 13 May 1920, and 1918–20, *passim*; *Rundbriefe 3*, p. 13; Marinelli, *Katalog*; Huppke; see also Jones II, p. 221; Jones III, pp. 9, 31–40, 48, 49; and particularly discussion of the publishing company in Freud/Eitingon; also the regular reports in the 'Mitteilungen

des Internationalen Psychoanalytischen Verlags' in *IZ*, vol. 7 (1921), pp. 533f. and thereafter; see also Zerfass and Huppke with numerous illustrations and detailed bibliography⟩.

90 AF

[Vienna] 23 September 1918

Dear Papa,
I will give Dr Sachs the most important mail. Here everything is fine and nothing new. I am looking forward to seeing you again soon.[1]
With many greetings,
Your Anna

1 In Budapest. For Anna, it was the first Psychoanalytical Congress that she experienced in person (Gay, p. 436, is incorrect when he claims that Anna did not attend this Congress). Martha and Ernst Freud were also guests, 'the only occasion on which any of Freud's family (except of course the professional Anna Freud) attended any psychoanalytical Congress' ⟨Jones II, p. 222⟩. The Freuds 'lived in the pleasant Gellért Hotel on the left bank of the Danube (Buda), from where the small local boat, the *Propellor*, as it was called, took them over to the right bank. Anna Freud, who also came from Vienna to the Congress, was my guest' ⟨Lévy, p. 14⟩.

91 SF[1]

To spend as soon as you can buy anything with it.
Papa
Congratulations for 3 December 1918

1 Unlike Freud's other letters, this birthday greeting on the front of an envelope, presumably containing money, was written in the Latin alphabet.

1919

92 SF[1]

Frl Anna Freud
Vienna
Berggasse 19[2]

[Postmark: Salzburg 15 July 1919, 9 [o'clock]5 h[3]

Not so bad after all, both ladies[4] sitting in the corridor. Mama just debarked.

Affectionately,
Papa

1 Picture postcard: 'Salzburg – view of the castle, Hoher Göll and Untersberg'.
2 The address is crossed out and replaced by 'Bayrisch Gmain bei Reichenhall, Gasthof zur Post', which Anna had already left for; see 93 SF and note 2.
3 The shaky handwriting indicates that the card was probably written without a firm support. Freud was on the way to Bad Gastein, where he planned to stay until 12 August (see 106 SF). 'Minna is coming along to Gastein on the direct orders, which don't seem unobjectionable to me, of her physician Prof. Braun [. . .]' ⟨Freud/Ferenczi II, 817 F, 10 July 1919, p. 214; Freud/Jones, letter 248; Freud and Minna Bernays to Ernst, 19 July 1919⟩.
4 Martha Freud and Minna Bernays. Martha had had severe influenza in May (not March as Jones III, p. 9, incorrectly states), followed by pneumonia, the effects of which were still being felt; she convalesced in Sanatorium Parsch (see 99 SF and note 1) ⟨Freud/Ferenczi II, 813 F; Freud/Jones, letters 241, 244, 246, 248⟩.

93 SF[1]

Frl Anna Freud
Bair. Gmain
bei Reichenhall
Posthotel[2]

[Sender (handwritten):] Villa Wassing[3]

Badgastein, 15 July 1919

My dear Anna,
What an adventure! I had to stand until I nearly dropped. Mama and Aunt had it a little better and were able to sit some of the time in the corridor on the famous stools and some of the time in the compartment. Left Mama in a flurry in Salzburg to be at 7.45 in G.[astein] and 8.30 in front of the house, where very well received. Big rest day tomorrow. Dr Brecher[4] was already at the station.

Hope you receive this card very soon and had a peaceful journey.
Greetings to Marg.[arete] from me and send news soon, very soon
to your good
Papa

1 Postcard.
2 Anna had been spending her holidays here since 17 July with Margarete Rie (see 94 SF, note 2). For comments on Bayerisch-Gmain, see, e.g., 98 AF and note 2.
3 See 73 SF, note 2.
4 Guido Brecher (1877–?), doctor of medicine, working as a general practitioner in Vienna since 1903. 'Assistant doctor at the general hospital, general polyclinic and Rudolfinerhaus in Vienna', since 1907 member of the Vienna Psychological Wednesday Society ⟨*Badgastein. Liste* 1907, preface; *Minutes I*, pp. 3, 146; Mühlleitner, p. 53⟩. He worked in winter as a spa doctor in Merano (see 181 SF and note 10), and in summer from 1906 to 1937 in Bad Gastein at different spa establishments or hotels *Badgastein. Liste* 1907, 1912, 1919–22; preface⟩. In October 1938 he was denied permission to stay there on racial grounds, but had already left his apartment and practice in St Johann in Pongau shortly before; nothing appears to be known about his later fate ⟨Fellner, p. 436 – I thank Laurenz Krisch for this reference; Krisch [2002], [2003]⟩.

94 SF[1]

Anna Freud
Posthottel
B[ayerisch] Gmain

Bad Gastein, 20 July [1919]

We are here very comfortably without news from you.[2]
Papa

1 This telegram was not in the transcription; it was kindly copied for me by Gerhard Fichtner, who discovered it in LoC, SF (then E 1,16). During my research there (2002) it was put in the right place in Cont. 2.
2 Freud had in the meantime heard from Martha by phone 'that Anna passed Salzburg with Margaretl Rie on the 17th on their way to Bair. Gmain' ⟨Freud and Mina Bernays to Ernst, 19 July 1919⟩.

95 SF

PROF. DR. FREUD

BGastein, 21 July 1919
Vienna, IX. Berggasse 19

My dear Anna,
After three and a half wonderful days today proper letter-writing weather has arrived and yesterday your express letter, which I was very pleased to receive.[1] If our stay survives the trial by rain, everything will be all right until we can meet to stay in Badersee.[2] Today I received the first card from Mama after three teleph.[one] calls. My impression is that she is not living in the lap of luxury.[3] The doctor[4] has all my books in his library but she had them all at home as well, and hasn't got fat from them. At all events, life here would be even less to her liking.

We are very comfortable here. We are eating meat again, which must have very special juices, and are getting used to the real value of the krone. Altogether it is no more expensive here than in Vienna. As Aunt is following her lifestyle[5] much more consistently than if Mama were here, I am alone on all the paths and walks, which I like quite a lot. In the meantime she enjoys my very pleasant room, which is next to hers. We are together for the two main meals. Our restaurant is four minutes from the house. I was once in Prossau[6] for lunch but met a brother of Riesz[7] and wife, good people, who went to Italy for 15[8] years and know everything as well, and love it as much as I do. The rain today didn't stop me from going to a special place and picking the magnificent white orchids (Platanthera bif[olia]),[9] which are so incomparably fragrant. Mama certainly missed something at the next change.[10]

The time left after the walks I devote to the manuscript of 'Beyond the Pleasure Principle', which I brought with me and which is developing well here.[11] There is a lot about death in it, but unfortunately without literature[12] and practical experience it is very difficult to say anything definitive about it.

Rank has already written from the headquarters[13] for the first time bad news about Toni's appearance and mood; he is apparently quite gaunt and unrecognizable.[14] It is therefore highly unlikely that he will come to Gastein and perhaps we shouldn't even wish him to.[15]

There is a very nice reading room here where you can sit when curiosity about what is happening in the world gets too much for you. There are fresh newspapers every two days.

All in all we are thus very comfortable here. The strawberries are still blooming. Mushrooms have not yet emerged, perhaps the other Herr Riesz[16] will come for a game of tarock.

I am curious to hear how you like Reichenhall, where there is so much to see and buy. If you find the gravestone of Barbarossa[17] in St Zeno's you can then tell the children in the fourth class about it.[18]

I presume you have given my regards to Dr Ortenau.[19] You know that he advanced some money for the supplies.

Tell me all about your life and how you are getting on with Marger.[20][etl], who is no doubt busy going back and forth between you and Frl Neff.[21] Please thank her on my behalf for her regards. Don't write so much, however, that it spoils your day.

Affectionately,

Papa

1 Missing.
2 A small lake, at the time part of Unter-Grainau, now belonging to Grainau bei Garmisch-Partenkirchen; see 105 AF, note 3. The holiday together there was planned from 13 August (after Martha's spa cure) ⟨Freud/Jones, letter 246⟩. For the actual course of the second half of the holidays, see 106 SF.
3 She 'wanted originally to go straight through from Parsch but apparently got held up' ⟨Freud and Minna Barnays to Ernst, 19 July 1919⟩.
4 An uncle of Siegfried Bernfeld; see 99 SF.
5 'My sister-in-law is with me . . . Suffering as she is, she will lead a sedentary life there' ⟨Freud/Jones, letter 246, 8 July 1919, p. 351⟩. See 14 AF and note 4.
6 Prossaualp im Kötschertal, a side valley from the Gasteiner Ache (1271/1295 m) which links to many mountain huts and walking tours; from Bad Gastein it is approx. two and a half hours' walk ⟨Baedeker [1923], p. 424; Freytag-Berndt⟩.
7 Probably Ludwig Riesz, manufacturer, Vienna, and Josefine Riesz, Vienna; both were staying at Hotel Austria on 1 July ⟨*Badgastein. Liste* 1919, serial nos 590 and 591⟩. See below, and 102 SF and note 4.
8 Not clearly legible; it could also be '25'.
9 Lesser butterfly orchid; see 142 SF.
10 Changing clothes; see 83 SF and note 5.
11 'A second [work] with the mysterious heading "Beyond the Pleasure Principle" is in process.' 'In it I am saying many things that are quite unclear, out of which the reader has to make the right thing. Sometimes one can't do otherwise' ⟨Freud/Ferenczi II, 794 F, 17 March 1919, p. 335; 800 F, 31 March 1919, p. 341⟩. *Beyond* is Freud's '[. . .] metapsychological work containing as it does an outline of the forthcoming structural model of the psyche, introducing the new dualism of instinctive drives (death drives versus life drives) [. . .]', that was to 'startle the world of psychologists' ⟨Grubrich-Simitis [1993], p. 185; Jones III, p. 9⟩. See 112 SF and note 7.
12 This was later sent by Rank (see 100 SF and note 12).
13 After his return from Krakow, he once again 'plunged into work with his long-accustomed zeal' ⟨Freud/Ferenczi II, 780 F, 1 September 1919, p. 321; 769 F⟩.
14 Anton v. Freund had been operated on for a testicular sarcoma in early 1918. He subsequently suffered from neurotic symptoms, which Freud treated on several occasions through analysis ⟨Freud/Ferenczi II, 723 Fer, 730 Fer, 733 Fer and *passim*; *Rundbriefe 2*, p. 274, note 4⟩. Since early 1919 metastases of the tumour had occurred; see 96 AF, note 6).
15 In any case Anton v. Freund was refused an exit visa from the Hungarian authorities for Gastein, as were Ferenczi and his wife, Gizella (married since 1 March 1919, see 287 SF and note 5), who wanted to visit Freud together ⟨Freud/Ferenczi II, 791 Fer, 818 Fer, 819 Fer, 820 F; Freud/Jones, letter 246⟩. See 106 SF, note 6.
16 Julius Riesz, see 102 SF and note 4.

17 Written [Rothbart] this way. There is of course no Barbarossa gravestone at St Zeno's in Bad Reichenhall but an (interesting) high relief in the cloister apparently showing Emperor Frederick I (Barbarossa), who contributed considerably to the building of the monastery in 1170 through a local donation ⟨Schnell, p. 30 (with ill.); recent research has, however, questioned this attribution in part (thanks to Johannes Lang, Stadtarchiv Bad Reichenhall)⟩. Freud might have been referring to this or to one of the legends about the emperor, according to which deceased rulers slept in the mountain until their return; Barbarossa is usually said to be sleeping in the Kyffhäuser, with Charlemagne in the Unterberg (the mountain range between Salzburg and Berchtesgaden); in the various legends, however, the two are often switched ⟨Huber, pp. 27–9, 30–42; *Reader's Encyclopedia*, p. 97⟩.

18 Anna was expecting a class of forty-two children after the holidays, 'a large fourth class, which will probably give me a lot to do. But it is still the same children as two years ago; I have had them now since the second class and I am looking forward to it' ⟨Anna to Kata, 7 October 1919⟩. See ill. 12.

19 Gustav Ortenau (1864–1951), doctor of medicine, pneumologist, health councillor, spa doctor in Bad Reichenhall from 1890 to 1938. He made a great contribution to the spa and was highly appreciated by its inhabitants; nevertheless, his licence to practise medicine was withdrawn because he was Jewish and he had to flee to Switzerland. Some of his furniture has been preserved in the Ortenau Room of the Ethnographical Department of the Israel Museum in Jerusalem, including Heinrich Heine's writing desk, which had come into his possession at one time through historical family connections ⟨Leonhardt, pp. 210, 216–20, 223–6, 231f.⟩.

20 Written like that.

21 Gretl Neff; see 96 AF. She could be connected with Margarete Rie's acting studies. Since 16 June 1912, the Oberbayerische Bauerntheater Direktion Josef Meth had been playing in the theatre of Hotel Deutsches Haus and 'would also play for the next decades [until the 1920s]' ⟨Amman, pp. 79f.⟩. It is possible that a 'Marg. Neff' mentioned in various editions of the *Bühnenjahrbuch* gave a guest performance ⟨1918 (vol. 29) in Herzogl. Hoftheater in Meiningen; 1919 (with address; vol. 30, p. 224) as 'Königl. Schauspielerin' [royal actress] in the Schauspielhaus on Schillerplatz, Berlin; 1920 (vol. 31), ibid.⟩. In a letter to his wife, Olga, Arthur Schnitzler also mentions a (young) 'Frl [Margarethe] Neff playing "Erna" in his tragicomedy *Das weite Land*' ⟨Schnitzler [1981], Prague, 31 October 1911, pp. 678f., 973⟩. In the *Salzburger* theatre archives from around 1919, there is no mention of the name Neff, which does not mean, however, that she did not make guest appearances. ⟨I am grateful to Alma Scope, Salzburger Museum Carolino Augusteum, 17 September 2001, for information about Salzburg.⟩

96 AF

Bayr. Gmain, 24 July 1919

My dear Papa,

I have just woken up from a long sleep. Before lunch I climbed up to pick a large bush of rhododendrons and two martagon lilies behind the house, and afterwards felt that I deserved a long afternoon nap. The flowers will travel to Salzburg for Mama's birthday, and the courier who will bring them is – Ernst. He sent us a telegram, saying that he would be arriving here tomorrow lunchtime on the way to Salzburg, and Margaretl and I intend to receive him in our best dirndl scarves and aprons and to hold on to him at least for the afternoon.[1]

Life here continues as agreeably as it started in the first few days. The weather is not holding but our good mood is all the more so. I can no longer understand why I was so unhappy and listless in Vienna recently. Here I feel so well and peaceful and have discovered that there are no unpleasant things that I could think about. Nor am I afraid, as I have been in the last few years, when I think about school. This time I am really getting some rest. We always take breakfast in bed, sleep late, especially when the weather is bad, rest after lunch and also go to bed early. Then there is all the food, so it is really a rest. Now all we need is some sunshine.

Margaretl is very pleasant company and we have become friends remarkably quickly. She is so considerate and dear, but always so pretty and graceful in all situations that our shared room has only advantages. She doesn't go 'back and forth' so much, at least not at the moment. I think her work with Gretl Neff is not starting until next week[2] and the Neff parents are difficult to put up with, so she is staying well out of their way. She has something incredibly delightful in her manner and I wish I could have been like her. The only thing is that she is not very energetic and almost always has a headache and palpitations. Do you think it will stop? I told her that I was in analysis with you,[3] because she often talks about her therapy, and I didn't think it was fair that I knew about her and she not about me.

It often occurs to me here that in fact not much is required for a pleasant life. But why doesn't that work usually?

There are very nice shops in Reichenhall but so far Margaretl has not let me spend a lot of money. She says that I am too extravagant, but I think I will rebel some time. In Vienna money doesn't go very far and here there is not only whipped cream, bacon and ham sandwiches but also books, stones, vases, etc. I am not ashamed to say, however, that for the time being it is the food that tempts me most.

In the night before you left Vienna I had a terrible dream. I dreamt that the fiancée of Dr Tausk[4] rented the apartment at Berggasse 20 opposite us to shoot you, and whenever you went to the window she appeared opposite at the window with a pistol. I was very frightened and always rushed to the window as well. I was very happy that you left early the following morning and could escape her that way. Can that have been the purpose of the dream: to transpose the unpleasant feeling at your departure into a pleasant one?

I have read another Bennet[5] here, 'Anna of the Five Towns'. I want to stop reading now, however. Margaretl has brought too many books and like Martin I 'can't resist'.

I am glad to hear that you can take such nice and peaceful walks and I have a good feeling at the same time, knowing that you are nevertheless not alone. Perhaps the card school will get together; it's just right for a summer that promises to be as rainy as this one.

I am always immensely delighted to receive your letters and cards and all the news about yourself, and can't have enough of them. I was very shocked to read the news about Toni F., however. I had always believed that it was a mistake and cannot believe the opposite.[6] I intend to write to Katá[7] from here about Rank.[8] But when I think *about it*, I am always afraid of and for her.

I send you lots of greetings and a kiss.

Your Anna

Margarete sends her sincere greetings.
Hasn't Jones sent any work that I could translate here?[9]

1 In October 1918 Ernst 'had gone back to Munich to complete his technical studies', and in March 1919 'amidst the turmoil of the revolution [i.e., the Soviet Republic from 7 April to early May 1919] has earned his diploma [as architect] with distinction' there, working since then without pay in Munich ⟨Freud/Jones, letter 222, 10 November 1918, p. 325; letter 248; Freud/Ferenczi II, 768 F, 808 F, 20 April 1919, p. 348, 811 F; Freud/Andreas-Salomé, 2 April 1919, PS⟩. See 103 AF, note 4.

2 See 101 AF.

3 She began in 1918: 'Annerl's analysis is getting very fine' ⟨Freud/Ferenczi II, 765 F, 20 October 1918, p. 302; see also Peters, p. 34; Young-Bruehl, pp. 80, 103, 114–17; Gay, pp. xvii, 435, 439f.⟩. It lasted 'nearly four years' ⟨Young-Bruehl, p. 107⟩. In autumn 1923, Freud ordered control analyses in preparation for the first patients of her own ⟨Anna to Eitingon, 27 May 1923⟩. In 1924, she began 'a bit of renewed analysis' with interruptions until mid-1925. 'It should also be useful for my own analytical practice' ⟨Anna/Lou, letter 170, 5 May 1924, pp. 303f., and letters 171–4, 176, 178, 179, 182–5, 193, 211, 218, 224, 232; Young-Bruehl, pp. 122f., 124⟩. Later on, Anna occasionally requested individual sessions of 'follow-up analysis' from her father; see, e.g., 261 SF, note 2; also Introduction, pp. 7, 12.

4 Viktor Tausk (1879–1919), doctor of law, doctor of medicine, had worked as a lawyer until 1905, then as a writer and journalist. He started studying medicine in Vienna in 1908 and established himself there as a neurologist in 1914. He became a member of the Vienna Psychoanalytic Society in 1909. He served from the start of the war as a doctor in the field. On 3 July 1919 (three weeks before Anna's letter), he shot himself shortly before the marriage to his fiancée, the concert pianist Hilde Loewi ⟨Freud/Andreas-Salomé, 1 August (also 25 August) 1919; Freud/Ferenczi II, 817 F (here incorrect date of death); Freud 1919*f*; Mühlleitner, pp. 343–5; *Protokolle II*⟩.

5 Written like that. E. [still] Arnold Bennett (1867–1931), English novelist and playwright. The '"Five Towns" stories, all of them, . . . are in the first rank of English novels' (*Twentieth Century Authors*, p. 119). The novel *Anna of the Five Towns* was reprinted several times in the 1950s and 1960s, but does not appear to have been translated into German. It is possible that Freud himself told Anna about this writer (see the thirtieth lecture by Freud in 1933*a*, p. 49); Jones states that 'he had always been fond of Arnold Bennett' ⟨Jones III, p. 458⟩.

6 See 95 SF, note 14. After months of fluctuating health, v. Freund's condition deteriorated so badly that he had himself admitted in September 1919 to the Cottage-Sanatorium in Vienna. His family had always thought that a recovery was possible ⟨e.g., Freud/Ferenczi II, 820 F; 1918 and 1919 *passim*; Freud/Jones, particularly letters 237, 256, 257, 261; Freud/Abraham, 1 December 1919, 15 December 1919; Kata to Freud, 27 October 1919⟩. Freud also wrote to Ludwig Binswanger that 'your own fate gave me hope for him for a year and a half. . . . He underwent the same operation as you, but did not escape a relapse' ⟨Freud/Binswanger, 122F, 14 March 1920, p. 150⟩. Freud visited Toni regularly in the Sanatorium until he died on 20 January 1920. 'We buried him on 22 January' ⟨ibid; Freud/Ferenczi III, 830 F; Freud/Eitingon, 162 F; Freud 1920*c*⟩. On 6 November 1921, his body was transported to Budapest, where he was buried next to his first wife ⟨Freud/Ferenczi III, 893 Fer⟩.

7 Written like that.

8 See PS to 103 AF.

9 In early 1919, Anna had translated Ernest Jones's essay 'Anal-erotic Character Traits', this time citing her own name (see 60 AF, note 7) ⟨*IZ*, vol. 5 [1919], 69–92; Freud/Ferenczi II, 787 F; Freud/Jones, letters 229, 232⟩. Her translation of Jones 1920*a* appeared in 1921 and of Jones 1922*b* in 1923.

97 AF[1]

Prof. Dr. S Freud
Bad Gastein
Villa Wassing

[Bayerisch Gmain,] 25 July 1919[2]

Dear Papa! The anticipated visitor has arrived.
Affectionate regards,
Anna [in their own handwriting:] Margarete
Ernst

1 Coloured picture postcard written in pencil: 'Bayr. Gmain bei Bad Reichenhall', also with a picture of the Posthotel. A cross marks the door and window of the attic with flowers on the balcony; above it, written by Anna, 'our room'. See 105 AF and note 2.

2 Postmark 'Grossgmain', 25 July 1919; the old stamp of the k. k. Österreische Post [Imperial Austrian Post Office] is printed over with 'Deutschösterreich' [German Austria].

98 AF

[Bayerisch] Gmain, 28 July 1919

My dear Papa,
First: You must *without fail*[1] write again *poste restante* to Grossgmain. Your last letter took five days and that shouldn't happen when it need only take a day. Everything has been arranged perfectly and the postwoman is in agreement. I don't collect the mail any more myself either. A very nice

Salzburg doctor's family (Dr v. Hueber, who claims to admire you very much) has moved from here to Gr. G. and comes twice a day to eat. The two boys always collect our mail and bring it with them. So everything works perfectly and I am very happy to get the letters so quickly. If you address the letters here, they go via Munich.[2]

Since Ernstl's visit we have had a second, from Norbert Rie, who turned up quite unexpectedly.[3] He was looking for an apartment for his family and rented one for them in Grossgmain, about twenty minutes from us. Like all compromises, I don't find it particularly sensible. Margaretl is happy but with mixed emotions. After having taken her leave once, she would – I think – have liked to continue[4] to enjoy her new independence. For better or worse, she now has to start going back and forth. They are not meant to be coming, by the way, until the end of the week.

I have such an awful lot to write today that I don't quite know where to begin. I am very pleased to hear that they have caught the Hungarian scoundrel;[5] Rank once again showed how energetic he is. Aunt writes that[6] Uncle Eli[7] has announced another delivery; that's almost uncanny. When we departed from the station on the morning you left, Uncle Alexander told me a lot about Uncle Eli's beginnings and family stories from the distant past. Now I understand why you didn't dissuade Mama from accepting the delivery from him.[8]

I am receiving a lot of mail here and must tell you about some of it. I have a letter from little Vera Freund in which she writes that she is coming to Vienna in the autumn and asks whether I would like her to come, and if I can help her study, etc.[9] I wrote straight back, saying yes to everything, but I don't really understand it. Does the idea come from Toni in the event that he becomes ill? Does she want to come to us?[10] Have you heard anything about a plan of this sort, or is it perhaps her own idea?[11]

Then I had a very interesting, completely businesslike[12] letter from Jones. I will enclose it for the sake of simplicity. He assumes that I can also translate German–English. Do you think that is possible? At first I thought no, but then I tried a bit with your lectures, which Margaretl has with her, and I think it wouldn't be so difficult. I would get better with time, and at first Jones would have to check it. Of course, I don't want to embarrass you or myself. But I would be really pleased if I could do it. Which of the works is he talking about? Do you think I could ask Rank to send them[13] to me? In that way[14] I would also naturally have far more opportunities than if I restricted myself to English–German. (Do you think I am asking too much of Jones?)

Yesterday I was at Thumsee Lake and was quite taken with its beauty.[15] I went rowing, of course, and just didn't want to leave. If we only lived there, I would always go to it. I didn't have many other memories of it – except that I immediately found the spot where we always fished and where the stream collapsed during the floods.[16] I would like Margaretl to come there as well. She can't walk very far, but Regine Pachmayr, whom I visited in Kirchberg, said she would take us there by car some time.[17]

Unfortunately, long walks also make me tired. I have these descending pains in my legs, which no doubt are due to my being so thin. It is thus better for me to lead a restful lifestyle for the time being.

I have become more determined here in my plan to buy a small house.[18]

Write to me again soon. In the meantime I[19] send you lots of greetings and a kiss.

Your Anna

I don't know why I keep making mistakes today.[20]

1 Underlined twice.
2 For the complicated relationship between the two Gmain communities – the German Bayerisch Gmain and the Austrian Grossgmain (to distinguish it from Kleingmain near Salzburg) – see Lang and Schneider, pp. 6, 243ff., 365ff., 467–71, and elsewhere.
3 Norbert Rie (1897–?), brother of Margarete (Freud 1985*c*, p. 275, mistakenly referred to as 'Georg'). The stay in Grossgmain mentioned subsequently did not come about. See 103 AF.
4 The word 'begin' is crossed out.
5 Unknown.
6 The word 'Rank' deleted after this word.
7 Eli Bernays (1860–1923), brother of Martha Freud, married to Freud's sister, Anna ⟨Stammbaum Lange: Freud Family, 'Genealogical Tree', p. III⟩.
8 Jones writes at length in Freud's biography about Martha's close relationship with her brother, Freud's relationship with his brother-in-law fluctuating between friendship and crisis, and the friendly contacts between the Freud and Bernays families even before Freud's connection with Martha. Freud's brother, Alexander, will have told Anna, amongst other things, about a fierce argument over Martha's dowry, which was partly administered by Eli and not made available by him in the way Freud had wanted at the time. (For details, see Albrecht Hirschmüller's appendix to Freud/Bernays, p. 343.) Later, however, Freud helped with the Bernays family's financial problems connected with its emigration to America and took in Leah, one of the first-born daughters, until she and her sister Judith could be brought to New York; by the same token, Eli Freud and his family sent money on several occasions during the war and post-war years ⟨Jones I, pp. 112, 114, 128–33, 150–2; II, p. 225; III, p. 5; Freud 1985*c*, letter 18, 31 October 1892; Bernays [1967], p. 22; Young-Bruehl, p. 31f.; see also Freud-Bernays, A.⟩.
9 There are no indications in this correspondence to support Young-Bruehl's claim (p. 79) (without corroboration) that Anna had already acted as 'a kind of informal resident tutor' in 1917. Harmat (p. 63) mentions that v. Freund's daughter was 'mentally ill'. She later lived for some time in the household of Eva Rosenfeld as a foster-child ⟨Bittner, p. 14; Heller, p. 76; Anna/Eva, letter 4⟩.
10 This sentence was written afterwards between the lines.
11 See 100 SF and note 3.
12 This refers to the start of Anna's work in the new *Verlag* [publishing company] (see 100 SF, note 6), which was to have an English branch (see 100 SF, note 4) ⟨Freud/Jones, letter 229 and 1919–20 *passim*; Marinelli; List, pp. 39, 40f.; see also Jones III, pp. 31–4, 37–40, 48, 49f.⟩.

13 Written 'Sie'.
14 The word 'ich' [I] deleted.
15 The lake is approx. ninety minutes' walk from Bad Reichenhall. It is 'a typical mountain lake: the steep sides of the Gerbersberg and Heuberg almost reach the woody shores of the lake' ⟨*Bühler*, p. 85⟩. Today the property and lake belong to the descendants of Eugen Pachmayr; see notes 16, 17.
16 In summer 1901, when Anna was five and a half years old, the family spent a holiday at Thumsee. They had rented the house of the deceased owner. The children of the two families made friends with one another at the time (Freud 1985*c*, letters 269, 270). Among them was the nephew of the owner of the Thumsee, Eugen Pachmayr (1886–1963); a close relationship going beyond childhood developed between him and Mathilde Freud ⟨Gödde [2003]⟩.
17 Regine Pachmayr, née Steinhaus (1887–1945), married Eugen Pachmayr, now doctor of medicine in Munich-Pasing, in 1913; he was co-heir of Kirchberg [castle] in Reichenhall ⟨Gödde [2003]⟩. Her husband's uncle, Dr. med. Eugen Pachmayr (1834–95), then spa doctor in Bad Reichenhall and also owner of Bad Kirchberg, had made it highly respected and economically prosperous ⟨*Biographisches Lexikon*, p. 35; thanks to Johannes Lang, Stadtarchiv Bad Reichenhall⟩.
18 See 36 AF and note 6.
19 Written afterwards over the deleted word 'and'.
20 See notes 4, 6, 10, 13, 18; also 65 AF, note 4.

99 SF

PROF. DR. FREUD — Bgastein, 29 July 1919
Vienna, IX. Berggasse 19

My dear Anna,

I won't make any attempt to surprise you. I am sure you have already heard that I was in Parsch[1] on Friday with Mama and that I met Ernst there on Saturday and brought him back here, whence he departed yesterday, Monday. I expect you realized that was also the reason for the interruption in our correspondence. In addition, I was inundated with mail during those days, including the strangest news, which it took me hours to deal with yesterday.[2]

I found Mama to be looking well, cheerful and very contented. The doctor is refined, considers himself an analyst and is a real uncle of Dr Bernfeld, who is also expected there.[3] On the only evening I was in Parsch, I was obliged with a delegation of guests (including Mama and the doctor, of course) to go to a Wildgans evening[4] at the Mozarteum[5] given by a Frl Willner, herself a guest at the establishment. It was not boring for an instant, which says a lot. She spoke very well, including the most terrible: In memoriam.[6] I had the same impression of Wildgans as the occasional reading had given me. A rich and easy life, but he likes to use too many words, often borders on the trivial and sometimes touches on things without following them up completely.

Amongst other news, Uncle Eli sent some money, the reason for it to be explained in a letter that is on its way; there is also a cable from Edward[7] about authorization for his translation[8] of the lectures (this time given!), congratulations for an apparent academic promotion about which I know nothing more, but which is no doubt very trivial,[9] the arrival of 'Everyday Life' as vol. 3 of our library,[10] several urgent demands by the Dutch[11] to obtain an entry permit so as to give a lecture in Leiden,[12] Utrecht and Amsterdam, which I will not be able to do because of the October date,[13] the loden cap I forgot in Vienna, etc.

I was very pleased to read all your news. I will stop now so as to get this letter posted. I would just like to say that we are well, there is a little too much rain, two weeks have already passed, unfortunately, a few thousand already gone.[14] Herr Jul. Riesz is meant to be arriving on 2 August.[15]

More soon, look after yourself, affectionate regards to Margaretel, write again very soon,

Papa

1 Sanatorium Parsch, a 'hydropathic establishment; director Dr Bernh. Schwarzwald', higher up over the town of Parsch (on the Salzburg–Hallein railway line, 5 km outside Salzburg), was a ten-minute walk. A cog railway ran from Parsch up the Gaisberg, the 'most rewarding viewpoint in the vicinity of Salzburg' ⟨Baedeker 1925, p. 384⟩. Freud had travelled there on 27 July for his wife's birthday.

2 'As a result of the difficult communication with the current central management in Budapest [i.e., with Ferenczi and Anton v. Freund], the *Vienna Branch Association* in the person of its chairman Prof. Dr Freud and its secretary Dr Otto Rank will take temporary charge of the affairs of the International Psychoanalytical Association and will do their best to maintain communication with the central management' ⟨*IZ*, vol. 5 [1919], p. 230 (July 1919); Freud/Ferenczi II, 805 F, 817 F⟩. This might have been one of the reasons for Freud being 'inundated with mail'. See also 101 AF and note 9.

3 Siegfried Bernfeld (1892–1953), D.Phil., psychologist and educator, worked from the start of the First World War as a pioneer in educational reform and was a charismatic leader within the socialist-, pacifist- and feminist-oriented youth movement. In May 1918 he organized the major Zionist Youth Rally in Vienna. He had been a guest listener in the Vienna Psychoanalytic Society since 1915 and became a member in 1919. In 1922 he established an analysis practice in Vienna, and taught in 1923 at the Vienna Psychoanalytic Training Institute and from 1925 at the Berlin Institute. He was particularly interested in the socially critical aspects of psychoanalysis. He also became a 'major historian of psychoanalysis' and the 'first scientific Freud biographer'. In 1937 Bernfeld emigrated to the USA where he worked in psychoanalysis until his death ⟨Grubrich-Simitis [1981], (quotes pp. 37f., 46); *Protokolle IV*, p. XIX; Fallend and Reichmayr; Mühlleitner, pp. 36–8⟩. Anna had met Bernfeld in connection with his preparations for establishing the Baumgarten children's home, which opened on 15 October 1919; and in the early 1920s he was a member of an informal working group established by Anna Freud at Berggasse 19. 'Many of us had for years been listening to the inspiring lectures for teachers and youth leaders by Siegfried Bernfeld' ⟨*Writings I*, p. viii; Young-Bruehl, pp. 99–101⟩.

4 Anton Wildgans (1881–1932), Austrian poet and dramatist; in 1921–3 and 1930–1 he was director of the Burgtheater in Vienna. On 8 February 1919, six months before the date of this letter, his tragedy *Dies irae* had premiered there.

5 Short for the Salzburg Internationale Stiftung Mozarteum und Akademie für Musik und darstellende Kunst [International Mozarteum Foundation and Academy of Music and Performing Arts].

6 Poem written in 1917, originally published under the title 'In memoriam' and in 1929 given the title 'De profundis! Im memoriam F. P. Die Stimme eines Geistes' ⟨Wildgans, pp. 139–48⟩. The poem is part of a 'major reckoning with the problem of sexuality. . . . This cruel series of poems about the torment of the enslavement of emotional drives culminates in a terrible obituary on the suicide of a fellow-pupil Friedrich Parkos, who was a victim of this enslavement' ⟨Rommel, p. 400⟩.

7 Edward Louis Bernays (1891–1995), third child of Anna and Eli Bernays, Dr h. c. of the University of Boston. Together with his wife Doris Fleischmann, he developed public relations in New York until it was recognized at universities in the USA as a profession. He was known internationally as the 'father of public relations' and taught at various universities ⟨Stammbaum Lange: Freud Family, 'Genealogical Tree', p. III, and 'Bernays Family', table IIa, p. 116, text to IIa: pp. 47, 47a, 48, 49, 49a; Bernays [1967], pp. 7–18; see also Freud-Bernays, A.⟩.

8 Spelling mistake in the original. In his recollections Edward Bernays devotes a chapter to this translation ⟨Bernays [1967], p. 178; see also Jones III, pp. 9f.; Freud/Jones, letters 266, 269, 278, 280, 281, 283⟩. See also 107 SF and notes 8, 11 and 12.

9 On 16 July 1919, the Faculty of Medicine at the University of Vienna agreed to a proposal that Freud be made an ordinary university professor. The investiture by the President of the National Assembly took place on 23 December 1919, with the official confirmation by the Dean's Office on 7 January 1920 ⟨Gicklhorn, pp. 46f. with documents D37 and D39, pp. 127f., 130⟩. See also 106 SF.

10 The series 'Internationale Psychoanalytische Bibliothek' in the newly founded *Verlag*; vol. 3 contained the 6th expanded edition of *The Psychopathology of Everyday Life* (1901*b*).

11 The local group Nederlandsche Vereeniging voor Psycho-Analyse, which had existed since 31 March 1917 ⟨*IZ*, vol. 4 [1916/17], p. 217⟩. The next Psychoanalytical Congress was to take place the following year in the Netherlands; see 123 AF/SF, note 1.

12 The 'first official [i.e., academic] recognition' of dream interpretation and psychoanalysis came from Leiden in 1914: Gerbrandus Jelgersma, rector of the University of Leiden, and 'the most respected psychiatrist in Holland', spoke in praise of psychoanalysis in his official speech on the 339th anniversary of the founding of the university on 9 February 1914 and had invited Freud even then to give lectures ⟨Freud 1914*d*, p. 33; Freud/Abraham, 11 February 1914; Jelgersma [1914]; Freud/Ferenczi II, 456 F; Freud/Jones, letters 177, 192; *IZ*, vol. 2 [1914], p. 203; Jones II, p. 118⟩.

13 The lectures were to have been given in the second week of October at which time Freud was obliged to work in Vienna ⟨Freud/Jones, letter 248; Freud/Eitingon, 145 E⟩. He returned on 24 September ⟨Freud/Ferenczi II, 820 F⟩.

14 'Parsimony is no[t] part of our programme this year, it would not help us'

⟨Freud/Jones, letter 246, 8 July 1919, p. 351⟩. For discussion of the financial difficulties after the war, see, e.g., Jones III, pp. 3–5.

15 See 102 SF and note 4.

100 SF

PROF. DR. FREUD B Gastein, 30 July 1919
Vienna, IX. Berggasse 19

My dear Anna,
I confirm receipt of your express letter [98 AF] and agree with you. Unfortunately, it is often a disadvantage to be correct. A letter from me [99 SF] with all kinds of news is currently wandering around and will arrive later than this one. I won't repeat anything that I wrote there, however.

Toni wrote only that Vera had sent you a wistful letter and added that she would have to wait a long time for an answer. He has sent her to Dubowitz[1] in Ofen.[2] That is all I can do for her this year, he says.[3] You know, perhaps, that I suggested to Frau Margit D.[ubowitz] that she take in the little girl, just in case. I believe she is the right person for it.

The letter from Jones appears to have confused you. I find the offer very honourable and promising. You will struggle a bit at first and he will have some things to correct, but I think it will work and then it will be exactly what you wished for. You can go ahead and write to Rank for the works in question.

Rank is very keen on taking a most active part in the English company (I mean the journal[4]) and he wants to invest our money there, when we have it,[5] and I am giving him a free hand. Then you would be in the thick of it.[6]

Jones's letter is altogether very good and serious; perhaps he was right about Loe after all.[7]

Eitingon[s] wrote today that they have rented from 24 August to 5 September on Eibsee, not far from us, and are happy to be so close by.[8] The Berlin group has decided to open a polyclinic,[9] which Eitingon will head with Simmel.[10] Very sensible. So only good and friendly things are coming from that side as well.[11]

I have spoken to Rank about my interest in Schopenhauer;[12] he discovered the nice small edition on thin paper at Sachs and sent it to me. Reading it helps me with the work that I have brought with me.[13]

In spite of the rain and cold we are very contented here. Aunt complains a bit but is in a good mood.

There is a 'girlfriend' living in house no. 20 opposite. For your dream interpretation, you should also consider jealousy as well.

I send you my affectionate greetings and hope that you have good and interesting news.

Papa

PS: E.[rnest] J.[ones] letter enclosed. Can you send Ernstl some toys from Rehll?[14]

1 Dr Hugo Dubowitz and his wife Margit, née Garami. Margit Dubowitz, sister of the Hungarian Social Democrat Ernö Garami (1876–1935), later became a child analyst and in 1930/31 headed a psychoanalytical advice centre in Budapest ⟨Freud/Ferenczi II, 770 Fer, note 3⟩. She was a friend of Toni and looked after him towards the end of the year until his death ⟨ibid., 824 F, 825 F⟩. It was Hugo Dubowitz who drew Ferenczi's attention to an essay by Ludwig Börne, whose own early finding Freud mentioned thereafter in connection with the technique of free association ⟨'A Note on the Prehistory of the Technique of Analysis', 1920*b*, pp. 264f.⟩.

2 Hungarian 'Buda', former capital of Hungary on the right bank of the Danube; united since 1872 with Pest on the opposite side of the river to form Budapest, henceforth the capital of Hungary.

3 At the beginning of 1918, Anton v. Freund had asked Ferenczi to look after Vera if he died so that 'the little girl should have access to me whenever [she wants], as she formerly had to her father' ⟨Freud/Ferenczi II, 730 Fer, 17 February 1918, p. 266⟩.

4 In December 1918, Jones had already suggested the publication of an English-American journal or an English-language edition of *IZ*. It was to be published by a branch of the *Verlag* that was to be established, the International Psycho-Analytical Press, or 'Press' for short. During 1919, the idea gradually took shape amid drawn-out negotiations and meetings in Switzerland and Vienna. The first issue of this *Journal* appeared in July 1920; see 113 AF and note 2 ⟨Freud/Ferenczi II, 787 F; Freud/Jones, letters 223–59 *passim*; Jones III, pp. 12–18, 37–40, 48, 49–52; *Rundbriefe 1*, 5 October 1920/W with detailed editorial note 8, pp. 56f.⟩.

5 From the funds that v. Freund had donated (see 89 SF, note 2) only a small part had reached Vienna at that time. Jones took half of it back to England after a visit to Vienna in September (see 106 SF, end of note 6). There was a protracted tug of war with the city of Budapest regarding the transfer of the remaining money, which the foundation claimed for itself and confiscated. Only years later (1926) was a small amount of 10,000 Swiss francs again made available ⟨Freud/Ferenczi II, 762 F–828 Fer *passim*, III, e.g., 829 F and ff, 1083 F; Freud/Abraham, 3 October 1919; *Rundbriefe 1*, e.g., pp. 41–3, 48–51; Jones III, pp. 34–6, 136⟩.

6 This is what occurred. Through proofreading, translation, editorial and secretarial work, Anna gradually became more deeply involved in her 'second' area of work (see 108 AF and note 8): 'Besides (actually it's still half-secret) I am in the process of getting a second job working in a psychoanalytic publishing company. It will probably start at the end of October or beginning of November. . . . I already have quite a lot to do and have also done a translation (into English) of one of Papa's essays together with one of the two Englishmen who were here [Jones and Hiller, see 106 SF, note 6]' ⟨Anna to Kata, 7 October 1919; Mühlleitner (pp. 147 and 148) quotes an undated letter of thanks by Freud to Eric Hiller, which could have been written at this time or in the following two years.⟩ (This translation by Anna appears not to have been printed, however; it is not in Grinstein or in the translator information in the *Standard Edition*.) Anna was under some strain 'from her two professions' ⟨Freud/

Ferenczi II, 824 F, 3 December 1919, p. 371⟩. At Eitingon's instigation, she was also paid from May 1920 onwards for her work ⟨Freud/Eitingon, 176 E; see also Jones III, pp. 49f.; Freud/Abraham, 2 November 1919⟩. See 130 SF.

7 Probably a reference to Loe's sensitivity (see Freud/Jones, e.g., letters 231–57 *passim*, particularly 234); see also this correspondence 107 SF–111 AF, 155 SF–159 SF, 161 SF–163 SF, 185 SF–187 SF, also 42 SF, note 5. See also Appignanesi and Forrester, pp. 237–9.

8 The Eibsee at the north-west foot of the Zugspitze is only around 8 km from the planned holiday location of Badersee near Garmisch-Partenkirchen. From there, the Eitingons and Freuds got together ⟨Freud/Eitingon, 142 E; Freud/Ferenczi II, 820 F⟩.

9 For the Berlin Psychoanalytische Poliklinik und Lehranstalt – 'the first of its type at all' – Eitingon made available RM 16,000 a year from his private assets ⟨Schultz and Hermanns, p. 61⟩. It was opened at Potsdamerstr. 29 on 14 February 1920. Ernst Freud (as consultant architect) and Mathilde and Robert Hollischer (as Freud's representatives) attended the opening ceremony ⟨Freud/Eitingon, 154 F, p. 177, 161 E, 164 E, 166 F⟩. Apart from therapy, the clinic was devoted to systematic theoretical and practical training, which gradually developed into an independent branch of psychoanalysis (see 203 SF, note 2, second paragraph) ⟨Freud/Abraham, 3 October, 7 December, 29 December 1919, 13 March 1920; Freud/Ferenczi III, 837 F; Eitingon [1920], [1922]; *IZ*, vol. 8 [1922], p. 106; Jones III, pp. 21f.; Bannach, pp. 32f.; *Berliner Psychoanalytisches Institut*; Freud 1923*g*, 1930*b*; Schröter [2004], pp. 7–10⟩. For corresponding Viennese institutes, see 151 AF and note 5, and 166 SF, note 7. A Hungarian 'great teaching and treatment institute' had already benefited from a further donation by v. Freund to the city of Budapest ⟨Freud 1920*c*; Freud/Ferenczi II, 761 Fer, 827 F. p. 376⟩. It was not established, however, until 1931 ⟨Freud/Ferenczi III, Fer 1206 and Enclosure 1; *IZ*, vol. 17 [1931], p. 434; vol. 18 [1932], p. 141⟩.

10 Ernst Simmel (1882–1947), doctor of medicine, with his own practice from 1913 in a working district of Berlin. He had already cited works by Abraham, Breuer, Freud and Jung in his dissertation in 1908. He was committed to welfare and public health from an early age, and in 1913 founded the Verein Sozialistischer Ärzte [Association of Socialist Doctors] with Karl Kollwitz and Ignaz Zadek in Berlin. In the First World War he was a military doctor, ending up as director of a field hospital for war neurotics, whom he treated in part using psychoanalytical principles; he reported on it at the Congress in Budapest. After that he was already planning to set up a psychoanalytical clinic. This idea was not put into practice until 1927 (see text after 255 SF). In 1933 Simmel emigrated via Switzerland to the USA, where he collaborated in Los Angeles and San Francisco in the setting up of psychoanalytical institutions and was active until his death in 1947 ⟨Simmel [1919]; Schulz and Hermanns; Freud/Ferenczi III, 1244 F; Jones III, p. 190⟩.

11 'You were the first envoy to appear to a lonely man, and should I ever be abandoned again, I am sure you will be one of the last to stand by me' ⟨Freud/Eitingon, 39 F, 7 January 1913, p. 81⟩.

12 Rank had earlier 'studied the life as well as the works of Arthur Schopenhauer' ⟨Lieberman, p. 9⟩. Freud was reading him now 'for the first time' ⟨Freud/Andreas-Salomé, 1 August 1919, p. 99⟩. For Freud's critique of Schopenhauer, see Gödde [1999], pp. 331f. (with reference to Freud 1925*d*, p. 86).

13 *Beyond the Pleasure Principle* (1920*g*); Freud mentions Schopenhauer in chapter VI of this work, which he wrote later.

14 No toy shop by this name (which is otherwise quite common in Bad Reichenhall) can be identified, although at this time there was a company owned by Johann Riehll at Ludwigstr. 26 ⟨thanks to Johann Lang, Stadtarchiv Bad Reichenhall⟩.

101 AF

[Bayerisch Gmain] 2 August 1919

My dear Papa,
I will soon have to get larger writing paper and a thicker pen because there are more and more parts to me. One part is already a teacher, the second wants to become a translator, the third has to do with stories,[1] and the fourth is me in person: each would have different things to say in every letter and that's very difficult to manage. Today I have decided, however, to start with the fourth.

I have had one and a half wonderful days with Margaretl on König[s] see,[2] with the kind of magnificent weather that has been in particularly short supply this year. It was not until yesterday evening, when we were already in our beds in Gmain, that some soothing rain came again after our long exertions. I rowed Margaretl without an oarsman to Bartholomä and the Saletalpe and back, and don't even have aching arms today, just a few blisters from rowing. We had lunch at Obersee and picked strawberries on Bartholomä,[3] just like in the old days.[4] Our hosts had given us food to take with us, with enough meat and sausage for Shere Khan, the tiger, and Bagheera, the black panther,[5] to go on a day trip together. We nevertheless managed to eat it all. The Drexls, our hosts, are very nice people altogether. Recently the two of us – we have both become huge eaters here – ordered another pancake after lunch because the meal was only a light pastry and we were not quite full. They didn't make us pay for it because 'they were so ashamed that we were still hungry'. I'm sure Austrian hotelkeepers are less sensitive in that regard!

Margaretl has already started to work now,[6] and during that time I usually go for a walk and then I can't imagine going back to Vienna at all. I dreamt (yesterday) that it was the first day of school in the autumn and the children wouldn't follow me. That is always a sign of a lot of things. Why am I always so happy when I have nothing to do? I do like working; or does it only seem so? If the English journal gets very big and if my translations are successful and I earn a lot of money, I will buy a small house in the country and only work there, and only very nice people will be allowed to visit.[7] That is one of the plans I have been making here. Or I'll go next summer to a König[s]see farmer and work in the fields. Or I'll go up to the Stanger farm[8] in the mountains and spend the summer learning to make butter and cheese. Or I'll learn baking at Fischers. Am I imagining things or is that the old summer aversion to school coming back?

I have already written to Rank to ask for the two works. As the East came to nothing, he apparently wants to try it with the West.[9] Actually, I am also leaning more and more in that direction. I am very curious to find out if anything good comes out of the English newspaper.

I am always particularly pleased to hear all of your good news. I am sorry that you had to turn down the Dutch offer.[10] It would have been very nice, just a month earlier, and I would like to have come with you. I was also very pleased about the translation cable[11] and the news from Berlin. The main thing is that everything starts moving again.

I dreamt today that I was in our building in Berggasse and couldn't find the apartment; it was very frightening. I think you are right with the last dream interpretation. The only time I spoke with the 'friend' at Berggasse 20 was during the *shooting* in Hörlgasse. Aunt said at the time that I shouldn't talk to her.

I am trying to acquaint Margaretl with the Rilke things. We continue to get on very well. I am receiving lots of mail here. It is almost easier to communicate in writing than orally.

I will have to save everything else for another letter. Anni Rosenberg,[12] who arrived yesterday, offered to be my messenger to Austria, and opportunities like that have to be taken advantage of.

I have also gone through perhaps not thousands but certainly hundreds in the two weeks. But at least it has been enjoyable.

With a kiss,
Your Anna

1 See 105 AF, 132 AF (also 45 AF and note 12). Peters, who points out Anna Freud's early 'expressiveness', reports that Anna had begun at this time 'to work on a never-ending story [. . .]. It was the story of a large family with many children, no doubt fictional, but very realistically described' ⟨Peters, pp. 10, 17⟩. In discussion of Anna's attempts at writing, Young-Bruehl looks in particular at the connections between Anna's poetry and her analysis; see 114 AF and note 1 ⟨Young-Bruehl, pp. 81–90, 93–5, 97f., 104–9; also Peters, pp. 24f.⟩. Anna herself mentions to Kata Lévy that she has 'written all kinds of things', that lots of stories were already complete, which she would show to her (and only her) ⟨Anna to Kata, 31 October 1918, 29 May, 7 October 1919, 21 February 1920⟩. The 'nice stories' – connected with Anna's 'daydreams' – were a recurring topic in conversations between her and Lou Andreas-Salomé ⟨Anna/Lou, e.g., 1922–5 *passim*⟩.

2 Königssee (600 m), south of Berchtesgaden, is regarded as one of the most beautiful Alpine lakes. It is famous for its steep, sometimes almost vertical, cliffs emerging from the water, which are characteristic of the lake and the landscape in general ⟨Köhler, p. 30⟩.

3 St Bartholomä, green foothills on the west bank protruding far into the Königssee at the foot of the 1,800 m east face of the Watzmann, with a Baroque pilgrimage church and a former hunting lodge; starting point for various tours (see 257 AF and note 3). The Saletalpe (also Salletalm) forms the south end of Königssee. From there it is a fifteen-minute walk to the secluded Obersee, a lake that an Ice Age terminal moraine separated from Königssee ⟨Köhler; *Bühler*, pp. 145–7⟩. For mention of rowing, see 102 SF, note 2.

4 Freud mentioned Anna's first acquaintanceship with this impressive mountain lake to Wilhelm Fliess: 'You should have seen Annerl on the Königssee!' ⟨1985*c*, 1 August 1899, p. 364⟩. The Freuds had spent further holidays on Königssee and in Berchtesgaden, 1902–4, 1908 (see 3 SF, 4 SF) and, most recently, 1915 (see 66 SF, note 1, 68 SF/MF and note 6) ⟨Tögel [1989], pp. 152–4; Gödde [2003], pp. 62–4; Jones II, pp. 203f.⟩.
5 Characters from Kipling's *Jungle Book*; see 17 AF and note 8.
6 See 96 AF.
7 See 36 AF and note 6.
8 Possibly a farm on the Gmain. On an old map there is a farm marked 'Stangerer' ⟨*Bühler*, regional map, k3⟩; there is no trace of it today. On living in the country, see Introduction, p. 1 and 79 AF, note 6.
9 Freud had already expressed a wish for a 'shift to the West', in that case Zurich, because of his dissatisfaction with the Vienna group ⟨Freud/Jung, 270 F, 1 September 1911, p. 442⟩. Following the success of the Budapest Congress in 1918, Freud and his colleagues had hoped that Budapest would become the main centre of psychoanalysis. Rank had even decided to move there with his wife ⟨Jones III, p. 8; Freud/Abraham, 27 August 1918; Freud/Jones, letter 222; Freud/Ferenczi II, 774 Fer; List, p. 37⟩. But the situation changed after the war, when Hungary was cut off from regular communication with other countries ⟨Freud/Jones, letter 237; Jones III, pp. 8, 18⟩. At a meeting in March/April 1919 in Switzerland to revive psychoanalytical activities and to develop the *Verlag*, Rank, Sachs and Jones agreed on the 'orientation towards the West' ⟨Freud/Abraham, 18 May 1919, 3 October 1919, p. 404, 2 November 1919; Freud/Ferenczi II, 805 F, 12 April 1919; Freud/Jones, letter 229; Jones III, p. 12–14⟩; this in fact occurred and resulted in Ferenczi informally handing over the presidency to Jones at a further meeting in Vienna in late September 1919 ⟨*IZ*, vol. 5 [1919], pp. 328–31; Freud/Abraham, 3 October 1919; Jones III, p. 18⟩. See 99 SF, note 2. The official change in the organization was completed the following year at the Hague Conference; see 123 AF/SF, note 1.
10 See 99 SF and note 11.
11 From Edward Bernays, see 99 SF and note 8.
12 Anny Rosenberg (1898–1992), an early childhood friend of Anna, daughter of Judith and Dr Ludwig Rosenberg (see 105 AF and note 4). She studied medicine in Vienna, was awarded a doctorate in 1923 and became a psychoanalyst specializing in the analysis of children. She joined the Vienna Psychoanalytic Society in 1925. For a time she was socially active as a member of the Communist Party and in a Vienna sex-counselling centre. In 1936 she went to the Netherlands, where she married the psychiatrist Maurits (Moritz) Katan (a first marriage in 1926 to Otto Angel had been dissolved in 1928). She emigrated with her family to the USA in 1946 and worked as a doctor in Cleveland, Ohio, until 1965, where she devoted her energy to setting up several institutes for research into child analysis. She had a professorship in child analysis from 1955 to 1964 and was co-founder of the Cleveland Center for Research in Child Development. 'She was the last of that second generation of analysts who gather about Anna Freud in Vienna and helped establish the foundations of child analysis' ⟨Obituary in *IJ*, vol. 74 [1993], p. 834. Also DBA N. F.; Mühlleitner, pp. 27f.; Fallend [1995], p. 302; see also Freud 1985*c*, letter 29 and note 1, and letter 107; Young-Bruehl, pp. 40, 52; Jones I, p. 362, note 2⟩.

102 SF

PROF. DR. FREUD

Bgastein, 3 August 1919
Vienna, IX. Berggasse 19

My dear Anna,

Telegram[1] and letter about König[s]see received. I am very pleased that you were so intrepid and had so much good fortune.[2] But wasn't the rowing on the lake too much for you?

Your various personalities, I think, are coming alternately into their own. You understand that those that have been neglected during the year sometimes make themselves heard.

There is little to report from here. The mail, which was so interesting for a while, is tailing off. The day is dominated by the news that the madness in Budapest has been dealt with.[3] Rank is now certain to experience some very interesting things. He has been silent in the last few days.

Herr Jul Riesz[4] arrived yesterday, and today, because of the weather, we had the first very long round of tarock. It rains every day under all kinds of pretexts – thunderstorms, cloudbursts, drizzle, at all events rain. And yet it is astonishing how quickly the time passes, over half already! The meals are becoming markedly more expensive, but they just taste so good.

It was very nice of you to send toys to the children.[5] There is nothing to buy here. The standard price, if you find something you like, is 650 kr.

Enjoy yourself, affectionate greetings, also to Margar.[ete]

Papa

1 Missing.

2 Because of its situation protected by the mountains, the Königssee was generally regarded as 'calm', and 'most rowing visitors prefer to exercise themselves' on the lake, 'whose beauty is only discovered from the water.' But severe thunderstorms could suddenly occur that were life-threatening even for experienced rowers. And even the motorboats that had appeared on the lake in 1909 were not spared ⟨*Königssee*, pp. 40, 41, 42; Hinterbrander, chs III and IV: 'Storms and types of wind' and 'Storm experiences'⟩. Anna experienced such a storm there and once her Uncle Alexander nearly drowned ⟨Freud M. [1999], p. 82⟩. 'The Königssee is not to be trifled with at such moments' ⟨Anna/Eva, letter 13, 7 July 1929, p. 119⟩. In his recollections, Martin Freud describes how bold and intrepid Anna had been even as a child in her adventures on water and concludes: 'We Freud children had inherited a precious gift from both our parents: we enjoyed freedom from fear. Anna had received a big portion' ⟨Freud M. [1999], p. 141⟩.

3 On 21 March 1919, the Revolutionary Governing Council under Béla Kun replaced the Hungarian National Council of Count Károlyi, turning the post-war Hungarian republic into a communist-socialist soviet dictatorship, which only survived 135 days, however, before being overthrown when Romanian troops marched in during the first days of August 1919. Freud could not know that the 'madness' was not to end there: 'After the unbearable "Red terror", which lay heavy on one's spirit like a nightmare, we now have the White one', which was also anti-Semitic ⟨Freud/Ferenczi II, 819 Fer, 28 August 1919,

p. 365 and note 1; 821 Fer, 20 November 1919, p. 368; Lendvai, pp. 380f.⟩. On 24 November 1919, a new government was formed, and in March the following year Miklós Horthy was elected head of state and regent, and declared Hungary to be a 'monarchy with vacant throne', setting up a dictatorship that lasted twenty-five years and marched 'in step with Hitler' to its downfall ⟨Lendvai, pp. 373–405; Ploetz [1980], p. 997; Freud/Ferenczi II, 774 Fer, 823 Fer⟩.

4 'Julius Riesz, manufacturer, with son, Vienna, Hotel Astoria' is the entry in the guest list. The next number says: 'Frau Mathilde Riesz, manufacturer's wife, with daughter, Vienna', also staying at Hotel Astoria ⟨*Badgastein. Liste*, 1919, 2 August, serial nos 2076, 2077⟩. See 95 SF and note 7, and 99 SF and note 15.

5 Ernstl and Heinerle Halberstadt (see 127 AF and note 3).

103 AF

Bayr. Gmain, 5 August 1919

Dear Papa,
Not very much to report from here this time either. Most of the time we do nothing, climb up a little to pick alpine roses and lie in the heather and feel the time passing. That is something I still haven't quite come to terms with.[1] I was so pleased today to receive your letter of the 3rd. We are suffering less from this summer's rainy caprices; every day there are a few fine hours. I'm very glad to say that the rowing on König[s]see had no after-effects whatsoever. But I can't get fat although I eat such a lot and lead such a quiet life. And I am afraid that all the benefits of the rest will disappear just as quickly as they did last year.

The Ries can't come here; they were refused entry permits so they rented on Grundlsee[2] instead. For the time being they are still in Vienna.[3]

Please write to me in your next letter how you plan to travel to Badersee. I would really like to spend two or three days in Munich, and Margaretl would love to come for this time as well before going to Grundlsee. Do you feel like it? Ernst could show us around a bit.[4]

My different personalities leave me in peace now. But I dream every night very vividly and strangely. For example, yesterday: 'I murdered somebody or something like that. As punishment I was put into a large room where there were many people who could do with me what they pleased. The people wanted to tear me to bits and throw me out of the window. I was frightened but not excessively. There was also an elderly gentleman among them who suddenly took something down from the wall and gave half of it to me so that I could defend myself; that way I was able to drive the people back. Then I was guarded by two soldiers pointing their weapons at me. And then came the strangest thing: I was suddenly told the true cause of Napoleon's death. He had also been guarded in this room like me. Like me he had been standing at the open window and wanted suddenly to climb out to go to the toilet. The soldiers thought he was attempting to escape and shot him. They told me not to do the same.' I believe I could think up a lot of things to say about that. It seems that most of my dreams have something terrible in them, killing, shooting or dying.

Write me a long letter soon. Margaretl sends her regards.
With a kiss,
Your Anna

I have written to Kata and sent the letter to Rank.[5]

1 'When I was still tiny [. . .] I always yearned for everything to stand still and last for ever, as if it were only in that way that there would be space and peace to expand,' wrote Anna (shortly after her father's first cancer operation) to Lou Andreas-Salomé ⟨Anna/Lou, letter 101, 12 May 1923, also letters 102, 103⟩. She had clearly spoken about it earlier with Freud; see Anna's letter in 122 AF/MF (see also Freud 1916*a*). In summer 1920 she dealt with the question of impermanence in several prose pieces, which Young-Bruehl connects with Anna's analytical work ⟨Young-Bruehl, pp. 94f.; the same subject also occurred in prose pieces that Anna sent to her brother Ernst, e.g., 11 January 1920⟩.
2 The Freuds also spent a long summer holiday there later; see 271 AF and note 2.
3 The claim by Young-Bruehl – 'That summer [1919] Anna Freud spent mostly with the Oscar Rie family' and with Margarete 'hiking and sailing on the Königssee' – does not tally with these letters (see also 96 AF, 98 AF) ⟨Young-Bruehl, p. 86 – with no sources⟩. It was not until the following summer that Anna was invited to the Ries, in Altaussee not Königssee; see 107 SF–122 AF/OF.
4 After studying, Ernst continued to live initially in Munich before moving on 8 December 1919 to Berlin, where he finally established himself as an architect (see letterhead 165 AF) ⟨Anna to Kata, 29 May 1919; Freud/Sam, 27 October 1919; Freud/Abraham, 1 December 1919; Freud/Ferenczi II, 825 F⟩.
5 There is no letter from this time in the correspondence between Anna and Kata available to me.

104 SF[1]

Frl Anna Freud
Grossgmain
bei Salzburg
Poste restante

B Gastein, 8 August 1919

Dear Anna,
Martin is free and should have arrived in Vienna the evening before last.[2] Our travel plans are still uncertain because we have to wait for our passports, which might specify 15 August for the border, whereas Aunt is bound to 13 August. I would then remain the two days in Salzburg with Mama. If anything comes of Munich, Marg.[arete] is naturally welcome.[3]
Affectionately,
Papa

1 Postcard.
2 'Martin's arrival in the best condition was a great relief' ⟨Freud/Ferenczi II, 820 F, 5 September, 1919. p. 367⟩. On 7 December of the same year, his thirtieth

birthday, Martin married Ernestine Drucker (1896–1980), daughter of the Viennese lawyer Dr Leopold Drucker ⟨Stammbaum Lange: Freud Family, 'Genealogical Tree', p. I; Freud/Ferenczi II, 824 F, 825 F⟩. She was a speech therapist, teacher at the special education school in Vienna and lecturer at the University of Vienna, and 'worked in this field all her life in three languages, achieving considerable professional success in Vienna, Paris, and New York City', as her daughter Sophie Freud reports. She obtained a PhD after going back to university in New York at 'the age of fifty-nine' ⟨Freud, Sophie, p. 332⟩. Martin's father-in-law had obtained a position in a bank for him. He writes in his memoirs: 'Turning my back for the time being on the law, I found employment in one of the newly founded banks. . . . None of them could last long; and thus I changed employers a number of times. . . . Finally, I succeeded in making a living by writing articles on economic subjects for newspapers in Austria and Germany' ⟨Freud M. [1999], p. 199; see also Mühlleitner, pp. 104f.; Freud/Ferenczi III, 1092 F⟩.

3 For the final travel plans, see 106 SF.

105 AF

[Bayerisch Gmain] 9 August 1919

Dear Papa,

I received your card of the 8th today and have a lot of questions to ask you. That's why I'm sending this letter express.

Mama had already informed me of Martin's arrival. I sent him a telegram to Vienna straightaway and would, of course, like to see him as soon as possible. Are you planning on a meeting in Salzburg?[1] I am surprised that you have to cross the border on a specific day. I had no restriction, as the lady at the consulate explicitly pointed out to me. I had several days to choose from. I would be happy to spend two days here with Aunt if she really has to cross on the 13th and you on the 15th.

From my window here I can climb directly into a carriage of the Munich evening train[2] and could therefore meet you on the way. Just send me a telegram as soon as you know something for sure.

Should I cash the entire 1,000 marks of my letter of credit? I don't need it all for my personal requirements but perhaps you need marks. The bank charges 2.45 kr.

Can you please send me the full Badersee address?[3]

I have already been in touch with Rank. He doesn't agree with the selection that Jones has made for translation and wants me to inform him diplomatically by letter and make other suggestions.

I haven't had a good time since my last letter and was even confined to bed for a day. It was a stomach upset that has still not completely cleared up. Dr Rosenberg[4] came and brought me bismuth. I think I have lost all the weight I gained and naturally don't look very good.

But I myself am fine. I have finally written the great children's story.[5]

The weather is splendid at last.

I hope to hear all about you again soon and remain with a kiss,

Your Anna

1 Yes. 'I have already seen Max in Salzburg; he looks well, unbroken' ⟨Freud to Max Halberstadt, 19 August 1919⟩. Martin then met the family in Badersee, from where he undertook mountain tours, e.g., to the Zugspitze ⟨Freud to Paul Federn, 25 August 1919, LoC, The Papers of Paul Federn⟩.

2 The Posthotel was right next to Bayerisch Gmain Station and the window marked on the postcard (97 AF) was indeed right on the tracks. The hotel has subsequently changed hands several times and has been renovated and enlarged. The attic room in which Anna and Margarete stayed no longer exists.

3 The independent 'Badersee' consisted at the time only of a small lake and a hotel on the shore, without a more exact address but with its own mail-coach connection to Garmisch-Partenkirchen. This still exists today as a tourist attraction, but the old building has been replaced by an extensive hotel complex ⟨Hotel am Badersee brochure, 2000⟩.

4 Ludwig Rosenberg (1861–1928), doctor of medicine, paediatrician; he had been one of Freud's assistants at the Kassowitzisches Institut and was one of his tarock partners ⟨Jones I, p. 362; Jones III, p. 148⟩. His wife, Judith ('Ditha' [1870–1952]), was Oscar Rie's sister ⟨DBA N. F.⟩. Rosenberg had attended a session of the Vienna Psychoanalytic Society as a guest in 1912 ⟨*Minutes IV*, p. 101⟩. He appears as 'friend Leopold' in Freud's famous dream of 'Irma's injection' ⟨Freud 1900*a*, p. 112⟩.

5 See 101 AF.

106 SF

PROF. DR. FREUD BGastein, 10 August 1919
Vienna, IX. Berggasse 19

My dear Anna,

This is the last letter before our meeting. The passports have arrived and generously allow us to cross the border any time after the 10th. We are thinking of leaving on Wednesday the 13th and picking up Mama in Salzburg. Aunt will leave earlier,[1] and we will travel from 6 to 9 to Munich, where Ernst is expecting us. What will you do? Will you join us in Freilassing or will you travel on your own to M.[unich]? You should be able to manage Freilassing, I think.

The last few days here have been quite different with lots of socializing. Lots of colleagues, even a visit from Prof. Wenckebach[2] (who confirmed something about a promotion[3]), daily tarock rounds with Herr Riesz and then so-called 'family reunion', session with Frl Wassing,[4] who is a painter and requested this favour, and the most splendid summer weather for three days. Enchantingly beautiful.

The main event is Martin's return, about which I have not yet had any news from Vienna, only a mention in a letter from Oli of his arrival and his immediate plans, and the news in a letter from Margar.[ete]'s father that he had visited them. I probably won't see him again before the end of September.[5]

I would be very pleased if Marg.[arete] were to stay on until Munich. Perhaps we will spend an extra day there. It will be up to Ernst.

So that's all for the first summer act. Hopefully the second one[6] will also be pleasant.

Affectionate regards,

Papa

1 For Bad Reichenhall ⟨PS by Minna Bernays to Freud's letter to Ernst, 19 July 1919⟩.

2 Karel Frederik Wenckebach (1864–1940), Dutch-German specialist in internal medicine, 1914–29 professor in Vienna, renowned specialist in cardiovascular diseases, researcher in the anatomy and physiology of the heart ('Wenckebach phenomenon') ⟨Fischer, I., 1932/33⟩.

3 See 99 SF and note 9.

4 Dr Wassing had a daughter, Anna (1896–1926) ⟨Internet, 8 September 2005: 'Anton Wassertrilling Charlotte Jallowetz'; <http://www.geocities.com/okouneff/Anton-Charlotte.htm> [link now broken]; provided by Wolfgang Kloft⟩. It was not possible to identify whether she was the painter ⟨thanks to Laurenz Krisch⟩.

5 See 105 AF, note 1.

6 At Badersee, where they met the Eitingons and others (see 100 SF and note 8). Ernst visited his family again at Badersee; Ferenczi and Jones, who also wanted to come, were unable to obtain exit permits (see 95 SF, note 15) ⟨Freud/Jones, letters 245, 247; Jones III, pp. 12f., 16–18⟩. On 9 September Freud travelled with the family and the Eitingons via Munich to Berlin ⟨Freud/Ferenczi II, 820 F⟩. From there, by the 13th, they wanted to be in Hamburg with Sophie, Max and the children ⟨Freud to Martin, 7 September 1919⟩. On the return journey Freud met Eitingon and Abraham, again in Berlin. He had to cross the border in Salzburg by 24 September at the latest so as to arrive back finally in Vienna on 26 September ⟨Freud/Jones, letter 250; Jones III, p. 10⟩. Then Freud met Jones for the first time in five years, when Jones visited him with Hiller (see 100 SF, note 6); on this occasion, together with Rank, Ferenczi and v. Freund, they discussed above all the pending organization questions (see 101 AF, note 9) ⟨Jones III, pp. 16–18⟩.

Departure of the Sons from Berggasse 19 (End of 1919)

Martin, Oliver and Ernst were together one more time in their parents' home towards the end of the year: 'I now have all my three sons together for a short time. Martin is marrying on the 7th inst., and the following day Ernst will be leaving for Berlin . . .' ⟨Freud/Abraham, 1 December 1919, p. 409⟩. Oliver, who had found a temporary position in the summer, was looking for work. After applications for the Dutch colonial service in the East Indies had been unsuccessful, he went to Hamburg and Berlin to continue looking in Germany (see 115 SF and note 4). Minna, who was ill and could not survive the Viennese winter without heating, spent the months in Bad Reichenhall and was not expected back in the near future: 'So we are only three and very lonely' ⟨Freud/Ferenczi II, 825 F, 2 December 1919, p. 373; Freud/Jones, letter 248; Freud/Eitingon, 154 F; Freud/Sam, 27 October, 24 November 1919⟩.

Sophie's Premature Death (1920)

The sad mood of parting in the family at the end of the year was intensified at the start of the following year by an incisive stroke of fate. Only a few days after the death of Anton v. Freund (see 96 AF, note 6), Sophie died in Hamburg on 25 January in the flu epidemic that was raging in Germany at the time: 'snatched away from glowing health, from her busy life as a capable mother and loving wife, in four or five days, as if she had never been' ⟨Freud to Oskar Pfister, 27 January 1920, 1963*a*, p. 74⟩. 'Since I am profoundly unbelieving, I have no one to blame, and I know that there is no place where one can lodge a complaint. [. . .] My wife and Annerl are severely shaken in a more human sense' ⟨Freud/Binswanger, 14 March 1920; Freud/Ferenczi III, 833 F, 4 February 1920, pp. 6f., 837 F⟩. The effect that this loss had on Max Halberstadt is evident in many places in this correspondence.

1920

107 SF

PROF. DR. FREUD

22 July 1920
Vienna, IX. Berggasse 19

My dear Anna,

I am very happy to hear that you are able to enjoy the 'country' so much.[1] It's horribly hot here. I have only now had an hour free and during it have to sit for Königsberger, who is working very well.[2]

Two pieces of news for you! The first you can see from the enclosure.[3] I'm sure, like me, you will interpret it to mean that she will not be seeing us in The Hague.[4] It shouldn't be taken too seriously because (1) we don't have the time between Gastein and The Hague,[5] and (2) we won't get passports, or at least not without a great deal of time and effort that I can't afford. I won't reply, of course, until the promised letter from Davy has arrived.[6] Incidentally,[7] there is another possible interpretation. Could the curious 'pofpler' perhaps be 'together'?

Second, Edward has sent the book[8] and promised # 275 for Amsterdam,[9] the whereabouts of which I have already inquired about. The presentation is undistinguished; the translation,[10] as Jones rightly notes, careless,[11] but generally with the right tone. Some serious misunderstandings, the worst being the treatment of the examples of slips [*Fehlleistung*] and dreams, which were not replaced by new ones but translated and artificially changed, which removed all of their persuasiveness.[12] Jones, who wants to do the English version together with Allen & Unwin, will no doubt do a better job of it. The foreword by St.[anley] Hall is generally flattering.

Postscript to the first Jones story: Does 'returning together' [English in original] mean that they are to go with us or just that the two of us should then go to Holland?

Otherwise, as I said, it's high time for a holiday.[13] Martin and Esti returned in a very happy mood.[14] Kata has finally worked it out of her system.[15] She is very kind, organizing a car to the station for us. We fear that Lajos will not obtain permission to pick her up from Vienna. The Ferenczi[s] have had to abandon Aussee and are probably going to Lake Balaton.[16] For Mama's birthday[17] we are planning a fine lunch with ice cream. On Sunday I am travelling to Tulln again.[18]

Give my warmest regards to Frau Mela and Margaretl[19] and accept my best wishes for your stay in Aussee. Don't go on long walks unaccompanied. Write to me soon, when it rains.

Papa

1 A letter by Anna from Altaussee appears to be missing. She had been spending her summer holidays there (not in Gmain as stated in Young-Bruehl, p. 90) since 17 July with the family of Oscar Rie at the house Puchen 39, rented by the Rie family as their holiday home; see 109 SF, 111 AF note 5 ⟨Freud/Ferenczi III, 848 F, 850 F⟩. The Freuds had originally wanted to spend the holidays together with the orphaned children of Sophie and Max Halberstadt (see text following 106 SF), somewhere in Bavaria, but 'Bavaria does not admit foreigners' ⟨Freud/Andreas-Salomé, 9 May 1920, p. 102; Regulation [of 20 March 1920] on Entry and Residence, Bayr. Staatszeitung und Bayr. Staatsanzeiger 76 (2nd sheet), 8th year, Munich, Wed., 31 March 1920, p. 111, official section; quoted in Murken (1982), note 12 (p. 14)⟩.

2 Paul Königsberger (1890–[after 1941]), a sculptor friend of Ernst Freud, born in Vienna, student of Prof. Bitterlich in 1912–13 ⟨archive of the Academy of Fine Arts, Vienna, 25 October 1999; Freud to Martin, 22 July 1920; see also *Rundbriefe 2*, p. 154, note 2⟩. Eitingon asked him to make a bust of Freud, who assumed that it was for Eitingon himself. The following year, however, it was presented to Freud by the committee members on the occasion of his sixty-fifth birthday. Jones later (4 February 1955) gave a copy to the University of Vienna, where it was installed in the Arkadenhof. Eitingon had a further copy made for himself. ⟨Freud/Eitingon, 209 E; Jones II, p. 15; Jones III, pp. 26, 242; Freud/Ferenczi III/1, 850 F, 870 F; Freud/Jones, letter 308; Freud/Abraham, 2 May 1921; ill. in *Freudiana*, p. VIII (18) between pp. 8 and 9⟩.

3 Missing; probably an invitation from Loe Jones to Anna to come to England before the Hague Congress. See Appignanesi and Forrester, p. 239 and note on p. 508; Young-Bruehl, pp. 143–4.

4 Loe had wanted to visit the Freuds during the Congress in The Hague. See Jones to Freud: 'Loe had a dictatorial neurotic talk with me about your going to Holland. She always wants to arrange everything as she thinks it should be, or not at all. I hope that her visit to Holland to see you will not exclude the possibility of your coming to England' ⟨Freud/Jones, letter 271, 24 April 1920, p. 375⟩. See also 100 SF, note 7.

5 'On 30 July I am going to Gastein with Minna, and at the end of August [30 August] with Anna to Holland by way of Berlin–Hamburg' (see 121 SF) ⟨Freud/Ferenczi III, 848 F, 17 June 1920, p. 29⟩.

6 Herbert Jones; see 108 AF, note 1.

7 Spelt incorrectly (without umlaut) in German.

8 The translation of Freud's *Vorlesungen* (1916–17*a*), entitled *A General Introduction to Psychoanalysis* (New York: Boni & Liveright, 1920). The title page states: 'Authorized Translation With Preface By Stanley Hall'. The translator was a 'doctor of psychology at Columbia University, a Miss Hoch'; Cora

Senner from New York, who had apparently been trained by Freud, checked the translation ⟨Bernays [1967], p. 179⟩. See 99 SF and note 8.

9 Freud frequently used the number sign for dollars. With Jones's assistance, Freud had been able to open accounts in the Netherlands for foreign currencies ⟨Freud/Jones, e.g., letters 286 with note 1, 288–91, 297–302, 310, 335–7, 340, 392–5 and elsewhere⟩. A year earlier he had already 'accumulated a sum of money in London' ⟨Freud/Binswanger, 120 F, 25 December 1919, p. 146⟩. See also 153 AF, 187 SF.

10 Abbreviated in the original German letter.

11 'The translation is loose and rapidly done, full of vulgar Americanisms. [. . .] The translator [. . .] makes such mistakes as using "suppression" for "Verdrängung" in spite of our efforts to make "repression" a technical term distinguished from suppression' ⟨Freud/Jones, letter 280, 9 July 1920, p. 385⟩. See also Jones III, p. 9f., and comments about a glossary in note 3 to 157 SF.

12 Freud also complained of this in his reply to Edward Bernays: 'You can tell the unnamed translator that I appreciate the difficulties in translating slips and dreams, but do not consider his solution of inventing similar examples to be correct. Such inventions do the author an injustice and rob the description of its validity. The only right way would have been to replace the untranslatable examples of slips of the tongue, puns in dreams, etc., by *ones from his own analytical experience*. . . . To do this, of course, the translator would have to have been an analyst himself' ⟨Bernays [1967], p. 184⟩. See also Bernays [1980], p. 34f. and note 1. Jones later had a new translation done for the British public (see 163 SF and note 5). Freud's concerns about the translation of his works in general are discussed by Ilse Grubrich-Simitis [1993], pp. 20f. and note 7, and note 1. Jones, by contrast, regretted that Freud showed a certain carelessness in this regard, which he had repeatedly admonished ⟨Jones III, pp. 52, 139f.⟩.

13 The holidays this year were particularly late, partly for financial reasons ⟨Freud/Eitingon, 178 F, point 6, p. 206⟩.

14 From their honeymoon; see text following 106 SF.

15 Kata Lévy had been analysed by Freud for several weeks from the end of April/beginning of May ⟨Freud to Kata, 8 April and 16 August 1920; Freud/Ferenczi, III, 841 F, 850 F⟩.

16 This idea also came to nothing. They spent the summer 'in a small, not very luxurious, but quiet boarding house with ample cuisine in the immediate surroundings of Budapest (in the "Cool Valley")' ⟨Freud/Ferenczi III, 851 Fer, 15 August 1920, p. 32; 846 Fer, 849 Fer⟩.

17 On 26 July; then Martha spent the weeks until 25 August with Mathilde and Robert Hollitscher in Goisern before meeting Anna in Altaussee ⟨ibid., 850 F; Jones III, p. 26⟩. See also 109 SF and note 6, 122 AF/MF.

18 Perhaps to visit a patient in this town 31 km north-west of Vienna ⟨Freud/Jones, letter 287, 4 October 1920⟩, where a friend of Freud, Doz. Dr Bonvicini, ran an institution for the emotionally disturbed, which, for example, Freud recommended to his sister, Rosa, in 1922 to recover from the shock of the suicide of her daughter 'Mausi' ⟨Freud to Victor Heller, 23 August 1922, LoC SF, Cont. 12⟩.

19 Melanie Rie and her daughter, Margarete, had gone on ahead. Dr Rie and the second daughter, Marianne, followed on 27 July; see 108 AF.

108 AF

Alt-Aussee, 27 July 1920

Dear Papa,
You tell me to wait for a rainy day to write to you, but after receiving your two communications today at the same time,[1] I have so much to write that I must disregard the weather. I can't wait for you to be out in the country as well; you must be very tired, and it is clear from your letter how hot and frightful it is in Vienna.

I hope you read Herbert Jones's letter straightaway before forwarding it. You can probably imagine how delighted I was to receive it and how much my old attachment to Loe,[2] which appears to become stronger in periods of inactivity, reacted to it. I don't need to tell you that I would be indescribably happy to visit England. I don't think it will be possible *before* the Congress, but Herbert himself suggests that we meet Loe in Holland beforehand and then travel to England with her. We would then have one or two weeks (and perhaps they would invite me to stay longer). England is already entered in our passports and I'm sure Rank could organize the visa, perhaps through a visa fixer or Miss Muret (or Murray).[3] I would be very happy if you would decide to come. I am also very pleased to read that Loe has *not* given up the idea of seeing us in Holland. And her silence can probably be explained by her and Kobu's illness.[4] I shouldn't say any more for now about this English plan because I am so full of it at the moment that I could go on for ever.

I am glad to hear that you finally have the English translation, but it should be the last one that we leave completely to others like that. It's good that Jones is revising it for England; but how much better would it have been if he had had a proper one done in England under his supervision and our Verlag had published it for America. The American-French cousins of Ries say that your things are really widely read and well known in America; everyone must therefore think that Edward will do a fabulous deal. The 275 dollars coincide nicely with the English plan and could be used for the crossing to London.

By the way, I would never have interpreted 'pofpler' as 'together' as you so rightly did. I read it as 'congress', which shows how poor I still am at interpretation.

Please give Königsberger my address in Aussee so that he can show me your head when he comes here with it,[5] and ask Kata where I can write to her after 1 August.[6]

And now the news from here: my good mood of the first few days is holding up and is even getting stronger. I feel so much better and happier than in the last months that I cannot emphasize the difference enough. Living with Margaretel is just as agreeable as last year, except that we sleep separately,[7] which is very pleasant. Dr Rie's wife is particularly kind and delightful to me and I therefore feel very much at home. I sometimes go shopping, much to the satisfaction of the household, and will soon be able to tell the difference between shoulder and rump. We eat very copiously and well. Dr Rie is arriving today with Marianne.

Sometimes I help in the field and get extra milk for it from the farmers. I *never* go on long walks alone and in fact don't go walking very much at all. Nor can I persuade myself to go swimming in the lake, although most people do so.

The revision is proceeding well between Rank and myself.[8]

I'll write about everything else in a letter to Gastein, where you will be hopefully in four days, and *hopefully* you are just as enthusiastic about England as I am.

With a kiss and many affectionate greetings.

Anna

[In Margarete's handwriting]

Sincerest greetings, dear Professor. If only you were finally away from Vienna and the work as well! I am enjoying living together with Annerl even more than last summer, if that's possible, and am more grateful than I can say to you for entrusting us with this child, who is so loved and not only by me. I sincerely wish you a relaxing time.

Margarete

1 Presumably 107 SF and the letter mentioned in it from Herbert Jones with details of the invitation to England. Ernest Jones would also have liked to meet Freud in England: 'I wish we knew if there were any hope of seeing you here after the Congress; it would be an enormous pleasure' ⟨Freud/Jones, letter 284, 20 August 1920, p. 389; also letters 271, 278⟩.

2 See AF 45. Young-Bruehl speaks of Loe Kann Jones as the third of Anna Freud's 'collection of beautiful and good maternal older friends' ⟨Young-Bruehl, p. 86, although she confuses 1919 and 1920 on several occasions⟩.

3 Possibly Dr Jessie Murray, whom Jones mentions in his *Rundbrief* of 2 November 1920 as 'now deceased' ⟨*Rundbriefe 1*, p. 141 and note 8; see also Schröter (1996), p. 1162⟩.

4 Jacobus Kann (1872–1945), Loe's brother, who lived in the Netherlands; see 110 SF ⟨Freud/Eitingon, 174 F, note 6⟩. During the war he had provided the Freuds with food and cigars, and helped to ensure that the correspondence with Anna and Jones in England could be maintained. At the end of 1919, Loe suggested that Freud emigrate from Austria and take over her brother's house in The Hague ⟨Freud/Jones, letters 255, 257; Young-Bruehl, p. 78⟩.

5 See Anna's letter in 122 AF/MF and note 11.

6 In Anna's letters to Kata that were left to me, there is only one letter in 1920, on 21 February, and a fragment of a letter from the Netherlands (undated).

7 See 97 AF, note 1.

8 The proofreading for the journals in the *Verlag* and for the new *Journal* in 'Press'; see 100 SF, notes 6 and 4. 'An invaluable, though at the time apparently incidental, gain was the enlisting of Anna Freud's help in the English department in Vienna, work which brought her closer to psycho-analysis than ever before and which foreshadowed her future career' ⟨Jones III, p. 50f.⟩.

109 SF[1]

Frl Anna Freud
c/o Dr O. Rie
Alt-Aussee
Styria
Puchen 39

[Sender (handwritten): V.[illa Dr.] Wassing]

B Gastein 31 July 1920

Everybody arrived yesterday safe and sound.[2] Busy settling into the old rooms.[3] Weather overcast but rest delightful. Last week very tiring. Ferenczi and Lajos as well.[4] Write to me as soon as Dr arrives and tell me how he is.[5] Thank Marg.[arete] and give everyone my sincere regards.

Papa

Mama is travelling[6] with Hitschmann[7] and Königsberger.

1 Postcard.
2 Jones (III, p. 26) says incorrectly '20 July 1920'. In the guest list the arrival of Freud and Minna Bernays is given as 31 July ⟨*Badgastein. Liste* 1920, serial nos 590, 591⟩.
3 In the same house as the previous year. See 73 SF, note 2.
4 See 110 SF. On 18 July 1920, Ferenczi wrote: 'Unfortunately I didn't succeed in getting the Hungarian passport. The exit prohibition is valid only for Austria' ⟨Freud/Ferenczi III, 849 Fer, p. 30⟩. It is possible that Lajos Lévy was in Vienna for a 'short analysis' while meeting his wife ⟨Freud to Kata on 18 July 1920 could be interpreted in this way⟩.
5 Dr Rie had had dysentery and was expected in Altaussee. See following letters.
6 To Goisern, see 107 AF and note 17, also 112 AF and note 10.
7 Eduard Hitschmann (1871–1957), doctor of medicine, the Freuds' family doctor for a while. He was a member of the Vienna Psychoanalytic Society from 1905 and played a decisive role in the psychoanalytical movement; he also headed the psychoanalytical out-patients' department in Vienna until it was closed by the Nazis in 1938. Thereafter he emigrated first to England and then, in 1940, to Boston, Massachusetts ⟨*Minutes I*, pp. XXXIVf. (with incorrect year of death); obituary in *IJ*, vol. 39 (1958), p. 614f.; Mühlleitner, pp. 149–51⟩.

110 SF

PROF. DR. FREUD

BGastein, 1 August 1920
Vienna, IX. Berggasse 19

My dear Anna,
Thank you very much for your express letters of Thursday and Friday, both of which I received today, Sunday.[1] I was quite concerned and tried hard to dissuade him from travelling,[2] but he would have none of it, and

then I asked Mariandl in the morning to send for Zweig.[3] I don't know whether she managed to do that. I hope that he will recover under Mela's care and Dr Jung's treatment,[4] but it must be a difficult time for you. Of course, I also think it right that you shouldn't leave now but rather share everything with them.

You appear to regard the trip to England as a certainty, but I don't think so at all. As I understand from the letter, Loe wants us in England only before the Congress and not afterwards, because she wants to spend some time with her terminally ill brother, and we will probably have the greatest difficulties with the visa. Rank had to wait for a week in Rotterdam when he tried to get one.[5] At all events, it looks as if we shall be seeing Loe again for certain. I am sure you will write to Herbert that there won't be enough time between Gastein and the Congress for England, particularly as I cannot possibly avoid visiting Marie and Sam[6] in Manchester, or wherever they are, even if we postpone Berlin and Hamburg until after the Congress. So I'm not at all sure about England.[7] I have an uneasy feeling in general about the near future that it will be impossible to make any long-term plans.

We have the same rooms as before and the old home comforts in Gastein. I have already had two baths and went today on the first long walk; very tired, almost certainly from the baths, but also from the whole difficult year.[8] I have just looked at the notes I brought with me for work,[9] but I'm in no hurry to get started. The last days in Vienna were complicated by the visit of Lajos and Ferenczi. Kata left safely,[10] and will write to you first and give a reply address. The food here is excellent and we are only now realizing how badly we ate in Vienna. The prices are high but lower than in Vienna[;] altogether we should manage with 300 K per person, which means we need £1 a day, and I have brought £55 for possible purchases on the black market.

There are lots of familiar faces here, and even the 'government' appears to be represented,[11] at least I greeted Tandler[12] and recognized Fritz Adler in the train.[13]

The peace is delightful, not even an organ grinder. I love the noise of the waterfall.[14] But it is cold, overcast and rainy.

I look forward to your further letters.

Affectionate regards,

Papa

1 Neither letter survives.

2 Spelling mistake (without umlaut) in the German.

3 The gastroenterologist Dr Walter Zweig.

4 Probably Rudolf Jungh, doctor of medicine, Medizinalrat [senior medical officer], spa doctor and attached to the Radiology Institute in Salinenspital in Bad Aussee ⟨Perfahl, p. 28⟩. In the 1916 Annual Index for Community Services in Aussee, a Dr Rudolf Jungh is listed as 'kaiserlicher Rat' [imperial councillor]. ⟨Thanks to the Styrian Provincial Archive, Department ID, Graz, 23 August 2002.⟩

5 November 1919, when he travelled on an administrative trip from the Netherlands to England ⟨Freud/Ferenczi II, 823 Fer and note 3, 824 F, 825 F, 827 F, III 829F; Jones III, p. 18⟩. Jones believed that it was largely Rank's own fault that he had to wait so long in the Netherlands because all the involvement with the political atmosphere of Vienna had made him lose contact with the outer world ⟨Freud/Jones, letter 255⟩. This comment presaged much deeper conflicts in which personal animosities between publishing colleagues and committee members became entangled with material and institutional problems. See, for example, 163 SF, 181 SF and note 5.

6 See 42 SF and notes 10 and 12.

7 The visit to England and to the relations in Manchester was indeed cancelled. See text after 123 AF/SF.

8 Reference to the two deaths in January 1920; see 96 AF, note 6, and text after 106 SF.

9 *Group Psychology and the Analysis of the Ego* (1921*c*), the work that Freud mentioned for the first time in a letter to Ferenczi in May 1919: 'With a simple-minded idea [*Einfall*] I attempted a φα foundation for group psychology. Now that should rest' ⟨Freud/Ferenczi II, 813 F, 12 May 1919, p. 354⟩. 'In Gastein I want to compose my intention on mass psychology into a short book' ⟨Freud/Abraham, 14 May 1920, p. 423; Freud/Jones, letter 283; Freud/Ferenczi III, 852 F; Jones III, p. 44f.⟩.

10 See 107 SF and note 15.

11 Entries in *Badgastein. Liste* for 1920 include for 26 July: 'Karl Seitz, President of the National Assembly, with wife' and 'Dr Otto Bauer, State Secretary (ret.), with wife' (the brother of Ida Bauer, who became known as Freud's patient 'Dora' [1905*e*]); he was regarded as one of the most influential people in the First Republic; see 246 SF, note 3 ⟨Weissensteiner, pp. 185–90; Braunthal; Appignanesi, p. 47⟩.

12 Julius Tandler (1869–1936), doctor of medicine, professor of anatomy in Vienna, at the time Under-Secretary of State for Public Health (1919–20), later head of the Health and Welfare Department; between 1920 and 1934, he introduced pioneering social reforms, which 'soon attracted international attention and acclaim' ⟨Czeike [1984], p. 211 f. and figs 408, 409; also Czeike [1999], p. 54; Weissensteiner, pp. 123–6; Sablik [1983]⟩. Tandler and Freud had a number of points of contact: among other things, they both belonged to the steering committee of an endowment for a Vienna children's home that American doctors and Freud's sister Anna had set up with Eli Bernays ⟨Freud/Ferenczi III, 841 F; Jones III, p. 5; Molnar [1996], pp. 113–14⟩. The claim by Sablik (1985, p. 12) that Tandler and Freud had co-edited the *Zeitschrift für Sexualwissenschaft* in 1918–19 cannot be verified; the source cited by Sablik (1983) mentions only Tandler as co-editor and nowhere else in the volumes is there any reference to Freud as co-editor. In 1924, Tandler presented Freud with the *Bürgerrecht* on his sixty-eighth birthday and in 1926, on the occasion of his seventieth birthday, the diploma giving him the freedom of the city of Vienna ⟨*IZ*, vol. 10, 1924, p. 210; vol. 13, 1927, p. 80; Freud/Abraham, 4 May 1924, p. 501; Jones III, pp. 107, 130⟩. See also Freud's letters to Tandler in 1925 (in 1960*a*) and 1931*g*. After the violent suppression of the Social Democrats in 1934, Tandler was arrested and in 1936 summoned as an adviser for hospital reform to Moscow, where he died a short time afterwards.

13 Friedrich Adler (1879–1960), Austrian socialist. During the First World War

he opposed the war policy of the Austrian Social Democrats and on 21 October 1916 shot Minister-President Count Karl von Stürgkh as a 'fighting signal', but was pardoned after his conviction. 'Our inner conflict here is perhaps nowhere so plainly revealed as it is by the extremely notable trial of Fr. Adler. He happens to have been born precisely in the rooms [in Berggasse 19] in which we live' ⟨Freud/Abraham, 20 May 1917, p. 350; see also Freud, 1960*a*, p. 379⟩. He later became secretary-general of the Labour and Socialist International in Zurich. Freud had met his father, Victor Adler (1852–1918), the socialist leader, while a student and played an inglorious role in a dispute with him; the experience later figured in a dream that Freud analysed in *The Interpretation of Dreams* ⟨1900*a*, pp. 209ff., 213, 214⟩.

14 See 72 SF, note 4, and 152 SF.

111 AF

[Altaussee] 4 August 1920

Dear Papa,

I am writing to you today for the very first time with a real feeling of relief. The improvement, noticed first only by the doctor and followed by another few bad days and nights, has now finally reached the patient. Dr Rie is gradually beginning to return to his normal self again; he is regaining his appetite and is finally starting to look like his old self. The loss of blood has stopped, and with the opium, which he has to take in spite of his great reluctance to do so, he is able to gain longer periods of rest. I visited him in his room today for the first time in several days. The danger has passed, and you can imagine how the entire house is breathing again and beginning to become more cheerful.

Dear Papa, I was so appalled that Dr Rie was already ill in Vienna and no one here knew anything about it. I find it terribly wrong. Promise me that if you are ever ill and I am not there that you will write to me immediately so that I can come. Otherwise I could never have any peace anywhere. I meant to ask you in Vienna before leaving but in the end I didn't dare.

I think that the post office here waits until there are a few letters so that it's worthwhile delivering them. I have been writing to you practically every day. Only once did Rank send me such an endlessly long revision that I didn't have time to write. Your telegram and express letter both arrived today at the same time.[1] You have to pay again for the express delivery but it saves almost twenty-four hours[2] so I am very happy when you do it.

I am very pleased to hear that you are finally in Gastein and that you are eating well. Hopefully the tiredness will soon pass and also the 'uneasy feeling[']. After all, you don't have any real reason for it, do you?

I don't want to say much more about England. Herbert writes that he hopes we will be coming over with Loe, so they also appear to be counting on it. But I don't want to persuade you to do anything you don't want to do yourself. Besides I've promised someone – I can't remember who – not to be bothered if England doesn't work out if only Dr Rie gets well again and doesn't die. And even if it doesn't make sense, I want to keep the promise, at least until he gets completely well again. I'm also not in favour of England *before* the Congress.

With the last revisions I had an article by Pierce Clark about compulsive neuroses. Is it nonsense, or do I not understand it properly?[3]

I presume you are coming to Ischl for 18 August, aren't you?[4] Wouldn't you like to visit us here for a day? It would be so nice, and there are always plenty of spare beds to sleep in. I think the Ries would be delighted. By then Rie should also be well again. And Aussee is so beautiful that I don't need to go anywhere else any more.

Marie[5] is really helpful and provides us with everything that we can't otherwise get for Dr Rie. As a result I have acquired a completely undeserved reputation for being a good housekeeper.

Write to me again very soon; I hope that you will now only have good news to report.

With a kiss,
Anna

1 The telegram (perhaps to the Rie family) is missing.
2 Corrected from 'days'.
3 L[eon] Pierce Clark (1870–1933), doctor of medicine, American neurologist and psychiatrist. The reference is to the essay 'A Study of Primary Somatic Factors in Compulsive and Obsessive Neuroses' (1920), which Jones sent to the *Verlag* for publication in the *Journal*. Freud had already answered on 16 July: 'As for Pierce Clark's paper which you sent I will not venture to advise it should be repudiated, but [it] is very bad, worthless Adlerism, based on analysis not reaching into the period of first childhood and therefore most shallow and superficial' ⟨Freud/Jones, letter 281, p. 386, and also p. 278⟩.
4 For the birthday of Freud's mother; see following letters to 117 SF, 120 AF.
5 Marie Rischawy. Starlvilla, Puchen 52, where the guesthouse was located, was on the outskirts of Altaussee, while Puchen 39, the 'Wirthskasperlgut', as it was called, where Anna was living with the Ries, was about fifteen minutes' walk away in the countryside outside the town. ⟨Thanks to Johannes Linortner, Altaussee, and the Styrian Provincial Archive Department ID, Graz, 23 August 2002.⟩ See also 72 SF, note 2, and 122 AF/MF.

112 SF

PROF. DR. FREUD [Bad Gastein,] V. Wassing, 7 August 1920
Vienna IX, Berggasse 19

My dear child,

Have just received your express of the 4th. Since your telegram[1] I no longer doubted the outcome and was relieved. Fortunately, Margaretl's sad letter of the 2nd arrived on the 6th after the telegram. Please be so good as to deliver the enclosed card to the doctor.

So that you see what a deep impression your admonition made,[2] I should tell you – if I haven't done so already – that I spent some of the first week in

Gastein with an upset stomach, although admittedly it wasn't as bad as the doctor's dysentery and has now passed and been replaced by a huge appetite. It was either something endemic here[3] – Frau Blau[4] had a similar complaint and Wassing claims to have seen several cases – or a random expression of the normal affliction after putting work aside. But enough, it's over, and life here is turning out to be extremely agreeable and can gradually be enjoyed again. In the mornings a long walk on my own, return with some, never very many, mushrooms, then the midday decision where to spend the 200 K for lunch, then into the afternoon, while 'the companion'[5] is sleeping, work on the new paper[6] or revision of the old one[7], and then after 6 p.m. a tame walk through the town, to the railway station to enjoy the misery of the new arrivals, the reading room, and finally the dining room. After dinner, more creative writing but no longer until 1.30 a.m., because the bath attendant wakes me up at 5.30 a.m. I carry on sleeping from 6 to 8 a.m.

The weather alternates between magnificent and – interesting. The visitors here are said to be mixed: 50 per cent Jewish men and 50 per cent Jewish women.

The most delightful aspect is the peace and quiet. Spend time only with Jul. Riesz and wife, who are charming as ever and have fully shared our interest in the illness in Aussee, but no tarock games. I am pleased that the new work is going well because I only have these few weeks for it. I have abandoned the idea of visiting Ischl on the 18th. Because of the miserable transport connections, it would take up three whole days, which would compromise the spa cure and rest. I will leave Gastein a day earlier and go to Ischl from Salzburg, which is easier.[8]

You are right about Pierce Clark; it's a very stupid work. A book from a supporter[9] has found its way here from Los Angeles, Calif., which I envy at least for its weather.

Today the first letter from Mama in Goisern arrived, which describes the horrors of the journey but also reports that she is quite content with the stay.[10]

Keep well, regards to all, thank Margar.[ete] for her dear letter and write again soon.

Your old papa

1 Missing.
2 See also 277 SF and note 9.
3 See 184 SF.
4 Unknown.
5 Minna Bernays; the entries in the spa guest list often said 'with companion' (instead of the name).
6 *Group Psychology and the Analysis of the Ego* (1921*c*).
7 *Beyond the Pleasure Principle* (1920*g*). Freud reported to Ferenczi on 12 May 1919 that he had completed the draft, but, as can be seen from the above comments (and 95 SF), he continued thereafter to work on the manuscript; during Ferenczi's visit to Vienna at the end of September 1919 they also discussed it ⟨Freud/Ferenczi II, 813 F, 817; III, 848 F, 850 F; also Freud/Jones, letter

248; Freud/Andreas-Salomé, 1 August 1919⟩. See Ilse Grubrich-Simitis ⟨1993, pp. 183–91, quotation p. 187⟩ for detailed discussion of this 'reworking process that was no doubt multilayered and involved several phases' with 'the composition of an entirely new chapter, constitutive of the structure of the work'. See also Jones III, pp. 42–4. The book appeared in early December 1920 ⟨Freud/Abraham, 28 November 1920, pp. 42–4⟩. For the second edition of *Pleasure Principle*, see 142 SF and note 8.

8 See 117 SF, 121 SF.

9 Unknown.

10 See 107 SF, note 17.

113 AF[1]

Prof. Dr. S. Freud
Bad Gastein
Villa Wassing

[Altaussee,] 7 August 1920

Dear Papa,

The recovery is proceeding slowly, interrupted repeatedly by pain and misery, which Dr Jung[h] finds quite natural. Albert Hammerschlag is now also here and visits often. I received news for the first time today from Mama and am pleased to hear that it is so good. How is Aunt? You don't write anything about her.

How did you like our first English number?[2] Rank urged me today to start translating the *Review*,[3] which I in fact began yesterday. But it's almost a shame to do anything here because the togetherness with everyone is so cosy that I don't feel like 'withdrawing'.

Greetings to you and Aunt.
Anna

Have you sent a telegram replying to Loe? I'd like to know before I answer.

1 Postcard.

2 'The first number of our *Journal* ought to have come out today. Perhaps it did. It appeals to me as very rich and dignified' ⟨Freud/Jones, letter 281, 16 July 1920, p. 386⟩. This first number contained Freud's essay 'A Difficulty in the Path of Psycho-Analysis' (1917*a*) in English. The introduction was in the form of an open letter, in which Ferenczi, as president of the International Psychoanalytical Association, explained why the journal had been founded and the relationship between the English and German versions. At the same time he announced the handing over of responsibility to Jones (see 101 AF, end of note 9). In an editorial, Jones explained the particular circumstances and modalities of the new journal.

3 *The Psychoanalytic Review* (ed. White and Jelliffe) – the first psychoanalytical journal in English – existed from 1913 (1958–69 hon. ed. Theodor Reik) ⟨Freud/Jones, PS to letter 152⟩. The journal changed its subtitle several times until 1962; from vol. 50 (1963) onwards it had its earlier title again (see list of abbreviations). Apart from original contributions, it also contained translations of

other psychoanalytical papers and articles from the *Journal*. White had asked Freud from the beginning for an article, which Freud refused, because he saw the undertaking as competition to the *Zeitschrift*. In later years he changed his mind, however ⟨Freud, 1976*l*; Jelliffe (1983), Part I, p. 61f., Part II, pp. 194–6, 229, 230f. and *passim*⟩. See 236 SF.

114 AF

Aussee, 9 August 1920

Dear Papa,
I was particularly pleased to receive your express letter today and also at the fact that you admitted having an upset stomach and now appear to feel better. Regrettably, I had to hold back the enclosed letter to Dr Rie – with the agreement of the rest of the family – because although the improvement is acknowledged by all the doctors, his subjective condition has become very wretched again, so that for the time being he can only be sympathized with and there is not yet anything to congratulate him about.* He himself is very despairing and still has so much pain that you can hear him groaning loudly for hours (last night was particularly bad again), and he even cries very often. Otherwise, I believe, he would have very much welcomed a letter from you (and curiously enough any expression of sympathy). The doctors repeatedly insist that the danger is over; if only we could see some improvement.

Today I attempted with Margaretl to interpret a dream she had had. We didn't get as far as I would have liked, but we made a little progress. She was very proud that she had been able to write to you and appears in general to be able to do more this year than before. She is trying to learn how to ride a bike, carries rucksacks full of bread and even went swimming today. So at least she's trying a few things again. Now she is doing something else that is quite remarkable. I gave her a few things to read that I have written in the last few weeks,[1] and she is now rehearsing so as to be able to recite them nicely.[2] It doesn't have any sense otherwise, but she can then at least read them out to me as the author and 'only audience'[3] in one. I work every day for quite a while translating the not very amusing *Review*, which consists mainly of 'vague phrases', as Reik,[4] for example, comes up with.

What are you writing your essay about?[5]

I am very well here, except for one thing: I can't bring myself to undertake anything. If I'm not out on an errand or the like, I just lie in the hammock or deckchair in the field and feel no desire to go anywhere. I went collecting mushrooms with Alfred Rie's family[6] (measly pickings that you would ignore, but there are no boletus here any more), but I found the walking difficult and quickly became tired. Afterwards I declined the offer

---

* Because he feels bad, he gets annoyed when someone says that he is looking well.

of an excursion to the Loser.[7] Do you think I should force myself so as to get back into practice? But I still feel the after-effects of this winter[8] in the form of fatigue, backache and general laziness. I haven't been able to bring myself to go swimming, although almost everyone else does. My attempts at socializing[9] are no different. As soon as a lot of people are around, I get terribly bored. However, the people whom the Rie children[10] meet are much younger than I am, and that makes a difference.

Apart from that everything is fine.

I am pleased that you take my exhortation seriously (unless you are just amused by it) and that I now know exactly what you do during the day. You cannot imagine how much I think about you. I am looking forward very much to our joint trip.[11]

I understand why you cannot come to Ischl for the 18th and was already wondering how you would manage it. But can't you leave Gastein two days early and come here to pick me up and spend a day?[12] Dr Rie should be better by then. The doctors reckon that with the necessary convalescence to regain his strength, it could take perhaps another three weeks before he is fully fit.[13]

I must close now – it's a very late and dark hour that I am attempting to illuminate with two candles – although I could quite easily carry on writing.

Write to me again soon!
With a kiss
Anna

1 Including poems ⟨Young-Bruehl, pp. 81–7⟩. See 101 AF and note 1.
2 Margarete Rie was training to be an actress ⟨Young Bruehl, p. 52⟩. See 161 SF and note 11.
3 Reference to Nestroy's expression 'only audience' (also the 'one' or the 'other audience'). See Freud's letters to Wilhelm Fliess, 19 September 1901, 11 March 1902 ⟨1985*c*, pp. 450, 457⟩.
4 Theodor Reik (1888–1969), D.Phil., received his doctorate in 1912 with a psychoanalytical thesis on Flaubert. He became a member of the Vienna Psychoanalytic Society in 1911 and in 1918 became its second secretary and librarian; in 1919 (and not 1915 as Reik himself incorrectly claims), Freud designated him as one of the winners of a prize awarded for 'outstanding works, one each in the field of medical and applied psychoanalysis' ⟨Freud, 1919*c*, p. 268; Reik, 1942, p. 89⟩. He was Rank's assistant for a short time in the *Verlag*. He practised in Vienna until 1928, then in Berlin, where he also taught at the Psychoanalytical Institute. In 1933 he emigrated to the Netherlands and from there in 1938 to the USA, where – as a lay analyst – he had difficulties. He nevertheless continued to practise analysis and publish there. He was made honorary publisher of the *Review* for life in 1958 ⟨Titles of the *Review*; Marinelli, p. 16; Mühlleitner, pp. 260–3; *Minutes IV*, p. XVIII⟩.
5 *Group Psychology and the Analysis of the Ego*; see 112 SF and note 6.
6 The family of Alfred Rie (1862–1932), an older brother of Oscar Rie, and his wife Johanna, née Karplus (1879–1931) ⟨Molnar [1996], p. 100⟩.

7 See 141 SF. The Loser (1,838 m), one of the mountains near Altaussee with a famous view. Today the Salzkammergut Panoramastrasse goes past the Loser-Hütte to a restaurant at 1,600 m.
8 In which Sophie died (see text following 106 SF). Anna's complaints were probably also connected with her general health, which had suffered since the winter of 1917 during the war ⟨Young-Bruehl, pp. 78f., 91–2; Freud/Ferenczi II, 642 F, 646 F, 648 F, 649 F, 686 F, 690 F, 762 F, 824 F; III, 837 F; Freud/Eitingon, 178 F⟩. See also 127 AF.
9 See 28 SF and note 2.
10 Including the 'the Ries' American-French cousins'; see 108 AF.
11 To the Congress in The Hague and then possibly to England; see 123 AF/SF and note 1, and the text after 123 AF/SF.
12 See 117 SF to 121 SF, particularly 119 SF, point 2.
13 The letter card from Freud to Oscar Rie had the following content:

BGastein, 7 August 1920

Dear Oscar,
I congratulate you sincerely on your recovery and urge you to promise in the general interest to refrain in future from rash undertakings like your trip while suffering miserably from dysentery. I'm sure Mela will agree.
Warm greetings to both of you.
Freud

⟨Loc SF, Cont. 39⟩

115 SF[1]

PROF. DR. FREUD [Bad Gastein,] 10 August 1920
Vienna, IX., Berggasse 19

My dear Anna,
A card will have to do. I have so much to write, reply to, correct, draft that I can't really enjoy the weather.

Today also a publisher from Madrid, who inquired back in 1918;[2] lively correspondence with Rank on passport and Congress matters.[3]

We are in the best of spirits, fully contented. In fact I am working very hard. Unfortunately, it will soon be over. Aunt is very mobile and well. Oli is dutifully keeping in touch,[4] received word today from him, Ernst[5] and Mama, and everything fine. Lucie and her husband[6] are in Berlin. Dr Drucker[7] has suddenly been taken ill with an unknown complaint. Martin's new position appears to be set.[8] As you know, I won't be going to Ischl on the 18th. Affectionate greetings to you and all the Rie[s]. Take care of the doctor!

Affectionately,
Papa

1 Letter card with printed letterhead.

2 Biblioteca Nueva, Madrid, which was to publish the Spanish edition of Freud's works, *Obras Completas des Professor S. Freud*, 1922–34; see 133 SF, 166 SF and notes 4 and 5.
3 This refers to the preparations for the Congress in The Hague; see 123 AF/SF.
4 After searching in Vienna in vain, Oliver found a job in Berlin with the help of Eitingon: 'We are very happy about it and he is completely changed' ⟨Freud/Eitingon, 180 F, 10 July 1920, p. 209, 178 F, point 4; Freud/Ferenczi III, 833 F, 837 F⟩. See also PS to 125 SF and note 21. Oliver lived temporarily with the Eitingons in Berlin and in Ernst's apartment; see 131 AF ⟨Freud/Eitingon, 163 E⟩.
5 Ernst became engaged to Lucie ('Lux') Brasch (1896–1989) in the spring; she was a student of classical philology, 'a Jewish girl of good family who is described as highly cultured and intelligent' ⟨Freud/Sam, 22 April 1920; Zohlen, p. 80⟩. Martha came from Hamburg to the wedding in Berlin on 18 May, and Anna travelled as an 'ambassador of the family' from Vienna ⟨Freud/Sam, 27 May 1920; Freud/Ferenczi III, 844F⟩. A month later the couple visited the family in Vienna: 'Ernst was here with his wife Lux, who won everyone's heart' ⟨Freud/Ferenczi III, 848 F, 17 June 1920, p. 29; Freud/Sam, 16 June 1920⟩.
6 This 'Lucie' is Leah ('Lucy'), the second daughter of Anna and Eli Bernays (1886–1980; see 98 AF, note 8), married since 1904 to Felix Wiener (1873–1930), sales representative. The couple had two sons (see 150 SF and note 3). ⟨Stammbaum Lange: Freud Family, 'Genealogical Tree, p. II; see also Freud-Bernays, A.⟩
7 Martin Freud's father-in-law; he was staying with 'spouse and [2] daughters' at Haus Germania ⟨*Badgastein. Liste* 1920, serial no. 2855⟩. See also 117 SF.
8 At Treuga, a Dutch-Austrian commercial company; see 117 SF and 104 SF, note 2.

116 AF

[Altaussee,] 12 August 1920

Dear Papa,
Now I realize for the first time how difficult it was for the poor war reporters, whom everybody complained about so much. It's just not possible to keep up with events, and so everything is always wrong. After having reported to you that Dr Rie was getting better, he took a turn for the worse again; and barely had the news of his deterioration reached you when this changed and now he's fine – almost recovered. He sat with us for the first time today on the veranda in a deckchair and has started to have a human existence again; he speaks, eats and only complains that he can't sleep. He is estimated to have lost 15–18 kg and looks much older than before. The pain has stopped since yesterday.

The two girls were immensely pleased to receive your letter.

Today I have been wearing my new blue dress for the first time,[1] because we have been invited to tea by the Winters[2] at the Auspi[tz] villa.[3] I allowed myself to be tempted by the promise of good food.

I am travelling on the 17th to Mama[4] and on the 18th to Ischl. I am taking leave from here, although I have been told that the 'guesthouse' doesn't like it when guests stay away for so long. We are now catching up on all of the good mood that has been missing.

Please send my affectionate regards to Aunt. She will be receiving a letter tomorrow.

Anna

1 See 74 AF, end of first paragraph.
2 The 'multimillionaire' Josefine Winter (1873–1943), daughter of Rudolf Auspitz and cousin of Valerie Karplus (see 74 AF, note 1) ⟨Schnitzler [1985], p. 100⟩. She was the widow of the Viennese surgeon and poet Dr Joseph [also Joseph v.] Winter (1857–1916) ⟨ibid.; Winter, pp. 42, 91–3, 100 and *passim*⟩. As Anna writes of 'Winters' in plural, it is to be assumed that one or more of the children were also in Altaussee. Oscar Rie (who could not yet take up the invitation himself) was also connected with the Auspitz villa as a doctor, having treated both Josefine and her children ⟨Winter, pp. 68, 75⟩.
3 The extensive country residence of the Viennese economist, industrialist and banker Dr Rudolf Auspitz (1837–1906) on the banks of Altaussee Lake, a magnificently furnished 'really feudal' property 'for only two or three summer months each year' that 'to this day [is] referred to only as "Auspitz Villa"' ⟨*Beiträge*: '50. Mitteilungsblatt des Burgvereins Pflindsberg, Altaussee', Dec. 1993, pp. 2 and 3⟩. The family and relatives, together with their households, staff and children's tutors, spent their holidays there (see 74 AF, note 1). Apart from their own staff, they also employed local workers, gardeners and craftsmen; through marriages amongst the servants there were several connections between the localities (see also 2 SF, note 2, 125 SF and note 15). After the annexation of Austria in 1938, the property was confiscated under the Jewish racial laws and used by wartime organizations. After restitution the community acquired the property; the villa underwent several alterations and now houses the spa and municipal administration ⟨*Beiträge*: ibid., pp. 2–5 (with ill.)⟩. The earlier architecture can no longer be seen.
4 To Goisern; see 107 AF and note 17.

117 SF

PROF. DR. FREUD — BG. [Bad Gastein,] 15 August 1920
Vienna, IX. Berggasse 19

My dear Anna,

Thank you for your two letters, the latter with the news that the doctor is finally well again so that a more cheerful mood should now also return. Following your first letter, I wrote to him in another tenor. I hope not to have done any harm.

I am not very happy to hear about your fatigue, but I think it's quite understandable as a consequence of all the hard work during the year. In this way you can justify your intention of giving up school.[1] Do not force yourself but try to rest.

Here we are past the halfway mark in our stay and the intimate atmosphere has also gone. We have social obligations and I tremble at the thought of not completing the draft version of Group Psychology.[2] An American journalist[3] visited us and turns out to have been close to the Bernays family, a friend of Felix[4] and Edward for seventeen years; he used to be a lawyer and liberal councillor in Vienna before a disaster occurred. We have been seeing more of Drucker[5] because of his illness. After a few days of mysterious fever he has recovered and is travelling tomorrow with everyone to Millstadt. Like us, they are very pleased at Martin's new position with Treuga, a large new Dutch-Austrian trading company, where he is to start work as a management secretary with a much higher salary and better future prospects.[6] I received the news from Ophuijsen[7] that we have FL 3,600 in Holland (= 65 × 36 = K 234,000),

195
390
2340
1 1

that we will also spend honestly.

Emden says that Kati[8] has become engaged to a young gynaecologist in The Hague. We should take a few thousand krone and bring her something nice. Uncle and Sophie[9] are arriving in Gastein on the 20th. Their friends (Director Stein, etc.[10]) are already here.

I am thinking of leaving on Saturday, 28th, Salzburg–Ischl, and of picking you up in Salzburg on the 30th. I will send a telegram to confirm, of course.[11] I cannot yet determine the other details of the journey. The Committee is asking that we arrive in The Hague in the evening of 5 September.[12] Will we be able to manage it?[13]

Eitingon wants to accompany us from Hamburg and Abraham from Bremen. It should be very interesting.

Send my sincere regards to all the Rie[s] and in the remaining two weeks try to do as many as you can of the things you have not yet done. I will write to Ischl today to cancel for the 18th.

Affectionate regards,
Papa

1 Anna indeed gave up her position as a teacher at the end of the 1920 school year. See 120 AF, 127 AF.
2 But see 119 SF.
3 Unidentified.
4 Felix Wiener, Edward Bernays' brother-in-law.
5 See 115 SF and note 7.
6 See 115 SF and note 8.
7 Johan H. W. van Ophuijsen (1882–1950), Dutch psychiatrist, co-founder of the Dutch Psychoanalytic Society and its president for several years. After 1935 he lived and worked in New York ⟨*IZ*, vol. 5 [1919], p. 146, and vol. 6 [1920], p. 376; *Rundbriefe 1*, p. 9, note 7⟩. As treasurer of the Dutch group, he was one of the organizers of the conference in The Hague. The travel

expenses for participants from Budapest, Vienna and Berlin to The Hague were covered in part by a donation of $5,000 that a New York relative of Eitingon had provided for psychoanalysis ⟨Freud/Ferenczi III, 844 F; Freud/Eitingon, 174 F⟩.

8 Probably the daughter of the Emdens; there is a 'Frl K. van Emden, The Hague' after 'Frau A. van Emden, The Hague' in the guest list at the Hague Conference ⟨*IZ*, vol. 6 [1920], p. 378⟩.

9 Alexander Freud and his wife; see 119 SF and note 4.

10 Unidentified. Although the *Badgasteiner Liste* contains several guests with this name for the period in question, the entries do not permit a reliable identification. Alexander's 'friends' possibly included members of the Vienna Verein der Tarifeure, which he strongly supported through talks and articles in his magazine ⟨Kursidem, unpublished, p. 6⟩. The members of Alexander's regular table ['Stammtisch' or, more poetically, 'Tafelrunde'] sent Freud flowers and a congratulatory telegram on his seventieth birthday ⟨Freud to Alexander, 14 May 1926⟩.

11 See 121 SF.

12 Jones wrote to Freud: 'Rank, Sachs, and I arrive at The Hague on the 5th. I hope it will be possible for you to do the same, as there is so much to discuss' ⟨Freud/Jones, letter 284, 20 August 1920, p. 390⟩.

13 No, Anna and Sigmund Freud did not arrive in The Hague until the morning of 7 September 1920. Beforehand they visited Sophie's widower, Max Halberstadt, and the two orphaned grandchildren, Ernstl and Heinerle, in Hamburg. They met Eitingon there and travelled together with him to the Netherlands ⟨Freud/Eitingon, 181 E; Jones III, p. 26⟩. See text after 123 AF/SF for details of the return journey.

118 AF

[Altaussee, between 15 and 19 August 1920][1]

Dear Papa,

1) When do you think you will be leaving Gastein?
2) Would it be possible for you to pick me up here? It would be a nice compensation for the Ries, who have had to put up with me all summer.
3) Do you have the first issue of the English journal with you?
4) If so, would you mind if I asked you for some translation information? I don't always understand the Americans completely.[2]
5) Have *you* replied to Loe?

With a kiss,
Anna

1 Dating is on the basis of Freud's reply in the following letter.

2 The translators of the articles taken from the *Review* and the *Journal* for the *Zeitschrift* are not named. They could be original works or edited articles.

119 SF[1]

Frl Anna Freud
c/o Dr O. Rie
Alt-Aussee
Styria
Puchen 39

B Gastein, 20 August 1920
[Postmark: 21 August 1920]

My dear Anna,
Answers

1) I will let you know as soon as I have passports. Probably leaving the 30th of this month (28th from here).[2]
2) Travel to Aussee impossible, however much I would like to. We are meant to be in The Hague in the evening of 5 September.
3) Int. J. of ΨA impossible to obtain in Gastein.
4) Always willing to provide information.
5) I have not been able to reply to Loe because she hasn't written to me.

News:

(a) Group psychology finished.[3]
(b) Uncle, Sophie, Harry[4] arrived today in rain and mist.[5]

Affectionately,
Papa

1 Postcard.
2 Added later between the lines.
3 1921*c* (see 117 SF). Freud revised the script again in early 1921 but said of it: 'and what was added was not well done' ⟨Freud/Ferenczi III, 876 F, 19 July 1921, p. 60⟩. The work was published in mid-July 1921; see 142 SF.
4 Sophie and Alexander Freud's son, Otto Heinrich (1909–68), later doctor of law ⟨Stammbaum Lange: Freud Family, 'Genealogical Tree', p. IV; Molnar [1996], p. 144⟩.
5 See 117 SF and note 9. They lived in Villa Glück auf. The entry in the guest list (somewhat later) reads: 'Herr Alexander Freud, editor, with spouse and son' ⟨*Badgastein. Liste* 1920, serial no. 5116⟩. It is not possible to determine where they arrived from. According to Young-Bruehl, Anna met her cousin Edward in Salzburg in 1920 when he was visiting their uncle Alexander and had gone on walks with him ⟨Young-Bruehl, p. 95, without indication of source⟩. Anna makes no mention of it in this correspondence (unless it is these very letters that are missing). In his memoirs (1965), Edward Bernays says nothing of such a meeting; nor is there any mention in Freud/Bernays A.

120 AF

Aussee, 21 August 1920

Dear Papa,
There is no end to the illnesses in the house. Now that the doctor is finally getting about and conducting himself like a healthy person again, there is a minor bout of gastric flu going about in the house. The doctor's wife had it for a day, then the cook, and on my return from Ischl I found Margaretl with high fever and the same condition. She has still not yet quite recovered. It's as if a personal divine fate has been entrusted with looking after the Ries' holiday. As I don't belong, it has left me untouched for the time being.

I found Mama to be well when I met her in Goisern.[1] She looks fresh and is very comfortably installed. Food and company quite average. By contrast, it's a long time since I have seen Mathilde in such an unhappy state, in a very bad mood, very dissatisfied and physically wretched. It was nevertheless a very pleasant day there. I spent the night at Mama's and on the 18th had a delightful carriage ride with Mama and Math to Ischl.[2] Large, lively but very copious family meal; Mausi, who appears to miss us,[3] very tender; very good news again from Rosi;[4] and then after having to kiss various aunts I returned here and, much to my pleasure, found your long letter.

I am in full agreement with all the information and am particularly happy to hear of Martin's new position, which will hopefully get him away somewhat from the D. atmosphere.[5] I am always willing to spend money in Holland, or at least won't ever object to it. So far, I have not regretted giving up the school for one single minute.[6]

As I have to travel through Ischl in any case, perhaps I could meet you there. Have you heard anything about Frau Eitingon's Italy plans?[7] I still haven't had enough of the summer and wish, on the contrary, that it were 15 July and could start over.

I'm a bit muddled because I'm sitting with the family while writing today.

Affectionate greetings from
Your Anna

1 See 116 AF.
2 For grandmother's birthday.
3 Cäcilie Graf spent some time during spring with the Freuds in Vienna ⟨Anna to Sam, in: Freud/Sam, 7 March, 20 April 1920⟩.
4 See 125 SF, 128 SF. In 1913, Rosi Winternitz had already suffered a 'schizophrenic episode' and felt the after-effects for a long time afterwards ⟨Young-Bruehl, pp. 73, 193–4⟩. In late September 1919 she travelled to New York at the invitation of her uncle, Eli Bernays, but suffered another attack a short time afterwards and needed treatment at a hospital there ⟨Freud/Sam, 24 November 1919; Freud to Eli Bernays, 20 October 1919, LoC SF, Cont. 1; Anna/Lou,

letter 346⟩. She later returned to Vienna and in 1923 married the poet Ernst Waldinger, D.Phil. (1896–1970) ⟨Anna/Lou, letter 78; Stammbaum Lange: Freud Family, 'Genealogical Tree', p. IV⟩.
5 Perhaps 'Drucker' atmosphere.
6 But see 127 AF.
7 Mirra Jacovleina Eitingon, née Raigorodsky (1877–1947), a Russian actress married to Eitingon in 1913 ⟨Schröter [2004], pp. 5f.; Neiser, p. 9; Lockot, p. 324⟩. See 137 SF and note 3 for a planned invitation of Anna to Merano.

121 SF[1]

Anna Freud
c/o Rie
Puchen 39

B Gastein 24 [August 1920][2]

Arriving Ischl Saturday [28 August] evening expect you and Mama there Sunday depart[3] early Monday.
Papa

1 Telegram.
2 The telegram was classified in the LoC under 1922, but from the contents it clearly belongs here.
3 Via Berlin–Hamburg to the Netherlands ⟨Freud/Ferenczi III, 848 F⟩.

122 AF/MF

[Altaussee,] 25 August 1920

Mama is dictating to me because she has been stung by a wasp and cannot write.

Dear husband,
We arrived here safely this lunchtime in streaming rain and the customary Alt-Aussee mud.[1] Marie reserved a delightful room for me,[2] the stove was lit immediately so that the freshly scrubbed room would be dry by night. The Loser, Trisselwand and Tressenstein can hardly be made out in the mist.[3] As we were leaving, I was stung so badly by a wasp that I ran to the doctor in great pain. He bandaged the sting and at the same time announced that he intended to apply for membership of the p.a. [psychoanalytic] association. The departure from Goisern was a touching experience for all concerned; I have grown very fond of it. I plan to be in Ischl on Sunday with Annerl and hope to meet you there hale and hearty. I send

you both my sincerest regards and look forward to the promised letter from Aunt.

Your loyal wife

Dear Papa,

As you can see, even in the summer occasions present themselves for practising as a secretary;[4] without Erika,[5] however, it's not that easy, especially as Mama doesn't trust me with her fountain pen.[6]

Margaretl is on the road to recovery. She went today to Salzburg to 'Jedermann'.[7] I helped Mama unpack and settle in here. As per telegram, I shall arrive in Ischl on Sunday and look forward to seeing you and to the trip.[8] Nevertheless I'm sorry to have to leave here – you know I don't like transience;[9] I really enjoyed staying with the Ries.

Yesterday I received a nice present from Frau Mela:[10] a delightful old Biedermeier bottle and matching drinking glass; for no particular reason, which I always prefer.

Everything else will wait until next week. Yesterday I took a look at the Königsberger bust so as to get used to the sight of you again.[11] It is still very good.

With a kiss

Your old Anna

1 Altaussee is notorious for its overcast and damp climate, with rain, thunderstorms and even severe flooding ⟨Freud, M., pp. 52, 60–3; Winter, pp. 51, 66, 79; Freud/Bernays, letter 148 Mi; Schauer; Stephan⟩.
2 Marie Rischawy in her guesthouse.
3 For Loser, see 114 AF, note 7; Trisselwand (1,755 m) at the eastern end of Altaussee Lake; Tressenstein (1,201 m), opposite Loser, on the southern shore, above the col to the neighbouring Grundlsee Lake.
4 See 100 SF and note 6.
5 The brand name of the typewriter was 'Erika' ⟨Jones II, p. 125⟩.
6 The letter is written with a violet crayon.
7 *Jedermann. Das Spiel von Sterben des reichen Mannes*, adapted 1903–11 by Hugo von Hofmannsthal. The premiere took place in Berlin in 1911. It had been performed in front of the cathedral at the first Salzburger Festspiele since 22 August 1920. The first performance was a charity event and the actors received only presents (*lederhosen* for Werner Krauss as Death, for example). Jedermann: Alexander Moissi; director: Max Reinhardt; wardrobe: Alfred Roller; musical direction: Bernhard Paumgartner ⟨Kleindel, p. 325; Kaut; Weissensteiner, pp. 157, 162⟩.
8 Via Hamburg to the Congress in The Hague; see 117 SF and note 13, 123 AF/SF.
9 See 103 AF and note 1.
10 Melanie Rie.
11 Probably in Goisern, when she picked up her mother, whom Königsberger had accompanied there; see PS to 109 SF.

123 AF/SF

[The Hague,[1] 10 September 1920[2]]

[Anna's handwriting][3]

Dear Papa, I hope you are eating sparingly and not drinking wine. I'm doing the same with the drinking.
Regards

[Freud's handwriting]

I'm only making an exception for champagne, which is not a wine, and am crossing out every course from the programme. Be careful and look after yourself.
Papa

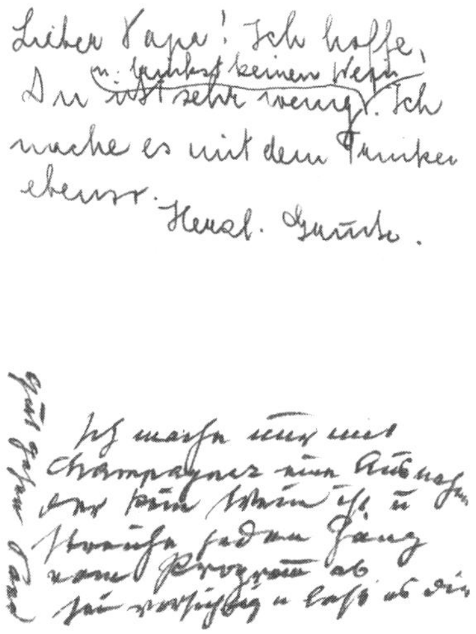

III Hague Congress, 1920 (exchange of notes)

[1st place card, front, printed][4]
'Fräulein Anna Freud'

[Back, Anna:] Do you eat pineapple?
[Underneath, Freud:] Yes

[2nd place card, front, printed]
'Prof. Dr. S. Freud'

[Back, Freud:] Just sent back a course. Further news to follow.[5]

1 Freud and Anna arrived in The Hague on the morning of 7 September. The Sixth International Psychoanalytic Congress took place there from 8 to 11 September 1920 in the building of the artists' society Pulchri Studio 'under the chairmanship of the most recently elected president of the Society Dr S. Ferenczi ⟨*IZ*, vol. 6 [1920], p. 377⟩. It marked 'in more than one way [. . .] the beginning of a new era for the psychoanalytic movement' ⟨Sachs, p. 152⟩. It was the first really international Congress after the First World War. Jones's presidency, which he had assumed temporarily in autumn 1919 (see 101 AF and end of note 9), was officially confirmed and the updated statutes were formally approved ⟨*IZ*, vol. 5 (1919), pp. 142–5, 328–31; ibid., vol. 6 (1920), pp. 376–402; Jones III, pp. 26–9; for the drawn-out preparations, see Freud's correspondence, particularly Freud/Abraham, 13 April to 10 June 1920; Freud/Jones, letters 243, 254, 257, 259, 282, 283; Freud/Ferenczi III, 849 Fer–851 Fer⟩. For the course of the Congress, see Ludwig Binswanger's impressive diary records, printed in editorial comments: Freud/Binswanger, p. 151 (see also ill. 11).

2 The date can be inferred from the menu of Restaurant de Deux Villes, The Hague (see note 3); it is in the same folder as the other parts ⟨LoC SF, Cont. 2, 'Miscellaneous related material, 1891–1920, n.d.'⟩.
3 This and the next note – both written in pencil – are together on a torn-off, loosely folded sheet on the back of which is written 'Prof. Freud' in Anna's handwriting; the word 'Prof.' is crossed out and replaced by 'Frl' in Freud's handwriting. It is thus an exchange, probably during a function of some kind: 'The British group of those attending the Congress entertained Freud and his daughter at a luncheon' ⟨Jones III, p. 29⟩. The copy of the note was not in the package of transcripts, but was kindly made available by Gerhard Fichtner, who found the sheet in the LoC in Washington, USA.
4 In my research in the LoC I found the following evidently connected place cards, on the back of which were further messages written in pencil. On Anna's place card the name is crossed out and 'Prof. Freud' written above it in Anna's handwriting. See also a similar question-and-answer interchange on the programme of the Budapest Congress in 1918 (ill. 11/12 in Freud/Ferenczi II/2, German version, between pp. 144 and 145).
5 These messages, if written at all, have not survived.

After the Hague Congress (September 1920)

Freud and Anna intended to travel to England after the Congress (see 107 SF–111 SF). 'I did my best to procure them permits [. . .]. Freud received his, but his daughter's was so delayed [. . .] that they had to renounce the plan. Instead van Emden and van Ophuijsen accompanied them on a tour around Holland. [. . .] The pair left Holland on September 28, but separated in Osnabruck. Anna went to spend some weeks with her little orphaned nephews in Hamburg, while Freud proceeded via Berlin to Vienna, getting home on September 30,' writes Jones ⟨Jones III, p. 29; Freud/Jones, letters 285, 287⟩. As the trip did not take place, the visit to Freud's nephew Sam and his family also did not occur (see 110 SF and note 6) ⟨Freud/Sam, 22 July, 18 September, 20 September, 2 October, 15 October 1920⟩.

124 SF[1]

Frl Anna Freud
c/o Halberstadt[2]
Hansastrasse 1
Hamburg
Germany

Vienna, 2 October 1920
[Postmark: 3 October 1920]

Dear children,
Affectionate greetings from the first family evening on Saturday with Robert and Math (instead of a tarock game) with the rest of Eitingon's provisions.[3]

Papa

[In their own handwriting]

Best regards, why no letter? Robert

Very best regards, and Annerl should write a letter herself, telling us everything.

Affectionately, Math

My dearest Annerl, thousand greetings, I hope to hear from you in detail soon. Papa very alert, thank goodness, already had six hours on Monday. Math and Rob. with us this evening. I will write to you soon. Greetings to Max and Frl. Jakob.[4]

Your Mama

1 Postcard; the sender, 'Freud, IX Berggasse 19', is added in Martha's handwriting.
2 After Sophie's death, Anna devoted herself to her two boys (see text after 123 AF/SF); on 7 November Oliver accompanied her from Hamburg to Berlin, where she stayed alternately with the Eitingons and the Wertheims (see 129AF to 137 AF). She returned to Vienna between 10 and 13 December ⟨Freud/Eitingon, 190 E, 191 F⟩.
3 Freud had also visited the Eitingons on the return journey from the Netherlands to Vienna ⟨Freud/Eitingon, 187 E⟩.
4 Elsewhere also 'Jacob', the help that Max had engaged for the children and household after Sophie's death: 'My brother-in-law doesn't want to leave the children and wants to keep up the house as much as possible. He has already found a housekeeper and wants now to give her some time to get used to the house and the children. [. . .] My brother-in-law appears quite despairing and broken' ⟨Anna to Kata, 21 November 1920; also Freud/Sam, 15 February 1920⟩. Immediately after Sophie's death, Max had received help from his widowed sister-in-law, the wife of his brother, the paediatrician Dr Rudolf Halberstadt, who had been killed during the war ⟨Freud/Ferenczi III, 832 F⟩.

125 SF

PROF. DR. FREUD 5 October 1920
Vienna, IX. Berggasse 19

My dear Anna,
This won't be a long letter. After two days of work I'm as tired as I was on 15 July. I am fully booked and have had to turn away some patients. As compensation for our failed trip to England,[1] I hear for four hours a day the beautiful and unfortunately often unclear sound of the English

language[2] and have only answered half of the hill of letters on my desk. In Holland it would have been a respectable mountain and might have been called Lange Brievenberg.

I was very pleased to receive your letter.[3] That's exactly how I imagined your impact on the orphaned house. Continue to make it comfortable for them and yourself.

Yesterday we visited the Ries. I'm sure you will be interested to hear about that first of all. Margaretl, who had already visited us earlier, looks well and now knows when the incredible difficulties with passports, certificates, invoices, etc., will finally be over,[4] Friday morning. As a farewell gift I brought her a small girl's head with a pigtail, which is all I could find that would be suitable for her in the collection. Afterwards I began to have doubts that it might have belonged to you from way back. If so I will make it up to you. The doctor is well. Unfortunately, the Leischings arrived shortly after us.[5]

At a meeting with Rank and Sachs it was decided that Jones's textbook should be translated[6] by you.[7] Rank also brought up the book of children's quotes again and found out that it is to be edited by Hug,[8] you and himself. Hug is to provide observations from the children's corner in *Imago*;[9] you are to collect new material and should start soon.[10] I also enclose proof of your new interest,[11] around 7 Dutch guilders. Lampl[12] brought your box. Mama, who is very well, has promised really to spend 200 fl on purchases.[13] I have not yet seen Maus. Rosi has apparently lost or given up her position in N[ew] York.[14]

We have a new Marianne from Aussee, who is very intelligent but probably won't stay. Everything is being done to keep her. She is to be paid 600 K.[15] My first day of work yesterday was worth 10,000 K. As the krone is steadily losing value, I will soon be a millionaire.[16] In this way the boldest wishes are coming true even by day.[17]

The French publisher yesterday paid 1,500 frcs for the translation[18] of the lectures,[19] which makes around 15,000 K for my part, etc., etc.

Affectionate greetings to Max and the little ones and my best wishes also to you yourself.

Papa

P. S. Ernst and Lux are in S. Vigilio[20] until the 10th of this month. Oli is hoping to come to Romania in about six weeks.[21] The Eitingons are expecting you.[22]

1 See text after 123 AF/SF.

2 'The chaps all whisper or mumble' ⟨Freud/Ferenczi III, 855 F, 31 October 1920, p. 37⟩. Freud complained in a number of instances of fatigue and 'lack of productivity' that analysis in a foreign language caused him: 'Nine analytic sessions daily have become a greater strain because of the shift to English (5 sessions). I note with surprise how greatly the effort of listening and inwardly translating uses up one's free energy' ⟨Freud/Abraham, 28 November 1920,

p. 434, 31 October 1920, pp. 432f.; see also Freud/Jones, letters 269, 288; Freud/Ferenczi III, 857 F; Freud/Sam, 28 January 1920, 25 July 1921⟩. On the other hand, he would not have been able to exist without the foreign patients; this income was life-saving for the entire family ⟨Jones III, p. 4; Freud/Jones, letter 269; Freud/Ferenczi III, 862 F⟩. See also 126 SF, 128 SF and note 4.

3 Missing.

4 Spelling mistake (no umlaut) in German. Margaret Rie was no doubt preparing to leave to continue her training as an actress. See 161 SF and note 11.

5 Eduard Leisching (1858–1938), D.Phil., art historian, and his wife, Hedwig, widowed Singer, née Bunzel (1871–1944). Leisching was director of the Austrian Museum of Art and Industry from 1909 to 1925 (appointed 'Hofrat' in 1911), then until 1934 permanent adviser on art to the Vienna city authorities. He was a strong supporter of local crafts and taught art history and aesthetics at the School of Arts and Crafts (*Kunstgewerbeschule*). He deserves particular credit as founder and organizer of adult education in Vienna; he founded the Vienna Adult Education Association in 1887, and initiated public university lectures by renowned academics and the establishment of public libraries, the Wiener Volksheim and the Volksbildungshaus (adult education centres) ⟨Leisching⟩.

6 Spelling mistake (no umlaut) in German.

7 Anna's translation of Jones 1920*a* was published in 1921 as *Therapie der Neurosen*. There is no translator's name on the title page; see 144 AF, note 6, and 60 AF, note 7.

8 Hermine Hug-Hellmuth (pseudonym), née Hug von Hugenstein (1871–1924), D.Phil., teacher, 1913 member of the Vienna Psychoanalytic Society. She was the first child analyst (since 1919 in the remedial department of Vienna Children's Hospital) and had given a paper in The Hague on techniques of child analysis. In 1919, *A Young Girl's Diary*, published anonymously by her, appeared in the *Verlag* (its authenticity was subsequently questioned). Until her death (she was murdered by her nephew) she gave talks and courses for members of social and educational professions, and headed the education advice centre at the Psychoanalytical Clinic in Vienna, founded in 1923 ⟨Mühlleitner, p. 163f.; *Protokolle IV*, p. XXI⟩.

9 Hug-Hellmuth was responsible for the column 'The Nature of the Child's Soul' in *Imago* ⟨introduction in *Imago*, vol. 1 [1912], p. 285f.; further contributions by her on this subject in 1912–14, 1917, 1921⟩.

10 This refers to a project to collect evidence of the early sexual knowledge of children, which Lou Andreas-Salomé mentions in a letter to Freud and in which Anna was also involved: 'Here Daughter-Anna has again scored a direct hit' ⟨Freud/Andreas-Salomé, 26 June 1922, p. 115⟩. Ferenczi describes evidence of this type from the everyday life of a child and comments: 'This small contribution definitely belongs in the children's collection' ⟨*Rundbriefe 2*, 11 April 1921, pp. 139f.⟩. The project was never completed, however: 'It seemed difficult to know what to do about it,' wrote Lou ultimately, on 5 August 1922 ⟨Freud/Andreas-Salomé, p. 118⟩.

11 Missing. Some sheets with financial summaries from later years are reproduced as annexes to 154 SF.

12 Hans Lampl had taken part in the Hague Congress as a guest ⟨*IZ*, vol. 6 [1920], p. 378⟩. As in the following year, he 'couldn't find a position as a bacteriologist', he began training in 1921 as a psychoanalyst at the Berlin Poliklinik,

where he also taught from 1922 onwards ⟨Anna to Eitingon, 20 April 1921; Eitingon [1922], p. 508⟩. See also 151 AF and note 2.

13 See 149 AF and note 3.

14 See 120 AF, note 4.

15 See 2 SF, note 2. She did indeed remain not much longer than a year. 'The second event was the departure of our Marianne, who could telephone so well but was too intelligent for a maid. She is now learning dressmaking so as to become independent' ⟨Anna to Kata, 21 December 1921⟩.

16 See 130 SF, note 3.

17 Reference to Freud's theory about the wish-fulfilling tendency of (nocturnal) dreams.

18 Spelling mistake (no umlaut) in German.

19 Freud's lectures at Clark University, USA, in 1909, *Five Lectures on Psycho-Analysis* (1910*a*). The translation by Yves Le Lay, entitled *Origine et développement de la psychoanalyse*, appeared in three instalments in *Revue de Genève*, in December 1920 and January and February 1921, accompanied by a long introduction by Édouard Claparède, professor at the University of Geneva ⟨*IZ*, vol. 7 [1921], p. 109⟩. On receipt of the first part, Freud wrote to Claparède on 25 December 1920, pointing out some inaccuracies ⟨Cifali-Lecoultre, pp. 298f., 304⟩. The claim in *IZ* and by Cifali-Lecoultre (p. 291) that it was the first translation of a work by Freud into French is based on an error. On various occasions, however, Freud himself also used the misleading formulation 'first French translation' (see, e.g., 149 SF and note 4; also Freud/Ferenczi III, 882 SF). In 1913, however, Freud's essay *The Claims of Psycho-Analysis to Scientific Interest* (1913*j*) was published simultaneously in German and French ⟨*Scientia. Internationale Zeitschrift für wissenschaftliche Synthese*, vol. XIV, year VII [1913], no. XXX1, Supplement, pp. 157–67, 236–51, translated by M. W. Horn, Nifflheim–Grossharthau–Dresden⟩. See also 43 SF and note 11.

20 Presumably San Vigilio, 3 km to the west of Garda, from where Freud wrote in 1908 to the family: 'The site is one of the most beautiful on Lake Garda, the most beautiful altogether' ⟨2002*b*, p. 270⟩. See also 128 AF and note 7.

21 For his job in Berlin, which Eitingon obtained for him (see 115 SF and note 4) ⟨e.g., Freud/Eitingon, 189 E, 207 E⟩. The trip was postponed, however, until 13 March 1921 ⟨Freud/Ferenczi III, 870 F⟩. Oliver visited his family in Vienna on the way ⟨Freud/Eitingon, 201 F, 202 E, 207 E⟩. See also 138 SF and note 1.

22 See 129 AF and note 5.

126 SF

PROF. DR. FREUD 12 October 1920
Vienna, IX. Berggasse 19

My dear Anna,

Received your two letters.[1] As far as your confidential letter is concerned, the situation doesn't worry me. It can only do Max good if he has the possibility again of some tenderness,[2] and he will just suffer a renewed loss if you behave imprudently, which I doubt will occur. Don't concern yourself about a harmless friendship.

I will write to him directly about money. You shouldn't limit your own spending.

It's quieter here. I have currently reduced the number of hours to six and am thus really reserving some time for expected foreign patients.

The tempest in the practice has calmed. My stomach is now behaving again properly through two bottles of Karlsbader, but with salmon and pears.

News: Jones[3] has a little girl.[4] He announced it in the Committee circular.[5] Everything well,[6] drop him a line.

The negotiations on the sale of the Verlag to Kola[7] appear to be drawing to a favourable conclusion. For us a great advantage, freedom from worry and great expansion of our scope of action.[8] Your position not affected, of course, only prospect of increased salary.

Pribram,[9] who was here today, says that I was expected in Cambridge on 27 September. Why didn't they write? The interest, particularly in *Totem and Taboo* [1912–13*a*], is said to be extremely great. Pribram has undertaken to edit all of the articles relating to Austria for the next supplement to the *Encyclopaedia Britannica* and intends to give due attention to me and ΨA.[10]

In the last few days the London Rothschild, head of the house, visited me on the recommendation of the sister of Frl Schiff.[11] He is quite meshugge and probably beyond help and also rejected the treatment.[12] I'll be interested to see if I receive the 10 guineas I charged him.

I'm having problems with decorating your room. Mama is absolutely against it, probably because she doesn't want to invest any more in an apartment that she would willingly exchange tomorrow for one in Döbling[13] or the Cottage.[14] She forgets that there is nothing to be had.[15] But I can't force her; I have always let her have her way in the house. The only possibility is for you to write to her yourself and insist on it.[16]

Affectionate greetings to you, Max and the children.

Papa

1 Neither letter can be found in the papers.

2 Max did not marry again until three years later; see 162 AF, note 7.

3 In 1917 Jones had married the singer and composer Morfydd Owen, who died tragically in 1918 ⟨Freud/Jones, letters 219, 221, 520; Jones [1959], pp. 254–6⟩. On 9 October 1919 he married Katherine Jokl, a former fellow student of Sophie, in Zurich ⟨Freud/Jones, letters 253, 265⟩.

4 Gwenith Jones (1920–28) ⟨*Rundbriefe 1*, 7 October 1920/L, p. 72; also Freud/Jones, letter 288⟩. She died at the age of seven of severe double bronchopneumonia ⟨Freud/Jones, letter 520⟩.

5 As a reaction to the distancing of Adler and Jung from Freud, a group of his closest supporters – Ferenczi, Jones, Rank, Sachs and Abraham – formed a 'Secret Committee' in 1912 to defend the basic principles of psychoanalysis; in autumn 1919 Eitingon joined them at Freud's request (for Anna's membership, see 156 AF and note 1) ⟨Freud/Jones, letters 80, 94; Freud/Ferenczi I, 320 F, 395 F, 397 Fer, 398 F; Freud/Abraham, 13 May 1913; Sachs, pp. 151ff.; Jones II, pp. 172–88, Jones III, pp. 19f., 106f., 143f., 197. For the history of the Committee and the group, see Wittenberger [1992], [1995, part C]; Fallend [1995], pp. 41–50.⟩

The members of the Committee corresponded with one another initially without any fixed rules, and after the Hague Congress of 1920 continuously in the form of 'Rundbriefe' (circular letters) ⟨*Rundbriefe 1*, p. 7; Jones III, p. 30⟩. For details of the symbol of a 'ring of covenant', see 129 AF, note 5, 174 AF, note 5.

6 German 'Alles gut geht'.

7 Richard Kola (1872–1939), one of the wealthiest and most influential Austrian bankers in Vienna who – following a 'pet idea' – wished to expand his powerful financial empire of paper mills, printing and publishing companies through the addition of a 'Vienna book publishing company in grand style' by buying up existing publishers ⟨Kola, pp. 188ff.; quotes pp. 279, 270⟩. This Rikola Verlag AG was constituted on 2 December 1920 ⟨Hall, vol. II, pp. 310–47⟩.

8 Through this affiliation the shareholders of the *Verlag* hoped for relief from the enduring financial difficulties. 'The sale of the Verlag to Kola [. . .] could assure Rank's immediate future, give us back half a million in cash, and permit the greatest possible expansion of our activity, so that we can publish what we want and what seems worthwhile' ⟨Freud/Ferenczi III, 853 F, 11 October 1920, p. 34; also Freud/Jones, letters 288, 293–5; *Rundbriefe*, *passim*⟩. The negotiations broke down ⟨*Rundbriefe 2*, 11 March 1921, p. 104⟩, but this proved in the end to be a good thing because Rikola Verlag was unsuccessful for want of publishing know-how: 'Rikola was created on the stock exchange not in a publishing office' ⟨Hall, vol. II, pp. 326, 336–46⟩.

9 Alfred Francis Pribram (1859–1942), D.Phil., professor of history at the University of Vienna, member of the Institute of Austrian History Research, known for his meticulous research of source material. He was regarded internationally as '*the* Austrian historian' and belonged to the 'intellectual elite of Austria at the time' ⟨Zouzelka, pp. 15–17, 133, 190f.; quotations pp. 49, 191⟩. His *Urkunden und Akten zur Geschichte der Juden in Wien* was published in 1918. Freud had met him at Josef Breuer's house and they had become friends thereafter (see 75 SF, note 2) ⟨ibid., p. 48⟩. In the summer he spent several weeks as a guest at St John's College, Cambridge ⟨Freud/Jones, letters 288, 289⟩. The claim by Fallend that Pribram attended a meeting of the Vienna Psychoanalytic Society as a guest on 30 November 1921 is not corroborated by the minutes in *IZ*, vol. 7 (1921), p. 531 (perhaps it is based on a handwritten list of those present) ⟨Fallend [1995], pp. 344, 216 and notes 53 and 54⟩.

10 The 11th edition of the *Encyclopaedia Britannica* (1910–11) had not contained an entry on psychoanalysis. Freud wrote that his name could be found in the supplement (1913), however ⟨Freud/Sam, 28 November 1920⟩. The 12th edition (1922) was an unchanged reprint of the 11th edition with three additional volumes in which 'psychoanalysis was duly mentioned in four places': 1. in a short and somewhat unreliable biography of Freud, 2. under 'medicine', 3. under 'psychical research', 4. under 'psychotherapy'. This marked 'an important milestone in the history of the psychoanalytical movement concerning the canonization as it were of psychoanalysis' ⟨*Rundbriefe*, 18 February 1923/Vienna; see also Zouzelka, p. 133⟩. (Strachey's claim in the *Standard Edition*, vol. 20, p. 261, that psychoanalysis was still not mentioned in the new edition is incorrect.) For the 13th edition, in 1926, Freud was asked to write an article himself, which he did (1926*f*). For the 14th edition, Jones (1929) wrote an article about Freud ⟨Freud/Jones, letters 530, 531⟩.

11 Helene Schliff, sister of Prof. Dr. med. Arthur Schliff (1871–1953), son-in-law of Josef Breuer and translator of Freud's French work 1895*c* ⟨Hirschmüller

[1978], p.48 (with different year of death); Stangl, pp.121–7⟩. Freud gave her a copy of *The Interpretation of Dreams* with the dedication 'Fräulein Helene Schliff by courtesy of the author' ⟨*Sigmund Freud Museum*, p.58, ill. 143 – with thanks to Gerhard Fichtner⟩.

12 Freud's letter to Ferenczi of the previous day also indicates that no treatment took place. It is not possible to determine which member of the British branch of the banking family is referred to ⟨Freud/Ferenczi III, 853 F⟩.

13 Döbling, on the edge of the Vienna Woods, beneath Hermannskogel; formerly a suburb, later the 19th district with 'some magnificent' villas from the first third of the nineteenth century ⟨Czeike [1984], p.112⟩.

14 See 16 AF/OF and note 7. Freud's mother also lived there ⟨Freud/Andreas-Salomé, 12 January 1922, p.111 and note, p.231⟩.

15 For years Freud had teased his wife: 'My plan for old age is made: not Cottage but Rome. You and Minna will like it just as much' ⟨Rome, 20 September 1912, in: 1960*a*, p.301⟩. Martha Freud's wish for an apartment outside the inner city was partly fulfilled: in 1931 and 1932 the family spent the summer months in Pötzleinsdorf (see 287 SF and note 2), in 1933 in Döbling (4 May–30 September) and in 1934–7 in Grinzing (28 April–13 October 1934; 18 April–18 October 1935; 18 April–17 October 1936; 24 April–16 October 1937) ⟨Molnar [1996], pp.148, 158, 169, 170, 176, 183, 191, 199, 207, 217, 223⟩.

16 See 128 SF–130 SF, 138 SF.

127 AF

Hamburg, 22 October 1920

Dear Papa,

I was very pleased to hear from Mama that Frl Dellisch really had the hour with your patient. Perhaps the good pay and better life that goes with it will be the best cure for her.[1] I very much enjoyed your last letter and all the good news, and would have answered long ago if I hadn't felt so unwell. Just like last winter, I once again have all kinds of minor abdominal pains, with the tiredness they produce when walking and the like. I know from Fleischmann[2] what it is, but I am very unhappy that it has recurred after I felt very well the whole time. Now there's not much left of the recuperation in Holland. Today I am lying on the sofa to get well and hope that it will soon be fine again.

Heinzi[3] fell head first out of his pen in a moment of inattention this morning but fortunately damaged neither himself nor the floor. With his boundless energy he is almost impossible to watch over and control, but is becoming sweeter and gentler by the day. He already talks a lot. Yesterday I bought a pair of shoes for each of the children and a new rain cape for Ernstl,[4] all with mother Halberstadt's assistance.[5] I had Max give me some more money today. Now that I no longer have the Dutch prices to hand, everything seems incredibly expensive here (a pair of shoes for Ernstl – 125 marks). The children will be getting coats from a seamstress in the house and I hope that before I leave they will have a complete children's wardrobe.

I have phoned Eitingon twice on Sunday evenings, and yesterday I had a delightful letter from Frau Wertheim,[6] who invited me to spend a week with her as a guest. The Eitingons have also sent me chocolate. She has been confined to bed for fourteen days, incidentally, and is not well at all.[7]

I have not heard anything directly from the Cottage-Lyzeum. I feel so out of everything now, without having been able to find a replacement that does me good.[8] I have received a couple of corrections from the publishers but not heard much else otherwise. I have written to Loe and Herbert[9] from here.

Write to me again soon.
Affectionately,
Anna

1 Anna's former teacher colleague (see 86 AF and note 6), who was now living in Vienna 'in miserable financial circumstances', had applied in vain (in Berlin, through Eitingon) for a position as a tutor ⟨Anna to Ernst, 11 February 1920⟩. Anna continued later to be concerned about her well-being ⟨e.g., Anna to Eitingon, 16 March 1925; correspondence between Anna Freud and Josephine Dellisch, 1946 ff., LoC AF, Cont. 17⟩.
2 Carl Fleischmann (1859–1941), doctor of medicine, Viennese specialist in obstetrics and gynaecology, 1902–29 senior consultant in the Gynaecology Department of Rothschild Hospital and hospital director from 1910 to 1924 ⟨Fischer, I. 1932/33; DBA N. F.⟩. He had tended Martha Freud when Anna was born, and operated on Mathilde in 1912 (see text following 18 SF/MF) ⟨Freud 1985*c*, letter 83; Freud to family, 3 September 1912 (printed in part in 2003*e*); see also Gödde [2003], p. 233⟩. He died in exile in London ⟨Schnitzler [1981], pp. 840, 352, note 6⟩.
3 Heinz Rudolf Halberstadt (1918–23), called Heinele (also Heinerle), the second son of Sophie and Max Halberstadt. For details of his early death, see 195 SF ⟨Stammbaum Lange: Freud Family, 'Genealogical Tree', p. II⟩.
4 See 54 SF and note 1.
5 Mathilde Halberstadt, née Wolff ⟨Weinke, p. 111⟩.
6 Martha Wertheim, née Meschelsohn (1870–1953), married to Wilhelm Wertheim (1859–1934), co-owner of the renowned Wertheim family department stores in Berlin ⟨Ladwig-Winters, p. 407 and elsewhere, genealogical table, p. 489⟩. She was particularly friendly with Minna Bernays (see, e.g., PS to 132 AF). She was forced to emigrate in 1938. 'In later years she lived dependent on nursing care in England' (see 135 AF, note 5) ⟨Ladwig-Winters, p. 420⟩. Anna accepted the invitation; see 129 AF, 131 AF, 132 AF, 135 AF.
7 Mirra Eitingon was ill with a severe liver and gallbladder complaint.
8 But see 120 AF.
9 Loe and Herbert Jones, see 107 SF, 108 AF.

128 SF

PROF. DR. FREUD — 26 October 1920
Vienna, IX. Berggasse 19

My dear Anna,

Received your sad express letter today. I am very sorry to hear that the complaint has recurred. It looks as if plenty of rest is the only way to help, possibly a radical Franzensbad cure.[1] At all events, you should go to see Fleischmann right after you arrive here.

The fact that you regret the school and cannot find a satisfactory replacement is also just a temporary consequence of your bad mood at being ill. I can handle the reproach very well. Be happy that you can rest a little. Max has written to me very gratefully about what you are doing in Hamburg. Shortly after receiving this letter you will no doubt be exchanging Hamburg for Berlin.[2] It will be very quiet this time at Eitingon's and in any case you should not let yourself be rushed around too much.

As far as your room is concerned, a matter that you don't mention at all at the moment, you should either cheerfully resign yourself to it or have a serious conversation with Mama about it. It would not be very useful to keep quiet about it and then be dissatisfied for a year.

After having lectured you so thoroughly, I shall now pass to lighter matters. I was very sorry for Heinzi and had already intended to concern myself properly with him after you left. But adventures like that often occur when the mother is there and you have to rely on the guardian angel and the elastic cranium of children. It's a pity that he's such a boisterous donkey.

There is an enormous amount of business and projects here that are still waiting completion. Perhaps Kola will take you on in the Verlag.[3] Rank is splendid as ever, but I don't see much of the others. I have a lot to do and can now consider myself quite rich. But all of my English patients except one are leaving before Christmas. Perhaps new ones will come; I don't know.[4]

The good mood from Holland is also gradually disappearing with me too and my eagerness for work is returning in its place.

The prospects for the family at Uncle Eli's are not good and most, including Mausi, are in dire straits.[5] Stupid news of disaster[s] has apparently been received from Rosi again.[6] Ernst sent a telegram today from Anacapri.[7] The reply cost 74 K, but that's still much less than a guilder.

I send you my greetings and commiserations. There is always something to worry about. Write soon. Tell Max that I have received his letter and wish the three of them all the best for Christmas.

Papa

1 Spa in western Bohemia, today: Fratiskovy Lázne; 450 m altitude on the northern rim of the Cheb Basin in a moor landscape. Franzensbad was widely known for its moor bath cures, particularly for women's complaints and rheumatism; it was also regarded as the 'most outstanding heart spa in Austria' ⟨Zörkendörfer, p. 161; Reinl⟩.
2 See 124 SF, note 2.
3 Spelling mistake (no umlaut) in the German.
4 See 125 SF and note 2. The 'English' included not only patients but also and above all students training with Freud; additionally, foreigners from other countries – France, Switzerland, India, America – came to study psychoanalysis in Vienna (see 156 AF, 157 SF, 163 SF). Special courses 'on selected chapters

of psychoanalysis' were organized for them and taught by Rank, Ferenczi, Abraham, Sachs, Röheim and others ⟨*IZ*, vol. 7 (1921), p. 398; also *IZ*, vol. 8 (1922), p. 106; Kardiner, pp. 82–8; Oberndorf, pp. 138–51; *Bloomsbury* [1995], pp. 53–5; Freud/Jones, *passim*; see also, e.g., Freud/Ferenczi III, 876 F, 892 F; Freud/Abraham, 9 and 25 December 1921; Gay, pp. 387–9⟩. Apart from income in stable currencies, Freud wanted psychoanalysis to be disseminated by the students in their own countries either through direct communication or through the translation of psychoanalytic literature. Shortly after the start of their analysis, for example, Freud suggested to both Stracheys that they translate some of his works (see 157 SF, note 3, and 196 SF and note 9).

5 It is not clear whether this refers to financial support. After emigrating to New York, Eli started out selling products and gradually 'worked his way up nicely' before finally earning a respectable fortune on the corn exchange. His income was always dependent on bank crises and stock-exchange fluctuations ⟨Freud-Bernays, A., e.g. pp. 66, 118, 125, 165, 166, 169, quotation p. 71⟩. The previous year Freud had said in praise: 'Eli . . . is providing nicely for the passive female members of the family' ⟨Freud/Sam, 24 November 1919⟩. It is possible, however, that he had to be persuaded on occasion to send money, see, e.g., 130 SF.

6 Rosi was to remain Anna's 'problem child' for some years to come, as she wrote eleven years later to Lou Andreas-Salomé after a recurrence of her illness ⟨Anna/Lou, letter 346⟩. See also 120 AF and note 4.

7 Place on Capri. Ernst and Lucie were travelling in Italy 'without a fixed address' ⟨Rank on 21 October 1920 in: *Rundbriefe 1*, p. 101⟩. They were intending to remain there until the end of November ⟨Freud/Sam, 15 October 1920⟩. See also the PS to 125 SF.

129 AF[1]

Hamburg, 1 November 1920

Dear Papa,

Now I have a letter from you and one from Mama to reply to. I've been meaning to do so for two days but have not been able to get round to it. Today I am in Max's studio and am using his typewriter.

I realize from reading your 'letter of commiseration' that I had written a real complaining letter like Edith,[2] although that was not at all my intention. On the contrary, I had intended to do quite the opposite. But your diagnosis is quite correct that my bad mood came from my poor health and that is also why it is now over. I am completely well again, except that I'm freezing terribly. It's bitterly cold here with an easterly wind, which I can't say I am particularly fond of. The heating in the apartment works excellently but outside it's so cold that I keep thinking that I'm completely naked.

I'm very annoyed that you call Heinzl a 'donkey'. You have no idea how intelligent and funny he is. His boisterousness is just a natural reaction to having to sit still and being tied down, which he has to endure because of his crooked little legs. Incidentally, Max is going with him this week to a real orthopaedist, trying again to find out what can be done. Heinz is beginning to talk a lot, curiously in complete sentences, like 'What was that?' when a noise gives him a fright, 'Where is she then?' when he is looking for someone, or 'Daddy, look at that' when he wants you to admire something. Besides, he teases everyone quite delightfully and is getting more and more handsome. The day before yesterday Max took photos of him in the studio so you should be getting pictures soon. It was not easy to take his picture because he was very agitated.[3] Mama will be able to see his new winter coat in one of the pictures; blue with black fur.

Ernst is also having an unusually good phase. In fact I find it quite unfair when people just say that he is unamiable and difficult. Perhaps the new school is also doing him good; at all events, he is very communicative and quite delightful. Once he told me of the long stories he thinks up in the afternoon when he's supposed to be taking his nap; in fact, he thinks a great deal and has a lot of imagination. Every evening before he goes to sleep I have to tell him a story in the dark room, and recently made a great impression with the child Roland slaying the giant.[4] Perhaps too great, because I have noticed that he believes everything, gets easily excited and then afraid. He's no hero. After the story of Roland, he said first: 'I couldn't have killed him; I'm not strong enough.' And when I said to him that you get strong by eating a lot, he said: 'I would be strong enough, but you also have to have the things.' These 'things' are the shield, spear, sword, etc. He gets on very well with Heinz now and hasn't pushed or hit him for weeks. In fact he likes playing with him a lot, talks to him, sometimes feeds him and takes him around very nicely by the hand so that he doesn't hurt himself. He recently said to him one morning: 'Tell me, Heinzl, are you Daddy's favourite?' I asked him in return: 'Whose favourite are you, Ernst?', to which he answered promptly 'Aunt Anna's and Mummy's and Daddy's.' So it looks as if he doesn't resent the little one as long as there is someone there who likes him at least as much. He is very well liked in school and they treat him nicely. Yesterday at supper we were making up funny rhymes and his contributions were very witty and clever. His best effort was: 'Wenn Ernst Strümpfe anziehn soll, wird Fräulein Jakob doch ganz doll' ['When Ernst has to put on stockings, Fräulein Jakob gets quite worked up']. He means that he is so annoying that no one can stand it. But I don't mind; he has it from me. He can now read quite well. He recently surprised me by reading the title of a book nearby: T-o-t-e-m a-n-d T-a-b-o-o. Then he also spelled out the author. When I asked him who that was, however, he beamed and said: 'Aunt Anna'. I appreciated the compliment.

I have been spending a lot of time lately with Max, also in the studio. I feel so sorry for him that he will be completely alone again. His mood is so bad that it sometimes gets to me too and I have then to make an effort to remember that I have no reason to be as gloomy as he is. But he is really such a poor thing and doesn't have anything to interest or distract him a little.

Oli called yesterday and will probably pick me up. I am leaving next Saturday [7 November] for the Eitingons[5] and then for a few days to the

Wertheims.[6] I haven't written any more about my room because to be honest I don't really know what I should say. One factual reason is that the wallpaper has now been there for twelve years and is terribly grubby. As for emotional reasons, I have wanted to change it for years. If that doesn't move Mama, then I will really have to resign myself to it or have it done when I'm there at my own expense and under my own supervision, which I probably won't do but will prefer the good old Austrian solution of making do. But it's still a great pity.[7]

I shall be in Vienna by the end of November at the latest.[8] And I can't let you celebrate my birthday without me. I hope that you will be missing me a lot by then.[9]

Affectionately,
Anna

1 This letter was typed with only the signature 'Anna' written by hand. Typing errors were corrected without mention in the transcription.
2 Probably Edith Rischawy.
3 Max was a 'specialist in children's photographs and was therefore extremely popular and sought after in bourgeois Hamburg society' ⟨Herbert Pardo in: Weinke, p. 112⟩.
4 In his ballad *Roland Schildträger* Ludwig Uhland (1787–1862) relates a fictional episode from the childhood of Roland who, according to an old French saga, was the nephew of Charlemagne and later the bravest of his twelve paladins; in the story, the boy slays a giant with his sleeping father's weapons and takes from his shield a strength-giving jewel, sought after by King Charlemagne, so as to bring it to his uncle ⟨Uhland, vol. 1, pp. 185–91; also *Klein-Roland*, ibid., pp. 152–6, *Roland Schildträger*, ibid., pp. 185–91, and *König Karls Meerfahrt*, ibid., pp. 201f.; also Schleussinger⟩. As a child, Anna had also imagined herself as a heroine performing heroic deeds ⟨Young-Bruehl, p. 50⟩.
5 The Eitingons had already invited Anna for Christmas in 1919, but she was prevented from travelling by a rail strike ⟨Freud/Eitingon, 157 F⟩. She was not able to respond to the invitation until May 1920, when she travelled to Ernst's wedding. On that occasion she gave him the committee 'ring of covenant', with Freud's accompanying words (see 174 AF, note 5): 'Anna is finally bringing you the ring that you have been entitled to for so long. I took it off my own finger. . . . You are more deserving of it than anyone. Wear it also in memory of me, to whom you have become such a valuable friend and dear son' ⟨Freud/Eitingon, 174 F–176 F, quotation (16 May 1920), p. 200⟩.
6 On 15 November; see 132 AF.
7 After her return from Berlin, Anna 'was allowed to set up the two boys' rooms' ⟨Freud/Ferenczi III, 860 F, 25 December 1920, p. 43; also Freud/Sam, 24 December 1920⟩. See 130 SF; 'both rooms have turned out really well, much better than I had imagined . . . Everyone who comes in is quite surprised,' wrote Anna to her brother Ernst with a detailed description of the new interior design, her life and work there (26 January 1921).
8 On 15 November; see 132 AF.
9 See 132 AF, 264 SF.

130 SF

PROF. DR. FREUD

5 November 1920
Vienna, IX. Berggasse 19

My dear Anna,
Welcome to Berlin and thank you for your nice letter in which I learned first of all something proper and gratifying about the children. It is sad about Max and he can't be helped. The marks I send him are not enough either to bring about the radical change[1] in his situation that a move[2] or change of job would. In such cases we just have to wait for the famous 'time' to heal all.

The continuing devaluation of our krone has made me very rich.[3] I already own 1,600 m[ille], in other words over 1½ million but unfortunately only – let's say wedding balls,[4] if you remember them. You have also become richer, as 2,000 K from the Felix–Edward shipment are for you, so little that it would be unfriendly not to accept it. Incidentally,[5] Felix has also written that he has managed to get Uncle Eli to send 250,000 K.[6] It is now expected.

I have just received a telegram from Aunt, saying that she will be arriving Tuesday morning (9th of this month).[7] She is willing to take your room. This, I think, will satisfy your original wish to have two adjacent rooms, and the dirty wallpaper will no longer bother you. Please write *straightaway* whether my memory is correct and that you are happy with this.

Today six packages also arrived from Sam,[8] lots of good and useful things that you will also see when you come. I am now making sure that there is no scrimping with food.

You will now once again be at the source and will be able to find out everything you need about the state of the *Verlag*, the negotiations with Jones and Kola, and anything else you wish to know. I doubt that you have any shortage of translation work.[9] You won't be able to keep up with my English so easily, because I have five hours of practice every day.[10] But there is a limit to what I can learn.

The popularity in England and America seems to continue to grow. I have not had a reply from Edward yet about my suggestion.[11] That is why I haven't yet written a line of 'Popular Scraps' [original in English].

I send you my affectionate and ask you particularly to greet all of the Berliners and your hosts in particular.

Papa

1 Abbreviated in German.
2 Abbreviated in German.
3 See 125 SF. The collapse of the multinational Austrian empire destroyed its economic basis. The value of the krone had dropped considerably and was to continue to do so (100 Swiss francs were worth 567 Kr. in 1919,

2,702 Kr. in 1920, 12,200 Kr. in 1921 and 360,000 Kr. in 1922, which led to enormous price increases and brought Austria to the brink of disaster (see 179 AF and note 5). It was not until 1922 that the League of Nations Loan (Geneva Protocols, 4 October 1922) slowed down the depreciation. This held up the currency but not the economic situation. The beneficiaries were foreign banks, while large parts of the population led a sparse existence ⟨Weissensteiner, pp. 114, 116–18, 128f.; Kleindel, pp. 326, 327; Braunthal, pp. 31, 55. 62⟩.

4 Pellets or pea-sized coloured candy balls often with aniseed, fennel or coriander seeds inside. It was an old Viennese custom, which probably still existed at the start of the First World War, for guests to throw these pellets at the bride and groom at a wedding (like confetti, derived from the Italian word, which originally meant confectionery). ⟨Thanks to Elisabeth Groschopf, Vienna, 19 October 1999, with exhaustive evidence of the custom and bibliographical references.⟩

5 Spelling mistake (no umlaut) in German.

6 See 128 SF, note 5.

7 Minna Bernays had been staying in Merano ⟨Freud/Sam, 15 October 1920⟩.

8 Freud/Sam, 5 November 1920. In a letter of 27 October 1919, Freud had told his nephew about the post-war shortages in Austria; since then Sam had been sending food packages to the Freud family, often with great difficulty, until the situation gradually improved in 1921 ⟨Freud/Sam, letters until 1921, *passim*⟩.

9 Spelling mistake (no umlaut) in German; see 100 SF, note 6.

10 See 125 SF and note 2.

11 In early October, Freud wrote to Edward: 'As I have now developed a taste for it . . . I suggest the following arrangement. . . . I could, for example, write four popular scientific articles a year for a magazine selected by you. If these articles prove successful, they could be published later in the form of a small book entitled "Popular Psychoanalysis", or something similar. They should be written in an easily understandable but original manner. I can already tell you the first one I should like to write: "Psychoanalysis should not be used in polemic arguments" . . .' ⟨Bernays [1967], p. 185f.⟩. The idea came to nothing, however, because Freud could no longer accept the 'completely different way in which an American and a European editor treat the same question' ⟨ibid., pp. 186–90⟩.

131 AF

Berlin, 12 November 1920

Dear Papa,

I was very pleased to receive your letter of the 5th and Mama's card that Sopherl[1] brought today. I presume that you will have already heard from Tom himself about her engagement; she didn't want me to write about it to you before her letter.[2] The groom[3] makes a good and intelligent impression. He is a young Jewish scripture scholar and I'm very happy for Tom. I wish Mausi had also got this far, but not with her Lampl.[4] It's Tom's birthday next week and I would like to give her a proper present for the two events together.[5] Yesterday I was at the ps.a. [psychoanalytic] meeting to listen to a paper by Dr Müller.[6] Although only three candles were lit because of the strike, it was very nice and interesting. Only Sachs is puffed up, playing the omnipotent Jewish god, dishing out praise and criticism, and making jokes in the public meeting that he had not dared to do in Vienna.[7] But he feels quite happy and that is possibly the main thing. Little Frl Schott,[8] Hug's student, is already doing child analyses. You see, everyone can do much more than me.

Dr Eitingon's wife is much better and she went out for a drive yesterday for the first time, but she still remains lying down most of the day.[9] On Monday I'm moving for a few days to the Wertheims and will then come back here again. I see Oli almost every day and he makes a really good impression at the moment.[10] Life in Ernst's empty apartment is not very comfortable for him, however.[11]

I'm happy with the room change and will try to make it as nice as possible for myself. I am also very happy to hear about the rapid arrival of my trunk. I have the key myself so the unpacking will have to wait for me.

The Eitingons have a good chance of obtaining a large new apartment,[12] and I am happy for them, although I believe that guests are also well enough looked after in the old small one.

At all events, you can still write to me at this address. With a kiss,

Anna

[Lengthways in the margin]:

I have now become very fat and weigh more than ever.

1 Alexander's wife had travelled to Berlin to her recently widowed sister-in-law, Marie Freud; see 134 SF and note 1 ⟨Freud/Sam, 5 November 1920⟩.

2 Martha Gertrude Freud (1892–1930), who called herself 'Tom', third daughter of Freud's sister, Marie, married her fiancé in Berlin on 21 June 1921 ⟨Murken [1982], p. [5]; [2004], p. 80; Stammbaum Lange, Freud Family Tree, p. IV⟩. She was 'an illustrator bordering on genius of children's books, some of which she also wrote', a highly gifted artist with various creative activities ⟨Murken [2004], pp. 85, 94f., 92⟩. And yet she had no success: 'in spite of her great gifts, Tom Seidmann was a deeply unhappy person,' wrote Anna years later ⟨ibid., p. 95⟩. After the death of her husband, she put an end to her own life on 7 February 1930. 'Broken much too early by reality, she leaves behind an oeuvre that . . . deserves to be as widely known, as "Stuwwelpeter"' ⟨Obituary in *Vossische Zeitung*, Berlin, no. 36 of 11 February 1930, quoted in Murken [1982], p. [12]; a detailed tribute to Tom's life and work can be found in Murken [2004]⟩.

3 Jankef (also Jankew; Jakob) Seidmann (1892–1929), from Wisnitz (now Wiśnicz) in Bukovina ⟨Murken [2004], p. 87 and note 2⟩. He published above all translations of Jewish religious philosophers and had contact in Berlin with Gershom Sholem, Chaim Nachman Bialik and other Jewish writers who had emigrated from Soviet Russia. 'He was a master of Hebrew and introduced Tom to this language'; some of Tom's children's books also appeared in Peregrinverlag, which he founded, 'an indication of the harmonious and intensive collaboration between the couple' ⟨Murken [1982], p. [9]; [2004], pp. 87–9⟩.

But Jankew was unlucky in his business affairs; he went bankrupt and took his life in shock on 19 October 1929 ⟨Murken [2004], pp. 91, 95; Anna/Eva, letter 21⟩.

4 Young-Bruehl concludes from this remark by Anna that Mausi was not happy with 'her Lampl' ⟨Young-Bruehl, p. 97⟩. In fact the rest of her life was unhappy. Entangled in a love affair, she took her life in Vienna on 18 August 1922 ⟨Freud/Jones, letters 376, 378; Anna/Lou, letters 13, 39–73, *passim*; Young-Bruehl, p. 97 and notes 61, 62⟩.

5 Oliver and Anna gave Tom a woollen jacket for her birthday (see 135 AF) – a precious gift in view of the difficult economic conditions in Berlin at the time ⟨Freud/Abraham, 6 December 1920⟩.

6 'Dr. phil. K. Müller as guest' spoke at this meeting about 'Psychoanalysis and Morality' ⟨Müller, K., 1920⟩. On 24 September 1920 he had already delivered a paper entitled 'From the Analysis of a Painter'; on 21 December 1920 he was admitted as an extraordinary member of the Berlin group ⟨*IZ*, vol. 7 (1921), p. 118; the title 'From the Analysis of a Painter' is questionable because in the same place a paper with an identical title by Simmel is listed; nor is there any evidence of publication⟩. K. Müller is the same person as Carl Müller-Braunschweig (1881–1958), scientist and humanities scholar, who was to act as trustee when the Vienna Psychoanalytic Society was dissolved on 20 March 1938. He had become interested in psychoanalysis in 1908 and visited Freud for the first time in Vienna in 1910. Following his membership, he was active in the Society and taught from 1923 at the Berlin Institute. He was one of the people who kept the psychoanalytic idea alive during the Nazi era; after the war, he helped rebuild the Berlin Institute and the German Psychoanalytic Society, and was chairman of the Society in 1956 ⟨Bannach, p. 37; Dräger, pp. 41, 48f.; Maetze, pp. 54f., 57–63, 67; Lockot, pp. 118–26, ch. 6.7 and elsewhere; *Minutes IV*, pp. 303f.⟩.

7 Hanns Sachs moved to Berlin in 1920, where Abraham arranged for him to deliver talks on psychoanalysis and carry out teaching analyses ⟨Freud/Abraham, 10 June, 21 June, 27 June, 28 November, 6 December 1920 and elsewhere⟩. Regarding Anna's observations, Jones says: 'Sachs has evidently some infantile regression and has been behaving in Berlin, as I hear, rather like a youth visiting a *Grosstadt* for the first time. . . . I read it as being largely a reaction from years of exile, illness and dependence; his restoration to full life, an important standing, and an unexpectedly strong financial position, has carried him a little off his feet' ⟨Freud/Jones, letter 326, 11 October 1921, p. 441; see also Freud/Ferenczi III, 1045 Fer, p. 244⟩.

8 Ada Schott (1897–1959) worked from 1922 as a child analyst in the Poliklinik. In 1925 she married Carl Müller-Braunschweig ⟨Lockot, pp. 121, 342, note 9 (thanks for the oral indication of the year of birth); Eitingon [1922], p. 508; *IZ*, vol. 8 (1922), p. 528; Bannach, p. 38; Maetze, p. 66⟩.

9 See 127 AF and note 7; also 167 AF and note 9.

10 See 125 SF and note 21. See also Freud/Eitingon, e.g., 187 E–189 F; Anna/Lou, letter 172, p. 310.

11 Ernst and his wife, Lucie, spent long periods in Italy at the time (see PS to 125 SF, also 128 SF and note 7, and 137 SF).

12 At Rauchstr. 4; see 167 AF and note 7.

132 AF

Grunewald, 16 November 1920

Dear Papa,

Yesterday a new welcome phase started in my nomadic life, which I am enjoying more and more. I am living at the moment with the Wertheims[1] in a room that Aunt has stayed in several times, with its own bathroom and other necessities that are normally shared with other people.[2] The weather is so mild that you can walk in the park without a coat, and I don't find Grunewald so melancholy; quite the contrary. Today I did errands in the car and found it much more convenient than even the emptiest tram. With all the extra space here, I often think of the small and confined apartment of Max and the children, and hesitate between the desire to be a Bolshevist and a millionaire. As I don't have to decide for now, however, I am enjoying all of the good things.

On Sunday I went to see *Tannhäuser*[3] with Oli. It was the first time I'd heard it and I was very enthusiastic. For the price of the tickets that Eitingon got for us you could have bought a small house in German-Austria. But he wouldn't let us pay for them even though we asked to.

Dr Eitingon's wife is now much better, and we spent the whole week very agreeably together. I really feel at home with them and have had all the peace and quiet there that I have wished for since the summer. The doctor is unfortunately very busy and runs around from morning till evening, toiling away at least as much as you do.[4] I am reading your new work here with great pleasure.[5] I really like the idea of the ego ideal.[6]

I have finally started here in Berlin to write the new story[7] that has been worrying me all summer. It will be a little different from all the earlier ones; also more detailed. I'd like to finish it before coming to Vienna.

I am particularly happy that I became unwell[8] yesterday without any abnormal sequelae whatsoever and this time appear to be tolerating it well. So all this lazing around and being spoiled has had a good effect. I even have breakfast in bed here and feel no urge at the moment to become a useful member of human society again. But perhaps it will come back soon.

Herr Wertheim keeps asking me insistently what the story with Serbia was about, although I can't give him any precise information.[9] But I talk a lot with Frau Wertheim and get on very well with her. I am also revelling in the many flowers here. Even orchids are flowering now in the greenhouse.

The Eitingons want to pick me up from here on Saturday,[10] since the Wertheims collected me from Güntzelstrasse. They are afraid that otherwise I will get too accustomed to the large rooms and space.

After the different ways of living that I have got used to successively since I left Vienna, I feel that I will be 100 years old in a few months and not just ending the first quarter-century. But as I feel very well at the moment, I am quite willing to do the remaining seventy-five years.

I send you a kiss and am still waiting for one of you to write how much you miss me[11] before I come home.

Affectionately,

Anna

A letter for Aunt from Frau W[ertheim] is enclosed.

1 In Max-Eyth-Strasse in Dahlem ⟨Ladwig-Winters, pp. 189, 380, note 145⟩. See 135 AF, note 5. The parts of the city and the administrative districts overlap. The property at the time belonged to Dahlem but the inhabitants preferred to call it Grunewald, not least because it sounded like the neighbouring villa colony, known as the 'millionaires' colony'. ⟨I am grateful to Karl-Heinz Metzger, head of the press office of Charlottenburg-Willmersdorf district office, for this information.⟩

2 See 12 AF and note 4.

3 *Tannhäuser und der Sängerkrieg auf der Wartburg*, romantic opera in three acts (Dresden, 1845; Paris version, 1861) by Richard Wagner (1813–83).

4 Apart from his private practice, Eitingon devoted all his energies without pay to consultancy, treatment and teaching activities at the Berlin Poliklinik ⟨Eitingon [1922]; see also Freud/Eitingon, 190 E⟩.

5 *Group Psychology and the Analysis of the Ego* (1921*c*). A few years later Anna recommended to her friend Eva Rosenfeld that she read it: 'because with it I did a huge portion of my own analysis. Everything was suddenly there, my old daydreams and everything I wanted' ⟨Anna/Eva, letter 4, around September 1927, p. 113⟩. (See also Introduction, p. 7 and note 67.)

6 Freud states in *Group Psychology* that he had introduced the concept of the 'ego ideal' earlier (1914*c*, 1916–17*c*); as an aspect of the ego, as a psychological agency 'which may cut itself off from the rest of the ego and come into conflict with it . . . so that a man, when he cannot be satisfied with his ego itself, may nevertheless be able to find satisfaction in the ego ideal which has been differentiated out of the ego' ⟨1921*c*, pp. 109f.⟩. Continuing this idea, he says: 'But the ego ideal comprises the sum of all the limitations in which the ego has to acquiesce' ⟨ibid., p. 131⟩. In the later development of his structural model of the mind, in *The Ego and the Id* (1923*b*), it is then transformed into the 'superego' ⟨see editorial remarks on 1916–17*g* in *S. E.*, vol. XIV, p. 240, 3rd paragraph⟩.

7 See 101 AF and note 1.

8 Familiar and still common expression at the time for menstruation. See 135 AF, also 127 AF–129 AF.

9 Not clearly identifiable. Perhaps Herr Wertheim's question related to the recently concluded political dispute about the unification of Carinthia in the years 1918 to 1920. After the war the newly created Yugoslavia tried to bring part of the bilingual areas of southern Carinthia and Styria under its control, and its troops had made repeated incursions into the south of German-Austria. After two years of bitter resistance, the Carinthians finally managed with American aid to achieve an assurance in the Treaty of Saint-Germain-en-Laye (2/10 September 1919) that the inhabitants should decide for themselves whether they wished to maintain their territorial integrity and remain part of Austria or whether they wanted to join the Serbian-Croatian-Slovenian state. The hard-fought referendum took place on 10 October 1920, with the decision to remain part of Austria. 'This freedom fight was one of the most important

and concluding acts in the establishment of the Republic [Austria] in 1920' ⟨Wurte [1985], p. XVIII (also *passim*, e.g., pp. XXX, 55, 59, 74, 76, 147, 159f., 320); also Weissensteiner, pp. 54–9; Kleindel, p. 325; Braunthal, p. 38; Ploetz [1980], pp. 855, 949⟩. During this summer Freud was in Bad Gastein and Anna in Altaussee, but they did not mention those events in these letters (although letters are missing from the October days in question, see 126 SF and note 1).

10 Anna remained a few days longer, however; see 135 AF.

11 See 129 AF.

133 SF

PROF. DR. FREUD 18 November 1920
Vienna, IX. Berggasse 19

My dear Anna,
This should be the last letter because it is your birthday in two weeks and we expect you here earlier, and communication by mail is so tedious. I hope you continue to feel well and full of energy in Berlin and will still bring some of your extra fat back with you. Here you can look forward to a rise in salary and some translation work,[1] first for Jones. When the first financial statement from the Verlag is available, we shall decide what to do next, probably without taking account of a possible merger with Kola. Dr Radó from Budapest[2] is to be engaged to relieve Rank, an assistant for the accounts. Frau Fischer, who used to work for Heller, has been hired on probation, and Hiller is to move to Vienna to represent the English business.[3] Reik will be removed and I shall probably find another position for him independent of the Verlag.[4] Rank gives me hope that the financial statement will be very good.

Thanks to our devaluation, I have now passed the second million mark.[5] Yesterday I celebrated a reacquaintance with the dollar,[6] which I haven't seen since 1909.[7] Edward is not supporting my ambitions to become rich and hasn't replied to my proposal. By contrast, the Spanish publisher has done its accounts and should soon pay me 350 pesetas, equivalent to about 24,000 K, for my part.[8] Max should also be getting money again soon from the Verlag.[9]

As you can see only business news occurs to me. There is really very little science, and as far as the family is concerned you can tell me more than I can report to you. I congratulated Tom right away and hope it proves to be the right thing. So the poor, silly Gretel[10] is really failing. Good news from Ernst and Lux from Anacapri. He has already put on weight and accepts the need to do something about his catarrh. He hopes, however, that the trip to Italy will overcome it, but it is not likely to happen. Don't forget to ask Sachs to give you or me directly *precise information about the cost of the sanatorium in Davos*.[11] Ernst wants it to help him with his decision.[12] He can no longer write to him (E.) directly.

Of course we are looking forward to your coming home. All these old people, it's quite depressing. Perhaps you can travel with Aunt Sophie[13] and avoid the untamed Czechoslovakia in that way.

Affectionate greetings to you, the Eitingons and all friends and relatives,
Papa

1 Spelling mistake (no umlaut) in German. See 125 SF and note 7.

2 Sándor Radó (1890–1972), 'a very talented young law student, who recently became a medical student in order to learn psychoanalysis' ⟨Ferenczi to Freud on 27 May 1911 in: Freud/Ferenczi I, 222 Fer, p. 283⟩. He was one of the founder members in 1913 of the Hungarian Psychoanalytic Society and became its secretary ⟨ibid., 394 Fer, 12 May 1913 and note 1⟩. During the Soviet Republic in 1919 he had a certain influence for a time in university circles and used this, amongst other things, to obtain a professorship for Ferenczi in psychoanalysis, but had to leave Hungary after the change in government ⟨ibid., II, 802 Fer, 812 Fer, 814 Fer; *IZ*, vol. 5 (1919), p. 228; Harmat, p. 77; Freud/Ferenczi III, 855 F⟩. In autumn 1922 he moved to Berlin, where until 1931 he worked amongst other things as a lecturer at the Institute and later in the education committee. In 1924 he took over Rank's *Verlag* business for a time after Rank's split from Freud (see 43 SF, note 9) ⟨Freud/Jones, letter 441⟩. He became editor-in-chief of *IZ* and, in 1927, of *Imago* until he emigrated to New York in 1931. There he set up a Psychoanalytic Institute on the Berlin model and in 1944 became professor of psychiatry and head of the first Columbia University Center for Psychoanalytic Training and Research, and continued to carry out analysis even after his retirement ⟨Alexander [1966]⟩. See also Freud's letters to Radó (1995*c*).

3 Eric Hiller (1893–?), Jones's office assistant, had already been in Vienna in 1919 on *Verlag* business (see 106 SF, end of note 6) and attended the Hague Congress in September 1920 as a (non-practising) founder member of the British Psychoanalytical Society ⟨*IZ*, vol. 6 (1920), p. 377⟩. He arrived in Vienna in December 1920 and was 'taken over [in the Vienna group] from the London group' ⟨*IZ*, vol. 7 (1921), p. 400; Freud/Jones, letters 293, 294; Jones III, pp. 32, 34, 38, 50⟩. The collaboration with Hiller was not very profitable, however (see 160 AF and note 5, also 181 SF, note 5), and in March 1923 he returned to England, where he joined the London group again from 1924 to *c.* 1928 ⟨Mühlleitner, p. 147f.⟩.

4 Freud had already complained on a number of occasions about Reik's incompetence and unreliability ⟨Freud/Jones, letter 183; Freud/Ferenczi II, 824 F⟩. He therefore offered him 'the position of literary director, with responsibility for reviews and the annual report', and tried (in vain) to accommodate him in Berlin ⟨Freud/Abraham, 28 November, 6 December 1920⟩. On 1 January 1921, Reik set up an international central office for psychoanalytic literature as a scientific information centre ⟨Reik, 1976, p. 105; *IZ*, vol. 7 (1921), p. 110; *Rundbriefe 2*, p. 18⟩.

5 See 130 SF and note 3.

6 The currency in which Freud's American students paid (see 128 SF, note 4).

7 The year in which Freud gave five lectures on psychoanalysis (1910*a*) to mark the twentieth anniversary of the founding of Clark University in Worcester, Massachusetts, USA.

8 In 1922 the first translations by Luis Lopez-Ballesteros y de Torres appeared; see 115 SF and note 2, 166 SF and notes 4 and 5.

9 For photography which he did for the *Verlag* ⟨Freud to Max, e.g., 27 July 1919 and elsewhere⟩. See also 138 SF, note 4.
10 Freud used the term 'silly Gredl' in the meaning of 'silly billy'; see, e.g., Freud/Bernays, letter 118 S; see also 181 SF.
11 Sachs had been in a sanatorium in Davos for some time in 1918 for a – fortunately curable – pulmonary tuberculosis ⟨Freud/Ferenczi II, 759 F; Jones II, pp. 223f.; Freud/Binswanger, 117 F; Harmat, p. 65⟩.
12 Ernst decided on a cure in Arosa ⟨Freud to Ernst, e.g., 7 October, 7 November, 15 November 1920; Freud/Sam, 21 January 1921⟩. See 87 SF, note 7.
13 See 134 SF.

134 SF

PROF. DR. FREUD 21 November 1920
Vienna, IX. Berggasse 19

My dear Anna,
Yesterday an express letter arrived from Tom complaining about Aunt's[1] condition and asking urgently for advice as to what is to be done with her. You can imagine how easy it is to give such advice from a distance. They are unfortunately all so helpless and inept; there must be a complicated situation in the house because Aunt Sophie, instead of helping, which is otherwise so much her way, is constantly sending telegrams asking to be recalled. She appears not to be able to stand it there and we don't know why. (All this is confidential and to be treated with discretion!)

I would therefore request that you ask around in our circle, best of all with our trusted family curator Eitingon, which doctor it is most useful to consult so as to assess and make a decision on a heart complaint of this type (or is it just migraines) and then tell Tom that this doctor should really be fetched. He shouldn't be an official authority who acts on a single occasion but a doctor who carries out treatment himself. But do it in a way that the poor harassed man[2] does not feel the need to take on yet another task. One cannot sacrifice everything and everyone for one's family. Besides, it's not his speciality at all.

It is unlikely that you will be able to intervene successfully either, because anyone who is so unintelligent that they cannot obtain advice themselves will not usually be able to accept advice from others. But do it anyway for my sake. I can't do anything else from here. I imagine that there is no chance of Aunt travelling to Vienna at the moment.

I don't have much new to report since my last letter. The best news was your letter and the good news about your stay in Berlin, which, by the way, will soon be giving way to a stay in Vienna.

Affectionately,
Papa

1 In this case Freud's sister, Marie ('Mitzi/Mizi/Mizzi/Mietzi') (1861–1942), is being referred to. More details on her life can be found in Tögel [2004*b*]. Her

husband, Mauritz ('Morris/Maurice') Freud (1857–1920), a distant relative, died of a heart attack on 7 September while Freud was in the Netherlands ⟨Murken [2004], p. 86⟩. Freud visited her on his journey back and reported to Sam: 'The conditions at Berlin after Morris' death are so intricate that nobody can say how rich or rather how poor they are' ⟨Freud/Sam, 15 October 1920; also 27 May and 2 October 1920; Freud/Jones, letter 287⟩. See 135 AF. Freud said of this sister to Wilhelm Fliess in 1898: 'None of us has a relationship with her; she has always been isolated and rather peculiar. In her mature years this has manifested itself in pathological parsimony, while the rest of us are all spendthrifts' ⟨1985*c*, 27 April 1898, p. 311⟩. See Freud's letters to her, 2004*d*.

2 Eitingon.

135 AF

Dahlem, 21 November [1920]

Dear Mama and Papa,

This letter is from me (Anna) and not from Oliver as it seems at first glance.[1] But Papa knows that since I have become a secretary other people have to write letters for me and in this way I hope that I will be able to continue to put up with my new job. Oli is eating with me today because it's Sunday and I am currently having my afternoon rest.

I was very pleased to receive the letter of the 15th from Mama and Aunt; I'm not keen on sending the key for the trunk, and the revision might have to wait until my return. The baby things for Esti[2] are also in it.

I'm not sure whether I will be able to leave on the date originally planned (1st).[3] I feel so comfortable here that I might add on a few days. I was completely well this time again after four days;[4] I don't have any pain whatsoever when walking and feel much better than I have done for a long time.

I am still at the Wertheims. I was unable to bring myself so quickly to part from the 'palace and grounds'[5] in which I otherwise live only in my imagination,[6] from my bathroom and the other pleasant things here. Asserting their right as a branch of the family, however, the Eitingons are now beginning to insist energetically on my return. We had a small party here on Wednesday (a public holiday here)[7] at which Oliver and I both had a very good time. Oliver went afterwards to Tom's birthday celebration. We are both developing social skills.[8]

We gave Tom a really beautiful woollen jacket for her engagement and birthday, which she was indescribably happy about. Soferl will give you more information about the situation in Bambergerstr.;[9] apart from Tom's engagement it is quite sad and Aunt Mietzi is also physically in a very pitiable condition. But Tom is really happy, and Oliver and I believe that Jankew means the best. They should not have any worries for the moment thanks to a large transfer from New York.[10]

I recently visited Abraham for lunch; it was quite nice and I was very amiable. I'm like that most of the time now.[11]

A short while ago I received the first letter from Ernsti written by himself. It was so delightful that I cannot bring myself to send it to you; the spelling is still a bit poor.

My various outfits are admired as much here in Grunewald as I admired those of Dr Eitingon's wife in Güntzelstrasse. I can no longer decide whether I am a lady of fashion obsessive about her clothes or basically just an averagely dressed primary school teacher. It's all relative. I have become very friendly with Elschen[12] and am teaching her lots of bad habits as I find her a little too well brought up at the moment.

We are swimming here in begonias, chrysanthemums, cyclamens and even orchids. I wish you something from all of them.

Affectionately,

[Anna's handwriting] Anna

PS Please remind Mathilde that I really need my sofa throw this year. She said she wanted to dye hers.

1 With the exception of Anna's signature, the letter and PS are in Oliver's handwriting.
2 Martin's wife was expecting her first child, Anton Walter Freud (see 159 SF, note 8) ⟨Freud/Sam, 15 October, 5 November 1920⟩.
3 Anna did not leave on that date; see 136 SF, 137 SF.
4 See 132 AF and note 8.
5 Wilhelm Wertheim owned several properties in Dahlem (see 132 AF, note 1), one of which 'had an area of 17,291 m^2, which was an enormous size, even for those days. On it was the villa designed by Messel with annexes such as a coachman's lodge, gardener's lodge and orangery, . . . also listed as a "palace".' The entire property was confiscated by the Nazis in their persecution of the Jews. Goebbels' *Stiftung für Bühnenschaffende, Deutsche Tanzschule und Deutsche Tanzbühne* (Foundation for Theatre People, German Dance School and German Dance Theatre) 'purchased' the Messel villa and grounds in 1938–9 for 'cultural' purposes. It no longer exists. ⟨Ladwig-Winters, pp. 410f., 417–19 – with thanks for further oral information.⟩
6 See 36 AF, note 6.
7 Day of Prayer and Repentance.
8 See 28 SF, note 2.
9 Freud's sister, Marie, had an apartment at Bamberger Strasse 5, Berlin-W ⟨postcard from Freud of 14 September 1912, from San Cristoforo to Marie Freud, LoC SF Cont. 1 (now Freud 2004*d*)⟩.
10 See 128 SF, note 5.
11 Reference to something Anna said as a child at the birthday of Aunt Minna: 'On birthdays I am mostly a little bit good' ⟨Freud 1985*c*, 27 June 1899, p. 357⟩.
12 Elsa Harmening, née Barckmann, later married 'Z.' (1911–93), an adoptive daughter of the childless Wertheims ⟨Ladwig-Winters, pp. 407f.; further details about Elsa (including a photo 'Wilhelm and Martha Wertheim with Elsa and others in front of the orangery', p. 409) in ibid., pp. 189, 292, notes 613 and 614, pp. 295, 408–16, 420⟩.

136 SF[1]

[3 December 1920]

Happy Birthday 1920
Papa

1 The text, in Latin letters, is written on the front of an envelope, which was presumably prepared for the event that Anna should be at home for her birthday. See 137 SF.

137 SF

PROF. DR. FREUD

6 December 1920
Vienna, IX. Berggasse 19

My dear Anna,
So I have to write you another letter after all! I'm sure you will have understood that the absence of letters from us on your birthday had to do with our uncertainty about your return.

You are right: a birthday cannot be postponed. It's possible for the presents but not for the feelings. I can see from you how old I am, because you are as old as psychoanalysis. Both have caused me concerns but I basically expect greater joy from you than from it. I am sure you will also be willing to promise not to torment me for nine hours a day.

Naturally, I don't yet understand some of your allusions.[1] It is nice and honourable that you have been able to keep up and intensify all your relationships. I am sure they didn't make it difficult for you.

Now for some news. Mama and Käthe Brasch[2] were delightful and quickly earned a front seat in the gathering of relatives. Käthe has undertaken to inform you that we have no objection if you want to spend a few more weeks with Frau Mirra in Merano. You will receive so much money for your birthday that you will easily be able to afford it.[3] The condition, of course, is that she is unaccompanied. I hope you still have time to think about it, and then you can travel with her directly.[4] A telegram arrived this morning saying that Ernst and Lux will be arriving tomorrow in the morning or evening.[5] The Brasch[es] were inconsolable that they already had tickets. Ernst's room is ready for him.

Eitingon will have told you from the circular letter[6] that I have turned down an invitation to go to New York for six months.[7] The only tempting aspect was that I could have travelled (?) and spent half of the time with him.[8] Otherwise the shabbiness of the invitation, from Edward naturally with the best intentions, just annoyed me. #[9] 10,000 guarantee, of which 5,000 for the journey and expenses, albeit with the freedom to earn more through greater torment, if I can stand it. Don't tell me that the 5,000 that I would take with me are 2½ million K. The tax there and here would have taken so much away that there would have been little more left than I could earn in Vienna. A million K is nothing more than a hollow sound; in reality it is just # 2,000. At another time, no American would have dared to make me such an offer.[10] They are banking on our dalles[11] and want to buy us cheaply.

I send you affectionate greetings. Write soon about the prospects for our seeing each other again.[12]

Papa

1 A letter from Anna appears to be missing.
2 Ernst's mother-in-law, Elise Brasch, née Belgard, and her daughter, Käthe ⟨envelope, FM London; correspondence between Ernst and Lucie Freud, Exeter, Box X 503⟩. The Brasches had interrupted their return journey to Berlin from a holiday in Rome to visit the Freuds in Vienna ⟨Freud to Max Halberstadt, 5 December 1920⟩.
3 See 136 SF.
4 The plan did not come to fruition. Eitingon accompanied his wife himself. He had originally intended to visit relatives in New York while she was taking the cure but was unable to obtain a visa ⟨Freud/Eitingon, 190 E, 191 F⟩.
5 Grammar mistake in German.
6 *Rundbriefe 1*, 5 December 1920/W, p. 198.
7 'Don't accept for me,' Freud cabled to his nephew, Edward, explaining in more detail in a subsequent letter. The invitation was from Scofield Thayer, editor-in-chief and publisher of *Dial* – perhaps not quite selflessly, since Thayer came the following year (through Edward's brokering) as a patient himself to Vienna ⟨Bernays [1967], pp. 186–91, 193⟩.
8 See Freud/Eitingon, 190 E.
9 See 107 SF, note 9.
10 'The American offer has shown in its paltriness how hollow, indeed, all assertions of popularity, esteem, and the like are' ⟨Freud/Ferenczi III, 860 F, 25 December 1920, p. 43⟩.
11 Yiddish for poverty, misery.
12 Anna was back home on 13 December; see 124 SF, note 2.

1921

138 SF

PROF. DR. FREUD

29 June 1921
Vienna, IX. Berggasse 19

My dear Anna,
I am enclosing the most recent letter from Oli,[1] which arrived on the 25th, and am writing to him myself today.

Your reports, letters and telegram[2] were naturally of the utmost interest to us. We hope that the good news continues, also with regard to your dear hay.[3] It would be very nice if the two poor souls were to have a proper good time in Aussee. Send Max my sincere regards and tell him that I will soon be able to send him cigars, also that 9,000 mk from the Verlag and 1,300 from Frankfurt are waiting for him for the beginning of August.[4]

You will, of course, want to hear the news from here. The patients will be holding the line until the evening of 14 July.[5] I successfully asserted your claims with the *Verlag*.[6] You can have an issue of the journal (IV) sent to you in Aussee if you want. The Group Psychology has been promised to me before I leave.[7] Heller appears worn out and wants to sell us everything he still has on analysis.[8] Rank has new Englishwomen;[9] we will be seeing each other twice more.

The demolition is going on busily at home and since yesterday the wallpapering of your former room as well.[10] Since Marianne left, the dynasty of Fanny, grandmother and granddaughter has been managing the household very virtuously, but yesterday came a telegram from M. in which she says that she is not staying and asks if she can come back. Lucie has been a welcome visitor on several occasions, today to say farewell.[11] On Sunday we even went on an excursion up Kahlenbergstr from Beethovengang and met Martin coming down, with whom we stopped for a spritzer. We didn't see the Strauss monument until the evening. Bronze is no fabric for trousers.[12] An ice cream there costs 50 kr. Ernst writes that he is already building two houses and regards himself as a busy architect;[13] he has put his wife in charge of his correspondence, which she deals with as if it were her own.

The first 200 cigars from Lampl have arrived via the mission and the others will apparently be coming in the next few weeks. Figdor[14] has done a good job in delivering.

We received news today of how sadly our relatives in Odessa are going under.[15] Jascha[16] died a year and a half ago of spotted fever, Anna Deiches (the eldest[17] sister) has managed to make it to Krakow with a nine-year-old granddaughter. The Russian prince, her son-in-law,[18] has also died. You see, a colourful series of news.

Mama insists that we don't celebrate her birthday and that I don't come to Aussee on the 26th.[19] I am sorry on Ernsti's account but as I would need three days for the trip, of which I could only spend half a day with you, I will probable concede. We will celebrate the birthday here and have already bought a very nice woollen coat (10 mK). We are still looking for a comfortable armchair.

The weather is occasionally very heavy, which makes the English guessing game[20] while[21] carpets are being beaten [English in brackets after the German][22] into hard work. But that will also pass.

I wish you and the two men a wonderful time and send my affectionate greetings,

Papa

1 'Dissatisfied letters from Oli. He doesn't seem to be able to get used to the unreliability of the situation in Romania' ⟨Freud/Eitingon, 212 F, 31 July 1921, p. 257; see also 211 E, 217 E⟩. See PS to 125 SF and note 21; also 141 AF. Oliver returned shortly afterwards 'and was in Berlin again from August' ⟨Freud/Eitingon, 210 F, note 4; 216 F⟩.

2 The letters and the telegram are all missing. Anna was on her summer holiday with Max and his elder son, Ernstl, in Altaussee, in the guesthouse belonging to her sister-in-law, Marie Rischawy (see 139 F, 143 SF), where Martha joined them on 17 July (see 144 AF). (For the summer plans that year, see, among others, Freud/Ferenczi II, 868 F, 876 F; also Freud/Jones, letters 318–25).

3 Anna's hay fever (see 140 AF).

4 Freud repeatedly obtained commissions from the *Verlag* (see 133 SF, note 9) for Max and helped him otherwise by sending money regularly, here the fee from a Frankfurt patient ⟨Freud to Max, 15 February 1920 and ibid., *passim*⟩.

5 On the following day, Freud left with Minna Bernays for Bad Gastein (see 142 SF).

6 Freud represented Anna's wishes vis-à-vis Jones regarding translations: 'I think it would be nice if you could reserve some work in this line for Anna, who now is in excellent health and threatens to go back to school, if we don't give her work' ⟨Freud/Jones, letter 327, 6 November 1921, p. 443⟩.

7 The promise was kept (see 142 SF); the *Verlag* published an initial print run of 5,000 copies ⟨Marinelli, p. 19; there are also (pp. 19–22, 27) further statistics on publications and print runs⟩.

8 Until the founding of the *Verlag* Heller still had publication rights for psychoanalytical literature, which were redeemed whenever reprints were planned. Apart from books, this also applied to articles in *IZ* and *Imago*. Buchhandlung Heller also continued provisionally to manage the distribution

of printed works ⟨Marinelli, pp. 12f., 16, 19; Zerfass and Huppke, pp. 17f. [no. 46]⟩.

9 Three female lay workers from Brunswick Square Clinic, London ⟨Schröter [1996], p. 1166; for details of this polyclinic, see ibid., pp. 1162–7; thanks to Michael Schröter⟩.

10 See 126 SF and note 16; 130 SF.

11 Lucy Wiener, who was preparing to move to Berlin ⟨Freud/Sam, 25 July 1921; also Bernays [1967], p. 191⟩. See also 149 SF, 150 SF, 167 AF.

12 The monument to Johann Strauss the Younger (1825–99), famous operetta composer and 'Waltz King'; it was erected by Edmund Hellmer in the Stadtpark, Vienna, in 1921 and shows the composer in gold-plated bronze, holding a violin in his hand and standing in front of a marble arch with sheets and dancing couples in relief on it ⟨Czeike [1999], p. 197⟩.

13 See 164 AF and note 4 and letterhead to 165 AF.

14 M. Figdor, a brother in the B'nai B'rith lodge. From congratulations sent by Martha and Sigmund Freud on 5 August 1938 to M. and Melanie Figdor, on the occasion of their son's marriage, it would appear that the families had been friends from earlier years ⟨LoC SF, Cont. 25; thanks to Ernst Falzeder⟩.

15 Two brothers of Freud's mother (and families) lived in Odessa: 'Freud's favourite uncle' Hermann (Herz) Nathansohn (1822–95) and Nathan Nathansohn (*c.* 1825–?) ⟨Krüll, table 3, p. 234 and note 37⟩.

16 This could be Jakob [Jascha], one of the sons of Hermann Nathansohn ⟨Krüll, ibid.⟩. Apart from the name Jakob, Krüll has no further details; see, however, a mention in Mathilde Freud's youthful letters ⟨Gödde [2003], pp. 64, 73, 282, 292, 301, 365⟩.

17 Spelling mistake (no umlaut) in the original. Anna Deiches, Jascha's 'eldest sister', was possibly one of 'several daughters' of Hermann Nathansohn; a cousin of these daughters (and hence of Freud), Heinrich Nathansohn (1858–?), was a lawyer in Krakow. He was the son of another brother of Freud's mother, Adolf Nathansohn (*c.* 1830–62), who died in Vienna ⟨Krüll, p. 234 and note 37⟩.

18 Unknown.

19 Martha was sixty on 26 July and spent her birthday in Aussee; see 142 SF and note 6.

20 The analysis sessions in English.

21 Spelling mistake (no umlaut) in the original.

22 See 170 AF and note 6, 177 AF and note 7.

139 AF

[Altaussee,] 4 July 1921

Dear Papa,

Max has decided spontaneously to visit you for a day and I tended to encourage rather than discourage him, in spite of the stress that the journey will probably cause for him. I think that at present it is almost more important for him to have something to look forward to and to have company and a change. Don't keep him for too long, however, so that he can carry on gaining weight here.[1]

I can already say with a degree of certainty that the plan of having the two of them come here was a good one. I think we will not find it so easy to part from Ernstl in the middle of the summer and will probably want to keep him until September.[2] Perhaps you could speak with Max about it.

I talk to Ernstl every evening and find him much more trusting than I expected. He has started telling me his made-up stories again and apart from that talks a lot and with great tenderness about Sophie. As far as I can tell, he has arrived in his questioning at the point where he is asking what his father had to do with the birth of the child. In between are all the mysteries of dying and being dead. How much can he already be told at this age?

Yesterday he related to me a nice extract from his 'story': Heinerle, who is certainly too young for him in real life, is already three and a half years old in it.

Thank you again for your long letter with all the good and bad news. I would like the issue of the journal and, of course, also *Group Psychology* when it appears. Today I received 2,000 kr from Hausmanns[3] for my private session.

If Max does not abandon his idea of coming to Gastein, would you mind if I came with him?[4] I think Edith[5] would look after Ernstl in my place for two days and Mama would also already be here by then, of course.[6]

I hope very much that your patients no longer torment you too much and that you have a good time with Max. Affectionate greetings,

Your Anna

I have given Max 4,000 of the 10,000 K because he wanted to buy all kinds of things here and needed around 4,000 K provisionally for the journey and joint expenditures, but I still have plenty of money of my own in reserve.

1 After a visit of a week to Vienna, Max returned to Altaussee on 11 July; see 140 AF.
2 See 146 SF and note 5.
3 Unknown.
4 Freud advised Anna against accompanying Max, who also ultimately abandoned the idea; see 142 SF, 144 SF with Anna's footnote; see also 73 SF, note 1.
5 Edith Rischawy.
6 Martha arrived on 17 July; see 144 AF.

140 AF

Aussee, 10 July 1921

Dear Papa,

If you have been counting the hours or days, you must be down to quite a small and hopeful number by now. I think that this will be the last letter I write to you from here [to Vienna] and hope that you will let me know that you have arrived safely in Gastein. If you still have time to go into town in Vienna, Ernstl and I have a request: could you send us *Hirzepinzchen*? I think he would find it huge fun. He is not one himself, however.[1]

Max sent a telegram announcing his arrival tomorrow evening, and I am very curious to hear what he has to say. The week alone with Ernstl has not done either of us any harm. We get on excellently and absolutely peacefully and never have any conflicts, and I am proud that he has not yet cried. I believe that in some things we have misjudged him in the past; he is neither very fully formed in his character nor independent or unapproachable. He only appears alien to me for some moments when he gets caught in a strange and quite silly mood, which he thinks is funny, and consists mostly of turning words around and talking nonsense. Oli used to be like that sometimes as a child.

Today he asked me while we were out walking what 'parting' [Scheiden] means, from the song 'Winter ade, Scheiden tut weh' ['Goodbye winter, parting is painful']. I explained it to him, adding that parting doesn't have to be painful, and I asked him if he had been sad to leave Hamburg. He laughed and said: 'Not at all!' Or when he has to leave Aussee. That appeared to affect him and he said 'Oh, yes!' and asked how long he would still be staying, and started to calculate and was very upset to find out that August comes right after July. I had to comfort him and assure him that his departure had not yet been fixed for certain. His appetite is improving and he is even developing a certain passion for whipped cream and pastries. He argues at least twice a day with Mariechen Blitz, which naturally calls for the same number of reconciliations. They are quite inseparable, and I have made friends with the mother.[2]

Helene arrived today with the boys,[3] who I hope will be a pleasant addition to the stay here, which is a bit lonely. The weather is fine and my hay fever at the moment quite tolerable.

I look forward to hearing from you soon.

Your Anna

1 *Hirzepinzchen*, stories (in verse with irregular rhymes) by Marie v. Ebner-Eschenbach (1830–1916). The little prince, who is vain and bossy, undergoes a change of character following a number of chastening trials and is able to regain the love and acknowledgement of his family and friends.
2 Possibly holiday guests in Marie Rischawy's guesthouse; see 'Dr Blitz's wife' in 141 AF.
3 Helene Gebert with her two sons Karl and Fritz (see 72 SF, note 2).

141 AF

Aussee, 14 July 1921

Dear Papa,
I wish you a pleasant journey tomorrow and a safe arrival in Gastein. Hopefully the weather will stay as fine as it looks like being at the moment and it will be as nice there as it is here.

Today Max and I were with Dr Blitz's wife on the Loser and came back home in good form and not too tired with rhododendrons and gentian. I was quite happy to be up the mountain again after so many years and to find that I am no longer quite such a poor climber as I used to be.[1] That's all thanks to the 'excess energy'.[2] I left Ernstl for the day with Helene and Edith, because Max had so much wanted to go on the walk and had been in a good mood so little in the last few days that I didn't want to dissuade him. And the little one has behaved here so impeccably that everyone is enthusiastic about him and is willing to look after him every day if necessary. He even made his own bed this morning, although no one asked him to do so. He is becoming nicer, fresher and cheekier every day and is clearly flourishing here. He is also eating at least twice as much as he did at the beginning, and the day before yesterday after a copious supper he stayed seated at the table and said: 'I think there's something more.' You can only appreciate this properly if you had seen him eating in Hamburg. I'd love to see him put on some weight, but that obviously can't happen so fast.

Helene Gebert feels at home here and we enjoy each other's company.

We are looking forward to Mama's arrival.[3] I received the letter you enclosed from Oli[4] today and thank you for it. He now seems to have got over the experiences in Berlin.[5]

I hope to hear from you soon and send affectionate greetings to you and Aunt.

Your Anna

1 See 114 AF and note 7.
2 Reference to Maurice de Guérin's story *The Centaur* (1840). Ernst had given Anna the book (translated by Rilke) as a present and she wrote to him: 'You see, if I really give up school . . . it will be so as one day to have excess energy like the centaur. The emotion and the freedom in which it lives and its desire always to experience life are incredibly likeable. I am sometimes almost afraid that my whole life will pass me by without my noticing' ⟨12 March 1920, FM London⟩. See Anna/Lou, letter 44, p. 74; letter 58, p. 101f. See also 23 AF, note 4, 79 AF, note 6, and Introduction, pp. 1f.
3 See 144 AF.
4 See 138 SF and note 1.
5 The unsuccessful wooing of Henny Fuchs, whom he married after all two years later; see 192 AF and note 8 ⟨Anna/Lou, letters 70, 91⟩.

142 SF

PROF. DR. FREUD — Gastein, 16 July 1921
Vienna, IX. Berggasse 19

My dear Anna,
The change in my existence is incredible. I haven't spoken a word of English since lunchtime the day before yesterday, and today have done nothing except to pick three white orchids[1] – the grass has already been cut – and have not earned anything. The journey was apparently quite

comfortable, but the heat was so bad that neither of us has yet got rid of the feeling of having boiled. Gastein was delightful yesterday evening and today until 2.30 p.m., our rooms were waiting for us and we were already settled in the same evening.[2] Now a protracted thunderstorm has erupted; it is already 5 o'clock and it is still thundering and raining, probably for the whole of next week. But that's fine as well.

I am writing to you today mainly for two things. First, Mama is quite miserable but could not be persuaded to consult a doctor and yet has quite immoderate ideas about the severity of her condition.[3] I hope very much that rest and care in Pension R.[ischawy] will do her good, but I would ask you at the next opportunity to get Dr Jung[h] to pester her and if possible to get a more uninvolved person like Marie R.[ischawy], Frau Zinner[4] or even Max to get her to accept being a patient. We ourselves have no influence over her. I think it is just her old intestinal catarrh, and measures like massage, baths, etc., would probably be quite useful along with her diet.

The second thing is to ask you not to accompany Max here.[5] The journey from Aussee to Gastein takes a whole day (if you're lucky) and then there's another day soon afterwards. The journey is extremely arduous, as we have been able to observe from all the people who didn't travel from Vienna with a reserved seat. In addition, Gastein is overcrowded (in our guesthouse, for example, there is not even a small room free now) and the threat of bad weather makes it senseless to come here on a short visit. Max will just have to chance it and he could be unlucky, but at least he doesn't have to travel back to Aussee. As you know, in view of the difficult journey Mama has absolved me directly from visiting her for her birthday, as I had wanted.[6] You will hopefully be well rewarded for your restraint. There is still Gastein as well.[7]

On the last day the *Group Psychology* (1921*c*), *Beyond*,[8] your Jones,[9] and the Stärcke[10] all arrived. Here there was a letter waiting from Varendonck[11] and his French thesis on the development of consciousness.[12] He now has a PhD from the Sorbonne, but I shall write to him and tell him not to be so agitated and to want to discover so much.[13]

I have not taken any work and only two books (textbooks) with me, and would be interested to see whether complete idleness and gentle boredom are not the most radical ways of resting. The year was really not easy and next year won't be either. Letters, corrections and the like don't count as work.[14]

Mama is bringing 100,000 kr, perhaps no longer untouched. It won't be enough. Let me know *in good time* when it is running out so that I can arrange for Martin to replenish the stocks.

Gastein is, of course, not cheap, but given the devaluation of the krone this is not surprising. A meal costs 750 kr per person. Aunt says that in Germany she paid 40[15] marks for less. Our first meal while the weather was still fine was under trees with a splendid view, not far from the house. Cart from the train yesterday only 300 kr; Aunt's ability to walk is still very modest.

Thank you very much for all the news, particularly about the child. I hope you continue to remain 'flourishing'.

Give my sincere regards to Max; he should come unless it looks too bleak.[16]

Affectionately,
Papa

1 See 95 SF and note 9.
2 In other words they had settled in at Villa Wassing (see 109 SF and note 3), where they remained until 14 August (see 150 SF).
3 'The boys loved to tell the story of her reaction to the suggestion from the governess that a doctor should be called to see a feverish Freud child. She snapped: "How can I telephone the doctor, I don't yet know myself what is the matter with the child?" ⟨Young-Bruehl, p. 38⟩.
4 The housekeeper in charge of the staff. She lived next door 'where Frau Rischawy's brother Dr Hollitscher was also staying'. 'To all of us she was Frau Resi.' ⟨Thanks to Frau Pep Pucher, owner of the neighbouring house, Puchen 1973, for the kind information, 24 June and 8 July 2002.⟩
5 See 139 AF and note 4.
6 See 138 SF and note 19.
7 See 73 SF, note 1.
8 1920*g*, second reprint.
9 Anna's translation of Jones 1920*a*; see 125 SF, note 7.
10 August Stärcke (1880–1954), doctor of medicine, Dutch psychiatrist and neurologist, doctor at the Hospital of the Willem Arntz Foundation in Den Holder near Utrecht. He did not do analysis but carried out research and communicated it to the Dutch medical profession; amongst other things, in 1916 he translated Freud's *Psychopathology of Everyday Life* (1901*b*) into Dutch. From 1911 to 1917 he was a member of the Vienna Psychoanalytic Society and then of the Dutch society, which he co-founded. For the work *Psychoanalysis and Psychiatry* (1921), mentioned here by Freud, he received a prize for outstanding psychoanalytical work ⟨Freud 1921*d*) (*Minutes III*, p. XVII; Spanjaard⟩.
11 Julien (also Julian/Juliaan) Honoré Marie Varendonck (1879–1924), initially a primary school teacher, later a triple PhD, pioneer of psychoanalysis in Belgium where, amongst other things, he founded a 'Cabinet de Psychanalyse' to treat abnormal children and neurotic adults. He was an extraordinary member of the Nederlandsche Vereeniging voor Psycho-Analyse. In 1922 he delivered a paper at the 7th International Psychoanalytic Congress in Berlin. He died unexpectedly of a trivial operation. ⟨*IZ*, vol. 8 (1922), p. 112, and Congress report, ibid., pp. 488–91 with paper in full; *IZ*, vol. 10 (1924), p. 429; Federn, P. [1924]; *The National Union Catalog*, vol. 630, p. 95.⟩
12 *L'évolution des facultés conscientes* (1921*a*). It is prefaced by Henri Bergson's statement that the investigation of the unconscious was the main task of the century that was starting. ⟨I thank Stéphane Michaud, Paris, for this information.⟩
13 An earlier work by Varendonck (1908) had already been reviewed in 1909 by Eduard Hitschmann in the Vienna Group (*Minutes II*, p. 148 and note 7). In 1920 Freud had presented Varendonck's *The Psychology of Day-Dreams* (1921*b*), which at the time was not yet in print, in his contribution

'Ergänzungen zum Traumlehre' (Freud 1920*f*) at the Hague Conference. Anna later translated the book into German – with the indication 'authorized translation by Anna Freud' – under the title *Über das vorbewusste phantasierende Denken* (1922) (see 161 SF). Freud had written an introduction (in English) to the original edition (1921*b*), the first part of which was included by Anna as 'Geleitwort' in the German edition (probably Freud's own translation).

14 Thus Freud did not count as 'work' the writing of a paper on 'psychoanalysis and telepathy', which he presented to the Committee members during a trip together to the Harz (see 153 AF, note 2). From the dating of the manuscript (published posthumously and abridged) and a brief reference to it (1941*d*, pp. 177, 191), it is clear that it was written during this time in Gastein (also from Freud/Eitingon, 212 F). ⟨For confirmation of the date and a detailed comparison of the published version with the manuscript, see Grubrich-Simitis [1993], pp. 259–75; also Strachey [1955].⟩

15 The zero is not clearly legible; it could also be a nine.

16 But see 139 AF, note 4.

143 SF[1]

Frl Anna Freud
Alt-Aussee
Styria
Pension Rischawy

Gastein, 18 July 1921
[Postmark: 19 July]

My dear Anna,
Don't forget to give Max my small rucksack and a medium-sized one, or perhaps you can send it straightaway COD. Mama didn't pack one for me and there aren't any to buy here.

Telegram gratefully received.[2]

Fine, hot, thunderstorms.

Affectionately,
Papa

1 Postcard.

2 Missing. It probably contained news of Martha's arrival in Altaussee (see 144 AF).

144 AF

Altaussee, 18 July 1921

My dear Papa,
I see that Mama has written you an eight-page letter and that you therefore know all of the details of her departure, journey and arrival. She arrived with a bad migraine and did not look very well at all, but felt much better today than I would have expected. Frau Zinner has promised to take personal responsibility for Mama's diet and feeding up, and appears

to know what she is doing very well. If there is a recurrence, however, we have decided to inform Dr Jung[h]. For the time being, however, Mama will just lie quietly and rest in the deckchair; she appears to have over[1]-exerted herself in the last few days in Vienna. By the way, Dr Maxim. Steiner[2] is here at the Seehotel. Should we ask him to look at Mama, or will he have forgotten all that?

Max decided today not to travel to Gastein.* After his last journey here from Semmering, he is reluctant to put up with the stress of travel in Austria and fears that the signs of recovery he has acquired here would be lost again. He is also counting on seeing you in Hamburg and fears that particularly if the weather is bad, the meeting in Gastein might not be so pleasant.[3] So he will be leaving here for Frankfurt on Thursday [21 July]. I find that he has not recovered as much as I would have liked, and his mood in particular is very bad and gloomy, perhaps more than you might have noticed in Vienna.[4] That has also been oppressing me the whole time, because my own mood is generally only enough for one person and seldom for two. We have had only a visit of two days from Dr Rosenthal[5] from Hamburg, who passed through Aussee on a tour of the Dachstein, and that appeared to have markedly bucked up Max's spirits, but only for the duration of the visit.

I thank you for your nice long letter of the 16th. The thunderstorm while you were writing it cannot have been worse than the one when it arrived here. I only just managed to get myself and my belongings from my balcony, which was flooded with water. But the cool temperature was long overdue, as it has been intolerable in the last few days.

I thank you also for my copy of *Group Psychology*, which I was very glad to receive. By contrast, with the best will in the world I cannot summon up any auntly affection for the Jones book.[6] I have already had news directly from Dr Varendonck and am pleased at his success.

The two things in your letter are dealt with by the above. I will certainly look after Mama as well as I can and keep you informed. Now I also have a 'thing' to discuss with you that I have thought and been concerned about a lot recently, namely Ernstl. Max's imminent departure has naturally turned the conversation to Ernstl's return, and he would like to know in advance when and how it is to take place. We have not finalized anything yet but I have spoken at length with him and know his feelings, and nothing that I write to you today is against his wishes.

I am sure you can already guess that I can hardly imagine separating from Ernstl after so short a time as would be the case in mid-August and that I would like to keep him with me as long as possible. In the short time that he has been here he has become so much more cheerful and open and is so visibly happy that it would really be a shame to send him back to the old circumstances so soon. We are getting very used to one another and

* I had long abandoned the idea of accompanying him.

that will only be of benefit over a long period. He is also very worried about the thought of leaving. Although I had not spoken about it in the last few days he said at bedtime today, for example: 'When you write to Grandpa, leave the letter open. I want to ask whether I can stay longer.' I don't know whether he will actually do it, but that was his intention. The day before yesterday someone asked me how long we are staying in Aussee, and I said without thinking of him 'until mid-August'. Thereupon he tugged my arm and said: 'I thought you wanted to write to Frl Lehmann[7] to ask if she would allow me to stay here longer.' It's not just his enjoyment of the holidays because he said yesterday: 'It's so wonderful here. If the school was here and the children and Frl Jacob and Heinerle, we could stay forever.' I have also been wondering whether it might not be possible to bring him to Vienna for six months or perhaps until Easter, and I would like to tell you how this idea came about. I have had plenty of opportunity here to observe Max's relationship with Ernstl: Max endeavours to be very nice[8] to him and sometimes manages very well. In general, however, he can't put up with him[9] for more than ten minutes and then becomes so impatient that ultimately both of them lose their temper. That, of course, is when Ernst becomes grouchy. I have just had to make sure that the two are kept apart, because Max can only make a little progress in recovering if the child is not around him, and Ernstl can only enjoy himself a little when Max is not nearby. I didn't think it would be so bad, but Aunt will confirm that I am not exaggerating. Max tries as hard as he can and he should not be reproached; he is much too wretched himself to be able to do otherwise. All this means, however, that in Hamburg Ernst is reliant exclusively on Frl Jacob, whose limitations as an educator we both know. Added to that is the fact that he is not an everyday child, highly sensitive and in need of tenderness and, at least for the moment, far too soft for a boy and always ready to feel rejected. I think that many of his characteristics, as you have always said, can be explained by his particular life, and Sophie's death now plays a not unimportant role.

I am writing all this today because I understand from Mama that you intend to send him back with Helene[10] Gebert.[11] The only advantage of that would be that someone else and not us would have the trouble with the return journey, and it would be a bit much to ask Helene, even though she would certainly do it. This doesn't make up for the many great disadvantages for Ernst. I think we should keep him at least for the summer, and then either Mama or I could bring him with you to Hamburg[12] or, even better, bring him back to Vienna, from where I could take him back to Germany during the year. A few months would make a difference for him. I would, of course, make it my responsibility to ensure that he was no trouble for Mama. Here, too, I am the only person who looks after him, and if he went to school, I could easily manage it, given my self-employment and the frequency of my evening outings in Vienna. I am writing this not in an impetuous moment but after having given the matter a great deal of thought. I could easily make up the difference between the schooling in Hamburg and Vienna. He would not be much of an expense at home; I could also promote him to co-owner of my 100 pounds.

I am very relieved that you now know exactly what I think about the matter and hope that you will soon write to me with your views. I know you don't have as much sympathy for Ernstl as you do, e.g., for Heinzl, but I think that is because you have only ever seen him fleetingly and that you can only really appreciate him if you know him more intimately. Basically he is a poor child who has had to put up with a lot and whom we could perhaps help a little for later.

I am still 'flourishing' and am gradually taking on the colour of a negro from the Congo. My hay fever[13] is gradually retiring exhausted from the ring and my handkerchief consumption is coming back down into single figures again. Please excuse the many small slips of the pen in this letter. After Ernstl went to bed it it grew quite late so I am writing into the night, and perhaps it really was a case this time of 'darkness and uncertainty that robbed me of the time'.[14]

Please give my sincere regards to Aunt. I shall write to her soon.

With a kiss.

Your Anna

1 Written over the deleted 'excessively'.

2 Maximilian Steiner (1874–1942), doctor of medicine, dermatologist and urologist, member of the Vienna Psychological Wednesday Society since 1907; he practised and taught psychoanalysis in Vienna until his emigration to England in 1938, where he continued working ⟨Freud/Jones, letter 660, p. 761⟩. Freud wrote a preface (1913*e*) to Steiner's *The Psychical Disorders of Male Potency*. When Freud was diagnosed with cancer of the palate in 1923, he consulted Steiner, who recommended excision ⟨*Protokolle I*, p. XXXVIII; Schur, p. 350; Mühlleitner, p. 318⟩.

3 See 139 AF and note 4. For the meeting in Hamburg, see 153 AF, note 2.

4 When Max had visited a short time before; see 139 AF and note 1.

5 Probably Prof. Dr. med. Felix Rosenthal (1885–1939/1952?). He spoke the funeral oration at Sophie's burial ⟨Freud/Eitingon, 163 F⟩. In 1930 he became head of internal medicine at the Jewish Hospital (and for a time medical director of the entire hospital) in Hamburg, and remained so until his emigration to London in 1938. He died there the following year ⟨Lindemann [1981], pp. 65, 94, and [1997], pp. 68, 71, 74. Thanks to Angelika Voss and Christiane Adam, both Hamburg. See also Fischer [1962]⟩. According to the inscription in the picture gallery of the Jewish Hospital in Hamburg, Dr Rosenthal died in 1952 ⟨information kindly provided by H. Jepsen, Jewish Hospital, Hamburg⟩.

6 Anna seems to have had a lot of trouble with this translation; see two letters from Freud to Jones: 'As for niceties Anna is not responsible this time, she has not yet found a good style for sober stuff, as she may develop hereafter.' And a few weeks later (with a hint of self-justification): 'Your translation is finished, not bad I hope yet it could be better I am afraid; not equal to the care you are spending on my papers. A more fascinating subject would have challenged the ability of the translator to a higher amount of effort' ⟨Jones/Freud, letters 299, 7 February 1921, p. 409; 304, 18 March 1921, p. 416⟩. Is this the

reason perhaps that Anna did not have her name on the title page (unlike with Varendonck)? See 125 SF, note 7. However, Freud's comment in his letter to Jones of 2 October 1921 – 'My daughter was very much flattered and pleased by your present' – could refer to a gift of thanks by Jones for Anna's efforts ⟨Freud/Jones, letter 325, p. 440⟩.

7 Unknown; presumably Ernstl's teacher.
8 Corrected.
9 The word 'uh' deleted before this word.
10 'Mama to' deleted before this word.
11 She had been in Altaussee since 10 July; see 140 AF and note 3.
12 'Wie[n]' deleted before this word.
13 Misspelling corrected.
14 Reference to Freud's analogy to back up his thesis that physical circumstances facilitate mistakes but do not cause them: 'Suppose that one dark night I went to a lonely spot and was there attacked by a rough who took away my watch and purse. Since I did not see the robber's face clearly, I laid my complaint at the nearest police station with the words: "Loneliness and darkness have just robbed me of my valuables"' ⟨*Introductory Lectures on Psychoanalysis* [1916–17*a*], p. 45; a slightly different version had already been published in 1907 in *The Psychopathology of Everyday Life* [1901*b*], p. 21⟩.

145 AF

[Altaussee,] 20 July 1921

Dear Papa,
I am accompanying Max tomorrow on his departure as far as Ischl, visiting Grandma and returning in the evening. Ernst has so many friends amongst the other children that he can do without me during the day. Mama has already recovered surprisingly well in the short time, looks much better and has so far not been troubled by her intestines. Yesterday Dr Steiner visited us by chance and asked in detail about her health. Frau Zinner is taking excellent care of her diet.

Otherwise nothing new except for a letter from Mathilde, who is now quite well again.

With affectionate greetings,
Your Anna

146 SF

PROF. DR. FREUD — BG. [Bad Gastein,] 22 July 1921
Vienna, IX. Berggasse 19

My dear Anna,
Right after reading your letter, in which you presented your request so honestly, I realized that it would not be possible. The first reasons that occurred to me were the most immediate emotional ones but not the strongest; these emerged later in discussion with Aunt, but were certainly valid as well from the outset.

You know that I am especially fond of Heinele. My first thought was that it would be unfair to him to separate the children for six months, a long time for both of them at this age, and that we should not make them both only children. Their togetherness is the only thing left that they really have.[1] Then, being fairer to Ernsti, I said to myself that he wouldn't benefit much from living with three old people, with you as the only[2] counterbalance, and all that would happen as a result of the interruption would be that he would be torn away from his regular situation so would be even unhappier when he returned. And that brought me to the decisive argument, consideration for Mama, who will be sixty years old, has worked so hard all her life and is entitled now to ask for some respite. You know how she almost instinctively opposes every new person at the family table, even a guest for one evening, which is merely an expression of her fatigue and weakness. A seven-year-old child would be a new and difficult task for her; even if you devoted yourself exclusively to him, it is inconceivable that Mama would not be completely aware of his presence, his education, perhaps even his minor ailments. If she had to, she would also certainly look after him; it is sad that this question comes up at all, but as long as it is not a necessity but rather a dubious benefit for the child, consideration for his grandmother is an insurmountable obstacle.[3] I think we should drop the idea.[4] It is obviously no problem for him to come with us to Seefeld[5] and for us to bring him back then.[6] You will just have to make sure that you write to the sanatorium in good time so that we can find a place for him.

I would have replied to you two days ago, but I was – quite literally – too lazy to do so in the humid heat of those days. Only this afternoon has our good Gastein air been breathable again. Otherwise we are doing excellently, as you will have read from Aunt's letters. The two rucksacks[7] have just arrived, for which I thank you sincerely. No news or delivery yet from Verlag or Rank.

Affectionate greetings,
Papa

1 The following year the children were separated after all: as Heinerle was particularly frail, Mathilde and Robert took him in September 'at least for a year' (see 188 AF, note 7, 189 AF and note 4) ⟨Freud 1985*d*, 14 November 1922, p. 290; Freud to Kata and Lajos Levy, 11 June 1923, in: 1960*a*, pp. 348–9; Martha and Minna to Freud, in: Freud/Bernays, letter 181 Ma/Mi⟩. He flourished in Vienna and had soon 'put on 3 kg' ⟨Anna/Lou, letter 61, 3 December 1922, p. 110, also letters 46, 71 and elsewhere; Freud/Ferenczi III, 917 F⟩. His happiness was short-lived, however: after less than a year, Heinerle died of meningitis; see 195 SF and note 2 ⟨see also Gödde [2003], pp. 173–5⟩.

2 Grammatical error in the original.

3 Freud wrote to Max on this subject on 6 August 1921: 'I would like to have agreed to your plan for Vienna . . . but consideration for yourself, Heinz and above all Grandma, who needs to be treated with a lot of care, spoke quite plainly against it. Even if you still have difficulty putting up with the children now, their absence – especially Ernsti – would make you even more cranky.'

4 Only after incisive changes in Max's living conditions (see 162 AF, note 7) was the idea taken up again; in 1928 Anna managed to have Ernstl taken in by Eva Rosenfeld and admitted to the school in Hietzing. In Vienna he found new 'brothers and sisters' and a 'second family' with the Burlinghams (see 244 AF and note 2), to whom he remained attached henceforth; see 211 SF and note 4 ⟨Freud, W. E. [1987], pp. 200f., 208–10; Freud to Max, 23 August 1927–1 December 1929; Freud/Sam, 6 December 1928; Anna/Eva, letter 6 and note 5; Heller, p. 66; Young-Bruehl, p. 136⟩. In 1931 he transferred to the progressive Schulfarm Insel Scharfenberg (Tegler See) but had to flee back to Vienna in 1933, where he took his school-leaving examination in 1935. In 1938 he emigrated to London, where he studied psychology and became a psychoanalyst. He lived in Germany again from 1983 ⟨Freud, W. E. [1988], pp. 14–16; Freud/Ferenczi III, 1244 F, 2 April 1933; Molnar [1996], pp. 96, 103, 145, 186f; *Freud-Vorlesungen*, p. 232⟩.

5 Where the second part of the holidays were to be spent; see 153 AF, note 1.

6 Freud brought Ernstl back himself; see 153 AF, note 8.

7 See 143 SF.

147 AF

Altaussee, 4 August 1921

My dear Papa,

The heat and a couple of days of infirmity are the only reasons I have not written to you for so long. I had the feeling that I was breaking up into my constituent parts and just lay there like a fish on dry land, gasping for air without being able to do anything. Today it's pouring again and cool, and I am quite amazed to discover that there is still something, quite a lot actually, left of me.

I cannot say very much in reply to your letter. I cannot and certainly will not deny that the reasons you cite are justified and serious; none of them had escaped me either. It is just that this is a case that, much more clearly than other cases, has two sides. Our disagreement is due to the fact that you take greater account of the disadvantages of Vienna and I of the household in Hamburg. But even as I was writing the first letter I had already decided not to attempt to persuade you any more once I had heard your opinion. I am just pleased that you will at least have the opportunity in Seefeld of getting to know and better appreciating Ernstl. It doesn't necessarily mean anything if perhaps he doesn't make such a good impression on you the first day. He is always shy and reserved, particularly when he feels he is being observed by new people, and doesn't then make the best impression. In reality, however, he is so delightful and decent that I could not wish for a different or better son of my own.[1] Mathilde, who hasn't seen him since Hamburg, also finds him surprisingly changed for the better and is delighted by him. He has made great progress,[2] especially since Max's departure from here.[3]

My conversations with him have so far had concrete results and, I believe, clear up a hitherto unexplained and less sympathetic trait. I am sure you will remember Aunt and I telling you about his great physical anxiety[4] and caution; for example, that he is always scared of catching a cold, of getting stomach ache, and that the most reliable way of preventing him from doing something naughty is to tell him that it is damaging. Sometimes with a child as small as this it is comical, and he would seem to have similarities with some Hamburg relation, Julius Philipp,[5] I think. Recently he said to me, when I was trying to find out why he is afraid of the dark (which he is), in another context, that Sophie had told him that if he played with his member he would get very ill; apparently this was long ago. Does that explanation make sense? The fear, he says, began in Schwerin with a dream, which I don't yet really understand, however.[6] He distracts himself before going to sleep, like I used to (and Sophie as well, by the way), with a continuing story and now insists on saying it out loud to me – instead of thinking it silently to himself. I discover all kinds of things about him in this way, but have yet to understand the real meaning and salient features. I can see with Ernst, however, how difficult it must be to find out more about a child if you don't spend all your time with him from morning to evening.

I am enclosing a letter from Max I received two days ago. He seems once again to be in a terrible mood and condition, and I blame myself for advising him to come to Aussee if he took so little benefit back with him.[7]

Mama, who was recovering marvellously, has been less satisfactory again the last two days. One afternoon she suddenly had 37.2 and felt miserable, was better again the next morning, but no longer looks so good and enjoys her food much less.

I am currently busy for the first time analysing a dream in writing and it is going much better than I thought. I hope to finish it today (dreamt and begun yesterday) and am curious to see how it turns out.[8] The only thing is that it is practically impossible in this terribly noisy house to find an hour and a place where you can be alone and undisturbed at all.

I am looking forward very much to seeing you again and hope that you have been able to cool down and rest in the meantime.

With a kiss,
Your Anna

1 For Anna's repeated great concern about Ernstl, see, e.g., Anna/Eva and Anna/Lou (letter 120, 17 August 1923 and elsewhere).

2 Freud wrote to Max after seeing Ernst in Seefeld: 'I am writing to you mainly about Ernstl, who gives me great pleasure and I am willing to take back my earlier reservations. . . . He is a really decent and sensible little person and we are on the best of terms. . . . He is polite and endearing, cheerful, sometimes boisterous, obedient, and makes hardly any difficulties. . . . As you can see, Ernstl does not need to be overshadowed by Heinerle' ⟨Freud to Max, 20 August, 31 August 1921⟩.

3 On 21 July; see 144 AF.

4 Spelling mistake in the original. 'It seems to be such a good aim: making the child fearless and comfortable with everything' ⟨Anna/Lou, letter 305, 11 December 1927, p. 551⟩.

5 Probably a Wandsbeck cousin of Martha and Minna, who with his younger brother, Oscar (sons of Elias Philipp, the brother of Martha and Minna's mother, Emmeline), had founded the Philipp Company in England ⟨Molnar [1996], p. 166; see Appendix by Albrecht Hirschmüller in Freud/Bernays, p. 232, and 115 S, note 11, ibid.⟩. See also 158 AF and notes 3 and 5.
6 See 150 SF.
7 Freud had initially thought: 'We are extremely happy to have persuaded you to make this trip' ⟨Freud to Max, 16 June 1921⟩.
8 See 151 AF and note 4.

148 AF

[Altaussee,] 4 August 1921

Dear Papa,
Mama called me away as I was about to seal today's letter, to show me the news that has just arrived from Ernst of the birth of little 'Gabriel'.[1] That's why I forgot to enclose Max's letter. I am doing so now and am also sending a second one that arrived today and is also meant for you. I don't understand why he has no news from us; needless to say, I wrote so that the letter would be there on his arrival.
Affectionately,
Anna

1 Stephan Gabriel, the first son of Lucie and Ernst Freud, born on 31 July 1921 in Berlin ⟨Freud/Sam, 6 August 1921⟩. After having had three grandsons, Freud would dearly have liked a granddaughter ⟨Freud/Jones, letters 306, 322⟩.

149 SF

PROF. DR. FREUD

Gastein, 4 August 1921
Vienna, IX. Berggasse 19

My dear Anna,
Out of pure fear that a letter doesn't come from you today, I am writing to you first. We had 30° in the room yesterday and today 7°. A white powdered kuglhopf[1] rises before me that I recall being green. The first effect of this fall, which can only be compared with that of the krone, is a strange feeling of misalignment. We had eighteen glorious, usually too hot, days. Hardly has the – burning is not quite the right word – desire been fulfilled than we long for what was before. Hopefully it will change one more time before we meet in Schwarzach-St Veit on the 14th.[2]

I am sure Aunt has written all about our life here. I therefore only ask you to squeeze out of Mama some information about your financial requirements *as soon as possible*.[3] Everything else will be easy to arrange.

The first French translation[4] (of the five lectures) has arrived. Rank is writing faithfully; the Verlag is sending corrections. The increase in the exchange rate has made us richer by several million. Tomorrow I will finally be going into the forest to find out whether God has created any mushrooms. Until now even the smallest climb has been impossible.

What do you think of the Berlin child? Do you know more about it than we do? I'm still afraid that it will be called Kurt Rolf Waldemar. A Hebrew name would be much less terrible.[5]

On the social front Lucie,[6] who is very dear, is dominating the field. I am sure you have heard about Emden,[7] Mr Snyder[8] and Selma Kurz.[9]

And now I would finally like to hear from you. Affectionate regards to all and enjoy yourselves,

Your Papa

1 Written like this. There is no mountain of this name in the Gastein region. From Haus Wassing, however, a hemispherical silhouette of the Stubnerkogel can be seen and the upper part, on which only grass grows, resembles a guglhopf when it is covered in snow. ⟨I thank Laurenz Krisch, Bad Gastein, for this explanation.⟩

2 In order to travel together via Innsbruck to Seefeld ⟨Freud to Oscar Rie, 4 August 1921, in: 1960*a*, p. 340⟩. See also 150 SF, 153 AF and note 1.

3 'Mother . . . was always rather parsimonious in everything that did not concern Father. This had been a grim necessity in her younger days, an attitude of mind towards spending money which had become second nature' ⟨Freud, M. [1999], p. 93; also p. 44⟩. See, e.g., 5 MF/SF and note 6, 125 SF; but see also 151 AF (2nd paragraph), 177 AF and note 5.

4 Spelling mistake (no umlaut) in the original. Freud used the same formulation in a letter of the same day to Oscar Rie ⟨1960*a*, p. 340⟩. See 125 SF, note 19.

5 Freud notified his mother, Amalie, of Gabriel's birth in the form of congratulations on her birthday: 'To my dear mother in the name of her most recent great-grandchild Gabriel Freud, born 31 July 1921, Berlin Sigm 18 Aug 1291' (slip of the pen for '1921') ⟨LoC SF, Cont. 2⟩.

6 'Lucy' Wiener, who had previously lived for a while in Davos and now lived in Berlin ⟨Freud/Sam, 21 January, 25 July 1921; Freud/Bernays, A., p. 174⟩. See 138 SF and note 10.

7 'Van Emden also visited three times from Salzburg, the last time for two days with his wife. That way I could pay back at least a small amount of last year's hospitality [at the Hague Congress]' ⟨Freud/Eitingon, 214 F, 12 August 1921, p. 259⟩.

8 Carl Snyder (1869–1946), American economic scientist and statistician at the Federal Reserve Bank, who was extensively self-taught; he studied scientific subjects (e.g., Snyder [1907], [1917]). ⟨Research by Gerhard Fichtner, whom I thank for this information.⟩ He might have visited Freud in Gastein (see 'eight persons' in 152 SF).

9 The coloratura soprano Selma Kurz (1874–1933), a celebrated Viennese opera singer, engaged at the Court Opera from 1899 to 1929. She was married to Prof. Josef Halban (who later treated Marie Bonaparte; see 238 SF and note 3). She interrupted a concert tour to the USA in early 1921 for health reasons and was obliged to go to Bad Gastein for 'a thorough examination and cure before the summer season' ⟨Halban, pp. 174f.⟩. She had been staying since 20 July with her husband at Hotel Austria ⟨*Badgastein. Liste*, 1921, no. 89, serial no. 4848⟩.

150 SF

PROF. DR. FREUD Gastein, 4 August 1921
Vienna, IX. Berggasse 19

My dear Anna,
I sent off Ernst's letter yesterday by express and am enclosing Oli's at his request.[1] Please don't lose it, etc.

I was very pleased to receive your letter – on your account and Ernstl's as well. (But you forgot to enclose Max's letter.) I am sure you have found the right reason; now you should just follow it up further. The dream that started his fear could be one that Sophie recorded when he was three years and five months old. He woke up quite distraught and said: 'Tonight Daddy had his head on the bowl. Why did Daddy have his head on a bowl?' It took a long time to calm him down. In other words, a real castration dream, transferred to the father.[2] Make use of this.

It is very sad that Heinerle had an accident but it has no consequences. You know, I take it, that he fell over and broke his collarbone?

Your letter says nothing of your new nephew.

Here still incredibly fine, but too hot for me and the mushrooms. Lucie dominates the field; her boys[3] are arriving tomorrow. Aunt will write to you about the travel details. I think I will be arriving on the 14th in Innsbruck before you, and will meet you at the station after I have inspected the rooms. I know nothing of Maus's intentions.[4]

With affectionate regards,
Papa

1 See 138 SF, note 1.
2 See 147 AF and note 6. Freud included this dream in 1919 in the 5th edition of *The Interpretation of Dreams* ⟨1900*a*, ch. VI, E, example 5a, p. 366; instead of 'bowl' the published version says 'plate'; also the editorial note, ibid., p. 350⟩.
3 Frederick Bernays Wiener (1906–96) and Walter Wiener (1907–2000) ⟨Stammbaum Lange: Freud Family, 'Genealogical tree, p. II; Tögel, [2004*a*], p. 206⟩. 'My second daughter [Lucy] went [in 1919] with husband and sons to Germany. The boys were put up in Switzerland and learned French there. The older grandson went back to America in 1920 as he wanted to go to an American college,' reported Freud's sister, Anna ⟨Freud-Bernays, A., p. 174⟩.
4 She was in Seefeld for some of the time ⟨Freud to Max, 31 August 1921; Freud/Ferenczi III, 882 F, 887 Fer⟩. See also 153 AF.

151 AF

Altaussee, 7 August 1921

My dear Papa,
I am enclosing another letter from Max, once again not very good news, I'm afraid. They say that a broken collarbone (read Max's letter before mine), as Max describes Heinerle's, is not very serious or painful and

heals quickly, but I would have wished the boy a more undisturbed recovery, and Max really didn't need this extra concern. I am all the more happy that Ernstl is thriving so well and just become more fearful when I hear this kind of thing. With the best will in the world, I can't always be by him and it is not really possible to prevent a child from falling over.[1]

Thank you very much for your letter, which I was delighted to receive yesterday. It crossed mine as both were written on the one cold day. I have been trying for a long time to get Mama to utter something about our financial situation, as she has been calling it for a couple of days, and have even had some success. To improve my external appearance, which is probably not a bad idea, she gave me a very pretty dirndl apron and old shawls. I hope you will admire them as well, because I was very happy to receive them.

As one rainy day is not enough to catch up with everything that has been omitted during the fourteen sunny days, I forgot all kinds of things in my last letter that I wanted to tell you. First something very nice that Ernstl said: on a card to Frl Jacob (whom he calls Tante [Aunt] Martha) he wanted to write Tante with 'nn' and – as usual in such matters – didn't believe me when I told him it wasn't correct. Finally, I pronounced slowly 'Tan-te', and then suddenly he got it. 'I see now. Tante has one "n"; only Anna has two.' Isn't that very flattering for me? Mama recently wanted to wash him as a surprise while I wasn't there, but he wouldn't allow her to and said to me: 'You know, I thought it would be much too tiring for such an old lady.' Math is quite surprised how well he can walk, climb and clamber, and spends a lot of time with him.

I also forgot to tell you that Lampl arrived here a few days ago. He is very fulfilled and happy with the psychoanalytical work and praises Sachs to high heaven.[2] I am with him a lot and we get on very well, but also have the opportunity every day to confirm our last year's assessment of him and to be pleased that we were so right.[3]

I have been thinking a lot about the dream I described to you.[4] I have put together over twelve pages of my thoughts and think that I now understand it quite well. If I am not wrong, it goes back to the primal scene that you told me about. Now, finally, I believe you that if you analyse dreams on your own you have to do it in writing.

Yesterday I had the first migraine in my life and I hope it is the last.

Vera, who lives in Markt with the Vidors, comes over sometimes during the day. She has changed very little.

To my surprise, Lampl told me about a polyclinic in Vienna that you have never mentioned to me.[5] I'm afraid that I haven't started the Varendonck corrections yet.[6] And who is Mr Snyder?

I was delighted to hear about the Berlin child. But it is difficult to believe births and deaths when one hasn't seen them with one's own eyes and felt their consequences. So they simply have to be accepted from afar without being able to do more than write a letter.

To my astonishment, I even received a letter from Margaretl; she is also complaining about the heat, but otherwise thinks very highly of Seefeld.[7] Kurheim has already confirmed the accommodation for Ernstl.[8]

This time next week we will be meeting. With a kiss and regards to Aunt.

Your Anna

1 Spelling mistake (no umlaut) in the original.
2 He was studying teaching analysis in Berlin with Hanns Sachs, who worked at the Psychoanalytical Institute from 1920 until his move to Boston in 1932 (see 131 AF, note 7) ⟨Sachs, p. 154; Mühlleitner, pp. 199, 280⟩.
3 Lampl had wooed Anna, who rejected him as a suitor but remained friendly with him. He married Jeanne De Groot in 1925 ⟨Anna/Lou, letters 148, 208, 209, 224–6, 228; Young-Bruehl, pp. 95–9⟩.
4 In 147 AF (and note 8).
5 In summer 1920 the Vienna local group had expressed the wish to set up a psychoanalytical polyclinic on the Berlin model. Freud opposed the idea saying that 'Vienna has no qualification to become a centre' ⟨Freud/Ferenczi III, 855 F, 31 October 1920, p. 37; previously also Freud/Abraham, 4 July 1920, p. 430⟩. But other Viennese analysts (particularly Hitschmann, Federn and Helene and Felix Deutsch) stubbornly pursued the plan against considerable resistance by the Vienna medical profession. On 22 May 1922 it opened 'on the quiet' (in the out-patient building of the Herzstation Verein, Pelikangasse 18) under the direction of Eduard Hitschmann ⟨*IZ*, vol. 8 (1922), p. 234; Deutsch, H. [1925], pp. 522f.; Hitschmann [1925], pp. 521f., 1932; Jones III, p. 90⟩. Detailed description (based on careful study of source material) with reproduction of statutes, work regulations and instructions in Fallend [1995], pp. 107–30. See Kage for the role of out-patient departments in the recognition of psychoanalysis by the medical profession.
6 See 144 AF, note 6.
7 The Ries were already there on holiday ⟨Freud to Oscar Rie, 4 August 1921, in: 1960*a*, p. 340⟩.
8 See 146 SF and note 6.

152 SF[1]

Frl Anna Freud
Alt-Aussee
Styria
Pension Rischawy *Express*[2]

Gastein, 10 August 1921

Dear Anna,
Max sent a telegram yesterday: Heinzl back bloomingly cheerful.

I transferred 50 m to Bk f ObÖst[3] in Salzburg on 5 August. Send me a telegram *at once if no* notification has yet arrived, but ask first at the bank (in Aussee).

The Emden[s] arrived yesterday;[4] there are now eight of us at table.[5]

Weather remains fine, yesterday a thunderstorm for a change, after which the waterfall was *chocolate brown*.

Affectionate greetings,

Papa

1 Postcard.
2 In red crayon at an angle on the address side.
3 Bank für Oberösterreich.
4 See 149 SF and note 7.
5 Freud, Minna Bernays, Lucy Wiener with the two boys, van Emden and wife. It was not possible to determine whether Mr Snyder (see 149 SF) was the eighth person. He is not listed in the *Badgasteiner Liste der Kurgäste und Passanten* for 1921.

153 AF

Seefeld,[1] 20 September 1921

Dear Papa,

Yesterday two letters arrived for you that I know you were waiting for. We don't want to forward them as it is so uncertain whether you will get them.[2] I will tell you briefly, therefore, what they say.

1) Edward wrote on 29 August:
[English original] 'I sent to Amsterdam a few days ago to be credited to the account of E.[rnest] J.[ones][3] Fl. 3,205.81. This is royalty on the book up to and including June 30th. It amounted in dollars to $997.65. – To date therefore the sales of copies in the last year amount to 5,803. I hope to have another royalty report for you at the end of the year.'[4]

2) Henry S. King & Co, London S. W. 1, 9, Pall Mall, wrote on 15 September:
[English original] 'We are in receipt of your letter of the 7th instant. Are we to understand that we are to send a cheque for £60 drawn *in favour of* Mrs Zoe Jones[5] at the address given?
You simply state that we are to send to the address of Mrs Zoe Jones, £60, but you do not say in whose favour the cheque is to be drawn.'

There is also a delightful letter from Lou Salome,[6] in which she basically accepts the invitation.[7]

We are travelling down to Innsbruck on Friday [23 September] and on Saturday with the day express (like Maus) to Vienna.

We do not have any word yet from Hamburg, although Ernsti left almost a week ago.[8]

Otherwise we are very well.

With affectionate greetings,

Your Anna

1 A high plateau in Tyrol, west of the Karwendel mountains; the 'Seefelder Sattel', popular summer holiday resort, mountain spa (1,180 m) and winter sports resort ⟨Baedeker, 1923, p. 34; Freud/Jones, letter 322⟩. Freud spent the rest of the summer holidays there from 15 August at Pension Kurheim with Martha, Anna and Ernstl (and some of the time with Maus, see 150 SF, note 4) ⟨Freud/Jones, letter 320; Freud/Ferenczi III, 876 F, 882 F⟩.

2 Freud left Seefeld on 14 September for Berlin and Hamburg to visit his children and grandchildren. As there was no Congress that year, the committee members met in Berlin on 20 September to continue together to a 'private congress' ⟨Freud/Eitingon, 212 F–218 F, 221 E, note 1, quote 214 F; *Rundbriefe 2*, 8 September 1921, pp. 239f.; Freud/Abraham, 2 May, 8 May, 21 July, 8 August 1921; Freud/Ferenczi III, 870 F, 876 F, 880 Fer, 888 Fer, 889 Fer; Freud/Jones, letters 297, 298, 317, 320–5⟩. See Jones: 'We had planned making a ten days' tour of the Harz region. [. . .] Every day there were walking expeditions, and we were all impressed with Freud's swift and tireless capacities in this pursuit. [. . .] Freud read to us two papers he had specially written for the occasion': [1941*d* (see 142 SF, note 14), and 1922*b* (see 175 SF, note 1)] ⟨Jones III, pp. 85, 429–31⟩. Freud was back in Vienna on 30 September ⟨Freud/Ferenczi III, 891 F⟩.

3 See 107 SF and note 9.

4 Edward Bernays had been clearing up irregularities by publishers Boni & Liveright regarding sales calculations for the American translation of Freud's *Lectures* (1916–17*a*) ⟨Freud/Jones, letter 310⟩.

5 Misinterpretation by the bank for 'Loe'.

6 Lou[ise] Andreas-Salomé (1861–1937), writer, analyst. She studied philosophy, history of art and theology in Zurich. In 1887 she married the Orientalist F. C. Andreas and moved with him in 1903 from Berlin to Göttingen (see 167 AF and notes 11 and 12). She was acquainted with many famous intellectuals of her time – including Nietzsche and Rilke – and was 'one of the most important women in the history of ideas' in Europe at the time ⟨Mühlleitner, p. 24⟩ (see ill. 15). She went to the 3rd Psychoanalytic Congress in Weimar in 1911 as a guest and attended Freud's lectures at the University of Vienna and the Wednesday discussions of the Vienna Psychoanalytic Society in the winter semester of 1912–13 during her analytical training with Freud. 'I have come to know her very closely and must say that I have never before met with such an understanding of ψα,' is how Abraham introduced her ⟨Freud/Abraham, 28 April 1912, p. 150⟩. From 1913 she practised and taught psychoanalysis while pursuing her writing activities. She remained a close friend of Freud and his family until her death ⟨Andreas-Salomé [1951], [1958]; *Protokolle IV*, p. XIX, *Minutes IV*, pp. 107, 108 and note 1, and elsewhere; Gicklhorn, p. 155 (although Lou's name is absent from the list of listeners), p. 169; Freud 1937*a*; Michaud⟩.

7 'And now like a wish-dreaming teenager I picture to myself every day a little of what it will be like when I shall really and truly be your guest,' wrote Lou Andreas-Salomé in her reply of 13 September 1921 to Freud's invitation ⟨Freud/Andreas-Salomé, 13 September 1921, p. 108⟩. Since the end of the war both had longed for a meeting, as Lou had written most recently with greetings to 'your daughter Anna, whom I have so long wanted to meet' ⟨ibid., 6 September 1921, p. 107⟩. The meeting took place on 9 November (the salon in Berggasse was converted into a guest room) and the two women became

friends ⟨Freud/Ferenczi III, 895 F; Freud/Eitingon, 223 F⟩. 'She was a delightful guest and in general an outstanding woman. Anna worked on analysis with her, visited many interesting people and profited greatly from her presence,' wrote Freud to Ernst on the day of her departure on 20 December 1921. Anna soon repaid the visit; see 167 AF – 169 AF. See also Anna/Lou correspondence.

8 Freud took Ernstl with him on his journey to Berlin and Hamburg and brought him back to his father. Martha had wanted to accompany him on this journey, but was still 'in need of respite' (see 146 SF and note 3, 142 SF, 147 AF) and Freud therefore travelled alone with Ernstl ⟨Freud to Max, 6 August, 31 August, 5 September, 10 September 1921; Freud/Eitingon, 214 F, 216 F, 218 F⟩.

154 SF[1]

[3 December 1921?][2]

Contribution
to marriage fund or
independence[3]

1 This is an envelope; the text, undated, is written on the front in the Latin alphabet. The copy and two other undated sheets – shown as annexes to this letter – were in the transcriptions of Freud's manuscripts at the end of 1920 (the originals are now in LoC SF, Cont. 2, folder 'Anna Freud, Miscellaneous related material').

2 The envelope is possibly connected with the list printed here for Anna's birthday, 'Anna's assets and dowry'. A further unsigned sheet, with nothing except the note '1st half of dowry £500', could also belong to it (see also 125 SF and note 11).

3 Various other letters by Freud show that he repeatedly thought about Anna's independence. He wrote, for example, to Eitingon: 'Anna is fine, by the way. She is cheerful, hardworking and inspired. I would like just as much for her to stay here as I would for her to have her own home, *provided that it's also the same to her*.' And later, 'Anna, incidentally to my delight . . . is blooming and cheerful; I just wish she would soon find a reason to exchange her attachment to her old father for a more permanent one' ⟨Freud/Eitingon, 208 F, 24 April 1921, p. 252 (my emphasis); 223 F, 11 October 1921, p. 267; also Freud/Sam, 7 March 1922, 19 December 1925⟩. Or to Lou Andreas-Salomé: 'I have long felt sorry for her for still being at home with the old folks . . . but on the other hand, if she really were to go away, I should feel myself as deprived as I do now' ⟨13 March 1922, p. 113⟩. For discussion of Freud's ambivalence in this context and of Anna's 'father complex', see, e.g., Gay, pp. 437–43 and Grubrich-Simitis [2005], pp. 273f.; see also Introduction, p. 6.

154 SF – 1st enclosure

[Sheet without letterhead, everything – with the exception of the words 'of which' in the right-hand column – written in the Latin alphabet]

Anna's assets and dowry

3 December 1921

3 Dec 21

£ 556 + lire 1000 + # 20 + fl 10 + 2 sover[ei]g.[n]

	– £ 500	Martin – #20
	£ 56	0
4/1 22	– 3	
19/2	£ 51 2	
	+£ 200	
	£ 251	
24/2	– 7	
	£ 244	
8/3	– £ 2 to me	
	£ 242	
8/5	– £ 2	
	£ 240	
31/5	– 205	
	35	
13/6	– 3	
	32	
29/6	– 5	
	£ 27	

1 Oct 22

£ 27, fl 10. lire 1000.

3/X	– 2
	25
– £ of which	1000
3/XII	– 100
	900
25/XII	– 100
	800
14/X	– 200
	600
	– 25
17/X	575
13/2	– 300
	275
21/2	– 250
	25
17/4	– 20
	5
13/5	– fr 5[?][1]
	– fl 10

[1] The five not clearly legible.

1 Freud, *c.*1906, at the beginning of the correspondence © Sigmund Freud Copyrights/The Marsh Agency

2 Family photo, 1909: the six children, Oliver, Sophie, Mathilde, Anna, Martin, Ernst, with their 'two mothers', Minna Bernays and Martha Freud © Freud Museum, London

3 Robert Hollitscher, married to Mathilde Freud © Freud Museum, London

4 Mathilde Hollitscher, née Freud, as a middle-aged woman © Freud Museum, London

5 Freud, *c.*1912, at around the time of Anna's visit to Merano © Sigmund Freud Copyrights/The Marsh Agency

6 Anna, *c.*1912, at around the time of her visit to Merano © Freud Museum, London

7 Sophie Halberstadt, née Freud

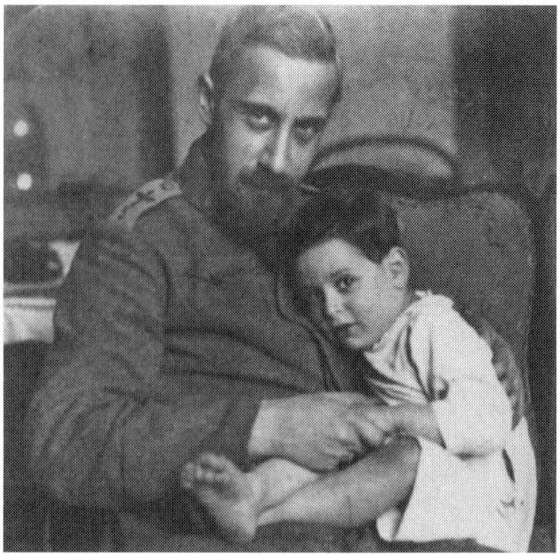

8 Max Halberstadt and son Ernstl, *c.*1916–17

9 Anna with Heinerle and Ernstl Halberstadt, the two sons of Sophie and Max, in Hamburg, 1922 © Freud Museum, London

10 Freud with Evchen Freud, daughter of Henny and Oliver, Semmering, 1927 © Sigmund Freud Copyrights/ The Marsh Agency

11 Freud and Anna, at the 6th International Psychoanalytic Congress, The Hague, 1920 © Sigmund Freud Copyrights/ The Marsh Agency

12 Anna with conventional school class, 1919 © Sigmund Freud Copyrights/The Marsh Agency

13 Anna with dog Wolf and 'Hietzinger schoolchildren' (including Tinky Burlingham with short blonde hair), *c.*1927–8 © Freud Museum, London

14 Dorothy Burlingham, Schneewinkl, 1929 © Sigmund Freud Copyrights/ The Marsh Agency

15 Lou Andreas-Salomé, *c.*1903 © Lou Andreas-Salomé Archiv, Göttingen

16 Marie Bonaparte with chow-chow Topsy © Sigmund Freud Copyrights/ The Marsh Agency

17 Anna, *c.*1931 © Sigmund Freud Copyrights/The Marsh Agency

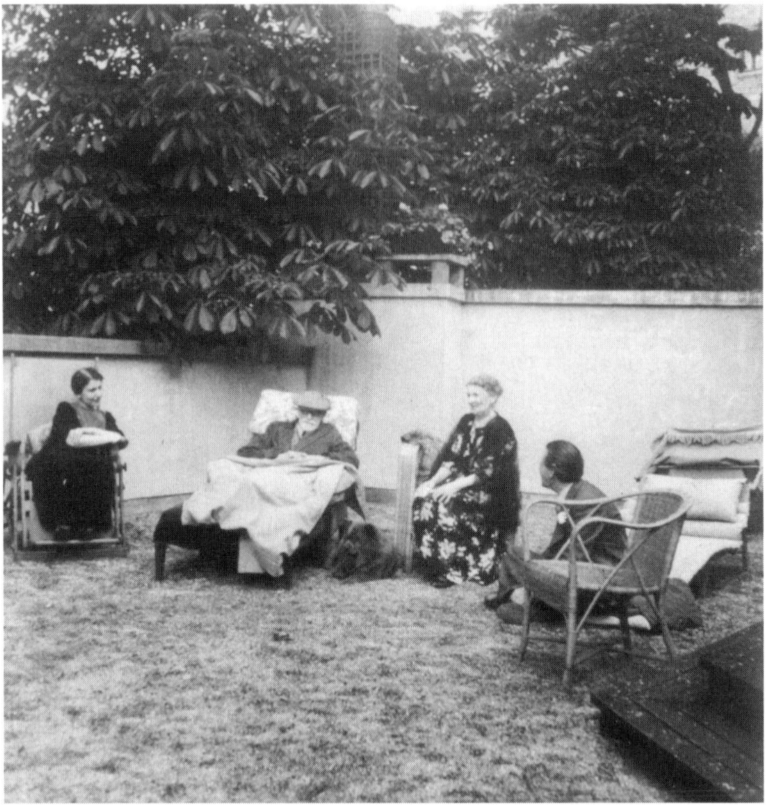

18 Anna, Sigmund, Martha and Ernst, on their way to exile in London, 1938, on the roof terrace at Marie Bonaparte's, Paris © Sigmund Freud Copyrights/ The Marsh Agency

154 SF – 2nd enclosure
[Folded double sheet, written on one side only, Latin alphabet]

Deposits

4/X	Asch[1]	# 125	[entire line crossed out in red pencil]
5/X	Blumg[2]	# 350 # 20	[line until '350' in red pencil, the rest crossed out again in black pencil]

1 Joseph Jefferson Asch (1880–1935), doctor of medicine, American urologist, pioneer in the field of cystoscopy, clinical director of Lenox Hill Hospital, New York. He was one of the first to recognize the connection between clinical medicine and psychoanalysis, and became a member of the New York Psychoanalytic Society. He was a student of Freud in 1921–2; during this time he supported Freud, amongst other things treating Frink, who became ill during his own analysis (see 156 AF, note 10) ⟨Freud/Jones, letters 330, 434; see also Schnitzler [1984], pp. 306, 912, note 10; obituary: Asch⟩.

2 Leonard Blumgart (1881–1959), doctor of medicine, American psychiatrist, member of the New York Psychoanalytic Society from 1914 and president from 1942 to 1946. He was in Vienna from October 1921 to mid-February 1922: 'His analysis was excellent, as far as it went' ⟨Freud/Jones, letter 342, 5 February 1922, p. 458, letter 306, 12 April 1921, p. 418; Freud's letter to L. Blumgart, 1962*a*; Lorand [1960]⟩.

1922

155 SF

PROF. DR. FREUD

Tuesday, 7 March 1922
Vienna, IX. Berggasse 19

My dear Anna,
Received your very pleasing news;[1] I assume you are less interested in my reactions to your letters than you are in news from here so that you can continue to share our lives.

I can confirm first of all that you are sorely missed. The house is very empty without you and there is no complete substitute anywhere. There is very little news but I shall nevertheless report it conscientiously.

First there is the letter from H. J.,[2] called Davy, which I enclose and which I shall speak about at the end of this letter. Then a dear letter from the other Lou, who confirms receipt of your letter in a PS. My M[. . .] went to her for a cure after all.[3] I believe you learnt whilst you were still here that Jones has had a son.[4] By contrast, I am wearing my English shoes for the first time today,[5] delay because of the move in the Verlag.[6] Yesterday evening I had dinner at Urbantschitsch and walked home in blissful peace between midnight and 1 o'clock in the morning. Spring made its appearance here on Sunday. The same afternoon Rank came to work and in the morning Frau X Y-Z with husband and doctor, whose melancholy appears finally to be lifting. I think that's everything.

I took the liberty of opening the letter from H. J. to you, because you would in any case have shown it to me right away. I think a response is necessary. For all its friendly tone,[7] it is very forced and the shift in relations from the personal[8] to the literary is too clear. I will write a letter to *her* and enclose it with this letter. If you are in agreement, you can send it off from where you are. I don't want to go it alone because they are your friends as well. The comment that *he* can't write to Rank also affects the relations with us.[9]

Send my affectionate regards to Max, the two naughty[10] boys and mother Halberstadt.

Papa

1 Correspondence from Anna missing. After a short stay in Berlin she had been in Hamburg since 4 March to replace the housekeeper Frl Jacob, who was suffering from sciatica, in the family of her brother-in-law, Max Halberstadt (see ill. 9) ⟨Freud/Andreas/Salomé, 13 March 1922; Anna/Lou, letters 9, 11⟩. She remained there until 18 April; see 164 AF; see also 160 AF and note 7.
2 Herbert Jones.
3 Freud/Andreas-Salomé, 2 March 1922, pp. 111f. See also Anna/Lou, letter 23 and elsewhere.
4 Mervyn Ioan Gower, born 27 February 1922 ⟨Freud/Jones, letters 321, 347, 350⟩.
5 Because of the poor quality of post-war Austrian goods, Freud had asked his nephew to obtain a good pair of shoes from England ⟨Freud/Sam, 5 February–15 May 1922⟩.
6 When the *Verlag* was founded, Otto Rank's apartment at Grünangergasse 3–5 in Vienna's 1st district had been the head office and workshop ⟨Marinelli, p. 16; List, p. 37⟩. After several moves it had now found a 'definite and satisfactory home' at Andreasgasse 3, 7th (not 3rd) district ⟨Freud/Andreas-Salomé, 13 March 1922, p. 113; *Rundbriefe 2*, pp. 50, 58, 72, 235, 250, 261, 278, 300; sender's address on envelope 28 July 1922, ORC; Freud/Ferenczi III, 891 F, 1063 Fer, note A⟩. It was not finally furnished until May ⟨*Rundbriefe 3*, pp. 30, 40, 58, 80, 129⟩. The *Verlag* remained in Andreasgasse until 1928 before moving to Haus der Börse (1., Börsengasse 11) and in 1936 to Berggasse 7, where it was liquidated by the Nazi occupation forces on 15 March 1938 ⟨Freud/Ferenczi III, 1124 F; Marinelli; Mühlleitner, p. 383⟩.
7 Spelling mistake (no umlaut) in the original.
8 Spelling mistake (no umlaut) in the original.
9 See 100 SF and note 7 and other references.
10 See 28 SF and note 8.

156 AF

[Hamburg,] Sunday, 12 March 1922

My dear Papa,
Thank you for your letter, which has just arrived, and the various pieces of news. Of course, I want above all to hear news from you because otherwise I will be completely out of touch when I return. Here you could almost forget as well that there is such a thing as psychoanalysis and everything associated with it. I wish I could at least get a Committee letter[1] so as to keep in touch.

I am in full agreement with your reply to Loe and have already addressed it and sent it off.

His letter is so far from reality – as his letter last year was as well, incidentally – that it no longer makes any sense to continue relations on *this* basis. I had the feeling at the time, when it was decided in Holland that we wouldn't be going to England,[2] that we would no longer see or hear much from her. I don't think she will reply either; and of course I would be all the more pleased for that reason if she were to after all.[3] She spoke to me about Rank in the same way in Holland, but didn't want you to know about it. She assured me at the same time on several occasions that her relationship to us was quite different from the relationship to Rank and that the two were independent. I believe I have already mentioned that to you.

I also received a particularly nice letter from the other Lou the day before yesterday, a whole collection of books of hers and the promised manuscript of Rilke's elegies.[4] I was immensely pleased to receive everything and will thank her today.[5]

I have written to Mama with the news of the house and all the housekeeping details that are only of interest to her. I am sitting at the moment with Heinerle, who is suffering terribly from chickenpox and is very unhappy.

I found everything in Berlin very good. Oliver makes a relatively good impression and is captivated and fulfilled by his analysis[6] and is currently postponing all other activities and plans.[7] He is still limping a lot, by the way, and his minor accident appears to have been less pleasant than he wrote. I have also spoken with Eitingon as I intended about the matter of his analysis. He claims to have known that I would think like that and even wrote a very nice letter to me here in Hamburg about it. I am very happy that he is his old self again.

[Continuation 13 March 1922]
Since I wrote the first line of the last paragraph it is now Monday, because it's not so simple to write letters here. Dr Lippmann[8] was just here to look at Heinerle and promised that he would soon be healthy again; he said I should be happy that the children chose this disease and not a more serious one for my visit. But they take everything so seriously: yesterday evening Heinerle had 39.9 and today he has a temperature of 40, but is now very dear and well-behaved. When I wanted to know something from him earlier, he lifted up his nightdress and said 'Ask the pox!' I am sleeping at the moment in Ernstl's bed and he in mine, because Heinerle often needs something and it would otherwise disturb Ernstl too much.

The household is going excellently except that today a pastry didn't rise properly, which is very annoying. But I think the flour here is not right.

Max is very happy to be rid of Frl Jacob for a little while.

He has incidentally concluded a great deal, which he is very happy about. The day before yesterday he was informed that he will be receiving provisionally 10,000 M for the fifteen photographs signed by you! He promptly gave me a whole box of langues de chat. But he says that he can't keep it for himself and will write to you about it.

Ditha[9] writes on a card that you have invited Dr Frink for 1 May.[10] Is that right? Or did I read the name incorrectly?

How are the Stracheys[11] and how is my typewriter?

Write soon.

Sincerely,
Your Anna

1 See 126 AF, note 5. At the end of 1924 Anna became a member of the committee (instead of Rank). 'The new member, my daughter and secretary, appreciates the recognition,' wrote Freud in his *Rundbrief* article on 15 December 1924 ⟨*Rundbriefe I*, pp. 25f.⟩. For her 'Ring of the Nibelungen', see 174 AF, note 5.

2 See 107 SF–111 AF, text after 123 AF/SF.

3 See 161 SF.

4 As a present for Anna's twenty-sixth birthday, which occurred during Lou's visit to Vienna, Lou transcribed the *Duino Elegies* that had been completed at that time ⟨Anna/Lou, letters 6–11, with editorial comments, pp. 684, 686, 688⟩. Pfeiffer describes the Third Elegy (1912–13) and the imaginary 'Letter from a Young Worker' (1922) as the greatest witnesses . . . to the very intensive effect of Freud's theories on Rilke ⟨Pfeiffer [German version], p. 255, 3rd note on p. 57⟩. See also 168 AF and note 9.

5 Anna/Lou, letter 11.

6 With Franz Alexander; see 163 AF ⟨Freud/Eitingon, 225 E⟩.

7 'The dashing start he has made goes on,' wrote Eitingon to Freud on 16 February ⟨Freud/Eitingon, 230 E, p. 276; Anna/Lou, letter 172, p. 310; Gay, p. 429, note †⟩.

8 Arthur Siegfried Lippmann (1884–1950), professor of medicine and surgery, specialist in internal medicine, employed since 1908 at the Hamburg St Georg General Hospital, from which he was dismissed in 1933 because of his Jewish origins. He also had a private practice and had earlier treated Sophie Halberstadt there (Freud 1997*e*). He had made a name for himself for his research, particularly into children's diseases. In 1938 he emigrated with his wife to Australia, where he worked until his death as a doctor and researcher ⟨Andrae, pp. 32–66, 110; *Hamburger Ärzteblatt* 5/98, pp. 172f.; *Reichsmedizinkalender für Deutschland*, part II, Leipzig (1926–7); Fischer, I. [1962]; I thank the Hamburg scientists mentioned individually in the Acknowledgements⟩.

9 Judith Bernays (1885–1977), later married name Heller, the oldest daughter of Freud's sister Anna and Eli Bernays. She worked for a time in the *Verlag* and also translated some of Freud's works into English (e.g., 1893*f*, 1898*a*, 1904*a*, 1905*a*) ⟨Freud/Jones, letter 353; see also the editorial preface by Strachey to the Freud translations in volumes 3 and 9 of the *Standard Edition*⟩. See 159 SF, note 6.

10 Horace Westlake Frink (1883–1936), doctor of medicine, American psychiatrist, founder member of the New York Psychoanalytic Society and president in 1913 and 1914. Freud thought him to be extraordinarily talented and appreciated him as an outstanding pioneer of psychoanalysis in the USA. From March to June 1921 he had been analysed by Freud and now wished to continue. He terminated the second phase in July before returning again in November for a few weeks (until 23 December 1922) and again in early 1923. He then became president of the New York group again. His career ended tragically, however, through an unfortunate love affair and divorce – in which Freud was also involved (see 181 SF and note 15, 184 SF) – and recurrent attacks of an earlier psychotic disease (see 154 SF, annex 2, note 1) ⟨*IZ*, vol. 7 (1921), p. 398; vol. 9 (1923), p. 249; vol. 23 (1937), p. 331; *IJ*, vol. 18 (1937), pp. 109, 119; Freud/Ferenczi III, 860 F, 913 F, 1088 Fer, 1094 Fer; Dupont, p. xxv; Freud/Jones, *passim*, e.g., letters 194, 327, 353, 356, 359, 376, 433–5, 443; *Rundbriefe*, e.g., vol. 1, pp. 102f., vol. 3, pp. 167, 181, and 15 February

1925; Oberndorf [1936]; Jones II, p. 98; Jones III, pp. 39, 89 (with incorrect year of the first analysis), pp. 111f. (dates different from this correspondence); Edmunds; Gay, pp. 565f. with note; Roazen [1976], pp. 377–80; for more recent literature, see letter 181 Ma/Mi, note 5, in Freud/Bernays⟩.

11 James Strachey (1887–1967) and Alix Strachey, née Sargant-Florence (1892–1973), both associated with the Bloomsbury Group, an influential group of British intellectuals, writers and artists in the first third of the twentieth century. Recently married, they had been having a teaching analysis with Freud since October and November 1920, respectively, which they completed at the end of June 1922 ⟨Freud/Jones, letters 353, 364, 367, 370⟩. Alix had had life-threatening 'serious influenza with purulent pleurisy' ⟨Anna/Lou, letter 9, 26 February 1922, p. 22; letters 10, 13; *Bloomsbury* [1995], pp. 89f.; Freud/Jones, letters 342, 347⟩. (See also PS to 157 SF.) In 1920 both Stracheys had already begun to translate works by Freud. After their return to England in autumn 1922 they became members of the British Psychoanalytical Society ⟨*IZ*, vol. 8 (1922), p. 531; Freud/Jones, letters 274–342, passim; De Clerck, pp. 22–8; Bloomsbury [1995], e.g., pp. 4–8, 26–30; Strachey [1966], p. xxi⟩. James Strachey later became the leading translator of Freud and editor of the first commented edition of his psychoanalytical works, *The Standard Edition of the Complete Psychological Works of Sigmund Freud.*

157 SF

PROF. DR. FREUD 19 March 1922
Vienna, IX. Berggasse 19

My dear Anna,
I am very pleased that you approved of and sent off my letter. I don't think there will be a reply either.[1] But that will just prove that it is time to break off. One has to be able to tear oneself away sometimes and should not continue to drag things around that have evidently outlived their purpose.

You insist on news from here. Aunt will already have reported to you on the minor events. I have little to add. It is a markedly quiet and empty time, little mail, few signs of interest in the world at large, no books, no manuscripts. I had an incidental inquiry from the University of Dublin, asking if I wanted to lecture there for a week.[2] I also have the impression that the Verlag is not doing anything at the moment but enjoying its nice new premises;[3] the promised new publications are not yet here, and I have heard nothing about the translations of *Pleasure Principle* or *Group Psychology*.[4] The other English books don't seem to be making any progress; I don't know what I should say about it. Nothing would most likely be the best. They are probably supporting the strike in their way, which is still keeping all bookshops and publishing companies closed.[5]

Some changes in the practice.[6] You were still here when Mrs Riviere arrived,[7] and so far she has not been bad at all. Meyer[8] and Kardiner[9] are leaving at the end of the month and will be replaced by Dr Blum from Zurich,[10] who is already here, and Tansey,[11] for whom the indefatigable Rickman[12] has organized accommodation. He will occupy the rooms of the late botanist Wiesner[13] and use his library. Frink will indeed be here on 1 May; he apparently cannot hold out.

Our finance controller Dr Young has been keeping away from me, which is not very polite, because there are good reasons for him to come.[14]

Your typewriter does not grip the paper any more. It is being repaired, which we shall naturally pay for.

As you know, I wanted to go with Mama to Karlsbad. Both authorities, Edelmann[15] and Steiner, were against the idea and Aunt has therefore rented with Wassing for July.[16] The other summer plans are still cooking.

Altogether, what you write about the boys is much more interesting than everything going on here. Heinele is a very amusing scoundrel but should certainly be capable of taming. For Ernstl the summer in Seefeld[17] appears really to have been a turning point.

I hope that you settle into this phase of your life as well as in the previous one, and send my affectionate greetings,

Papa

P.S. I am surprised to discover that I am going this evening to *The Marriage of Figaro*[18] in the Redoutensaal.

[Vertically in the margin]

The Strachey[s] are still in the sanator[ium]. She is well and I sent her a basket of flowers 'on behalf of Lou A.'.[19]

1 But see 161 SF.
2 See 159 SF.
3 The slowness of the *Verlag* and the 'Press' was partly to do with the difficulties in the translation work. This subject also takes up considerable space in the correspondence between Freud and Jones ⟨Freud/Jones, e.g., letters 280, 289–335, 342, 351–64, 382, 433, 494–9, 515, 550; Freud's article in the *Rundbriefe* on 26 November 1922, vol. 3, pp. 231–5, is just one example⟩. In 1927 Jones was still complaining: 'In the course of years we have gathered in London three or four people . . ., no sign of an adequate translation has yet appeared anywhere except in their hands' ⟨Freud/Jones, letter 494, 27 January 1927, p. 609⟩. Besides himself and Joan Riviere, these three or four reliable translators included James and Alix Strachey. During their first translations these two established a glossary of specialist terms, which Jones (1924) together with them, Joan Riviere and Anna Freud added to (see 107 SF, note 11) ⟨Freud/Jones, letters 321, 340, 342; *Rundbriefe 2*, 11 December 1921, p. 311; Hughes, p. 265; for a revision under Jones's direction, see *IZ*, vol. 21 (1935), pp. 143, 308⟩.
4 Both appeared that year, however: *Beyond the Pleasure Principle* (1920*g*), translated by C. J. M. Hubback with a preface by Jones (1920*a*); *Group Psychology and the Analysis of the Ego* (1921*c*), translated by James Strachey. Freud had long been interested in the translation of these works into English ⟨Freud/Jones, letters 310, 316, 318–20, 324⟩.
5 See 170 SF, note 4; 179 SF and note 5.

6 Spelling mistake (no umlaut) in the original.

7 Joan Riviere (1883–1962), British lay analyst, founder member of the British Psychoanalytical Society since 1919 ⟨*Rundbriefe 1*, p. 25; Freud/Jones, letter 339⟩. She was analysed by Jones from 1916 to 1921 (with a one-year interruption) and attended the Congress in The Hague in 1920 ⟨*IZ*, vol. 6 (1920), p. 377⟩. Even then she was working on the translation of Freud's writings and became one of his most committed and reliable translators ⟨Freud/Jones, letters 301, 316, 339–83, *passim*; Freud 1992*l*; Freud to Edward Bernays, 14 September 1923, quoted in Grubrich-Simitis [1993], p. 34, note 1⟩. Her analysis with Freud began on 27 February 1922 ⟨Freud 1992*l*, 5 February 1922; Freud/Jones, letters 321f., 339, 342 ('25 February' here either a typing or printing error)⟩. After the Salzburg Congress in 1924 she underwent further analysis for six weeks with Freud ⟨Freud 1992*l*, 24 March 1924⟩. Although after 1924 in England, she became a major supporter of Melanie Klein's theories, she remained in personal contact with Freud ⟨Hughes, p. 268; also Freud/Jones, letters 511, 512, pp. 634ff.; see also Gast [1996]⟩.

8 Monroe A. Meyer (1892–1939), doctor of medicine, American psychiatrist, member of the New York Psychoanalytic Society whose business he managed from 1932 until his death. He came to Vienna in autumn 1920 for training ⟨*IZ*, vol. 7 (1921), p. 398; Membership Roster of the New York Psychoanalytic Society; Freud/Jones, letter 306 (in note 2 by error 1919); Kardiner, pp. 16, 17, 70, 92; obituary in *IJ*, vol. 21 (1940), pp. 114f.⟩.

9 Abram Kardiner (1891–1981), doctor of medicine, American neurologist and psychiatrist, practising psychoanalyst after his return to New York in 1922. His analysis with Freud began in October 1921 and ended on 1 April 1922 ⟨Kardiner, p. 67 and *passim*; Freud/Jones, letters 306, 342⟩.

10 'Zurich' spelt incorrectly (no umlaut). Ernst Blum (1892–1981), doctor of medicine, neurologist, initially in Berne, then in Zurich. Member of the Swiss Society for Psychoanalysis, in which he was a member of the expert committee ⟨*IZ*, vol. 7 (1921), p. 521; vol. 9 (1923), pp. 132f.; *Schweizerisches Medizinisches Jahrbuch* 1973; *Historisches Lexikon* 1998⟩. Freud arranged accommodation for him in the apartment of his friend Pribram ⟨Blum [1956]⟩.

11 (Sir) Arthur George Tansley (1871–1955), British biologist and phytoecologist, who coined the term 'ecosystem' in 1935; professor at Cambridge University. He knew James Strachey through his membership of the Bloomsbury Group. He was a supporter of psychoanalysis and had given a lecture in 1920 at the British Society for the Study of Sex Psychology on 'biological aspects of Freud's sexual theory'. In 1925 he became a member of the British Psychoanalytical Society. Jones told Freud that he would be arriving in March 1922; he started his analysis on 1 April ⟨Freud/Jones, letters 307, 310, 353; Jones III, p. 119; *Rundbriefe I*, p. 94⟩.

12 John Rickman (1891–1951), doctor of medicine, British psychiatrist, member of the British Psychoanalytical Society, in which he was later to play an important role. He was analysed by Freud from Easter 1920 to autumn 1922. At the time he worked occasionally in the *Verlag* and with Anna translated some of her father's works for the *Collected Papers* ⟨Freud/Jones, e.g., letters 262, 266, 269, 275, 316, 327, 330–4, 342, 352, 353, 370, 386; *IZ*, vol. 7 (1921), p. 119, vol. 8 (1922), p. 531⟩. He later underwent a further analysis with Ferenczi, during which some of the aspects of the alienation between Freud and Ferenczi came to light (see 287 SF) ⟨Freud/Jones, letter 546; Freud/Ferenczi III, 1132 Fer; 1172 F⟩.

13 Julius Ritter von Wiesner (1838–1916), professor at the Mariabrunn Forestry Academy and from 1873 in Vienna. He worked in the field of phytoecology and physiology and in raw material sciences, and published many fundamental botanical works ⟨Molisch⟩.

14 George M. Young (1882–1959), British diplomat who had been staying temporarily since 1920 in the British mission in Vienna to supervise a loan that Britain had given to Austria. At the time, after initial analysis by Jones, he had consulted Freud at Jones's suggestion. Jones recommended him as a highly intelligent and extremely cultured 'typical Englishman', by far the most capable and interesting person he had ever analysed. Young terminated the analysis with Freud after a few months because he was sent on a mission to Innsbruck. He returned to Vienna thereafter, but not to Freud ⟨Freud/Jones, letters 288, 289, 297–9, 301, 347, 353⟩.

15 Adolf Edelmann (1885–1939), doctor of medicine, specialist in internal medicine in Vienna. He was made (life-long) director of the S. Canning Child Clinic in Vienna in 1930 but was dismissed after the annexation by the Germans in 1938. As a Pole by birth, he returned to Warsaw, where he died a short time afterwards ⟨Fischer, I. [1962], [2002]⟩.

16 In Bad Gastein.

17 The previous year; see 153 AF, note 1.

18 Opera by W. A. Mozart, libretto by Lorenzo da Ponte. An aria from this opera played a role in a dream by Freud, which he analysed in *The Interpretation of Dreams* ⟨1900*a*, pp. 208–18, 431–4⟩.

19 Lou Andreas-Salomé, who met the Stracheys during her stay in Vienna at the end of 1921 and was very taken particularly with Alix, had asked about her health ⟨Freud/Andreas-Salomé, 2 March 1922, p. 113; 13 March 1922, p. 114; Anna/Lou, letter 10⟩.

158 AF

Hamburg, 23 March 1922

My dear Papa,

Thank you for your letter and all the news. I am astonished to read that really nothing has been happening in Vienna in my absence, like when you are called to the phone while dining and say before going out: 'Don't talk about anything interesting while I'm gone'. It's surprising that not even the Verlag has managed anything new. I think it spends all its time sending me English revisions; but if it doesn't buck up its ideas, I shall also stop working so quickly.

The news of the minor indisposition of my typewriter doesn't surprise me. It already had a tendency to do that, and I had also warned Dr Rickman about it. He should now try to get it repaired as quickly as possible (but not pay for it, of course), but shouldn't use the time in between for a rest from work; I can read his handwriting very well.

I am secretly hoping for a reply from Loe after all. I cannot understand that such things can simply come to an end. We have remained the same; why hasn't she? Or were we simply an artificially sustained exception after the war to her hatred of Germans that could not be kept up for ever? If she doesn't write, my reluctance to accept assistance from her – in 1918 or whenever – might well have been right.[1]

From the other Lou I had again a particularly delightful, rapid and personal reply to my letter, which gave me much pleasure. I don't want to abandon the idea of going to Göttingen, even if it means that the visit to Berlin will be a very short one. Dr Eitingon says of her that when you tell her something she understands it better than yourself. For example, she also made a few utterances about my stay here, about which I had only written to her briefly and vaguely, speculating how I must be feeling. And she was quite right; except that I wouldn't have been able to say it as clearly as she did.[2]

There is not much news to relate from here. The weather is murderous, still around 0° and a biting wind. The day before yesterday we were at Helene[3] and Julius Philip[p]'s[4] for dinner. It was quite nice but the way home was so terrible that I couldn't warm up again until the following morning. Yesterday Dr Obermann[5] came to dinner, and we also see the Rosenthals quite often.[6] I am very tolerant towards everyone here, with the pleasant feeling that they in fact have nothing to do with me and that in a short time I will see nothing more of them.[7]

Max's mood is unchanged, very dispirited and depressed, and like last year I am being somewhat infected by it again despite myself. Unfortunately, he has little joy in his work either, and in the evening too little strength and freshness to summon up a real interest in anything unconnected with his work.

Nothing to report from the children at present. Heinerle is not difficult to 'tame' and for the time being he is more of an internal revolutionary. If you tell him not to do something, his first reaction is 'But I would really like to'; his second, if you continue to look sternly at him, the tempestuous and gentle demand: 'Please be friends with me!' As you can see, he hasn't yet managed to make himself completely independent of his environment. He is extremely intelligent and plays for hours with lots of imagination, taking all possible roles, appearing in turns as the milk, butter and egg man, 'young gentleman', little girl or the different people from Hohegeiss.[8] Each one is announced out loud, and he speaks so incessantly that one wonders how a human throat can stand it. He only knows two times for the moment: 'yesterday', which covers all of the past (e.g., 'But yesterday you said I could', if he is not allowed to do something), and 'Monday', which covers all of the future and consoles him for every refusal (e.g., 'But on Monday I'm allowed to again').

Write to me again soon. Affectionate greetings in the meantime from,
Your Anna

When are we [sic] meant to be in Dublin?

1 See 161 SF, 162 AF and notes 1 and 2; see also 100 SF, note 7.
2 See Lou to Anna on 18 March 1922 and Anna's reply on 26 March ⟨Anna/Lou,

letters 12, 13⟩. The first visit to Göttingen took place from 24 April to 4 May 1922 (see 167 AF⟩.

3 Possibly the 'Mrs Philipp, wife of your wife's cousin here [in London]' mentioned in the Freud/Jones correspondence, who might have been staying temporarily in Hamburg with her husband ⟨letters 326–8, pp. 442–4⟩.

4 See 147 AF and note 5.

5 Julian [N.] Obermann (1888–1956), D.Phil., Privatdozent [outside lecturer] in Semitic languages and cultures, history of religion and history of the Orient in the Philosophy Faculty in Hamburg, in 1923 professorship at the Jewish Institute of Religion in New York. ⟨I thank Dagmar Bickelmann, Hamburg, for the latter information.⟩ In 1928–9 he taught at Columbia University and in 1931 at the Jewish Institute of Religion as 'distinguished Sterling professor of Semitic languages' ⟨Heller, p. 83; *Kürschner* 1928–9⟩. On 4 December 1920 (in *Rundbriefe 1*, p. 206, note 7, incorrectly '20 December') he spoke at the Berlin Psychoanalytic Society on 'religious problems and psychoanalysis' ⟨*IZ*, vol. 7 (1921), p. 118⟩. He might also have been one of the guests in Bad Gastein mentioned by Freud in 152 SF. 'Two of your friends have already visited us. Dr Obermann is coming this evening for dinner,' Freud wrote on 6 August 1921 to Max Halberstadt. And on 19 February 1922 he reported: 'I have just read the manuscript of a new book by Dr Reik, "Der eigene und fremde Gott" in which . . . Dr Obermann could find the solution to many of the puzzles that are tormenting him.' Between 1913 and 1929 Obermann was linked with Eva Rosenfeld in a 'poetically and spiritually' inspired 'passionate friendship and turbulent romantic love affair'. Anna did not hear of it until 1929 ⟨Heller, pp. 82f.; Bittner, p. 21; Anna/Eva, letters 11–13 and note 5, letter 9 and note 2, letter 11, note 1⟩.

6 Spelling mistake (no umlaut) in the original.

7 See 28 SF, note 2.

8 Hohegeiss, in the western Harz, south of Braunlage on the edge of the Upper Harz, where the children were to spend their summer holidays with Martha and Frl Jacob. See 172 MF/AF, note 3.

159 SF

PROF. DR. FREUD 27 March 1922
Vienna, IX. Berggasse 19

My dear Anna,

I shall reply straightaway. It takes long enough for an answer to come.

The outcome with the first Loe is not so difficult to understand. We did not need to change, but she has come increasingly under the influence of her husband, who was clever enough not to demand a sudden change[1] and who was very keen to tear her away from all her earlier relationships because he does not want to be reminded of her 'past'. A very understandable expression[2] of jealousy, which no one should in fact be ashamed of.[3]

You should certainly not give up the idea of visiting the other Lou and should not think about when you will be coming home.

Still very little news. This week Meyer and Kardiner will be substituted by Blum (Zurich) and Tansley (Cambridge). The replacement will be made as promptly as the changing of the guards. I recently complained to Jones and suggested that we include a snail next to the sphinx in the coat-of-arms of the Press. He will no doubt feel very insulted.[4] Riviere, who is very clever, recalls how bad he is at organizing and making good use of people.

For Dublin a date has not even been mentioned. Otherwise just unimportant rejections: articles, lectures, other forums, congresses.

Eitingon asked in his last letter if he should come to Vienna on 6 May. I reluctantly agreed on the grounds that every pretext that brings him here is acceptable.[5] You can oppose the idea if you think that he won't be hurt, but be careful!

Nothing new at home either. Ditha is touchingly virtuous and inefficient.[6] Esti ran off yesterday without saying goodbye in a hardly justified fit of rage but was already back today to apologize. She is quite unusually hot-headed.[7] Martin is not wrong when he says that he hasn't hit the jackpot, but is behaving very respectably. The boy[8] is well again but not very intellectually precocious for one year (3 April). Today I paid 1,661,000[9] K in taxes.

The way you write about Heinerle is delightful. With so much tenderness, the morality will come of its own accord. It's a pity about Max. Difficult to help! By the way,[10] has he sent the two pictures to New York and Calcutta?[11]

The weather is bitterly cold, although not as bad as where you are. There was some magnificent snow a few days ago. People are dying en masse. The summer plans are very unclear. An inquiry has been written to South Tyrol,[12] e.g., Madonna di Campiglio from 1 August to 8 September. How would you feel about spending July with Ernstl in Seefeld?[13] Although he would have to be brought there and picked up again. In the mountains it's not much fun for him for now, and you should also take some weeks off.[14]

Affectionate regards to you, Max and the little ones.

Papa

1 Spelling mistake (no umlaut) in the original.
2 Spelling mistake (no umlaut) in the original.
3 Freud himself had been extremely jealous during his engagement ⟨letters to his fiancée, Martha Bernays, in 1960*a*⟩.
4 Jones did not feel insulted (see 163 SF and note 7); in his reply he explained in detail the difficulties with his co-workers, particularly Hiller, and the failings of the printers and suppliers ⟨Freud/Jones, letters 351, 352, and again emphatically in 354⟩. For the growing conflict in the *Verlag* and 'Press', see 181 SF, note 5.
5 Freud/Eitingon, 231 E, 232 F.
6 Judith Bernays (see 156 AF, note 9). She was living with the Freuds at the time; see 165 AF, note 3. On the 'efficiency' of her work, see Freud/Jones, letters 354, 356, 364; see also 160 AF.
7 Esti's daughter, Miriam Sophie Freud (born 6 August 1924), recalls: 'My first mother was (or became in her disastrous marriage) an unhappy and bitter woman' ⟨*My Three Mothers and Other Passions*, p. 3⟩. See also her epitaph,

'Mother and Daughter', ibid., pp. 327–39. See also Anna/Lou, letter 75; Molnar [1996], p. 55 (6 January 1930).

8 Anton ('Toni/Tonerl') Walter (1921–2004), Esti and Martin Freud's first child ⟨Freud/Jones, letter 306; I thank Christfried Tögel for the year of death⟩. He was named after the 'unforgettable Toni Freund' ⟨*Rundbriefe 2*, p. 139; Freud to Kata, 28 March, 4 April 1921⟩. In 1938 he emigrated with his father to England and was interned in Australia in 1940. He joined the Pioneer Corps on his way back to England and later the Special Operations Executive. In early 1945 he was parachuted into Austria 'and liberated the airfield in Zeltweg on his own'. In December 1946 he was demobbed with the rank of major and lived in London, where he worked as a chemical engineer ⟨Molnar [1996], p. 64; Freud/Ferenczi III, 857 F, note 1⟩.

9 The two figures before '1,000' are difficult to read as they have been corrected and crossed out. For the devaluation of the currency, see 179 SF and note 5.

10 Spelling mistake (no umlaut) in the original.

11 The Indian Psychoanalytical Society was founded in Calcutta on 22 January 1922 ⟨*IZ*, vol. 8 (1922), p. 500; Freud/Jones, letter 344⟩. See also Freud's letters (1956*i*) to Girindrarsekhar Bose, the founder of this group.

12 Spelling mistake (no umlaut) in the original.

13 Full stop instead of question mark in the original.

14 The summer plans were changed again several times; see 160 AF, 161 SF, 166 SF, 187 SF; for the final dates and places, see 170 AF, notes 2 and 5, 172 MF/AF, note 3, 174 AF, note 10, and 188 AF, note 7.

160 AF

[Hamburg,] Sunday, 2 April 1921

Dear Papa,

I thank you very much for your letter and I shall answer you straightaway as well, at least in the first somewhat longer, quiet hour on Sunday after dinner, when the others are sleeping. Yesterday and the day before were somewhat unsettled days; Ernsti is on holiday again, then I had to go to the police to extend my residence permit, then it was washing and ironing day, and finally visitors yesterday evening. On one afternoon I was also invited with Ernsti to Frl Lehmann's for tea.

I enclose a letter from Jones, which I received today through the Verlag. Ditha will be pleased at the praise for her translation.[1] I don't know Jones's style well enough to decide whether it is a friendly or an offended letter; most likely the latter. I find that his fear of 'duplication' [in English] is not justified, because in a letter to you he explicitly described the first volume of the collection as still free.[2] I find the idea of having Bryan translate something by you outrageous. Bryan doesn't know German and as everyone knows after his Abraham translations he is a notoriously bad translator;[3] Dr Rickman will confirm it. I have already written back to Jones, referring to this letter to you and promising that Ditha will provide the titles of her translations herself. Do you want to tell her? And perhaps Dr Rickman can do the same. I am very disappointed, incidentally, that Dr Rickman has not been working in my absence; since my departure I have not received more than five pages of translation from him. Is there some reason for this? And can't you push him?[4] If he were to work, the whole volume could be done by the summer. Instead the English publishers senselessly and unintelligently send me the same essays with the second, third and fourth revisions instead of just giving me the galley proofs and sending everything else – as agreed – to Ditha, which would save a lot of time and postage. But Hiller still seems to be preoccupied.[5] I was very amused about the snail in the coat-of-arms. No one says such nice things here.

I also wanted to write to you about the summer plans. Ernstl is counting on staying with us, and Max could probably be persuaded; it's not possible to make proper plans with him. I think, however, that if Max is to spend some time with us again, it should definitely not be during the time when you are not there. I already saw last year that it wasn't the right thing and have an even stronger feeling here that there would be little sense for him to be dependent on me; not to mention the fact that it is not always easy for me either; when you are there it is, of course, quite different. And who will collect and bring back Ernsti if not Max? Why are you writing about Seefeld, by the way? Isn't Mama meant to be going to Karlsbad on 1 July?[6] I have had another very nice letter from Lou in Göttingen in which she proposes – as our time together now will only be short and not sufficient to work[7] – that I spend July with her in Göttingen. I would like to do so. And then all of us, possibly with Max and Ernsti, could meet somewhere on 1 August. Do you think that would be possible?

I have now been here for four weeks but cannot yet say when I will be leaving. It will probably be another two or three weeks, then a few days in Berlin and a few days in Göttingen. I cannot possibly miss your birthday and for that reason I am less strict about Dr Eitingon, especially – as he has promised – if he meets to travel with me.

Heinerle's bedwetting is beginning to concern me; he fixes on it too energetically and consoles himself too easily when his surroundings are not to his liking. Today, in response to my coaxing and questions as to why he does it, he said: 'Because I like it.' I think that's a bit much and I will try to put more energy into the matter from now on; it will probably not do much good.[8]

The differences between the two children are very interesting. Ernst always asks at the table: 'Is Minna served already?' Yesterday Heinz, while eating with his right hand, reached for the rest of the pudding in the bowl with his left hand and said with a beaming smile: 'Give me that, then Minna will have nothing!' Max said recently at the table: 'I'm full.' Ernstl said sympathetically: 'Don't force Daddy', at which Heinz said: 'Daddy *has to* eat everything!' Heinz also unhesitatingly claims that everything belongs to him, especially when the real owner is out of hearing range. I still predict that in later life he will forge the bills of exchange and Ernst will pay them.

Max has sent the pictures (Calcutta, NY).

Write again soon,

Your Anna

1 See 159 SF, note 6.
2 Freud/Jones, letter 336, but see also letter 328. The reference is to the *Collected Papers*, the first collection of Freud's work in English ⟨Freud/Jones, letters 327, 334⟩.
3 Clement A. Douglas Bryan (1878–1955), doctor of medicine from Leicester. He was secretary of the Psycho-Medical Society, London, co-founder and vice-president in 1913 of the London Psychoanalytical Society, and one of the only practising British psychoanalysts of the time. From 1919 to 1937, he was secretary and treasurer of the British Psychoanalytical Society ⟨year of death according to the minutes of a scientific meeting [FSD/92]; for this information I thank Polly Rossdale, Archives of the British Psychoanalytical Society, 17 November 2004⟩. Jones appreciated Bryan's reliability and described him as one of the two 'leading analysts in England'. He worked most industriously as a translator but his style and grammar were weak, even if he was constantly improving ⟨Jones II, p. 116; Jones III, p. 39; Freud/Jones, letters 141, 331, 354 (the quote pp. 470f.)⟩. He translated the following works by Freud: 1908*a*, 1908*c*, 1909*a*, 1916–17*c*, 1919*g* (editorial preface to these works by James Strachey in vols 9, 14 and 18 of the *Standard Edition*). He also translated parts of the *Selected Papers of Karl Abraham* (1927–50) and Abraham and Harnik ⟨Grinstein, vol. 1, pp. 265f.⟩.
4 'He has an Oriental idea of time,' judged Jones in a letter to Freud ⟨Freud/Jones, letter 395, 5 April 1923, p. 518⟩.
5 See 133 SF and note 3. For Hiller's involvement in the conflicts between the 'Press' and the *Verlag*, see also 163 AF, 184 SF, 185 AF ⟨Freud/Jones, letters 352, 379, 380, 382, 383; *Rundbriefe 1*, p. 56 and notes 7 and 8⟩.
6 The doctors had advised against this; see 157 SF.
7 Because Anna stopped once again in Berlin before her visit to Lou (25 April–4 May) ⟨Anna/Lou, letters 13–19⟩.
8 In her later works, Anna discussed the problem of bedwetting as part of toilet training on several occasions, particularly in connection with the early loss of the mother; see, e.g., 1927d ⟨*Writings I* [1927*d*], p. 55, *Writings I* [1930], pp. 98–100, *Writings IV* [1953], pp. 512–15, *Writings VIII* [1965], p. 121, *Writings III* [1971], p. 201f.⟩.

161 SF

PROF. DR. FREUD 4 April 1922
Vienna, IX. Berggasse 19

My dear Anna,
I am once again answering your letter right away. Rank is coming tomorrow and there is at least some news. Above all, your Varendonck is here; it's quite impressive.[1] I hope they send you a copy soon. Even more interesting, there is a reply from Lou.[2] Not very friendly, a little crazy and just as we suspected. But still friendly as a gesture. You can't argue with her as you would with another cool-headed person; her strength is in her impulsiveness,[3] which now serves her Christian, anti-German Davy. I shall now make an effort to compose a cordial but dignified reply and will send it to you with her letter. I have not managed in the

last few days as I was suffering again from catarrh, which has only been helped by the cauterization today. On Sunday morning I went by car to Sanator[ium] Purkersdorf[4] (100,000[5] K) and in the afternoon was at Frau Schiff's.[6]

It was Tonerl's birthday yesterday but he slept through my congratulatory visit. He got lots of presents. His mental development seems to suffer under the influence of the nanny. Fortunately, he has time. Esti has rented in Spital aS [am Semmering].

The cigar situation has improved. Figdor[7] has brought some again from Holland and Schmideberg[8] is looking out for the telegram from Emden indicating the departure of the next – and last – children's train.[9] Marianne[10] has successfully completed her doctoral viva. Margarethl has been engaged for the autumn at the Raimundtheater[11] – finally some glimmers of light amongst our friends.

Ditha was red with bliss at the praise from Jones, like a boarding-school girl. She will write to him directly. I don't know why the scoundrel Rickman is not working and I will talk to him tomorrow. He will take a week's holiday before Easter to collect wife and child[12] from Antwerp. I shall read out your justified criticism of the Press activity to Rank tomorrow.

The new ones are doing well. Riviere is sharp and very shrewd, and Tansley is an amiable scholarly type.

The weather is dreadful; people are saying 'Frierjahr' [freezing year] instead of 'Frühjahr' [spring]. The plans for the summer are refusing to prosper and there has been no progress since the last letter. I approve of your plan to spend July in Göttingen, but what is Mama to do in the meantime,[13] and most important, *where* are we to meet on 1 August with Max and Ernstl?[14] I am more optimistic about Heinerle's future. He will become very moral; his great amiability will assure him of that. His naughtiness is closely linked to his intellectual vitality. Being well behaved is dull [English word used in original] from the outset. Of course, it would be good if he were finally to become toilet-trained. Try by arousing his ambition and with some energy. Of course, if you tell him that we cannot take him in summer unless he is toilet-trained, he might pull himself together and then we will have to do it!

I wish you further success in your difficult position and send my affectionate greetings, also to Max and the boys,

Papa

1 Anna's translation of Varendonck (1921*b*); see 142 SF and note 13. Ferenczi was 'quite delighted with the book by Varendonck' ⟨Freud/Ferenczi III, 902 Fer, 15 May 1922, p. 80⟩.

2 From Lou Jones; see 155 SF – 157 AF. See also 100 SF, note 7.

3 See 42 SF, note 5; also 163 SF, 100 SF, note 7.

4 Freud could have been visiting a patient there. Many illustrious persons went for a cure to 'Sanatorium Purkersdorf Dr Victor Zuckerkandl', but it served

for the most part for the treatment of neurological diseases. Frau 'Berta Zuckerkandl was known personally to Professor Freud . . . but the findings of psychoanalysis were not included in the sanatorium therapies, although a good number of the "neurotics" were typical of the patients recruited by Freud' ⟨Etzersdorfer, pp. 103f.⟩. In 1904–6 the architect Josef Hoffmann designed a new kurhaus for the sanatorium, which became famous as an outstanding Vienna Jugendstil 'Gesamtkunstwerk' [total work of art]; this 'milestone in European architecture' remains a cultural monument today ⟨*Purkersdorf*; Etzersdorfer; Müller, D.⟩.

5 The figure is not clearly legible; it could also be 200,000.

6 See 126 AF and note 11.

7 See 138 SF and note 14.

8 Walter Schmideberg (1890–1954), Austro-Hungarian cavalry captain with an early interest in psychology. He met Eitingon (who introduced him to psychoanalysis), Ferenczi and Freud during the First World War, and he was able to use his military position to perform several similar 'courier services' as now ⟨see Freud/Ferenczi III, 891 F, 901 Fer⟩. He became a member of the Vienna Psychoanalytic Society in 1919. He moved to Berlin in 1922, where he had a psychoanalytical practice and was actively involved in the Berlin group. He married Melitta Klein in 1924 (daughter of Melanie Klein, who later became an analyst herself). They emigrated to England in 1932 but separated after the Second World War. Schmideberg went to Switzerland and worked there until his death ⟨*Protokolle IV*, p. 314 (here incorrectly 'Schmiedeberg'); *IZ*, vol. 6 (1920), pp. 112, 124; vol. 7 (1921), p. 532; vol. 8 (1922), pp. 117, 248, 528; Freud/Jones, letters 607, 619; Glover; Mühlleitner, pp. 289f.⟩.

9 This train was organized by an international children's aid association to transport "children from starving Austria abroad" ⟨Freud 1960*a*, p. 514, note 2 [German version]⟩.

10 Marianne Rie.

11 Margarete Rie. The theatre dedicated to the Viennese dramatist and actor Ferdinand Raimund (1790–1836) at Wallgasse 18–20 originally showed mainly popular pieces and operettas; in 1921–4, however, director Rudolf Beer inaugurated an 'ambitious and courageous programme' ⟨Weissensteiner, p. 156⟩. Several famous actors and actresses began their career at the Raimundtheater, including Hansi Niese, Paula Wessely, Attila Hörbiger and Karl Skraup, or made guest appearances (Adele Sandrock, Eleonora Duse). The theatre has been renovated and has belonged since 1987 to Vereinigte Bühnen Wien GesmbH. Its repertoire now consists of operettas and musicals. ⟨I thank Christiane Mühlegger-Henhapel, Austrian Theatre Museum, Vienna, for her kind information.⟩ For details of Margarete's roles, see letter 181 Ma/Mi, note 8, in Freud/Bernays.

12 Lucy Rickman, see 174 AF and note 6.

13 She went with Ernst and Heinerle to Hohegeiss; see 172 MF/AF, note 3.

14 The meeting with Max and Ernstl did not come about; Freud did not see the grandchildren again until mid-September, when he travelled with Anna to the Congress in Berlin (see 183 AF, note 3) and chose to go via Hamburg (see 188 AF, note 7). For further aspects of the summer, see 159 SF, note 14.

162 AF

Hamburg, 10 April 1922

My dear Papa,
Your Lou letter has just arrived – a short time after your own letter – and is now in an envelope next to me waiting to be posted. I was astonished to read her letter and almost frightened at her hardness, unfairness and bitterness, particularly the latter, for which I cannot find a reason anywhere. Her claim that we showed a lack of sympathy for Davy is difficult to understand – sometimes it was more a case of too much. And her distinction between providers of assistance (I wish we had never seen or eaten it)[1] is petty and quite unlike how she used to be. But what the war has to do with a purely human relationship, I will never understand, however many pages of explanation are written. Your reply is very good and proper and could not be otherwise; perhaps it will help to salvage a bit of the old friendship and take the sad aftertaste away from the way things have turned out. It might be a good idea to write a detailed letter to him to deal with the matter of the outstanding debt, because she suggests that he is the person concerned by the money matter, and he is so proper that he would certainly not make any difficulties if you were to explain the recent improved turn in our situation. I am fairly sure, but you will be able to judge even better. It is probably better that his letter to me remains unanswered. (It is now evident that she has really changed. And do you know what the initial signs were? The first was her petulant letter to me after Ernest Jones took my luggage,[2] and the second was his quite strange reaction to the news of Sophie's death.)

Do you have any news of Kata, by the way? I wrote to her from here,[3] but I haven't had a reply, which worries me at a time when relationships thought to be solid come unstuck like this.

I am getting really dear letters from the other Lou, which in the closed-off world here are almost like refreshing visits. (Can you ask Rank if she was sent a Varendonck (which she is interested in)? I arranged it (with Storfer)[4] before my departure, but don't trust the Verlag as it still hasn't sent me a copy either.)

I thank you for another of your detailed and newsy letters, which I always enjoy and look forward to as the most interesting event of the week here. Along with the letters from you and Lou, there was also a telephone call from Dr Eitingon and a really nice evening visit to Dr Foerster[5] and wife. He makes a very good impression as an analyst and never says anything stupid or exaggerated; and his wife is a simply wonderful singer.[6]

Everything is very quiet in the house, except for the noise that the children make. Max's mood and physical condition (the two are the same with him) are not very gratifying; I just see him tired and lying on the sofa all the time. I spoke to him yesterday evening and tried again to encourage him, like last year and in the summer, to spend more time with Ernsti, who would be so receptive to any stimulus from him and who is not really stretched intellectually by Frl Jacob and Minna. But it is to no avail. Max cannot put up with either of the children for more than five minutes and likes it best if they are already in bed when he comes home. He just wants peace and quiet, and advice like this makes him restless at most and puts him in a bad mood. But I nevertheless make an effort at least once a year.[7]

Max is always very pleased to hear that you console us about Heinerle's naughtiness by talking about his intelligence; both are unusually well developed. Added to that is a really huge appetite recently, which suits him very well. When food comes through the door, he shouts happily from far away: 'Yes, please!' And then it is a real pleasure to feed him. I naturally tell myself that this is the result of my not very frugal menus, because Ernstl is now also eating well. But there too Heinzl's character is evident. Whereas other children need to be coaxed to eat the last spoonfuls with: 'One for Mummy, one for Daddy', etc., with him you have to say: 'This is Minna's, this is Ernstl's, this is Aunt Anna's . . .' and then he eats it all up happily. Yesterday he was crying at the table so we sent him to Minna to finish eating, and after he had consoled himself he said to her: 'Fine, now Daddy can sit alone in the dining room and we can eat comfortably out here.' Or when Ernst throws him out of the children's room because he won't leave him in peace, he closes the door from the outside and says punitively: 'Now you can stay alone inside.' So he is always on form. The word he says most is a drawn-out 'why', as an expression of his doubts and disbelief at all of the commands and prohibitions. The chickenpox scabs have finally dropped off his head; he has had a haircut and looks delightful but still pale. He is always dirty or grubby and with the blackest hands he strokes his face, causing smears of dirt on his cheeks the next time he cries. His bedwetting cannot be taken lightly any more. After three proud dry nights, he once again soaked the bed for a week and on some nights, after I had changed the sheets at 2 or 3 o'clock, a second time before morning. Today I managed for the first time again to keep him dry, albeit after picking him up four times, at 9, 11, 1 and 5 o'clock. I think that I am more deserving of the reward he receives in the morning. During the day his bladder is not weak at all and he gets nothing more to drink after 4 o'clock, etc. He has no ambition and he quickly gets over having been naughty. I really don't know what to do any more. Is there no remedy? Dr Rosenthal speaks of electricizing but I don't know what you think of that. It is meant as a deterrent.

That's all of the interesting news from here at the moment – by land and by sea. Today I am going to the hospital again to try to get Frl J.[acob] to give me some kind of a date.

With a kiss and many greetings,
Your Anna

1 'Loe is still supplying the greater part of our sustenance by means of her shipments from The Hague,' wrote Freud to Ferenczi on 15 March 1920 ⟨Freud/Ferenczi III, 837 F, p. 13⟩.

2 When Ernest Jones travelled to Switzerland in early 1919 on *Verlag* business (see 100 SF, note 4), he took most of Anna's luggage with him (see 47 SF, note 6), which Loe was very indignant about. Jones advised Freud at the time to get Anna to write a thank-you letter to placate her ⟨Freud/Jones, letter 234, 17 March 1919, pp. 336f.⟩. See 100 SF, note 7.

3 Missing from the collection of letters from Anna to Kata available to me. The correspondence continued, however, until Kata's death (and afterwards with her son, Peter Lambda).

4 Adolf (Albert) Josef Storfer (1888–1944), journalist and editor (with law degree), who published the first legal psychoanalytical study in 1911 ⟨Freud/Abraham, 18 December 1910 and note 3 – the last sentence of this note is based on an error⟩. In 1919 he moved from Budapest to Vienna and switched from the Hungarian to the Viennese Psychoanalytic Society. In July 1921 he replaced Reik as Rank's assistant in the *Verlag* and took over from Rank as managing director on 1 January 1925, a position he retained until he was replaced by Martin Freud (16 January 1932) ⟨Freud/Ferenczi III, 1001 F, 1219 F; Freud 1992*i*, pp. 119f.; Freud/Eitingon, 691 F and note 4⟩. (For the disastrous financial situation of the *Verlag* at the time, see Martin's description in Freud, M. [1999], pp. 199f.) Storfer managed to escape to China at the end of 1938, where he founded a German émigré newspaper, *Die Gelbe Post*; in the first issue he printed fragments from six letters he had received from Freud between 1910 and 1935 ⟨Freud 1939*d*⟩. In 1941 he was obliged to flee again, this time from the Japanese, to Australia, where he lived in Melbourne until his death ⟨Mühlleitner, pp. 334–6; Jones III, pp. 32, 117, 144, 165f., 180f.; Scholz-Strasser; Freud/Eitingon, *passim*⟩.

5 Rudolf Hermann Foerster (1884–1924), doctor of medicine. With 'thorough neurological and psychiatric training', psychoanalyst, initially in Berlin, later in Hamburg ⟨Abraham [1924]⟩. He joined the Berlin group as a medical student in 1913 and presented a talk there on 29 November 'on the analysis of a paranoia' ⟨*IZ*, vol. 2 (1914), p. 410⟩. Even after moving to Hamburg in November 1919, he remained an external member of the Berlin Psychoanalytical Society until his 'premature death' ⟨Abraham, H. [1971], p. 24; Freud/Abraham, 16 October 1923, p. 474; I thank Dagmar Bickelmann, Hamburg, for additional information⟩.

6 Anna later took singing lessons herself: 'I have had an unfortunate love of singing since I was a very small child and have only now found the courage [. . .] but I don't want others to know. They would just laugh at me.' Soon, however, it was 'no secret any more' ⟨Anna/Lou, letters 213, 1 February 1925, p. 404; 232, 12 May 1925, p. 442; 264, 4 December 1925, p. 492; also 211, 212, 259, 271⟩. See also 48 SF, note 3.

7 The following year – after Heinerle's death (see 195 SF and note 2) – Max found another partner: Bertha Katzenstein (1897–1982), who had started work in his studio a short time previously as a clerk. They married on 20 November 1923 and their daughter, Eva, was born on 5 April 1925. Ernstl left his father's home in 1928 (see 146 SF and note 4). Max remained in Hamburg with his wife and daughter until 1936; when their economic and social circumstances deteriorated increasingly with the boycott of Jewish businesses in Germany, they emigrated to the Union of South Africa ⟨Freud 1992*i*, p. 197, 1 February, 4 February 1936; Freud/Jones, letter 652, 2 March 1937⟩. He died on 30 December 1940 in Johannesburg without 'having been able to take up his former occupation

fully' ⟨Weinke, pp. 112, 116f., 129, the quote p. 117 (Stammbaum Lange, Freud Family, 'Genealogical Tree', p. II, incorrectly gives Bertha's year of birth as 1894)⟩.

163 SF

PROF. DR. FREUD

13 April 1922
Vienna, IX. Berggasse 19

My dear Anna,
This time I really have to reply without delay, otherwise you might no longer be in Hamburg when the letter arrives. (Yesterday was a meeting of the Association; the number of guests is getting more and more out of hand.)

I am very pleased that you are in agreement on the whole with my reply to Loe. I think you can take your time answering Davy's letter, unless he has sent you a book again.[1] There is nothing I don't understand about this development; it is how I imagined it would be. The exaggeration[2] in her passion, all his inclinations; his hate of the Germans and no doubt an antipathy towards Jews. Passion was her strength, she never had judgement, and she was always unapproachable in analysis. (Instead of judgement I should perhaps say self-criticism.[)]] We can still like her, but at a distance. I don't think I could have expressed my willingness to repay more insistently. People with so much money are not impressed when you as a poor man rattle your coins; much more so if you appear to care as little about small amounts as they do themselves. The acceptance at the time doesn't bother me; it was done in good faith. The chapter will soon be closed.

Some small news from here. Polon,[3] the last of the Mohicans, is leaving tomorrow and his successor, Jeanne de Groot,[4] has already announced herself. The new ones, Riviere, Tansley and Dr Blum, continue to prove themselves agreeable and interesting. The English translation[5] of the *Lectures*, which was published on 11 April, is awaited daily. As you know, the translator is Riviere. I will be closed for Easter from Saturday to Tuesday. On Tuesday evening a Press meeting[6] is scheduled here: Hiller, Rank, Mrs Riviere, Strachey, Rickman, to discuss whether there is an alternative to this snail's pace. Jones, whom I turned to first, has replied in an unusually gentle and pleasant tone. He foresees Hiller returning to England and you taking over his position as head of the Verlag! (With #144 per annum.) He doesn't appear to consider any other possibilities for you.[7]

I have passed on your Varendonck message. Something happened yesterday that was like a class III textbook case with a moral background. In the morning I sent Mama to Augenfeld[8] with a #50 note for Aunt Mitzi, who is travelling to Berlin, and in the evening I received the same amount unexpectedly from the Verlag. Some weeks ago an American magazine requested an article from me. I refused to write something new but said that if they wanted to translate and publish[9] some trifle (*Dreams and Telepathy*), which is appearing in *Imago*, they could arrange it with Rank. I heard nothing further until I received half the fee, #50, from Rank yesterday for this essay.[10] If I were paid like that for every article, we would be rich people today.

An outstanding article for the magazine has arrived from Dr Alexander,[11] Oli's analyst,[12] which I shall probably award the prize at the Congress.[13] The first issue of both the magazine and *Imago* have now appeared.

So much for science. At home the arrival of spring has improved everybody's mood, without any progress having been made in the plans for the summer. Toni is becoming very cheeky and wild but remains quite stupid. Ditha is extremely[14] virtuous, makes herself useful and looks terrible. A new safety lock, Salvo, was fitted today to the door of the practice (15,000 K).

Electric [English in original] for Heinerle is of course nonsense. It is occasionally useful but the only certainty is that it costs money. There is nothing unduly worrying about the matter; it is quite in keeping with the little chap's character and he shouldn't be exposed so early to such serious traumata. It will probably clear up soon of its own accord. He will realize at some point that he is not socially acceptable and will break the habit. Don't make things difficult for yourself now. The remedies available are ultimately more damaging than the disorder, because they are all based on discipline.

Yesterday I had a very dear letter from Kata.[15] Complaints and requests for advice because of Rozsi's uselessness and lack of skill at bringing up children. Another person for whom nothing can be done, elemental abnormality. It's strange that such a fine specimen should have chosen two such useless women.[16]

I might already have told you of Schmideberg's inability to wrest from the Hungarian doctor the cigars sent in the Dutch children's train by Emden, and his unhappiness regarding it. It might still be possible to rectify matters on 10 May when the train returns.[17]

We are now very curious to hear more news from you. You have really been away long enough. I wouldn't object at all if you could be back by the beginning of May.

One more thing: I leaned on my nephrite paper knife with my elbow and broke the handle off from the blade. Can you write the address of your master gluer on a card so I can ask him first?

Affectionate greetings to you and the three men.

Papa

1 Two years previously, Herbert Jones had given her a 'long promised volume of poems'. 'They are love poems, sonnets, incredibly beautiful and clear in their language. He has learnt a lot in these five years and I am very happy,' wrote Anna at the time to her brother Ernst (12 March 1920).

2 Spelling mistake (no umlaut) and abbreviated in the original.
3 Albert Polon (1881–1926), doctor of medicine, American neurologist and recognized psychoanalyst, member and ultimately secretary of the New York Psychoanalytic Society. There he gave a talk in May 1921 on 'Bergson and Freud: Some Points of Correspondence' ⟨*IJ*, vol. 2 (1921), p. 485; Freud/Jones, letter 324⟩. His analysis commenced in October 1921 ⟨Freud/Jones, letter 306; Meyer⟩.
4 Jeanne de Groot (later Lampl-De Groot) (1885–1987), doctor of medicine. She had already become acquainted with psychoanalysis during her studies in Amsterdam; from 1922 onwards she attended meetings of the Vienna group as a guest. Her training analysis with Freud lasted until 1925, after which she moved to Berlin and completed her training at the Berlin Institute, where she subsequently also taught (1932–3). She married Hans Lampl in Berlin in 1925. In 1933 the family emigrated, initially to Vienna, and then at the end of May 1938 to the Netherlands. Both Lampls continued their analysis work in secret. After the Second World War, together with colleagues, they organized the re-establishment of psychoanalysis in the Netherlands. Jeanne de Groot was awarded several honorary titles; she became renowned for her research into femininity and the analysis of children. Anna, Jeanne, Dorothy Burlingham and Marianne Kris (née Rie) were friends and called themselves the Four Old Ladies of Psychoanalysis ⟨Lampl-De Groot, p. 58; Mühlleitner, pp. 202–4⟩.
5 The new translation of 1916–17*a* with a preface by Jones (1992*c*) was entitled *Introductory Lectures on Psychoanalysis I* (see 107 SF, notes 8, 11 and 12). The version of the *Lectures* published under the same title in the *Standard Edition*, vol. 15, in 1961 is another new translation, this time by James Strachey.
6 'Press' in Latin, 'sitzung' [meeting] in Gothic script.
7 See Freud/Jones, letter 354, 10 April 1922, p. 472. See also 159 SF, note 4.
8 Felix Augenfeld (1893–1984) ⟨Internet, 8 September 2005: 'Felix Augenfeld', <http://www.archinform.net/arch/58380.htm>; information supplied by Wolfgang Kloft⟩, an architect friend of Ernst and Lucie. He later renovated the apartment above the Freuds for Dorothy Burlingham, who moved there in 1929 (see 281 AF, note 3). At Mathilde's request, he designed a specially shaped tilt-and-swivel chair adapted to Freud's sitting and reading habits, which he used until the end of his life (see 'Epilogue' after 298 SF). It can be seen in the Freud Museum in London ⟨Gödde [2003], p. 178; Molnar [1996], p. 79; *Sigmund-Freud-Haus*, p. 55, no. 290. Ill., e.g., in Günther, p. 108, and Engelman, pp. 54, 56⟩.
9 Spelling mistake (no umlaut) in the original.
10 The 50-dollar remittance was accompanied by a letter from Rank of 11 April 1922; the fee was for providing the article (1922*a*) to 'Mr Wilson Pance for single publication in McCall-s [sic] Magazine' ⟨ORC; LoC SF, Cont. 39⟩. Freud writes that he had heard nothing more but he (probably later) checked the translation and rejected it with a 'two-page list of objections' (undated); he recommended that it be redone because it was 'so bad, so full of mistakes and so poor in understanding' ⟨quoted in Grubrich-Simitis [1993], p. 20, note 7, where 'Wilson Vance' is cited as the translator⟩. In a perusal of all issues of *McCall's Magazine* for this period in the Library of Congress, no relevant publication could be found ⟨LoC, Sign. TT500.M2, vol. XLIX, October 1921 – September 1922⟩. In spite of the down payment *this* translation appears not to have been published.

11 Franz Alexander (1891–1964), Hungarian doctor of medicine (Göttingen), student of Ferenczi, later of Hanns Sachs in Berlin where he had also been practising as an analyst since 1921, and soon to become an important figure in the Berlin Institute. He met Freud, who appreciated his great talent, during a visit to Vienna in 1925. In 1930 Alexander moved to the USA, founded a psychoanalytical institute in Chicago, which he directed for twenty-five years, and thereafter headed the psychiatric and psychoanalytical research centre at Mount Sinai Hospital in Los Angeles until his death. During this time he was also professor of psychiatry at the University of Southern California. He was one of the pioneers of psychosomatic medicine ⟨Grotjahn, pp.384–8; Harmat, pp.244–6; Kurzweil, pp.45, 52 and 322, note 9⟩.
12 See 156 AF and notes 6 and 7.
13 This work by Alexander (1922) did not ultimately receive an award, as no prizes were given at the Congress in the autumn (Stärcke and Róheim had received the prize in 1921; see Freud 1921*d*). Instead Freud announced a new competition on the subject 'The relationship of analytical technique to analytical theory' ⟨1922*d*; *IZ*, vol. 10 (1924), p.106⟩.
14 Spelling mistake (no umlaut) in the original.
15 Freud replied to her at 'Easter 1922' ⟨Freud to Kata⟩.
16 'Freund suffered one calamity after another; his first wife took her life, his daughter was mentally ill. His second marriage cannot have been so balanced either, as he kept a girlfriend' ⟨Harmat, p.63; see also Freud/Ferenczi III, 836 Fer, 866 Fer⟩.
17 See Freud/Ferenczi III, 901 Fer.

164 AF[1]

Prof. Dr. S. Freud　　　　Berlin, 19 April 1922
Vienna IX Berggasse 19

Dear Papa,
Your letter was forwarded to me here today. Unfortunately, I don't know the house number of my glue man[2] and can only describe its location. He lives in Lange Gasse on the odd-number side between Schönbornpark and Josefstädterstrasse. The shop has one door, a dark hole in, I think, a projecting house. Above the door is a long Italian-sounding name and on the doorpost there is normally a sculpture hanging. I hope you can find it from this description. Ernst reckons that the knife will need a narrow mounting, like my broken pendant did.

I have been with Ernst and Lux since yesterday. Gabriel has become even more handsome since my last visit.[3] This morning I visited three of Ernst's very elegant houses.[4] I want to be in Göttingen on the 25th.[5]

Lots of greetings to everyone!
Anna

1 Postcard.
2 Herr Kleiner; see 166 SF.
3 Beginning of March; see 155 SF, note 1.

4 Ernst had made a good name for himself in Berlin during the 1920s, which was the great era for architecture. 'Some of his buildings still stand today.' He obtained his first commissions amongst other things thanks to Lux's social connections, e.g., Haus Maretzki and Haus Levy-Hofer (both 1921 in Dahlem); in 1925 he also designed Lampl's 'house with surgery' whose material and design were 'different from conventional private houses of the time'. 'From this time on Ernst Ludwig Freud was known in Berlin as an architect whose buildings were discussed in professional journals and general magazines' ⟨Zohlen, p. 80; ill. 'country house' and 'tobacco warehouse' in Hajos and Zahn, pp. 45, 80; list of major works after 1921 in ibid., p. 113⟩. In 1926 Ernst was invited by Chaim Weizmann, president at the time of the Zionist organization, 'to Jerusalem in the spring to build Dr Weizmann's villa' ⟨Freud/Ferenczi III, 1085 F, 13 December 1926, p. 289⟩.

5 See 167 AF.

165 AF

ARCHITECT ERNST L. FREUD DIPL. ING.
BERLIN W. 10 REGENTENSTR. 11, TELEPH. LÜTZOW 9584[1]

Berlin, 20 April 1922

Dear Papa,

Yesterday I was at the Eitingons for dinner and also tried to dissuade him gently on your behalf from travelling to Vienna, but without success. He seems determined and stresses that he only spoke to you in the autumn under unfavourable circumstances and would like to see you again, to which I could, of course, say nothing in reply. His wife had naturally long abandoned the idea of the trip, and from the outset I never thought it was realistic. Dr Eitingon will arrive in the afternoon of the 5th and stay for the 6th and 7th. I shall probably meet him on the way and travel with him. I think it would nice – and only fair – if we were to put him up like we did Abraham and Ferenczi.[2] I am quite willing to give him one of my rooms or, if you think it's more practical, to put Ditha in there for that time.[3] As I will not yet have completely unpacked and put things away and have not been used to having much room on my travels, there will be more than enough space.

The weather here is cold, bleak and cheerless. I am invited for lunch today with Helene Gebert and in the afternoon with Frau Wertheim. I am already very curious to go to Göttingen.

Lots of greetings to everyone.

Anna

1 Printed letterhead. The letter is typed with only the signature written by hand.

2 For Eitingon's visit and journey with Anna, see 166 SF–168 AF; see also Freud/Eitingon, 235 E, 236 F, 238 E.

3 Judith Bernays, who was working at the time in the *Verlag*, had been living since the beginning of 1922 temporarily (until 16 May) in the salon, which had been converted into a guest room for Lou Andreas-Salomé (and then for Ferenczi and Abraham) ⟨Anna/Lou, letters 7 [p. 17], 22; Freud/Abraham, 9 December

1921, 25 December 1921; Freud/Ferenczi III, 895 F; *Rundbriefe 3*, pp. 9, 16, 23, 30⟩. Perhaps Freud was attempting in this way to avoid being forced to have the room occupied: 'I will soon be putting up the English section in our former living room, which I have persuaded my good wife to clear in view of the danger of requests for accommodation,' he wrote on 11 November 1921 to Eitingon ⟨Freud/Eitingon, letter 223 F, p. 267⟩. See also 166 SF.

166 SF

PROF. DR. FREUD 24 April 1922
Vienna, IX. Berggasse 19

My dear Anna,
First of all, welcome to Göttingen and warm greetings to your new friend, who will hopefully be as durable as she is splendid.

You were able to write frequently from Hamburg, where you were a housewife with her hands full; it is typical of Berlin that you hardly had any time to write, unless there is a letter in the post this morning.

Today the enclosed letter from Varendonck arrived in which he thanks you for your translation work.[1] So you are certain to have a harebrained champion at the Congress.[2]

Another event today is the arrival of the *Spanish* translation of *Everyday Life*,[3] as you know by Don Luis Lopez Ballesteros y Torres, a luxurious translator's name for such a plebeian man as your father. The publisher has also written, with genuine Spanish courtesy. The best thing, however, is a line on the back cover of the book, which says 'Obras completes I', i.e. collected works![4] A second volume is scheduled for this year, for which they are asking for a photograph.[5]

Other news: Grandmother has not been well after a fainting fit. Ditha has started analysis[6] with Frau Dr Deutsch[7] and will be moving to a guesthouse on 15 May. Mama has bought me two new hats, each costing exactly £1. The cost of my new shoes to be made by Jellinek, modelled on the English ones, cannot yet be determined and is still a matter for speculation [English in original]. Kleiner has taken the nephrite knife to repair. Lampl told me that there would be five boxes of cigars coming through W. Pick but only two have arrived so far. The last delivery from Holland, for which the cavalry captain,[8] who has been called for his doctoral viva, fought so bravely, appears for now to have been mislaid. By contrast, Rank managed to smuggle in 600 through the Verlag as literature. Result: surplus instead of shortage. The little de Groot is as old as you but still looks younger, seems nice, still very timid. You will have the opportunity on your return to practise being nice[9] as Mrs Riviere, the proud English translator, is also counting on it. I don't know what to say about the fact that you are only coming with Eitingon, but I hope you have plenty of interesting impressions and experiences. It will be difficult for Eitingon to stay with us because we can't send Ditha away so soon before she is to move out, or lumber you with her. We will get an extra-nice room for him at the Regina.[10] It is, of course,[11] a great relief that Mirra is not coming too.

The plans for the summer look like this: July free for everyone (Aunt already away in Abbazia), on 1 August meeting of us three to travel to Karersee, H.[otel] Latemar, where this time nice south-facing rooms have been promised (in a fond letter from the owner). Then on 1 September or a few days earlier for a short stay at the Baltic bathing resort, where Max should come with the two rascals. On 25 September Congress in Berlin. What do you think? The plans have not yet been finalized.[12]

With affectionate greetings to you and Frau Lou,

Papa

1 Spelling mistake (no umlaut) in the original here and twice more in the next paragraph.
2 See 183 AF, note 3.
3 Freud 1901*b*.
4 See 133 SF, note 8.
5 The second volume was to contain Freud's writings 1905*d*, 1910*a*, 1901*a* and 1920*g* ⟨*IZ*, vol. 8 (1922), pp. 237, 525; ibid., vol. 10 (1924), p. 481⟩. In a letter of thanks written in Spanish (1923*h*), Freud praised the translator particularly for the elegant style and the great understanding and correct reproduction of the difficult psychoanalytical concepts. In the same year he added a footnote to his 'History of the Psychoanalytic Movement' with specific mention of the collected works as evidence of the 'lively interest in Spanish-speaking countries' ⟨1914*d*, pp. 33f., note 1⟩.
6 Ditha had already begun to read Freud's works in America in 1989 and had received advice in letters by Freud about studying his writings and psychoanalysis ⟨Freud to Judith Bernays, 5 December 1909, 28 August 1911, LoC, Cont. 12⟩. On 17 May she moved into a guesthouse in the Cottage ⟨Anna/Lou, letter 22⟩.
7 Helene Deutsch (1884–1982), doctor of medicine, psychiatrist, married to Dr Felix Deutsch. She was one of the first women to study medicine in Vienna and until 1918 was head of the women's psychiatric department at Wagner-Jauregg Clinic. After her training analysis with Freud she opened her own practice in Vienna, became a member of the Vienna Psychoanalytic Society in 1918 and soon took on a leading role in the movement. In 1924 she collaborated in the setting up of the Training Institute in Vienna, which she headed until 1934 (and in which Anna was secretary) ⟨Anna/Lou, letter 206; *IZ*, vol. 11 [1925], p. 254; Deutsch, H. [1925], [1944] (particularly ch. X, 'Sigmund Freud')⟩. See also Freud/Ferenczi III, 899 F. She was one of a select group of colleagues whom Freud invited to meetings at his house after he contracted cancer ⟨Heenen-Wolf, p. 159⟩. In 1934–5 she emigrated with her son and husband to Boston, where she continued her analysis work and teaching. In the 1970s she was also politically active. She was an extremely versatile analyst and one of the most important and highly esteemed women in the history of psychoanalysis ⟨Mühlleitner, pp. 75–7; *IZ*, vol. 5 (1919), p. 149; Deutsch, H. [1994]; Roazen [1989]⟩.
8 Schmideberg.

9 Spelling mistake (no umlaut) in the original.
10 Freud frequently had guests staying at Hotel Regina, near the Votiv-Kirche (today Sigmund-Freud-Platz), which was just a few minutes' walk away.
11 Spelling mistake (no umlaut) in the original.
12 See 159 SF, note 14.

167 AF

Göttingen, Tuesday evening [25 April 1922]

Dear Papa,
Getting to Göttingen is relatively easy, but from here to Vienna is difficult even for an old timetable specialist like Oliver.[1] He finally found the route via Leipzig to be the most practical and the only one that doesn't involve an overnight stay, which it is better to avoid given the hotel situation today. I have been in Göttingen a few hours, will remain eight days, leave at lunchtime on Thursday, 4 May, via Goslar and Halle (like you in September[2]), arrive at 7 o'clock in the evening in Leipzig, where Dr Eitingon will be waiting for me (also like you in September) and will continue with him (hopefully with less excitement) at 10 o'clock, so that we should arrive in Vienna in the early afternoon (2.10) on 5 May. Dr Eitingon wanted to send you a telegram about getting a room but as there is enough time he left it to my letter. So he is definitely coming without further confirmation. We will have lunch in the train so you don't have to save anything for us, and no one needs to meet us either at this inconvenient time.

Unfortunately, the past is not as quick and easy to describe as the future. If you run around enough, you can pack so much into a week in Berlin that it will not fit into a single letter. I will wait to talk to you in person to tell you about Gabriel, who is really particularly delightful, and his proud and loving parents. Teddy[3] has become very nice and kind, taking me to places and picking me up several times, and behaving in a very manly and friendly manner. There is far too much to eat: a Sunday lunch with Frau Brasch, an evening in my honour with Gerda,[4] tea with Frau Wertheim and with Lucy,[5] lunch with Helene,[6] etc., etc. Best of all were three days or rather evenings and nights with the Eitingons, where one still feels completely at home even in the new apartment.[7] He is quite unchanged and without doubt one of the best people and friends that we have. He intimates that he himself now has a number of concerns and difficulties that are oppressing him somewhat and he is very much looking forward to visiting you. Her recovery, it would appear, is very superficial, and the slightest little thing would probably be sufficient for her to revert[8] to her old condition. It was nevertheless as always with her as well, except for a stronger feeling that she is sick and that she cannot be counted on as with a healthy person.[9]

I can only briefly sketch in telegram form what it's like in Göttingen; it is now so late that even you would be going to bed. So: very well put up in a very nice room with a professor's family,[10] met by Frau Lou with flowers and sweets, a walk to her very small, not very prosperous-looking house,[11] a very nice and fine evening meal with her, a long discussion afterwards, as if we had just stopped yesterday in Vienna, a night-time walk back with the very nice and friendly Professor Andreas,[12] now very sleepy as the amount of sleep I had in Berlin would hardly fill up a single night, and looking forward to continuing tomorrow.

With[13] greetings and kisses,
Your Anna

Please ask Ditha[14] to tell the Verlag not to send anything else, then I won't have to inform it specially.

1 See 16 AF/OF and note 14.
2 On his journey to the Harz; see 153 AF, note 2.
3 Theodor Freud (1904–23), son of Marie and Moritz Freud ⟨Stammbaum Lange: Freud Family, 'Genealogical Tree', p. IV⟩. He died in a swimming accident the following year; see 197 SF and note 2.
4 Gerda, née Brasch, a sister of Lucie ⟨Lucie Freud to Felix Augenfeld ['Grockchen'], 2 October 1939; LoC SF, Cont. 12⟩. She married Karl Mosse in 1919 ⟨thanks to Albrecht Hirschmüller for this information⟩.
5 Lucy Wiener.
6 Helene Gebert.
7 Rauchstr. 4, where the Eitingons moved from Güntzelstr. 2 on 29 April 1921, which Ernst as an architect also helped to design ⟨Freud/Eitingon, 204 E, 207 E, 211 E, 213 E⟩. See 131 AF and note 12.
8 Spelling mistake (no umlaut) in the original.
9 For Mirra Eitingon's illness/state in general, see Freud/Eitingon, *passim*; see also 131 AF and note 9, 137 SF.
10 Frau Gudrun Bruns with her three children in Nikolausberger Weg 61. 'You are living on the edge of the city that is close to us, so we can cross the fields to get to one another' ⟨Lou to Anna in Anna/Lou, letter 16, 11 April 1922, p. 39⟩. See also 169 AF. The family was in the throes of moving to Königsberg [Kaliningrad]. Prof. Oskar Bruns (1878–1946), until 1922 Privatdozent [outside lecturer] and senior physician at the medical clinic in Göttingen, had already left (31 March 1922); his wife and children followed him on 13 September 1922 ⟨thanks to Herr Lohmar, Stadtarchiv Göttingen, registration of residents, 10 November 2000⟩.
11 'Haus Loufried', Herzberger Landstrasse 101. A large apartment block stands on the site today with just a plaque to recall the house:

Lou Andreas-Salomé
Writer
1903–1930
Friedrich Carl Andreas
Iranist
1903–1930

The lost country idyll is replaced by a block of stone with the following verse chiselled into it:

du heller himmel über mir dir
will ich mich vertrauen
Lass nicht von Lust und Leiden hier
den Aufblick mir verbauen
Lou Andreas-Salomé

12 Friedrich Carl Andreas (real name F. C. Bagratian) (1846–1930), German Orientalist; he lived seven years in Persia, then in Berlin, and had been professor of Oriental Philology in Göttingen since 1903. He studied the Iranian language from antiquity to the present in all dialects and published fundamental works on old and middle-Iranian traditions. For his marriage to Lou, see Andreas-Salomé [1951], pp. 199–216, 287–90.
13 From this word a long arrow points to an empty space bottom left. At some distance from the tip of the arrow is the first PS. The reason is unknown; perhaps Anna had left room for Lou to add something.
14 See 156 AF and note 9.

168 AF

Göttingen, 27 April 1922

Dear Papa,
Thank you very much for your letter, which was waiting for me today up at Frau Lou's. There is always so much news in them that I am almost getting impatient at not being in Vienna already and in the thick of it. I would have come before Dr Eitingon, but after having waited it out so dutifully in Hamburg and having survived Berlin so happily I did not want to cut short the stay with Lou, which is something special and unique in its way. Besides it is also a particular pleasure for me to travel with Eitingon. But then I will stay put again and only wish (very selfishly) that this work season had not just two months to run but at least six, so that I could get something proper done. I hope Grandmother is well when I arrive.

I am ashamed to say that I didn't really manage to write from Berlin because I never had the fortunate coincidence of having a desk, chair, paper, ink, pen and some peace and quiet all in one place. Life there is like a whirlwind and it's a wonder how the people endure it. Here, by contrast, the day has the normal twenty-four hours and allows time as a consequence for all kinds of things.

I would be glad to practise friendliness and look forward to all new acquaintanceships.[1] My poor Varendonck appears to be really very weird. I am highly impressed by the Spanish complete works and also the choice of South Tyrol for the summer holidays.[2] I have become frugal again in Germany, travel third class and always look first on the right-hand side of the menu if I have to eat out. But that will no doubt cease again in Vienna where there is no sense in saving. I was very surprised and interested at the news about Ditha.[3] I am sorry that Dr Eitingon cannot stay with us. I would have been happy to take in Ditha; I have been living out of a suitcase since Hamburg and would just postpone the start of a regular and unpacked life for two and a half days. But whatever you think best.

Today I visited our Bernays relations[4] with Frau Lou and am meant to be eating potato dumplings [Kartoffelklöse] there tomorrow lunchtime, which I hope are what we call 'Erdäpfelknödel'. They live just a few houses away from where I am staying.[5]

Frau Lou has cancelled one of her analyses while I am here so that apart from an hour in the morning and two in the evening she is completely free for me. We talk endlessly, just like in Vienna, but this time with a much more limited aim, in keeping with the short time. I brought a plan and a kind of idea to Göttingen for a short piece of work, which she is helping me with. If you agree, it will be my guest lecture in the Vienna Psychoanalytic Society, as I would very much like to become a member.[6] Of course, you shouldn't expect too much of it, but working on it alone brings me a lot of pleasure. Today, the first day on which the weather has been better, with only three short rain showers, I went on a splendid walk in the forest, field and hills.

Incidentally, I also had a perhaps fanciful idea as to how we could help Frau Lou financially for a while and at the same time do a good turn for another person;[7] but I prefer to wait until Vienna to tell you about that. Lou's hair has now grown back to normal,[8] and she looks much better and younger. It is quite impossible to keep up with the speed of her thoughts and she can keep going long after everything has become confused in my head. I have also seen new Rilke things here,[9] and everything is very nice in general.

And despite all this, the time in Göttingen is so abundant that I have finally managed again to do like the eagle owl and sleep almost 'twelve hours a day'.

I send everyone my affectionate greetings.

With a kiss,

Your Anna

1 See 28 AF, note 2.

2 See 159 SF, note 14.

3 This could refer to Ditha's analysis or her moving out of Berggasse. Anna might also have learnt already, however, that Judith was getting engaged ⟨Freud/Bernays, letter 177 Mi⟩. See 175 SF and note 8, 181 SF.

4 In Göttingen at the time were:

1. Paul Isaak Bernays (1888–1977), son of a cousin of Martha and Minna (Julius Bernays, 1862–1916, married to Sara Brecher, 1867–1953). Paul, a mathematician and philosopher, spent the years 1909–34 in Göttingen and from 1917 to 1933 assisted David Hilbert (with whom he wrote, amongst other things, *Grundlagen der Mathematik*). He was a 'Privatdozent' [outside lecturer] in 1919 and titled professor in 1922; in 1934 he emigrated to Zurich, where he worked at the ETH and remained until his death. He was unmarried, frequently changed residences between Berlin and Göttingen, and lived at the time in Nikolausberger Weg 43.

2. Isaac Bernays (1861–1924), D.Phil., historian. He was a cousin of Martha and Minna (uncle of Paul Isaak) and had already lived in Göttingen as a student in 1894–7. He worked as city archivist in Strasbourg from 1898 until the Armistice and returned to Göttingen on 2 February 1919, where he lived with his wife, Marie Elisabeth Emilie, née Feldmann (1857–1931), in Nikolausberger Weg 44; he died in Göttingen in 1924. As Anna speaks of her 'relatives' in the plural, the invitation to eat was probably from this family ⟨Stammbaum Lange: Bernays Family, 'Genealogical Tree IIa', p. II 7, text to IIa: pp. 43, 44, 44a; Specker. Thanks to Herr Lohmar, Stadtarchiv Göttingen, registration of residents⟩.

5 See 167 AF, note 10.

6 On 31 May 1922 Anna gave a guest lecture in the Vienna group on the subject 'Beating Fantasies and Daydreams'. 'I think Papa was also content and enjoyed my "start",' she wrote afterwards to Lou ⟨Anna/Lou, 31 May 1922⟩. Freud commented beforehand to Eitingon that he would feel like Brutus 'judging his own sons' and added 'she could be making a decisive step' ⟨Freud/Eitingon, 240 F, 19 May 1922, pp. 286f.⟩. The work (1922) appeared under the title 'Beating Fantasies and Daydreams'; for the autobiographical background, see Young-Bruehl, pp. 110f. Anna became a member of the Vienna Psychoanalytic Society on 13 June 1922. Lou was also admitted on 21 June 1922, exceptionally without having presented a paper ⟨*IZ*, vol. 8 (1922) pp. 247f., 245; Anna/Lou, letters 24, 25, 31; Freud/Andreas-Salomé, 26 June 1922⟩.

7 Possibly a reference to Anna's idea mentioned in a later letter from Göttingen to Eitingon: 'I have not given up my idea of having Edith do a training analysis with Frau Lou but merely postponed it until Edith is a little older and has got past her special approach to analysis' ⟨Anna to Eitingon, 20 July 1922⟩. Anna then made the connection ⟨Anna/Lou, letters 64 (p. 116, 148 (p. 266) and note pp. 742f.⟩. See also 177 AF and note 8.

8 In summer 1921 Lou had been ill with a high fever, which, as she wrote to Freud, 'made me lose all my hair, so that I wander around in a cap like an old granny' ⟨Freud/Andreas-Salomé, 6 September 1921, p. 107; see also Anna/Lou, PS to letter 6⟩.

9 Lou had already notified Anna in March of a new 'production storm' by Rilke ⟨Anna/Lou, letter 12, 18 March 1922, p. 30; also letter 13, p. 33⟩. Anna was 'deeply and affectionately attached to Rilke's work and, through her later friend Lou Andreas-Salomé, to him personally' ⟨Peters, p. 8, also p. 24f.⟩. Freud had mentioned earlier in a letter to Lou that Anna 'knows his poems, some of them by heart' ⟨Freud/Andreas-Salomé, 1 April 1915, p. 28; see also Young-Bruehl, pp. 47, 128⟩. At the age of seventy-five she quoted 'poets such as Rainer Maria Rilke, who sees the move toward death as one of the main purposes of life' in her final paper on aggression at the 27th International Psychoanalytic Congress in Vienna ⟨1972, in *Writings X*, p. 173⟩.

169 AF

Göttingen, 30 April 1922

Dear Papa,
In spite of the dreadful weather it's basically getting better and better[1] here in Göttingen. I spend all day up at Frau Lou's, writing my little piece, and

read it to her bit by bit. She says I am doing it completely on my own, but I think that she inspires me in a strange and occult fashion, because when I am alone I know nothing about these things. I am very curious to see whether you will approve of the result.

'My new friend', as you write, is really splendid, and I still find that the way I came to know her is quite uncanny. On the other hand it is easier, simpler and more natural to live with her than with all but a few people that I know. Also, the more time I spend with her, the younger, livelier and more intimate she becomes, and discusses and develops such interesting things every day that I realize for the first time all that there is in the world.

Apart from that Göttingen is very nice, quite Mama's idea of a small university town with front gardens and green trees. I cannot spend any money here because when I am not up at Frau Lou's I have to eat alternately at the Bruns or Bernays.[2] I also have the greatest difficulty paying for my room with Prof. Bruns's wife (the mother of little Mai from the narcissism essay).[3] I fear therefore that I will leave here with more marks than when I arrived, a worrying situation in these times.

I am already looking forward very much to Vienna and everything there, particularly after this nice end to my trip.[4]

With many greetings to you and all,

Your Anna

1 Grammar mistake in original.
2 Anna uses the Yiddish word *teg-essen*: to eat alternately at different people's houses (a good deed that used to be offered particularly to Talmud students) ⟨Wolf, p. 184⟩.
3 Andreas-Salomé, 1921.
4 For the homeward journey route, see 167 AF.

170 AF[1]

Prof. Dr. S. Freud
Bad Gastein
Villa Wassing[2]

[Vienna,] Saturday, 1 July [1922][3]

Dear Papa,

I have just collected our tickets; if there is not a new strike[4] we will be travelling on *Tuesday*.[5] I will send a telegram to Berlin tomorrow, notifying our arrival. Here everything is in order, in other words everything is upside down and being beaten.[6] The indefatigable[7] Dr Rickman was here yesterday evening while we were out at the station to collect the letter, and came again today at 6 a.m., getting us out of bed. A very nice letter from Max with the children's measurements; we still have to buy something for them. We have really purchased the green evening dress; it is wonderful and the gentleman in the shop said that he appreciates such exclusive customers, as his brother-in-law is also a neurologist.

Unfortunately, Jellineks made my shoes too short and are keeping them themselves. Mama's ear is better today; we are all in a very good mood and looking forward to the journey. The platform guard yesterday was quite unbribable. Aichhorn[8] and Trude[9] were here with me yesterday.

Greetings from us.

Your A.

1 Postcard.

2 Freud began his cure here on this day (until 31 July), accompanied by Minna, who until then had been spending her holiday in Abbazia since 19/21 May ⟨Freud/Jones, letters 356, 364; Freud/Bernays, letters 177 Mi–179 Mi⟩.

3 Postmark: 2.VII.2 – the last digit of the year is illegible.

4 'Since I last wrote we have all of the strikes that one could possibly imagine: first post, telegraph and telephone strike and now [. . .] a tram strike' ⟨Anna/Lou, letter 32, 29 June 1922, p. 60⟩. See 157 SF, 171 AF, 179 SF and note 5.

5 Anna travelled with her mother on 4 July first to Berlin, where they stayed with the Eitingons. For the onward journey, see 172 MF/AF and note 3 ⟨Anna/Lou, letter 22⟩.

6 The beating of furniture and carpets, which Freud found intolerable; see 138 SF, 177 AF.

7 This might refer to a characteristic of Rickman that Anna mentioned in a letter to Lou Andreas-Salomé. She connects it with Rickman's membership as a Quaker of the Society of Friends, comparing him with the 'goodwill to fellow-men' in Aichhorn and Eitingon and asking about a connection with psychoanalysis: '[. . .] aren't such people always greatly attracted by analysis?' ⟨Anna/Lou, letter 9, pp. 22f.; Lou's reply: letter 10, pp. 24f.; see also Freud/Ferenczi III, 1097 Fer, p. 312⟩. See also 174, note 9.

8 August Aichhorn (1878–1949), Prof. h. c., pioneer in the application of psychoanalysis to juvenile delinquents. He was a schoolmaster and remedial teacher, devoting himself fully from 1909 to juvenile welfare, and in 1918 established 'a juvenile home for asocial Viennese children and juveniles in Oberhollabrunn', which he directed until its closure in 1923 ⟨Aichhorn, A. [1923], pp. 190, 192⟩. Later he established educational advice centres and welfare institutions in Vienna. Anna had met Aichhorn in January 1922 (in Steinlechner, p. 80, incorrectly as 1921) in his institute with 'thieves, vagabonds and slashers' and reported enthusiastically on him to Lou Andreas-Salomé ⟨Anna/Lou, letter 7, 18 January 1922, p. 14⟩. See 26 AF, note 5. (See also Freud's Preface (1925*f*) to *Aichhorn's Wayward Youth* (1925).) Aichhorn became a member of the Vienna Psychoanalytic Society in October 1922 and had his own analysis practice, thereafter functioning as a training analyst ⟨*IZ*, vol. 8 (1922), p. 536; Mühlleitner, p. 21⟩. In subsequent years he introduced Anna privately to his specialist discipline ⟨Anna/Lou, e.g., letters 148, 150⟩. From May 1924 Aichhorn, Bernfeld and Willi Hoffer met regularly at Anna's to exchange pedagogical experiences, thoughts and plans ⟨Anna/Lou, 1924, from letter 172, 1925, *passim*⟩. Aichhorn also advised Anna on the establishment of the Hietzing school (see 208 SF and note 7) and taught there temporarily. After the Second World War he ran and revived the Vienna society

and became its president ⟨Aichhorn, T.; Anna Freud [1951]⟩. In 1947 he was made a professor in recognition of his contribution to psychiatry and juvenile welfare ⟨Mühlleitner, p. 22⟩.

9 Gertrud Hollstein, née Baderle; see 26 AF and note 5.

171 AF[1]

Monday morning [Vienna, 3 July 1922][2]

Dear Papa,

We were delighted to receive your card just now,[3] and Mama was particularly pleased with the matching shirts. Hopefully, we can make better use than you of our sleeping car tomorrow. Yesterday was a quiet day; we started packing our suitcases and had dinner in the evening at Café Reichsrath with Math and Robert. You are quite right never to do it. The stove setter is here today and is lifting off the tops of all the stoves; the apartment increasingly resembles a fortress.[4] It is still smouldering here, but the trams have been running again since this morning.[5] I am sending some post with this letter.

Regards to you and Aunt.

Your A.

1 Postcard sent as a letter (address side is empty), probably so as to include with the mail to be forwarded (see end of letter).

2 This card was right at the end of the correspondence. It is the same kind of postcard as 170 AF and 173 AF; to judge by the content, handwriting and stroke thickness, it most probably belongs here.

3 Missing; probably addressed to Martha (but also not in LoC SF, Cont. 10).

4 See 16 AF/OF, note 4.

5 There had also been a tram strike; see 170 AF, note 4, and 179 SF and note 5.

172 MF/AF[1]

Prof. Dr. S. Freud
Bad Gastein
Villa Wassing

Berlin, 6 July,[2] [1922]

Dear All,

We are sitting on the veranda at the Eitingons drinking black coffee; it is so boiling hot that everything experienced in Vienna fades by comparison. The days are nevertheless very pleasant, although we are not looking forward very much to the journey tomorrow.[3] Phoned Max again yesterday evening.

[In their own handwriting]

Greetings before my departure. I received your card and new supplies.[4]

Your Lampl

Have already sent telegrams to everyone, unfortunately travelling again tomorrow.

Sincerely, Anna

Best regards, Oliver

Sincerely, Max Eitingon

Sincerest greetings, Mirra

1 Postcard, Martha Freud's handwriting.
2 Written erroneously '7 July'; the postmark is: '6.7.22 8-9 N.' (afternoon).
3 Martha and Anna travelled together some of the way on 7 July (see 177 AF, note 1) ⟨Anna/Lou, letter 30⟩. Then they separated: Martha continued to Hohegeiss, where Frl Jacob and the two Hamburg grandchildren were already waiting (see 174 AF–188 AF). The children and Frl Jacob also remained there a few days longer than Martha, who left at the beginning of August for Obersalzberg near Berchtesgaden via Göttingen ⟨Freud to Max, 20 June, 6 August 1922⟩. Anna visited Lou Andreas-Salomé in Göttingen, where she remained until the beginning of August; see 173 AF–188 AF.
4 Cigars; see 166 SF.

173 AF[1]

Prof. Dr. S. Freud
Bad Gastein
Villa Wassing
Austria
Salzburg

Friday evening, [Göttingen, 7 July 1922]
[Postmark: 8.7.22 910 V. {morning}]

Travelled coolly and very comfortably with Mama, splendid accommodation here,[2] very comfortable and cosy, tired and very contented, hope you and Mama are the latter too. More tomorrow. Money arrived.[3]

Your Anna

1 Postcard with handwritten sender: 'Address: Göttingen, Herzberger Landstr. 110, c/o Frau Prof. Petersen'.
2 'In the only house opposite us [. . .] there are two small interconnecting rooms available looking out on to the wooded hill, they are really in the middle of the countryside and right behind the house you have completely undisturbed forest where you can picnic, walk barefoot, and everything' ⟨Lou to Anna in Anna/Lou, letter 26, 3 June 1922, p. 52; letter 30⟩. See also 6 AF, note 9.
3 Because of foreign-exchange restrictions Anna had sent German currency in advance via a Munich bank ⟨Anna/Lou, letter 31⟩. See 177 AF.

174 AF

Göttingen, 8 July 1922[1]
Saturday evening

My dear Papa,
I hope you have received our meagre correspondence to date: two cards from me from Vienna, one from Mama and a joint card from Berlin, and my short very sleepy card yesterday evening. I expect Mama will already have written in detail from Hohegeiss.[2] We got on very well during our journey together and were actually quite sorry to part. Mama recovered visibly from the moment Berggasse was behind us and survived the visit to Berlin very well. If the rail connections allow I shall also check for myself how she and the children are getting on in Hohegeiss;[3] as the crow flies we are not so far apart.

Everything here was quite unexpectedly and undeservedly in fine order. My two rooms are delightful; my hostess, the young, very fine and educated widow of a professor of Greek, has taken me in with full board and appears to have the best intentions for me. So I have everything I could possibly wish for – except perhaps electric light. But it is, of course, not as cheap as I was hoping; I am paying 200 marks a day. It is a lot, I think, but for the price everything is first class. My three windows look out on to a fruit orchard and just behind me the forest begins.

Lou decorated my rooms with roses of all colours from her garden and also provided chocolate, your picture on the wall and even stamps to write letters on my desk. Today I didn't feel well and was a little lethargic so we just lay on deckchairs in the garden, which is overgrown with cherries, blackcurrants,[4] gooseberries and flowers. We are both looking forward very much to the coming four weeks. As you can see, I feel so well here too that – if I didn't like my two rings from you so much[5] – I would almost feel like sacrificing one.

I trust that Mama has written to you a lot about Gabriel. He has developed incredibly since May and is becoming more and more amazing. He really is incredibly more than Lucy Rickman.[6] Apart from his really serious beauty and glowing health, the surprising thing about him is his adult, human reaction to his surroundings. There is absolutely nothing of the animal-like in him that our Tonerle had – half little monkey, half little donkey. He trusts us completely and, as Ernst says, has a strong sense of family. He can't stand Christians, it is said. Lux does not have any maids at the moment and is somewhat vexed. Both were very nice.

We have been testing out hotel Eitingon[7] for you and have had the best possible experience. It has everything you could need, more than enough space, peace and quiet or company, solitude or family life, depending on your needs. Meals can also be brought up to the room on request, hot and cold baths, shower at any time of the day, transport tickets obtained for you and – something we were obliged to try out – departure even in the early morning with the greatest punctuality and ease. It is thus to be recommended in every respect. And finally, you are also provided with victuals and chocolate and are not even allowed to pay for the car.

The doctor's wife is quite well; she participates in everything and seems, outwardly at least, to make a cheerful impression. He doesn't look too good and labours greatly with six hours of work at home and three to four in the polyclinic; he starts at eight o'clock, and intends to keep this up until the Congress.[8] For our sakes he has taken an afternoon off after five o'clock to drive us to Wannsee. Frau Eitingon claims that the million you gave up for him in May impressed him so much that he is now seeking opportunities to put himself out to the same extent for our family.[9]

I had a long evening conversation with him, and there are lots of things going round in my head that I would like to talk to you about; I'll save it for Berchtesgaden.[10] But I don't think that what we thought in the autumn, that her illness would make him give up psychoanalysis and distance him from us, will ever happen; and the friendship with him will never end as it did with Loe – unless we do something to make it happen. Or do you disagree? He cannot treat her any differently because that's how he is; and if he were otherwise we probably wouldn't like him the way we do.[11]

Perhaps you can understand what I mean amongst all this nonsense.

Give my regards to Aunt and write again soon.

Your Anna

[In the margin]:

Oli makes a very good impression and is looking forward to the summer with us.[12]

1 Written erroneously as 9 July 1922.

2 Yes, she had written the same day ⟨Martha to Freud, 8 July 1922; also other letters from Hohegeiss⟩. 'My poor wife is freezing in the Harz with our little boy. The arid nest is called Hohegeiss. . . . Around the 4th we all intend to be together on the Salzberg' ⟨Freud/Ferenczi III, 908 F, 21 July 1922, p. 84⟩.

3 See 176 AF and note 2, 177 AF.

4 'Ribiseln': Austrian for 'Johannisbeere'.

5 Six years later (probably for her birthday on 3 December 1928) Anna received a second symbolic ring from her father: the 'Nibelungenring' or 'Bundesring', which were given initially only to committee members (see 126 SF, note 5, 129 SF, note 5), whose significance changed over the years, however, so that other intimates were considered ⟨Jones II, pp. 174f.; Freud/Ferenczi II, 813 F, 815 Fer; Grosskurth; Wittenberger [1995], pp. 212–16 and note (also further considerations on the 'ring story' as a whole)⟩. 'Now I also have a ring and wear it all the time,' wrote Anna to Eitingon on 12 December 1928 ⟨the incorrect statement in Jones III, p. 18, Peters, p. 38, and Young-Bruehl, p. 92, that Anna obtained the ring in May 1920 was corrected by Wittenberger [1992], pp. 55–7⟩. See also Appendix 3.

6 The little daughter of Mrs and John Rickman (see 161 SF and note 12), who was apparently the same age as Gabriel.

7 Familiar joking reference ⟨e.g., Freud/Eitingon, letters 207 E, 245 F; Freud/

Andreas-Salomé, 8 September 1922⟩. For the warm welcome, see Freud's letter of thanks of 10 July 1922 ⟨Freud/Eitingon, 246 F⟩.

8 See 183 AF, note 3.

9 Eitingon had visited Freud for his birthday in May (see 159 SF, 160 AF, 167 AF) ⟨Freud/Eitingon, letters 235 E, 238 E⟩. Freud had given up an entire Saturday for him and had not therefore seen any students or patients ⟨ibid., 239 E; on Eitingon's '(excessive) kindness', see, e.g., Anna/Lou, letter 172, pp. 309f. and elsewhere; see also 170 AF, note 5; Schröter [2004], document appendix XIII, p. 977, Young-Bruehl, pp. 123, 127–32⟩.

10 The family was to come together for the rest of the holidays at the Obersalzberg (where Freud had already sought accommodation in 1915; see 48 SF, note 2): Freud and Minna came from Gastein on 1 August; see 187 SF ⟨Freud/Bernays, letter 177 Mi; Martha to Freud, 27 July 1922; Freud/Eitingon, 241 E, 248 E⟩. Martha and Anna arrived on 4 August 'very late at night in the pitch dark [. . .] after many delays and some problems in Munich' ⟨Anna/Lou, letter 35, 5 August 1922, p. 62⟩. See also 182 AF, 188 AF. Oliver, Mathilde and Robert, Ernst and Lux, Lux's mother, Edith and Freud's brother Alexander followed later ⟨Anna/Lou, letters 37, 44⟩. Minna travelled subsequently from Berchtesgaden to Bad Reichenhall, and Martha followed her there on 8 September; both returned to Vienna for the Jewish New Year festival (29 September) ⟨Anna/Lou, letter 44; Freud/Bernays, letters 180 Ma/Mi, 181 Ma/Mi⟩. Freud and Anna remained until 14 September, then spent a day in Munich and were 'on the 16th in Hamburg and the 20th in Berlin' for the Congress ⟨Anna/Lou, letter 43, 6 September 1922, p. 73⟩. See 183 AF and notes 3 and 7, 188 AF, note 7.

11 For Anna's relationship to Eitingon, see, e.g., Young-Bruehl, pp. 117f., 130–5; Anna/Lou, *passim*; Anna/Eva, letters 24, 25, 47; Bittner, pp. 17f.

12 Oliver arrived at Obersalzberg on 5 August ⟨Freud to Max, 6 August 1922⟩. He also compiled the itinerary for Martin and Anna; see 182 AF, 188 AF.

175 SF

PROF. DR. FREUD — Bgastein, 10 July 1922
Vienna, IX. Berggasse 19

My dear Anna,

I am writing you a few words to confirm receipt of your first card from Göttingen, which sounds very pleasing. I hope everything will be as you wish it.

Here very nice, comfortable, quiet and worry-free. Finally an opportunity to work. I have already finished one essay[1] and drafted a second.[2] The natural surroundings with which I am so familiar do not excite me so much this year, but yesterday we were on the Nassfeld, which is the equal of any of our Alpine summer beauty.[3] There are no mushrooms to be found yet, but I have nevertheless managed to bag a couple. The food is excellent, the prices fabulous,[4] impressive, as long as one reduces them through conversion. Altogether we are spending 80,000 K a day, but in truth it is barely £1. Aunt spent more in Abbazia alone; but it did her an enormous amount of good.[5]

I trust you know that you are already a hundred-fold millionairess. Don't be too proud of it, however.

I received a letter from Rank before he left for Seefeld. Kurt Redlich[6] is here and Dr Morgenthau,[7] and of course the Hellers (the new couple),[8] but the incognito existence has been less disrupted than in earlier years. Today we met Prof. Königstein[9] by chance[10] at the station. He is staying here for eight days, brought by an American doctor.[11]

Aunt is at the concert today, I of course not.

Give my sincere regards to Frau Lou and have a good time, interrupted only by the occasional letter.

Your Papa

1 Probably 'Some Neurotic Mechanisms in Jealousy, Paranoia and Homosexuality' (1922*b*). The essay contained 'approximately that which you heard in the Harz', as Freud wrote a short while afterwards to Ferenczi ⟨Freud/Ferenczi III, 908 F, 21 July 1922, p. 84⟩. It would thus appear that Jones's claim that the work had already been written in January 1921 ⟨Jones III, p. 86 and note 2⟩ can only refer to the version read out in the Harz (see 153 AF, note 2), which Freud must have revised somewhat as well as changing the title ⟨Grubrich-Simitis [1993], p. 166⟩.

2 'Remarks on the Theory and Practice of Dream-Interpretation' (1923*c*) ⟨Freud/Ferenczi III, 908 F⟩. See also 178 SF, 179 SF.

3 A 'long high valley surrounded by mountains, some snow-covered' south-west of Bad Gastein ⟨Baedeker [1923], p. 426⟩. Today the area can be reached by lift and has become part of an extensive skiing region called Sportgastein ⟨signposts in Bad Gastein⟩. See also 199 SF.

4 See 179 SF and note 5.

5 See Minna to Freud from Abbazia in Freud/Bernays, letters 177 Mi–179 Mi.

6 Kurt Redlich, Edler von Vežeg (1887–1939), originally of Brno, student in Vienna from 1905; later a Viennese industrialist and patron of Hugo Heller's publishing and artistic activities. Jones II (p. 46) mentions a 'von Redlich' in his list of participants at the Salzburg Congress ⟨Freud/Jung, 141 F, note 2, p. 223⟩. He is entered in the guest list as 'factory shareholder from Vienna' and he was staying at Hotel Bellevue ⟨*Badgastein. Liste* 1922 (29 June), serial no. 3357⟩.

7 George L. Morgenthau (1862–1934), doctor of medicine, otolaryngologist in Chicago. He spent several months in Vienna in the years 1921 to 1929 for training in psychoanalysis. He was a guest at meetings of the Vienna Psychoanalytic Society in December 1921 and January 1922, and became an extraordinary member in 1931; he also belonged to the Chicago Psychoanalytic Society ⟨Mühlleitner, p. 231⟩. He was staying in Gastein with his sister Selma at Hotel Astoria ⟨*Badgastein. Liste* 1922 (2 July), serial no. 3721⟩.

8 Ditha Bernays, who married in Vienna on 26 June (see 168 AF, note 3), and her husband, Victor Heller (1873–1947), D.Phil., consultant at the Ministry of Finance in Vienna, the brother of Freud's publisher Victor Heller ⟨comment by K. R. Eisler on Freud's letter to Victor Heller of 27 May 1916, LoC SF, Cont. 12; Stammbaum Lange: Bernays Family, 'Genealogical Tree IIa', p. II 5, text to IIa: p. 47⟩. The young couple stayed at Villa Dr Schneyer ⟨*Badgastein. Liste* 1922 (28 June), serial no. 3320⟩. They lived in Austria until the occupation in 1938 and then returned to the USA ⟨Anna/Lou, note to letter 56, p. 708⟩.

9 Leopold Königstein (1850–1924), doctor of medicine, professor of ophthalmology in Vienna, an old fellow student of Freud and one of his few *Du* friends. The regular tarock evenings took place in his apartment (see 7 AF, note 5). In a letter to Wilhelm Fliess (16 June 1899), Freud described the Königstein family as 'the only warm friends we have here' ⟨1985*c*, p. 356⟩; Königstein was staying in Gastein in the Kaiserhof ⟨*Badgastein. Liste* 1922 (10 July), serial no. 4484⟩.

10 Spelling mistake in original.

11 'Dr Robert Kunitzer with wife, New York, Kaiserhof' ⟨*Badgastein. Liste* 1922 (10 July), serial no. 4484⟩. See 181 SF.

176 AF[1]

Prof. Dr. S. Freud
Bad Gastein
Villa Wassing
Austria
Salzburg

[Göttingen,] 11 July 1922
[Postmark: 12.7.22 9–10 V. {morning}]

Dear Papa,
Today I received news for the first time from Mama. Unfortunately, she appears not to have been so lucky with her accommodation and board as me. I will go over there tomorrow[2] to look around a bit. If all goes well, I can even return the same evening. I am still very well and am waiting to become smarter; if not here, then I fear it will be never. I have not heard anything from you yet and it is impossible here to get any news about Austria. Write me a long letter!

Your Anna

1 Postcard with handwritten sender: 'Freud bei Petersen Göttingen, Herzberger Ch. 110'.

2 In a letter from Martha to Freud from Hohegeiss '12/VII Wednesday' (continued on 13 July), Anna added the following lines:

> 'I am settling into my sleeping quarters here, everyone in the cold and mist but quite happy and reconciled. More tomorrow from Göttingen. Regards, your Anna.' ⟨LoC SF, Cont. 10⟩

177 AF

Göttingen, 13 July 1922

My dear Papa,
I returned an hour ago from my trip to Hohegeiss, which lasted from Wednesday morning until Thursday lunchtime. Although we are really not far apart, the journey in both directions took four to five hours.[1] It is good to see that the travel here in Germany is hardly worse than what we

saw in Holland; the trains are almost never late and at no station do you need to arrive earlier than one minute before the train departure. The only bad thing is what I see of the passengers; I don't know whether they are really all anti-Semites, but they look it. And I can hardly think of any other country where one has a stronger feeling of being among 'foreigners'.

Hohegeiss doesn't look so bad to me on the whole. Mama has got over her initial horror at the house, which has many shortcomings, is on good terms with the waiter, owner, etc., and has managed to get all she needs. The place must be very nice when the weather is fine. It has clear mountain air, which makes one hungry and eager to go on walks; when the weather is bad like yesterday, however, it is very cold. In many ways the place and view are reminiscent of Seefeld. For Mama slightly less solitude might perhaps have been better. But we can hardly consider changing sites and accommodation now. The connections from Hohegeiss are difficult, and besides Mama is happy to have overcome the initial feeling and to have some peace. It would also be still quite impossible for Heinerle in a quality hotel. If the weather is propitious, I am sure Mama will be fine here; the children have all the space to play that they could want. For the time being Mama still has problems with her ear, which this time persist despite the mountain air.

What I fail to understand are Mama's money matters. Either Max did not receive the large money dispatch or else the notification that it was for Mama. His first sign of life arrived in Hohegeiss yesterday, in which he announced that he was sending Mama two dispatches of 2,000 M; ridiculous amounts compared with Mama's weekly outlay! I immediately wrote him a long letter from Hohegeiss and asked about the dispatch for 'Ditha Bernays'.[2] Mine arrived before me in Göttingen and was kept for me by Frau Loe.[3] I will come and visit Mama again for two or three days on 25 July.[4] At all events, it was not as bad here as I expected. She is not really 'economizing' and even intends to indulge in carriage rides.[5]

Naughty Heinerle refused to acknowledge me at first and even later he appeared visibly embarrassed to call me aunt. As he was going to sleep he demanded: 'I want Fräulein Freud to come again and play ball with me', and once he called me away from Ernstl's bed while I was saying good-night: 'You sitting over there, come to me!' When I left he was quite affectionate again and wanted to go with me.[6] Ernstl was affectionate and as familiar with me as ever and really wanted me to stay with him. Both look quite well and are very nice. Heinerle makes a pretty picture in lederhosen, a miniature adult, albeit with a will of very adult strength. Frl Jacob is a good soul; unfortunately she has the same effect on me as lengthy carpet beating has on you:[7] a mixture of rage and despair.

I was very pleased to find your letter on my return because mail is the only thing missing to make my well-being here complete. I don't want to exult too much about my 100 mi[llion]. In any case I have no idea about the Austrian exchange rate; there is no information here. I have even become thrifty here again, as always in Germany, and really couldn't decide whether to travel 3rd or 4th class to the Harz, but ultimately opted for 3rd. Frau Loe unfortunately lives in very impoverished circumstances and I don't have the slightest possibility of 'doing' anything for her.[8]

One more thing: do you think that it is possible to find an inkwell in Gastein that looks even remotely like my old marble one and is not too expensive? I no longer have mine and I am looking for a replacement.

I hope to hear from you again soon and send a kiss to you and best regards to Aunt.

Your Anna

1 Martha described her journey from Berlin to Hohegeiss in a letter to Freud on 'Saturday', 8 July 1922: We 'left together [. . .], split up at lunchtime, Annerl on to Göttingen, me from Nordhausen to Ellrich and from there met by a small omnibus, which took almost two hours to get here.' See 172 MF/AF, note 3.
2 As cover name for the transfer. The explanation is to be found in 183 AF.
3 See 173 AF and note 3.
4 For her birthday; see 185 AF.
5 See 149 SF and note 3.
6 Heinerle's wish was soon to be fulfilled in another way; see 146 SF, note 1.
7 See 138 SF and note 22.
8 See 168 AF and note 7, 180 AF and note 1.

178 SF

PROF. DR. FREUD — Bgastein, 14 July 1922
Vienna, IX. Berggasse 19

My dear Anna,
I expect you have received my first letter. I am enclosing two cards and will keep the stamp from one of them. It was very good of you to go and help Mama right away. I expect you to report frankly on your experiences.

I am sure that the stay in Göttingen will be good for your intelligence. About that I have no worries. Here nothing new, except that I have now finished the second essay.[1] I am not happy with the style of either of them: all those hours in English have apparently spoiled it. Königstein is still here in the retinue of a genuine dollar billionairess[2] (copper!) and we played tarock together once. Since yesterday Aunt has had lumbago following the change in weather from searing heat to pouring rain.

It is impossible to avoid talking about prices.[3] Today I exchanged £10 for over 1.1 million K. Every day something goes up, coffee or bread or ham. You need also to be prepared for price rises. Money can still be had.

The Verlag has been very good. Yesterday it sent me *Dream*[4] in a new separate edition. By contrast, the Press is as lethargic[5] as ever, and neither no. 2 of the *Journal*[6] nor any of my translations[7] have arrived.

My affectionate regards to you and Lou. I am more likely to send cards than letters.

Your Papa

1 See 175 SF and note 2.
2 Written thus. The 'copper magnate' (see 181 SF) was 'Frau Carrie Guggenheim, with chambermaid, New York'. She was staying at the Kaiserhof ⟨*Badgastein. Liste* 1922 (10 July), serial no. 4483⟩. The huge Guggenheim family group owned tin, gold and copper mines in North and South America, and extensive diamond, nitrate and rubber fields in Africa; it had a dominant influence worldwide on all associated industries. The name is well known in particular, however, for its important philanthropic foundations, the most prominent of which is perhaps the Guggenheim Museum for Modern Art in New York, whose distinctive round building was designed in 1936–7 by Frank Lloyd Wright. Sixteen years later, in October 1938, another renowned member of this art-sponsoring family, Peggy Guggenheim (1898–1979), was to exhibit contemporary children's art in her London gallery, including drawings by Freud's sixteen-year-old grandson, Lucian Michael (1922–2011), one of the most famous figurative painters in the United Kingdom ⟨Tacou-Romney, p. 90⟩.
3 See 179 SF and note 5.
4 The second part, 'The Dream' of *Introductory Lectures on Psychoanalysis* (1916–17*a*), appearing as a special reprint entitled *Vorlesungen über den Traum*.
5 Spelling mistake (no umlaut) in the original. For the ill-feeling between *Verlag* and the 'Press', see 181 SF and note 5.
6 The *IJ* appeared at the end of the month; see 187 SF.
7 Spelling mistake (no umlaut) in the original. On this problem, see, e.g., 107 SF and notes 11, 12; 157 SF, note 3.

179 SF[1]

Frl Anna Freud
c/o Petersen
Herzberger Landstrasse 110
Göttingen
Germany

Bgastein, 15 July 1922

My dear Anna,
Just to confirm receipt of your worthy letter of 13th. Don't understand Max and thought to have arranged everything well. Wrote to him today by express and asked for telegram explanation but until then they could be impounded in Hohegeiss.[2]

Here bad, very bad weather. Have completed two works[3] and should be getting new ideas, but they won't come.[4] Have a lot of letters of refusal to write and patients to keep away. Aunt and Königstein are suffering from lumbago, the former getting better. You are already at 140 million. There is no end to it.[5] Is there really nothing we can do for Lou?[6]

Affectionately,
Papa

1 Postcard.
2 Freud to Max, 15 July 1922. See 183 AF.

3 See 175 SF and notes 1 and 2.
4 But see 181 SF and note 4.
5 Because of the continuing inflation (see 130 AF and note 3), there had already been strikes, unrest and even looting in Vienna in 1921. In spite of a change of government the price of food, coal and clothing continued to rise without end: 'A shirt that had cost 8 Austrian krone in peacetime was now [1922] 30,000 times more expensive' ⟨Weissensteiner, pp. 114, 116–18, 129f.; Kleindel, pp. 236, 327⟩. The Austrian economy was close to collapse and 'a wild fermentation among the working masses presaged the most serious social upheavals' ⟨Braunthal, p. 55; Freud/Jones, letter 367⟩.
6 See 183 AF.

180 AF

Göttingen, 15 July 1922

My dear Papa,
For the last two days it has been raining with a curious, economical consistency, as if it didn't want to stop before 15 September. It's all right for me here in Göttingen but I feel terribly sorry for Mama and the children, who are no doubt freezing in Hohegeiss.

My hostess is now expecting two Danes, who are coming here to do some work with Prof. Andreas. I have already moved but within the apartment and have actually made a good swap: a large room with glass veranda and view of the city below me. I continue to be treated excellently and am probably getting fatter and fatter. My only grievance is that apart from corrections from the Verlag, your short letter and cards from Mama, I have been getting no post whatsoever. I think it's the postman's fault, however, and I will try to bribe him tomorrow.

With Frau Lou we have started again to talk about the various complicated things that were already bothering her in the autumn in Vienna. At the same time, she tells me such interesting things that we keep on getting distracted. M[. . .] is still here but now for an unpaid session; apart from that there is only one other person – hopefully paying – who comes once or twice a week. As she has no prospects for analysis in the autumn either, Frau Lou contacted Eitingon a few days ago to ask whether he thought she could find work in Berlin in the autumn after the Congress. Do you really not know any paying patients for her? Her English is probably not good enough, but she speaks French. I am curious to see what Eitingon says.[1]

Everything is ripening in the garden, and my insides are already quite mistrustful of all the fruit we eat from the bushes. If it doesn't rain tomorrow, I am supposed to start picking one of the cherry trees.

With a kiss and lots of greetings,
Your Anna

1 See 183 AF.

181 SF

PROF. DR. FREUD

[Bgastein], 17 July 1922
Vienna, IX. Berggasse 19

My dear Anna,
I am glad to hear that you are otherwise doing so well and I shall do everything I can to assuage your hunger for post. In fact, I don't have much material and my main preoccupation is still one of bewilderment at the whereabouts of Mama's money. I would like to hear that everything is in order. I wrote to Max a while ago but must, of course,[1] wait a long time for an answer.

Apart from that, everything is untroubled and quiet here. The daily price inflation is having a great impact on our foreign exchange. We are very rich. Martin says that your £ have already had 22 little £. As for my research, I can only report that I have already sent off my two new works.[2] One of them should appear in the third magazine issue for the Congress.[3] In my free time I am mulling over something new.[4] The Verlag is working very well, the Press at snail's pace as ever. The guns are silent.[5] The Rundbriefe are saying nothing.[6]

Some small gossip. Eight days ago Königstein moved into the Kaiserhof as a guest of Dr Kunitzer, himself the personal physician of a copper magnate from New York, Mrs Guggenheim.[7] Königstein[8] has finally acknowledged that there is something as nice if not nicer than the Vienna Woods.[9] We have already played tarock together twice. Of course, Mrs Guggenheim wanted me to give her a consultation and to treat her here. Through direct rudeness and various dark threats I have managed to persuade the multimillionairess, who is said to be even more 'exact' (mean) [English in original] than she is rich, to forego it.

The outcome in two other cases is not so certain. A spa doctor here,[10] who spends the winter in Merano, has induced me to examine a lady from Merano, who is arriving after the 20th. The enticement was that poor Dr Brecher would start a cure with her and could then continue it in Merano. Threatened penalty therefore only 200 lire, but it might not have to be. There is another case that looks more serious. Dr Fritz G. Steiner[11] wrote a while ago on behalf of a Dutch bank director friend of his, whose sister-in-law from America wants to be treated. The day before yesterday he sent his secretary to Gastein just to ask me whether and for what fee I would be willing to travel to Switzerland to treat the patient, who had been unsuccessfully treated for a long time in New York by an alleged but unnamed student.[12] Answer: there is no question of me travelling to Switzerland. Above all, I don't know what this woman[13] has and whether she is a suitable case at all for treatment. She is supposed to be arriving here by 30 July so that I can make an assessment. For this consultation the higher penalty of #300. This might also come to nothing as well.[14]

Less avoidable and also for less money is another visit announced by telegram from Mrs Bijur, who is in Innsbruck with Frink. She is a rich Jewish woman, now widowed, whom he is supposed to marry, although he is still not quite sure.[15] I know that he feels worse because of 'transference',[16] which gives him a reason to make the visit, and I have invited both of them.[17]

Ditha and Dr Heller are very discreet and pleasant when we see them. We cannot yet say whether he realizes what kind of a disaster he has married. Every time she comes she forgets something important that he has to come back for.

After a few nasty föhn days the weather has changed completely and as with you it rained valiantly for two days, with snow on the mountains, and today was the most brilliant mountain landscape with delightfully fresh air, in other words authentic Gastein.

We really have to talk about[18] poor Lou in Berlin. There must be something that can be done.[19] Give her my affectionate regards and continue to enjoy yourself.

Papa

1 Spelling mistake (no umlaut) in the original.
2 See 175 SF and notes 1 and 2.
3 1992*b*.
4 *The Ego and the Id* (1923*b*): 'Besides that, I am occupied with something speculative, which is a continuation of "Beyond", and will either become a small book or nothing' ⟨Freud/Ferenczi III, 908 F, 21 July 1922, p. 84; see also Anna/Lou, letter 37, p. 65⟩.
5 This choice of words by Freud gives an indication of the hostile tone that the increasing ill-feeling between the employees of the *Verlag* and the 'Press' – and also to some extent between the (sometimes identical) members of the committee – had taken at that time. The discord was connected in part with translation issues and production difficulties but was also due to the differences in the abilities and characters of those involved (see 200 SF, note 5). Jones explains the background – from his point of view – and refers to the combination of personal incompatibilities and the obstacles to the production of books and magazines in Austria at the time ⟨Jones III, pp. 31–4, 37–9, 48–52, 57; see also Freud/Ferenczi III, 913 F; *Rundbriefe 3*, e.g., Freud's contribution, 26 November 1922, pp. 231–5; see also Wittenberger [1955], particularly Part C; and also 196 SF and note 11⟩.
6 They were mainly involved during the summer break with preparations for the Berlin Congress (see 183 AF, note 3) and only took up discussion of the disagreements thereafter ⟨*Rundbriefe 3*, from 15 October 1922⟩.
7 See 178 SF and note 2.
8 Spelling mistake (no umlaut) in the original.
9 Freud himself had a 'strong dislike of the famous Wienerwald, with the solitary exception of the Cobenzl. His children, who were all fond of it, could never drag him there' ⟨Jones II, p. 429⟩.
10 Guido Brecher; see 93 SF, note 4. In 1922 he had a surgery in Hotel zum Hirschen ⟨*Badgastein. Liste* 1922, Introduction⟩.
11 Unknown.

12 Abraham A. Brill ⟨Freud/Ferenczi III, 908 F, note 7⟩.
13 German 'Gredl': see 133 SF, note 10.
14 See 184 SF, note 2.
15 This connection with Angelika Bijur, a former patient of Frink, whose husband died in May 1922, posed a difficult conflict of conscience for both partners. They did get married, but Frink, who had two small children from his abandoned wife, suffered an intensification of his manic-depressive states and had to abandon his career. The marriage to Angelika did not bring the hoped-for recovery: they divorced after three years. After several periods of hospitalization, Frink was cured only to the extent that he could lead a secluded life with his children ⟨Edmunds, pp. 42–8⟩. See 156 AF, note 10, for further sources.
16 Spelling mistake (no umlaut) in the original.
17 Frink and Angelika Bijur came to Gastein on 21 July ⟨Freud/Ferenczi III, 908 F⟩.
18 Spelling mistake (no umlaut) in the original.
19 See 183 AF and note 6.

182 AF

Göttingen, 18 July 1922

My dear Papa,
Thank you for the letter and card. My mail situation here is beginning to get better. I received a long letter from Mama today without mention of the money, but with complaints about the weather that is also terrible here in G. Oli has written in detail with discussion of our itinerary to Munich,[1] and the Verlag sends at least one sign of life every day, which always means a visit to the post office, which is so far from here that it is a regular excursion. An old patient is returning to Frau Loe tomorrow so she will have more to do, unfortunately also unpaid. But she jokingly calls the practice her private out-patient clinic and has no choice but to accept it. We take advantage of all breaks in the rain to go for walks, pick flowers and berries, regret that the time is passing so quickly and get on better and better. It is a pleasure to talk to her, one that is more and more enjoyable and appreciated every day.

What are your two papers about?[2] And are you not in a good mood or is that just my impression from your letters?[3] Is Gastein not as nice as usual? Would it be possible for you to send me a copy of the *Presse*? I have heard nothing about Austria for fourteen days so even the oldest will contain news for me.

Have you heard anything from Grandma?[4] Please send me her address. Please tell Aunt that I sympathize with her lumbago and will write directly to her soon.

With a kiss,
Your Anna

The people are also complaining here about the sharp increase in prices, but I think my host is too decent to charge me more.[5]

1 For the onward journey to Berchtesgaden/Obersalzberg; see 174 AF, notes 10 and 12, 188 AF.
2 See 175 SF and notes 1 and 2.
3 According to Gay (p.438), Freud did indeed confide soon afterwards to Rank 'that his health was uncertain'. In his correspondence with Ferenczi he wrote of 'hoarseness' and 'strains of the Gastein cure' ⟨Freud/Ferenczi III, 907 Fer, p.83, 908 F, p.84, 909 Fer, p.86⟩. See 183 AF, note 9.
4 'My mother, who is very unsteady with her eighty-seven years, is said to be doing better in Ischl' ⟨Freud/Ferenczi III, 908 F, 21 July 1922, p.84⟩.
5 See 178 SF.

183 AF

Göttingen, 20 July 1922

My dear Papa,
First of all, I have heard from Mama that Max has confirmed to her that he has 50,000 DM and that she has already received 13,000. This problem seems thus to have been successfully resolved.[1]

Thank you for your long and detailed letter, which I received this morning. The postman has finally realized that I am not someone to be passed over and wakes me up every morning with all kinds of things, mostly either from you or Mama. I had left the choice between sun and post to chance, and after having dealt with the latter I hope confidently for the appearance of the former.

From here there is one piece of good news affecting Lou. As I told you,[2] she wrote to Eitingon to ask whether there might be any analysis for her in Berlin that would enable her to stay there for a longer time. He replied yesterday that he could not yet say anything definite about patients, but that she could stay (and probably take meals) in his apartment and then look into everything else at her leisure. He and his wife are leaving right after the Congress,[3] and the apartment – looked after by Frau Schirmer[4] – will be empty. (I'm not sure whether Schmideberg will be living there as well.)[5] Frau Lou naturally has all kinds of reservations, but is basically delighted at the freedom of movement and lack of worries that it will offer. She also hopes that she will find patients she can bring back here. Would it not be easier for you to refer someone to her in Berlin than here? At all events she is full of plans and enterprise.[6] At the moment we are preserving self-picked berries in a very primitive way and have excellent conversations about psychoanalytical and also quite unscientific things from her pre-analysis time. I am currently attempting to secretly smuggle in sugar for preserving, which she doesn't allow herself, but don't yet know whether I will succeed.

I have discovered genuine baumkuchen at a cake shop here[7] and intend to order one and take it with me for Mama's birthday.[8] In Berlin I bought her a beautiful coat-like black and white woollen shawl from the family money, which she wanted for her birthday. As it comes from you, she might already have thanked you for it.

Don't let the patients irritate you and leave all millionairesses in their madness – they don't have anything else to do. It is nice above all when one doesn't need them.

Will you give a paper at the Congress?[9] I hope so.

With a kiss,
Your Anna

1 See 177 AF, 179 SF and note 2.
2 180 AF.
3 The 7th International Psychoanalytic Congress took place in Berlin from 25 to 27 September 1922 ⟨Congress report in *IZ*, vol. 8 (1922), pp. 478–505⟩.
4 Not identified.
5 Yes; see Lou's report from Berlin ⟨Anna/Lou, October 1922⟩.
6 Lou stayed at the Eitingons from the time of the Congress until 31 January 1923 and also found patients ⟨Anna/Lou, letters from August 1922 to 27 January 1923⟩. Freud also helped her by sending money ⟨Freud/Andreas-Salomé, 8 September 1922⟩. From 1923 onwards he regularly sent her monthly funds through Eitingon ⟨Freud/Eitingon, 283 F, 294 E; Anna to Eitingon, 2 November 1923⟩. In 1930 he gave her 1,000 marks from his Goethe Prize money ⟨Freud/Andreas-Salomé, 22 October 1930⟩. See also 168 AF and note 7, 177 AF.
7 Konditorei-Café Cron & Lanz (since 1876), still known today for its baumkuchen [layered cake] and other exclusive confectioneries. ⟨I thank Inge Weber, Göttingen, for this information.⟩
8 See 185 AF.
9 Freud had on several occasions expressed his 'deep reluctance' to deliver a paper of his own ⟨Freud/Eitingon, 249 F, 17 August 1922, p. 293⟩. Also to Ferenczi: 'Your encouraging me to speak at the Congress does not penetrate easily. What is aggravating in the symptom of hoarseness is the fact that I am so very much in agreement with it. . . . I simply don't want to. There also has to be a transition to the later Congresses without me' ⟨Freud/Ferenczi III, 908 F, 21 July 1922, p. 84⟩. As it transpired, because of his illness (see 197 SF, note 3) this was to be the last Congress that he attended. He did in fact deliver a paper: 'Something about the Unconscious' (1922*f*), which contained excerpts from the work he was writing at the time (*The Ego and the Id*) (see 181 SF and note 4).

184 SF

PROF. DR. FREUD

Bgastein, 22 July 1922
Vienna, IX. Berggasse 19

My dear Anna,
After having received your letter, I am writing back straightaway so that the postman doesn't lose his respect for you.

There is very little to report from here, except that I have already given Mrs Bijur (Frink's future wife) two hours and that the American managed by Dr F. G. Steiner has announced[1] that she is coming to Berchtesgaden.[2] Perhaps also that because of a stomach upset yesterday, I have started drinking Karlsbader today and shall therefore take my baths in the evening. This is the third year that I have had these tummy aches in Gastein, and those in the know say that it is very common[3] and is due to the water.[4] At all events the bottle of Mühlbrunn, which costs 4,400 K, is starting to have its effect.

Arriving at the same time as your letter was an official document from Hiller, announcing[5] a further delay[6] with the two translations. He managed to discover that the indexes for both of them were very bad and has made new ones that will be sent to London, etc. But they should be ready for sale [English in original] at the Congress. Both you and Eitingon appear to be profoundly convinced that I will be delivering a paper at the Congress. I know nothing about it yet.[7]

In Mama's last letter was the sad news that Fanny[8] has been diagnosed with cancer of the axillary glands.

I am really delighted at Eitingon's offer to Lou. It is nice when someone has something to offer.

I don't know what you want of the weather. Here it is beautiful. Through the payment from Alcan for the *Interpretation of Dreams*,[9] I was able send Max 33,000 Mk again. So don't economize but enjoy life.

With affectionate greetings,

Papa

1 She did indeed go there, although Freud initially wanted to refuse: 'Here on the Salzberg another American is fighting for treatment, she would certainly have paid $50 a day, since she was accustomed to giving Brill $20 in New York for *half* an hour. . . . But she won't accomplish anything, I won't sell the time here' ⟨Freud to Rank, 4 August 1922, quoted in Freud/Ferenczi III, 908 F, note 7, p. 84⟩. It is possible that he decided to treat her after all, because Anna wrote to Lou on 12 August that Freud's work 'was unfortunately interrupted by Americans who have settled in Berchtesgaden and can still reach him here as well' ⟨Anna/Lou, letter 37, p. 65; see also Freud/Jones, letters 373, 376⟩.

2 In other words for Obersalzberg (see 174 AF, note 10).

3 Spelling mistake (no umlaut) in the original.

4 See 72 SF, note 4, 112 SF.

5 See 157 SF and note 3; 160 AF and note 5; 181 SF and note 5.

6 Spelling mistake in the original.

7 See 183 AF, note 9.

8 The Freud family's domestic help. She continued initially to take care of the house: 'The house is the same as ever; even Fanni is her old self' ⟨Anna/Lou, letter 47, 10 October 1922, p. 78⟩. See 185 AF and note 9.

9 The French translation of *The Interpretation of Dreams* (1900*a*) by Librairie Félix Alcan, Paris, did not appear, however, until 1926 ⟨*G. W.*, vol. II/III, p. 701⟩.

185 AF

Göttingen, 27 July [1922], afternoon

My dear Papa,

I have just returned from Mama's birthday[1] half a day earlier than planned because I had the most pleasant travelling companions: Max, Ernst, Lux and I rode half the way together, then Max left and Ernst and Lux came with me to Göttingen, and from there on to Würzburg; from there they are planning to spend fourteen days on Lake Constance. Mama's birthday was quite a celebration, with a candlelit table on the evening before, a fine lunch ordered by Ernst and real wine, which made me quite drunk. Even the weather was tolerable enough for one afternoon for us to go for a walk, albeit with chattering teeth; and the dining room was heated in celebration. Each of us had a present for the children as well and they were quite excited as a result. Both now look well and fresh, eat very well and are very amusing. Heinerle is really entrancing in his moods that switch from rage one minute to amiability the next. Now the stay only has a week to go, at least for Mama.[2] Unfortunately, there are no prospects for an improvement in the weather. In the last few days the newspapers have been making a lot of the below-average temperatures; it is supposed to come from a deep depression somewhere. Hopefully we will have the subsequent manic phase when we are in Berchtesgaden. (The newspapers are also talking about something else: a general exodus of foreigners from Bavaria for fear of political unrest![3] I don't know whether it is true or not.)

Now, however, the reason why this letter is so solemnly registered and comes express. On my return I found the enclosed news from Loe and H. J.,[4] quite unexpected, as you can imagine. Please read it, send it back and write soon telling me what you think; I don't want to delay answering. It's not possible in August but perhaps before or after the Congress, so that I could travel with our Englishmen (Strachey or Rickman)?[5] *In theory* it's not very far: if you leave Berlin or Hanover in the morning, you can be at the Hook by 11 p.m. and at 9.30 a.m. the following morning in London. But I would need to get the visa in Munich or Berlin. Regardless of what comes of it, if anything, I was nevertheless immensely pleased to receive the letter. (I know of one pleasant travelling companion: you, if you accept the invitation to Cambridge.)[6]

Do not think that I already see myself in England, however. I am clearly aware of all the difficulties and am just curious to know whether you are as surprised as me. I am sure you know that apart from all the difficulties I would be interested.[7]

The corrections to the first half of my paper[8] have also just arrived. Hiller is really stupid with his delays; with such short books the indexes are not so important. I would like to have Rank's address.

So now you have a full account of the impressions that assailed me on my return to G. Frau Lou and I are quite sad that we only have a week left. I feel that I have only got to know her properly for the first time during this visit.

I dreamt a whole night long about our good and my very dear Fanni. She was quite silent, however, and didn't respond to anything, and as I recall from the dream interpretation, that is not a good sign.[9]

In spite of the rain I propose to make the somewhat tedious journey down to the post office so that the news gets to you soon.

With a kiss,
Your Anna

1 From Hohegeiss; see 177 AF.
2 See 172 MF/AF, note 3, 174 AF, note 10.
3 Martha also wrote on the same day: '[. . .] I read in the German newspapers that people are fleeing from Bavaria and cancelling their reservations for August (I don't know why)' ⟨to Freud, 27 July 1922⟩. On 18 July 1922 the Reich government proclaimed the Reich Protection Act to counter the civil-war-like unrest, which extended from the post-war revolution in Germany to the separatist movement in Bavaria. In response to this 'encroachment on the legal sovereignty of the *Länder*' Bavaria adopted its own emergency decree, in which 'all jurisdiction of the state constitutional court was removed in favour of the Bavarian people's courts', resulting in the threat from Berlin of emergency intervention ⟨Kraus, pp. 657–99, quotes pp. 675, 678⟩. The following year Lou was even afraid that her patients would believe that they had to leave, since 'in these days one cannot be certain that the German man-in-the-street will not go berserk' ⟨Freud/Andreas-Salomé, 10 August 1923, p. 126⟩. The conflicts continued to escalate, culminating in the Hitler putsch ⟨Ploetz [1980], pp. 923–7⟩.
4 An invitation to England from Loe and Herbert Jones; see 187 SF, 188 AF; see also 100 SF, note 7.
5 They had returned to England after their analyses ⟨Freud/Jones, letter 367⟩.
6 See 187 SF.
7 The trip to England did not take place; see 188 AF, note 2.
8 See 168 AF and note 6.
9 '[. . .] then psychoanalysis will tell us that in dreams dumbness is a common representation of death' ⟨Freud 1913*f*, p. 295⟩. Fanny died in January 1926; Anna reported at length on her death ⟨Anna/Lou, letter 269, p. 500⟩.

186 SF[1]

Frl Anna Freud
c/o Petersen
Herzberger Landstrasse 10
Göttingen
Germany

Bgst. [Badgastein], 29 July 1922
[Postmark: '30.7.22 VIII']

Message following the initial enthusiasm. I fear that you will have great difficulties with the visa and might not get it at all if not[2] in Vienna,[3] so I would suggest that you don't accept unconditionally and that you leave yourself a way out otherwise an acceptance and subsequent cancellation would probably be followed by insults. As long as these travel conditions exist, it is not a pleasure trip.

Affectionately,
Papa

1 Postcard.
2 Spelling mistake (no umlaut) in the original.
3 See 188 AF, note 2.

187 SF

PROF. DR. FREUD

Bgastein, 29 July 1922
Vienna, IX. Berggasse 19

My dear Anna,

I am sending back the letter, which I was also very pleased about, without delay. Of course, I have no objections at all to this adventure. It is quite easy for me to deal with the difficulties that I can solve. You have enough money to get to The Hague and you can get as much as you need from Kobus, as I have my account with him.[1]

The problems with the visa are your affair entirely. Nor is it pleasant to travel alone. My invitation to Cambridge is for Easter and will in any case come to nothing.[2] The main point is a different one, however. Your invitation is for two weeks between the end of July and the end of August. So you won't be able to go after the Congress. You would have to decide whether you prefer to travel from Hanover on the way to Holland or later from Berchtesgaden. From around 15 August to the end and then to Berlin – or back.

If you postpone the trip and come with Mama to Berchtesgaden, take into account that we have rooms there from *1 August* and you should thus be there as soon as possible, perhaps early on the 4th.[3] I just wrote yesterday to Mama about this.

I enjoyed your report of the birthday. My letter and telegram appear not to have arrived in time.[4]

Dr Federn[5] was here for one and a half hours, a bit too long. We already have train tickets and are leaving early on Tuesday, 1 August, arriving hopefully in Berchtesgaden at 4 o'clock.[6] Feeling well, weather fine again today. Rank's address is Seefeld no. 87. *Journal* II has arrived here for you. I won't write to you again from Gastein unless anything special happens.

Affectionate greetings to you and Frau Lou.

Papa

1 See 107 SF, note 9.

2 'On Sunday an Englishman is supposed to come, who will negotiate with me in vain about a series of lectures in Cambridge' ⟨Freud/Ferenczi III, 908 F, 21 July 1922, p. 84⟩.

3 See 174 AF, note 10, 188 AF.

4 'I only received your dear letter of the 24th this morning. The telegram, which I was very pleased to get, arrived on time' ⟨Martha to Freud, 27 July 1922⟩.

5 Paul Federn (1871–1950), doctor of medicine, specialist in internal medicine, psychoanalyst. He was an active Socialist, member of the Austrian Social Democratic Party and committed supporter of a critical application of psychoanalysis for social reform. He had met Freud in 1902 and was a member of the Psychological Wednesday Society from 1903. He soon proved to be 'one of Freud's most trusted adherents in the Vienna Psychoanalytic Society'

⟨Gay, p. 176⟩. He was one of the leading teaching analysts and vice-president from 1924 to 1938. He was also Freud's replacement with 'authorization for all aspects of his practice' and remained connected with Freud for his entire life. He made a name for himself scientifically in the field of ego psychology and the theory and treatment of psychoses. In 1938 he emigrated with his family to the USA, where he worked as an analyst and became a member of the New York Psychoanalytic Society ⟨Federn, E. [1971], quote p. 725; ibid., [1974]; Plänkers and Federn, pp. 75, 82–8, 92–103; *Protokolle I*, pp. XXXVf; see also Mühlleitner, pp. 90–2⟩. See 291 SF.

6 See 174 AF, note 10.

188 AF

Göttingen, 31 July 1922

My dear Papa,

Thank you for your speedy reply. I will send an answer right away to England. I will attempt to storm the English consulate on my way through Munich, possibly staying there half a day longer than planned. I cannot do anything from here as the nearest English consulates are in Hamburg and Munich and I don't want to risk waiting for weeks somewhere on the way – as we had to back then in The Hague.[1] That way I can wait quietly in Berchtesgaden for the matter to be processed. I don't really expect to be successful in such a short time, but just the idea of travelling has been quite pleasurable.[2]

I need to wait to see what Mama decides about our arrival in Berchtesgaden.[3] She had already reserved rooms in Munich and wanted to meet me here.[4] Our journey and our meeting with Oli[5] have been well planned.

Frau Lou sends her best regards; I am unwilling to leave and wish I could take her with me.[6]

I'll send you a telegram when I hear from Mama or meet her.

Everything else orally.[7]

See you soon.

Your Anna

1 See text after 123 AF/SF.

2 Indeed, Anna was unable to make the journey as her visa application was turned down ⟨Anna/Lou, letter 35⟩.

3 See 174 AF, note 10.

4 She did so, getting to know Lou's husband and their home at the same time ⟨PS by Martha to Anna's letter to Lou of 5 August 1922, Anna/Lou, letter 35⟩.

5 See 174 AF and note 12.

6 They saw each other again at the Congress in Berlin; see 183 AF.

7 The journey to the Congress in Berlin was also fixed orally. It was via Hamburg (see 174 AF and note 10) so as to make good the postponed meeting with the grandchildren (see 161 SF, note 14) ⟨Anna/Lou, letter 43; Freud to Max, 13 September 1922⟩. Freud and Anna were accompanied on

the return journey to Vienna on 29 September by Frink and Angelika Bijur, who had attended the Congress as guests ⟨Freud to Max, 1 October 1922; Edmunds, p. 44⟩. They took Heinerle with them to live with Mathilde (see 146 SF, note 1) ⟨Anna/Lou, letters 45, 46; Freud to Max, 6 August, 1 October 1922⟩.

1923

189 AF[1]

Family
Prof. Freud
Vienna IX
Berggasse 19

[Frankfurt,] 25 March [1923], afternoon

I am unexpectedly in the Frankfurt Palmengarten. I will be able to continue travelling this evening and will be in Göttingen[2] *very early*. It is hot and summery and there are huge camellias in the Palmenhaus. The Passauer Wolf[3] was a nice tame lamb; but really full. I would be very interested to hear news of Heinerle![4]

Anna

1 Coloured picture postcard: 'Frankfurt a. Main. Palmengarten–Blumenparterre'; written in pencil without sender.

2 At the home of Lou Andreas-Salomé, whom she was visiting 'for Easter week' ⟨Freud/Ferenczi III, 922 F, 19 March 1923, p.97⟩. As the trains in Germany at that time did not run reliably, she was able to determine some of the route only in the train itself. She set off from Vienna on Saturday 24 March, spent the night in Passau, and had planned to be in Göttingen in the early evening of the 25th ⟨Anna/Lou, letters 85, 88–90⟩. See 191 AF–194 SF.

3 The 'Passauer Wolf' in Bahnhofstrasse was the leading establishment on the square at the time. It has now been demolished and a Hypo-Bank built there in its place. The present-day hotel at Rindermarkt 6–8 has the same name, referring to the wolf in the Passau coat-of-arms, but otherwise there is no connection with the former establishment. ⟨I thank Dr Armin Leebmann, Rotthal-Münster, and Franz Mader, Passau, for their kind information.⟩

4 Heinerle, who had recovered extremely well over the winter in the care of Mathilde and Robert (see 146 SF, note 1), had developed a fever a few days before Anna's departure. Jones states that he had contracted tuberculosis the previous year in the country [in Hohegeiss?] ⟨Jones III, p.96⟩. On this occasion he recovered (see up to 194 SF), but he became ill again at the end of May ⟨Freud to Kata and Lajos Lévy, 11 June 1923 in: 1960*a*, p.348⟩. See 195 SF.

190 SF[1]

Frau Lou Andreas
for Anna Freud
Herzberger Landstrasse 101
Göttingen
Germany

Vienna, 25 March 1923
[Postmark: '26.III.23']

Dear Anna,
I hope your journey was without mishap. The postal strike is over. Heinerle still has fever but doesn't[2] look seriously ill and Rie isn't worried. The glands on his neck are swollen today, which would seem to indicate an infection of the tonsils.[3]

Spring really looks as if it has arrived.

Affectionately,
Papa

1 Postcard.
2 Sign reversing the words in original.
3 This infection resulted in the 'enucleation of the tonsils' ⟨Anna/Lou, letter 93, 18/19 April 1923, pp. 173, 175⟩. Shortly afterwards Freud himself had to undergo an operation on the mouth ⟨Anna/Lou, ibid., p. 175⟩. See 197 SF and note 3.

191 AF[1]

Familie
Prof. Freud
Vienna IX
Berggasse 19

[Göttingen,] 26 March 1923

Dear All,
I arrived safely today after thirty-six hours, not tired at all from the journey and ready for action. I am living again at no. 110, but this time a floor lower.[2] Everything unchanged and very comfortable at Lou's; fortunately she is now almost completely free. The garden is showing the first signs of spring. The victuals proved very useful and have all been eaten.

Send me a word by telegram when Heinerle is better.

Your Anna

1 Postcard.
2 The previous year she had stayed with the Petersens on the first floor; see 173 AF, notes 1 and 2; this time, as the Petersens were away, she was staying on the ground floor with the Trümpers ⟨Anna/Lou, letters 90, 91⟩.

192 SF[1]

Frau Lou Andreas
for Anna Freud
Herzberger Landstrasse 101
Göttingen
Germany

Vienna, 27 March 1923

My dear Anna,
Heinerle has 37.5 and is said to be very chirpy. We put together your journey from the telegram[2] and card. I'm sure you will take a different route home.[3] Mama had migr.[aine] yesterday, me today. Yesterday Wock[4] visited in the evening[;] he has an excellent appetite. Two deliveries came for you today from England,[5] little Hans from Strachey and some of the ψα movement from Riviere.[6] I will write her a card[7] to excuse you. I think Mama is well enough to travel to the wedding[8] in Berlin.[9] Ernst will have to represent us. Enjoy yourself and send my affectionate regards to Frau Lou.

Papa

1 Postcard.
2 Missing.
3 See 189 AF, note 2, and 193 AF and note 3.
4 Handwriting unclear; it could also be 'Nock' or – very badly written – 'Walter'; that would refer to little Anton Walter, called 'Tonerl' in these letters. Neither he nor his sister Sophie can recall a nickname. Sophie Freud says: 'We always called him "Walter".' ⟨Thanks for oral information, 2001.⟩
5 Corrections of work for the *Verlag*.
6 The English versions of Freud's *Analysis of a Phobia in a Five-Year-Old Boy* (1909*b*), translated by Alix and James Strachey for vol. 3 of the *Collected Papers* (not published until 1925), and *On the History of the Psychoanalytic Movement* (1914*d*), translated by Joan Riviere for *Collected Papers*, vol. 1 (published in 1924).
7 Postcard of 27 March 1923 ⟨Freud 1992*l*, p. 273⟩.
8 'Oli married the girl who turned him down two years ago [see 141 SF and note 5]. My wife and Martin were at the wedding as a delegation and brought with them very friendly impressions' ⟨Freud/Ferenczi III, 927 F, 17 April 1923, p. 102; Anna/Lou, letter 91⟩. (The assertion by Young-Bruehl, p. 115, that Anna went to Oliver's wedding and was relieved 'to find him so well and happy' is incorrect; see also 193 AF.) Freud did not meet his new daughter-in-law until Christmas 1923 in Vienna ⟨Freud to Abraham, 4 January 1924, p. 479⟩. Oliver's wife, Henny, née Fuchs (1892–1971), the daughter of a Berlin doctor, was a teacher and painter ⟨Stammbaum Lange: Freud Family, 'Genealogical Tree', p. I⟩. The two lived initially together in a room in Duisburg, where Oliver worked for Thermosbau A. G., Sonnenwall 77: 'Much good mood and modesty will be demanded of the young woman' ⟨Freud/Ferenczi III, 927 F, 17 April 1923, p. 102; 922 F; 977 F (p. 176); Anna/Lou, letters 144, 148⟩. See 211 SF and notes 6 and 7.

9 She was accompanied by Martin and stayed there from 7 to 16 April 1923 ⟨Anna/Lou, letters 91, 93⟩.

193 AF[1]

Prof. Dr S. Freud
Vienna IX
Berggasse 19

Göttingen, 28 March 1923

Dear Papa,
I thank you very much for the telegram[2] and your card; perhaps Heinerle is already getting better. I have been very worried about him. It's a pity that Oli's wedding is so late and cannot be coordinated with my visa. I will probably travel back via Berlin after all.[3] With the train connections as they are, it is shorter than going via Frankfurt or Würzburg. The Eitingons will not be there, by the way, as I have been informed by Lampl that they are leaving for Berchtesgaden on Friday.

Here it is magnificent spring weather and yesterday we went on a long walk. Having to leave again so soon is not at all easy.

How many days are you taking off?[4]

Anna

1 Postcard.
2 Missing.
3 She did this and spent a long 'and enjoyable' day in Berlin 'divided between Henny, Tom and Lampl' ⟨Anna/Lou, letter 91, 6 April 1923, p. 168⟩.
4 Over Easter (Easter Sunday was 1 April).

194 SF[1]

Frl Anna Freud
c/o Prof. Petersen
Herzberger Landstrasse 110
Göttingen
Germany

Vienna, 29 March 1923
[Postmark: '30.III.23']

My dear Anna,
The week is nearly over. This is the last card that I will risk. Heinerle's fever is almost gone.[2] Nothing new from Oli, and no other news worth reporting. The Polish *Dream* has come out.[3] Ferenczi might be coming over Easter.[4] We have tickets for Pallenberg[5] on Sunday evening. Martin and Esti have gone to Schladming.[6] The weather is beginning to become overcast.

Looking forward to seeing you,

Papa

1 Postcard.
2 'My little grandson here is the most ingenious child of this age (four years) that I have ever seen. He is also correspondingly thin and sickly, nothing but eyes, hair and bones' ⟨Freud/Ferenczi III, 927 F, 17 April 1923, p. 102⟩.
3 *On Dreams* (Freud 1901*a*), translated into Polish by Beate Rank, published by the *Verlag* as the first volume of the series Polska Bibljoteka Psychoanalityczna, 1923 ⟨*G. W.*, vol. II/III, p. 702; *Katalog*, p. 87⟩.
4 He postponed the visit until Whitsun ⟨Freud/Ferenczi III, 925 Fer, 928 Fer, 930 Fer; Anna/Lou, letter 103⟩.
5 Max Pallenberg (1877–1934), Austrian actor, one of the most well-known character actors of his time. Hugo von Hofmannsthal wrote the title role of his comedy *Der Unbestechliche* for him; the premiere took place on 16 March 1923 in Raimundtheater; the tickets for Easter Sunday (1 April) might also therefore have been for one of these performances.
6 Holiday and winter sports resort in Styria in the upper reaches of the Enns, the gateway to the Dachstein-Tauern region.

195 SF[1]

Present
from
Heinerle

19 June 1923[2]

1 Loose sheet without letterhead; Freud's handwriting; the first two words are in Gothic and the name 'Heinerle' in Latin letters. The sheet was probably enclosed with a keepsake in memory of Heinerle.
2 This is the day Heinerle died ⟨Freud/Ferenczi III, 933 F⟩. He became ill with high fever again at the end of May. Only after several days of unclear diagnosis did it become evident that he was suffering from disseminated tuberculosis and thus could not be saved. During this time Anna moved in with Mathilde to help care for Heinerle. She wrote at length to Lou about the course of the disease ⟨Anna/Lou, letters 105–11⟩. Freud admitted to his friends Kata and Lajos Lévy and Ferenczi: 'I find this loss very hard to bear. I don't think I have ever experienced such grief' ⟨11 June 1923 in: 1960*a*, p. 349⟩. 'I have never had a depression before, but this must be one now' ⟨Freud/Ferenczi III, 936 F, 18 July 1923, p. 109⟩.

196 SF

PROF. DR. FREUD [Bad Gastein,][1] 12 July 1923
Vienna IX, Berggasse 19

My dear Anna,
All letters and deliveries arrived,[2] very happy about the good postal service.[3] Thank Jeanne[4] as well for her[5] kind and cheerful letter (slip of the pen instead of an answer)!

It is so hot that we do not go out before 6 p.m. I'm glad that the postbox is right next to the house.

Not much news. Aunt is apparently recovering very well[6] and is all the more keen to prolong the stay in Gastein. I am very sorry that Mama is still having trouble with eczema.[7] Hopefully the inactivity will finally do her some good.

A letter today from Martin. He wanted to bring his wife and child[8] via Trieste to Mallnitz but the child had a fever and started vomiting on the way, so he left them at Parkhotel Villach. From there he received a comforting telegram that everything was all right again[;] the child appears simply not to have been able to put up with travelling in the heat. Martin himself must be in a bad way because he carried out a simple commission from me wrongly.

I don't know whether Esti is still in Villach and would not particularly welcome her appearance in Annenheim[,] but I doubt that she will come.

The revision of the pathologies[9] is extremely tedious. The Stracheys are probably giving themselves unnecessary trouble[10] as the Press seems to be disintegrating.[11]

Keep well; I shall write again soon.

Papa

1 Freud was here on a cure from 1 to 30 July 1923, with Minna Bernays ⟨Anna/Lou, letter 111; Jones III, p. 103⟩.
2 Anna's mail missing.
3 Between Bad Gastein and Annenheim on the Ossiacher See in Carinthia (north of Villach), where Martha, Anna and Ernstl had been staying in the Kurhotel since 6 July. Anna took the two-and-a-half hour journey from there to visit her father from 8 to 10 July ⟨Anna/Lou, letters 111–14; Freud (and Minna Bernays) to Max, 7 July 1923⟩.
4 Jeanne de Groot, 'the young Dutch doctor [. . .] has joined us and it's doing me a lot of good' ⟨Anna/Lou, letter 114, 11 July 1923, pp. 202f.⟩.
5 Corrected in German from 'Ihren' (= your). The comment in brackets at the end of the sentence is in reference to this.
6 Minna had been treated for a heart condition for four weeks in April and May in the Cottage-Sanatorium. Her condition was very unstable for a time and as a result Anna had considered accompanying her father to Bad Gastein instead of her. But she abandoned this wishful idea again when Minna felt somewhat better after convalescing in Bad Reichenhall ⟨Anna/Lou, letters 93, 98, 111; Freud/Ferenczi III, 929 F; Freud/Bernays, intermediate text, p. 294; Young-Bruehl, p. 123⟩.
7 'Eczema on both hands' ⟨Anna/Lou, letter 111, 29 June 1923, p. 199⟩.
8 Esti and Tonerl.
9 Freud was working at the time on the translations by Alix and James Strachey of his five major descriptions of pathologies (1905*e*, 1909*b* and 1922*c*, 1909*d*, 1911*c* and 1912*a*, 1918*b*) (see 128 SF, end of note 4, 157 SF, note 3). They appeared in 1923 in vol. 3 of the *Collected Papers* ⟨see also *Bloomsbury* [1995], 16 January 1925, p. 185 and note 3⟩.
10 Spelling mistake (no umlaut) in the original. According to Anna, the trouble

must have been worthwhile, however, as she had been working the previous year on the 'correction of Strachey's wonderful translation of Papa's pathologies' 〈Anna/Lou, letter 49, 17 October 1922, p. 83〉.

11 The complications between the *Verlag* and the Press (see 181 SF, note 5, 200 SF, note 5) had further degenerated in 1922 and there was talk of a separation, which was ultimately effected 〈Freud/Jones, letters 382–6, 395, 401, 403, 406–13, 415–23, 428–30, 433f.; Freud/Ferenczi III, 913 F, 917 F; Freud 1992*l*, 2 July, 14 July, 8 August 1923〉. On 25 September 1924 Freud admitted in a letter to Jones: 'The final success of the Press is a matter you may be proud of, I have given up all hope of such an issue [. . .]' 〈Freud/Jones, letter 434, p. 552〉. See also Jones III, p. 56.

197 SF

PROF. DR. FREUD BGastein, 13 July 1923
Vienna IX, Berggasse 19

Dear Loved Ones,
Was hugely delighted with Mama's card – she knows how to write after all. I still firmly intend to travel to you at 9.32 on Monday [16 July].[1]

Unfortunately, the next letter was from Lux, saying that Theo[2] had a fatal accident while bathing on the 10th of this month. There is apparently absolutely no question of it having been deliberate and they are blaming the effect of the heat on his brain, which was affected by his last illness. He dived, failed to resurface and was not found until twenty minutes later. It's a little too much for one season.[3]

The same post brought a dear and cheerful card from Henny from the 8th.

Aunt's recovery is making excellent progress. I just had a powerful reaction again. It is frightfully hot for Gastein, but enchantingly beautiful. Impossible to walk or to work.

I don't know how Aunt Mitzi will get over this accident. I am still insensitive to anything new.

Affectionate greetings to you both, Ernstl and Jeanne.
Papa

1 He did 〈Anna/Lou, letter 116〉.

2 Theodor Freud ('Teddy'), the eighteen-year-old son of Freud's sister, Marie, in Berlin. See also Murken [2004], pp. 87f.

3 The deaths of Heinerle and Teddy were not the only shadows cast by the 'season'. In spring Freud's own cancer, which was ultimately to lead to his death, was discovered. His suffering began on 21 April with the extirpation of a tumour in his mouth, which was to be followed in subsequent years by over thirty further operations (see also text after 201 SF/AF). 〈There is some dispute in the literature about the date of the first operation: Anna to Lou (letter 93): 'Saturday morning' (= 21 April); Jones III, p. 94, 'the 20th'; Schur, p. 348, 'the 20th'; Freud/Jones, letter 398, p. 521, 'the 28th'; Freud/Ferenczi III, 929 F, 'April 28'; Freud/Eitingon, 278 E, note 1, '21 April'〉. There are also conflicting versions of the course of the disease 〈Jones III, pp. 94–101; Pichler; Schur, ch. 13; Deutsch, F.; Gay,

pp. 418–28⟩. The correspondence between Anna and Lou (letters 93–103, 114–72 and elsewhere) show Anna's great concern and emotion, which she refrains by agreement from mentioning in these letters (see 198 SF and notes 1 and 5).

198 SF

PROF. DR. FREUD BGastein, 21 July 1923
Vienna IX, Berggasse 19

My dear Anna,

It is good that we agree so well.[1] Now I shall wait for a letter, if one comes at all.[2] If he doesn't write, I will naturally be free.[3]

I do not propose to give in to your wish for the time being.[4] You should not prematurely take on the sad role of nursing old, ailing parents. Hopefully you will be spared it altogether.[5] I will make the concession, however, of summoning you at once by telegram if he wants to keep me in Vienna for any reason, although I believe it highly unlikely.

I am returning the dear letter from Lou.[6] Your comments on Jeanne[7] coincide completely with a remark by Ruth.[8] She is here, by the way,[9] and has met me three times at Wenger[10] to go for a walk, otherwise very nice and discreet. She is still affected from having seen parents and husband[11] again and prefers a few more days rest to the company in Annenh[eim].

No news at all from Uncle and Martin in Berlin. It also rained here for two days but today it's glorious again.

What is happening for Mama's birthday??

Affectionate greetings to all of you and acknowledgement to Ernstl for his letter of thanks.

Papa

1 A letter from Anna is missing; Freud might be referring to an oral agreement during his visit to Annenheim; see note 5.

2 This is presumably a reference to a letter from the laryngologist Univ.-Prof. Dr. Marcus Hajek (1861–1941), who carried out the first excision in Freud's palate. Without telling him the truth about the malignant findings, he had allowed Freud to go on his usual summer holidays while insisting at the same time that Freud should report to him regularly about his health and that he should return to Vienna at the end of July for a check-up; the latter was ultimately thought unnecessary after all ⟨Jones III, p. 97 (with the incorrect date 'mid-June' for Freud's inquiry to Hajek from Gastein, where Freud did not arrive until 1 July); see also Freud/Ferenczi III, 938 Fer⟩. See Freud's letter from Bad Gastein to his son Ernst of 28 July 1923: 'My condition has improved considerably here and I have also been let off having to come to Vienna to have the operation wound looked at' ⟨Freud/Children, p. 349⟩. For details about Hajek, see Schnitzler [1985], p. 300.

3 Possibly a reference to the plan 'in September, if all goes well, for three weeks' ⟨Anna/Lou, letter 56, 16/17 November 1922, p. 100⟩. See 201 SF/AF and the following text.

4 Anna had no doubt wanted to accompany Freud to Vienna for the check-up.

5 It turned out otherwise, and Anna ultimately became Freud's main carer after

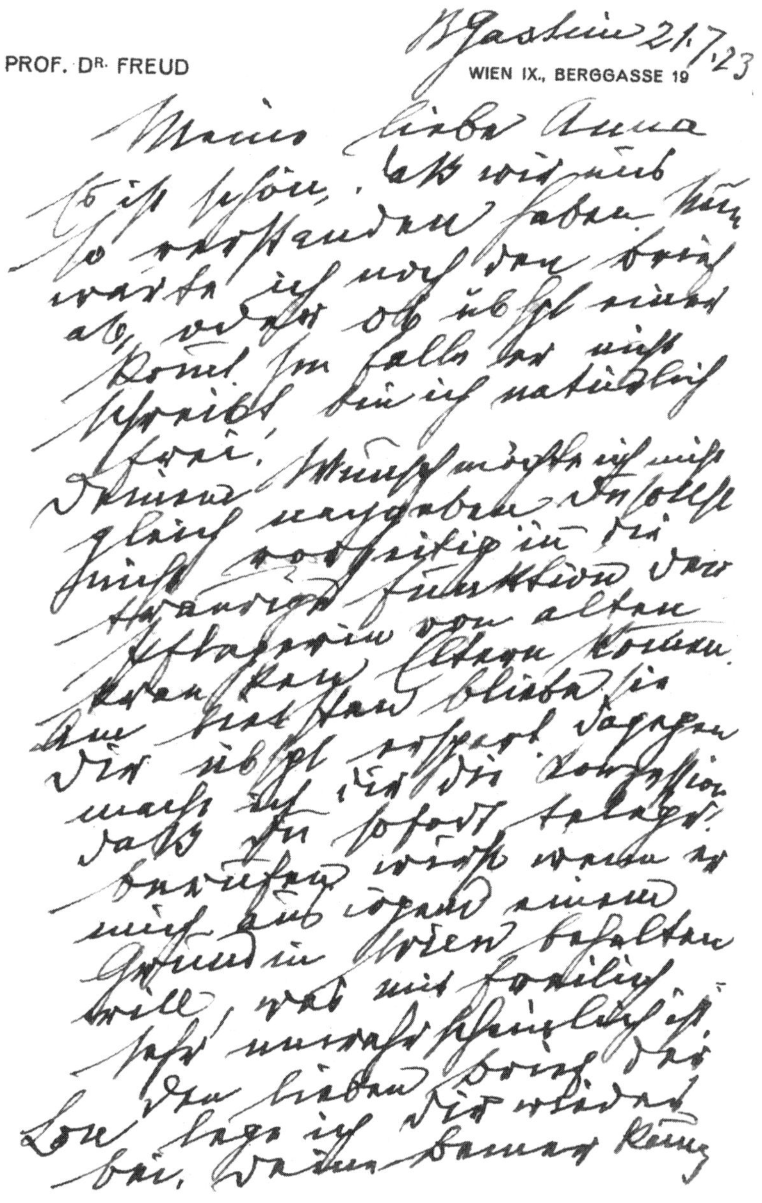

IV Freud's letter of 21 July 1923

all: 'He made a pact with her at the beginning that no sentiment was to be displayed; all that was necessary had to be performed [. . .] with the absence of emotion [. . .]. This attitude, her courage and firmness, enabled her to adhere to the pact even in the most agonizing situations' ⟨Jones III, p. 101; see also Lou to Anna in Anna/Lou letter, 130, p. 232⟩. From 1929 Max Schur provided additional medical care as Freud's personal physician; see 277 SF and note 8. 'Their watchful care and their skill in detecting the earliest signs of danger undoubtedly prolonged Freud's life by years' ⟨Jones III, p. 154⟩.

6 Anna/Lou, letter 112, 3 July 1923.

7 Jeanne de Groot, see 196 SF and note 4.

8 Ruth Mack-Brunswick, née Mack (1897–1946), doctor of medicine, American psychiatrist and psychoanalyst, who had been studying with Freud since 1922 in Vienna where she then opened a practice. Until 1938 she worked in psychoanalysis on both sides of the Atlantic and was a member of both the New York and the Vienna Psychoanalytic Society, from 1929 at the Training Institute. In 1938 she returned to the USA, had her own practice in Washington and worked as a training analyst at the New York Psychoanalytic Institute. She died under tragic circumstances at the age of forty-eight (see 296 SF and note 6, 297 SF and note 4). Anna made friends with her and she soon became very closely attached to the family. Amongst other things, Ruth helped Oliver and his wife, Henny, with their emigration from France to America; see 208 SF, note 3 ⟨Mühlleitner, pp. 214f.; Roazen [1976] pp. 420–35 (also [1993], [1999]); Young-Bruehl, p. 127⟩.

9 Spelling mistake (no umlaut) in the original.

10 Café und Gasthaus Wenger on Kaiser-Wilhelm-Promenade, not far from Villa Wassing ⟨Baedeker [1923], p. 422⟩.

11 Ruth was still married at the time to her first husband, the heart specialist Herman Blumgart, brother of the American psychiatrist Leonard Blumgart, who had had a training analysis with Freud; see 154 SF/2, note 2. For details of her relationship at the time to her father and her marital difficulties, see Roazen [1976], p. 422. At the end of March 1928 Ruth married for the second time to Mark Brunswick (see 228 SF, note 6), a cousin of her first husband. Freud and Oscar Rie were the witnesses ⟨Jones III, p. 148⟩. Her father, Julian Mack, a reputed jurist in the USA, married Mark Brunswick's mother after the death of his first wife ⟨Roazen [1976], pp. 422–3⟩.

199 SF[1]

Frl Anna Freud
Annenheim
am Ossiachsee
Kurhotel

BGastein, 23 July 1923

Dear Loved Ones,
I have suddenly been feeling much better since yesterday and so today I went with Ruth up the Nassfeld[2] (on foot), without exertion but with lots of rhododendrons and twelve vanilla orchids.[3]

The yellow jacket has proved its worth excellently. A dear card from Henny arrived, otherwise silence on all fronts.

Ossipov[4] and Dostoyevsky[5] arrived yesterday. Aunt is no longer so brilliant at the moment. Letter from Jeanne received with thanks.

Affectionate greetings to all,

Papa

1 Postcard.
2 See 175 SF and note 3.
3 '*Kohlroeserl* (*Nigritella nigra*), a small, dark-purple flower, almost black, with a peculiarly strong and sweet perfume' had a particular significance for Freud and his wife, Martha: 'When she was still a bride, she had been on the Schneeberg with her young and handsome husband and they had spotted a clump of these flowers. He had climbed a steep, grassy slope to gather some for her. Throughout her life, until she was driven from Austria, the sight and the scent of the *Kohlroeserl* brought back this happy period in her life' ⟨Freud, M. [1999], p. 85⟩. On the next page Martin describes a perilous adventure experienced by Freud while picking these flowers.
4 *Tolstoy's Childhood Memories* (1923*b*). Anna had worked the previous year on the 'thorough correction of the Ossipov manuscript' ⟨Anna/Lou, letter 49, 27 October 1922, p. 82. See also *Rundbriefe*, 28 February 1923/W, 1st paragraph⟩. Ossipov had already delivered a lecture on 17 June 1922 to the Czech Medical Society on 'Tolstoy's emotional suffering' (1923*a*). Nikolai Yegrafovich Ossipov (1877–1934), doctor of medicine, Russian psychiatrist, who co-founded the Moscow Psychoanalytic Society in 1911 and was its first president, visited Freud in 1910 and in 1911 translated his *Five Lectures on Psychoanalysis* (1910*a*) into Russian ⟨Freud/Abraham, note 4, pp. 111f.⟩. After the October Revolution in 1918 he was obliged to flee from Russia and settled in Prague in 1921 ⟨*Rundbriefe 2*, pp. 73f. and elsewhere⟩. See Fischer, E. for further details of Ossipov's life and his importance for the spread of psychoanalysis in Russia and Czechoslovakia. The publication of the correspondence between Freud and Ossipov by E. and R. Fischer, H.-J. Rothe and H.-H. Otto is in preparation. ⟨I thank Hans-Joachim Rothe, Frankfurt, for details and information.⟩
5 J[olan] Neufeld, *Dostoyevsky: Sketch for a Psychoanalysis* (1923). Freud mentioned this work in his own essay on Dostoyevsky as an 'excellent book' ⟨1928*b*, p. 194⟩.

200 SF[1]

Frl Anna Freud
Annenheim
am Ossiachsee
Kurhotel

BGastein, 25 July 1923

My dear Anna,

Your last letter[2] is fortunately out of date. I intend to travel to you on Monday morning [30 July].[3] Have the concierge check the itinerary so that we make the connection in Trento.[4] Math wrote today and is looking forward to seeing us all,[5] but is thinking of meeting in Bolzano.

Affectionate greetings,

Papa

1 Postcard.
2 Missing.
3 The holidays continued 'only after a lot of changing our minds,' wrote Anna to Lou. 'At first Mama didn't want to travel at all, but in the end Papa fetched her' ⟨Anna/Lou, letter 118, 5 August 1923, p. 209⟩.
4 For the onward journey together to Lavorone in Trentino, where the extended family with Ernstl stayed at Hotel du Lac: 'at 1,100 m altitude on a beautiful and remarkable high plateau with a small warm lake [. . .]. We have been here twice before [1906 and 1907] [. . .] and every time I think back to a tree, a path or a spot, it makes me happy to be that much older, more independent and no longer "little"' ⟨Anna/Lou, letter 118, 5 August 1923, p. 210⟩. (See also 11 AF/EF and note 9.) The family left Lavorone at the end of August; Eitingon took Ernstl back to Berlin when he returned on 30 August (see note 5): 'and after dinner Mama, Papa and I are leaving; Mama for Merano to Tante Minna, we directly to Rome' (see 201 SF/AF) ⟨Anna/Lou, letter 122, cont. 31 August 1923, p. 217; 'see also Jones III, p. 103⟩. Martha and Minna returned to Vienna around 21 September ⟨Freud 2000*b*, 11 September 1923⟩.
5 Apart from family members and many guests, Freud also visited the committee members, who had met after Freud's operation (without Freud) on 26 August in nearby San Cristoforo, for an initial discussion and consideration of the internal tensions (see 181 SF, note 5; 196 SF, note 11) ⟨Jones III, pp. 97f., 103⟩.

201 SF/AF[1]

[1–21 September 1923]

[Front]

	Rome[2] morning	afternoon	evening
1.	–	Corso	–
2.	Forum, Cap[itol]	Pincio	–
3.	Palatine	Gianicolo Vatican	–
4.	Museo naz[ionale]	Pantheon Coloss[eo] P[iazza] Navona Maria s[opra] Min[erva] G[iordano] Bruno	
5.	Mus[e] Vatic[ani]	Moses Bocca dl [della] Verità 2 temples Port[ico di] octav [Ottavia] carcer.	
6.	Museo capitol[ino]	Janus Palatine	
7.	Sistina Stanze [di Raffaello]	Protest. cemetery S[an] Saba S[anta] Sabina	

		Aventino
		cestius
8.	S[ant'] Angelo	Caec. [Cecilia] Metella
		Via appia [antica]
		Columbar[ia]
9.	Villa Giulia	S[an] Paulo [fuori le Mura]
		tre fontane
10.	Vatican	[Monte] Celio
	Loggia	Via Latina
	Bibliot[ecai]	(tombe)

[Reverse]

	morning	afternoon	evening
11.	Laterano	–	cinema
12.	M[onte] Tarp[ea]		–
	Arcoeli	Ponte Molle	
	Mus[eo] Kirch[eriano]		
13.	Tivoli	Villa d'Este	
14.	Doria	–	–
15.	Pinacoteca vatic[ano]	Prassede	
	S[anta] Maria d[el]	Maria magg[iore]	
	Popolo	S[anta] Croce	
		S[an] Lorenzo	
		[fuori le Mura]	
		Eurysaces	
16.	Zool. Gardens	Maria s[opra] Min[erva]	
	Gall[eria] Borgh[ese]	Maria dell[a] pace	
		Cam[era di] commerc[io]	
		Isola Tevere [Tiberina]	
		Palaz[zo] Farnese	
		Spada	
		Cancellarie [Cancelleria]	
		Massimi [Massimo]	
17.	Corsini	P[orta] Pia	
	Farnesina	Gesù	
		S[an] Clemente	
18.	–	Shopping	
		(silver chain)	
19.	Campo di [de'] Fiori	Via Appia [Antica]	
		San Sebastiano	
		Hermes excavations	
20.	Via Nazionale, leather	M[on]te Mario,	Fontana Trevi
	purchases	Camil[l]uccia	
21.	Shopping	Palatine	departure[3]
		Café [Caffe] Aragno	

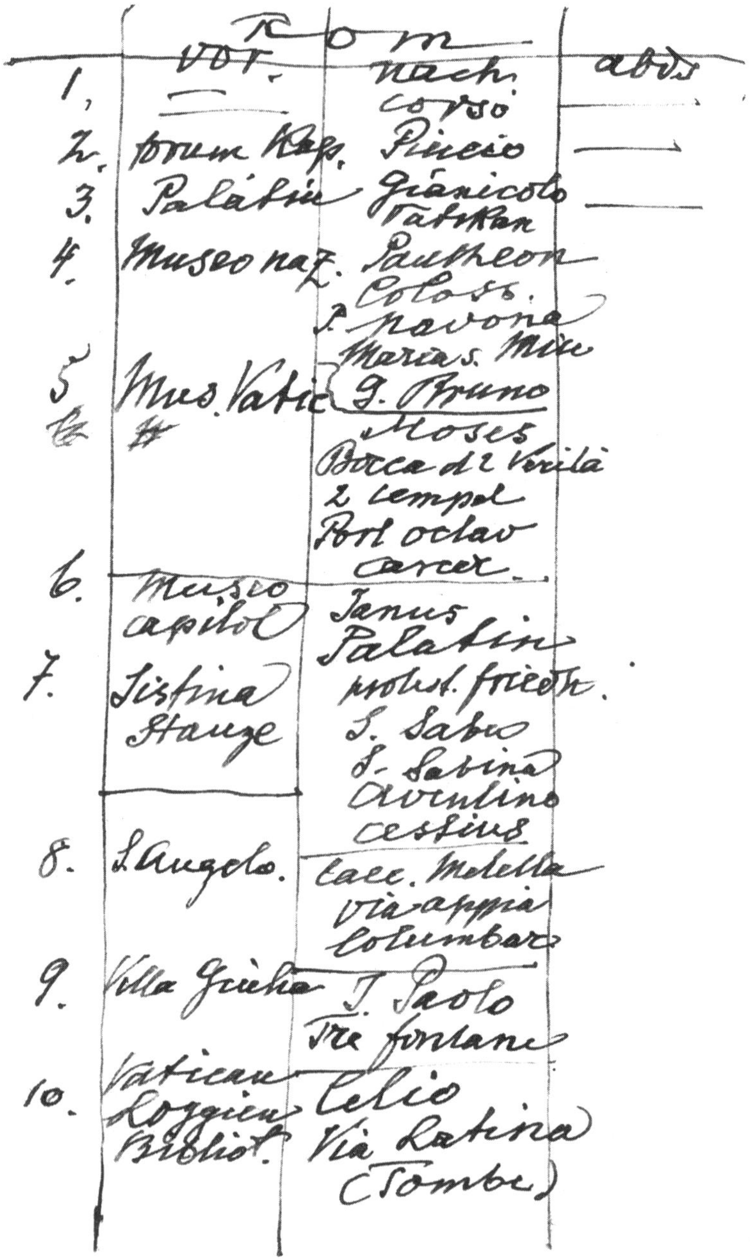

Rom

	vorm.	nachm.	abds
1.	—	Corso	→
2.	Forum Rom.	Pincio	→
3.	Palatin	Gianicolo Vatikan	—
4.	Museo naz.	Pantheon Coloss. P. navona Maria s. Mine G. Bruno	
5.	Mus. Vatic.	Moses Bocca d. l. Verità 2 tempel Port octav carcer	
6.	Museo capitol	Janus Palatin	
7.	Sistina Stanze	protest. friedh. S. Saba S. Sabina Aventino cestius	
8.	S. Angelo.	Caec. Metella via appia Columbar.	
9.	Villa Giulia	S. Paolo Tre fontane	
10.	Vatican Loggien Bibliot.	Celio Via Latina (Tombe)	

V 'Travel Diary', Rome

	vor.	nachm.	abends
11.	Laterano	—	Kino
12.	M. Tarp. Aracoeli Mus. Kirch.	Aq. acet. Ponte molle	—
13.	Tivoli	Villa d'Este.	—
14.	Doria	—	
15.	Pinacoteca vatic. S. Maria d. Popolo	Prassede Maria magg. S. Croce S. Lorenzo. Eurysaces	
16.	Zool. Gart. Gall. Borghese	Maria s. Min " dell pace Cam. commerc. Isola Tevere Palazz. farnese " Spada " Cancellaria Massimi	
17.	Corsini farnesina	P. Pia Gesù S. Clemente.	
18.	—	Einkäufe (Silberkette)	
19.	Campo di Fiori	Via Appia, San Sebastiano	
20.	Via Nazionale, Ledereinkäufe	Ausgrabg Hermes. Mte Mario,	Fontana Trevi
21.	Einkäufe	Gianicolo Palatin Café Aragno	Abreise

1 This sheet was not in the transcriptions. Gerhard Fichtner discovered it in another bundle in the Library of Congress and kindly gave me a copy. Following the rearrangement of Freud's papers, it is in LoC AF, Cont. 162. The entries are transcribed here without comment (see facsimile on p. 320f.). Detailed explanations can be found in Appendix 1, p. 412ff. (See also Freud's letters from this trip to the family, 2002*b*, with numerous illustrations, Tögel [2002].)
2 See 200 SF, end of note 4, and the following text.
3 Freud had booked the return journey early: 'We have a simple splendid return journey from 8.35 [in the evening] to the next morning but one in the same sleeping car via Tarvisio and had already reserved before your letter (from 19–21, depending on what's available [. . .]' ⟨2002*b*, 1 September 1923, p. 383⟩.

Freud and Anna in Rome (September 1923)

Freud described his 'longing for Rome' as 'deeply neurotic' ⟨1985*c*, 3/5 December 1897, p. 285; also pp. 332, 368⟩. At all events, the city had symbolic significance for him at several levels ⟨Jones II, p. 18; particularly impressively Grubrich-Simitis [1995a]⟩. It is perhaps not therefore surprising that he decided in the very week after his operation in April (see 197 SF, note 3) to carry out a plan that he had long been harbouring: to visit Rome with Anna. Although the doctors had originally denied the diagnosis to him and his family, he suspected the truth, as did Anna soon afterwards ⟨Jones III, p. 97f.; *Rundbriefe*, 1 May 1923; Freud/Ferenczi III, 929 F, 970 F; Anna/Lou, letters 98, 100, 120; Deutsch, F.; Schur, pp. 357, 361, 499⟩. '"Allowing" Freud to see Rome once more and to show it to Anna was the most humane and constructive action of all those months' ⟨Schur, p. 361⟩.

The trip was an exhilarating experience for both of them: 'We are having a really nice time here. . . . Anna is enjoying herself completely and is managing perfectly and is open to all aspects of the Roman polydimensionality. I feel better here than ever – since April – and even have hours of complete contentment' ⟨Freud/Eitingon, 283 F, 11 September 1923, p. 331; also 285 F⟩. Anna: 'Papa . . . has instructed me on everything so well and has made me so familiar with all of the beauty, antiquities and curiosities that I feel after the second week that I belong here, as if I had been with him on the many occasions that he has seen it all before' ⟨Anna/Lou, letter 124, 16 September 1923, p. 222⟩.

Anna studied Italian for several months in advance to prepare herself for the trip ⟨Anna/Lou, letters 61, 115⟩. They stayed at Hotel Eden in Via Ludovisi 49 at the southern end of Villa Borghese, where Freud had already stayed previously (see 35 SF, 38 SF) ⟨Anna/Lou, letters 122, 124⟩. See also Anna's description of the hotel in Appendix 2.

Autumn (1923)

On their return, Freud's doctors informed him of the malignancy of the tumour, which had grown in size in the meantime. Radical surgery was required, which was performed in three sessions on 4, 11 and 12 October in Sanatorium Auersperg, where he was accompanied by Anna. This time the surgery was carried out by Prof. Pichler, the renowned jaw surgeon from the University of Vienna, who was to treat Freud henceforth (see 215 SF and note 6). He also made the first prostheses for him, which needed constant adjustment, however, calling for further interventions. It was not until 2 January 1924 that Freud was able to work in his practice again ⟨Anna/Lou, letters 128, 148, 172; Schur, pp. 361–6; Jones III, pp. 99–105⟩.

These events were a decisive turning point in the life of both Freud and Anna, and without a doubt were instrumental in her final decision to remain in her father's house ⟨see Anna/Lou, letter 204, pp. 384f.⟩. The interruption in the continuity and character of the correspondence reflects this caesura.

1924

202 SF[1]

One year, one pound
3 Dec 1924[2]
Papa
with affectionate wishes[3]

1 Front of an envelope, all written in Latin alphabet.

2 Anna had a particularly large number of guests for this birthday: 'Everybody wanted to celebrate what was better this year than last.' Her aversion to birthday presents also began to change: 'I no longer feel ashamed, as I used to be, when someone gives me a present; do you remember how appalled you used to be? I now see how nice it is to be showered so undeservedly, really to be a real "recipient", in other words' ⟨Anna/Lou, letter 204, 4 December 1924, p. 384; also letter 320⟩.

3 This is the only surviving document for 1924 in the correspondence; since Freud's operation Anna had not left her father at all for any lengthy periods. She had resumed her own analysis (see 96 AF and note 3) and continued working hard to become a psychoanalyst. At the end of the year she became a member of the 'Secret Committee' (see 156 SF and note 1) and apart from her practical activities also helped with the organization of the Vienna Psychoanalytic Training Institute and became its secretary, the first of her official positions ⟨Anna/Lou, letter 206⟩.

1925

203 SF[1]

anna freud, ritters parkhotel, Bad Homburg v. d. Höhe[2]
semmering 1[3] 2/9 1925 15.30

sincere welcome to everyone
papa

1 Telegram.
2 Anna was at the 9th International Psychoanalytic Congress in Bad Homburg (3–5 September 1925). Freud, who had already missed the 8th Congress in Salzburg at Easter the previous year on account of a serious bout of influenza ⟨*IZ*, vol. 10 (1924), p. 211; Freud/Jones, telegram 425, p. 543; Anna/Lou, letter 164; Freud/Ferenczi III, 954 F⟩, wanted to participate this year, but ultimately did not feel strong enough. Anna read out the work written for the Congress, 'Some Psychical Consequences of the Anatomical Distinction between the Sexes' (1925*j*), in his place ⟨Jones III, pp. 107, 108, 115, 118f.; Anna/Lou, letters 224–43 *passim*; *IZ*, vol. 11 (1925), pp. 506f.⟩. It was decided amongst other things at this Congress to make psychoanalytical training stricter and more standardized; the relatively unregulated training courses were replaced by an International Teaching Commission, chaired by Eitingon, to coordinate the branch societies ⟨*IZ*, vol. 5 (1919), p. 138; vol. 8 (1922), p. 539; vol. 10 (1924), p. 231; vol. 11 (1925), pp. 515–20, also pp. 525f.; first summary report: Eitingon [1927]); see 251 SF, note 2; in October 1925 Anna was elected secretary of the Training Committee of the Vienna group ⟨*IZ*, vol. 11 (1925), p. 120⟩.
3 So as not to travel too far from Vienna and his jaw surgeon, Pichler, Freud had been spending the summer since 30 June 1925 at Villa Schüler in Semmering ⟨Anna/Lou, letter 240; Freud/Abraham, 1 July 1925; Freud/Eitingon, letter 338⟩. He had already spent some weekends there before and in 1924 stayed there at Easter (14–24 April) and in the summer (8 July–29 September) ⟨Freud/Jones, letters 424–6; Freud/Ferenczi III, 954 F, 967 F, 970 F, 979 F; Freud/Eitingon, 295 F, 306 F; Freud/Abraham, 4 July 1924; Anna/Lou, letters 162, 164, 167⟩. He made several more visits there until 1928; see 244 AF, note 2, 250 SF.

204 SF[1]

anna freud, ritters parkhotel, Bad Homburg v. d. Höhe
semm[e]ring 1 3/9 1925 12.00

everything fine not coming monday to vienna[2] mathilde expected evening weather overcast wolf[3] good sad
[unsigned]

1 Telegram.
2 Freud normally travelled every ten days or so to Prof. Pichler's surgery in Vienna to check the prosthesis ⟨Anna/Lou, letter 242; Jones III, p. 116⟩.
3 Anna's Alsatian dog, which she had owned since 1 June: 'some big news. Papa is giving me a dog before the summer so that I will have some company when walking. . . . In fact I think of my dog in those nice stories [see 101 AF, end of note 1], which can now come true.' Wolf soon became 'a recognized housemate' (see ill. 13) ⟨Anna/Lou, letter 236, p. 449; 220, 3 March 1925, p. 416 (1st quote); 240, 4 July 1925, p. 457 (2nd quote); also 1925 passim⟩. It lived 'over eleven years'; it is thought to have died in 1936 ⟨Freud/Jones, letter 632, p. 739; Molnar [1996], p. 206⟩.

205 SF[1]

anna freud, parkhotel, Bad Homburg v. d. Höhe
semmering 1 4/9 1925 11.10
[taken down 12 noon]

pleased at your news[2] mathilde arrived weather cold overcast rainy even without lectures
[unsigned]

1 Telegram.
2 Missing.

206 SF[1]

Anna Freud, Parkhotel, Bad Homburg v. d. Höhe
Sem[m]ering 1 5/9 1925 15.20
[taken down 16.35]

Everything fine weather brighter all your news welcome[2]
Goodbye[3]
[unsigned]

1 Telegram.
2 Missing.
3 On 6 September Anna and Eitingon travelled back from Frankfurt to Semmering, where the family remained until 29 September. On 1 October Freud started working again in Vienna, with six patients ⟨Anna/Lou, letters 251, 253; Jones III, p. 118⟩.

207 SF[1]

Good
for sitting on
for many hours[2]

3 Dec 1925
[unsigned]

1 Sheet without letterhead, Freud's handwriting; everything written in Latin letters.
2 This time Anna's birthday present was an armchair ⟨Martha Freud to Lucie Freud, 18 December 1925, FM London, Box 27⟩.

1926

208 SF[1]

Frl Anna Freud
c/o Dr Val. Rosenfeld[2]
Vienna XIII
Wattmanngasse [11]

Berlin, 27 December 1926

The strongest impression from Berlin is little Evchen,[3] an exact replica of Heinerle, rectangular face with coal-black eyes, the same temperament, facility of speech, intelligence, fortunately looks stronger, was uncomfortable and not gracious at first. Both houses[4] very pleasant. Spoke only briefly with Eitingon, this afternoon at greater length. Mirra was at the station. Your clothes suit Henny perfectly. Our accommodation magnificent, will incite me to take on new pat[ients]. Am meant to be seeing Einstein,[5] but otherwise hope for a quiet time. Am reserving a sleeping car today for Saturday, 1 January 1927. Sincere greetings to your hen party[6] in Hietzing.[7] Hope that you will get on with Wolf after all.[8] Met by Lux.

Papa

1 Postcard with handwritten sender 'Esplanade', the hotel in Berlin where Freud and Martha were staying (see 211 SF, postscript). They spent the New Year there from 25 December 1926 to 1–2 January 1927: 'On Christmas Day we – wife and I – intend finally to go to Berlin to see the big and the small children. . . . I only know one of my four grandsons, and he was a year old at the time' ⟨Freud/Ferenczi III, 1085 F, 13 December 1926, p. 289; Anna/Lou, letter 287⟩. In addition to the four Berlin grandchildren – Stephan Gabriel (born 21 July 1921), Lucian Michael (born 8 February 1922), Clemens Raphael (born 24 April 1924) and Evchen (see note 3) – 'Ernsti came as the fifth from Hamburg' ⟨Anna/Lou, letter 292, 3 January 1927, p. 536⟩. See 211 SF and note 4. It was Freud's first trip after his major operation. Anna would like to have accompanied him but had an injured toe. At first she complained to her father that he had 'left her in the lurch', but when her parents returned safe and sound 'everything was all right again' ⟨Anna to Eitingon, 21 December 1926, 3 January 1927; Anna/Lou, letters 290–2⟩.

2 Valentin Rosenfeld (1886–1970), doctor of law, lawyer in Vienna, married since 1911 to Eva Rosenfeld (see note 6). He had already attended Freud's lectures in 1906–7 and drawn Eva's attention to him. He consulted Freud before his marriage because Eva was his cousin ⟨Ross, p. 26⟩. 'So that I won't be so alone in Berggasse I'm moving with Wolf to Eva Rosenfeld in Hietzing,' wrote Anna to Lou on 21 December 1926 ⟨Anna/Lou, letter 290, p. 534⟩.

3 Eva Mathilde, the daughter of Henny and Oliver Freud, born 3 September 1924 (see ill. 10) ⟨Stammbaum Lange: Freud Family, 'Genealogical Tree', p. I⟩. Freud was very fond of her. 'Eva to Nice', he noted on the last day of his entries in his diary (Freud 1992*i*, p. 41), when she visited him once more to say farewell in London (24 July–25 August 1939) (see 257 SF, note 14). She died in 1944 while undergoing surgery in Nice, where her parents had put her in the care of friends during their own flight to Spain from occupied France (see 198 SF, note 8) ⟨Molnar [1996], pp. 261, 263; note by Anna about Eva Freud, undated [1944?], in LoC AF, Cont. 158⟩.

4 The families of Ernst and Oliver. See 211 SF and note 7.

5 Albert Einstein (1879–1955) was teaching at the time at the Prussian Academy of Sciences in Berlin and was also director of the Kaiser Wilhelm Institute (see 210 SF).

6 The togetherness of Anna and Eva. ⟨Thanks to the translator, Nick Somers, for pointing out the misreading 'Heuparty' in the original German.⟩ Eva Marie Rosenfeld (1892–1977) looked after foster-children and live-in helps in her house, whom she trained at the same time in domestic work and gardening. 'Eva's model household was remarkable nonetheless for its [. . .] spirit' ⟨Heller, p. 65; details of Eva Rosenfeld in Ross⟩. She met Anna in 1924 ⟨Anna/Lou, letter 202, p. 380⟩. They soon became very close and were joined later by Dorothy Burlingham (see Anna/Lou correspondence; see also 158 AF, end of note 5) ⟨Ross, pp. 25–33; Young-Bruehl, pp. 135–7; Burlingham, M., pp. 128 f.⟩. In 1931 Eva moved to Berlin-Tegel and worked for Ernst Simmel as head housekeeper at his sanatorium ⟨Ross, pp. 38–40⟩. After the sanatorium closed, she continued from Berlin the training in analysis that she had started with Freud in 1929 (see 287 SF and note 17). In 1936 she emigrated to London and worked there as an analyst and member of the British Psychoanalytical Society. The close friendship with the Freud family became more distant – for some time Eva had favoured the theories of Melanie Klein – but was never abandoned ⟨Ross, pp. 33–48⟩.

7 Hietzing, a middle-class suburb of Vienna, was the location of the house and property of the Rosenfelds, who made the site available in 1927 to permit the fulfilment of a joint idea by Dorothy Burlingham, Eva and Anna: the founding of a private school whose progressive curriculum was based on the 'project method' (see 82 AF, note 3). Peter Blos (see 215 SF, note 3) and Erik H. Erikson were the teachers, and August Aichhorn, Siegfried Bernfeld and others also taught there for a time ⟨Erikson, pp. 91–4⟩. Under Eva's supervision, the children formed an 'extended family' with all the adults; '[. . .] Anna Freud was concerned [. . .] with something like a reformed and improved life-style, or rather an "alternative way of life" on the basis of psychoanalysis' ⟨Bittner, p. 14⟩ (see ill. 13). In many respects the school was a 'precursor of future creative cooperation between Anna Freud and Dorothy Burlingham' in England, including the Hampstead Child Therapy Clinic, the psychoanalytical institute now called the Anna Freud Centre ⟨Freud, W. E. [1987], pp. 212f.⟩. The school

was closed in spring 1932 ⟨Bittner, pp. 10f., 12–19; Ross, p. 32; Heller, pp. 67, 78–90; Burlingham, M., pp. 183–9, 230 f., 232f.; see also Young-Bruehl, p. 136; Anna/Lou, letter 305⟩.

8 'I had quiet holidays with Eva and Wolf. She taught me how to cook' ⟨Anna/Lou, letter 292, 3 January 1927, p. 536⟩.

209 SF[1]

Frl Anna Freud
c/o Dr Val. Rosenfeld
Vienna XIII
Wattmanngasse [11]

Berlin, 28 December 1926

My dear Anna,
Very comfortable and will very soon be over. Very bad weather, no activities. Yesterday discussed with Eitingon your trip[2] and the Reich[3] affair. He had expressly forbidden St.[4] from doing what he did.[5] The relationship won't last long. Regarding your trip, he was only amenable to the argument that you should not trouble yourself too much.[6] He has received a long letter from Ferenczi.[7] Aunt Mitzi is just coming.
Affectionately,
Papa

1 Postcard.

2 In November Anna had held a four-part course at the Psychoanalytical Training Institute in Vienna on the technique of child analysis and the difference from adult analysis, and Eitingon had suggested that she give a lecture on it to the Berlin society ⟨Anna/Lou, letter 285, p. 528; also letter 287⟩. But Anna declined because of the impending publication of the series. Her hesitation also had to do with the fact, however, that she did not want to 'tussle' with Melanie Klein, who rejected her ideas and had therefore strongly attacked them (see 216 AF, note 2) ⟨Anna to Eitingon, 7 November, 21 December 1926⟩. After the book (1927*a*) had appeared, Eitingon again urged Anna and she finally agreed to a lecture and discussion evening (19 March; 1927*c*) ⟨Anna to Eitingon, 13 February 1927 – in the original '1926' by mistake; Anna/Lou, letter 297; *IZ*, vol. 13 (1927), p. 367⟩.

3 Wilhelm Reich (1897–1957), doctor of medicine, psychoanalyst, member of the Vienna Psychoanalytic Society while still a student, member of the Training Institute since 1925; assistant in the out-patients' department and deputy head from 1928. In 1922 he inaugurated the Technical Seminar, which he headed from 1924 onwards ⟨Reich [1927*c*], English edition (1973), p. 60, 1927*a*, 1927*b*⟩. He was regarded as an outstandingly gifted theoretician and clinician; 'As a teacher and seminar leader he was the most competent I have ever met' ⟨Raknes, p. 54⟩. As a member of the Communist Party he endeavoured to link social criticism and psychoanalysis, and moved for that reason to Berlin in 1930 but fell out with both institutions, which subsequently ostracized him ⟨Modena, pp. 316f., 327; Boadella, pp. 78–82; Raknes, p. 54; Jones III, p. 204; Briehl, S., p. 435; Fallend [1987], pp. 75–81; see also Fallend [1995], p. 309, and pp. 293,

299–317; Fallend [1998]; Fallend and Nitzschke. See also Freud/Ferenczi III, 1218 Fer–1220 Fer⟩. Reich fled first to Scandinavia in 1933 and then to the USA in 1939. There he continued the biophysical experiments on vital energy ('orgone'), which he had commenced in Europe, but came into conflict with American justice and was put into prison, where he died in 1957 ⟨Mühlleitner, pp. 257–9; Boadella; Raknes; Briehl⟩.

4 Probably Storfer, managing director of the *Verlag* at the time.

5 Storfer had accepted money from Reich ⟨Freud/Eitingon, PS to 416 F⟩, possibly to cover the costs of the printing of Reich's manuscript of *The Function of the Orgasm* (1927*c*), whose publication by the *Verlag* was a subject of controversial discussion ⟨Freud/Eitingon, 391 F, 392 E, 394 E, 414 F–417 E⟩.

6 'Anna was in Berlin for two days to give a lecture. She is working really well, but fanatical like all women, and she makes herself much too tired' ⟨Freud/Ferenczi III, 1092 F, 25 March 1927, p. 304⟩. See also 212 SF, note 2.

7 Ferenczi was on a lecturing and teaching visit of several months to the USA ⟨Freud/Ferenczi III, 1081 Fer–1095 Fer; *IZ*, vol. 13 (1927), p. 335⟩.

210 SF[1]

Frl Anna Freud
c/o Dr Valent. Rosenfeld
Vienna XIII
Wattman[n]gasse [11]

[Berlin,] 29 December 1926

M D[2] Anna,
Einstein was very interesting, cheerful, happy; we talked for two hours, more about analysis than relativ[ity theory].[3] He is reading at present, and naturally[4] is not convinced.[5] He looks older than I expected – 48 years![6]

Weather bad, we walk the same two streets all the time.

Affectionately,
Papa

1 Picture postcard with pre-printed sender 'Hotel Esplanade, Berlin' and a picture of the hotel's interior garden.

2 Capital letters in the original. It looks from the card as if Freud wrote originally 'L Anna' [Liebe Anna] and added the M in front afterwards.

3 'He came to Ernst's with his wife in order to see me . . . understands as much about psychology as I do about physics, and so we had a very good conversation' ⟨Freud/Ferenczi III, 1087 F, 2 January 1927, p. 292⟩.

4 Spelling mistake (no umlaut) in the original.

5 See Einstein's letter to Freud on his eightieth birthday: 'Until a short time ago I was only aware of the speculative force of your thought and of its powerful influence on our contemporary view of the world, and was unable to make up my mind about the intrinsic truth of your theories. However, I recently happened to hear about [. . .] cases which convinced me that any differing explanation [. . .] was excluded. This gave me pleasure' ⟨full facsimile in Molnar [1996], p. 200f.⟩. Freud replied: 'I really must tell you how delighted I am to learn of the change in your judgement, or at least a move in that direction' ⟨Freud 1960*a*,

3 May 1936, p. 424; also in Jones III, p. 217⟩. The *first* surviving exchange between them dates from 1929 ⟨Grubrich-Simitis [1994]; see Freud/Eitingon, letters 622 E and 623 F⟩.
6 Einstein turned forty-eight on 14 March 1927.

211 SF[1]

Frl Anna Freud
c/o Dr Val. Rosenfeld
Vienna XIII
Wattmanngasse [11]

HOTEL ESPLANADE BERLIN W. 30 December 1926
BELLEVUESTRASSE[2]

My dear Anna,
One can already see the journey.[3] Still all kinds of things to do. Max and Ernst[4] are coming at lunchtime. The Lampl[s][5] are already back. Probably going to Fuchs[6] tomorrow. This evening a mass visit to the Russian Fledermaus with Eit[ingon] is planned. Yesterday we inaugurated the hospitality in Oli's new apartment.[7] Evchen was very affectionate. Weather gruesome. Lots of talk about influenza. Ernst wants to go this afternoon to a private collection of old gold jewellery, but there is nothing to buy there.

Affectionate greetings,
Papa

[In Martha's handwriting]

Thousand greetings and thanks for your card;[8] except for the weather everything delightful.
Mama

1 Postcard.
2 Pre-printed card head with vignette ('E') over the hotel name. The date is added by hand.
3 According to Ernst Freud, a phrase of little Sophie's, frequently quoted in the family ⟨Freud 1960*a*, p. 438, note 1⟩. See also 219 SF.
4 Ernstl, who after his father's remarriage (see 162 AF, note 7), felt 'very left out' 'was a lonely little boy and suffered a lot', until he was allowed to move to Vienna in 1928 (see 146 SF and note 4) ⟨Freud, W. E. [1987], pp. 200f.⟩. Freud took every opportunity to see him.
5 Hans Lampl and Jeanne de Groot had now married; see 163 SF, note 4.
6 Oliver's parents-in-law (see 192 SF, note 8): Gertrud Fuchs, née Boas (1867–March 1944) and Paul Fuchs (1861–1942), doctor of medicine, health officer in Berlin. Both were killed in Theresienstadt. The address at the time of the transport on 14 July 1942, given in *Gedenkbuch Berlins*, is Berlin-Wilmersdorf, Lietzenburger Str. 41–42. ⟨I thank Almuth Kliesch, librarian at the Institute

of the History of Medicine, Berlin, for her extensive research.⟩ Freud gave the address in 1924 as Lützowstr. 95 ⟨Freud/Ferenczi III, 979 F, 13 September 1924, p. 179⟩.

7 'Oli finally has his own place to live' ⟨Freud/Ferenczi III, 1085 F, p. 289; see 192 SF and note 8⟩. The apartment was in Berlin-Tempelhof, 'Theodor-Fran[c]ke-Str. 6, I[st floor], T[elephone] Südr. 4447' ⟨Berlin Address Books 1928–33 (no entry from 1934); I thank Veronika Liebau, Archive for the History of Tempelhof and Schöneberg, 19 August 2003, and Regine Lockot, Berlin, for kind assistance.⟩

8 Missing.

1927

212 SF[1]

VIENNE, 8 April 1927
[Receipt stamp: Milano[2] Centro 8.4.27 10[H]30)

ALL WELL[3] AGAIN EXPECT FINE REPORTS GREETINGS TO THE TRAVELLERS[4]
[unsigned]

1 Telegram without address.
2 Anna was away for a longer period for the first time since Freud's mouth operation (see 202 SF, note 3) and was taking an Easter holiday in northern Italy with Dorothy Burlingham (see note 4). She was in urgent need of relaxation; in 1925 she had already confided to Lou that she was 'stressed and tired from thousands of things behind and ahead' of her, and her own practice and commitments had grown quickly and took up more and more of her energies ⟨Anna/Lou, letter 255, 6 October 1925, p. 476 and elsewhere⟩. Now Freud himself had insisted that she take a break (see 235 AF): 'Our next task is to persuade her that she should allow herself plenty of time for rest and relaxation this year' ⟨Freud/Eitingon, 423 F, 22 March 1927, p. 506⟩. See also 209 SF and notes 2 and 6.
3 In spring 1926 Freud had already spent some time in the Cottage-Sanatorium for a heart complaint (see 223 AF and note 2, 228 SF, 238 SF, note 7). Now Freud's health was 'if anything worse this year than in the last' and he was admitted again on 14 April, this time with Martha and Minna; they remained until 28 April (see 219 SF–249 AF) ⟨Jones III, p. 144; Freud/Eitingon, 423 F–426 F⟩. For Freud's heart condition in earlier years, see Schur, ch. 2.
4 Anna and her travelling partner: Dorothy Burlingham (1891–1979), daughter of the wealthy American glass artist Louis C. Tiffany. She had separated from her husband, Dr Robert Burlingham, who suffered from a manic-depressive syndrome with psychotic episodes requiring multiple hospitalization ⟨Heller, p. 76f.; Ross, p. 29⟩. In 1925 she came to Vienna from New York to have her ten-year-old son, Bob, treated by Anna Freud for asthma and related symptoms ⟨Anna/Lou, letter 257, p. 479⟩. She settled permanently in Vienna with her four children and soon began analytic treatment and training herself, initially with Reik and from 1928 with Freud (not 1927 as frequently cited) ⟨Freud/Ferenczi III, 1128 F, 11 July 1928, p. 342⟩. A very close friendship developed between the

two families. Freud later described her as 'our symbiosis' ⟨Freud/Binswanger, 167 F, 11 January 1929, p. 195; Freud to Ruth, 16 September 1929⟩ (see ill. 14). Anna and Dorothy remained lifelong professional and personal companions. They worked together on child psychology research, founded the private school in Hietzing with Eva Rosenfeld (see 208 SF, note 7), and lived together even after the emigration of the Freud family to London, where they – alongside many other psychoanalytical activities – founded the Hampstead Nurseries war children's home (with courses for childcare assistants and educators) in 1940 and the Hampstead Child Therapy Course and Clinic (training programme and children's clinic) in 1947 ⟨Burlingham, D., particularly chs 7–9, pp. 220–3, 228f., 233; Bittner, pp. 11, 13f.; Ross, pp. 29f.; Heller, pp. 74–8; Anna/Lou, *passim*; Anna Freud [1971]; see also Young-Bruehl, pp. 132f., 134–9; Freud, W. E. [1987]; Mühlleitner, pp. 55f.⟩.

213 AF

ANNA FREUD [8 April 1927][1]

Milan, 9 p.m. in bed

Vienna IX, Berggasse 19 [2]

Dear Papa,

Instead of the Scala, we are already in bed because the first day was as full as a whole holiday. Journey excellent on the lines of 'you can travel much cheaper but . . .'. Fattening diet in the dining car, very punctual arrival, no different from Vienna–Berlin. Hotel de la Ville very friendly, nice room over hellish din, bathroom well worn. Cathedral in the morning; roof, tower quite dizzying, everything like Aunt's lace, unfortunately too well anchored to bring back, really beautiful. Weather like in Dianabad,[3] have bought galoshes. Lunch in the hotel, rest. Then Maria delle Grazie, *Last Supper*,[4] thought a lot about Mereschkowski.[5] Afterwards gardens, magnolias, Corso, dinner, bed. Communication unarticulated sounds, issued by us with less intelligence than they are understood by the Italians. Thought a lot about Rome.[6]

Tomorrow probably Como, will wire on arrival. Very pleased to receive your telegram, wish you were here.

More tomorrow, all the best to everyone. Mama's and Aunt's flowers travelled well, enjoyed the farewell at the station very much.

Your Anna

[In Dorothy's handwriting in English]

Dear Professor Freud,

This first day has been a lovely one. I have a fondness for Milan already and many pictures in my mind that I won't lose. We were so glad to hear that you were feeling better. Even here I miss our Ford trips.[7] With love to you all.

Dorothy Burlingham

1 See 223 AF: 'Today a week since we left Vienna.' The correspondence from this trip was not arranged chronologically in the transcription bundle.
2 Printed letterhead; city and street crossed out. The letter and Dorothy's postscript are written in pencil.
3 The Dianabad swimming baths in Vienna, built 1841–3, had a special method of water supply: 'The brackets holding the cast iron girders for the gallery ended in lions' heads from which water flowed into the baths' ⟨Kräftner, p. 113⟩. The streams of water can be clearly seen in a steel engraving from 1841 ⟨ill. 249 in Czeike [1984], p. 136⟩. Although this construction was lost during the remodelling in 1913–17, Anna must have seen it when she went swimming. ⟨I thank Susanne Winkler, Wien Museum; Ferdinand Opll, director of Municipal Department 8, City Archives; and particularly Felix Czeike, Vienna, for assistance, information and material.⟩
4 In the refectory of the monastery of Santa Maria delle Grazie is Leonardo da Vinci's mural *The Last Supper* (1495–7).
5 The German translation of his book (1902–3) was one of Freud's main sources for his study of Leonardo (1910*c*).
6 See 201 SF/AF and Appendixes 1 and 2.
7 Dorothy Burlingham had acquired the habit of taking Freud for a drive in the morning before work in her Model T Ford ⟨Freud/Ferenczi III, 1085 F; Jones III, p. 129; Anna/Lou, letter 275; Burlingham, M., p. 192; Schur, p. 391⟩. Anna herself did not learn to drive until 1932 from Dorothy's chauffeur, Herr Wimmer ⟨Burlingham, M., p. 237⟩.

214 SF[1]

Vienna, 9/4 21.55
[Receipt stamp:] Cernobbio,[2] Gr. Hotel Villa d'Este
10.4.27 8.55

Very pleased telegram[3] all well mathilde princess[4] uncle[5] departed won new vase[6]
[unsigned]

1 Telegram.
2 Locality on the west bank of the southern tip of the western arm of Lake Como.
3 Missing.
4 Marie Bonaparte (1882–1962), Princess George of Greece and Denmark – 'great-granddaughter of Napoleon's brother Lucien, a really bright, mature woman with a good critical sense, who, partly out of interest in the cause, partly because of her own neurotic remnants, has found her way here by way of Laforgue' – had been in analysis with Freud since 1925. 'She is not an aristocrat at all, but a real person, and the work with her is going excellently' ⟨Freud/Ferenczi III, 1031 F, 18 October 1925, p. 232⟩. 'The analysis is the most "gripping" thing I have ever done. *Ich bin*, as they say in German, *gepackt! aber vollständig*,' she wrote to Laforgue on 10 October 1925 ⟨Bertin, p. 157⟩. She did indeed become a loyal and energetic supporter and friend of Freud and his whole family (see ill. 16). Soon she was practising analysis herself and published numerous psychoanalytical works, translated several of Freud's works

into French and promoted the spread of psychoanalysis in France. She was a member of the International Psychoanalytical Association and co-founder of the Société psychoanalytique de Paris (1926). In 1938 she organized and financed the emigration of Freud and his relatives from Austria to London (see text after 295 SF and ill. 18). Even after Freud's death she remained in constant contact with Anna until her own death ⟨Bertin, *passim*; Loewenstein⟩. Freud's comment in the telegram refers to Marie Bonaparte's departure for Pallanza on Lago Maggiore, cf. 229 AF–231 AF.

5 Alexander Freud.

6 Written 'gewommen' instead of 'gewonnen' in handwritten transcription of the telegram.

215 SF[1]

Wien 11 14
[Receipt stamp:] Cernobbio, Gr. Hotel Villa d'Este 11.4.27
17

Both letters[2] read with pleasure daily telephone to siebergasse[3] winterstein[4] neue presse discussed your book[5] pichler[6] braun[7] cook departed[8]
[unsigned]

1 Telegram.

2 Only Anna's (213 AF) appears to have been preserved.

3 Should be Silbergasse. Dorothy, who had originally rented a villa with extensive grounds in autumn 1925 in Braungasse in the suburb of Dornbach, had moved in late September 1926 to Silbergasse 55 near Hohe Warte in Unterdöbling, another spacious villa, the Silber-Schlössl, with extended grounds. An American couple, Ruth and Arthur Sweetser (see 259 AF and note 2), lived for a year with their four children together with her in the house, and looked after the family and the entire property when Dorothy was away (see postscript to 216 AF) ⟨see Freud/Ferenczi III, 1081 Fer and note 9⟩. For the children they had hired a joint educator and home tutor, Peter Blos (who was shortly to become director of the Hietzing school, see 208 SF, note 7); until then a Swiss chalet on the property, which they called 'the farm', served as a school ⟨Burlingham, M., pp. 152, 154–6, 164f., 181, 189⟩.

4 Alfred Freiherr von Winterstein (1885–1958), D.Phil., had initially studied law, then philosophy and the history of art. He had been a member of the Vienna Psychoanalytic Society since 1910, published works on the application of psychoanalysis to problems of philosophy, literature, humour, etc., practised as an analyst and also wrote literature. After the Second World War he was active in the revival of the Vienna Psychoanalytic Society and was its president from 1949 to 1957 ⟨*Protokolle III*, pp. XVIf.; Mühlleitner, pp. 366–8⟩.

5 Anna Freud (1927*a*); see 216 AF and note 2.

6 Johannes (also Hans) Pichler (1877–1949), doctor of medicine, 1919 professor of dentistry, one of the founders of jaw surgery, since 1914 head of the oral surgery ward in the 1st Surgical University Clinic in Vienna ⟨Engelhardt [2002]⟩. See text 'Autumn 1923' after 201 SF/AF.

7 Ludwig Braun (1867–1936), doctor of medicine, professor of cardiology in

Vienna ⟨Engelhardt [2002]⟩. He was, as Freud wrote (1936*d*), one of his 'closest and warmest friends' and occasionally a medical consultant. He gave the oration to celebrate Freud's seventieth birthday in the B'nai B'rith lodge ⟨Freud 1926*j*⟩.

8 Written 'abgekeist' instead of 'abgereist'.

216 AF

ANNA FREUD VIENNA IX, BERGGASSE 19[1]

Cernobbio, Villa d'Este

Monday evening [11 April 1927]

Dear Papa,

Very pleased to receive your telegrams, post here very good. Curious about Winterstein's article,[2] unfortunately no newspapers here. I hope that you don't miss Pichler too much; you are probably feeling the effects of the radiation by now. The absence of Braun and cook is probably not so bad.

Today was a special day; we found a second place where you could stay without difficulty (first: Villa d'Este, second: Villa Serbelloni in Bellagio).[3]

Slept long because raining outside. Then suddenly brighter, took motorboat under the bluest of skies, waves, sailed along the lake, an hour to Bellagio, past all villages, waterfalls, parks, villas. Cold, mountains snow-white, some snow down to the lake. Bellagio delightful, climbed right up to Villa Serbelloni, ate outside up there, first hot sun, view of both arms of the lake at once. Walked in the park, southern plants, palms, camellias, rambling roses, cacti. Asked about rooms but too attached to Villa d'Este. Down to the village, lots of shops, bought things for the children,[4] hard to resist. Returned quite tired and excited, dinner, bed. Found telegrams.

Could not be nicer anywhere. Leaving further plans to time and weather.

All the best for the move.[5] I wish at least that you had the view from our window. Greetings to Mama and Aunt.

Your Anna

[In Dorothy's handwriting in English]

Dear Professor Freud,

We are indeed having a lovely time. It's[6] been so beautiful today on our way to + from Bellagio, besides Bellagio itself. It is lovely that you call up the children each day + I do appreciate it. The children have written dear letters, and I have also received telegrams so I feel very happy about them. With greetings to Mrs Freud + Tante Mina[7] – affectionately

Dorothy Burlingham

1 Printed letterhead; place and street crossed out.

2 As part of a longer report about new publications, Winterstein wrote (1927): 'Anna Freud [. . .] makes a valuable contribution [. . .] in a specialist area, the

application of analysis to teaching.' In the 'passionate discussion' [with Melanie Klein, see 209 SF, note 2] on the analysis of children, he continues, can be heard Anna Freud's 'calm voice', which speaks from practical experience, and he concludes: 'Anna Freud shows us how she thinks and feels amongst other things in the careful formulation that takes account of the real situation.' See also Introduction, p. 122, and note 11. In some parts of her book (1927*a*) Anna does in fact discuss theoretical and technical differences ⟨*Writings I*, pp. 6f., 36–40, 45⟩; see also Anna's lecture in Innsbruck (1927*b*; see 252 SF and note 4) and her correspondence with Lou Andreas-Salomé about the book ⟨Anna/Lou, letters 296, 297, 301, 302, 303; also Freud/Eitingon, 422 E and notes 1 and 2; Freud/Jones, letters 502, 503⟩. For detailed discussion of these debates, see, e.g., Peters, pp. 79–100.

3 Locality in the centre of Lake Como at the point of separation of the western and eastern arms (Lago di Lecco).

4 Probably for the Sweetsers' children and for Dorothy's four: Robert (Bob; 1915–70), Mary (Mabbie; 1917–74), Katrina Ely (Tinkey; 1919–98, see ill. 13) and Michael (Mikey; 1921–2003) ⟨Burlingham, M. pp. 136, 144, 147, 309, 310 (with thanks for oral addition of data for Tinkey and Mikey, 18 June 2004)⟩.

5 To Cottage-Sanatorium; see 212 SF, note 3.

6 Like this in the original.

7 Minna Bernays. Muriel Gardiner recalled that 'Mina' was the name of one of Dorothy's former housekeepers and cooks ⟨Burlingham, M., p. 207⟩.

217 SF[1]

Wien 12/4 14.40
[Receipt stamp:] Cernobbio, Gr. Hotel Villa d'Este 12.4.27
16.45

Fond greetings from wolf[2] and family
[unsigned]

1 Telegram.
2 Anna's dog.

218 AF

ANNA FREUD VIENNA IX, BERGGASSE 19[1]
Cernobbio, Villa d'Este
Tuesday evening [12 April 1927]

Dear Papa,
Almost went to Lugano but discovered at the last moment that my passport has only a single-entry visa for Italy. Concierge reckoned that I could have had difficulties coming back. Could not risk being cut off from Villa d'Este – change of plan.

Finally fabulous weather. In the morning balcony door and windows opened in various directions, wind and sun like on a ship's deck. Difficult to get up.

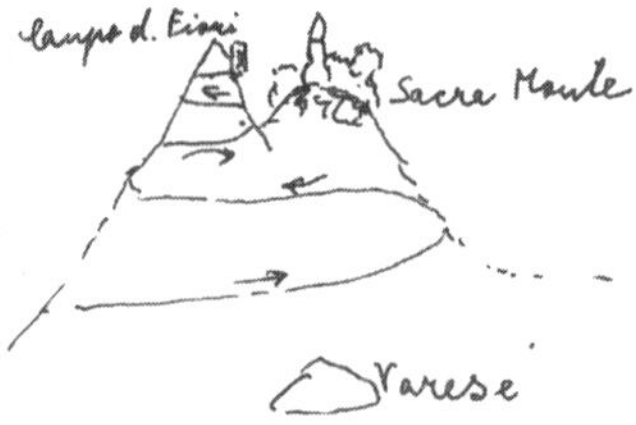

VI Drawing in Anna's letter of 12 April 1927

By car via Varese to Campo dei Fiori, one and a half hours from here, steep hill, 1,200 m high.[2] Lunch in Sacra[3] Monte halfway up, large pilgrimage site with twelve chapels,[4] each with a different view. Small old town on top of the hill like near Rome.[5]

Seen: Lago di Lugano, Lago Maggiore, Lago di Varese, three small shallow lakes. Drove past beautiful[6] parks.

Long walk at the top, primroses, liverwort, like in the Vienna Woods. Returned completely windblown and burnt, found telegrams,[7] *very* pleased, especially with Wolf's, very intelligent dog,[8] always knew. Would have enough water here,[9] but would be the only one.

Enclosed card[10] shows our house and garden. X our room.

Rest day tomorrow.

All the best to all.

Your Anna

(Bad handwriting because already in bed)

1 Printed letterhead; place and street crossed out.
2 Famous viewpoint approx. 15 km north-west of Varese; today a mountain railway goes up to Monte Campo de Fiori (1,226 m).
3 Written like this in the original.
4 Santa Maria del Monte.
5 For example, in Etruria; see middle of second paragraph of Anna's 'Jottings', Appendix 2.
6 Spelling mistake in original.
7 Only one contained here (217 SF); the other is probably for Dorothy.
8 'Anna's Alsatian . . . was used to travelling with us in open taxis in the Prater, and when we lost it once there it simply jumped into one of these taxis, had the driver read its address from its collar and was promptly dropped off at Berggasse' ⟨Freud, W. E. [1987], p. 206⟩.
9 'Wolf takes me every morning – between eight and ten – down to the Danube Canal . . . but unfortunately he often goes into the water and brings all kinds of odours back home' ⟨Anna/Lou, letter 255, 6 October 1925, p. 476⟩.
10 Missing.

219 SF[1]

Wien 13/4 16.10
[Receipt stamp:] Cernobbio, Gr. Hotel Villa d'Este 13.4.27
17.58

Can already see[2] great easter journey tomorrow Cottage sanatorium[3]
[unsigned]

1 Telegram.
2 See 211 SF and note 3.
3 See 212 SF, note 3. The Cottage-Sanatorium, founded in 1908 by Rudolf von Urbantschitsch, was 'one of the most well-known deluxe establishments in Europe; its facilities and social environment had to comply with the most demanding standards. For the Vienna school of medicine, which attracted patients from all over the world, the Sanatorium was a place where all prominent Viennese doctors could treat their rich clientele' ⟨Mühlleitner, p. 348⟩. See 76 SF and note 11. Freud also occasionally had other members of the family admitted there as patients ⟨e.g., Freud/Ferenczi III, 699 F; Anna/Lou, letter 93⟩.

220 AF[1]

professor freud
berggasse 19
wien

cernobbio, hotel villa d este 13 21/30
[Receipt stamp Vienna:] 13 APR 27 24

rest day sun rowed many hours in cause[2]
fair in como greetings
[unsigned]

1 Telegram.
2 Probably misread for 'canoe' (see 221 AF).

221 AF

ANNA FREUD

Wednesday evening Berggasse 19[1]
Cernobbio, Villa d'Este
[13 April 1927] Vienna IX,

Dear Papa,
Today sent the last telegram to Berggasse, hope to hear tomorrow that the move went well. Nothing in the Cottage-Sanatorium that you would not find nicer here: balcony, sun, rest, the view as an extra.

Most beautiful, peaceful day. Slept long, morning overcast, plans made for trip to Lago Maggiore. Took canoe[2], rowed to Como in three-quarters of an hour. Large fair. Main articles: bath dolls with coloured wool fringes.

Bought three, very cheap. Ate minestra and risotto in Italian restaurant. Sun came out, most beautiful clear weather. Back to canoe and pushed off with great assistance from the locals. Rowed along the shore for three hours in the sun, admiring all the private villas with incredible gardens from the water. 'Want one too . . .!'[3] Home at sunset, stiff from rowing. Had a large snack on the lakeside terrace instead of dinner, bought paste[4] in village, all fringed dolls hung up in the room. Effect: very homely.

Departure plans postponed again, too nice here. Very happy, getting on best.

Delighted to hear telegram news. A lift boy always en route between the main building and us.

Bought beach magazines. Not interested in other literature. Holidays a good invention. It's easy to get used to them.[5]

Greetings and plenty of kisses for you.

Your Anna

1 Printed letterhead; place and street crossed out.
2 English: paddleboat but probably a rowing boat.
3 See Introduction, p. 4 and note 25, p. 15; 7 AF and note 3.
4 Fine thick paste with fish, poultry, meat or vegetarian; usually conserved (e.g., anchovy paste). Could also be sweet baked confectioneries – paste dolci. See 235 AF.
5 See 56 AF, note 1.

222 AF[1]

prof. freub
cottagesanatorium
sternvvarstrasse[2] Vienna

cernobbio hotel villa d este 14 21/55
[Receipt stamp Vienna:] 14.4.27 23[57]

rowed all day sunburnt rowing blisters hope you accommodated satisfactorily
[unsigned]

1 Telegram.
2 Sternwartestrasse.

223 AF

ANNA FREUD

Thursday evening [14 April 1927]
Cernobbio, Villa d'Este
Vienna IX, Berggasse 19[1]

Dear Papa,
No telegram yet today, probably delayed because of the move. Hope you are well settled and happy. Weather reports from Vienna bad, hopefully the balcony is not as unusable as it was last year.[2]

Today six hours canoeing on the lake, up the left-hand shore to Brienno. Bought bread, cheese, oranges on the way, ate on the water. Result: totally burnt, totally stiff, very hungry. Ate dinner in the room, very sleepy.

Departure plans increasingly serious, but difficult to leave. Today a week since we left Vienna.

All the best for the Sanatorium, lots of greetings to Mama and Aunt.
Your Anna

[Picture postcard: 'Lago di Como – 7 – Primo e Secondo Bacino', presumably enclosed with the letter][3]

Today's boat trip!

1 Printed letterhead; place and street crossed out.
2 In February 1926, Freud had suffered a dangerous heart condition and after long hesitation had himself admitted to the Cottage-Sanatorium for treatment on 5 March, accompanied by Anna; she alternated with Martha in caring for him and slept in a neighbouring room ⟨Freud/Eitingon 372 F–376 E; Jones III, pp. 126–9; Schur, pp. 390–2 and notes 3 and 5; Freud/Ferenczi III, 1051 F–1057 Fer; Anna/Lou, letters 273, 275; Freud/Jones, letters 478, 482 (in this letter of 6 April, Freud states 'day before yesterday', i.e., 4 April, as return date in contrast to Freud/Eitingon, 377 F, Jones III, p. 127, and Tögel and Pouh, p. 145, which say 'Good Friday', i.e., 2 April)⟩. See 212 SF and note 3, 228 SF, 238 SF, note 7.
3 The card (undated) was at the end of the transcription bundle; it could also belong to 221 AF.

224 SF[1]

Vienna [Cottage-Sanatorium] 14/4 18.00
[Receipt stamp:] Cernobbio, Gr. Hotel Villa d'Este 14.4.27
20

Transfer old room like berlin esplanade[2] you appear to have forgotten Lago Maggiore[3]
[unsigned]

1 Telegram.
2 See 208 SF, note 1.
3 See 226 AF, 228 SF.

225 AF[1]

prof. frend
lottagesanatorium
sternwartestrasze wien

stresa 15 [1927] 17./30
[Receipt stamp Vienna:] 15 APR 21^{50}

folgsat [indecipherable] set off without delay have become island dwellers telegrams verbano baveno letter to verbano isola superiore[2] enthusiastic remaining here for now = warning
[unsigned]

1 Telegram.
2 One of the Borromean Islands (Isola Bella, Isola Madre, Isola dei Pescatori) in the bay between Stresa and Baveno in the middle section of Lago Maggiore (Lago Verbano), opposite Pallanza.

226 AF

ANNA FREUD

Friday evening [15 April 1927][1]
Pension Verbeno[2]
Isola Superiore (Pescatori)
Lago Maggiore
Vienna IX, Berggasse 19[3]

Dear Papa,
Your telegram worked wonders. Received it in the morning in bed,[4] jumped out of bed, packed, left. Travelled to Stresa, took a rowing boat there, first to Isola Madre then here. Found the right place here, a former private house, guesthouse for the last three years, managed by two ladies, everything white, clean, stone floor, light furnishing, running water, even bathroom. We have a room on the second floor with balcony and bathroom, full board, incredibly cheap. View of Pallanza in the distance with lots of lights, full moon over the water in our honour, the noise of incoming waves under us.[5] Much warmer than in Como, also the trees somewhat more advanced, in the gardens of Stresa incredible r[h]ododendrons in bloom as big as chestnut trees at home. Telegrams come from Baveno, post via Isola Madre. Everything unpacked and put away, vases set up. Bath dolls hung up. Will not leave without urgent need. Still some snow on the hills, views in all directions indescribably beautiful.

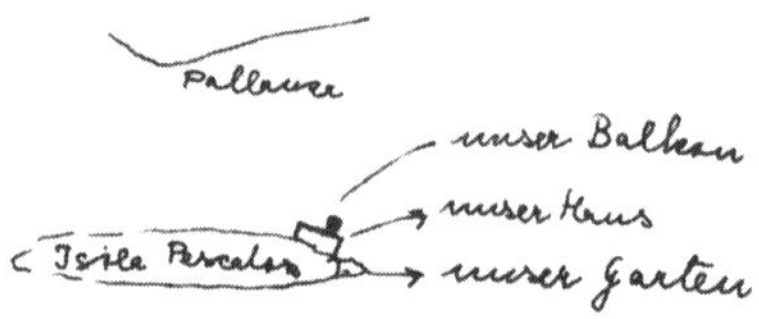

VII Drawing in Anna's letter of 15 April 1927

Big plans for tomorrow, want to take a boat trip, hesitating between other islands, Baveno, Stresa, Pallanza, Intra.

Didn't think that it would all be so beautiful.[6]

Greetings and kisses to you all.

Your Anna

1 The context puts this letter here in the chronology.
2 Should be Verbano; the name of the hotel can be seen on the picture postcard, 220 AF.
3 Printed letterhead; place and street crossed out.
4 According to the receipt stamp, the telegram (224 SF) had already arrived in Cernobbio at around 8 o'clock the previous evening.
5 See drawing: Pallanza – under balcony – our house – Isola Pescator[i] – our garden.
6 Freud and Aunt Minna had visited this region in autumn 1905 and reported to the family from there ⟨2002*b*, pp. 200–3, 206⟩. See 2 SF and note 4; 235 AF and note 6.

227 SF[1]

Vienna [Cottage-Sanatorium] 16 13.50
[Receipt stamp:] BAVENO 16.4.1927 18.50

Surprised[2] waiting to hear purchase of island letter underway pranzessig [princess] leaves monday[3]

1 Telegram.
2 Misspelt in telegram.
3 Marie Bonaparte, who was staying in Pallanza, actually left on Saturday (16 April); see 229 AF–231 AF.

228 SF

PROF. DR. FREUD [Cottage-Sanatorium] 16 April 1927
Vienna IX, Berggasse 19

My dear Anna,
Am taking the rare opportunity offered by your telegram today of writing you a letter. Very pleased to hear how your trip is going;[1] you both appear to be quite happy. Apparently not the most conventional visit, but a selection according to individual taste, no stress, but leisurely enjoyment. Would not have bothered you,[2] but it would just have been a pity about Isola madre and Isola bella.[3]

The weather where you are appears more merciful than elsewhere; Math is also complaining about the cold in Florence. The dear letters from Mrs B[urlingham] have removed any remaining concern that you are not the right travelling companions.

Nothing much of interest to report from here. We are living in a princely apartment: apart from the two rooms you know about,[4] the Baroque bedroom opposite and a dining room next door, bathroom, etc., of course.

The cures are boring[5] and tiring on account of their frequency; you need to be very healthy to put up with it all. Today is just the start of the third day, but it feels like a small eternity. The prosthesis is so-so; one can laugh, but it's not always a laughing matter. Ruth was here yesterday and brought a new coffee machine; I believe she intends to go next week to Berlin with Mark.[6] I sent you a telegram today about the princess.

The relocated tarock game is taking place here this afternoon. A book by Wittels,[7] *Die Befreiung des Kindes* [*Set the Children Free!*], has been published by Hippoktrates-Verlag in which I think you are not yet quoted.[8] By contrast, the report by Winterstein is very flattering.[9]

Martin has just called, back from the Rax.[10] I will therefore close this letter, which will get to you God knows when.

Enjoy what you can at your leisure and affectionate greetings to both of you.

Papa

PS Wire money transfer ready any time.

1 Spelling mistake (no umlaut) in the original.
2 See 224 SF.
3 See 235 AF, 241 AF. Freud cites Isola Bella in his discussion of cultural sites and the demands of beauty, cleanliness and order in 'Civilization and Its Discontent' ⟨1930*a*, p. 93⟩.
4 See 223 AF, note 2.
5 Freud had already complained earlier of this ⟨Freud/Ferenczi III, 1052 F, 1054 F; Freud/Eitingon 426 F⟩. See also 235 AF and note 2, 238 SF and note 11, 250 SF.
6 Mark Brunswick (1902–71), American composer, in Europe from 1925 to 1938 to further his musical education. He married Ruth (née Mack, divorced Blumgart) in 1928. He returned to the USA in 1938 and worked as a renowned and committed teacher at Black Mountain, Kenyon and Brooklyn College. From 1938 to 1945 he headed the Department of Musical Theory and Composition at Greenwich House Music School Settlement, and was professor of music from 1946 to 1965 in the Music Department of City College, New York, where he was an advocate, in particular, of contemporary music. He later had several positions in music companies; from 1937 to 1941, as chairman of the National Committee for Refugee Musicians, he helped with the integration of European colleagues arriving in the USA ⟨Brunswick [1971], [2002]; see also Roazen [1976], p. 424, also [1993], [1999]⟩.
7 Fritz Wittels (1880–1950), doctor of medicine, neurologist and psychiatrist, joined the Vienna Wednesday Society in 1907, but resigned in 1910 ⟨*Minutes I*, pp. 146, 153, in disagreement with Mühlleitner, p. 269; *Minutes III*, p. 2 and note 1⟩. In spite of differences of opinion, Freud appreciated his talents and wealth of ideas and therefore supported his return in 1927 to the Society,

where Wittels remained until 1936 ⟨*IZ*, vol. 13 (1927), pp. 371f.⟩. In 1924 he published a biography of Freud, which the latter reviewed critically in a letter with accompanying corrections ⟨Freud, 1924*g*, 1987*a*⟩. For later revisions to this book, see Molnar [1996], pp. 153f. Wittels emigrated to New York in 1932, where he continued to work ⟨*Minutes I–IV*, *passim*; Mühlleitner, pp. 369–72; Freud/Ferenczi III, 1054 F; editorial note to Freud, 1924*g*, p. 286⟩.

8 This is true: Anna is not mentioned in Wittels' book.

9 See 216 AF and note 2.

10 A mountain range in the Limestone Alps at the border of Lower Austria and Styria, north-west of Semmering with the Heukuppe, 2,007 m; popular excursion and winter sports region. The centre is the spa town of Reichenau an der Rax; a cable railway runs from Hirschwang to the Rax plateau (1,545 m).

229 AF

ANNA FREUD

Easter Sunday, early [17 April 1927]
Isola Superiore
Vienna IX, Berggasse 19

Dear Papa,
First telegrams arrived yesterday evening; the postal service working again. At Villa d'Este they promised to forward everything that arrived there. We are travelling over to Pallanza this afternoon to visit the princess.[2] It is not possible to inquire in advance because the island unfortunately has no telephone. Something strange happened yesterday evening. We slipped into bed for a moment right after dinner to warm ourselves up before letter-writing, because we were cold from the steamer, and both fell asleep with all the lights on. I hope I don't keep up this sleeping and eating rhythm in Vienna, otherwise I will have to severely limit all other activities. It is so beautiful here that one can't do anything else other than to look. We are living as if we were on a large boat on the ocean. Even when the weather is at its finest the water is so agitated that we can hear the waves crashing all night; they have white crests and the boats toss around so much that two old rowers like us have to rent an even older one for rowing. This is apparently very rare here and is very impressive. The house[3] has all comforts, even running hot water, and is very friendly. We went to Baveno yesterday morning to have our hair washed, in the afternoon in Stresa, a few hours just on the rocks at our beach.

I think the island is too expensive for us. But if you promise to come, perhaps we can buy it after all. There is a summer apartment here to rent. I would never need to go anywhere else if you were also here.

Greetings and kisses to you, Mama and Aunt.
Your Anna

[Picture postcard;[4] 'Lago Maggiore – Isola Pescatori'; handwritten arrow pointing to the window and garden terrace:]

Our balcony – current writing place[5]

1 Printed letterhead; place and street crossed out.
2 On 27 April 1927, Marie Bonaparte had brought her two children Pierre and Eugénie for a cure in Pallanza, under the care of their governess, and had travelled from there to Freud in Vienna to continue her analysis for a time; she was able to escape her many commitments only at irregular intervals. She had been visiting Pallanza for a week but was now back in Vienna, where she wanted to undergo surgery ⟨Bertin, pp. 307f.⟩. See 230 AF, 231 AF, 238 SF.
3 Written 'Haut' (= skin) instead of 'Haus'.
4 Probably enclosed with the letter (sorted elsewhere in the set of copies). Printed on the back of the card is 'Saluti dall' Isola Pescatori'. The picture side shows the island with several houses, a church further back and the large Verbano house in the foreground.
5 See 235 AF and note 7.

230 AF[1]

professor freud
lottagesanatorium
stermoaterstrasse vienna

pallanza 17 17/40
[Receipt stamp Vienna:] 17 IV 1927 21

visit to pallanza but princess departed[2] sincerest easter greetings
[unsigned]

1 Telegram.
2 See 227 SF and note 3.

231 AF

ANNA FREUD

Easter Monday, early [18 April 1927]
Vienna IX, Berggasse 19[1]
Isola Superiore

Dear Papa,
Yesterday in Pallanza, clear weather, storm and waves, but princess had already left on Saturday, and only Miss Croisdale,[2] little princess and dog. Miss C. very amiable, little princess very brown, but apparently not yet very strong,[3] dog (see below),[4] the most sheep-headed creature, cowardly, refuses to tussle, doesn't chase after cyclists, red eyes, scratches itself. Much smaller than Wolf, just hair. Pallanza nice but very noisy, lots of cars, dusty, shops unfortunately closed. Eden Hotel wonderfully situated on the tip, magnificent grounds. But nothing compared with the island.

Very good dinner, straight to bed, evenings and nights very cold, as the sun is the only source of heat.[5]

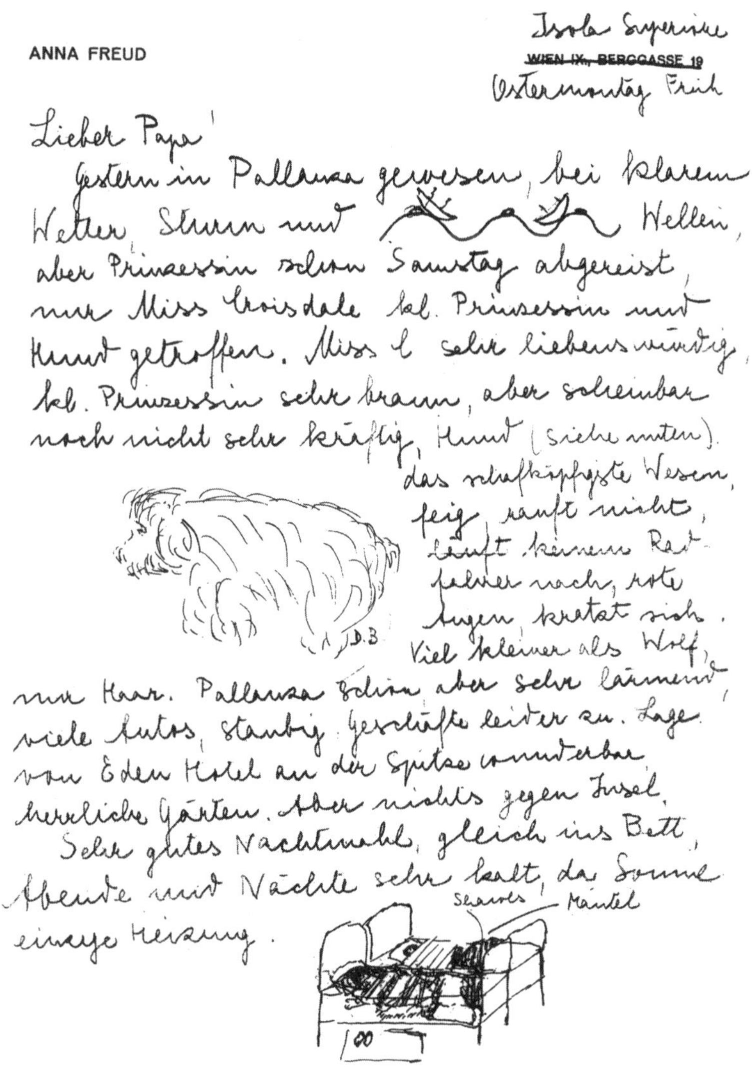

ANNA FREUD

Isola Superiore
~~WIEN IX., BERGGASSE 19~~
Ostermontag Früh

Lieber Papa!
Gestern in Pallanza gewesen, bei klarem Wetter, Sturm und Wellen, aber Prinzessin schon Samstag abgereist, nur Miss Croisdale, kl. Prinzessin und Hund getroffen. Miss C sehr liebenswürdig, kl. Prinzessin sehr braun, aber scheinbar noch nicht sehr kräftig, Hund (siehe unten) das schafköpfigste Wesen, feig, rauft nicht, läuft keinem Radfahrer nach, rote Augen, kratzt sich. Viel kleiner als Wolf, nur Haar. Pallanza schön aber sehr lärmend, viele Autos, staubig, Geschäfte leider zu. Lage von Eden Hotel an der Spitze wunderbar, herrliche Gärten. Aber nichts gegen Insel.
Sehr gutes Nachtmahl, gleich ins Bett. Abende und Nächte sehr kalt, da Sonne einzige Heizung.

VIII Anna's letter of 18 April 1927

The storm died down in the night, for the first time no surf, peaceful, slightly cloudy, rowing weather.

Look forward to mail today as there was no delivery yesterday because it was Sunday.

Greeting to all.

Your Anna

1 Printed letterhead; place and street crossed out. The letter appears to have been written in indelible pencil but a pen was used for the drawings; see facsimile VIII, illustration of the first page.
2 Violet Croisdale, called Croisy, the English governess employed in the house since 1913 to look after the children through their childhood and adolescence. In 1932 Marie bought her a house in England where she died in 1949 ⟨Bertin, pp. 209, 255, 262, 274, 313, 347, 390⟩.
3 The seventeen-year-old princess Eugénie had become ill with tubercular pleurisy at the end of 1926, which was the reason Marie Bonaparte brought her for long periods to the Italian lakes; she was still to suffer a number of years from the disease ⟨Bertin, pp. 305, 307f., 313, 320, and elsewhere⟩.
4 The pencil drawing was evidently done by Dorothy, as it is signed 'D. B.'; these initials are written, however, with the same pencil as the text. Anna might have added them afterwards.
5 See drawing 'Shawls, overcoats'.

232 AF

ANNA FREUD Tuesday, early [19 April 1927]
Isola Superiore
Vienna IX, Berggasse 19[1]

Dear Papa,
No telegrams for two days, probably because of the holidays. But children's telegrams came.

We rowed yesterday morning to Isola Madre and were taken on a tour there. Wonderful plants and trees, the most beautiful the giant rhododendrons in full flower; the gardener gave us camellias. It's a pity that we can't go around on our own and stay there. The Borromeo family[2] itself now lives there. The next island, close to Pallanza, S. Giovanni, is rented to an American family. In the afternoon, as not quite able to move at the time, lay in the sun until evening on the flat end of the islands, where the nets dry.

Early this morning the water as quiet as a mouse, sun haze so that it was difficult to distinguish the sea, sky and hills. Plans still undecided, breakfast waiting.

Thoughts about coming home. Dorothy reckons we don't need to be back before you come out of the sanatorium. Would like to know what you think.

I hope that you are saving all letters unwritten for me. Will be coming with plenty of fresh energy for everything.

Look forward very much to hearing from you.

Your Anna

1 Printed letterhead; place and street crossed out. The letter is written with indelible or normal pencil.
2 Descendants of the Milan noble family whose members built villas in the seventeenth and eighteenth centuries and laid out huge gardens on the hitherto bare islands.

233 AF[1]

professor freud
cottagesanatorun
sternvartestrasse Vienna

baveno 19º 11,15
[Receipt stamp Vienna:] 19 APR 27 16[52]

no news since saturday here nice and quiet
[unsigned]

1 Telegram.

234 AF[1]

professor freud
lottagesanatorium
sternwartestraze Vienna

laveno 19 17h15
[Receipt stamp Vienna:] 19 APR 1927 19[20]

very happy about letter[2] still contactable here motor boat excursion on lake glorious weather unfortunately not sendable[3]
[unsigned]

1 Telegram.
2 228 SF.
3 Misprint in telegram.

235 AF

ANNA FREUD

Wednesday, early [20 April 1927]
Isola Superiore
Vienna IX, Berggasse 19[1]

Dear Papa,
Received your letter yesterday lunchtime and was very pleased to read the detailed news. No telegrams since Saturday, but today I expect one again. It is quite unfair that I should get to see all these nice things while you are lying bored[2] in the sanatorium. I would have liked just as much to go with you if you had not been so against it[3] and I would have been quite happy to wait until we could travel together as in Rome.[4]

I am enclosing leaves from Isola Madre that the gardener gave to us. They are camphor.[5] We originally wanted to send the camellias but they would probably arrive quite black. And it is not possible to send the real thing. I am sure you have never seen them[6] as we are seeing them now, because in autumn they cannot all be in flower, lots of Japanese shrubs in yellow, white and red. The gardener says that one of the rhododendrons was brought to the island three hundred years ago and turned into a tree with a real trunk and branches like an oak. But I think if you left me on Madre Island for three hundred years I would also turn into something quite special; it is barely an achievement. I am writing in my nightdress in the sun on our balcony,[7] to the left Isola Madre, straight ahead Isola Bella. Despite the fact that it doesn't have a garden, our island is just as nice, perhaps even more picturesque.

Yesterday we went by motorboat to Santa Caterina, a monastery stuck on a rock looking out on to the water. Then a short walk over the rocks to the next tiny harbour, picked wild flowers, then stopped in Laveno, sent telegrams, bought paste[8] and home with the sunset. I go to sleep at 9 or 9.30.

Plans for today still uncertain.[9] Bought timetable; connection to Venice convenient. Only dates unsure. Is it really all right to stay away for so long?

Greetings and lots of kisses.

Your Anna

PS I'm peeling.

PS Dorothy B[urlingham] sends you lots of greetings. Her father has never yet offered to wire money to her.

1 Printed letterhead; place and street crossed out.
2 See 228 SF and note 5.
3 See 212 SF, note 2.
4 See 201 SF/AF and Appendixes 1 and 2.
5 Written 'Kampher'. *Dryobalanops camphora* (camphor); the leather-like leaves are pedunculated, egg-shaped, pointed, the flowers paniculated.
6 In 1905 on his trip with Minna Bernays (see 2 SF and note 4), during which they visited 'the two magic islands Madre and Bella' ⟨Freud and Minna to Martha, 9 September 1905, in Freud 2002*b*, p. 201⟩.
7 See enclosure to 229 AF and note 5.
8 See 221 AF and note 4.
9 See 237 AF.

236 SF[1]

Vien 19 11.40
[Receipt stamp:] Baveno 20 April 1927 11.30

Everything in order cold easter math Robert already back no example for[2] you beating fantasy[3] essay with jeleffe[4]
[unsigned]

1 Telegram.
2 Spelt 'feuer' (= fire) instead of 'für' (for).

3 'Beating Phantasies and Daydreams' (Anna Freud, 1922); Jelliffe [1927] (a slightly modified reprint of Jelliffe [1925]). See 238 SF and note 8, and 241 SF and note 3.

4 Smith Ely Jelliffe (1866–1945), doctor of medicine, American neurologist and psychiatrist, co-editor of the *Journal of Nervous and Mental Disease*, pioneer of psychosomatic medicine in America. In 1913 he founded *The Psychoanalytic Review* with William A. White (see 113 AF and note 3). He did not meet Freud, who initially mistrusted him, in person until August 1921 in Bad Gastein; they gradually became closer in the ensuing correspondence: 'I now often laugh in remembrance of the bad reception I gave you in Gastein because I had first seen you in company of Stekel' ⟨Freud to Jelliffe, 9 February 1939, in: Jelliffe [1983], p. 279⟩. In 1925 Jelliffe delivered a paper at the Bad Homburg Congress and then visited Freud in Semmering, and again in 1927. He was meant to meet Anna in Oxford in 1929 (see 257 SF–264 AF) ⟨Freud/Jones, letter 320, 27 July 1921, p. 434; Freud/Eitingon, 465 F, 13 September 1927; Jelliffe [1983], *passim*. See also Lewis, pp. 224–6⟩.

237 AF[1]

PROFESSOR FREUD
COTTAGESANATONIUM
STERNWATERSᵗRASSE VIENN

INTRA 20 17^H^15
[Receipt stamp Vienna:] 20 APR [1927] 19[10]

LAZING IN THE SUN ON THE WATER = GREETINGS =
[unsigned]

1 Telegram.

238 SF

PROF. DR. FREUD [Cottage-Sanatorium] 20 April 1927
Vienna IX, Berggasse 19

My dear Anna,
So I can write to you once more![1] How nice; I'm taking the first free moment that my many treatments permit. Braun's visit will interrupt me, but I hope you still get the letter on the island, where I once ate such delicious fish with Aunt. At that time it was not possible to stay there.[2]

Here there is enough news, but nothing of great import. The princess had minor gynaecological surgery today with Halban,[3] but it is not to be talked about. She is incognito at Loew. Ruth assisted and is travelling on Friday to Berlin with Mark, has a passport for the family. I am enclosing a small picture of Eva;[4] please bring it back. I find the similarity[5] more and more unsettling. Esti is apparently sick, Math and Robert have seen everything in Florence, complain about the city, people and weather. Harry came back alone today; he was with Uncle[6] in the sunshine in Venice.

I am going first today to Pichler in town and tomorrow I'm starting work with three hours.[7]

Your beating fantasies are referred to correctly and in great detail in Jelliffe's journal, probably by himself.[8] The same issue has a review of lay analysis by Brill,[9] polite but flat.[10]

Out of boredom[11] I am starting to write something.[12] I don't yet know whether it will be viable.

Ostwald[13] was complimentary about analysis in his Easter essay[14] for the N. Presse.

I greet you affectionately and hope that you prolong your stay.

Papa

1 See 234 AF.
2 See 235 AF and note 6.
3 Joseph Halban (1870–1937), doctor of medicine, surgeon and professor of gynaecology in Vienna (married to Selma Kurz, see 149 SF, note 9). Marie Bonaparte (under the pseudonym Narjani) had already written an essay on female frigidity in 1924, describing a surgical method which she was now having performed on herself. She remained until 2 May at Sanatorium Loew in Vienna. A further intervention of this type was performed in May 1930 (this time at the American hospital in Neuilly, once again kindly accompanied by Ruth Mack-Brunswick); a third operation followed in 1931 ⟨Bertin, pp. 265f., 298, 308, 314, 320–4; see also ibid., p. 275; Freud/Ferenczi III, 969 Fer, 970 F, p. 161; Freud/Eitingon, 633 F⟩.
4 Henny and Oliver's daughter, Eva, who reminded Freud of Heinerle; see 208 SF.
5 Incorrectly spelt (no umlaut) in the original.
6 Alexander Freud.
7 As in the previous year (see 223 AF and note 2), Freud again received patients in the sanatorium ⟨Jones III, pp. 134, 144⟩.
8 See 236 SF and note 3. Jelliffe was indeed the author ⟨information from author in *Review*, vol. 12 (1925), p. 108⟩. Freud and Anna must have missed Jelliffe's first article (1925). See 241 AF and note 3.
9 Abraham Arden Brill (1874–1948), doctor of medicine, neurologist and psychiatrist, professor at the Psychiatric Clinic at New York University. He learnt about psychoanalysis as Bleuler's assistant in Zurich in 1908, and between 1908 and 1910 was the first and only analyst in the USA. In 1910 he was lecturer in psychoanalysis at Columbia University. He was instrumental in introducing psychoanalysis to the USA, also through translations. In 1911 he founded the New York Psychoanalytic Society and was president on several occasions of it and of the American Psychoanalytic Association; the library of the New York Psychoanalytic Institute was named after him in 1947. After a period of reticence during the First World War and for some years afterwards, Brill once again turned to Freud and remained friendly with him until his death ⟨Jones II, pp. 45, 50; Jones III, pp. 39f., 181; Freud/Ferenczi III, 837 F and note 5; Romm, pp. 211–14, 217f.; Molnar [1996], p. 120⟩.
10 Brill [1927].
11 See 228 SF and note 5.
12 *The Future of an Illusion* (1927*c*).

13 Wilhelm Ostwald (1853–1932), scientist and philosopher, until 1906 professor of physical chemistry at the University of Leipzig, 1909 Nobel Prize winner. He was editor of *Annalen der Naturphilosophie* from 1901–14, and in 1910 asked Freud to write an article for it ⟨Freud/Jung, letters 190 F and 194 F⟩. His three-volume autobiography was just being published.

14 In this article – a tribute to the achievements of humanity in technology, sciences, politics and art – Ostwald also mentioned psychology, which he said was just beginning to be recognized as a science: 'Thus we can see only the beginnings of this psychotechnology; but they already give indication of the unforeseeable future significance for improving life and making it more attractive. *Freud's psychoanalysis* and *psychotherapy* are on their way to influencing the state of science' ⟨Ostwald, p. 2; emphasis in the original⟩.

239 AF[1]

PROFESSOR FREUD
COTTAGESANATORIUM
STERNWARTESTRASSE VIENNA

BAVENO 21 11
[Receipt stamp Vienna:] 21 APR [1927] 12^{35}

HAPPY ABOUT TELEGRAM ALL ROUND LAKE ONE GETS USED TOO EASILY[2] TO SUN BEAUTY DOING NOTHING
[unsigned]

1 Telegram.
2 See 56 AF, note 1.

240 SF[1]

WIEN 21 13/20
[Receipt stamp:] Baveno 22.4.27 [no time]
[Delivery stamp:] per posta

DOROTHYS SUGGESTION VERY SENSIBLE STAYING EASIER THAN RETURNING
[unsigned]

1 Telegram.

241 AF[1]

[Lago Maggiore, undated; c. 22 April 1927]

Dear Papa,
Yesterday on Isola Bella a white peacock fanned its tail before us, just like on the card. I don't understand why the oranges are ripe now and not in

autumn; I think just for the Germans on account of Goethe.[2] Everything else is as on the card only more beautiful. The peacocks on Isola Madre and Bella cry so loudly that we can hear it at night in our room like the wailing of cats.

I was very pleased to receive your telegram. I had been thinking that Math and Robert are so much more moderate in their enjoyment than I.

Does Jelliffe want to make me 'famous'[3] so that more people are interested in my book?[4]

Your Anna

1 Picture postcard (sent as letter): 'Lago Maggiore – Isola Bella – Giardino'. The colourful picture of the garden shows three white peacocks, one fanning its tail, under tropical plants. The text is written in very pale ink.

2 Reference to Mignon's song in Goethe's *Wilhelm Meister's Apprenticeship* (Book 3, Ch. 1):

> Know'st thou the land where the pale citrons grow,
> The golden fruits in darker foliage glow?

3 The delayed review in her opinion of her earlier essay (already translated into English in 1923) probably amused Anna. But see 236 SF and note 3, and 238 SF and note 8.

4 Anna Freud (1927*a*).

242 AF[1]

professor freud
cottage sanatorium
stermvarte strasse Vienna

pallanza 22 13
[Receipt stamp:] 22 APR [1927] 15[21]

hot rest day greetings
[unsigned]

1 Telegram.

243 SF[1]

Vienna 22 20.30
[Receipt stamp:] Baveno 23.4.1927 8.50

hot here too half working day three hundred eighty-eight copies mterz[2] sold.
[unsigned]

1 Telegram.

2 Illegible in handwritten telegram. The letters could also be 'interz' or 'niterz'. See Anna's comments in 244 AF.

244 AF

Saturday afternoon [23 April 1927]
Beach at Baveno

Very pleased to receive your letters yesterday to both of us,[1] Eva's picture and the telegram [240 SF], which then determined our plans. Eva really looks exactly the same and is a particularly attractive child. It would be nice if we had her with us in the summer. But I would also like it if Ernsti were to come to us. I have been thinking about it all here and I think the Burlingham children would be very pleasant company for him, in other words with us but also with children, which is not always so easy to arrange. We will have to discuss it all when I come home.[2] I am *very* curious to see what you are writing and hope something comes of it.[3] Have just collected today's telegram from the post office, the most important word unfortunately unintelligible and defies all my efforts to interpret it. Is it the copies of my book that have been sold?[4] Where would they find so many people to read it?

We are lying on the beach across from our island and are in the middle of making plans. We are leaving here tomorrow afternoon via Milan to Venice and will be in Vienna perhaps on Wednesday, probably Thursday.[5] It will depend on the sleeping-car situation. Your telegram and advice were the triggers. It is really much easier to give in here than to leave in the near future. And Berggasse doesn't tempt me as long as there is no one there. But I have earned so much money in the last one and a half years that the three or four days don't really matter – and I can make it up, particularly if I am to have two hours in the summer.[6] The pause now was very good; I have become much more sensible than I have been for a long time:[7] I hope, like the tan, it can be seen from the outside.

Dorothy was very pleased to receive your letter and thanks you. We have really had the most pleasant and unclouded relationship on this trip.

Today is the first half-day with no sun, but hardly less beautiful for all that.

I am sorry that Math and Robert did not have as much luck as we have.

I send you greetings and lots of kisses. I hope Wolf has not become too well behaved in Kagran.[8] I hope we can collect him on Friday.

Your Anna

1 Only the letter to Anna (238 SF) survives.

2 Anna's wish was fulfilled and both children were able to spend the summer holidays together with them: Freud again rented Villa Schüler in Semmering in the summer (from 16 June to 29 September) (see 203 SF, note 3) ⟨Freud/Eitingon, 401 F, p. 478⟩. The Burlinghams stayed, as in the previous summer when Peter Blos accompanied the children, in the neighbouring Villa Sophie, this time with Erik H. Erikson as minder, whom Dorothy and Anna had in the meantime hired as a teacher at the Hietzing school (see 208 SF, note 7) ⟨Freud/Eitingon, 387 F, 401 F; Jones III, p. 144; Freud/Ferenczi III, 967 F–979 F, 1061 F–1079 F, 1096 F–1107 F; Anna/Lou, letters 280, 301; Freud, W. E. [1987], pp. 210f.; Burlingham, M., pp. 158, 164, 184f.⟩. 'Living together between the two villas is proving to be very comfortable' ⟨Freud/Eitingon, 435 F, 20 June 1927, p. 518⟩.

Minna was also in Semmering at first; Oliver, Henny and Evchen (see ill. 10) arrived around the end of June and stayed until 18 July. Ernstl was probably taken back to Berlin by Eitingon after his visit ⟨Freud/Eitingon, 435 F, 437 F, 444 F, 445 F⟩ (see also 146 SF, note 4).
3 *The Future of an Illusion* (1927*c*); see 238 SF and note 12.
4 1927*a*.
5 See 249 AF.
6 Anna planned to take some patients with her to Semmering ⟨Anna/Lou, letter 301⟩.
7 See 209 SF, note 6; also 5 MF/SF, end of note 1.
8 District in the north-east of Vienna; Anna's dog, Wolf, was housed there at the Nausch kennels during Freud's stay in the sanatorium ⟨Freud, M. [1999], p. 195⟩. See also 277 SF and note 2.

245 AF[1]

PROFESSORE FREND
COTTAGESANATORIUM
STERNWARTESTRASSE WIENNA

BAVENO 23 17H15
[Receipt stamp:] 23 APR [1927] 18[55]

LEAVING ISLAND REGRETTABLY TOMORROW NEXT LETTERS AND TELEGRAM ADDRESS VENICE MAIN POST OFFICE ALL NEWS GRATEFULLY RECEIVED
[unsigned]

1 Telegram. Two versions were received; it was presumably thought that the first, addressed to 'Professore Pend', had not arrived. It did, however, arrive correctly in Vienna with the time stamp '18'. The text is the same, but with different misprints. This version contains the addition 'Ampliation', i.e., backup version.

246 SF[1]

WIEN 24 11/50
[Receipt stamp:] UFFICIO TELEGRAFICO VENEZIA
24.4.27 [time illegible]

YESTERDAY SILBERGASSE[2] CHILDREN NOT ARRIVED GARDEN FLOURISHING TODAY ELECTION[3] ABSTENTION[4] REGRET YOUR DEPARTURE LOOK FORWARD TO SEEING YOU
[unsigned]

1 Telegram.
2 See 215 SF and note 3.
3 The third parliamentary elections in the First Republic of Austria: the Social Democratic Party led by its mastermind, Otto Bauer (see 110 SF, note 11), lost

to the conservative list 'which included some of the National Socialists'. The Federal Chancellor, Ignaz Seipel, thus remained in office (until 1929) and with his policy 'took the polarization of the country into Marxist and anti-Marxist camps one step further. The stage was thus set for an even more conflictual political confrontation' ⟨Weissensteiner, pp. 185–90, quotations pp. 189 and 190; also ibid., pp. 195, 200, 314; more details in Braunthal, *passim*⟩.

4 This 'abstention' conflicts with the claim in Eschbach and Willenberg (p. 300 and note 14) that Freud signed an election appeal on 24 April 1927 in the *Arbeiter-Zeitung*, Vienna, with Alfred Adler and Karl Bühler. This claim is misleading, however. It is true that Freud was one of thirty-nine signatories to a declaration entitled 'a statement by Vienna's intellectuals' in which 'intellect' was given priority over any 'political dogma', acknowledging the great social and cultural achievements of the Vienna city council, which should be 'maintained and encouraged'. The concluding declaration says: 'The essence of intellect is above all freedom, which is now endangered and which we feel committed to protect. We will always be ready to struggle for greater humanity and to fight against inertia and atrophy' ⟨see Freud 1927*l*⟩. In 1933 Freud commented to Jones: '[. . .] a rightist dictatorship, which means the suppression of social democracy, [. . .] will not be an agreeable state of affairs' ⟨Freud/Jones, letter 606, 7 April. For Freud's political stance, see, e.g., Ekstein; Leopold-Löwenthal [1981], pp. 332f. and note 36; see also Plankers and Federn, pp. 76–8; for the change in his political interest in his youth, see, e.g., Gödde [1990], pp. 14f.⟩.

247 AF[1]

professor freud
cottagesanatorium
sternwartestrasse wien

venezia 24 23/55
[Receipt stamp and note:] 25/4 1927 1^{55}

arrived venice evening address britania as fourteen years ago[2] found st marks square on foot
[unsigned]

1 Telegram.
2 See 31 SF, 32 AF.

248 AF[1]

professor freud
lottagesanatorium
sternvvartestrasse Vienna

venezia 26 8/30
[Receipt stamp:] 26.IV.27 9^{22}

coincidentally saint mark name day large procession music sunshine see you thursday
[unsigned]

1 Telegram.

249 AF[1]

prof freud
cottagesanatorium
sternwartestrasse wien

venezia 26 23/10
[Receipt stamp:] 26.IV.27
[Delivery stamp:] 27 APR 24[34]

arriving berggasse thursday [28 April] eight morning
happy looking forward to seeing you
[unsigned]

1 Telegram.

250 SF[1]

anna freud tirolerhof innsbruck[2]

semmering[3] 31 August [1927]

here bad weather very quiet wolf bored[4] i would be too if i couldn't write[5]
greetings all friends from near and far[6] = papa

1 Telegram. This and the two following telegrams are classified in the LoC under 1919, but the forms were not printed until 1925.
2 Anna travelled from Semmering to the 10th International Psychoanalytic Congress in Innsbruck, taking place from 1 to 3 September and preceded on 31 August by 'Business Pre-Conference of Officials' and a meeting of the International Training Commission ⟨*IZ*, vol. 13 (1927), pp. 261, 468–500⟩.
3 The family had been here since 16 June; see 244 AF, note 2.
4 See 228 SF and note 5.
5 *The Future of an Illusion* (1927*c*).
6 As a 'greeting from Freud to the assembly', Anna read his essay 'Humour' (1927*d*) at the opening of the scientific sessions of 1 September ⟨*IZ*, vol. 13 (1927), p. 470; Freud/Eitingon, 455 E–457 E⟩.

251 SF[1]

anna freud tirolerhof Innsbruck

semering, 2 September [1927]

very pleased at latest news[2] today back to vienna again before visitors[3]
come all the best = papa

1 Telegram.

2 Documents from Anna missing. Freud's comments might refer to a greeting telegram from the Eitingons ⟨Freud/Eitingon, 461 E⟩. In his reply of 2 September (1927*i*), Freud voiced the expectation that the members 'will find the strength from the feeling of a shared task to agree on practical matters'. This warning arose as a result of a long-simmering disagreement about 'lay analysis' – the question of whether only doctors should be allowed to practise analysis – and the training regulations ensuing from it (see 256 AF, note 2, 259 SF and note 6; see also 203 SF, note 2) ⟨Freud 1926*e*, 1927*a*; *IZ*, vol. 13 (1927), pp. 53–235, *passim*⟩. The discord threatened on several occasions to split the Association. 'Things looked distinctly unpleasant at the meeting when suddenly above the hubbub a girlish voice rang out with the words: *Meine Herren, ich glaube wir thun ein Unrecht* [Gentlemen, I think we are committing an injustice]. It was this intervention by Anna Freud that saved the situation. . . . It was a historic moment in the dispute . . . and it meant that for the time being the crisis was over' ⟨Jones III, p. 318⟩. Only temporarily, however: a commission was formed and the decision postponed until the following Congress (see 256 SF and note 2, 237 SF and note 10, 259 SF and note 6). ⟨Details in *IZ*, vol. 13 (1927), pp. 480–4, 485, 492–6; see also Jones III, Ch. 9; Leupold-Löwenthal [1984]; Grubrich-Simitis [1993], pp. 230–8; Schröter [1996], [2002]⟩.

3 'In September after the Congress he had to put up with the strain of receiving many visitors' ⟨Jones III, p. 145; Freud/Eitingon, 447 F; Freud/Binswanger, 158 F, 159 B, 160 F⟩. Binswanger noted in his diary, in some cases verbatim, the various topics he had discussed with Freud. The moving expression of his feelings is typical of the significance of such discussions for Freud's visitors: 'I felt refreshed and elated from the visit, not only spiritually, but almost physically, and am pleased at last to have seen again the man who plays such a big role in my inner life' ⟨Freud/Binswanger, editorial appendix, p. 238⟩. See also 257 SF, note 13, 277 SF and note 4.

252 SF[1]

anna freud tirolerhof Innsbruck

semmering, 3 SEPT [1927] 8/15

alls well that ends well[2] very pleased at election result[3]
hope further success for you[4] mathilde arrived safely
tomorrow froeschnitzthal[5] with her and martin = papa

1 Telegram.

2 Comedy by Shakespeare (*c.* 1602–3); see 264 SF.

3 On 2 September, Eitingon was elected president and Anna Freud central secretary of the Association. This important position involved not only the organization and correspondence but also the editing of the correspondence journal, in which she reported on the Congress ⟨*IZ*, vol. 13 (1927), pp. 468–99⟩. The highly detailed description gives an idea of how Anna's zeal influenced not only her scientific and practical activities (see 209 SF and note 6), but also the psychoanalytical institution. See also 251 SF, note 2.

4 For her first paper at a Congress, which was to be delivered that morning: 'The Theory of Child Analysis' ⟨1928; paper: 1927*b*⟩. 'The idea of presenting a paper

is still difficult for me. . . . But the others are urging me to do it and Papa as well doesn't want me to give in and not do it. . . . I should soon be used to it' ⟨Anna/Lou, letters 307, 15 January 1928, p. 544, and 322, 20 February 1929, p. 568⟩. Anna had originally wanted to speak on the subject 'Training in Reality as Analytical Training', but Eitingon advised her against it in view of the controversy with Melanie Klein (see 209 SF, note 2) ⟨Freud/Eitingon, 428 E; see also Anna/Lou, letter 305⟩.

5 Presumably an excursion to Frossnitz-Tal.

1928

253 SF[1]

ANNE FREUD HOTEL BOURGOGNE PARIS[2]

WIEN 29 [February 1928] 14/20
[Receipt stamp: PARIS-CENTRAL 29.2.28 $15^{H}36$
PARIS 44 = 15.55

[in English]
ENTHUSIASTIC REPORTS FROM BUDAPEST[3] CHECK BURLINGHAM ARRIVED ALLRIGHT
[unsigned]

1 Telegram.
2 Anna's duties had further increased, particularly since the Innsbruck Congress; her health suffered so much – she had terrible headaches and extreme fatigue – that at her father's insistence she went to Paris for a week with Dorothy to rest ⟨Anna to Eitingon, 16 February 1928; Freud/Eitingon, 493 F⟩.
3 Anna had been invited by Ferenczi to deliver another paper to the Hungarian Association on Saturday, 25 February, which was very well received ⟨*IZ*, vol. 14 (1928), p. 429⟩. It was, as she wrote, about 'my form of child analysis' ⟨*Rundbriefe*: Vienna, 23 February 1928 (written by Anna), and Budapest, 6 May 1928, Archives of the British Psychoanalytical Society, London; Freud/Ferenczi III, 1117 Fer, 1118 F⟩. She returned to Vienna on the 26th, leaving the following morning for Paris with Dorothy. They returned on the evening of 4 March ⟨Anna to Eitingon, 21 February, 7 March 1928⟩.

254 AF[1]

professor freud neuf
Berggasse 19 wien

paris 2 [March 1928] $15^{h}25$
[Receipt stamp Vienna:] 2 MRZ [1928] 18^{20}

greetings from a joint visit to the monsters of notredame = marie[2] anna

1 This telegram was filed under 1918 (probably misreading of the time as the date; this form was printed in 1925). This is the most plausible position in the chronology. Freud noted a similar short visit by Anna and Dorothy to Paris (but with different dates), in the *Diary of Sigmund Freud*, on 15 and 17 April 1930 ⟨1992*i*, p. 5⟩.
2 Marie Bonaparte. 'The princess was incredibly nice and friendly in Paris. She regarded our visit as if it were her task to make it pleasant' ⟨Anna to Eitingon, 7 March 1928⟩.

255 SF[1]

ANNE FREUD HOTEL BOURGOGNE RUE BOURGOGNE, PARIS

WIEN 3 [March 1928] $10^{H}25$
[Two receipt stamps:] PARIS-CENTRAL 3.3.28 10
PARIS 44 R.DE GRENELLE 3.3.28 11.50

YESTERDAYS TELEGRAM PROBABLY NOT DELIVERED[2] NOTHING NEW GREETINGS PRINCESS LOOKING FORWARD TO YOUR RETURN[3]

1 Telegram.
2 Indeed; missing from the collection.
3 On Sunday evening, 4 March 1928.

Summer–Autumn 1928 and Berlin/Tegel (1928–30)

The Freuds again spent a summer in Semmering, from 16 June to 30 August 1928 (with the Burlinghams this time 'in the house next door' ⟨Freud/Ferenczi III, 1127 F, 1128 F, 11 July 1928, p. 342; Jones III, p. 149⟩. Freud's complaints had been gradually getting worse since spring, however. 'Pichler's attempts this year to get me a usable prosthesis turned out so badly that I have finally decided to break [with him],' he wrote to Ferenczi ⟨Freud/Ferenczi III, 1127 F, 19 June 1928, p. 341⟩; and on 1 July to Jones: 'Last week Prof. Schroeder of Berlin sent his assistant here to examine me. [. . .] We arranged that I should go to him in Berlin in September' ⟨Freud/Jones, letter 526, p. 648; see also Schur, p. 405⟩. The claim in Jones III, p. 150, that Schröder came to see Freud is incorrect, although the intention apparently existed ⟨Freud/Ferenczi III, ibid.⟩. On 30 August Freud, accompanied by Anna, put himself in the care of Prof. Dr Hermann Schröder (1876–1942), then department head at the Institute of Dentistry at the University of Berlin ⟨*Kürschner* 1928–9⟩. A new prosthesis had to be made and fitted; Freud was not able to return to Vienna until 31 October 1928 ⟨Anna/Lou, letters 310, 315⟩.

They stayed at Schloss Tegel, in which Ernst Simmel had opened a Psychoanalytical Clinic on 10 April 1927 for the hospitalized treatment of patients whose symptoms were too severe and advanced for out-patient treatment ⟨Simmel [1927]; Schultz and Hermanns, pp. 61–3; Hermanns and Schultz, p. 80; Brecht et al., p. 46 (with ill. of the invitation to the opening, through which various other references to the date in the literature may be corrected)⟩. See 100 SF, note 10. 'I found the most gracious reception at Simmel's Sanatorium. It is half an hour by car from the city centre, but beautiful and quiet, situated in a park a few minutes from Lake Tegel' ⟨Freud/Jones, letter 528, p. 649, also letters 526–32; Anna/Lou, letter 310; for details of the sanatorium in general, see Schultz and Hermanns; Hermanns and Schultz; Ross, pp. 37–40; on Anna's relationship to the sanatorium, see Bittner, pp. 19–21; Heller, pp. 90f.; Anna/Eva, letters 15–33, *passim*⟩.

For further treatments in Berlin/Tegel in 1929, see 257 SF, notes 6 and 8. A new prosthesis was also required in 1930; the stay in Berlin – again with accommodation in Tegel and Anna's accompaniment – lasted from 4 May to 24 July ⟨Freud 1992*i*, pp. 5, 7; Freud/Ferenczi III, 1185 F–1187 F, 1193 F; Freud/Jones, letters 551, 552, 555, 557; Jones III, p. 159; Anna/Eva, letters 22–33; Anna/Lou, letters 336–9; Molnar [1996], pp. 69, 76, 103f.; Burlingham, M. p. 211⟩.

1929

256 SF[1]

ANNA FREUD HOTEL MAYFAIR LONDON[2]
KOENIGSSEE OBY [Schneewinkl]1722 25 [July 1929] $9^{H}10$

[in English]
HERE VERY PEACEFULLY[3] EXCEPT THUNDERSTORM
VISITED MATHILDE[4] LOVE = PA

1 Telegram. Attached to this sheet is a handwritten vaccination certificate, which Anna presumably required to enter England and which was kept with the letters; it is reproduced in Appendix 4.

2 Anna left Schneewinkl on 22–3 July for the Congress in Oxford ⟨Freud to Martin, 23 July 1929⟩. She stopped first in London, where Jones had invited the American and European functionaries for a pre-conference on problems of lay analysis ⟨*Rundbrief*, Berlin, 4 June 1929 (Archives of the British Psychoanalytical Society); Freud to Ruth, 24 June 1929⟩. Freud stated his position in a letter to Ophuijsen of 26 May 1929, and emphasized in conclusion: 'The question of lay analysis is too vital for the decision to be left to a random majority at a congress. You and Jones are playing a dangerous game. [. . .] The first to leave the IPV [International Psychoanalytical Association] if it were to yield to the Americans on this issue of lay treatment am I, the author of "The Question of Lay Analysis"' ⟨Anna/Eva, letter 23, note 5, p. 135; the sending of the letter is mentioned in Freud/Ferenczi III, 1165 F⟩.

3 The Freuds and Burlinghams rented the 'Schneewinkllehen' in Schönau am Königssee from the Munich art historian Rudolf Berliner, as a summer residence for their extended families and guests; see 266 AF, note 2 ⟨Freud/Ferenczi III, 1161 F, 11163 F, 1169 F; Chaussy, pp. 195–8, ill. p. 201. For the fate of the property, which was confiscated in 1938 and subsequently used by Heinrich Himmler, see Chaussy, Ch. 21⟩. They had been there since 17–18 June: 'Martha, Lün and I are travelling the day after tomorrow, . . . Anna, Dorothy, Wolf and the children a day earlier' ⟨Freud to Ruth, 16 and 19 June 1929; Freud/Jones, letter 539⟩. (See ill. 14.) Apart from Dorothy's own children, Ernstl and other fellow pupils at the Hietzing school, including Victor Rosenfeld, spent their holidays there: 'For the children it is really paradise' ⟨Anna/Eva, letter 12,

30 June 1929, p. 118, letter 9 and note 3, letter 10 and note 2; Freud, W. E. [1987]; Burlingham, S., p. 196; Bittner, pp. 12f.⟩. Freud and Anna travelled on to Tegel on 15 September ⟨Freud/Ferenczi III, 1169 F⟩.

4 Reference to the unpeaceful mood that Anna had encountered at the pre-conference and Congress (see 257 SF, note 10); at the same time it may be taken literally: 'It's like a fairy tale. Two houses on a large meadow, surrounded by dense forest with a view of the mountains above it – Watzmann, Hoher Göll – no external noise to be heard, in the forest a murmuring stream and a pond, a long winding road through the forest for the car and still only 11 minutes' drive to the main square in Berchtesgaden' ⟨Freud to Ruth, 19 June 1929⟩.

5 She was spending the holidays in Bayerisch Gmain (see 257 SF) with her husband, Robert Hollitscher.

257 SF

PROF. DR. FREUD 25 July 1929
Schneewinkl
Vienna, IX. Berggasse 19

My dear Anna,
There was no time to write to London, because the letters don't travel as quickly as you. It is only the third day since your departure; if Ernst and Lux weren't here, it would be very sad,[1] not only for Wolf. The days have been very fine, hot as everywhere else; yesterday there were two thunderstorms in the early afternoon and late evening, and then it was not at all easy to entice Wolf away from his shelter in the lower closet. Between the storms I went with Ernst and Lux to visit Math-Rob in Gmain. Car driving is particularly pleasant at the moment! On the first day, the day before yesterday, the whole family, all six of us, showed Lux Bartholomae. Herr Wein was again our pilot.[2] It was once again quite magnificent, except that the crane flies on Barth[olomä] are particularly unabashed, probably because they know that they live in a nature reserve, where nothing can happen to them.[3] A telegram for Dorothy, saying [in English] 'at last arrived', came only today, quite significant.[4]

I provisionally terminated the new work today except for additions and corrections that can only be done in Vienna. I now have the impression that it was quite superfluous.[5] The prosthesis fluctuates between bad days and good ones; it's all right on the whole.[6] Braun, whom I asked whether Karolyi was up to protracted work, said in his very friendly reply that he was not very sick and I should put myself in his care[7] and spare myself the trip to Berlin.[8] My gallbladder problems are occurring with too much frequency; I have little desire to compete seriously with the German Reich chancellor.[9]

I wanted to tell you that you shouldn't get upset by Jones's torments[10] and the whole Congress; treat Oxford as an interesting adventure and simply be happy that you didn't marry Jones.[11] A very reassuring telegram just arrived from Eitingon, which hopefully will not be followed by disappointment.[12] At least it will be a distraction for you if I tell you about all of the minor events from the world of Schneewinkl.[13] I should also add that Oli sent some very good pictures of the house and the children. It's true that he is having a hard time as a photographer,[14] but he will make good. We had our daily thunderstorm again today; after a long search Lun[15] was found in the coal box. Lux met the Landauers[16] at the lake and thanked them for their kindness.[17] Yesterday I won around 9 M at tarock from Ernst and Lux; the ambitious woman has really retained something from the Tegel lessons. As a preliminary celebration of Mama's birthday, Ernst (maj.)[18] and Victor[19] angled[20] a small trout from our own pond.[21] Now you know everything and I send you affectionate greetings to Oxford.

Papa

1 'Ernst and Lux have taken advantage of Anna's absence and are living with us. [. . .] Like Wolf, I can hardly wait for her return. I write, and he spends half the day lying apathetically in his basket' ⟨Freud/Andreas-Salomé, 28 July 1929, p. 182⟩.

2 'Georg Wein was a Königssee boatman and wood carver.' He was also the janitor of Villa Schneewinkl, and his wife, Agathe, 'cooked for the Freud family and kept house' ⟨Chaussy, pp. 192, 196⟩. The 'pilot' could have been him – or another member of the extended family, who all operated motorboats as well. ⟨I thank Helene Hinterbrandner, Schönau, for the kind information.⟩

3 The Königssee and surrounding area (already since 1910 a 'flora conservation area') had been made a nature reserve in 1921 in which 'the collection, capture or killing of non-huntable animals of all kinds' was forbidden ⟨Local Police Regulations for Nature Reserves on Königssee, 18 March 1921, §4, in: *Nationalpark Berchtesgaden* [n.d.], p. 87; Zierl, pp. 9f.; Floericke, p. 34; Köhler, pp. 1f., 26, 28⟩. Today the area, with 'absolute' nature conservation, forms the foundation of the significantly enlarged Berchtesgaden Alpine and National Park, which was awarded the European Diploma of Protected Areas in 1990 ⟨*Nationalpark Berchtesgaden* [1990], [1991]⟩. Freud was familiar with the 'mother of nature reserve thinking', the Yellowstone Park idea (1872) ⟨Zierl, pp. 9f.; Floericke, p. 32⟩: in his 'Formulation on the Two Principles of Mental Functioning', he referred to it as a metaphor for the use of fantasy free from reality testing ⟨1911*b*, p. 222; also in 1924*e*, p. 187⟩.

4 'Dorothy is getting ready to leave at 11 o'clock,' wrote Freud on 23 July to Martin. It appears from a letter to Ruth Mack-Brunswick of 21 July 1929 ⟨Fichtner [2008*b*]⟩ that she travelled with three children to a sister in France, possibly out of fear because of the impending visit from her husband, who had come with his father from the USA to try to persuade Dorothy or at least the children to return. This attempt, like earlier ones, was unsuccessful ⟨Freud/Ferenczi III, 1133 and elsewhere; Burlingham, M., pp. 199–205; Heller, pp. 74–8; Anna/Eva, letter 12 and note 2⟩. See 281 AF and note 3.

5 *Civilization and Its Discontents* (1930*a*); 'It deals with civilization, sense of guilt, happiness and similar lofty topics, and strikes me, no doubt rightly, as very superfluous – in contrast to earlier works, which always sprang from some inner necessity' ⟨Freud/Andreas-Salomé, 28 July 1929, p. 181⟩.

6 Schröder had performed a 'long-anticipated adjustment' of the previous year's prosthesis from 11 to 22 March 1929; Anna had again insisted on accompanying her father in Martha's stead ⟨Anna/Lou, letters 322, 323; Anna/Eva, letter

8; Freud/Ferenczi III, 1159 F, 5 March 1929, p. 364, and PS to 1154 F⟩. Lou came to visit for a few days on the 14th ⟨Anna/Lou, letter 324; Anna/Eva, letter 6⟩.

7 Károlyi, a Hungarian dentist and assistant of Schröder, continued to treat Freud after the spring session: 'Your countryman Károlyi . . . is doubtless very bright and skilful, but up to now we are having little success, and I am not yet certain whether I won't have to make the great sacrifice of a trip to Berlin' ⟨Freud/Ferenczi III, 1165 F, 10 June 1929, p. 369; also 1164 Fer⟩. Károlyi's condition worsened, however, and he later had to decline treating Freud ⟨Freud to Ernst, 26 August 1929⟩.

8 Freud had to go to Berlin after all, and Anna once again accompanied him (from 15 September to 21 October 1929; see also 261 SF, note 2) ⟨Jones III, p. 155; Anna/Eva, letters 15–21⟩. (And again in 1930: see text after 255 SF.)

9 Prince Otto von Bismarck (1815–98), who suffered throughout his life from various illnesses, including persistent stomach cramps and bilious attacks ⟨Richter [1962], e.g., pp. 55, 198f., 200f., 236f.; Ulrich⟩.

10 Spelling mistake (no umlaut) in the original. In contrast to Freud, Anna and Ferenczi, Jones adopted a pro-American attitude to lay analysis and attempted to assert this in the discussions. Ferenczi reported 'on the whole extremely unpleasant and arduous' Congress in Oxford 'which friend Jones strove, where possible, to make even more disagreeable for us' ⟨Freud/Ferenczi III, 1168 Fer, 9 September 1929, p. 370; also 1177 F; see also Freud/Jones, letter 542; also letters 505, 506, 509; Freud/Ferenczi III, 1927–9, *passim*; Freud/Eitingon, e.g., 548 F; Jones III, p. 156⟩.

11 See 42 SF–45 AF; see also 251 SF and note 3.

12 Telegram of 25 July 1929 on 'satisfactory provisional understanding' at the pre-conference ⟨Freud/Eitingon, 552 E, 25 July 1929, p. 647⟩.

13 These included the many daily visitors whom Freud received alongside his living-in guests: 'Guests, guests of all kinds, dearest and most inconsequential' ⟨Freud to Ruth, 13August, 1 July 1929; Freud/Andreas-Salomé, 28 July 1929, p. 182; Jones III, p. 155; Freud/Eitingon, 551 E, 555 E (p. 649), 556 E; Burlingham, M., p. 196⟩. See 251 SF and note 3.

14 Oliver had practised this profession earlier: 'Oli photographs, enlarges, makes projectors and the like' ⟨Freud to Martin, 16 February 1919; also Anna/Lou, letters 44, 71; Jones II, p. 462⟩. After emigration with his family in 1933 to France (initially Paris), he later ran a photography shop in Nice ⟨Molnar [1996], pp. 181, 192, 210, 224; Freud/Eitingon, 809 E⟩.

15 Lün Yu (also Lun Yug), a black chow dog that Dorothy had given to Freud in June of the previous year ⟨Freud/Eitingon, 505 F⟩. It was run over by a train shortly after this letter was written; it tore itself away from the leash as Eva Rosenfeld was bringing it home from Berchtesgaden (see note 19) to Vienna ⟨Jones III, p. 150; Anna/Eva, letter 14; Burlingham, M., pp. 193f.⟩. Freud received another dog from Dorothy a few months later; see 273 AF and note 2.

16 Karl Landauer (1887–1945), doctor of medicine, psychiatrist, training as psychoanalyst in 1912 with Freud; 1913 member of the Vienna Psychoanalytic Society and of the German group from 1919. In that year he moved to Frankfurt where he practised as an analyst from 1923. He also devoted himself to building up institutions in south Germany and to interdisciplinary exchange with university clinics. He was co-organizer of the First German Meeting for Psychoanalysis in Würzburg in 1924, organized the Congresses in Bad Homburg

(1925) and Wiesbaden (1932) and, in close cooperation with the Institute for Social Research (under Max Horkheimer and Theodor W. Adorno), played an important role in the founding of the Frankfurt Psychoanalytic Institute, which he headed together with Heinrich Meng ⟨Brecht et al., pp. 50f.; Laier [1989]; for his friendship with Horkheimer, see Rothe [2004]⟩. At the opening, on 16 February 1929, a highly acclaimed series of lectures was inaugurated, to which Anna also contributed on 28 February with a lecture on the importance of psychoanalysis for teachers (1929*a*) ⟨Anna to Eitingon, 12 December 1928, 20 February, 5 March 1929⟩. Landauer kept up regular contact with Freud. In 1933 he was forced to flee with his family to the Netherlands. After several years working as a training analyst in Amsterdam, he was arrested in 1943 with his wife, Karoline, and daughter, Eva, and deported to Bergen-Belsen concentration camp in 1944, where he died of hunger in 1945. His family was rescued and emigrated to New York ⟨Landauer; Rothe [1991], pp. 13–23; Brecht et al., p. 56⟩.

17 Presumably the provision of cigars. Landauer's brother-in-law had a top-quality cigar commerce in the Netherlands ⟨I thank Hans-Joachim Rothe⟩. See also Freud's entry 'cigars from Landauer' in the *Diary of Sigmund Freud* ⟨1992*i*, 3 January 1930, p. 2⟩ and Freud/Eitingon, 743 E, 744 F.

18 Ernst major as opposed to Ernstl Halberstadt, who was now usually called Ernst as well.

19 Victor (Vicki) Rosenfeld (born 1919; later Victor Ross), son of Eva and Valentin Rosenfeld. He spent the holidays here with the other children; his mother was alternately at Grundlsee, Schönau (4–6 July), and from 8 July to the end of the month in Berchtesgaden, some of the time together with Julius Obermann. When Eva moved to Berlin in the summer of 1931, Victor attended the progressive school in Marienau until 1933 and then accompanied his mother on her long road to their emigration together in 1936 to London ⟨Anna/Eva, letter 32, note; I thank Victor Ross for checking all comments relating to him and his parents⟩.

20 A year later, Anna found an explanation for Victor's enthusiasm for fishing: 'I think I know what Vicki's fishing means. Ernst's boy, Gabriel [Anna's nephew], has the same thing. It is such a passion with him that the mere anticipation of it gets him excited in all sorts of ways. I'll tell you about it in Grundlsee' ⟨Anna/Eva, letter 28, 28 June 1930, p. 142⟩.

21 A pond which – as in Dietfeldhof or on Thumsee – belonged to the property was particularly appreciated as an asset in a holiday location ⟨Freud 1985*c*, letter 270, p. 447; Gödde [2003], ill. pp. 58, 59⟩.

258 SF[1]

ANNA FREUD LADY MARGARET HALL OXFORD[2]

KOENIGSSEE [Schneewinkl] 26 [July 1919] 17.20

[Receipt stamp and note:] OXFORD 26JY29 6.36 [p.m.]

[in English]
ENJOYED THE THREE WIRES[3] MAMAS BIRTHDAY
PLEASANT HEAT SEEMS BROKEN
[unsigned]

1 Telegram.
2 This was the venue of the International Psychoanalytic Congress from 27 to 31 July. It was the first Congress of analysts to be held in England: 'It is not easy to find a more interesting venue for a congress than this worthy home of old English culture and scholarship' ⟨Anna Freud in the introduction to the Congress report, *IZ*, vol. 15 (1929), pp. 509–42⟩.
3 See 259 SF and notes 3–5.

259 SF[1]

PROF. DR. FREUD [Schneewinkl] 26 July 1929
Vienna, IX. Berggasse 19

Four letters for you. From Ruth Sw.[2] a cheque for $280, which I am sending to Martin, who will hold the amount for you. Very pleased to receive teleg[rams] from you,[3] Eit[ingon],[4] Ferenczi.[5] Thank Brill for me.[6] Birthday[7] here in full swing. Affectionately,
Papa

1 Letter card.
2 Ruth Sweetser (see 215 SF, note 3), whose six-year-old daughter, Adelaide, was being analysed by Anna ⟨Burlingham, M., pp. 156, 164, 168f., 189; Young-Bruehl, p. 132⟩. This girl played an important role in the formation of Anna's theory of child analysis; she was the 'devil' in Anna's lectures and publications ⟨1927*a*, 1928; in *Writings I*, e.g., pp. 8, 17, 28, 33, 41–3, 61–4, 167–71, 172⟩.
3 Missing.
4 See 257 SF and note 12.
5 Ferenczi wired on 26 July [in English]: 'At last everything hopeful' ⟨Freud/Ferenczi III, 1167 Fer, 26 July 1929, p. 370⟩. This refers to the problem of lay analysis, in which Ferenczi was firmly on Freud's side. In a Congress paper on 28 July ⟨Ferenczi 1929⟩, however, there were the first hints of a technique bringing about a further development in psychoanalysis by Ferenczi. See his own description in Freud/Ferenczi III, 1223 Fer, and also earlier, e.g., III, 902 Fer, 15 May 1922, p. 80. Berman (p. 491) even indicates that the theoretical differences already existed in the earliest stages of the relationship between Freud and Ferenczi. See also below, 287 SF.
6 No final training proposal was elaborated at the Congress; the participants agreed to continue consultations until the following Congress; see 288 SF, note 4. A schism in the Association was avoided in this way ⟨*IZ*, vol. 15, pp. 524–8; Jones III, pp. 156f.⟩. 'The credit for allaying this danger is certainly due to you and Brill,' wrote Freud on 4 August to Jones. 'I have already thanked him and now thank you too' ⟨Freud/Jones, letter 541, p. 661⟩.
7 Of Martha Freud.

260 AF[1]

prof freud schneewinkel
berchtesgaden

oxford 26 [July 1929]
[Receipt stamp and note:] 27/7 29 10.26

more tradition than comfort[2] surviving = anna

1 Telegram.
2 Freud's comments on Anna's accommodation: 'I expect you know that the English, having created the notion of comfort, then refused to have anything more to do with it' ⟨Freud/Andreas-Salomé, 28 July 1929, p. 182⟩.

261 SF[1]

ANNA FREUD LADY MARGARET HALL OXFORD
KOENIGSSEE OBY [Schneewinkl] 27 [July 1929] 14
[Receipt stamp and note:] OXFORD 27JY29 3.38 [p.m.]

[in English]
SORRY YOU SUFFER[2] FOR THE GLORY OF THE NAME
[unsigned]

1 Telegram.
2 'Anna wished for some follow-up analysis after the excitement of the Congress' ⟨Freud to Ruth, 13 August 1929⟩. This was also later continued during the stay in Tegel ⟨Anna/Eva, letter 17⟩. Freud wrote to Ruth Mack-Brunswick on 15 May 1929 about such follow-up analysis: 'I [. . .] really emphasized the inadequacy of teaching analysis compared with a therapeutic one and recommended a periodic new analysis to wash out the adverse effects of analytical work.'

262 AF[1]

professor freud schneewinkel
berchtesgaden

oxford 29 [July 1929]
[Receipt stamp and note:] 29/7 29 12.40

lecture[2] very successful[3] no disgrace for family good atmosphere = anna

1 Telegram.
2 'Anna is having rather a hard time in Oxford; by this evening she will have given her paper and will then, I hope, take things more easily' ⟨Freud/Andreas-Salomé, 28 July 1929, p. 182⟩. The lecture was entitled 'A Counterpart to the Animal Phobias of Children' (1929*b*). Anna gave the same lecture the following year on 26 February to the Vienna group, where it was also discussed ⟨*IZ*, vol. 16 (1930), p. 547⟩. In *IZ*, vol. 15 (1929), p. 518, there is just a short review by the author. The content of the lecture was later included in Anna's book *The Ego and the Mechanisms of Defence* (1936).

3 [in English] 'Her Vortrag was certainly the most interesting and the most applauded of all; everyone was full of admiration for her gifts' ⟨Jones to Freud in: Freud/Jones, letter 542, 20 August 1929, p. 662⟩.

263 AF[1]

professor freud schneewinkel
bgaden

oxford 30 [July 1929]
[Receipt stamp and note:] 30/7 29 14.20

most peaceful business meeting[2] greatest unity re-elected[3] = anna

1 Telegram.
2 The Business Meeting on 30 July, at the beginning of which Eitingon as chairman of the Congress presented Jones with two commemorative issues of the *Zeitschrift* and *Journal* in honour of his fiftieth birthday, quoting Freud's oration (1929*a*); the Congress report does not indicate whether Anna read it 'at the formal celebration', as Young-Bruehl (p. 180) states ⟨*IZ*, vol. 15 (1929), pp. 509–42, the quote pp. 530f.; see also Freud/Jones, letter 534, p. 656⟩.
3 The entire central board was re-elected: Eitingon as president of the International Psychoanalytical Association, Ferenczi and Jones as board members, Anna as secretary and Ophuijsen as treasurer ⟨*IZ*, ibid., p. 542⟩.

264 SF[1]

ANNA FREUD LADY MARGARET HALL OXFORD
BERCHTESGADEN 31 [July 1929] 8.45
[Receipt stamp and note:] OXFORD 31JY29 11.50

[in English]
ALL FEELING LONELY[2] ALL S WELL THAT ENDS WELL[3]
[unsigned]

1 Telegram.
2 Anna had already jokingly hoped for this in 1920 (see final sentences of 129 AF and 132 AF).
3 See 252 SF and note 2.

265 AF[1]

professor freud schneewinkel
berchtesgaden
[Handwritten comment by Berchtesgaden post office] Schneewinkel?
london 1 [August 1929]
[Receipt stamp and note:] 1/8 29 14.33

everything finished[2] fly holland onward train wire arrival relieved see you again
[unsigned]

1 Telegram.
2 Misspelt in telegram.

266 AF[1]

professor freud schneewinkel
berchtesgaden

amsterdam 1 [August 1929]
[Receipt stamp and note:] 1/8 29 20.30

rapid stormy flight[2] to night train arrive berchtesgadn 17.50 says mathilde = anna

1 Telegram.
2 Anna flew for the first time in May (to rent Schneewinkl): 'Yesterday and the day before I flew properly, from here to Salzburg and back. . . . It was magnificent. We were 3,000 m over the entire Salzkammergut and the lakes and snow-capped mountains. One is much happier in the air than on the ground' ⟨Anna/Lou, letter 325, 10 May 1929, p. 570⟩.

267 AF[1]

freud berggasse 19
wien 9

koeln 18/12 [1929] 11.30
[Receipt stamp:] 18 DEC

as beast of burden in foggy cologne preliminary trip success outstanding[2]
[unsigned]

1 Telegram.
2 The reason for this trip is unknown.

268 AF[1]

freud berggasse 19 wien 9

essen 18 [December 1929] 2330
[Receipt stamp:] 18 DEC 1[2]

good over relieved tomorrow goettingen
[unsigned]

1 Telegram.
2 Time illegible.

269 AF[1]

freud berggasse 19 wien 9

goettingen 19 [December 1929] 2050
[Receipt stamp:] 19. DEC 29 22[2]

very pleased with lon[3] stopping nuremberg arrive saturday [21 December] early
[unsigned]

1 Telegram.
2 Time illegible.
3 Lou Andreas-Salomé had a foot injury which made her unable to walk for several months ⟨Anna/Lou, letters 330–5; Freud/Andreas-Salomé, 4 January 1930, p. 184⟩. It is unclear whether Anna's visit was in connection with it or whether she just took the opportunity on the way back from Cologne/Essen. There is no evidence in these letters that Dorothy Burlingham accompanied Anna on this trip, as Young-Bruehl, pp. 222f., writes (with no source reference).

1930

270 AF

Evening
Nauders, Tuesday [16 September 1930][1]

Dear All,
Austria is too small; we are already at the frontier.[2] The sun came out as we got out in Landeck. We travelled as far as Pfunds with the post bus, then hiked over Finstermünz to here. The walking is easy. Now we are waiting for the rucksacks[3] and will travel with them on to Reschen; tomorrow to Sulden.

The snow is very close, the air wonderful, everything very beautiful and peaceful. The telephone was very faint but understandable.

We are looking forward very much to what awaits us.

The first adventure was a beautiful young fox that ran across our path before we had even reached Salzburg.

We are very well.[4]
Greetings to all.
Anna

[In her own handwriting:] Dorothy

1 The classification of this letter is suggested by the course of the trip and is further confirmed by the penultimate sentence in 280 AF. Freud's entry 'Anna left with Dorothy', in *The Diary of Sigmund Freud* ⟨1992*i*, p. 6⟩, is dated 15 September. The undated letter from Milan quoted in the commentary in Molnar [1996], p. 82, belongs to 1927; see 213 AF and note 2.

2 'Anna . . . today went on a Swiss-Italian tour with her friend Dorothy,' wrote Freud on 16 September to Ferenczi ⟨Freud/Ferenczi III, 1195 F, 16 September 1930, p. 399⟩. They followed a similar route to the one taken by Freud and Minna Bernays in 1898 ⟨Freud 2002*b*, pp. 95–109⟩. Dorothy left her four children in Grundlsee in the care of a minder, Margot Goldschmidt. The statement by Burlingham, M., p. 216, that Dorothy drove Anna through Switzerland and Italy in her car at this time is incorrect.

3 'I have everything I need in my knapsack. Maybe that is all one ever needs'

⟨Anna/Eva, letter 34 [correct:] 17 September 1930, p. 150⟩. For Anna's earlier plan of doing a 'knapsack' trip, see 69 AF and note 6.

4 Anna had earlier complained repeatedly of exhaustion. Already under the greatest strain through her own increasing workload, she had overexerted herself in the previous months – also as the private companion and professional spokeswoman for her father (see Introduction, p. 9). In spring she moved with Freud to the Cottage Sanatorium from 22 April to 3 May, where he had 'fled' on account of heart and intestinal ailments ⟨Freud/Ferenczi III, 1187, 7 May 1930, p. 392⟩. Immediately afterwards she spent the months of May to July with him in Berlin-Tegel, while a new prosthesis was made (see end of text after 255 SF). Despite the pleasant surroundings, she had even yearned for 'some peace and quiet, which is not easy to come by, not even in Tegel' ⟨Anna/Eva, letter 22, 15 May 1930, p. 132⟩. The subsequent summer holiday in Grundlsee (see 271 AF and note 2) was also interrupted repeatedly by duties. From 27 to 29 August, Anna travelled to Frankfurt am Main to accept the Goethe Prize on her father's behalf: 'Anna will represent me and read aloud what I bring together about Goethe's relationship to analysis' ⟨Freud/Ferenczi III, 1193 F, 1 August 1930, p. 398; Freud 1930*d* and *e*; Jones III, p. 161f.; Freud to Martin, 25 August 1930⟩. And the day before her departure she was at the burial of Freud's mother, who had died on 12 September. 'Again, Anna represented, as in Frankfurt. Her importance to me can hardly be increased' ⟨Freud/Jones, letter 564, 15 September 1930, p. 677; see also Jones III, p. 162; 1992*i*, 12 and14 September, p. 7⟩. Dorothy also needed to convalesce, not least on account of tuberculosis, the treatment of which included exercise in the fresh air ⟨Molnar [1996], p. 67⟩. See also 281 AF and note 3.

271 AF[1]

Freud Rebenburg
Grundlsee[2]

Resia Adige[3] 17/9 1930 9 H 20 M

Beautiful morning off to Sulden happy
[unsigned]

1 Telegram.

2 Freud and some of the family spent the summer from 27 July to 27 September in the former estate of the aristocratic Rebenburg family, in the 'Archkogl' on the shores of the Grundlsee, near Aussee in the Salzkammergut ⟨1992*i*, p. 6; Freud to Ernst, 29 September 1930; Anna/Eva, 1930, *passim*, somewhat divergent data in Anna/Lou, letter 339, Freud/Ferenczi III, 1193 F, Jones III, pp. 161, 163; I thank the Steiermärkisches Landesarchiv, Graz, for information about Rebenburg⟩. 'My grandfather rented a huge house in Grundlsee. . . . The Burlinghams were living in one of the houses in the village as there was no neighbouring house next to the Rebenburgs' ⟨Freud, W. E. [1987], pp. 211f.⟩. See 277 SF, note 6. '[We have] found something particularly beautiful this year. It is generally agreed that we have never lived so well' ⟨Freud to Alexander, 8 August 1930⟩. As earlier in Semmering, Tegel and Schneewinkl, Freud and also Anna continued to treat some of their patients or students in their summer residence ⟨Jones III, pp. 110, 133f., 163; Anna/Eva, letters 5, 27, 32, 23, note 3; Anna/Lou, letter 240⟩.

3 Resia Pass (Reschenpass).

272 AF[1]

Freud
Rebenburg
Grundlsee

Solda Sgeltrude[2] 17/9 1930 15 H
[Receipt note;] 18/9 1930 8 H 30 M

Cold & beautiful tomorrow lunchtime Trafoi greetings
[unsigned]

1 Telegram.
2 Solda Santa Geltrude (St Gertraud, Sulden). 'It is very beautiful and at every stage of the way I leave a bit of unrest behind. I was at the house of a peasant woman who still spins and weaves loden cloth. But not while doing analyses' ⟨Anna/Eva, letter 34 [correct:] 17 September 1930, p. 150⟩.

273 AF[1]

Freud
Rebenburg
Grundlsee

Santa Geltrude Solda 18/9 1930 10 H

Blazing sunshine how is Jofi[2]
[unsigned]

1 Telegram.
2 Also yo-fie or Yofie, a new dog received by Freud as a replacement for Lün Yu ⟨1992*i*, 9 March 1930, p. 4⟩. Dorothy had brought it from Paris in September 1929, together with a 'second' Lün Yu, who was persecuted so jealously by Jofi, however, that Dorothy took it herself; see 287 SF, note 19. Jofi died in 1937 after an operation; Freud was then given back Lün Yu II and took it with him on his emigration to England in 1938 ⟨Freud/Andreas-Salomé, 23 March 1930; Burlingham, M., pp. 194, 205; Jones III, pp. 150, 226, 246; Molnar [1996], pp. 61, 214, 215, 237, 240, 252⟩.

274 AF[1]

Freud
Rebenburg
Grundlsee

Trafoi 18/9 1930 16 H 20 M

Wonderful morning Bagni Nuovi Bormio
[unsigned]

1 Telegram.

275 AF[1]

Freud
Rebenburg
Grundlsee

Bormio Bagni 19/9 1930 15 H 50 M
[Receipt note:] 19/9 1930 17 H 20 M

Drove through mist to Stilfse[r]joch on top sun and ice wonderful impression morning to lunchtime here sunny delightful[2]
News service brilliant post office St Moritz
[unsigned]

1 Telegram.
2 The transcription is in Gothic handwriting with only this word in Latin script with a U-shaped arc over the 'n' [of the German 'reizend'], indicating that it was probably misread (possibly 'hot and'?).

276 SF[1]

Frl Anna Freud
Poste restante
St. Moritz Bad
Engadin
Switzerland

Grundlsee
19 September 1930
[Postmark:] BAD AUSSEE 20.9.1930

My dear Anna,
As your telegram doesn't distinguish between village and spa, I am sending this card to the *spa* to inform you that the letter has been sent to the *village*. You will no doubt visit both places. Affectionate wishes for continued enjoyable travels.
Papa

1 Postcard with a small illustration on the sender side: 'Feldkirch – Vorarlberg'.

277 SF

PROF. DR. FREUD

19 September 1930
Grundlsee
Vienna, IX. Berggasse 19

My dear Anna,
There is little to say in addition to the telegrams.[1] Nausch didn't want to take Jofi at all, but I was right to insist.[2] I heard today that it has an

intestinal disorder and is playing happily with Wolf. Needless to say,[3] we miss the animal at every turn.

Everything has changed here through the departures and arrivals;[4] nothing is the same at all. The weather has been inconsistent, but not terrible; today, however, there was a strong sirocco. The three elderly ladies[5] had headaches and took medicine. The young ones, Ruth and Eva,[6] are just particularly tired, and I had a heart condition. Apart from that I have been well up to now and even my stomach is almost better.[7] It should be over by tomorrow. At least Ruth has not cancelled the missed visit that Dr Schur, her personal physician, wanted to make up.[8] I am reporting only to keep my promise[9] to be a reliable chronicler.

All of your mail is enclosed in this envelope except for the report[10] by Horney[11] and a colossal issue of a Spanish newspaper, *El Mundo*, which Marin[12] sent you from Habana.[13]

I hope you manage to do everything you have planned and have a pleasant trip.

Affectionate greetings to you and Dorothy
from Papa

PS I have sent a card to St Moritz-Bad.

1 Missing.
2 Nausch is the name of the kennels in Kagran where the Freuds housed their dogs when required (see 244 AF and note 8). Ernst appears to have brought Jofi to Vienna first ⟨1992*i*, 18 September 1930, p. 7⟩. From there it was taken by a veterinarian to Kagran: 'She was suffering and caused us concern' ⟨Freud/Eitingon, 610 F, 18 September 1930, p. 689⟩.
3 Spelling mistake (no umlaut) in the original.
4 Marie Bonaparte and Ernst Freud had departed. Eva Rosenfeld and Freud's sister Dolfi had arrived ⟨1992*i*, 17 September, 18 September 1930, p. 7⟩. In the previous weeks, apart from Mathilde, Alexander with Sophie and Harry, and Ernstl, who were all staying for a longer time, there had been a constant stream of visitors (see 251 SF, note 3) ⟨Molnar [1996], pp. 79–82; Freud, W. E. [1987], p. 211; Freud to Martin, 11 August 1930⟩. Gustav Freud (a relative now living in New York) also recalls a family visit in summer 1930 from Aussee to Rebenburg, which he made as a sixteen-year-old with his father. ⟨I thank him for this personal information, November 2002.⟩
5 Martha, Minna and Dolfi.
6 Ruth Mack-Brunswick and Marie Bonaparte had rented 'a small chateau together at the other end of the lake' ⟨Freud, W. E. [1987], p. 212⟩. Eva Rosenfeld, who frequently spent time in Grundlsee and had also arranged Freud's accommodation, was staying with her son in another rented house. ⟨I thank Victor Ross for the personal information, 22 June 2004.⟩
7 In spring Freud had had to spend some time in the Cottage Sanatorium on account of these ailments (see 270 AF, note 4).
8 Max Schur (1897–1969), doctor of medicine, specialist in internal medicine and psychoanalyst, had already met Freud at the start of his studies in the winter semester of 1915–16 and 1916–17 as a listener at his *Lectures* (1916–17*a*). From

1924 to 1930 he trained as an analyst and attended the Vienna Psychoanalytic Society as a guest in 1931, before joining the Society in 1933. In early March 1929 Freud had asked him to be his personal physician ⟨Schur, pp. 2, 407–9 (on p. 408 he states that his personal analysis started in 1925); Jones III, p. 154⟩. Schur had married in summer 1930 ⟨Mühlleitner, p. 294⟩; it is possible that the 'missed visit' is connected with this.

9 See 111 AF and 112 SF, second paragraph, and the end of 114 AF.

10 Horney [1930]; Anna later included this report in the 'Korrespondenzblatt' written by her in the *Zeitschrift*.

11 Karen Horney (1885–1952), doctor of medicine, psychiatrist and psychoanalyst with her own practice in Berlin, was secretary at the time of the local Berlin group, in which she played an important role. She worked as a training and control analyst at the Psychoanalytic Polyclinic and the Institute. Abraham had already written about her in 1912: 'The paper showed, for once, a real comprehension of the subject; unfortunately something rather infrequent in the talks in our circle' ⟨Freud/Abraham, 25 February 1912, p. 148⟩. She was the first public critic of Freud's theories of femininity. While remaining true to psychoanalysis, she gradually distanced herself from its orthodox idea of women and developed her own concept. In 1932, following an invitation by Franz Alexander, she went to the USA and became co-founder and deputy director of the Chicago Institute of Psychoanalysis. In 1934 she moved to New York, joined the Psychoanalytic Society there in 1935, taught at the New School for Social Research and turned her interest to the cultural influence on the development of the individual. After leaving the psychoanalytic group, she founded the Association for the Advancement of Psychoanalysis in 1941 and remained active until her death ⟨Rubins [1980]; Paris [1994]; Sayers, pp. 73–119⟩.

12 Unknown. It could be the Chilean author Juan Marín (1900–63), whose main work, *Paralelo 53° Sur* (1936), is a story of the fate of the mass of humanity ruled by greed, envy, alcohol and sex. It is possible that Marín, a correspondent of *El Mundo*, was at the award of the Goethe Prize in Frankfurt and had met Anna there. ⟨There is no list of participants in the Goethe Prize archive. I thank Elmar Stracke, Institut für Stadtgeschichte – Zeitgeschichte, Frankfurt, for his friendly information, 2 July 2003.⟩

13 Havana, capital of Cuba; Spanish La Habana [in full San Cristóbal de la Habana].

278 AF[1]

Freud
Febenburg
Grundlsee

Bormia[2] Bagni 20/9 1930 14 H 20 M

Rain staying overnight Poschiave[3] tomorrow still uncertain
[unsigned]

1 Telegram.
2 Correct: Bormio.
3 Correct: Poschiavo.

279 AF[1]

Freud
Rebenburg
Grundlsee

Pos[ch]iavo 21/9 1930 10 H 10 M

Cleared up new wanderlust[2] telegram Hotel Berninahospiz happy greetings [unsigned]

1 Telegram.
2 Dorothy's four children had also gone on a cheerful hiking tour during their absence – accompanied by their minder (see 270 AF, note 2) ⟨Margot Goldschmidt to Dorothy Burlingham, 20 September 1930, quoted in Burlingham, M., p. 216 (and note p. 534)⟩.

280 AF

Sunday, 21 September [1930]
In bed in Berninahospiz

Dear All,
I am sure you think we are going in a zigzag. From Bormio, which is quite delightful and where hot water comes right out of the rocks, we descended in a real Italian bus to Tirano and then right back up again to Poschiavo with the Bernina railway. It rained on that day. But today we woke up to blazing sunshine, put our rucksacks on the train and went up the Bernina road. It was quite magnificent, around five or six hours, but we gave ourselves the whole day.

Only the last quarter of an hour at the top of the pass was it icy with snow next to the road. So many snow-capped mountains and glaciers, that one is no longer amazed by them.

Now we are already in bed in the Bernina shelter, 2,300 m up, but quite warm and comfortable, having eaten a lot beforehand. The barometer has fallen a bit, but hopefully it won't be followed by bad weather, because tomorrow is meant to be the best part of the route.

I called yesterday because I hadn't received a telegram. Even if the line is bad, it is still great that it works at all. The connection from Bormio to Grundlsee took only fifteen minutes.[1]

We are very well. I am looking forward to receiving letters in St Moritz and hearing more from you all. Tomorrow we will have been away for a week.

Very many greetings to all,
Your Anna

1 In Vienna, Freud had already used the telephone before 1899 (albeit rarely). In a letter to Jung of 16 April 1909, he connected the telephone number of the time with an analysis of his number superstition ⟨Freud/Jung, letter 139 F, p. 219⟩.

281 AF

Monday evening [22 September 1930] in
Pontresina

Dear Papa,
I am very sorry to hear that you are having such bad weather. We are doing so well and I would have preferred that it were the same for you. I once again got your telegrams very quickly, yesterday in Bernina and today in Pontresina; just the second one to Bormio must have got lost.[1]

We had a wonderful day today. We left the Bernina shelter in the morning in the freezing cold with snow flurries and hiked down slowly to Pontresina. The sun never quite came out but also never quite disappeared, and the weather was good. We stopped a while in Morteratsch, which was the most beautiful sight we have seen so far. We climbed up to the glacier and were in a wonderful ice cave that had been carved out of the tongue. Three large St Bernards, one even a prizewinner, live there. All of the blueberry leaves are autumn red and all the trees golden yellow. With the strange rocks and ice, it is a magnificent mix.

We were at first shocked by Pontresina, so many more hotels than we would have liked. You would think at first that there was no space left.[2]

Dorothy is now very fit and has lots of stamina.[3] Every night we sleep in a different bed.[4]

I would like to do a hiking tour like this every year, perhaps in Scandinavia next time.[5]

Only in the night do I dream of unrest, sessions, patients and everything[6] I don't think about them during the day.

I send you a kiss and hope that you are very well.

Your Anna

Tomorrow we collect the mail in St Moritz.

1 None of Freud's telegrams during this trip have survived.

2 See Minna's impression of Pontresina in 1898 on her trip with Freud (270 AF, note 2): 'Until late into the night Pontresina [has] as much life as Kärnterstrasse at Christmas, with dazzling sunshine and incredible snowfields. . . . Apparently it rarely rains here, but starts to snow straightaway' ⟨Minna Bernays to Martha Freud, in: Freud 2002*b*, pp. 108f.⟩.

3 For details of Dorothy's impaired health, see 270 AF, end of note 4. Since summer 1929 she had been additionally affected by the visit of her husband to Schneewinkl and the associated problems with the splitting up of the family (see 247 SF and note 4). At the same time she had had to manage the decorations for a change of apartment; on 27 September 1929 she moved to Berggasse 19 (two floors above the Freuds) with two children ⟨Burlingham, M., pp. 205f.; Anna/Eva, letter 16 and note 1; Anna/Lou, letter 331⟩.

4 'We would have been happy to sleep in a different bed every night, which is Sigi's ideal,' wrote Minna on 6 August 1898 to Martha Freud ⟨in: Freud 2002*b*, p. 101⟩.

5 In 1923 Anna had already dreamt of a trip to Scandinavia together with Lou Andreas-Salomé, who even then had a list of ideas: 'For Sweden I suggest we start a joint diary, where we enter *everything* from the most sublime to the most ridiculous; people, routes, science, art impressions, visits, business, analysis of innocents abroad, etc.' ⟨Anna/Lou, letters 91 and 92, the quotation p. 170⟩.
6 Grammar mistake in the original.

282 AF[1]

Freud Rebenburg
Grundlsee

St Moritz 23/9 1930 12 H 50 M

Sympathize rain letters[2] found telegram St Moritz village although too grand
[unsigned]

1 Telegram.
2 To Anna: 277 SF.

283 AF[1]

Freud Rebenburg
Grundlsee

St Moritz 24/9 1930 10 H–M

Interesting impression onward hiking telegram Maloja thanks all reports[2]
[unsigned]

1 Telegram.
2 Dorothy also received news, e.g., from Margot Goldschmidt and the children ⟨Burlingham, M., p. 216⟩.

284 AF[1]

Freud Rebenburg
Grundlsee

Maloja 24/9 1930 18 H 30 M
[Receipt note:] 25/9 1930 8 H 30 M

Most magnificent route blazing sunshine greetings
[unsigned]

1 Telegram.

285 AF[1]

Freud Rebenburg
Grundlsee

Trentonoto[2] 26/9 1930 13 H 40 M

Change of scenery s Bristoforo[3] telephoto rain address Cristoforo Trento Lagohotel
Freud

1 Telegram.
2 A place or telegraphic address with this name could not be found in the Italian list for 1930; nor is there such a place in Italy today ⟨Rete Territoriale, consulente 1, Rome, 12 December 2000; I thank Roberto Berni, Rome, for this research with the Italian postal authorities⟩. It could have come from a misunderstanding of Trento and a following Italian word. Freud had already had difficulties in 1912 with sending a cable to Cristoforo: 'I have sent you a long telegram but S. Cristof (or similar) is not in the lists' ⟨Freud to family, 3 September 1912, note in 2003*e*⟩.
3 San Cristoforo.

286 AF[1]

freud berggasse 19 – wien 9

bolzano 28 11/25
[Receipt stamp:] 28 SPT [1930] 13^{29}

greetings until arrival[2] goodbye
[unsigned]

1 Telegram. This is the last surviving communication from Anna in this correspondence.
2 From Grundlsee; see 271 AF, note 2.

1932

287 SF

Frl Anna Freud
Hotel Rose
Wiesbaden
Germany[1]

PROF. DR. FREUD

[Pötzleinsdorf[2]] 3 September 1932
Vienna, IX. Berggasse 19

My dear Anna,

So[3] the Ferenczis came before 4 o'clock.[4] She[5] as kind as ever, from him an icy coldness. Without further ado or greeting he began: I want to read you my paper.[6] This he did, and I listened appalled.[7] He has regressed completely to aetiological views, which I held thirty-five years ago and have abandoned, that the regular cause of neuroses is crude sexual dreams in childhood; he uses almost the same words as I did back then. Nothing about the technique by which he obtained this material, in the middle comments about the hostility of patients and the need to accept their criticism and to admit his errors to them. The conclusions confused, artificial and unclear. The whole thing in fact stupid or seemingly so because it is so insincere and incomplete. By now[8] you will have heard the paper for yourself and will be able to form your own opinion.

While he was reading it, Brill arrived and later caught up the part he had missed. The paper appeared harmless to me and can only damage him; it will no doubt spoil the mood on the first day.

I asked just two questions. The first, which I told him listeners would also ask, was how he had arrived at these trance phenomena that the rest of us don't see. His answers were evasive, reserved; asked about his objections to Oedipus, etc., he said that Brill's statements[9] were ambiguous, admitted certain differences from his version, which he could not, however, understand.[10] Brill whispered to me: [in English] he is not sincere. The same as with Rank only much sadder.[11]

My second question was why he had read the paper to me. Here, too, his view[12] was quite cold, and it transpired that he wants to become president after all.[13] I told him that I would not influence the election. My only[14] objection to him is that in that case you could pass on the burden of your position.[15] I believe, however, that his paper will put the mood against him.[16]

The days are now quieter. The tarock game for this evening has also been cancelled. Eva[17] was not really palatable; Ruth made a great fuss[18] before she decided – just now – to leave. Lün is very naughty,[19] Aunt is now (this morning) on your property.[20] My ear and nose specialist[21] is discharging me next week. As if to mock our departure, the days here are of Italian beauty.[22] Enjoy[23] yourself as much as you can in Wiesbaden and don't take anything that happens gravely and seriously.

Affectionately,
Papa

1 Handwritten address on the envelope with date stamp '3.IX.32 15 Uhr' and Freud's printed sender's address. Although filed separately under 1933, the envelope belongs to this letter: Anna was in Wiesbaden at the 12th International Psychoanalytic Congress, which took place from 4 to 7 September 1932 ⟨*IZ*, vol. 18 (1932), p. 265; vol. 19 (1933), pp. 239–74; Jones III, p. 179⟩. On the journey there she visited Lou Andreas-Salomé in Göttingen on 1–2 September ⟨Anna/Lou, letters 365, 367⟩. She returned to Vienna on 8 September ⟨1992*i*, p. 15; Freud/Eitingon, 739 F⟩.

2 On 14 May Freud's household moved for the summer months to Villa Mauthner in Khevenhüllerstr. 6, in the outlying Vienna district of Pötzleinsdorf, which had already served the previous year as summer quarters ⟨1992*i*, pp. 10, 14; Freud/Ferenczi III, 1207 F and note A; Molnar [1996], pp. 98f., 106⟩. Freud could receive his patients there and was himself within range of a doctor. Limited by illness, he could no longer venture too far from Vienna ⟨Jones III, p. 169⟩.

3 Anna had learnt about the impending visit from Ferenczi on 2 September before her departure ⟨Freud/Ferenczi III, 1235 Fer, 1236 Fer⟩.

4 It was the last meeting before Ferenczi's death on 22 May 1933 (Jones III, pp. 190f., incorrectly gives the date of death as 24 May) ⟨Freud 1992*i*, p. 19⟩. He was suffering from pernicious anaemia, which Freud did not know of, however, until early October ⟨Freud/Eitingon, 742 F, 743 E; Jones III, p. 185; Schur, p. 431; also Freud/Ferenczi III, 1243 Fer; Ferenczi/Groddeck, 20 March 1933, p. 87 (German version)⟩.

5 Gizella, widowed Pálos, née Altschul (1866–1949), married to Ferenczi since 1 March 1919. ⟨I thank Emanuel Berman for correcting the dates; the dates given in Freud/Jones, p. 709, and Freud/Ferenczi I, p. 70, are incorrect.⟩ Freud admired Gizella enormously ⟨e.g., Freud/Ferenczi III, 1225 F⟩. 'His perceptive and good wife let me know that I should think of him as a sick child,' he wrote to Jones shortly before the Congress ⟨Freud/Jones, letter 596, 12 September 1932, p. 709⟩.

6 Ferenczi [1933]; he had changed the title of the paper several times since May 1931 ⟨Freud/Ferenczi III 1206 Fer/Enclosure 2, 1208 Fer/Enclosure; *IZ* vol. 19 (1933), pp. 242, 5–15⟩.

7 Freud was not completely unprepared (see note 9): certain differences,

apparently of a technical nature at first, had already spread at the latest by May 1929 to theoretical areas (see 259 SF, note 5) ⟨Freud/Ferenczi III, end of 1928 to 1933, *passim*, e.g., 1210 Fer (p. 417), 1233 Fer (p. 441); Anna/Lou, letters 357, 360. See also Freud/Eitingon, *passim*, e.g., 727 F, 730 F; Jones III, pp. 183–6⟩.

8 The Congress began on 4 September but the First Scientific Session with Ferenczi's paper took place 'at 9 p.m. on Saturday, 3 September' ⟨*IZ*, vol. 19 (1933) pp. 242–4⟩. It could have been brought forward as a result of the differences of opinion of Jones, Eitingon, Brill and Ophuijsen as to whether Ferenczi's paper could be prevented altogether ⟨Freud/Jones, letters 595 and 613; Freud/Eitingon, 731 E; Jones III, p. 185⟩.

9 Brill had visited Freud on 23 and 24 August, and had then travelled with Radó to Budapest; after their return, they reported to Freud on 28 August on Ferenczi's health and his new departures ⟨Freud/Eitingon, 727 F, 730 F⟩.

10 Ferenczi had noted his technical innovations and the resultant theoretical consequences in a 'diary' in 1932, which Freud learnt of only after Ferenczi's death. At that time he 'expressed his admiration for Ferenczi's ideas, until then unknown to him' ⟨Balint [1988], p. 219⟩. The book did not appear in German until 1988, with the title *Ohne Sympathie keine Heilung. Das klinische Tagebuch von 1932*.

11 Otto Rank had gradually distanced himself from Freud since the latter's illness in 1923, and split from him in a process that was extremely painful to both sides ⟨Freud to Rank, 25 August 1924, in: 1960*a*, pp. 357–8; Freud/Jones, letter 438, 5 November 1924, p. 559⟩. He developed his own concepts, left the Vienna group in 1928 and practised first in Paris, then in New York, where he settled finally in 1935 and continued on his way until he died, a month after Freud ⟨Mühlleitner, pp. 250–3; Taft; Lieberman; Zottl⟩. In both cases – Rank and Ferenczi – Freud insisted that the disputes were not of his doing ⟨1992*l*, 29 December 1924; Freud/Andreas-Salomé, 17 November 1924; Freud/Eitingon, 727 F; Freud/Jones, letter 596, pp. 708f.; Freud/Ferenczi III, 979 F, 995 F, 1211 F, 1238 F, 1241 F⟩.

12 'Ansicht', probably written by mistake instead of 'Antwort' (= reply).

13 In previous years Ferenczi had failed on several occasions, for internal strategic reasons, to obtain the presidency, as was his due (e.g., 101AF, note 9). In spite of the many doubts that had arisen in the meantime, he had originally agreed but then retracted his agreement ⟨e.g., Freud/Ferenczi III, 1043 Fer, 1044 F, 1172 F, 1173 Fer, 1175 F, 1191 F, 1192 Fer, 1205 Fer, 1210–2 Fer, 1223–6 Fer; Freud/Eitingon, 460 F, 728 F⟩. 'After long, anguished hesitation', he had finally decided that it was not compatible with his 'intellectual constitution' ⟨Freud/Ferenczi III, 1233, 21 August 1932, p. 441⟩. He was now hesitant again, but Eitingon had meanwhile decided: 'After everything that has happened Ferenczi can no longer be a candidate for election' ⟨Freud/Eitingon, 731 E, 30 August 1932, p. 827; see also Jones III, pp. 183–5⟩.

14 The position of this word in the original is moved by an arrow, probably to change the sentence structure in connection with the subsequently added *Du* [you].

15 Freud had suggested this 'drastic measure' to pull Ferenczi out of the isolation by taking over the presidency, and assured him of Anna's assistance as secretary ⟨Freud/Ferenczi III, 1223 Fer (PS), 1225 F, p. 433, 1226 Fer⟩. His hope that Anna would have less of a burden if someone else was elected was not fulfilled; see 289 SF and note 6.

16 This did not occur, as Jones and Eitingon subsequently reported to Freud ⟨Freud/Jones, letter 595; Freud/ Eitingon, 737 E, 740 F⟩.
17 Eva Rosenfeld, who had lived in Berlin since 1931, frequently travelled between Germany and Austria and continued her analysis ⟨Anna/Eva, letter 32, note, B48–51 with note⟩.
18 'It isn't quiet here: Brill is already in Vienna, Saturday Ernst is coming, Sunday Radó, Tuesday Levys, Jeanne just left, and Ruth is having fits' ⟨Anna/Eva, letter 52, 25 August 1932, p. 175⟩.
19 Lün Yu II (see 273 AF and note 2) no doubt missed its mistress, Dorothy, who (as in 1931) lived in the neighbouring Villa Casimir with her family, but was absent on 20 August; see 288 SF, note 3 ⟨Burlingham, M., p. 216⟩.
20 Anna and Dorothy had bought this 'property' together in autumn 1931, 'a small farmhouse . . . in Hochrotherd near Breitenfurt . . . we are doing it up' ⟨Anna/Lou, letter 359, 22 October 1931, p. 600; letter 360; Anna to Ernst, 22 November 1931. Heller, p. 75, Anna/Eva, letter 25, note 2, Burlingham, M. p. 216, Young-Bruehl, p. 136 and Molnar [1996], p. 109 incorrectly give the year of purchase as 1930.⟩ Hochrotherd had now been furnished: 'I . . . am out there every afternoon with Dorothy, Ernstl or the children' ⟨Anna/Lou, letter 363, 25 March 1932, p. 604; also Anna/Eva, *passim*⟩. Two years previously, the two had just rented a weekend refuge in Neuhaus, south-west of Vienna, which 'didn't agree' with Dorothy ⟨Anna/Eva, letter 45, undated, p. 165; Anna/Lou, letters 334, 344⟩. Hochrotherd was thus the first step in the fulfilment of Anna's 'house dream' (see 36 AF and note 6). After emigration Anna and Dorothy purchased a country residence on the east coast of England, and in 1965 a holiday home in Ireland ⟨Burlingham, M., p. 290f.; Anna to Kata, 15 April 1965⟩.
21 Perhaps Dr Joseph Neumann, who had already treated Anna for otitis in 1917 and Freud's sinuses in 1924 ⟨Freud/Ferenczi II, 686 F, 22 June 1917; III, 970 F, 979 F [1924]; Pichler, p. 503⟩. For details of the 'unending tiresome' side effects of the jaw operations – catarrh and otitis with difficulty in walking – see Pichler, pp. 504–7, 508, 511 (quote p. 505); Schur, pp. 433, 484, 490f.; Freud/ Eitingon, 746 F, 748 F. See also 298 SF and note 4.
22 'Unfortunately we had to go back to Berggasse already on 15 September' ⟨Anna/Lou, letter 357, 28 October 1932, p. 608⟩. Freud entered his return in *The Diary of Sigmund Freud* on Saturday, 17 September ⟨1992*i*, p. 15⟩.
23 The word 'Mass' deleted before this word.

288 SF[1]

ANNA FREUD HOTEL ROSE WIESBADEN

WIEN [Pötzleinsdorf] 16.35
[Receipt note Wiesbaden:] 03.IX.[19]32 17–32

= ALL WELL PROFOUNDEST PEACE[2] WISH YOU[3] SAME[4] SINCERELY
= PAPA

1 Telegram.
2 '. . . when I open my door I am in a large park-like garden . . . the acacias still

give off their scent, the lindens are just starting, blackbirds and larks hop or fly around, no loudspeakers or car horns disturb the peace' ⟨Freud/Eitingon, 655 F, 1 June 1931, p. 739⟩.

3 Apart from the other Congress participants, this doubtless refers to Dorothy, who also attended the Congress. Previously she had visited her father in New York and had travelled to Wiesbaden directly from there, where she met Anna on 3 September ⟨Burlingham, M., pp. 237, 238; Anna/Eva, letter 51⟩. They both returned to Vienna on 8 September ⟨Freud 1992*i*, p. 14⟩.

4 The Congress was not disrupted by Ferenczi's paper (see 287 SF and note 16); and an interim solution was reached in the discussion of lay analysis, once again postponing a uniform regulation ⟨*IZ*, vol. 19 (1933), pp. 253–6, 270⟩. No agreement was reached either at the following Congresses (Lucerne 1934, Marienbad 1936, Paris 1938) ⟨*IZ*, vol. 321 (1935), p. 308; vol. 23 (1937), p. 198; *IZ/Imago*, vol. 24 (1939), pp. 364–6, 368; Jones III, p. 323⟩. The events of the war and post-war period pushed the subject into the background. Its traces can still be found today, however, 'in the variety of training regulations by the individual psychoanalytical groups in the International Association and in the numerous international discussions on training and minimum standards' ⟨Leupold-Löwenthal [1984], p. 116⟩.

289 SF[1]

ANNA FREUD HOTEL ROSE WIESBADEN

WIEN [Pötzleinsdorf] 14.35
[Receipt note Wiesbaden:] 05.IX.[19]32 15–51

THANKS FOR ALL GOOD NEWS[2] CONGRATULATIONS JONES[3] RUTH[4] JEANNA[5] DISAPPOINTED AT YOUR STAYING IN OFFICE[6] HERE
PEACEABLE CONVERSATION WITH EINSTEIN[7] = PA

1 Telegram.

2 There is no news from Anna herself, but she co-signed Eitingon's telegram to Freud of 4 September ⟨Freud/Eitingon, 736 E⟩. She delivered her paper, 'Die neurotischen Mechanismen unter dem Einfluss der Erziehung' ['Neurotic Mechanisms under the Influence of Education'] (1933); it was not published separately and is only briefly described in the Congress report: 'Some examples of the interaction between internal and external world in the development of infantile neurosis'. Ideas from this paper are contained in Anna's book *The Ego and Mechanisms of Defence* (1936).

3 Jones succeeded Eitingon as president of the Association ⟨*IZ*, vol. 19 (1933), p. 273; Freud/Jones, letter 595⟩. Ferenczi was not a candidate (see 287 SF, end of note 13).

4 Ruth Mack-Brunswick gave a paper on 4 September on 'Observations on Male Preoedipal Sexuality' ⟨*IZ*, vol. 19 (1933), p. 244⟩.

5 Jeanne Lampl-De Groot spoke on 4 September on 'Instinctual Vicissitudes in Female Development' (ibid., published under the title 'Zu den Problemen der Weiblichkeit ['On the Problems of Femininity'], ⟨*IZ*, vol. 19 (1933), pp. 385–415⟩.

6 Anna was re-elected as secretary of the Association. See 287 SF and note 15 ⟨*IZ*,

vol. 19 (1933), p. 273⟩. In July she had considered resigning from the position, but was apparently dissuaded from doing so ⟨Anna to Eitingon, 5 July, 13 July 1932⟩. She at least managed to have Martin take over some of her work as secretary of the International Training Commission ⟨*IZ*, vol. 19 (1933), p. 253⟩.

7 This 'peaceable' conversation (on a non-peaceful subject) took place not in person but by letter; it was published in Paris in three languages under the title (in English) 'Why War?' ⟨1933*b*, editorial comments in *S. E.*, vol. XXII, pp. 197f.; there is also a summary of Einstein's letter to Freud⟩. On the day after his telegram Freud noted in *The Diary of Sigmund Freud*, 'Discussion Einstein ended' ⟨1992*i*, p. 15⟩.

290 SF[1]

PROF. DR. FREUD

3 December 1932[2]
Vienna, IX. Berggasse 19

Voucher[3]
for a writing desk
of choice up to
the amount of $100
Congratulations
from
Papa[3]

1 Letter card with printed heading.
2 The corresponding envelope also has the date '3 December 1932' in Latin script in Freud's handwriting.
3 This word is written in Latin script.

1933

291 SF[1]

PROF. DR. FREUD

12 March 1933
VIENNA, IX. BERGGASSE 19

Dear Anna,

As Dr Federn contacted you for an explanation of my relationship to him, I would ask you to tell him[2] that he is wrong to assume that anything has changed; my friendly disposition towards him and my appreciation of his achievements remain the same. The source of his error is perhaps that he gives too little consideration to my own motives, which have nothing to do with him. If, for example, he found that I was not sufficiently shocked by his intention of resigning as director of the Society,[3] he fails to take into account that his resignation would give me the desired opportunity to resign the presidency myself, which he had always prevented me from doing.[4] I want the Society to regain the freedom to govern itself. If he thinks, as I expect he does, that I am not sufficiently interested in his recent scientific work, he fails to consider that it is the regular technique I use so as not to disrupt, through my authority, the free development of opinions.[5]

Other complaints that you have intimated to me appear so trivial that I can explain them only as a result of a heightened sensitivity. He might bear in mind that my last action in this regard, his appointment as editor of the *Zeitschrift*,[6] was not exactly an expression of disdain or mistrust.

I have, of course, also noticed that he has been depressed and irritable in the last few months and have very much regretted that in this state he was involved in difficulties and unpleasantness that he would otherwise certainly have avoided.[7] What can his friends do but wait until the condition is over? I didn't think he needed to be handled so carefully[8] to the extent of withholding a minor criticism, for example, of his overzealousness[9] with regard to your Congress paper.[10] You told me that he admits himself to being depressed and dissatisfied. As an analyst he should know that the causes should not be sought in others, where they don't lie.[11] Let us hope that he resurfaces soon from the current[12] turbidity.

Freud

1 With the letter is an envelope with Freud's address as sender on the back and the note 'For Dr Federn' in Freud's handwriting. Freud apparently wanted Anna to forward the original to Paul Federn; the closing greeting would also indicate this.
2 Semi-colon instead of comma in the original.
3 As vice-president of the Vienna Psychoanalytic Society, Federn was its managing director.
4 'Every year my father resigned and every year he was re-elected, for fifteen years. When Freud once failed to advise him to remain in the position, my father was incredibly aggrieved' ⟨Ernst Federn in: Plänkers and Federn, p. 84⟩.
5 In spite of the different attitudes to the theory and practice of treating psychoses, 'Freud was convinced that Federn does nothing against the *cause*' ⟨Ernst Federn, ibid., pp. 87f., 93f., 96f., the quotation 98⟩.
6 In May 1932 Freud transferred the editorship of the *Internationale Zeitschrift für Psychoanalyse* from Berlin back to Vienna and appointed Federn and Heinz Hartmann as editors-in-chief ⟨Freud/Ferenczi III, 986 F and note 2; annual report of the board at the Wiesbaden Congress: *IZ*, vol. 19 (1933), p. 261 and title sheet; Freud/Ferenczi III, 1225 F, 1230 F; Freud/Eitingon, 709 F, 711 F, 714 F⟩. In 1935 Federn resigned from this post ⟨*IZ*, vol. 21 (1935), p. 329⟩.
7 'Federn is not always easy to keep under control,' wrote Anna to Eitingon on 11 December 1932. And a few months earlier Freud had commented: 'Federn has been making himself . . . highly unpopular recently through all kinds of foolishness' ⟨Freud/Eitingon, 709 F, 27 April 1932, p. 801; also 711 F⟩. See note 11.
8 'It is said of my father that he was already very depressive as a young man and that when he was older he had a post-operative psychosis. . . . My father then recovered completely, but this episode perhaps shows that his ego was not as strong' as Freud estimated here ⟨Ernst Federn in: Plänkers and Federn, p. 99⟩.
9 Spelling mistake (no umlaut) in the original.
10 Unclear; perhaps Federn had wanted to persuade Anna to provide a more detailed exposition of her paper at the Wiesbaden Congress (see 289 SF, note 2).
11 'The people in the Association were always arguing, something that disappointed Freud very much, because he thought that it wouldn't happen if they were analysed. Today we know that it isn't the case' ⟨Ernst Federn, ibid., p. 80⟩.
12 Spelling mistake (no umlaut) in the original.

292 SF[1]

Chinese jewellery[2]
(last century)
+ +

The two discs connected by a needle[3] can be separated and used on their own. The ornamentation is fine gold.

[In the side margin]

for 3 Dec 1933
affectionately Papa

1 Letter card without printed head, everything written in Latin script.
2 'We are getting ready now for Annerl's birthday. Papa has already a couple of delightful pieces of jade jewellery and from me she is getting a bookrest to put next to her chair' ⟨Martha Freud to Ernst and Lux in London, 29 November [1933], FM London, Box 31 A⟩.
3 The two '+' signs mark the needle perforations.

1935

293 SF[1]

Voucher
for a gold ring
from Löwy watchmakers
to be ♦ made by for
the attached stone
bearing an engraved ship with sail
and oars
for 11 November 1935 Freud

1 Back of a letter card with printed header. In the original there is a slot above and below the ♦ in which the gem was mounted. The card – the only correspondence for 1935 – was under the letters after the previous greeting card. Anna must have attached particular importance to the document for her to have kept it in this way. It is therefore included and left in the place, although the addressee must have been Dorothy Burlingham, whose birthday was 11 October. Facsimile and explanation, see Appendix 3.

1936

294 SF[1]

PROF. DR. FREUD

10 April 1936
Vienna, IX. Berggasse 19

Dear Colleague,
The uncertainty with our pat.[ient][2] prompts me to ask you to recommend a reliable nurse to take care of her. My daughter will not be able to do so on a long-term basis.
Yours sincerely,
Freud

1 Letter card. The addressee is unknown; Anna was probably meant to forward the letter.
2 Probably Minna Bernays; on 25 March she had undergone a glaucoma operation on both eyes, which still gave her considerable trouble at home ⟨Freud 1992*i*, p. 28; Freud to Marie Bonaparte, quoted in Schur, p. 478; Anna/Lou, letter 414; Jones III, p. 208⟩. Two days after this letter Freud noted in *The Diary of Sigmund Freud*: 'Minna still ill'. The provision of a nurse became unnecessary because on 15 April Minna had herself admitted to a sanatorium, from which she was discharged on 29 April ⟨Freud 1992*i*, p. 28⟩. Two further glaucoma operations followed two years later, which kept her for a long time in the sanatorium ⟨ibid., 2 and 11 March, p. 35; 12 April, p. 36; Freud 1968*a*, 21 March 1938; Freud/Jones, letter 661⟩. She continued to suffer from the ailment until her death ⟨Jones III, p. 208⟩.

295 SF[1]

Frl *Han*
(200 B.C.–200 A.D.)[2]
congratulates you sincerely on
3 December 1936
perhaps also one of the
women who like to
make themselves older[3]

1 Letter card without printed header or signature, Freud's handwriting, names and dates in Latin script. This is the last surviving piece of correspondence from the time before the emigration to London.
2 Figure from the Chinese Han dynasty, an antique that Freud gave to Anna for her birthday ⟨see Molnar [1996], p. 192⟩.
3 Joking reference to Anna's earlier wish to be older, 'no longer "little"'. 'I am constantly irritated that I wasn't born thirty or forty years earlier; then I wouldn't have been just a late appendage to you and Papa' ⟨Anna/Lou, letter 118, 5 August 1922, p. 210; letter 59, 24 November 1922, p. 104⟩. See also 200 SF, note 4. In a much later letter to Muriel Gardiner, Anna described a childhood scene in which she was once again unhappy at being too small and hence excluded, but had kept her complaint to herself: '. . . my father, who was watching the scene, praised me and comforted me. That made me so happy that nothing else mattered' ⟨Gardiner, p. 64; see also Freud, M. [1999], p. 55⟩.

Emigration (1938)

In the belief that National Socialism in Austria would not be on the same scale as in Germany, Freud had hoped until the last moment to be able to stay in Vienna ⟨Freud/Eitingon, 758 F; Freud/Jones, letter 606, p. 715; Freud/Ferenczi III, 1244 F⟩. But after the entry of German troops into Vienna on 11 March, SA members searched his apartment several times, occupied the premises of the Vienna Psychoanalytic Society and liquidated all psychoanalytical organizations. Martin was interrogated by the Gestapo several times and Anna even arrested, so that Freud had to fear for her life, and he eventually gave in to the insistence of his friends and agreed to emigrate: 'The advantage that emigrating will bring Anna is worth all our petty sacrifices' ⟨Freud/Jones, letter 662, 13 May 1938, p. 764⟩.

William Bullitt, US ambassador in Paris at the time (1936–40), took the initiative at the highest political level to obtain the necessary authorizations and ensure safe passage ⟨Schur, pp. 496f. and note; Jones III, pp. 235, 238, 242f.; Gay, pp. 623–6, 629⟩.

Jones arranged the immigration and work permit in England for Freud, his family and several accompanying persons. 'I am sometimes disturbed by the idea that you might think we believe that you simply want to do your duty, without our valuing the deep and honest feelings expressed in your activity,' Freud wrote to him on 28 April. He added: 'I assure you that this is not the case, that we recognize your friendship, rely on it, and fully reciprocate it. This is a rare expression of feelings on my part . . .' ⟨Freud/Jones, letter 661, p. 762⟩. Anna summed up her thanks in words: 'In calmer times I hope to be able to show you that I understand in full measure what you are now doing for us' ⟨3 April 1938, quoted in Gay, p. 627⟩.

With her untiring energy and helpfulness and with her international connections – practical and financial – Marie Bonaparte was indispensable to the family ⟨Jones III, p. 246; Schur, pp. 501, 503–5; Gay, pp. 623, 624f., 629f.; Bertin, pp. 347, 350⟩. Ernst Halberstadt, who managed as a German citizen to leave on his own without special requirements (see 146 SF, note 4), was also put up by her for several days on his way to England ⟨Freud, W. E. [1988], p. 16; Molnar [1996], pp. 232f.⟩. And later she housed Freud and his companions when they stopped over in Paris during the journey to London: 'The one day in your home in Paris restored our dignity and mood after we had been swathed with love for twelve hours' ⟨Freud to Marie Bonaparte, 8 June 1938, quoted in Schur, p. 564⟩ (see ill. 18).

The main burden of preparation was borne by Anna: 'And Anna has to look after everything, from the most important to the most trivial. She has no help. . . . It was not fair to leave Anna alone like that. . . . Martha is bearing up very well' ⟨Freud to Minna, in: Freud/Bernays, letter 199 S⟩.

After a gruelling period of waiting they were only allowed to leave in succession. Dorothy had already moved to Switzerland on 1 April and had been living since 9 April in Lugano. She had Minna, who was poorly, come to her and accompanied her to London later, around 20/24 May ⟨Freud to Ruth, 25 May 1938; Freud/Bernays, letter 195 S; Burlingham, M., pp. 262–4 (with differing travel date)⟩. Freud indicated the sequence of departures: Martin left on 14 May after he had 'sent off Esti and the children to Paris in advance' the evening before ⟨Freud/Bernays, letter 194 S; see Freud, Sophie, pp. 2–4⟩. Mathilde and Robert followed on 24 May. Freud, Martha, Anna and – instead of the sick Max Schur – the attending doctor Josefine Stross were the last to leave on 4 June, 'Paula [Fichtl] with us, Lün [see 297 SF, note 6] at least as far as Dover. . . . Ernst and my nephew Harry were already in Paris to welcome us. . . . Jones was at Victoria and . . . brought us to our new house . . . with a view of greenery and a delightful small garden enclosed by trees' (see 298 SF) ⟨Freud/Eitingon, 799 F, 7 June 1938, pp. 901–3⟩. This house in Elsworthy Road had been rented by Ernst, who had lived with his family in London since 1933 ⟨Jones III, p. 228⟩. It was a temporary address until the final abode at 20 Maresfield Gardens, Hampstead, London NW3, was found.

Details of the exodus have been written about by numerous authors, e.g., Jones III, pp. 233–44; Schur, ch. 12; Gay, pp. 622–9; Molnar [1996] (year 1938); Federn, E. [1988]. Freud himself described everyday life during the last days in Vienna in his letters, amongst others, to Minna: Freud/Bernays, letters 194 S–199 S.

1938

296 SF[1]

[39 Elsworthy Road, London NW3][2] 30 July 1938

[Without salutation][3]
Bullitt[4] was here today, very kind, and reckons that there won't be a war.[5] Ruth arrived yesterday evening, looks bad, is behaving sensibly.[6] Radium man[7] expected today.[8]

All right, don't work too hard,[9] greet Marie.[10] Paid Eitingon £50 unprompted.[11] (But you already known that.)

Affectionately,
Papa

1 Letter card written on both sides without letterhead, Freud's handwriting.
2 'We have really arrived in England, it is very nice . . . everything still strange and unreal' ⟨Freud to Jeanne, 13 June 1938; Jones III, p. 241⟩. 'The greatest change naturally is that we are now meant to live vertically while we were used to spreading ourselves horizontally' ⟨Freud to Ruth, 19 June 1938⟩. Freud could not at first use the upper floors 'without a sedan chair' ⟨Freud/Eitingon, 799 F, 7 June 1938, quotation p. 902⟩.
3 Anna had travelled on 29 July to the 15th International Psychoanalytic Congress in Paris, the first to take place in France (1–5 August 1938) ⟨*IZ/Imago*, vol. 24 (1939), pp. 360–70; Freud 1992*i*, p. 39⟩. She had obtained permission to travel 'with difficulty from the authorities' ⟨Freud to Jeanne, 26 July 1938⟩. On 2 August, as a greeting and on behalf of Freud, she read out an extract from his Moses book, 'The Advance in Intellectuality' ⟨1939*a*, Section C in part II of the third treatise, see *S. E.*, vol. XXIII, pp. 3f.; *IZ/Imago*, ibid., p. 364⟩. Jones was re-elected president and Anna as a member of the board and the International Training Commission (see note 9). The Paris group made Freud, Anna and Jones honorary members. Jones officially announced the forced liquidation of the Vienna psychoanalytical institutions, following the annexation of Austria ⟨see *Minutes IV*, pp. 303f., *IZ/Imago*, ibid., pp. 361, 366f., 369f.⟩.
4 William Christian Bullitt (1891–1967), American diplomat and journalist, amongst other things adviser to President Wilson during the Paris peace negotiations. He had known Freud at least since 1930; at the time they were

working together on a book about Wilson, which did not appear in print, however, until 1967 (Freud's introduction: 1966*b*) ⟨Gay, pp. 553–62; Jones III, pp. 160f.; Molnar [1996], pp. 71, 85, 87f., 185, 229, 237f. and elsewhere⟩.

5 'Bullitt is supposed to have said in Paris, we read, that the US did not think the conflict was of topical interest,' Freud reported to Minna on 26 May 1938 ⟨Freud/Bernays, letter 197 S⟩. There was great unease in England following the mobilization of Czechoslovakia on 20 May (as a response to the German territorial claims and troop concentrations). From 19 to 21 July in Paris, Britain and France had confirmed their solidarity in the face of Hitler's threats of war. In the subsequent weeks they negotiated the Munich Agreement of 29 September 1938 by which the German-speaking border regions of Bohemia, Moravia and Silesia were ceded to the German Reich 'to rescue peace' ⟨Ploetz [1980], pp. 866f.; see also Schur, p. 510; Freud to Marie Bonaparte, 4 October 1938, in 1960*a*, pp. 446–7⟩.

6 Ruth Mack-Brunswick, who had returned from America to be with her sick father, came from there to London on her way to the Congress in Paris ⟨Roazen [1976], p. 433⟩.

7 Dr Carter Braine ⟨Jones III, p. 247⟩.

8 Spelling mistake (no umlaut) in the original.

9 Anna had continued her psychoanalytical activities directly after the move. She was able to carry on working immediately. 'There are no restraints on the practice of analysis in England and our English group has given us a very cordial reception' ⟨Freud/Binswanger, 19 July 1938, p. 215⟩. She was accepted at once as a member by the British Psychoanalytical Society and Freud as an honorary member ⟨*IZ*/*Imago*, vol. 24 [1939], p. 366⟩. She said later in her 'Personal Memories of Ernest Jones': 'It cannot have been easy to persuade the British Society to open its doors to the influx of members from Vienna, i.e. to colleagues who held different scientific views from their own and could only be expected to disrupt peace and internal unity. . . . I have never ceased to be grateful to the British Society for their attitude at this crucial moment . . .' ⟨[1979] in *Writings X*, pp. 350f⟩.

10 Marie Bonaparte.

11 Eitingon had emigrated to Palestine in 1933–4, where he founded the Palestinian Psychoanalytic Association and the Psychoanalytic Training Institute in Jerusalem, which he financed for the most part himself. At the same time he was in close contact with European psychoanalytical activities. He visited Freud in London in August 1938 for the last time on the occasion of the Paris Congress ⟨Schröter [2004], pp. 25–31, 32; Freud/Eitingon, 800 E, note 2⟩. No further details are available about the reason for the payment of £50.

297 SF

PROF. DR. FREUD [39 Elsworthy Road, London NW3]
1 August 1938
Vienna, IX. Berggasse 19

My dear Anna,
Of course it's not the same when you are not here, although the telephone contact makes up for it a lot. It is as if you had your [in English] rooms in

Harley St[1] and came home dead tired in the evenings. You will have heard the main news from conversations; I can add some smaller items.

It was really terribly hot and oppressive yesterday. Mama tries to beat the weather with the trick of the thin suit[2] (what is it called?); it remains to be seen whether it will help her here too. Ruth, whom you will see before this letter arrives,[3] says she is depressed.[4] It is true that she gnashes[5] uninterruptedly. Jumbo is very nice, occasionally very enterprising, as selective as ever in its affection.[6] Not a day passes without the necessary Nazi excitement. There are rumours that the aunts have not been able to get their money from the fund.[7]

Yesterday a telephone commission from Harry[8] to insure Sophie's diamond jewellery heavily and send it to the bank in Zurich, which Ernst has done. Uncle is waiting in Z[urich] for his Viennese lawyer to whom the jewellery is to be given.[9] According to a bitter but humorous letter from him, something seems to have gone wrong, but he doesn't want to say what.[10] On our side a card from Anna[11] that the packing is almost complete. They went to the police to register (!). To register *what*? Then on the address side of the card a few lines written in pencil and carefully crossed out. What new nastiness is in the air here?

The Oxford ψtherapeut. Congress, chaired by Jung,[12] sent me the obligatory welcome telegram,[13] to which I responded[14] with a cool answer, prepared by Dr Bennet.[15] I have been made honorary president[16] somewhere, I don't know where. The radium man, Dr Carter Braine,[17] was a stolid Englishman; I didn't impress him and he wants to see me again on Thursday for a comparison.[18] My heart is behaving with nitroglyc[erin], but my greatest undertaking was a visit to Aunt.[19] I read in the newspaper that I have bought a house; I haven't seen it yet.[20]

A[. . .] has become sick under the pressure of analysis with a break in the treatment.

Don't take too seriously everything that goes on in Paris and send your hostess[21] my affectionate greetings.

Papa

1 Jones had his offices in Harley Street (Freud/Jones, *passim*).
2 Unclear.
3 At the Congress; see 296 SF, note 6.
4 Ruth Mack-Brunswick had been taking painkillers for years because of ill-health and had gradually become dependent ⟨Roazen [1976], pp. 430f.; Young-Bruehl, pp. 278–9⟩. 'Ruth is still here (until the 24th of this month),' wrote Freud on 22 August 1938 to Jeanne, 'and is having a bit of additional analysis, which should do her a lot of good. How incomplete all of my earlier analyses were!'
5 The Austrian dialect word 'kiefelt' is difficult to read. Freud also used the word in a letter to Ferenczi ⟨Freud/Ferenczi I, 96 F, 1 January 1910, p. 119⟩; Molnar [1996], p. 247, reads 'kichert' (giggle)⟩.
6 Freud's chow, Lün II, was put in quarantine for six months on account of Britain's strict immigration requirements for animals and could not be fetched

until December ⟨Jones III, p. 246; Molnar [1996], p. 252⟩. As a temporary replacement Anna had got a Pekinese called Jumbo, which was particularly attached to Paula Fichtl.

7 Freud and his brother Alexander had left money for their four sisters (Rosa Graf, Dolfi Freud, Marie Freud and Paula Winternitz) – who despite all efforts had not able to emigrate – to provide for them until the end of their lives ⟨Jones III, p. 231; Leupold-Löwenthal [1988], pp. 926–8⟩.

8 Harry had been in London in June for his and his parents' immigration but was now apparently travelling again ⟨Freud to Alexander, 22 June 1938 in 1960*a*, p. 444, and 17 July 1938 (LoC); Jones III, p. 242⟩.

9 Alexander's company had been put in the hands of a commissar on 21 March. He then tried to get to Davos with Sophie, where Harry was staying on account of illness; they were allowed to leave Switzerland (on 19 April), however, only after he had left his assets in trust with his lawyer, Dr Führer. The lawyer took the requested jewellery for himself ⟨Leupold-Löwenthal [1988], pp. 922–4; slightly differently in Molnar [1996], p. 248; see also Freud/Bernays, letter 196 S⟩.

10 Alexander's entire assets were ultimately confiscated after all and he was 'practically without means and reliant on help from friends and relatives' ⟨Leupold-Löwenthal [1998], p. 924⟩. On 4 September 1938, he arrived with his family in London ⟨Freud 1992i, p. 39; see also Molnar [1996], p. 259; Jones III, p. 247⟩. They emigrated in September 1941 to Canada ⟨Kursidem, unpublished, p. 8⟩.

11 Unknown; it could be a maid by the name 'Seidmann' who supervised the packing after their departure ⟨Freud/Bernays, letter 194 S⟩.

12 Jung as chairman of the International Medical Society for Psychotherapy, which organized the Congress (29 July–2 August), gave a welcome address entitled 'Views Held in Common by the Different Schools of Psychotherapy' ⟨Jung [1938]; Donn, p. 23; Jones III, pp. 198f.⟩.

13 'The Tenth International Medical Congress for Psychotherapy in session at Oxford extends you very hearty greetings. We recognize our indebtedness to you for your brilliant contribution to psychological medicine and wish you health, happiness, and tranquillity in your new surroundings in England' ⟨Donn, p. 24⟩.

14 Spelling mistake in the original.

15 Edward Armstrong Bennet (1888–1977), professor of medicine, doctor of natural sciences, British psychiatrist and analyst in London, chairman of the medical department of the British Psychoanalytical Society, supporter of Jung, with whom he was friends, and author of several books about him (e.g. [1963], [1985]) ⟨I thank Marion Palmedo for the research⟩. He knew Freud from a visit in 1932. Jung now requested him to ask whether Freud would accept a telegram from Jung and the Society ⟨Jung [1975], p. 188; Donn, p. 24⟩.

16 Spelling mistake (no umlaut) in the original. Freud disliked honours as mere conventions or concessions (e.g., 1960*a*, pp. 369, 443). He nevertheless accepted various honours over the years ⟨Jones III, pp. 165, 211, 213, 219, 253 and note 1; Freud/Jones, letters 636, 637, 653, 654; *IZ*/*Imago*, vol. 24 [1939], p. 366; Freud, M. [1999], p. 165⟩. 'What pleased me most was the visit of the two secretaries from the Royal Society who brought the sacred book of the Society for me to sign . . . the signatures from I. Newton to Charles Darwin. Good company!' ⟨Freud 1968*a*, 28 June 1938, p. 164⟩. Jones was able to use his election as Corresponding Member of the Royal Society – 'by far the highest

honour that any scientific man can attain' – in his efforts to obtain an entry permit for Freud ⟨Freud/Jones, letters 646 (p. 752), 647 (p. 753); Jones III, pp. 220, 237⟩.

17 Hyphenated in the original.

18 Radium had already been used in early stages of the disease and was now being kept up until the end ⟨Pichler, pp. 509, 514f., 520; Schur, pp. 357, 426, 449, 518–22⟩. The treatment bothered Freud considerably: 'The radium has once more begun to eat in, with pain and toxic effects, and my world is again what it was before – a little island of pain floating on a sea of indifference' ⟨Freud to Marie Bonaparte, 16 June 1939, quoted in Jones III, p. 258; see also Freud 1968*a*, 16 December 1934, p. 98; Molnar [1996], pp. 258f.⟩.

19 Minna was lying with a severe pulmonary infection in her room, which Freud must have gone upstairs to ⟨Freud/Eitingon, 799 F; Molnar [1996], p. 240; Freud to Alexander, 17 July 1938⟩. She was put in a nursing home during the move to the new house ⟨Molnar [1996], pp. 247f., 249; see also Freud to Marie Bonaparte, 4 October 1938, in 1960*a*, p. 447⟩. It was not until the end of the year that she gradually began to get better 'but she was not yet downstairs with me or upstairs with Anna' ⟨Freud to Ruth, 4 November, also 11 November 1938⟩.

20 'House purchase concluded,' Freud had written four days earlier in *The Diary of Sigmund Freud*. On 13 August he visited Maresfield Gardens for the first time ⟨Molnar [1996], p. 247 with ill.⟩. 'My own house! . . . Ernst . . . is installing a lift, making one room out of two or the other way round, translating the old sorcerer's two times table into architecture' ⟨Freud to Jeanne, 22 August 1938⟩. A glass door opened on to the garden from Freud's spacious and bright study, which he was still able to enjoy in the particularly mild autumn ⟨Jones III, pp. 246–8; Schur, p. 512; Molnar [1996], p. 248⟩. It was in this room that Freud died ⟨Schur, pp. 510, 526; ill. in Molnar [1996], p. XXV⟩. Today the house has been converted into a museum open to the public.

21 Marie Bonaparte.

298 SF

PROF. DR. FREUD [39 Elsworthy Road, London NW3]
1 August 1938
Vienna, IX. Berggasse 19[1]

My dear Anna,
As it is Wednesday today and you are flying back on Friday evening, this will be my last letter to Paris that you are sure to get. I am still awaiting a letter from you.[2] The telephone conversations make us almost forget what a trip otherwise means, but Math[3] still complains that she cannot understand you well on the phone.

It was also hot here, but the evenings in the garden with the magnificent view are delightful. I have survived the heat incredibly well, perhaps thanks to the nitrogl[ycerin] taken as a precaution. The catarrh has been disturbing my hearing again since yesterday;[4] I'll give it one more day before I treat myself to Dr Lux, who helped so rapidly last time (Lax?).[5] Schur is once again very well.[6] The fortunate circumstance that my only pat[ient] just gave me a cheque[7] has made it possible for me to pay his half-yearly invoice, as there is no more cash in the bank.[8] As you know, my other pat[ient A. . .] has severe angina – although not diphtheria – and is out of action for[9] some weeks.

Some better news: Harry just telephoned that the aunts have been paid their money for August and that it looks as if the matter might be settled.[10] Anna reports that everything has been packed and sent off[11] and believes naively that the first crates should already have arrived in London. We are waiting – twixt cup and lip[12] – to hear whether it has really been shipped.[13] Not until then will we feel rid of the Nazis. I have not yet been in the new palais. My hairdresser read in the newspaper that I had bought a house.

I successfully dissuaded Dorothy from travelling in this heatwave.[14] The children are leaving today.[15] She has made good progress and appears to feel much better. Jumbo remains wary of us and affectionate with Paula.[16]

My work for the holiday is proving to be an amusing occupation.[17] It is already twenty-six pages long and will be in three parts – the general, the practical task and the theoretical benefit. I still abide by the fiction that there is no need for it to be printed.[18] The unpleasant prospect looms before us of a homeless period between the two dwellings.[19] If Mr Kent really shows up in mid-September I don't know where we will receive him, but perhaps God will help and he won't come back.[20]

I hope that in spite of the heat and the countless papers[21] in Paris you have not had it too bad at Marie's[22] and I greet you, her and everyone most affectionately.

Papa

1 Address on the letterhead crossed out.
2 There are no letters from Anna after the end of September 1930.
3 Mathilde and Robert, who had lived initially in the house, later found their own apartment at 2 Maresfield Gardens, into which the Burlinghams also moved shortly afterwards ⟨Gödde [2003], p. 208; Burlingham, M., pp. 267–9⟩.
4 See 287 SF, note 21.
5 In the original this name is in brackets in the next line before the word 'hat' (in German), directly underneath 'Lux'. See also Freud/Jones, letter 662, pp. 763f.
6 Schur, who had not been able to emigrate with the Freuds because of an urgent appendix operation, did not arrive with his family in London until 15 June ⟨Schur, pp. 502, 507⟩. He continued his medical supervision of Freud right up to the end (see note 22) ⟨ibid., p. 529⟩.
7 Spelling mistake (no umlaut) in the original; 'cheque' written in English.
8 Schur had wanted to reduce his fee, but Freud refused: 'Dear Doctor, You are right; everything has changed. But . . . I wouldn't dream of starting to economize with, of all people, my doctor' ⟨26 July 1938, in 1960*a*, p. 446⟩.
9 Spelling mistake (no umlaut) in the original. ⟨For details of the closing of the practice, see Freud 1992*i*, 1 August 1939, with Molnar [1996], p. 263.⟩
10 Freud was no longer alive to learn of the terrible fate that the aunts met. After Marie Bonaparte's efforts to obtain French or Greek visas for the four women had failed, they remained in Vienna. In 1942 they were deported to Theresienstadt, where Delfi died of undernourishment on 29 September. The

other three were killed in Treblinka ⟨Tögel [2004*b*], p. 42 and note 18; Leupold-Löwenthal [1988], pp. 926–8⟩.

11 The removal by the Vienna transport company E. Bäuml was supervised by Dr Anton Sauerwald, the same commissar who had liquidated the Vienna Psychoanalytic Society on 20 March 1938 and the *Verlag* and out-patients' department ⟨Schur, pp. 498f., note 3; Jones III, pp. 237f.; Leupold-Löwenthal [1988], pp. 919–21; Marinelli, p. 28; Minutes IV, pp. 303f.; Molnar [1996], p. 245⟩.

12 The original (in German) is a quote from the poem 'König Ankäos' (1802) by Friedrich Kind (1768–1843).

13 It arrived a few days later: 'Our things have indeed arrived right down to the last small item . . . Furniture, books, antiques, everything in excellent condition' ⟨Anna to Eitingon, 26 September 1938; Freud 1992*i*, 7/8 August 1938, p. 39⟩.

14 In the original 'reissen' (tear) instead of 'reisen' (travel). 'Heatwave' written in English.

15 Dorothy lived in Norfolk Road, not far from Freud's temporary accommodation. Her children were alternately in the United States and with her. A week before Freud's move to his house, she moved into 2 Maresfield Gardens ⟨Burlingham, M., pp. 267–9⟩. At the end of August 1939 she travelled to the USA, but was not able to return to England immediately because of the outbreak of war; she did not come back until April 1940, after Freud's death ⟨ibid., pp. 271f.⟩.

16 Paula Fichtl (1902–89) ⟨*taz* newspaper, 2 April 1990, p. 17⟩. She had been the Freuds' housekeeper since July 1929 and emigrated with them to England, where she remained in the house until a few days after Anna's death in 1982 ⟨Berthelsen, pp. 24–7, 82–9, 174, 176⟩. '. . . our devoted Paula . . . was always there, always helpful and at pains to make one's life easy. . . . She appeared to understand the language of dogs and even almost to speak it' ⟨Freud, W. E. [1987], pp. 206f.; see also Berthelsen, pp. 45–7, 90 (a photo of Paula and Jumbo, ibid., before p. 65)⟩.

17 Spelling mistake (no umlaut) in the original.

18 *An Outline of Psychoanalysis* (1940*a*); the work was published posthumously and was regarded as 'unfinished'. See Grubrich-Simitis [1993], pp. 217–26, for a revision of this assumption.

19 The rental agreement for Elsworthy Road expired at the end of August but the new house had not been completely decorated; Hotel Esplanade served as an interim solution. Freud and Anna did not finally move into the new home until 27 September, after Martha and Paula had moved in on 16 September to complete the furnishing ⟨Molnar [1996], p. 248; Schur, p. 510⟩.

20 A Mr Kent had looked up Freud on 18 July ⟨Molnar [1996], p. 243⟩. A meeting cannot have taken place in mid-September because Freud had had another serious operation on 8 September. Pichler came specially from Vienna to London for it. It was the most serious operation since 1923 and Freud never fully recovered from it ⟨Schur, pp. 509–12⟩.

21 The Congress report lists thirty-two papers in seven scientific sessions. Anna did not deliver a paper, but chaired a symposium with Paul Federn on *Ego Strength and Ego Weakness* ⟨*IZ*/*Imago*, vol. 24 (1939), pp. 363f.⟩.

22 Marie Bonaparte invited Anna again for the following spring, but Freud had to refuse for her: 'You know that Anna won't be coming to the meeting in Paris

because she cannot leave me; I am growing increasingly incapable of looking after myself and more dependent on her. Some kind of intervention that would cut short this cruel process would be very welcome' ⟨28 April 1939, in 1960*a*, p. 454⟩.

The 'intervention' did not come of its own accord. On Thursday, 21 September 1939, Freud asked his personal physician ⟨Schur, p. 529⟩: 'My dear Schur, you certainly remember our first talk. You promised me then not to forsake me when my time comes. Now it's nothing but torture and makes no sense any more. . . . Tell Anna about this.'

Epilogue

Extract from a letter from Lucie Freud to "Grockchen" (Felix Augenfeld) of 2 October 1939 (LoC SF, now Cont 12)

This month has been eternally long and eternally painful. Papa actually started dying on 3 September. I wrote to you about this in my last letter. An injection by Schur delayed it at the time and he was therefore obliged to die before our eyes in full consciousness. My dear, I will spare you the details as it would be too painful for you. I will confine myself to the few positive moments. Until the end he was completely himself in the few hours and then minutes of the day when he was not sleeping or in pain. He was indescribably friendly and loving with all of us, touchingly patient in putting up with everything, and his gratitude for even the shortest respite from the suffering could be seen in his shining eyes. He wanted so much to continue living as long as there was even a glimmer of hope that he could overcome the illness. The wonderful thing about Annerl's care was not her self-sacrifice (she got used in the last weeks to doing without sleep completely) and not the exemplary effort that is so self-evident with her. The wonderful thing was he never saw her with anything but a happy expression on her face. A peaceful, cheerful, almost homely mood prevailed in the sick room (in the last four weeks he was downstairs in a bed with the doors open and a view of the garden). Perhaps the happiness that was really always to be seen in Annerl's expression is the explanation for the one thing about him that I couldn't understand: that without ever saying a word he accepted Annerl's self-sacrifice, almost to the point of self-destruction. I asked her and she confirmed my supposition that day or night he never said a word of thanks. Perhaps even measured against this unprecedented devotion he was still the giver?

It was only on Friday morning, when it became imperative for the first time to give him morphine and the doctor told us that he would not regain consciousness again and that he, the doctor, could not allow him to do so, did Annerl cry for the first time. Death was a release, not as bitter as the theatre of the closure preceding this hour. All of his children and Robert and I and Dr Schur and Dr Stross sat with him from Friday morning until Saturday around midnight. We sent Mama and Aunt upstairs after they fell asleep in their chairs on Friday night. Only Annerl and I didn't lie down at all. He slept for forty hours breathing peacefully. His heart wanted to continue beating. Finally it stopped, just before midnight.

We carried the bed upstairs again and his room with your chair, in which I sat sometimes during the nights, is like it was before. Only terribly empty.

Part II

Appendixes

Appendix 1

Travel Diary, Rome 1923[1]

Appendix to 201 SF/AF

	Rome *morning*	*afternoon*	*evening*
1.	–	Corso[2]	–
2.	Forum,[3] Cap.[4]	Pincio[5]	–
3.	Palatine[6]	Gianicolo[7] Vatican[8]	–
4.	Museo naz.[9]	Pantheon[10] Coloss.[11] P. Navona[12] Maria s. Min[13] G. Bruno[14]	
5.	Mus. Vatic[15]	Moses[16] Bocca d I Verità[17] 2 temples[18] Port octav[19] carcer.[20]	
6.	Museo capitol[21]	Janus[22] Palatine[6]	
7.	Sistina[23] Stanze[24]	protest. cemet.[25] S. Saba[26] S. Sabina[27] Aventino[28] cestius[29]	
8.	S. Angelo[30]	Caec. Metella[31] Via appia[32] Columbar[33]	
9.	Villa Giulia[34]	S. Paulo[35] Tre Fontane[36]	
10.	Vatican[8] Loggia[38]Bibliot.[38]	Celio[39] Via Latina[40] (tombe)	

11.	Laterano[41]	–	cinema[42]
12.	M. Tarp[43] Aracoeli[44] Mus. Kirch[45]	Aq. Acet.[46] Ponte Molle[47]	–
13.	Tivoli[48]	Villa d'Este[49]	
14.	Doria[50]	–	–
15.	Pinacoteca vatic.[51] S. Maria d Popolo[52]	Prassede[53] Maria magg.[54] S. Croce[55] S. Lorenzo[56] Eurysaces[57]	
16.	Zool. Gard.[58] Gall. Borgh.[59]	Maria s. Min.[13] Maria dell pace[60] Cam. Commerc.[61] Isola Tevere[62] Palaz Farnese[63] Spada[64] Cancellarie [Cancelleria][65] Massimi [Massimo][66]	
17.	Corsini[67] Farnesina[68]	P. Pia[69] Gesù[70] S. Clemente[71]	
18.	–	Shopping (silver chain)	
19.	Campo di Fiori[72]	Via Appia[32] San Sebastiano[73] Hermes excavations[74]	
20.	Via Nazionale,[75] leather purchases	Mte Mario,[76] Camiluccia[77]	Fontana Trevi[78]
21.	Shopping[79]	Palatine Café [Caffe] Aragno	departure[80]

1 This is a transcription of the facsimile shown on pp. 320 and 321 with additional explanations. (I thank Marion Palmedo, Victoria Palmedo and Robert Berni, Rome/New York, for their invaluable assistance in translating and compilation.)

The information is designed to enable readers to follow the intense visiting schedule that Anna and Freud undertook, some of it on foot, some by vehicle, from Hotel Eden ⟨Freud to family, 11 September 1923, 2002*b*, p. 383⟩.

Needless to say, the comments on the entries do not provide comprehensive information on the individual sites; they focus particularly on a selection of characteristic features that could shed light on the reasons Freud wanted to introduce Anna to these particular aspects of the city.

Unless otherwise specified, the information and quotes come from the following travel guides and city maps:

– Knopf Guides, *Rome*, New York 1944), 3rd revised and updated edition, November 1996.

- Corriere della Sera, *CityBook Roma*, Nuove Guide Visuali, Le Guide Peugeot/Mondadori, London – Milano, 1948.
- Guida d'Italia del Touring Club Italiano: *Roma e Dintorni*, 6th edition, Milan, 1962.
- E. Venturini, *Rom und der Vatikan*, Neuer illustrierter farbiger Führer mit grossen Stadtplan mit eingetragenen Denkmälern, Editrice Lozzi, Rome, undated [1991].
- E. Verdesi (Editore, Roma), *Nuova Pianta di Roma*, undated.

2 Via del Corso, one of the main streets in the city centre. It runs in a straight line from Piazza del Popolo to Piazza Venezia. Many princely and papal palaces line the Corso on both sides; halfway up is Piazza Colonna, 'behind which' Freud stayed at Hotel Milano in 1907 ⟨Freud to family, 22 September 1907, in 1960*a*; Jones II, p. 36⟩. Goethe, who lived at no. 18 on his first visit to Rome, describes the street in his *Italian Journey*. On this first outing in the afternoon of their arrival Freud and Anna went via the Spanish Steps (see Appendix 2).

3 Forum Romanum/Foro Romano, the valley at the foot of the Palatine and Capitoline Hills, was until the fall of the Western Roman Empire a centre of public life: marketplace and exchange, venue for gatherings, honours and encounters, court and site of political agitation. The word 'forum' today includes all of the vestiges of the Republican era and the various enlargements during the imperial epoch (imperial fora). In 1923 visitors still had access to all parts (as is mostly the case again today ⟨Seibt⟩). Via dei Fori Imperiali, which today crosses the site, did not exist then and was not built until 1932, with the loss of some of the ruins.

4 The Capitoline (il Campidoglio), the smallest of Rome's seven hills, once a holy place for the Roman gods, was a centre of religious and political power in antiquity; today the mayor of Rome and the city council have their offices in the Palazzo del Senatore (Senatorial Palace). In the sixteenth century, Michelangelo was commissioned to redesign the Piazza del Campidoglio and the adjacent buildings – the Palazzo dei Conservatori and the Palazzo Nuovo. He also designed the large flight of steps.

5 Monte Pincio, park above the Piazza del Popolo with particular charm; busts in honour of famous Italians line the paths, and the terraces offer some of the most popular views of the city, e.g., over the Tiber valley to the Vatican and the dome of St Peter's Basilica.

6 Palatino, the hill bordering the valley of the Forum to the south, is the legendary site of the founding of Rome (Roma quadrata). In ancient Rome it was inhabited by patrician families – the best preserved being the house of Livia from the first century BC – with temples and later imperial palaces; the High Renaissance gardens (Farnese Gardens) give it its distinctive park-like form today.

7 Monte Gianicolo (Janiculum), an extensive park on the west bank of the Tiber, bordered by the Vatican in the north and the Aurelian Walls in the west; at the top is a large terrace with an equestrian statue of Giuseppe Garibaldi and a famous panoramic view of the city.

8 Abbreviated designation for the supreme authority of the Roman Catholic Church, named after the papal residence since 1377 on Monte Vaticano. Vatican City, bordered by the Leonine Wall and the colonnade of St Peter's Cathedral, has been an independent city-state since 1929. The Vatican includes St Peter's Basilica and St Peter's Square, several palaces, extensive parks and

inner courtyards, and various administrative and service buildings. Apart from other institutions, it contains major art collections, libraries and archives, as well as considerable extraterritorial possessions (see notes 15, 23, 24, 30, 37, 38, 41, 51).

9 Museo Nazionale Romano (National Museum of Rome – also known as Museo delle Terme) contains valuable sculptures and paintings compiled from finds in Rome and Latium and from major collections by Roman nobles. The museum at that time was in parts of the former Baths of Diocletian opposite the entrance to the main railway station (see Anna's notes, Appendix 2). In the 1990s it was moved to the Palazzo dell'Ex-Collegio Massimo in Piazza del Cinquecento and Palazzo Altemps next to Piazza Navona. Only the Epigraphic Section, everyday culture and bronzes remain in the Baths ⟨Seibt⟩.

10 The Pantheon is the largest and most complete circular building and also the only intact vestige of Roman architecture from antiquity. The diameter of the impressive dome is even larger than that of St Peter's Basilica. Originally built as a temple, in 609 the site became a Christian church, Sancta Maria ad Martyres (today Santa Maria della Rotonda). It contains the grave of Raphael ⟨see Grubrich-Simitis [1995*a*]⟩.

11 The Coliseum, 'the most famous monument in the world', is a huge elliptical amphitheatre in which circuses and gladiator contests were held in ancient Rome. After lying in ruins for centuries, it was used again as a theatre for the first time in 2000 – this time for Sophocles' tragedies ⟨Seibt⟩.

12 Piazza Navona (Circo Agonale) is one of the largest and most important squares in Rome, with noble buildings along its sides and three magnificent fountains. It is built on the site of the antique Stadium of Domitian and retains the arena's elongated form. 'This square is the ceremonial hall of the Roman people' ⟨Raffalt, p. 26⟩. Daily and seasonal markets alternate with artistic events, folk festivals and entertainments of all kinds.

13 The church of Santa Maria sopra Minerva, built on the ruins of a Minervan temple, is a rare example of Gothic art in Rome. It has developed into a veritable treasure chamber including Michelangelo's *Christ the Redeemer*.

14 The monument to Giordano Bruno (1548–1600) in the centre of Campo de' Fiori (see note 72), formerly an execution site, recalls the burning of the philosopher here by the Inquisition in 1600.

15 Musei Vaticani (Vatican Museums): 'The Vatican buildings are a world of their own, a fantastic and grand building complex of over 11,000 rooms, halls, museums, galleries, libraries, chapels and corridors, courtyards and gardens, filled with immense art treasures of all kinds' ⟨Venturini, p. 124⟩. The part known officially today as 'museums' comprises the antique collections ⟨Speier, p. 45⟩.

16 Freud had been so impressed by Michelangelo's marble statue of Moses in the church of San Pietro in Vincoli (Basilica Eudossiana) on his first visit to Rome in 1901 that he discussed it in an essay (1914*b*). See also Grubrich-Simitis [2004].

17 Bocca della Verità (The Mouth of Truth) is an ancient marble fountain mask in the portico of the church of Santa Maria in Cosmedin (near the banks of the Tiber, south of Ponte Palatino). According to legend, it bites off the hand of those who put their arm in the open mouth and tell a lie.

18 This probably refers to the two Templi del Foro Boario in front of the church of Santa Maria in Cosmedin near the ancient Roman harbour, which amaz-

ingly survived the centuries only because they were transformed in the Middle Ages into Christian churches. They are regarded as rare examples of a mixed Greco-Roman architectural style. The rectangular Tempio della Fortuna Virile has been modified several times and was dedicated formerly to the harbour god Portunes or, according to other sources, Mater Matuta. The Tempio di Vesta (named because it resembles the vestal temple in the Forum, actually dedicated to Hercules Victor) is a circular building from the first century BC, said to be the oldest surviving marble structure in Rome.

19 Portico di Ottavia, close to the Theatre of Marcellus, is at the entrance to the Jewish ghetto. Only a few arches and columns in the foyer survive of the former extensive arcade court. It was part of a complex of columned halls used for religious ceremonies, political events and trading or general meeting places.

20 This is probably the underground Carcere Mamertino (Mamertine Prison) (church of San Pietro in Carcere) at the foot of the steps leading down from the Capitoline Hill to the Forum Romanum. The two connected dungeons of the Mamertine Prison (originally a cistern with access to the Cloaca Maxima) are underneath the church of San Giuseppe dei Falegnami. Prisoners of state were incarcerated there prior to their execution. According to an unconfirmed legend, St Peter was also imprisoned there for a while.

21 Museo Capitolino contains a rich collection of ancient marble busts and statues in a number of rooms in Palazzo Nuovo and Palazzo dei Conservatori, 'the oldest public collection in the world (1471)', including the famous statue of Cupid and Psyche, Spinario, Capitoline Venus, She-Wolf of Rome, the Mosaic with Drinking Doves from Hadrian's villa (Tivoli), mural paintings, and the Capitoline Painting Collection with sixteenth- and seventeenth-century masterpieces.

22 As there are but a few remains of the *temple* of Janus in the south of the Campidoglio (integrated in the church of San Nicola in Carcere), this entry probably refers to the Arco di Giano (*arch* of Janus) with its four entrances (Janus Quadrifons) at a crossroads at the edge of the former cattle market (Forum Boarium, today Piazza Bocca della Verità), offering shade to the dealers and citizens as they conducted their business.

23 The Sistine Chapel, the main chapel in the Vatican palace, has wall frescos by the great Quattrocento painters and Michelangelo's famous ceiling paintings and *The Last Judgement* on the altar wall. They were refurbished as part of a general restoration commenced in 1980 and now completed.

24 Le Stanze de Raffaello (Raphael's rooms) are the four private papal chambers in the Vatican palace with frescos by Raphael by order of Julius II, the most famous of which include *The Disputation of the Holy Sacrament* and *The School of Athens*.

25 The Protestant cemetery (Cimitero protestante – formerly English cemetery) is near Porta San Paolo, one of the main gates in the Aurelian Wall. 'This is perhaps the most atmospheric place in Rome' ⟨Siebenkirchen, p. 54⟩. It is the burial ground of non-Catholics, mostly foreigners, including Goethe's son, August: 'Accept me here, Jupiter, later let Hermes lead me, Quietly, by Cestius' Pyramid, down to Orcus' ⟨Goethe, *Roman Elegies*⟩. See also note 29.

26 The church of San Saba on the Piccolo Aventino, north-east of the Protestant cemetery near Piazza Gian Lorenzo Bernini, is a jewel with valuable architectural remnants from the seventh to eleventh centuries and works by the Cosmati from the thirteenth century.

27 Santa Sabina, church high on the Aventine Hill over the Tiber, is a well-preserved, sober early Christian basilica. It contains unusual testimonies from the early fifth to the ninth centuries. After enlargement in later centuries, it was restored to its original state in 1914 – for Freud, who had not been in Rome since 1913, a good opportunity for comparison. He might also have gone a few steps further with Anna to Piazza dei Cavalieri di Malta, to peep through the keyhole of the gate to Villa del Priorato di Malta to catch sight of the dome of St Peter's ⟨Merian, poster of Rome, back⟩.

28 The Aventine Hill, the most southerly of the seven hills of Rome, extends along the east side of the Tiber between Ponte Palatino and Ponte Sublicio. It is close to the ancient harbour and was originally inhabited by merchants, craftsmen, shopkeepers and small landowners, i.e., the common people. After the departure of the poorest inhabitants to the banks of the Tiber and over the river to Trastevere, it turned into a wealthier residential district.

29 The pyramid-shaped tomb of Caius Cestius (Piramide di Caio Cestio) is built into the Aurelian Wall close to Porta Ostiense. (The list for this afternoon might not be in the order of the visits, because the Protestant cemetery and the Cestius pyramid are directly adjacent.)

30 Castello Sant' Angelo (Castle of the Holy Angel), built as a mausoleum for the Emperor Hadrian, was once comparable with the Coliseum in terms of size and magnificence, but has undergone several incisive transformations over the centuries – into a fortress and bridgehead over the Tiber, refuge, citadel, prison, torture chamber and execution site, oil and corn store, residence and official building of various popes, connected by a gallery to the Vatican. Today the five floors up to the top viewing terrace are used as a museum. Ponte Sant' Angelo, parts of which date back to ancient Rome, is adorned with statues of angels by Bernini.

31 Tomba di Cecilia Metella (tomb of Caecilia Metella) is the burial site of the daughter of Consul Quintus Metellus Creticus. It is a huge cylindrical structure on a square base, rising up on Via Appia Antica (at kilometre 3). In the Middle Ages it was used as the foundations for a fortress watching over the road on both sides and serving as a prison. The ruins can still be seen today.

32 Via Appia Antica was one of the most important roads in the old empire to the southern provinces and to the Mediterranean and the Orient. Today it has this name from Porta San Sebastiano, the entrance to the city through the Aurelian Wall. This 'queen of roads' is lined with impressive monuments, villas, towers, tombs and the Catacombs, of which Freud – according to Jones – was most interested in the Jewish ones ⟨Jones II, p. 36⟩. See also note 73. Until the 1920s the surrounding land was an almost deserted steppe. Since then a mixture of houses has sprung up, and in the interests of traffic 'even its surface, the intact cobblestones from Roman times, has been sacrificed' ⟨Monelli, pp. 87f.⟩.

33 Columbaria, the urn niches in public cemeteries along the arterial roads of the early imperial era in which slaves and freemen were buried. Decorated arched chambers, sometimes let into the ground, contain stacked rows of niches resembling dovecots, sometimes carved directly into the rock. One well-preserved example is the Columbarium of Pomponius Hylas and his wife Pomponia Vitalinis, in Parco di Scipioni between Porta Latina and Porta San Sebastiano.

34 Villa Giulia is one of the largest of the summer residences set in contemplative garden landscapes and built by rich Roman families outside the city centre

since the Renaissance, some of which are open to the public. Villa Giulia, north of Piazza del Popolo, has housed the Etruscan Museum (Museo Nazionale Etrusco) since 1889.

35 The church of San Paolo fuori le Mura (St Paul's Outside the Walls) is a majestic basilica in large monastery grounds on Via Ostiense, south of Porta San Paolo and around 1.5 km outside the Aurelian Wall – on the site where the apostle St Paul is said to be buried (see note 36). On account of its size, magnificence and rich ornamentation, some of the site can be regarded as a modern wonder of the world; it contains architectural and artistic treasures from many centuries. Fragments of the original building can still be seen in the cloister.

36 The apostle St Paul is said to have been martyred in Abbazia delle Tre Fontane (a green oasis on Via Laurentina in the north-eastern corner of the EUR district). The church of San Paolo alle Tre Fontane commemorates the saint, who is said to have been buried later on Via Ostiense (see note 35).

37 Raphael's loggias are built on to the papal chambers and look down on the inner courtyard of San Damasco. Raphael completed work that had already been started and designed the ornamental elements, which were made by his students.

38 The Vatican library has a unique collection of precious documents, including a codex of the Bible from the fourth century, the famous Cicero palimpsest *De Republica* with the commentary *Super psalmos* by St Augustine. The walls are decorated with frescos and in one of the rooms are views of Rome from the Sistine era.

39 Monte Celio (Caelian Hill), one of the seven hills of Rome, is a greened hill with several churches and ancient relics. It extends south and south-east from the Coliseum and offers a panoramic view of the Palatine Hill, Forum and Coliseum as far as San Giovanni in Laterano. On the southern crest is the park of Villa Celimontana, laid out like an English garden, whose huge trees, flowers and fountains make it popular for walks.

40 Via Latina, an arterial road heading south-east, starts at Porta Latina and joins Via Appia Nuova at some distance from the city. Opposite the junction is the Archaeological Park whose southern border is formed by Via Demetriade. Here are the Tombs of the Valerii and Pancrazi, which are both richly decorated with mosaics and sarcophagi.

41 Until the papacy was transferred to Avignon in 1309 the Lateran was the residence of the popes in Palazzo Lateranense, which Emperor Constantine gave to the church. Alongside other extraterritorial possessions in this part of the city there is also Rome's cathedral, the massive Arcibasilica San Giovanni in Laterano (Archbasilica of St John Lateran), which is also the seat of the bishop of Rome and the ecumenical mother church for all Catholic churches in Rome and the world. In its baptistery 'Antiquity and Christianity meet'⟨Peterich [1957], p. 8⟩. 'The cloister is a masterpiece of Roman Cosmati art' (thirteenth century) ⟨Merian poster Rome, back⟩. The Lateran Accords were signed there in 1929, recognizing the full sovereignty of the Holy See and the Concordat. Today the rooms of Palazzo Apolistolico are used as museums (Musei Lateranense).

42 Anna probably went to the cinema with the daughter of the hotel operator, Nistelweck, whom she had met: 'Anna [. . .] is going out with her today,' wrote Freud on the same day to his family ⟨2002b, p. 383, with Tögel [2002], note 11⟩.

43 Monte Tarpea (also Rupe Tarpea – Tarpeian Rock) is a steep cliff on the

southern edge of the Campidoglio, named after the daughter of Tarpeius who, according to Roman legend, opened a city gate in the Capitoline Hill defended by her father to the Sabines and was pushed off the cliff as a traitor. Today this cliff, which is still dangerous, is fenced in.

44 The thirteenth-century church of Santa Maria in Aracoeli rises up from the highest point on the Campidoglio, on which the citadel of Rome used to stand. It became the national church of the aristocracy and the people of Rome, and in the Middle Ages it was the seat of the Senate. A wide and steep marble stairway with 124 steps, erected by the people in 1348 in thanks to the Virgin Mother for freeing the city of the plague, leads up to the basilica.

45 Museo Kircheriano (in Freud's day still in Via del Collegio Romano, now part of the Museo Preistorico et Etnografico Luigi Pigorini in Palazzo del Scienze, EUR), contains 'things from all over the world . . . from a Sioux costume to a Samurai sword, from a runic slab to African sculpture' ⟨Kircher; I thank Horst Peinlich, Department of Egyptology, University of Würzburg, for information and exhibition brochure⟩. Athanasius Kircher, S. J. (1602–80), scholar, collector and founder of Egyptology, taught from 1633 until his death at the Jesuit Collegio Romano and published 'fundamental works and summaries of the knowledge of his time' ⟨Kircher⟩. '*The Oedipus Aegyptiacus*' . . . is the best known of Kircher's Egyptian-Coptic studies' ⟨Brauen, p. 129, note 1⟩.

46 Fonte Acqua acetosa, on the southern tip of a tight northerly bend in the Tiber, with a well house over the source by Bernini. In Freud's day, it was still a rural area on the outskirts of the city at the start of the Campagna. Goethe once walked 'half an hour on foot in those days from his dwelling on Piazza di Spagna to drink from the aerated spring' ⟨Piwitt, p. 128⟩. Today there are sports fields in the midst of flyovers and the noise of urban motorways.

47 Ponte Molle, the popular name for the old Tiber bridge Ponte Milvio, at the crossroads of Via Cassia, Via Flaminia, Via Clodia and Via Veientana. In 312, the decisive battle between Maxentius and Emperor Constantine took place there. Constantine won 'under the sign of the Cross', leading to the recognition of Christianity as the state religion in 392.

48 Tivoli, classical Tibur, 30 km east of Rome in the Aniene Valley with its famous waterfalls, was already a popular summer residence for prominent Romans in imperial times. There are still remnants of villas, such as that of Pope Gregory or 'the red ruins below in the plain, among dark pines and clouds of cypresses: Hadrian's villa' ⟨Piwitt, p. 128⟩. Of the more recent buildings, apart from the church of Santa Maria Maggiore, the massive papal castle and the cathedral with its campanile, mention should be made of Villa d'Este, to which Freud and Anna devoted a whole afternoon.

49 The seat of the governor of Tivoli, Cardinal d'Este, incorporated in a former Benedictine monastery, is known above all for its grandiose terraced grounds and magnificent stairways, enchanting grottos, hundreds of springs, fountains, fish ponds and a central alley connecting shady paths. During the First World War, the property was taken over by the state and was opened to the public in the 1920s.

50 Palazzo Doria Pamphili is a splendid 'stone island' in the heart of Rome on Piazza del Collegio Romano. The Galleria Doria Pamphili contains antiques and a rich private collection of paintings from the sixteenth and seventeenth centuries, including choice items like the *Portrait of Pope Innocent X* by Velasquez and *Salome* by Titian. 'For those seeking the past in present-day

Rome a visit to the Roman museums is essential; this takes time, of course, since all epochs in history and art are dispersed throughout the different museums' ⟨Zschietzschmann, p. 19⟩. The reference might also be to an excursion to Villa Doria Pamphili behind the Gianicolo, the largest and most diverse park in Rome; its hilly landscape is full of cascades and grottos, a lake and numerous springs offering an unusually diverse habitat for flora and fauna.

51 Pinacoteca Vaticano, the famous collection of antiques and later paintings. The individual sections are housed in various rooms within the Vatican palaces.

52 Santa Maria del Popolo on Piazza des Popolo, one of the most interesting churches in Rome, with many impressive art treasures such as Chigi Chapel, designed by Raphael and decorated by other renowned artists, 'a jewel of the Renaissance', to mention just one example.

53 The church of Santa Prassede, next to the church of Santa Maria Maggiore near the main railway station, is famous for its mosaics, particularly those in the chancel and in St Zeno chapel, possibly the most important Byzantine work of art in Rome with its colourful ninth-century Carolinian mosaics. It is one of those 'old churches in the twilight off the beaten track, whose shabby façades give no indication of the magnificent interior, as if still keeping well-guarded secrets – and perhaps they do: in the darkness of Santa Prassede light suddenly falls through the side wing where the "garden of paradise", the Cappella di San Zenone, is located, a glazed focal point of its time' ⟨Modick, p. 95⟩.

54 Santa Maria Maggiore, the largest Roman church, dedicated to the Virgin Mary. Its Romanesque bell tower is the highest in Rome. In spite of many additions, the basilica has retained the form and character of the fifth-century original. Inside are precious mosaics, Cosmati floors and magnificent chapels belonging to various noble families, including one for Pope Sixtus V, the creator of Sistine Rome.

55 In a specially built chapel in the church of Santa Croce in Gerusalemme, not far from the Lateran buildings near Porta Maggiore, is one of the richest collections of relics, including allegedly a piece of the Cross and other items from the Crucifixion, which St Helen, the mother of Constantine, brought back from Jerusalem.

56 San Lorenzo fuori de Mura, which had a monastery and bell tower added in the twelfth century, was originally built by Constantine for the growing number of pilgrims coming to visit the grave of the martyr Lorenzo. As it was forbidden to bury the dead inside the city walls in ancient Rome, they were put to rest outside, next to the arterial roads. Freud and Anna saw this church before it was almost completely destroyed by bombs in 1943. It has now been extensively rebuilt.

57 This exceptional tomb of Marcus Vergilius Eurysaces and his wife, Atistia, was erected in 30 BC outside the walls next to Porta Maggiore. Eurysaces, a freed slave, was a baker by trade. Some of the architectural elements are shaped like dishes for dough, and there is a relief showing how bread is made.

58 The Zoological Garden is just to the north of Villa Borghese. 'The animals live where possible in their natural surroundings' ⟨Ente Provinciale Turisme – Roma; city map with descriptions of sights, undated, reverse⟩.

59 Galleria Borghese in the casino, at the highest point in the extensive Borghese villa complex, has a museum with numerous rooms on the ground floor, containing world-renowned sculptures. The painting gallery is on the first floor

and also has some of the most famous pictures in the world. The privately owned building and valuable collections were acquired by the state in 1902.

60 Santa Maria della Pace, on Piazza della Pace, has Raphael's famous fresco of the *Four Sibyls* over the arch of Chigi Chapel. The Bramante cloister, 'which inimitably reflects the spirit of the Renaissance', was added later.

61 Camera di Commercio (Chamber of Commerce) is on Piazza di Pietra in the same building as the stock exchange. It was originally built in the seventeenth century as a Vatican customs house on the site of Hadrian's Temple, constructed in 145 AD, with the integration of eleven 15 m marble Corinthian columns on a 4 m trass pedestal and part of the architrave above. The columns were originally part of the north wall of the temple, surrounding the cella or inner sanctum. When the customs house was remodelled in 1879 to accommodate the stock exchange and chamber of commerce, these elements were retained. A piece of the cella wall can still be seen behind the columns. It is possible that Freud wanted to show Anna this: as the stock exchange itself was not open to the public, he might have tried to gain access via the chamber of commerce. Some of the reliefs from inside the temple can be seen today in the Palazzo dei Conservatori.

62 Isola Tiberina was once the 'island of the sick' and retains this reputation today. A large part of the island is taken up with the Fatebenefratelli Hospital. The church of San Bartolomeo all' Isola stands on the site of a temple dedicated to Aesculapius, the god of medicine. Two old bridges connect the island with the mainland: Ponte Cestio (refurbished in the nineteenth century) with Trastevere, and Ponte Fabricio (almost completely intact) with Campo Marzio, the entrance to which is adorned by two four-headed busts of Janus.

63 Palazzo Farnese in the Renaissance district of Rome is 'called the most beautiful palace in the world on account of its harmony' ⟨d'Erme, p. 158⟩. The most renowned artists of the time were involved in its construction, headed by Michelangelo until his death. The charm of the highly structured architecture can be appreciated to the full in the masterly interior courtyard with its arrangement of columns and the bridge over Via Giulia. The palace was intended to 'demonstrate the magnificence of the provincial Farnese clan' ⟨ibid.⟩. Today it houses the French Embassy and the vast library of the École française de Rome.

64 Palazzo Spada is known for its colonnade and the elongated forced perspective gallery by Francesco Borromini, which is part of Galleria Spada. It contains one of the most important collections of seventeenth-century paintings in Rome, but also contains antiques such as the statue of Pompey, at whose feet Caesar is said to have fallen when he was murdered.

65 Palazzo della Cancelleria was the first major private Renaissance building in Rome. It was built over the remnants of the early Christian church of San Lorenzo in Damaso, whose granite columns can be seen in the interior courtyard. Today it belongs to the Vatican and is the seat of the Sacra Romana Rota, the highest appellate tribunal of the Roman Catholic Church.

66 Palazzo Massimo alle Colonne is a 'masterpiece of Romanesque architecture of the Cinquecento' ⟨d'Erme, p. 157⟩. The complex was built on the remains of the theatre of the emperor Domitian and follows the curves of the earlier building. One column from the ancient theatre on Piazza dei Massimi recalls the former building.

67 Palazzo Corsini on the edge of the Gianicolo contains galleries in its three large

wings. On the main floor is part of the Galleria Nazionale d'Arte Antica, one of the most important museums in Rome. The rest of the museum moved in 1949 to Palazzo Barberini. The park that used to belong to the palace has been turned into the botanical gardens of the University of Rome and has a wonderful cascade and a large number of indigenous and exotic plants, including the orchids and bromelias that Freud appreciated so much.

68 Villa Farnesina, whose grounds extend as far as the Tiber, is on Via della Lungara opposite Palazzo Corsini. It is perhaps the most well-known example of a Renaissance villa, 'a veritable work of architectural art'. Commissioned by Agostino Chigi, a rich papal banker, man of letters and patron of the arts, its rooms are adorned with mural and ceiling paintings by Raphael and other renowned artists. In the Salone delle Prospettive, for example, Peruzzi's trompe-l'oeil frescos make the walls appear to extend infinitely. The collection of valuable old prints in the Gabinetto delle Stampe is to be found in this building.

69 Porta Pia, the north-east entrance of the Aurelian Wall at the junction of Via XX Settembre and Corso d'Italia, replaced the ancient Porta Nomentana. It is the last architectural work by Michelangelo (1561–4) and characterizes the transition from late Renaissance to Baroque. Freud brought Ferenczi here in 1912 to witness 'the celebration of the capture of Rome' (1870), a commemoration held there regularly ⟨Freud 2002*b*, 21 September 1912, p. 269 (with ill.)⟩.

70 The architecture and decoration of Chiesa del Gesù, the Baroque mother church of the Jesuits in Rome, reflects the order's missionary activities and its support of the Counter-Reformation. It contains the grave of Ignatius Loyola, the order's founder, and Athanasius Kircher (see note 45).

71 From an archaeological point of view, the Basilica di San Clemente is one of the most interesting churches in Rome and offers a graphic illustration of the historical sequence of styles. The lower floor has the remains of first-century dwellings and a mithraeum; on the next level is a fourth-century lower church where councils were held in the fifth century, and an upper church from the twelfth century, which was subsequently modified. Together they form the three-storey San Clemente, near the Lateran. Remnants of earlier buildings were retained or reused every time the structure was modified, so that the different eras can all be seen, making the site 'a great attraction for students of Antiquity'. Some of the earlier elements were not discovered until 1938 and 1967, and were not therefore visible in 1923.

72 Piazza di Campo de' Fiori is one of the most atmospheric squares in Rome, with a market every morning except Sunday. During the Renaissance there were a number of print shops here and 'countless bookshops. . . . The address was also famous, however, for its guesthouses and taverns. . . . The guesthouses from this time can still be seen in two side streets off Campo de' Fiori' ⟨d'Erme, p. 158⟩. For a long time executions were also carried out here (see note 14).

73 *Porta* San Sebastiano (formerly Porta Appia) is a southern gate in the Aurelian Wall. It is the most monumental and best preserved of the Aurelian gates and has been refurbished and enlarged on several occasions. It is here that the most well-known part of Via Appia starts (see note 32). *Basilica* San Sebastiano is at the junction of Vicolo delle Sette Chiese and Via Appia. Work started in 1915 on the excavation of its catacombs, revealing an extensive grave complex.

74 There is no reference in the German Archaeological Institute in Rome to

German excavations of a Hermes statue or other signs of veneration of this messenger of the gods. ⟨I thank Alessandra Ridolfi, German Archaeological Institute, Rome, for her research and information.⟩ If no other groups made finds of this time, it could be that Freud and Anna visited a grave in the catacombs of San Sebastiano with the inscription 'Marcus Claudius Hermes' ⟨Knopf Guides, *Rome Italy* [1994], p. 327⟩.

75 Via Nazionale is a main transit and shopping street in Rome. It runs from Largo Magnanapoli near the Forum to Piazza della Repubblica.

76 From Piazzale Maresciallo Giardino, on the north-west outskirts of Rome, is a climb to the astronomical and meteorological observatory on Monte Mario (190 m), where the Copernicus Museum is also situated. In the Middle Ages pilgrims coming from the north, via today's Via Trionfale, obtained their first view here of the city and their destination, the Basilica of St Peter's. (See Anna's notes in Appendix 2.) Freud once described himself as a pilgrim to *Rome* ⟨[1900*a*] 1953, p. 194, note 1⟩. For Freud and Anna, it might have been a final view, with possibly a final walk on the Camilluccia on the eve of their departure.

77 Via Camilluccia is the continuation of Via Trionfale, leading north out of the city from the west side of Monte Mario. This arterial road is lined for several kilometres by villas, starting with Villa Mte Mario and Villa dei Massimi ⟨Verdesi, *Nuova Pianta di Roma*, undated, ill. 1–3⟩.

78 The Trevi Fountain, on the site of one of the earliest fountains in Rome and in a very picturesque area, forms a harmonious unit with the facade of Palazzo Poli. One might wonder whether Freud and Anna followed the tradition of throwing a coin into the fountain.

79 'Shopping will be difficult,' Freud reported to the family on 11 September. 'Anna has made friends with the daughter of the house and is going out with her today and will perhaps get some tips from her' ⟨2002*b*, p. 383⟩.

80 See 201 SF/AF, note 3.

Appendix 2

Notes by Anna on Return from Rome[1]

Appendix to 201 SF/AF

Vienna, 25 September 1923

The sheet of paper that I am inserting in front contains the notes on our Roman adventure. When I read them through, everything we experienced there comes to life again. I want to write down some of it from memory so as to hold on to it even better.

1 September

The journey from Florence to Rome was hot and uncomfortable, disturbed by a group of noisy, unpleasant Americans from Cincinnati, who kept on talking to us although we showed our lack of interest often enough. The woman thought we were Italians and wanted information about Roman pearls. Only when the man mistook the Appenine hills for the Urals was I able to reconcile myself to them. Just a sleepy glance at Florence in the early morning; hills that overlap like the background to lots of Madonna pictures. Then Etruria with villages on top of each hill. Papa made a special point of indicating Orvieto to me. Finally Latium and the Campagna. In many places the stubble fields were being burnt. Before that many small olive trees, between them endless garlands of grapevine. They look like rows of children extending their hands in play. Very few people to be seen.

Half an hour before arrival Papa pointed out the dome of St Peter's to me for the first time. How difficult the last barren bit of Campagna must have been for pilgrims coming on foot from the north to Vienna.[2]

A hotel bus was awaiting us, which made it very difficult to see anything. Instead of the street we kept on seeing ourselves in a large mirror. Papa showed me the Baths of Diocletian opposite the station. Then came large modern streets and after a very short time the Eden Hotel.

We had two nice comfortable rooms with a large bathroom, 119 and

120. The windows opened out south-west to Via de Porta Pinciana. Behind was the city wall with elevated gardens starting behind them.[3] From the buildings the side view of the church of S. Trinità del Monte and the two towers of Villa Medici could be seen; cypress trees and pines. We feared at first that the south-west sun would be too warm for us and wondered whether we should keep the rooms; but we needn't have worried. After some rearrangement the rooms were fine. Papa's desk had to be protected often from the wind; a vanity table with marble top was transformed into a card table. We didn't need to shut the curtains except to keep out the sun; no one could see in. In front of Papa's window were two particularly pointed cypresses which nodded very solemnly at the slightest breeze. They had been like that in 1913 as well, Papa said.

A disappointment and concern was the absence of our luggage. We couldn't change or get settled in and therefore went into the city after eating. We went first through Via Sistina, down the Spanish Steps to the Corso. The steps were very impressive; otherwise I was still very confused and dazed by the noise of the streets. We went to the luggage station but in vain. (We saw newspapers being unloaded.) We returned tired and annoyed and decided to try again in the evening. But dinner refreshed us and we changed our minds and went to bed. We were rewarded with the arrival of the luggage the following morning.[4]

1 These seven sheets, written in Anna's handwriting, are in LoC AF, Cont. 162, after the 'travel diary' reproduced in 201 SF/AF; see Appendix 1.
2 Presumably a slip of the pen for 'Rome'.
3 Villa Borghese, which was not south-west but north-west of Via di Ludovisi and of Via de Porta Pinciana; perhaps a window from a corner room opened to the west.
4 This is the end of the record. Anna cannot have felt like continuing because directly after their return the preparations had to be made for her father's radical surgery (see text after 201 SF/AF) ⟨Anna/Lou, letter 128⟩.

Appendix 3

Birthday Present for Dorothy Burlingham

Appendix to 293 SF

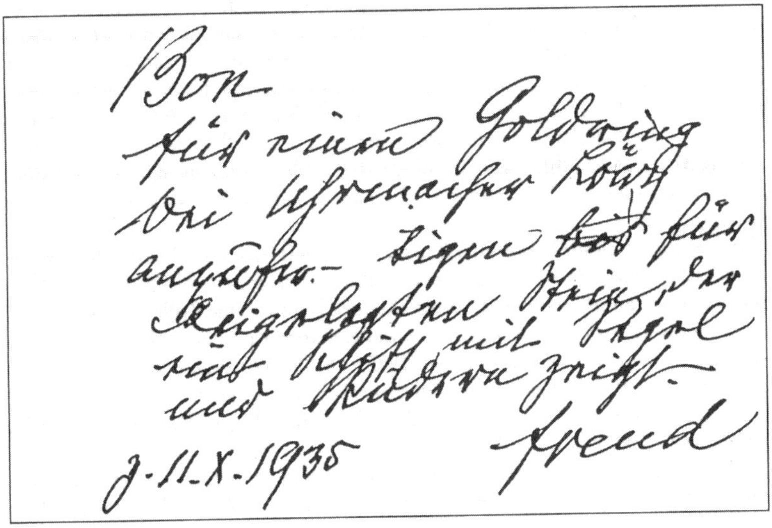

IX Voucher for Dorothy Burlingham

Voucher
for a gold ring[1]
from Löwy watchmakers
to be ♦ made by for[2]
the attached stone
bearing an engraved ship with sail[3]
and oars
for 11 November 1935 Freud

1 Freud had already given Dorothy a similar ring in 1929, whose gem showed a military and triumphal chariot with driver, which according to Michael Burlingham symbolized Dorothy's car and their morning drives together. As with the rings for committee members (see 174 AF, note 5), Freud once again chose an image that related to the wearer. The stone had broken, however, hence the replacement now ⟨Burlingham, M., p. 192⟩. Freud also gave jewellery to Anna's girlfriends on other occasions ⟨Ross, pp. 39f.⟩, and Anna herself had rings given to her by him (see 174 AF).

2 The slip of the pen before this word, and its subsequent correction, prompted Freud to write a small interpretive sketch, which he published in 1935 under the title 'The Subtleties of a Faulty Action' (1935*b*). He tried initially to explain the process stylistically – he had wanted to avoid repeating the word 'for', but in fact the mistake gained its purpose not by being made but only after it had been corrected. When he related it to Anna, she immediately saw how it went on: the repetition referred not to the word but to the act. 'You gave her a stone like that for a ring once before. . . . One doesn't like always to be making the same present.' The wish to avoid repetition referred obviously not to the word but to the giving of the present – the aesthetic pretext concealed an underlying instinctual conflict: 'I was looking for a motive for not making a present of the stone. . . . I wanted not to give the stone away at all. I liked it very much myself.'

Freud took this opportunity to show how one can easily be prematurely satisfied with a partial explanation and how many premises and dynamic determinants play a role in even a 'small mistake', in other words 'how complicated the most unobtrusive and apparently simplest mental processes can be' ⟨1935*b*, p. 234⟩. The incident seems to have been important for Freud as well; at all events he entered it in his *Diary*, while failing to note Dorothy's birthday ⟨Freud 1992*i*, 10 October 1935, p. 26⟩. Freud initially based his analysis on the use of 'bis' [= for, until] (in German) as a time-limit, but a comparison with his birthday present to Anna in 1932 also conjures up another meaning of the word, namely the limitation of a sum of money – see 290 SF.

3 Burlingham described it as a 'Viking longship'; Freud chose it as a symbol of Dorothy's long journey since leaving America ⟨Burlingham, M., p. 192⟩.

Appendix 4
Vaccination Certificates[1]

[Stamp] IX. BERGGASSE 19

Vaccination certificate

My daughter Anna Freud, born 3 December 1895, was vaccinated in her first year in my presence and has the normal vaccination marks on her left upper arm.

Prof. Dr Freud

Vienna, 13 October 1903

PROF. DR. FREUD

Scheewinkl
Vienna, IX. Berggasse 19
22 June 1929

Vaccination certificate

I confirm that Frl Anna Freud was once again vaccinated against variola (smallpox) on 10 June.

Prof. Dr Freud
at the University of Vienna

1 Anna kept these vaccination certificates with all of the correspondence (see 1 SF, note 1, and 256 SF, note 1). The first certificate is on a sheet with Martha Freud's initials MF as stamp and preprinted letterhead; the second is handwritten on a small-format sheet with Freud's preprinted letterhead.

Appendix 5

List of Places and Dates

Locations of correspondents and family members with dates (as far as can be ascertained from the correspondence)

Date	*Persons*	*Location*	*Source/reference*
1904			
end of June/beginning of July	Minna with children	Berchtesgaden/Königssee	1 SF + [3,4]
from 7 July	Martha as well		
12 July–28 August	Freud as well		1 SF[8]
29 August–10 September	Freud with Alexander	Greece, Athens	1 SF[8]
1905			
mid-July to at least 12 September	Martha with children (previously also Freud and Minna)	Altaussee	2 SF + [2,6]
3–23 September	Freud, Minna	Northern Italy, Switzerland	2 SF + [4]

1908			
7 July	Family	Berchtesgaden/Dietfeldhof	3 SF + [2]
16 July–31 August	Freud as well (also Ferenczi for some of the time)		
1–15 September	Freud	England	4 SF + [2-4]
15/17–21 September	Freud	(via Berlin) to Zurich (Jung)	4 SF + [2-4]
21–29 September	Freud, Minna	Northern Italy	4 SF + [2-4]
1909/1910			
27 December 1909 until after 6 January 1910	Mathilde, Anna	Semmering	5 MF/SF[1]
1–28 July	Minna, Sophie, Anna	Bistrai	6 AF + [1,2]
29 July	Minna, Sophie, Anna	Hamburg	6 AF + [1,2]
after 10 July until 29 July	Martha	Hamburg	6 AF + [1,2]
17–31 July	Freud, Oliver, Ernst	The Hague	
1–31 August	Freud, Martha and four children	Noordwijk	6 AF[13], 8 AF + [2]
	Minna	Hamburg	
31 August–24/26 September	Freud, Ferenczi	via Paris, Rome to Sicily/ return to Vienna via Rome	8 AF + [3]
31 August–13 September	Martha and four children	The Hague	8 AF + [4], 11 AF/EF[4]
14/16 September	Martha, Oliver, Sophie	return to Vienna via Berlin	11 AF/EF[4]
7 September	Ernst, Anna	return to Vienna	9 EF/AF
1911			
9–30 July	Freud (with van Emdens for some of the time)	Karlsbad	14 AF + [8]
15 July– ?	Martha, Minna, Sophie, Anna	Soprabolzano/Ritten	14 SF[2], 15 AF[13]
16 July– ?	Oliver as well		

Date	*Persons*	*Location*	*Source/reference*
1911			
? –15 September	Martha, Minna, three children	Klobenstein/Ritten	15 AF + [2, 13]
			16 AF[2]
31 July–15 September	Freud	Klobenstein/Ritten	
20 August–8 September	Ferenczi	Klobenstein/Ritten	
1–15 September	Martin	Klobenstein/Ritten	15 AF + [2, 13]
			16 AF[2]
8–15 September	Ernst, Mathilde	Klobenstein/Ritten	
15 September– ?	Martha, Minna, Sophie	Klobenstein/Ritten	16 AF[2], 17 AF
15–19 September'	Freud	Zurich/Küsnacht (Jung)	after 15 AF, 16 AF[2]
20–22 September	Freud, Jung	Weimar (Congress)	16 AF[2]
? –*c.* 30 September	Freud	Weimar, Hanover	16 AF[13], 17 AF[6, 7]
1912			
15 July–14 August	Freud, Martha	Karlsbad	18 SF/MF[4]
July	Minna with Sophie and Anna	Lovrana	18 SF/MF + [2]
15–30 August	Freud and family	Lago di Carezza	after 18 SF/MF
31 August–2 September	Freud, family and Ferenczi	Bolzano	after 18 SF/MF
2– after 14 September	Family	San Cristoforo	after 18 SF/MF
6–14 September	Freud, family and Ferenczi	San Cristoforo	after 18 SF/MF
15–27 September	Freud, Ferenczi	Rome	after 18 SF/MF
1912/1913			
End of October 1912? to	Anna	Merano	19 AF[1,7,9]
20 March 1913			32 AF[3]
21–26 March 1913	Freud and Anna	Verona, Venice	32 AF[3]
	Alexander and wife Sophie for some of the time		32 AF[5]

13 July–10 August	Freud, Martha, Minna, Anna	Marienbad	33 AF[2], 60 AF + [1]
before 27 July	visit from Sophie and Max		255 SF[4]
11 August–5 September	Freud, Martha, Anna (Abraham	San Martino di Castrozza	33 AF + [2]
15 August–5 September	and Ferenczi some of the time)		33 AF + [10]
5–9 September	Martha, Anna	still in San Martino	33 AF + [2]
9–15 September	Martha, Anna	Klobenstein	33 AF, 37 AF
5–8 September	Freud, Ferenczi	Munich (Congress)	33 AF[2], 33 AF +[10,11]
9–29 September	Freud, Minna	Rome	34 AF[4]
Christmas	Freud	Berlin and Hamburg (with Sophie and Max)	28 SF[5], 58 AF[9]
1914			
Easter	Freud, Ferenczi, Rank	Brionian Islands	40 SF + [2]
6–15 July	Anna	Hamburg	41 AF[1]
before 16 July– before 26 August		England (Arundel, St Leonard's)	41 AF[6], 46 SF + [4]
before 16 July–before 5 August	Minna	Cottage-Sanatorium	42 SF + [15], 46 SF + [4]
12 July–4 August	Freud, Martha	Karlsbad	41 AF + [2], 46 SF[4]
1915			
26–28 June	Freud, Minna	Berchtesgaden/Königssee	48 SF + [2]
before 10 July–before 12/14 August	Anna	Bad Ischl (grandmother)	49AF + [1], 70 SF + [1]
18 July–12 August	Freud, Martha	Karlsbad	50 SF, 51 SF
*c.*27 July	Mathilde	Berchtesgaden/Schönau	58 AF

Date	*Persons*	*Location*	*Source/reference*
1915			
*c.*7 August	Minna, Mathilde, Robert		66 SF 68 SF/MF
13 August–13/16 September	Freud, Martha, Anna, Mathilde (daughters only until 7 September)	via Munich to Schönau/ Berchtesgaden	66 SF[1] 67 AF[4] 68 SF/MF 69 AF[9] 70 SF + [1]
13/16–27 September	Freud, Minna	Berlin/Hamburg (Sophie)	67 AF[4]
29/30 September	Freud	Pápa (Ferenczi)	67 AF[4]
Christmas holidays	Anna	Hamburg (Sophie)	56 AF[4] 69 AF[6]
1916			
Easter	Anna, Rosi?	Hiking?	69 AF + [6]
Easter (23/24 April)	Freud	Mosty, Jablonica Pass, near Teschen [Český Těšín]	71 AF[8]
before 16 July	Minna, Anna	Weissenbach am Attersee	71 AF[7]
16 July–19 August	Freud, Martha, Minna, Anna	Salzburg	71 AF[7]
20 August–12 September	Freud, Martha, Minna	Bad Gastein	71 AF[7] 75 SF[7]
12–15 September		return Salzburg/Vienna	71 AF[7] 75 SF + [7]
14 August–*c.*10 September	Anna (Mathilde, Robert some of the time)	Altaussee/Marie Rischawy	71 AF[1] 74 AF, 75 SF
17 November–14 May 1917	Sophie with Ernstl	Vienna (parents' house)	75 SF + [8]

1917			
1 July–1 September	Freud, Martha, Anna (only until 19 August) (Sachs, Ferenczi, Rank some of the time)	Csorbató, High Tatra	76 SF + [1,4,6] 77 AF[2] 78 SF[3]
19 August to early September	Anna	Kotaj	76 SF[3] 77 AF + [1]
		return via Budapest?	79 AF + [1]
1918			
8–31 July	Freud, Anna	Quarry near Budapest	80 SF[2,10]
31 July–5 August	Anna	Quarry	80 SF[5] 81 SF
5–11 August		Budapest	82 AF
11 August–early September		Csorbató/Lomnicz	84 AF[1] 85 SF[1]
early September to 27 September		Vienna	84 AF[1]
1 August	Freud, Ferenczi with Willi (= Peter Lambda)	to Csorbató	80 SF + [2,5]
1–31 August	Freud, Martha, Anna (from 11 August) (some of the time with Ernst, Ferenczi, Kata)	Csorbató	80 SF + [2,5] 81 SF 87 SF[7] 82 AF[12,15]
1–25 September	Freud, Martha, Anna (only until early September)	Lomnicz	85 SF + [1] 84 AF[1]
early July–31 July	Martha	Schwerin	80 SF + [10]
1 August–25 September	Martha	Csorbató/Lomnicz	80 SF[10] 81 SF

Date	*Persons*	*Location*	*Source/reference*
1918			
25–29 September	Freud, Martha, Ernst	Budapest (Congress)	84 SF + [3,4] 86 AF[3] 87 SF[8] 88 SF 89 SF + [1]
27–29 September	Anna	Budapest (Congress)	86 AF[3] 90 AF + [1]
1919			
15 July–13 August	Martha	Salzburg, Sanatorium Partsch	92 SF + [4] 93 SF, 99 SF, 106 SF
15 July–13 August	Freud, Minna	Bad Gastein	93 SF 106 SF
17 July–13 August	Anna, Margarete Rie	Bayerisch-Gmain bei Bad Reichenhall	93 SF + [2] 94 SF[2] 106 SF
14 August–9 September	Freud, Martha, Anna (some of the time with Martin, Ernst)	Badersee	95 SF + [2] 104 SF[3] 105 AF[1,3] 106 SF + [6]
14 August to early 1920	Minna	Bad Reichenhall	106 SF + [1] after 106 SF
9–26 September	Freud, Martha, Anna, Eitingons	Munich–Berlin–Hamburg (Sophie)–Berlin–Salzburg–Vienna	106 SF + [6]

1920			
17 July–29 August	Anna, Rie family	Altaussee	107 SF[1,17]
30 July–28 August	Freud, Minna	Bad Gastein	107 SF[5]
			109 SF + [2]
			117 SF
			121 SF
20 August– ?	Alexander and family	Bad Gastein	117 SF
			119 SF
28–29 August	Freud	Bad Ischl	117 SF
			121 SF
*c.*31 July/early August–25 August	Martha, Mathilde, Robert	Goisern	107 SF[17]
			109 SF
			112 SF
25–29 August	Martha	Altaussee	122 AF/MF
30 August	Martha, Anna	Bad Ischl	121 SF
			122 AF/MF
30 August–6 September	Freud, Anna	Berlin	107 SF[5]
		Hamburg	117 SF[13]
		The Hague	117 SF[13]
		Congress	123 AF/SF + [1]
		Holland	after 123 AF/SF
		Tour	
29–30 September	Freud	Berlin, Vienna	after 123 AF/SF
29 September–7 November	Anna	Hamburg	after 123 AF/SF
7 November –10/13 December		Berlin (Wertheims, Eitingons)	124 SF +
			129 AF + [8]
			135 AF + [3]
			137 SF + [12]

Date	*Persons*	*Location*	*Source/reference*
1921			
10 July to after 18 July	Helene Gebert with children	Altaussee	140 SF
			144 AF
17 July–14 August	Martha		144 SF
15 July–14 August	Freud, Minna	Bad Gastein	138 SF + [5]
	(Lucy Wiener with children		141 AF
	some of the time)		142 SF
			150 SF
			149 SF + [2]
9/10 August	(v. Emdens etc., some of the time)	Bad Gastein	152 SF
14 August	Freud, Martha, Anna, Ernstl	Innsbruck	149 SF[2]
15 August–23 September	Freud, Ernstl	Seefeld	149 SF[2]
	(only to 14 September)		151 AF + [8]
	Martha, Anna		153 AF + [1,2]
	(Maus some of the time)		150 SF + [4]
			146 SF + [5,6]
14–20 September	Freud, Ernstl	Berlin, Hamburg	153 AF[2,8]
20–29 September	Freud, Committee members	Harz	153 AF[2]
1922			
1–3/4 March	Anna	Berlin	155 SF[1]
4 March–18 April		Hamburg	155 SF[1]
			164 AF
18–24/25 April		Berlin	160 AF[7]
			164 AF
			167 AF

25 April–4 May		Göttingen	165 AF + [2] 167 AF 168 AF
19/21 May–29 June	Minna	Abbazia	170 AF[2]
30 June/1 July to 31 July	Freud, Minna	Bad Gastein	157 SF 170 AF[2]
4–6 July	Martha, Anna	Berlin	170 AF + [5] 171 AF
7 July to early August	Martha, Ernstl, Heinerle, Frl Jacob	Hohegeiss	172 MF/AF + [3] 177 AF + [1] 174 AF[2] 188 AF
7 July to early August	Anna	Göttingen	172 MF/AF + [3] 173 AF 188 AF
1 August–14 September	Freud	Obersalzberg	174 AF[10] 187 SF
1 August – ?	Minna		174 AF[10]
4 August–8 September	Martha		174 AF[2,10]
4 August–14 September	Anna		182 AF + [1]
5 August– ?	Oli		174 AF[12]
later some of the time	Mathilde, Robert, Ernst and Lux, Lux's mother, Edith, Alexander		174 AF[10]
15/16–29 September	Freud, Anna	Munich Hamburg Berlin (Congress)	174 AF[10] 161 SF[14] 188 AF[2]

Date	*Persons*	*Location*	*Source/reference*
1923			
24 March–1 April ?	Anna	Passau –	189 AF + [2,3]
		Frankfurt –	191 AF
		Göttingen –	193 AF + [3]
		Berlin	194 SF
7–16 April	Martha, Martin	Berlin (marriage of Oli and Henny)	192 SF + [8,9]
20 April to after 10 May	Minna	Cottage Sanatorium	196 SF[6]
afterwards		Bad Reichenhall	196 SF[6]
1–30 July	Freud, Minna	Bad Gastein	196 SF + [1]
			200 SF
	(Ruth some of the time)		198 SF
			199 SF
6–30 July	Martha, Anna, Ernstl	Annenheim	196 SF + [3]
			200 SF + [3]
	(Jeanne some of the time)		196 SF + [4]
31 July–31 August	Freud, Minna?, Martha, Anna, Ernstl (only to 30 August)	Lavarone	200 SF + [3,4]
	(Mathilde some of the time)		200 SF + [5]
	Jones (1–25 August)		
	Committee members (27–30 August), etc.		
31 August–*c.*21 September	Martha	Merano (to Minna)	200 SF[4]
1–21 September	Freud, Anna	Rome	200 SF[4]
			201 SF/AF

1924			
14–24 April	Freud, Martha, Anna	Semmering	203 SF[3]
8 July–29 September	Freud, Martha, Minna, Anna (Mathilde some of the time)	Semmering	203 SF[3]
1925			
30 June–29 September	Freud, Martha, Anna (Mathilde some of the time)	Semmering	203 SF + [3] 206 SF[3] 204 SF 205 SF[2]
1–6 September	Anna	Bad Homburg (Congress)	203 SF + [3] 206 SF[3]
1926/1927			
5 March–2/4 April	Freud, Anna	Cottage Sanatorium	212 SF[3] 223 AF + [2]
17 June–29 September	Freud, Martha, Anna, Dorothy with children and Peter Blos	Semmering	244 AF[2]
25 December 1926– 1/2 January 1927	Freud, Martha, Ernstl (from Hamburg)	Berlin	208 SF + [1]
25 December 1926– 1/2 January 1927	Anna	Vienna/Rosenfeld	208 SF + [2,8]
1927			
18–20 March	Anna	Berlin	209 SF + [2,6]
7/8–28 April	Anna, Dorothy	Northern Italy	212 SF[2] 249 AF
14–28 April	Freud, Martha, Minna	Cottage Sanatorium	212 SF[3] 216 AF[3] 228 SF

Date	*Persons*	*Location*	*Source/reference*
1927			
16 June–29 September	Freud, Martha, Minna (start), Anna, Ernstl, Dorothy with children and Erikson	Semmering	244 AF[2]
end of June to 18 July	Oli, Henny with daughter Eva		
3 September– ?	Mathilde, Martin		252 SF
31 August–3/4 September	Anna	Innsbruck, Congress	250 SF
1928			
27 February–4 March	Anna, Dorothy	Paris	253 SF + [2,3] 255 SF[3]
16 June–30 August	Freud, Martha, Anna, Ernstl, Dorothy and family	Semmering	after 255 SF
30 August–31 October	Freud, Anna	Berlin–Tegel	after 255 SF
1929			
10/11–23/24 March	Freud, Anna (Lou 14 March– ?)	Berlin–Tegel	257 SF[6–8] 257 SF[6]
17/18 June–15 September	Freud, Martha, Minna, Anna, Ernstl, with school friends	Schneewinkl	256 SF + [3]
	Ernst and Lux		257 SF + [1]
	Martin, Oli, Dorothy and family		257 SF + [13,14]
	many visitors including Robert Burlingham and father (12August)		257 SF[13]
“Summertime”	Mathilde, Robert	Bayer. Gmain	256 SF + [5]
22 July–1/2 August	Anna	London, Oxford Congress	256 SF + [2] 265 AF 266 SF

15 September to after 21 October	Freud, Anna	Berlin–Tegel	257 SF[8]
18 December	Anna	Cologne, Essen	267 AF
			268 AF
19 December	Anna	Göttingen	269 AF
1930			
22 April–3 May	Freud, Anna	Cottage Sanatorium	270 AF[4]
4 May–24 July	Freud, Anna	Berlin–Tegel	after 255 SF
	Dorothy (some of the time)		270 AF[4]
27 July–27 September	Freud, Martha, Minna, Ernstl	Grundlsee	271 AF + [2]
	Dorothy and children with Margot Goldschmidt,		279 AF[2]
	Mathilde some of the time		277 SF + [4]
	Alexander with Sophie and Harry, Dolfi		277 SF + [4–6]
	Ruth, Marie Bonaparte, Eva Rosenfeld with Victor		
16–28 September	Anna, Dorothy	Knapsack trip to Italy and Switzerland	270 AF + [2,3]
			286 AF
27–29 August	Anna	Frankfurt, Goethe Prize	270 AF[4]
1931			
1 June–26 September	Freud household, Dorothy with family	Pötzleinsdorf	287 SF[2,19]
1932			
1/2 September	Anna	Göttingen	287 SF[1,8]
3–8 September	Anna, Dorothy	Wiesbaden, Congress	288 SF[1]

Date	*Persons*	*Location*	*Source/reference*
1932			
14 May–17 September	Freud household, Dorothy and family	Pötzleinsdorf	287 SF[2,22] 287 SF[19]
1933			
4 May–30 September	Freud household	Döbling	126 SF[15]
1934			
28 April–13 October	Freud household	Grinzing	126 SF[15]
1935			
18 April–18 October	Freud household	Grinzing	126 SF[15]
1936			
18 April–17 October	Freud household	Grinzing	126 SF[15]
1937			
24 April–16 October	Freud household	Grinzing	126 SF[15]
1938			
from 4 June	Freud and relatives (not his sisters) Dorothy and family	London (emigration)	after 295 SF 296 SF + [2] 297 SF + [7] 298 SF + [10] after 295 SF 298 SF[3,15]
29 July–5 August	Anna	Paris, Congress	296 SF + [3] 298 SF
from 4 September	Alexander and family	London (emigration)	297 SF + [8–10]

Part III

References

Abbreviations with Sources

Collected Papers — Sigmund Freud, *Collected Papers* (5 vols), vols 1, 2, 4 edited by Joan Riviere, foreword by Ernest Jones, vol. 3 translated and annotated by James Strachey; vol. 1 (New York, London, Vienna: International Psychoanalytical Press, 1924), vols 2–5 (London: The Hogarth Press and the Institute of Psycho-Analysis, 1924–50)

DBA N. F. — Deutsches Biographisches Archiv, Neue Folge

FM — Freud Museum, London, 20 Maresfield Gardens, London NW3 5SX

Grinstein — Alexander Grinstein, *The Index of Psychoanalytic Writings*, preface by Ernest Jones, vols 1–14 (New York: International Universities Press, 1956–75)

G. W. — Sigmund Freud, *Gesammelte Werke* (18 volumes and an unnumbered Supplement), vols 1–17 (London, 1940–52), vol. 18 (Frankfurt, 1968); Supplement (Frankfurt, 1987). The entire edition since 1968 Frankfurt: Fischer Verlag

IJ — *The International Journal of Psychoanalysis*, directed by Sigmund Freud, Official Organ of the International Psychoanalytical Association, edited by Ernest Jones (1920ff.)

Imago — *Imago, Zeitschrift für Anwendung der Psychoanalyse auf die Geiseswissenschaften*, published by Sigm. Freud (1912–1939), edited by Otto Rank and Dr. Hanns Sachs, last published vol. 26 (1941), in America continued by Sachs as *American Imago* until his death in 1947

IZ — *Internationale Zeitschrift für ärztliche Psychoanalyse*, Offizielles Organ der Internationalen

	Psychoanalytischen Vereinigung, published by S. Freud (1913–1939), edited by S. Ferenczi, O. Rank and E. Jones
Jb	*Jahrbuch für psychoanalytische und psychopathologische Forschungen*, published by E. Bleuler, Zurich, and S. Freud, Vienna, edited by C. G. Jung
Jb. Psychoanal.	*Jahrbuch der Psychoanalyse, Beitrage zur Theorie, Praxis und Geschichte*, edited by K. Dräger et al.
Journal	See *IJ*
Kürschner	*Kürschners deutscher Gelehrtenkalender*
LoC AF	The Library of Congress, Washington, DC, Manuscript Division, Sigmund Freud Collection, The Papers of Anna Freud
LoC SF	The Library of Congress, Washington, DC, Manuscript Division, Sigmund Freud Collection, The Papers of Sigmund Freud
ORC	Special Collections: The Papers of Otto Rank, Rare Books and Manuscript Library, Columbia University, New York, NY
'Press'	The Psychoanalytical Press, London
Ψ	Psycho-
ΨA	Psychoanalysis
ψa	psychoanalytical
Review	*The Psychoanalytical Review, A Journal Devoted to an Understanding of Human Conduct*, ed. and publ. by William A. White, MD, and Smith Ely Jelliffe, MD, first issue November 1913
S. E.	*The Standard Edition of the Complete Psychological Works of Sigmund Freud*, 24 vols, vols 1–23 edited by James Strachey in cooperation with Anna Freud, Alix Strachey and Alan Tyson (London: The Hogarth Press and the Institute of Psychoanalysis, 1953–74)
Standard Edition	See *S. E.*
Verlag	Internationaler Psychoanalytischer Verlag (Vienna, Leipzig, Zurich)
Zeitschrift	See *IZ*

Bibliography

Sigmund Freud

The chronological list is based on Ingeborg Meyer-Palmedo, Gerhard Fichtner, *Freud-Bibliographie mit Werkkonkordanz*, 2nd revised edition (Frankfurt: S. Fischer, 1999) and Alexander Grinstein, MD, *Sigmund Freud's Writings – A Comprehensive Bibliography* (New York: International Universities Press, 1977). The works marked with a double asterisk are not yet available in printed form and were classified by Gerhard Fichtner.

Unless otherwise indicated, for non-published letters by Freud, see 'Unpublished Material'.

The numbers in brackets after each entry refer to the letters or footnotes in which the work is mentioned.

Freud Illustrated Biography

Ernst Freud, Lucie Freud, Ilse Grubrich-Simitis (eds), *Sigmund Freud – Sein Leben in Bildern und Texten* (Frankfurt: Suhrkamp, 1976); available in English as Ernst Freud et al., *Sigmund Freud: His Life in Pictures and Words*, translated by Christine Trollope (New York: Norton, 1985) (text after 15).

Works

The works of Sigmund Freud are quoted from *The Standard Edition of the Complete Psychological Works of Sigmund Freud*, transl. from the German under the General Editorship of James Strachey, 24 vols (London: The Hogarth Press, 1953–74).

(1877*a*) 'Über den Ursprung der hinteren Nervenwurzeln im Rückenmarke von Amnocoetes (Petromyzon Planeri)', in *Sitzungsber. Akad. Wiss. Wien* (Math.-Naturwiss. Kl.), 3. Abt., vol. 75 (1877), pp. 15–27 (32, 75).

'On the origin of the posterior nerve-roots in the spinal cord of Amnocoetes (Petromyzon planeri)', abstract, *S. E.*, vol. 3, p. 228.

(1877*b*) 'Beobachtungen über Gestaltung und feineren Bau der als Hoden beschriebenen Lappenorgane des Aals', in *Sitzungsber. Akad. Wiss. Wien* (Math.-Naturwiss. Kl.), 1. Abt., vol. 75 (1877), pp. 419–31 (32, 75).

'Observations on the configuration and finer structure of the lobed organs in eels described as testes', abstract, *S. E.*, vol. 3, p. 227.

(1878*a*) 'Über Spinalganglien und Rückenmark des Petromyzons', in *Sitzungsber. Akad. Wiss. Wien* (Math.-Naturwiss. Kl.), 3. Abt., vol. 78 (1878), pp. 81–167 (32, 75).

'On the spinal ganglia and spinal cord of the petromyzon, abstract, *S. E.*, vol. 3, pp. 228–9.

(1881*a*) 'Über den Bau der Nervenfasern und Nervenzellen beim Flusskrebs', in *Anz. Akad. Wiss. Wien* (Math.-Naturwiss. Kl.), vol. 18, no. 28 (1881), 275f. (75).

(1882*a*) 'Über den Bau der Nervenfasern und Nervenzellen beim Flusskrebs', in *Sitzungsber. Akad. Wiss. Wien* (Math.-Naturwiss. Kl.), vol. 85 (1882), pp. 9–46 (75).

'On the structure of the nerve fibres and nerve cells of the river crayfish', abstract, *S. E.*, vol. 3, p. 230.

(1884*b*) 'Eine neue Methode zum Studium des Faserverlaufs im Centralnervensystem', in *Zbl. med. Wiss.*, vol. 22 (1884), pp. 161–3 (75).

'A new method for the study of the course of nerve fibres in the central nervous system', abstract, *S. E.*, vol. 3, p. 231.

(1884*d*) 'Eine neue Methode zum Studium des Faserverlaufs im Centralnervensystem', in *Arch. Anat. Physiol.*, Anat. Abt. (1884), pp. 453–60 (75).

(1884*f*) 'Die Structur der Elemente des Nervensystems', in *Jbb. Psychiatr. Neurol.*, vol. 5 (1884), pp. 221–9, lecture at the Verein für Psychiatrie une Neurologie, 1882 (75).

'The structure of the elements of the nervous system', abstract, *S. E.*, vol. 3, p. 230.

(1885*d*) 'Zur Kenntniss der Olivenzwischenschicht', in *Neurol. Zbl.*, vol. 4 (1885), pp. 268–70 (75).

'Concerning the knowledge of the intermediary layer of the olive', abstract, *S. E.*, vol. 3, p. 234.

(1886*b*) (with L. O. Darkschewitsch) 'Über die Beziehung des Strickkörpers zum Hinterstrang und Hinterstrangskern, nebst Bemerkungen über die zwei Felder der Oblongata', in *Neurol. Zbl.*, vol. 5 (1886), pp. 121–9 (75).

'On the relation of the restiform body to the posterior column and its nucleus with some remarks on two fields of the medulla oblongata', abstract, *S. E.*, vol. 3, p. 237.

(1886*c*) 'Über den Ursprung des N.[ervus] acusticus', in *Mschr. Ohrenhk.* N. F., vol. 20 (1886), pp. 245–51, 277–82 (75).

'On the origin of the acoustical nerve', abstract, *S. E.*, vol. 3, p. 238.

(1887*f*) 'Das Nervensystem', in Eduard Buchheim (ed.), *Ärztliche Versicherungs-Diagnostik*, section 5 (Vienna, 1887), pp. 188–207 (75).

(1891*a*) (with Oskar Rie) *Klinische Studie über die halbseitig Cerebrallähmung der Kinder* (Vienna, 1891) (16, 34, 75).

'Clinical study of hemilateral cerebral paralysis in children', abstract, *S. E.*, vol. 3, pp. 241–2.

(1891*b*) *Zur Auffassung der Apahsien – Eine kritische Studie* (Leipzing, Vienna: Deuticke, 1891) (71).

'On the interpretation of the aphasias, a critical study', abstract, *S. E.*, vol. 3, pp. 240–1.

(1893*b*) *Zur Kenntniss der cerebralen Diplegien des Kindesalters (im Anschluss an die Little'sche Krankheit)* (Vienna, 1893) (34, 75).

'Contributions to the knowledge of cerebral diplegias in childhood, in connection with Little's disease', abstract, *S. E.*, vol. 3, pp. 245–7.

(1893*d*) 'Über die familiären Formen von cerebralen Diplegien', in *Neurol. Zbl.*, vol. 12 (1893), pp. 512–15, 542–7 (75).

'On familiar forms of cerebral diplegias', abstract, *S. E.*, vol. 3, p. 247.

(1893*f*) 'Charcot †', *G. W.*, vol. 1, pp. 21–35 (156).

'Charcot', abstract, *S. E.*, vol. 3, p. 243.

(1893*h*) Contribution to: Ludwig Rosenberg, *Casuistische Beiträge zur Kenntniss der cerebralen Kinderlähmungen und der Epilepsie* (Vienna, 1893), pp. 92–111 (34).

(1893–4*a*) Signed lexicon entry in Anton Bum, Moriz T. Schnirer (eds), *Diagnostisches Lexikon für praktische Ärzte*, vol. 1 (1893) and vol. 3 (1894) (Vienna, Leipzig: Urban & Schwarzenberg) (75).

(1895*d* [1893–5]) (with Josef Breuer) Studien über Hysterie, *G. W.*, vol. 1, pp. 1–238 [without Breuer's contribution]; pp. 217ff., 221–310 [Breuer's contribution] (74).

Studies in Hysteria, *S. E.*, vol. 2.

(1897*a*) 'Die infantile Cerebrallähmung', part 2, sect. 2, in Hermann Nothnagel (ed.), *Specielle Pathologie und Therapie*, vol. 9 (Vienna: Holder, 1897) (75).

'Infantile cerebral paralysis', abstract, *S. E.*, vol. 3, p. 256.

(1898*a*) 'Die Sexualität in der Ätiologie der Neurosen', in *G. W.*, vol. 1, pp. 491–516 (156).

'Sexuality in the aetiology of the neuroses', translated by J. Bernays, revised translation in *S. E.*, vol. 3, pp. 263–85.

(1900*a*) *Die Traumdeutung*, *G. W.*, vol. 2/3 (16, 62, 71, 77, 105, 110, 150, Appendix 1, note 76).

The Interpretation of Dreams, *S. E.*, vol. 4, *S. E.*, vol. 5, pp. 339–627.

(1901*a*) 'Über den Traum', *G. W.*, vol. 2/3, pp. 643–70 (166, 194).

'On dreams', *S. E.*, vol. 5, pp. 633–86.

(1901*b*) *Zur Psychopathologie des Alltagslebens (über Vergessen, Versprechen, Vergreifen, Aberglaube und Irrtum)*, *G. W.*, vol. 4 (4, 5, 12, 65, 66, 99, 142, 144, 166).

The Psychopathology of Everyday Life: Forgetting, Slips of the Tongue, Bungled Actions, Superstitions and Errors, *S. E.*, vol. 6.

(1904*a* [1903]) 'Die Freudsche psychoanalytische Methode', *G. W.*, vol. 5, pp. 3–10 (156).

'Freud's psychoanalytic procedure', *S. E.*, vol. 7, pp. 249–54.

(1904*e*) 'Professor S. Hammerschlag [obituary], *G. W.*, Supplement, pp. 733f. (33).

'Obituary of Professor S. Hammerschlag', *S. E.*, vol. 9, pp. 255f.

(1905*a* [1904]) 'Über Psychotherapie', *G. W.*, vol. 5, pp. 13–26 (156).

'On psychotherapy', *S. E.*, vol. 7, pp. 257–68.

(1905*d*) 'Drei Abhandlungen zur Sexualtheorie', *G. W.*, vol. 5, pp. 27–145 (166).

'Three essays on the theory of sexuality', *S. E.*, vol. 7, pp. 130–243.

(1905*e*) [1901] 'Bruchstück einer Hysterie-Analyse', *G. W.*, vol. 5, pp. 161–286 (110, 196).

'Fragment of an analysis of a case of hysteria', *S. E.*, vol. 7, pp. 7–122.

(1906*f*) Answer to a questionnaire 'Vom Lesen und guten Büchern', *G. W.*, Supplement, pp. 662–4 (17, 20).

(1907*a*) 'Der Wahn und die Träume in W. Jensens "Gradiva"', *G. W.*, vol. 7, pp. 29–122 (6).
'Delusions and dreams in Jensen's *Gradiva*', *S. E.*, vol. 9, pp. 7–95.
(1908*a*) 'Hysterische Phantasien und ihre Beziehung zur Bisexualität', *G. W.*, vol. 7, pp. 191–9 (160).
'Hysterical phantasies and their relation to bisexuality', *S. E.*, vol. 9, pp. 159–66.
(1908*c*) 'Über infantile Sexualtheorien', *G. W.*, vol. 7, pp. 171–88 (160).
'On the sexual theories of children', *S. E.*, vol. 9, pp. 209–26.
(1908*e* [1907]) 'Der Dichter und das Phantasieren', *G. W.*, vol. 7, pp. 213–23 (20).
'Creative writers and day-dreaming', *S. E.*, vol. 9, pp. 143–53.
(1909*a*) 'Allgemeines über den husterischen Anfall', *G. W.*, vol. 7, pp. 235–40 (160).
'Some general remarks on hysterical attacks', *S. E.*, vol. 9, pp. 229–34.
(1909*b*) 'Analyse der Phobie eines fünfjährigen Knaben ["Der kleine Hans"]', *G. W.* vol. 7, pp. 241–377 (192, 196).
'Analysis of a phobia in a five-year-old boy ["Little Hans"]', *S. E.*, vol. 10, pp. 5–147.
(1909*d*) 'Bemerkungen über einen Fall von Zwangsneurose ["Der Rattenmann"]', *G. W.*, vol. 7, pp. 379–463 (196).
'Notes upon a case of obsessional neurosis ["Rat Man"]', *S. E.*, vol. 10, pp. 155–318.
(1910*a* [1909]) 'Über Psychoanalyse: fünf Vorlesungen gehalten zur 20 jährigen Gründungsfeier der Clark University in Worcester, Mass., Sept. 1909', *G. W.*, vol. 8, pp. 1–60 (18, 125, 133, 166, 199).
'Five lectures on psychoanalysis: delivered on the occasion of the celebration of the twentieth anniversary of the foundation of Clark University, Worcester, Massachusetts, September 1909', *S. E.*, vol. 11, pp. 9–55.
(1910*c*) 'Eine Kindheitserinnerung des Leonardo da Vinci', *G. W.*, vol. 8, pp. 127–211 (213).
'Leonardo da Vinci and a memory of his childhood', *S. E.*, vol. 11, pp. 63–137.
(1910*i*) 'Die psychogene Sehstörung in psychoanalytischer Auffassung: Beitrag zur Festschrift für Prof. Dr. Leopold Königstein', *G. W.*, vol. 8, pp. 94–102 (175).
'The psychoanalytic view of psychogenic disturbance of vision', *S. E.*, vol. 11, pp. 211–18.
(1911*b*) 'Formulierungen über die zwei Prinzipien des psychischen Geschehens', *G. W.*, vol. 8, pp. 230–8.
'Formulations on the two principles of mental functioning', *S. E.*, vol. 12, pp. 218–26.
(1911*c* [1910]) 'Psychoanalytische Bemerkungen über einen autobiographisch beschriebenen Fall von Paranoia (Dementia paranoides)' [Schreber], *G. W.*, vol. 8, pp. 239–316 (196).
'Psychoanalytic notes upon an autobiographical account of a case of paranoia (dementia paranoides)', *S. E.*, vol. 12, pp. 9–79.
(1911*j* [1910]) Translation with additional footnote to Putnam (1910) entitled 'Über Ätiologie und Behandlung der Psychoneurosen', in *Zbl. Psychoanal.*, vol. 1 (1911), pp. 137–54; footnote in *G. W.*, Supplement, p. 766 (49).
Included in editor's footnote to 'James J. Putnam (obituary)', *S. E.*, vol. 17, pp. 271f., note.
(1912*a* [1911]) 'Nachtrag zu dem autobiographisch beschriebenen Fall von Paranoia (Dementia paranoides)' [Schreber], *G. W.*, vol. 8, pp. 317–20 (196).
'Postscript to the case of paranoia', *S. E.*, vol. 12, pp. 80–2.
(1912*i*) Introductory passages to 'Über einige Übereinstimmungen im Seelenleben der Wilden und der Neurotiker', *G. W.*, Supplement, pp. 743–5 (27).

(1912–13*a*) *Totem und Tabu*, *G. W.*, vol. 9 (27).
Totem and Taboo, *S. E.*, vol. 13, pp. 1–163.
(1913*c*) 'Zur Einleitung der Behandlung (Weitere Ratschläge zur Technik der Psychoanalyse I)', *G. W.*, vol. 8, pp. 454–78 (77, 86).
'On beginning the treatment (further recommendations on the technique of psychoanalysis I)', *S. E.*, vol. 12, pp. 123–44.
(1913*e*) 'Vorwort' to Maxim[ilian] Steiner, *Die psychischen Störungen der männlichen Potenz* (Leipzig, Vienna: Deuticke, 1913); *G. W.*, vol. 10, pp. 451f. (144).
(1913*f*) 'Das Motiv der Kästchenwahl', *G. W.*, vol. 10, pp. 24–37 (28, 87, 185).
'The theme of the three caskets', *S. E.*, vol. 12, pp. 291–301.
(1914*b*) 'Der Moses des Michelangelo', *G. W.*, vol. 10, pp. 172–201 (Appendix 1, note 16).
'The Moses of Michelangelo', *S. E.*, vol. 13, pp. 211–36.
(1914*c*) 'Zur Einführung des Narzissmus', *G. W.*, vol. 10, pp. 137–70 (132).
'On narcissism: an introduction', *S. E.*, vol. 14, pp. 73–102.
(1914*d*) 'Zur Geschichte der psychoanalytischen Bewegung', *G. W.*, vol. 10, pp. 43–113 (6, 43, 99, 166, 192).
'On the history of the psychoanalytic movement', *S. E.*, vol. 14, pp. 7–66.
(1914*g*) 'Erinnern, Wiederholen und Durcharbeiten (Weitere Ratschläge zur Technik der Psychoanalyse II)', *G. W.*, vol. 10, pp. 126–36 (43, 87).
'Remembering, repeating and working through: further recommendations on the technique of psychoanalysis II)', *S. E.*, vol. 12, pp. 147–56.
(1915*a*) 'Bemerkungen über die Übertragungsliebe (Weitere Ratschläge zur Technik der Psychoanalyse III)', *G. W.*, vol. 10, pp. 306–21 (43, 87).
'Observations on transfer love: recommendations on the technique of psychoanalysis III)', *S. E.*, vol. 12, pp. 159–71.
(1915*b*) 'Zeitgemässes über Krieg und Tod', *G. W.*, vol. 10, pp. 324–55 (61).
'Thoughts for the times on war and death', *S. E.*, vol. 14, pp. 275–300.
(1915*c*) 'Triebe und Triebschicksale', *G. W.*, vol. 10, pp. 210–32 (54).
'Instincts and their vicissitudes', *S. E.*, vol. 14, pp. 117–40.
(1915*d*) 'Die Verdrängung', *G. W.*, vol. 10, pp. 248–61 (54).
'Repression', *S. E.*, vol. 14, pp. 146–58.
(1915*e*) 'Das Unbewusste', *G. W.*, vol. 10, pp. 264–303 (54).
'The unconscious', *S. E.*, vol. 14, pp. 166–215.
(1915*i*) 'Wir und den Tod', speech given on 16 February 1915 to the B'nai B'rith lodge in Vienna, in *Zweimonats-Bericht für die Mitglieder der österr. israel. Humanitätsvereine B'nai B'rith*, vol. 18 (1915), no. 1, pp. 41–51 (61).
(1916*a*) 'Vergänglichkeit', *G. W.*, vol. 10, pp. 358–61 (103).
'On transience', *S. E.*, vol. 14, pp. 305–7.
(1916–17*a* [1915–17]) *Vorlesungen zur Einführung in die Psychoanalyse*, *G. W.*, vol. 11 (72, 75, 107, 144, 153, 163, 178, 277).
Introductory Lectures on Psychoanalysis, *S. E.*, vols 15–16.
(1916–17*c*) 'Eine Beziehung zwischen einem Symbol und einem Symptom', *G. W.*, vol. 10, pp. 394f. (160).
'A connection between a symbol and a symptom', *S. E.*, vol. 14, pp. 339f.
(1916–17*g*) 'Trauer und Melancholie', *G. W.*, vol. 10, pp. 428–46 (54, 132).
'Mourning and melancholia', *S. E.*, vol. 14, pp. 243–58.
(1917*a* [1916]) 'Eine Schwierigkeit der Psychoanalyse', *G. W.*, vol. 12. pp. 3–12 (113).
'A difficulty in the path of psychoanalysis', *S. E.*, vol. 17, pp. 137–44.

(1917*b*) 'Eine Kindheitserinnerung aus *Dichtung und Wahrheit*', *G. W.*, vol. 12, pp. 12–26 (78).
'A childhood recollection from *Dichtung und Wahrheit*', *S. E.*, vol. 17, pp. 147–56.
(1918*a* [1917]) 'Das Tabu der Virginität (Beiträge zur Psychologie des Liebeslebens III)', *G. W.*, vol. 12, pp. 159–80 (82, 87).
'The taboo of virginity (contributions to the psychology of love III)', *S. E.*, vol. 11, pp. 193–208.
(1918*b* [1914]) 'Aus der Geschichte einer infantilen Neurose' [Der Wolfmann], *G. W.*, vol. 12, pp. 27–157 (196).
'From the history of an infantile neurosis' [the wolf man], *S. E.*, vol. 17, pp. 7–122.
(1919*a* [1918]) 'Wege der psychoanalytischen Therapie', *G. W.*, vol. 12, pp. 183–94 (77, 89).
'Lines of advance in psychoanalytic therapy', *S. E.*, vol. 17, pp. 159–68.
(1919*b*) 'James J. Putnam †', *G. W.*, vol. 12, p. 315 (49).
'James J. Putnam', *S. E.*, vol. 17, pp. 271f.
(1919*c*) 'Internationaler Psychoanalytischer Verlag und Preiszustellungen for psychoanalytische Arbeiten', *G. W.*, vol. 12, pp. 333–6 (89, 114).
'A note on psychoanalytic publications and prizes', *S. E.*, vol. 17, pp. 267–9.
(1919*f*) 'Victor Tausk†', *G. W.*, vol. 12, pp. 316–18 (96).
'Victor Tausk', *S. E.*, vol. 17, pp. 273–5.
(1919*g*) 'Vorrede' to Theodor Reik, *Probleme der Religionspsychologie*, part 1: *Das Ritual*, *G. W.*, vol. 12, pp. 325–9 (160).
(1919*h*) 'Das Unheimliche', *G. W.*, vol. 12, pp. 229–68 (15).
'The "uncanny"', *S. E.*, vol. 17, pp. 219–56.
(1920*b*) 'Zur Vorgeschichte der analytischen Technik', *G. W.*, vol. 12, pp. 309–12 (100).
'A note on the prehistory of the technique of analysis', *S. E.*, vol. 18, pp. 263–5.
(1920*c*) 'Dr. Anton v. Freund †', *G. W.*, vol. 13, pp. 435f. (80, 89, 96, 100).
'Dr. Anton von Freund', *S. E.*, vol. 18, pp. 267f.
(1920*f*) 'Ergänzungen zur Traumlehre', *G. W.*, Supplement, pp. 622f. (142).
'Supplements to the theory of dreams', *S. E.*, vol. 18, pp. 4f.
(1920*g*) *Jenseits des Lustprinzips*, *G. W.*, vol. 13, pp. 1–69 (95, 100, 112, 142, 157, 166).
Beyond the Pleasure Principle, *S. E.*, vol. 18, pp. 7–64.
(1921*a*) 'Preface' [in English] to James J. Putnam, *Address on Psychoanalysis* (London, New York: International Psychoanalytical Press, 1921), pp. III–V; *G. W.*, vol. 13, pp. 437f. (49).
(1921*b*) 'Introduction' [in English] to Varendonck (1921b); *G. W.*, vol. 13, pp. 439f. (142).
(1921*c*) *Massenpsychologie und Ich-Analyse*, *G. W.*, vol. 13, pp. 71–161 (110, 112, 114, 117, 119, 132, 138, 142, 157).
Group Psychology and the Analysis of the Ego, *S. E.*, vol. 18, pp. 69–143.
(1921*d*) 'Preiszuteilungen', *G. W.*, Supplement, p. 711 (142, 163).
'Award of prizes', *S. E.*, vol. 17, pp. 269f.
(1921*e* [1920]) Letter to Édouard Claparède (25 December 1920), *G. W.*, Supplement, pp. 750f. (125).
(1922*a*) 'Traum und Telepathie', *G. W.*, vol. 13, pp. 165–91 (163).
'Dreams and telepathy', *S. E.*, vol. 18, pp. 197–220.
(1922*b* [1921]) 'Über einige neurotische Mechanismen bei Eifersucht, Paranoia und Homosexualität', *G. W.*, vol. 13, pp. 195–207 (153, 175, 181).

'Some neurotic mechanisms in jealousy, paranoia and homosexuality', *S. E.*, vol. 18, pp. 223–32.
(1922*c*) 'Nachschrift zur Analyse des kleinen Hans', *G. W.*, vol. 13, pp. 431f. (196).
'Postscript (1922) to "Analysis of a phobia in a five-year-old boy"', *S. E.*, vol. 10, pp. 148f.
(1922*d*) 'Preisausschreibung', *G. W.*, Supplement, p. 712 (163).
'Prize offer', *S. E.*, vol. 17, p. 270.
(1922*f*) 'Etwas vom Unbewussten', *G. W.*, Supplement, p. 730 (183).
'Some remarks on the unconscious', *S. E.*, vol. 19, pp. 3f.
(1923*b*) *Das Ich und das Es*, *G. W.*, vol. 13, pp. 237–89 (132, 181, 183).
The Ego and the Id, *S. E.*, vol. 19, pp. 12–66.
(1923*g*) Foreword to Max Eitingon, *Bericht über die Berliner psychoanalytische Poliklinik (März 1920 bis June 1922)* (Leipzig, Vienna, Zurich: Internationaler Psychoanalytischer Verlag, 1923); *G. W.*, vol. 13, p. 441 (100).
(1923*h*) Letter to Luis Lopez-Ballasteros y de Torres (7 May 1923) [in Spanish], *G. W.*, vol. 13, p. 442 (166).
(1923*i*) 'Dr. Ferenczi Sándor (zum 50. Geburtstag)', *G. W.*, vol. 13, pp. 443–5 (8, 89).
'Dr. Sándor Ferenczi (on his 50th birthday)', *S. E.*, vol. 19, pp. 267–9.
(1924*e*) 'Der Realitätsverlust bei Neurose und Psychose', *G. W.*, vol. 13, pp. 3632–8 (257).
'The loss of reality in neurosis and psychosis', *S. E.*, vol. 19, pp. 183–7.
(1924*g* [1923]) Letter to Fritz Wittels (18 December 1923), *G. W.*, Supplement, pp. 754–8 (228).
(1925*d* [1924]) 'Selbstdarstellung', *G. W.*, vol. 14, pp. 31–96 (100).
'An autobiographical study', *S. E.*, vol. 20, pp. 7–70.
(1925*f*) 'Geleitwort' to A. Aichhorn [1925], *G. W.*, vol. 14, pp. 565–7 (170).
(1925*j*) 'Einige psychische Folgen des anatomischen Geschlechtsunterschieds', *G. W.*, vol. 14, pp. 19–30 (203).
'Some psychical consequences of the anatomical distinction between the sexes', *S. E.*, vol. 19, pp. 248–58.
(1926*e*) 'Die Fragen der Laienanalyse: Unterredungen mit einem Unparteiischen', *G. W.*, vol. 14, pp. 207–86 (251).
'The question of lay analysis: conversations with an impartial person', *S. E.*, vol. 20, pp. 183–250.
(1926*f*) 'Psychoanalysis: Freudian School' [article in English], in *Encyclopaedia Britannica*, 13th edition, new vol. 3 (London, 1926), pp. 253–5; German original, *G. W.*, vol. 14, pp. 299–307 (126).
(1926*j*) Address to members of the B'nai B'rith [letter to Salomon Ehrmann], *G. W.*, vol. 17, pp. 51–3 (61, 215).
(1926*k*) Unser Orden [letter to Friedrich Thieberger (27 January 1926]); complete facsimile in Gerhard Fichtner, '"Also ob" es Freud ware . . . Ein angebliches Freud-Gedicht und sein Zusammenhang mit Freuds Menschenbild', in *Jb. Psychoanal.*, vol. 33 (1994), pp. 49–71, the facsimile p. 52 (61).
(1927*a*) 'Nachwort zur *Frage der Laienanalyse*', *G. W.*, vol. 14, pp. 287–96 (251).
'Postscript to a discussion on lay analysis', *S. E.*, vol. 20, pp. 251–8.
(1927*c*) *Die Zukunft einer Illusion*, *G. W.*, vol. 14, pp. 325–80 (238, 244, 250).
The Future of an Illusion, *S. E.*, vol. 21, pp. 5–56.
(1927*d*) 'Der Humor', *G. W.*, vol. 14, pp. 383–9 (250).
'Humour', *S. E.*, vol. 21, pp. 161–6.

(1927*i*) Telegram to the participants of the 10th International Psychoanalytic Congress in Innsbruck (2 February 1927), *IZ*, vol. 13 (1927), p. 484 (251).
**(1927*l*) 'Eine Kundgebung des geistigen Wien: Zeugnis für die grosse soziale und kulturelle Leistung der Gemeinde Wien', [explanation] in *Arbeiter-Zeitung*, Vienna, vol. 40, no. 108, Wednesday, 20 April 1927, morning edition, 1; facsimile in H. Rüdiger Schiferer et al. (eds), *Alfred Adler: Eine Bildbiographie* (Munich, Basel: Ernst Reinhardt, 1995), p. 178 (246).
(1928*b* [1927]) 'Dostojewski und die Vatertötung', *G. W.*, vol. 14, pp. 399–418 (199).
'Dostoevsky and parricide', *S. E.*, vol. 21, pp. 177–94.
(1929*a*) 'Ernest Jones zum 50. Geburtstag', *G. W.*, vol. 14, pp. 554f. (41, 263).
'Dr. Ernest Jones on his 50th birthday', *S. E.*, vol. 21, pp. 249f.
(1930*a*) *Das Unbehagen der Kultur*, *G. W.*, vol. 14, pp. 419–506 (228, 257).
Civilization and Its Discontents, *S. E.*, vol. 21, pp. 64–145.
(1930*b*) 'Vorwort' to *Zehn Jahre Berliner Psychoanalytisches Institut (Poliklinik und Lehranstalt)*, *G. W.*, vol. 14, p. 572 (100).
(1930*d*) 'Goethe-Preis 1930: Brief an Dr. Alfons Paquet (3 August 1930)', *G. W.*, vol. 10, p. 291 (270).
(1930*e*) 'Ansprache im Frankfurter Goethe-Haus' (28 August 1930), *G. W.*, vol. 14, pp. 547–50 (270).
'Address delivered in the Goethe House at Frankfurt', *S. E.*, vol. 21, pp. 208–12.
(1931*g*) Letter to Julius Tandler (November 1931), *G. W.*, Supplement, p. 719 (110).
(1933*a* [1932]) *Neue Folge der Vorlesungen zur Einführung in die Psychoanalyse*, *G. W.*, vol. 15 (72, 96).
New Introductory Lectures on Psychoanalysis, *S. E.*, vol. 22, pp. 5–182.
(1933*b* [1932]) 'Warum Krieg?' [letter to Albert Einstein (September 1932)], *G. W.*, vol. 16, pp. 13–27 (289).
(1933*c*) 'Sándor Ferenczi †', *G. W.*, vol. 16, pp. 267–9 (8).
(1935*b*) 'Die Feinheit einer Fehlbehandlung', *G. W.*, vol. 16, pp. 37–9 (Appendix 3).
'The subtleties of a faulty action', *S. E.*, vol. 22, pp. 233–5.
(1935*c*) Letter to B'nai B'rith, in *B'nai B'rith Mitteilungen für Österreich*, vol. 35 (1935), no. 9/10, p. 193 (61).
(1936*d*) 'Zum Ableben Professor Brauns', *G. W.*, Supplement, p. 735 (215).
(1937*a*) 'Lou Andreas-Salomé †', *G. W.*, vol. 16, p. 270 (153).
'Lou Andreas-Salomé', *S. E.*, vol. 23, pp. 297f.
(1939*a*) *Der Mann Moses und die monotheistische Religion: Drei Abhandlungen*, *G. W.*, vol. 16, pp. 103–246 (296).
Moses and Monotheism, *S. E.*, vol. 23, pp. 7–137.
(1939*d* [1910–35]) Six letters to Adolf J. Storfer, in *Gelbe Post* (Shanghai), vol. 1 (1939), no. 1, pp. 9–11 (162).
(1940*a*) *Abriss der Psychoanalyse*, *G. W.*, vol. 17, pp. 63–138 (298).
An Outline of Psychoanalysis, *S. E.*, vol. 23, pp. 144–207.
(1941*d* [1921]) 'Psychoanalyse und Telepathie', *G. W.*, vol. 17, pp. 25, 27–44 (142, 153).
(1956*i*) Letters to Girindrasekhar Bose, in *Samiska: Journal of the Indian Psychoanalytical Society*, vol. 10 (1956), pp. 104–10, 155–66 (159).
(1960*a*) [1873–1939] Ernst und Lucie Freud (eds), *Briefe 1873–1939*, 3rd revised edition (Frankfurt: S. Fischer, 1980); available in English as Ernst Freud (ed.), *Letters of Sigmund Freud 1873–1939*, translated by Tania and James Stern (London: Hogarth Press, 1970) (Introduction, 1, 11, 15, 16, 18, text after 18, 19,

20, 39, 42, 47, 57, 61, 80, 110, 126, 146, 149, 151, 157, 159, 161, 189, 195, 210, 211, 287, 296–8, Appendix 1, note 2).

(1962*a*) Letter to Leonard Blumgart (12 May 1921) [in English; facsimile], in Martin Waugh, *Fruition of an Idea: Fifty Years of Psychoanalysis in New York* (New York: International University Press, 1962), pp. 89, 91 (154/2).

(1963*a*) Letters to Oskar Pfister, in Ernst Freud and Heinrich Meng (eds), *Briefe 1909–1939*, 2nd edition (Frankfurt: S. Fischer, 1960); available in English as *Psychoanalysis and Faith: the Letters of Sigmund Freud & Oskar Pfister*, translated by Eric Mosbacher (London: Hogarth Press, 1963) (Introduction, 13, 18, text after 106).

(1965*a* [1907–26]) See FREUD/ABRAHAM.

(1965*g*) Letter to the president of B'nai B'rith in Braila (22 April 1928) [in 1989*a*] (61).

(1966*a*) See FREUD/ANDREAS-SALOMÉ.

(1966*b*) 'Introduction' to S. Freud and W. C. Bullitt, *Thomas Woodrow Wilson, Twenty-Eighth President of the United States: A Psychological Study* (London: Weidenfeld & Nicolson, 1967) (296).

(1968*a*) Letters to Arnold Zweig, in Ernst Freud (ed.), *Briefwechsel* (Frankfurt: S. Fischer, 1968); available in English as Ernst Freud (ed.), *The Letters of Sigmund Freud & Arnold Zweig*, translated by Elaine and William Robson-Scott (New York: New York University Press, 1970) (Introduction, 294, 297).

(1971*a* [1909–16]) Letters to James J. Putnam, in Nathan G. Hale, Jr. (ed.), *James Jackson Putnam and Psychoanalysis*, German texts translated by Judith Bernays Heller (Cambridge, MA: Harvard University Press, 1971) (49).

(1974*a*) See FREUD/JUNG.

(1976*l*) Letter to William Alanson White of 17 July 1914 [English translation]; reprinted in Jelliffe [1983], pp. 195f. (113).

(1977*j*) Seven letters to Paul Häberlin, in Peter Kamm, *Paul Häberlin: Leben und Werd*, vol. 1 (Zurich: Schweizer Spiegel Verlag, 1977), pp. 254–7, 387f. (16).

(1979*d* [1937]) Letter to the president of B'nai B'rith in Vienna (October 1937), in Knoepfmacher, pp. 70f. (61).

(1985*a* [1915]) 'Übersicht der Übertragungsneurosen' [draft of 12th psychological essay of 1915], *G. W.*, Supplement, pp. 6345–51 (54).

(1985*c*) Jeffrey M. Masson (ed.), *Briefe an Wilhelm Fliess 1887–1904*, German version edited by Michael Schröter (Frankfurt: S. Fischer, 1986); available in English as *The Complete Letters of Sigmund Freud to Wilhelm Fliess 1887–1904*, translated by Jeffrey Masson (Cambridge, MA: Harvard University Press, 1985) (2, 5, 16, 34, 45, 49, 50, 52, 61, 74, 98, 101, 114, 127, 133, 134, 175, text after 201, 257).

(1985*d* [1903–26]) Letters to Anna von Vest, in Stefan Goldmann, 'Sigmund Freud s Briefe an seine Patientin Anna von Vest', *Jb. Psychoanal.*, vol. 17 (1985), pp. 269–95 (146).

(1987*a* [1923]) List of corrections to letter to Fritz Wittels (see 1924*g*), *G. W.*, Supplement, pp. 756–8 (228).

(1987*c* [1908–38]) Letters to Stefan Zweig, in Jeffrey B. Berlin et al. (eds), *Briefwechsel mit Hermann Bahr, Sigmund Freud, Rainer Maria Rilke und Arthur Schnitzler* (Frankfurt: S. Fischer, 1989) (Introduction).

(1989*a* [1871–81, 1910]) Letters to Eduard Silberstein, in Walter Boehlich (ed.), *Jugendbriefe an Eduard Silberstein 1871–1881* (Frankfurt: S. Fischer, 1989); available in English as Walter Boehlich (ed.), *The Letters of Sigmund Freud to*

Eduard Silberstein 1871–1881, translated by Arnold J. Pomerans (Cambridge, MA: Harvard University Press, 1990) (50).
(1992*a* [1908–38]) See Freud/Binswanger.
(1992*g* [1908–33] See Freud/Ferenczi.
(1992*i* [1929–39]) 'Kürzeste Chronik' [facsimile], in Michael Molnar, *The Diary of Sigmund Freud 1929–1939* (London: Hogarth Press, 1992) (57, 71, 74, 162, 208, 254, text after 255, 257, 270, 271, 273, 277, 287–9, 294, 296–8, Appendix 3).
(1992*l* [1921–39]) Letters to Joan Riviere [in English and translated into English], in S. Hughes, pp. 268–83 (157, 192, 196, 287).
(1993*e* [1908–39]) See Freud/Jones.
(1993*h* [n.d.]) Champollion (note about the meaning of infantile wishes), in Grubrich–Simitis [1993], p. 126 (62).
(1995*c* [1925–32]) Letters to Sándor Radó [translated into English], in Paul Roazen, Bluma Swerdloff, *Heresy: Sándor Radó and the Psychoanalytic Movement* (Northvale, NJ, London: Jason Aronson, 1995), pp. 151–73 (133).
**(1995*n* [1913]) Visiting card to Christov (V) Hartung von Hartungen (5 September 1913); facsimile in Albino Tonelli, *Ai confine della Mitteleuropa: il Sanatorium von Hartungen di Riva del Garda – Dai fratelli Mann a Kafka gli ospiti della cultura europea* (Riva del Gard, 1995), p. 346 (33).
(1996*g* [1911–38]) See Freud/Sam.
(1997*e* [1920]) Letter to Arthur Lippmann (15 February 1920), in S. Andrae, p. 110 (156).
**(2002*b* [1873–1939] Travel letters to the family, in Christfried Tögel with Michael Molnar, *Unser Herz zeigt nach dem Süden: Reisebriefe 1895–1923* (Berlin: Aufbau-Verlag, 2002) (Introduction, 1, 2–4, 6, 8, 11–14, 34, 125, 200, 201, 226, 235, 270, 281, Appendix 1, notes 1, 42, 69, 79).
**(2002*c* [1908]) Remarks about faces and people (13 September 1908), in Freud 2002*b*, pp. 250–5 (4).
**(2003*e* [1911, 1912]) Two letters to the family (12 July 1911, 3 September 1912), partially reproduced in Gödde [2003], pp. 162, 141f. [For other parts, see 'Unpublished Material'] (16, text after 18, 19, 71, 127, 285).
**(2003*l* [1885]) Letter to Rosa Freud (18 March 1885), full facsimile in Fichtner [2003] (16).
**(2004*d* [1888–1932]) Letters, postcards and telegrams to Marie and Moritz Freud, in Christfried Tögel, Michael Schröter, 'Sigmund Freud: Briefe an Maria (Mitzi) Freud und ihre Familie', in *Luzifer-Amor*, vol. 17 (2004), no. 33, pp. 51–72; the letters pp. 51–62 (text after 18, 134, 135).
**(2004*h* [1906–39]) See Freud/Eitingon.
**(2008*e* [1929]) Letter to Ruth Mack Brunswick (21 July 1929) [Facsimile in Fichtner (2008b)].
**(2010*e* [1858–1939]) See Freud/Children.

Correspondence

Freud/Abraham
Hilda C. Abraham and Ernst L. Freud (eds), *Sigmund Freud/Karl Abraham – Briefe 1907–1926*, 2nd revised edition (Frankfurt: S. Fischer, 1980); available in English as Ernst Falzeder (ed.), *The Complete Correspondence of Sigmund Freud and Karl Abraham 1907–1925*, translated by Caroline Schwarzacher with the col-

laboration of Christine Trollope and Klara Majthényi King (London and New York: Karnak, 2002) (6, 16, 18, 20, 41, 43, 45, 46, 56, 58, 61, 67, 74, 76, 78, 80, 81, 84, 87, 96, 99–101, 103, text after 106, 107, 110, 112, 123, 125, 126, 128, 131, 133, 151, 153, 162, 165, 192, 203, 277).

FREUD/ANDREAS-SALOMÉ

Ernst Pfeiffer (ed.), *Sigmund Freud/Lou Andreas-Salomé – Briefwechsel*, 2nd revised edition (Frankfurt: Fischer, 1980); available in English as Ernst Pfeiffer (ed.), *Sigmund Freud and Lou Andreas-Salomé – Letters*, translated by William and Elaine Robson-Scott (New York: W. W. Norton & Company, 1972) (Introduction, 12, 16, 36, 54, 71–4, 78, 80, 84, 89, 91, 96, 100, 107, 112, 125, 126, 153–5, 157, 168, 174, 183, 185, 257, 260, 262, 269, 273, 287).

FREUD/BERNAYS

Albrecht Hirschmüller (ed.), *Sigmund Freud/Minna Bernays – Briefwechsel 1882–1938* (Tübingen: edition diskord, 2005) (1, 6, 7, 14, 28, 33, 34, 45, 71, 74, 98, 122, 133, 146, 147, 156, 161, 168, 170, 174, 175, 196, text after 295, 296, 297).

FREUD/BINSWANGER

Albrecht Hirschmüller (ed.), *Sigmund Freud/Ludwig Binswanger – Briefwechsel 1908–1938* (Frankfurt: S. Fischer, 1992); available in English as Gerhard Fichtner (ed.), *The Sigmund Freud – Ludwig Binswanger Correspondence 1908–1938*, translated by Arnold J. Pomerans. Introduction, editorial notes and additional letters translated by Thomas Roberts (New York and London: Other Press, 2003) (5, 15, 16, 17, 96, text after 106, 107, 123, 133, 212, 251, 296).

FREUD/EITINGON

Michael Schröter (ed.), *Sigmund Freud/Max Eitingon – Briefwechsel 1906–1939*, 2 vols (Tübingen: edition diskord, 2004) (Introduction, 57, 76, 89, 96, 99, 100, text after 106, 107, 108, 114, 115, 117, 124, 125, 127, 129, 131, 132, 137, 138, 142, 144, 149, 153, 154, 156, 159, 162, 165, 167, 168, 174, 183, 197, text after 201, 203, 209, 210, 212, 216, 223, 228, 236, 238, 244, 250–3, 257, 277, 287–9, 291, text after 295, 296, 297).

FREUD/FERENCZI

Eva Brabant et al. (eds). *Sigmund Freud/Sándor Ferenczi – Briefwechsel*, 6 vols (Vienna, Cologne, Weimar: Böhlau); available in English as Ernst Falzeder et al. (eds), *The Correspondence of Sigmund Freud and Sándor Ferenczi*, translated by Peter T. Hoffer, 3 vols (Cambridge, MA: Harvard University Press, 1996).

Vol. I (1908–14): (3–8, 11, 14–16, 18, text after 18,19, 20, 28, 32–4, 37, 39–42, 52, 58, 60, 71, 77, 82, text after 82, 83, 99, 126, 133, 287, 297).

Vol. II (1914–19): (Introduction, 14, 36, 41–3, 46–50, 58, 59, 61, 66–9, 71–84, 87, 89, 91, 92, 95, 96, 99–104, 106, text after 106, 110, 112, 114, 123, 133, 174, 219, 287).

Vol. III (1920–33): (Introduction, 3, 6, 8, 43, 74, 76, 82, 83, 96, 100, 104, text after 106, 107, 109, 110, 112, 114, 115, 117, 119, 121, 123–6, 128, 129, 131, 132, 137, 138, 146, 150, 151, 153, 155–7, 159, 161–4, 165, 166, 170, 174, 175, 181–4, 187, 189, 192, 194–8, text after 201, 203, 208–15, 223, 228, 238, 244, 253, text after 255, 257, 259, 270, 271, 287, 291, text after 295).

FREUD/JONES

Andrew Paskausis (ed.), *The Complete Correspondence of Sigmund Freud and Ernest Jones 1908–1939* (Cambridge, MA: Harvard University Press, 1993); German original letters available in *Briefwechsel Sigmund Freud Ernest Jones 1908–1939*, transcribed and edited by Ingeborg Meyer-Palmedo (Frankfurt: S. Fischer, 1993) (Introduction, 14, 17, 18, text after 18, 19, 22, 27, 36, 39, 41–7, 60, 89, 91, 92, 95,

96, 98–101, 106, text after 128, 131, 133, 134, 138, 144, 148, 153, 154/2, 155–63, 170, 179, 184, 185, 196, 197, 202–4, 216, 223, 236, 246, text after 255, 256, 257, 259, 262, 263, 270, 287, 289, 294, text after 295, 297, 298).

FREUD/JUNG

William McGuire, Wolfgang Sauerländer (eds), *Sigmund Freud/ C. G. Jung – Briefwechsel* (Frankfurt: S. Fischer, 1974); available in English as William McGuire (ed.), *The Freud/Jung Letters – The Correspondence between Sigmund Freud and C. G. Jung*, translated by Ralph Manheim and R. F. C. Hill (Princeton, NJ: Princeton University Press, 1974) (3–6, 8, 11, 14–20, 33, 43, 101, 175, 238, 280).

FREUD/SAM

Thomas Roberts (ed.), *Vienna and Manchester – The Correspondence between Sigmund Freud and Sam Freud 1911–1938*, unpublished original manuscript, quoted with kind permission of Thomas Roberts (1995) (11, 18, 42, 45, 46, 103, text after 123, 124–6, 128–31, 133–5, 138, 146, 148, 149, 154, 155).

FREUD/CHILDREN

'Briefe und Karten an die Kinder', in Michael Schröter (ed.) with Ingeborg Meyer-Palmedo and Ernst Falzeder, *Sigmund Freud, Unterdess halten wir zusammen* (Berlin, 2010) (198).

Anna Freud

The works of Anna Freud are quoted from *The Writings of Anna Freud*, vols 1–8 (New York: International Universities Press, 1974–81). Works appearing only in German are quoted from *Die Schriften der Anna Freud*, vols I–X (Frankfurt: Fischer Taschenbuch Verlag, 1987).

Unless otherwise indicated, for non-published letters by Anna Freud, see 'Unpublished Material'.

The numbers in brackets after each entry refer to the letters or footnotes in which the work is mentioned.

Works

(1932) 'Schlagphantasie und Tagtraum', paper deliverecd on 31 May 1922 at the 20th session of the Vienna Psychoanalytic Society under the title 'Schlagphantasien und Tagträume', *Imago*, vol. 8 (1922), pp. 317–32 (168).

'The relation of beating fantasies to a daydream', *IJ*, vol. 4 (1923), pp. 89–102; 'Beating fantasies and daydreams', *Writings*, vol. I, pp. 137–57 (236).

(1927*a*) *Einführung in die Technik der Kinderanalyse*, four lectures given at the Teaching Institute of the Vienna Psychoanalytic Society (Leipzig, Vienna, Zurich: International Psychoanalytischer Verlag, 1927).

'Introduction to the technique of child analysis' (1929), *Writings*, vol. I, pp. 3–69 (Introduction, 209, 215, 216, 228, 238, 244, 259).

(1927*b*) 'Zur Theorie der Kinderanalyse', lecture at the 10th International Psychoanalytic Congress in Innsbruck, 1927, *IZ*, vol. 13 (1927), p. 477 (216, 252).

(1927*c*) 'Vortrag Frl. Anna Freud (Wien, a. G.): Zur Technik der Kinderanalyse', report on the meeting of 19 March 1927, *IZ*, vol. 13 (1927), p. 367 (209).

(1927*d*) 'Das Verhältnis der Kinderanalyse zur Erziehung', 4th of the 'Vier Vorträge über Kinderanalyse' (in 1927a).
'Child analysis and the upbringing of children', *Writings*, vol. I, pp. 50–69 (160).
(1928) 'Zur Theorie der Kinderanalyse', revised version of 1927b, *IZ*, vol. 14 (1928), 153–62; 'The theory of child analysis', translated by Nancy Procter-Gregg (1928), *Writings*, vol. I, pp. 162–75 (252, 259).
(1929*a*) 'Die Beziehungen zwischen Psychoanalyse und Pädagogik', 4th of 'Vier Vorträge über Psychoanalyse für Lehrer und Eltern', *Zeitschrift für psychoanalytische Pädagogik*, vol. 3 (1930), pp. 445–54.
'The relation between psychoanalysis and education', *Writings*, vol. I, pp. 121–33 (257).
(1929*b*) 'Ein Gegenstück zur Tierphobie der Kinder', lecture at the 11th International Psychoanalytic Congress in Oxford, 27 July 1929, *IZ*, vol. 15 (1929), p. 518; *Schriften*, vol. I, pp. 257–68 (262).
(1930) 'Vier Vorträge über Psychoanalyse für Lehrer und Eltern', lecture 2 'Das infantile Triebleben'.
'The instinctual life of early childhood', *Writings*, vol. I, pp. 91–104 (160).
(1933) 'Die neurotischen Mechanismen unter dem Einfluss der Erziehung', lecture on 5 September 1932 at the 12th International Psychoanalytic Congress in Wiesbaden; *Schriften*, vol. I, pp. 233–43 (289).
(1936) *Das Ich und die Abwehrmechanismen* (Vienna: Internationaler Psychoanalytischer Verlag).
The Ego and the Mechanisms of Defense, *Writings*, vol. II (1937) (7, 25, 262, 289).
(1951) Obituary 'August Aichhorn: 27 July 1878 – 17 October 1949', *IJ*, vol. 32 (1951), pp. 51–6; *Writings*, vol. IV, pp. 625–38.
(1953) 'Instinctual drives and their bearing on human behavior', *Writings*, vol. IV, pp. 498–527 (160).
(1965) *Normality and Pathology in Childhood: Assessments of Development*, *Writings*, vol. VI (22, 160).
(1967 [1964]) Doctoral award address, *Writings*, vol. V, pp. 507–16 (Introduction).
(1971 [1942]) with Dorothy Burlingham, *War Children* (London: Imago Publishing Co.) (47, 160, 212).
(1972 [1971]) 'Comments on aggression', *Writings*, vol. VIII, pp. 151–75 (168).
(1974) Introduction to 'Einführung in die Psychoanalyse – Vorträge für Kinderanalytiker und Lehrer 1922–1935', translated into German by Michael Schröter, *Schriften*, vol. I, pp. 3–8 (99).
(1979) 'Personal memories of Ernest Jones', *IJ*, vol. 60 (1979), pp. 271–3; *Writings*, vol. VIII, pp. 346–53 (41, 296).

Correspondence

Anna/Eva
Peter Heller (ed.), *Anna Freud: Briefe an Eva Rosenfeld* (Frankfurt: Stroemfeld/Nexus, 1994); available in English as *Anna Freud's Letters to Eva Rosenfeld*, translated by Mary Weigand with contributions by Günther Bittner and Victor Ross (Madison, CT: International Universities Press, 1992) (Introduction, 12, 58, 98, 102, 131, 132, 146, 147, 158, 174, 208, 212, text after 255, 256, 257, 261, 270–2, 281, 287, 288).

ANNA/LOU
Daria A. Rothe, Inge Weber (eds), '. . . *als kam ich heim zu Vater und Schwester' – Lou Andreas-Salomé – Anna Freud: Briefwechsel 1919–1937*, 2 vols. (Göttingen: Wallstein, 2001) (Introduction, 14, 16, 19, 26, 28, 29, 31, 36, 53, 73, 79, 96, 101, 103, 110, 120, 128, 131, 141, 146, 147, 151, 153, 155–60, 162, 165–8, 170, 172–5, 181, 183–5, 188–200, text after 201, 202–4, 206, 208, 209, 212, 213, 216, 218, 219, 223, 244, 252, text after 255, 257, 266, 269, 271, 281, 287, 294, 295, Appendix 2).

Translations

of Jones 1915 (60, 69, 74).
of Jones 1918 (96).
of Jones 1920*a* (96, 125, 142).
of Jones 1922*b* (96).
of J. J. Putnam (49, 60, 69, 74).
of Varendonck 1921*b* (142, 161).

Other Literature

ABRAHAM, Hilda
1971: 'Die Anfänge der psychoanalytischen Vereinigung in Berlin' in H. Abraham et al., *Psychoanalyse in Berlin – Beiträge zur Geschichte, Theorie und Praxis, 50-Jahr-Gedenkfeier des Berliner Psychoanalytischen Instituts* (Karl Abraham Institut) (Meisenheim: Anton Hain, 1971), pp. 11–25 (20, 162).
1976: *Karl Abraham: Sein Leben für die Psychoanalyse* (Munich: Kindler, 1976) (20).
ABRAHAM, Karl
(See also FREUD/ABRAHAM)
1924: 'Dr. Rudolf Foerster †', *IZ*, vol. 10 (1924), pp. 103f. (162).
1927–50: *Selected Papers of Karl Abraham, M. D.* (London: Hogarth Press and Institute of Psychoanalysis, 1927, 1942, 1950) (160).
ABRAHAM and HÁRNIK
Karl Abraham and J. Hárnik, 'Spezielle Pathologie und Therapie der Neurosen und Psychosen', in *Bericht über die Fortschritte der Psychoanalyse 1914–1919* (Vienna: Internationaler Psychoanalytischer Verlag, 1921), pp. 141–63 (160).
AICHHORN, August
1923: 'Über die Erziehung in Besserungsanstalten', in *Imago*, vol. 9 (1923), pp. 189–221 (170).
1925: *Verwahrloste Jugend – Die Psychoanalyse in der Fürsorgeerziehung; Zehn Vorträge zur ersten Einführung* (Vienna and Zurich: Internationaler Psychoanalytischer Verlag, 1925) (170).
AICHHORN, Thomas
'"Die Psychoanalyse kann nur dort gedeihen, wo Freiheit des Gedankens herrscht"', in *Luzifer–Amor, Zeitschrift für Geschichte der Psychoanalyse*, vol. 16 (2003), no. 31, pp. 106–23 (170).
ALEXANDER, Franz
1922: 'Kastrationskomplex und Charakter; eine Untersuchung über passagère Symptome', in *IZ*, vol. 8 (1922), pp. 121–52.

1966: 'Sandor Rado; b. 1890 – The Adaption Theory', in Franz Alexander, Samuel Eisenstein, Martin Grotjahn (eds) *Psychoanalytic Pioneers* (New York: Basic Books), pp. 240–8 (133).

AMMAN, Anneliese C.

Schliersee und sein Bauerntheater, Geschichte und Geschichten zum hundertjährigen Bestehen (Dachau: Verlagsanstalt 'Bayerland', 1992) (95).

ANDRAE, Matthias

Die Vertreibung der Jüdischen Ärzte des Allgemeinen Krankenhauses Hamburg–St. Georg im Nationalsozialismus, diss., University of Hamburg (1997) (156).

ANDREAS-SALOMÉ, Lou

(See also ANNA/LOU; FREUD/ANDREAS-SALOMÉ)

1921: 'Narzissmus als Doppelrichtung', in *Imago*, vol. 7 (1921), pp. 361–86; reprinted in Lou Andreas-Salomé, *Das 'zweideutige' Lächeln der Erotik*, Texte zur Psychoanalyse, edited by Inge Weber and Brigitte Rempp (Freiburg i. B.: Kore, 1990), pp. 191–222) (169).

1951: *Lebensrückblick: Grundriss einger Lebenserinnerungen.* From the estate edited by Ernst Pfeiffer. Quoted from new revised and enlarged edition with an epilogue by the editor (Frankfurt: Insel, 1974) (153, 167).

1958: *In der Schule bei Freud – Tagebuch eines Jahres 1912/1913.* From the estate edited by Ernst Pfeiffer (Zurich, 1958). Quoted from unabridged edition (Frankfurt, Berlin, Vienna: Ullstein, 1983) (33, 36, 153).

ANZIEU, Didier

Freuds Selbstanalyse und die Entdeckung der Psychoanalyse, 2 vols, translated from French by Eva Moldenhauer (Munich and Vienna: Verlag Internationale Psychoanalyse, 1990); originally published as *L'auto-analyse: son role dans la découverte de psychanalyse par Freud, sa fonction en psychanalyse* (Paris: Presses universitaires de France, 1959) (75).

APPIGNANESI and FORRESTER

Lisa Appignanesi and John Forrester, *Freud's Women* (London: Weidenfeld & Nicolson, 1992) (42, 74, 100, 110).

ARMBRUSTER, Karl

Die Tiroler Bergbah., ch. V, 'Die Rittnerbahn (von Bozen nach Klobenstein)', pp. 106–22 (Berlin, London, Vienna: Verlag für Fachliteratur, 1914) (14).

ARON, Willy

'Notes on Sigmund Freud's Ancestry and Jewish Contacts', in *YIVO, Annual of Jewish Social Sciences*, vol. 11 (1956/7), pp. 286–95 (77).

ASCH, Joseph Jefferson

Anon, 'In Memoriam Joseph Jefferson Asch, M.D., 1880–1935', in *The Psychoanalytic Quarterly*, vol. IV (1935), p. 630 (154/2).

ATLAS

Dr Ernst Ambrosius (ed.), *Andrees Allgemeiner Handatlas mit 221 Haupt- und 192 Nebenkarten* (Bielefeld and Leipzig: Velhagen & Klasing, 1914) (85).

BADGASTEIN. LISTE

Badgastein. Liste der Kurgäste und Passanten mit Jahresangaben und Lfd. Parteienzahlen (69, 74, 75, 93, 95, 102, 109, 110, 114, 117, 119, 149, 152, 175, 178, 181).

BAEDEKER, Karl

1923: *Handbuch für Reisende: Tirol, Vorarlberg und Teile von Salzburg und Kärnten*, 37th edition (Leipzig, 1923), p. 424 (72, 95, 98, 153, 175, 198).

1926: *Österreich: Handbuch für Reisende*, 30th edition (Leipzig, 1926) (39).

BALINT, Michael
1970: 'Einleitung des Herausgebers', in Sandor Ferenczi, *Schriften zur Psychoanalyse*, vol. 1 (Frankfurt: S. Fischer, 1970), pp. IX–XXII (8).
1988: 'Einleitung zum Tagebuch' in Ferenczi [1988] (German version), pp. 32–6 (287).
BANNACH, Hans-Joachim
'Die wissenschaftliche Bedeutung des alten Berliner Psychoanalytischen Instituts', in H. Abrahams et al., *Psychoanalyse in Berlin; Beiträge zur Geschichte, Theorie und Praxis* (Meisenheim: Anton Hain, 1971), pp. 31–9 (100, 131).
BEITRÄGE
Beiträge zur Kultur- und Heimatgeschichte des Ausseerlandes 1975–1994 (Literatur- und Heimatmuseum Altaussee, Kulturzentrum Steinberghaus [Altaussee], 1995) (116).
BENNET, Edward Armstrong
1961: *C. G. Jung* (London: Barrie & Rockliff, 1961) (297).
1985: *Meetings with Jung, Conversations Recorded During the Years 1946–1961*, 2nd edition (Zurich: Daimon, 1985) (297).
BERLINER PSYCHOANALYTISCHES INSTITUT
Zehn Jahre Berliner Psychoanalytisches Institut (Poliklinik und Lehranstalt), published by Deutsche Psychoanalytische Gesellschaft (Vienna, Leipzig and Zurich: Internationaler Psychoanalytischer Verlag, 1930) (100).
BERMAN, Emanuel
'Sandor, Gizella, Elma: a biographical journey', in *IJ*, vol. 85 (2004), pp. 489–520 (259, 287).
BERNAYS, Edward L.
1967: *Biographie einer Idee. Die Hohe Schule der PR. Lebenserinnerungen.* (Düsseldorf and Vienna: Econ, 1967) [contains extracts of correspondence between Bernays and Freud, pp. 179–202] (98, 99, 107, 119, 130, 137, 138).
1980: 'Uncle Sigi', in *Journal of the History of Medicine and Allied Sciences*, vol. 35 (April 1980), pp. 216–20 (107).
BERTHELSEN, Detlef
Alltag bei Familie Freud: Die Erinnerungen der Paula Fichtl (Hamburg: Hoffmann und Campe, 1987) (298).
BERTIN, Célia
Marie Bonaparte: A Life (New York: Harcourt Brace Jovanovich, 1982) (214, 229, 231, 238, text after 295).
BIOGRAPHISCHES LEXIKON
Bad Reichenhaller 'Biographisches Lexikon', dedicated to the city of Bad Reichenhall by the author W. Lossen, 1951 [typed manuscript] (98).
BITTNER, Günther
'Anna Freud's Letters to Eva Rosenfeld: A Reader's Response', in ANNA/EVA [1992], pp. 3–22 (98, 158, 174, 208, 212, text after 255, 256).
BLOOMSBURY
Perry Meisel, Walter Kendrick (eds), *Bloomsbury/Freud: The Letters of James and Alix Strachey 1924–1925* (London: Chatto & Windus, 1986) (27, 29, 86, 128, 156, 196).
BLUM, Ernst
'Das Menschenbild von Sigmund Freud – persönliche Erinnerungen', in *Schweizerische Zeitschrift für Psychologie und ihre Anwendungen/Revue Suisse de psychologie pure et appliquée*, vol. 15 (1956), pp. 141–7 (157).

BOADELLA, David
Wilhelm Reich: The Evolution of His Work (London, Boston and Henley: Arkana, 1985) (209).
BOLZINGER, André
1999*a*: 'Freud als Nervenpathologe, seine Rezeption in Frankreich vor 1910', in *Fortschritte der Neurologie und Psychiatrie*, vol. 67 (1999), pp. 337–46 (43).
1999*b*: *La reception de Freud en France* (Paris: Harmattan, 1999) (43).
BRAUEN, Fred
'Athanasius Kircher (1602–1680)', in *Journal of the History of Ideas*, vol. 43 (Jan–Mar 1982), pp. 129–34 (Appendix 1, note 45).
BRAUNTHAL, Julius
Otto Bauer: eine Auswahl aus seinem Lebenswerk (Vienna: Wiener Volksbuchhandlung, n.d. [1961]) (110, 130, 132, 179, 246).
BRECHT ET AL.
Karen Brecht et al. (eds), *'Hier geht das Leben auf eine sehr merkwürdige Weise weiter . . .' Zur Geschichte der Psychoanalyse in Deutschland*, exh. cat. ([Hamburg]: Michael Kellner, 1985) (text after 255, 257).
BRIEHL, Walter
'Wilhelm Reich, 1897–1957, Character Analysis', in Franz Alexander et al. (eds), *Psychoanalytic Pioneers* (New York and London: Basic Books, 1966), pp. 430–8 (209).
BRILL, Abraham A.
'Critical Review: Prof. Sigmund Freud: "Die Frage der Laienanalyse"', in *The Journal of Nervous and Mental Disease*, vol. 65 (Jan–Jun 1927), pp. 412–20 (238).
BROME, Vincent
Ernest Jones: Freud's Alter Ego (New York and London: Norton, 1983) (41, 42).
BRUNSWICK, Mark
Anon., 'Mark Brunswick, composer, is dead', in *The New York Times*, 28 May 1971, 36 (228).
BÜHLER
Bühler-Führer *Bad Reichenhall, Berchtesgaden und Salzburger Land*, 36th edition, vol. 98 (Bad Reichenhall, 1959) (98, 101).
BULLETIN
The Bulletin of the Hampstead Clinic, vol. 6 (1983), Part 1, Anna Freud Memorial Issue (297).
BURLINGHAM, D.
(See also Anna Freud [1971])
The Bulletin of the Hampstead Clinic, vol. 3 (1980), Part 2, Dorothy Burlingham Memorial Issue (212).
BURLINGHAM, M.
Michael John Burlingham, *The Last Tiffany: A Biography of Dorothy Tiffany Burlingham* (New York: Atheneum, 1989) (208, 212, 213, 215, 216, 244, text after 255, 256, 257, 259, 270, 273, 279, 281, 283, 287, 288, text after 295, 298, Appendix 3).
CHAUSSY, Ulrich
Nachbar Hitler: Führerkult und Hemiatzerstörung am Obersalzberg, 3rd revised edition (Berlin: Ch. Links, 2001) (256, 257).
CIFALI-LECOUTRE, Mireille
'Notes autour de la première traduction française d'une oeuvre de Sigmund

Freud', in *Revue international d'histoire de la psychanalyse*, vol. 4 (1991), pp. 291–305 (125).
CLARK, L[eon] PIERCE
'A study of primary somatic factors in compulsive and obsessive neuroses', in *IJ*, vol. 1 (1920), pp. 150–60 (111).
CREMERIUS, Johannes
'Einleitung des Herausgebers', in Karl Abraham, *Psychoanalytische Studien zur Charakterbildung; Und andere Schriften* (Frankfurt: S. Fischer, 1971), pp. 11–33 (20).
CZEIKE, Felix
1984: *Wien: Geschichte in Bilddokumenten* (Munich: C. H. Beck, 1984) (16, 110, 126, 213).
1999: *Wien: Kunst, Kultur und Geschichte der Donaumetropole* (Cologne: DuMont, 1999) (110, 138).
DE CLERCK, Rotraut
'"Der Traum von einer bess'ren Welt": Psychoanalyse und Kultur in der Mitte der zwanziger Jahre in Berlin und London', foreword to the German translation of *Bloomsbury* (Stuttgart: Verlag Internationale Psychoanalyse, 1995), pp. 9–40 (156).
DELAGO, Hermann
Dolomiten-Wanderbuch, 6th revised and enlarged edition (Innsbruck, Vienna, Munich: Tyrolia-Verlag, 1960) (2).
D'ERME, Elisabetta
'Durch die Stadtviertel der Renaissance', in *Merian: Das Monatsheft der Städte und Landschaften*, November 1991, vol. 11: 'Rom' (Hamburg: Hoffmann und Campe, 1991), pp. 157–9 (Appendix 1, notes 63, 66, 72).
DEUTSCH, F.
Felix Deutsch, 'Reflections on Freud's one hundredth birthday', in *Psychosomatic Magazine*, vol. 18 (1956), pp. 279–83 (197, text after 201).
DEUTSCH, Helene
1925: 'Bericht über das "Lehrinstitut der Wiener PsA. Vereinigung"', in *IZ*, vol. 11 (1925), pp. 522–4 (166).
1932: 'Lehrinstitut und Ambulatorium', in *IZ*, vol. 18 (1932), pp. 278–80 (151).
1973: *Confrontations with Myself: an Epilogue* (New York: Norton, 1973) (166).
DONN, Linda
Freud and Jung: Years of Friendship, Years of Loss (New York: Scribner, 1988) (297).
DRÄGE, Käthe
'Einige Bemerkungen zu den Zeitumständen und zum Schicksal der Psychoanalyse und der Psychotherapie in Deutschland zwischen 1933 und 1949', in H. Abraham et al., *Psychoanalyse in Berlin: Beiträge zur Geschichte, Theorie und Praxis* (Meisenheim: Anton Hain, 1971), pp. 40–9 (131).
DUPONT, Judith
(See also FERENCZI [1988])
'Ein frühes Trauma der psychoanalytischen Bewegung', introduction to Freud/Ferenczi III/1 (German version), pp. 9–42 (156).
EBNER-ESCHENBACH, Marie v.
Hirzepinzchen: ein Märchen (1890), 4th edition (Stuttgart, Berlin, Leipzig: Union Deutsche Verlagsges. [*c.* 1905]) (140).
EDMUNDS, Lavinia
'His master's choice', in *Johns Hopkins Magazine*, vol. 40 (1988), pp. 40–9 (156, 181, 188).

EITINGON, Max
(See also FREUD/EITINGON)
1920: 'Zur Eröffnung der Psychoanalytischen Poliklinik in Berlin;, in *IZ*, vol. 6 ((1920), p. 97f. (100).
1922: 'Bericht über die Berliner Psychoanalytische Poliklinik (März 1920 bis Juni 1922)', in *IZ*, vol. 8 (1922), pp. 506–20 (100, 125, 131, 132).
1927: 'Bericht über die Internationale Unterrichts-Kommission auf dem IPV-Kongress in Innsbruck', in *IZ*, vol. 13 (1927), pp. 480–9 (203).
EKSTEIN, Rudolf
'Sigmund Freud und die Politik', in Jörg Wiese (ed.), *Chaos und Regel: Die Psychoanalyse in ihren Institutionen* (Göttingen: Vandenhoeck & Ruprecht, 1992), pp. 204–15 (246).
ENGELHARDT, Dietrich v. (ed.)
Biographische Enzyklopädie deutschsprachiger Mediziner (Munich: K. G. Saur, 2002) (6, 215).
ENGELMAN, Edmund
Sigmund Freud: Wien IX. Berggasse 19 (Vienna: Christian Brandstätter, 1993) (163).
ERIKSON
Erik and Joan Erikson, 'Dorothy Burlingham's school in Vienna', in *The Bulletin of the Hampstead Clinic*, vol. 3 (1980), Part 2, Dorothy Burlingham Memorial Issue, pp. 91–4 (208).
ESCHBACH and WILLENBERG
Achim Eschbach, Gabi Willenberg, 'Karl Bühler', in Friedrich Stadler (ed.), *Vertriebene Vernunft II: Emigration und Exil österreichischer Wissenschaft* (Vienna and Munich: Jugend & Volk, 1988), pp. 97–305 (246).
ETZERSDORFER, Irene
Arisiert: eine Spurensuche im gesellschaftlichen Untergrund der Republik (Vienna: Kremayr & Scheriau, 1995), pp. 99–121 (161).
FALLEND, Karl
1987: 'Späte Kontakte: Reich – Trotzki – Briefe', in *Werkblatt* (Salzburg, n.d. [1987]), pp. 75–83 (209).
1988: *Wilhelm Reich in Wien: Psychoanalyse und Politik* (Vienna and Salzburg: Geyer-Edition, 1988) (209).
1995: *Sonderlinge, Träumer, Sensitive*, publication of the Ludwig-Boltzmann Institut für Geschichte und Gesellschaft, vol. 26 (Vienna: Jugend & Volk, 1995) (101, 126, 151, 209).
FALLEND and NITZSCHKE
Karl Fallend, Bernd Nitzschke (eds), *Der 'Fall' Wilhelm Reich: Beiträge zum Verhältnis von Psychoanalyse und Politik* (Frankfurt: Suhrkamp, 1997) (209).
FALLEND and REICHMAYR
Karl Fallend, Johannes Reichmayr (eds), *Siegfried Bernfeld oder die Grenzen der Psychoanalyse: Materialien zu Leben und Werk* (Basel: Stroemfeld, 1992) (99).
FEDERN, Ernst
(See also HEENEN-WOLF; PLÄNKERS and FEDERN; *PROTOKOLLE*; WITTENBERGER [1992])
1971: 'Fünfunddreissig Jahre mit Freud: zum 100. Geburtstag von Paul Federn am 13. Oktober 1971', in *Psyche*, vol. 25 (1971), pp. 721–37 (187).
1974: 'Marginalien zur Geschichte der psychoanalytischen Bewegung', in *Psyche*, vol. 28 (1974), pp. 461–71 (187).

1988: 'Die Emigration von Anna und Sigmund Freud: eine Fallstudie', in Friedrich Stadler (ed.), *Vertriebene Vernunft II: Emigration und Exil österreichischer Wissenschaft* (Vienna and Munich: Jugend & Volk, 1988), pp. 247–50 (text after 295).

FEDERN, Paul

1924: 'Varendonck †', in *IZ*, vol. 10 (1924), p. 203f. (142).

1933: 'Sándor Ferenczi, geb. am 16. Juli 1873, gest. am 22. Mai 1933', in *IZ*, vol. 19, (1933), pp. 305–21 (8).

FELLNER, Günter

'Die Verfolgung der Juden,' in Dokumentationsarchiv des österreichischen Widerstandes (ed.), *Widerstand und Verfolgung in Salzburg 1934–1945* (Vienna: Österreichischer Bundesverlag and Salzburg: Universitätsverlag Anton Puster, 1991), vol. 2, pp. 432–73 (93).

FERENCZI, Sándor

(See also FERENCZI/GRODDECK; FREUD/FERENCZI)

1910: 'Referat uber die Notwendigkeit eines engeren Zusammenschlusses der Anhänger der Freudschen Lehre und Vorschläge zur Gründung einer ständigen internationalen Organisation', in *Jb*, vol. II/2 (1910/1911), p. 48f. (8).

1929: 'Fortschritte der analytischen Technik', in *IZ*, vol. 15 (1929), p. 515 (259).

1933: 'Sprachverwirrung zwischen den Erwachsenen und dem Kind: die Sprache der Zärtlichkeit und der Leidenschaft', in *IZ*, vol. 19 (1933), pp. 5–15 (287).

1988: Judith Dupont (ed.), *Ohne Sympathie keine Heilung: das klinische Tagebuch vom 1932* (Frankfurt: S. Fischer, 1988); available in English as *The Clinical Diary of Sándor Ferenczi*, translated by Michael Balint and Nicola Zarday Jackson (Cambridge, MA: Harvard University Press, 1988) (287).

FERENCZI/GRODDECK

Correspondance (1921–1933) (Paris: Payot, 1982); available in German as *Sándor Ferenczi/Georg Groddeck: Briefwechsel*, translated by Joachim A. Frank (French) and Beatrix Geröli (Hungarian) (Frankfurt: Fischer Taschenbuch Verlag, 1986) (287).

FICHTNER, Gerhard

(See also FICHTNER and HIRSCHMÜLLER; FREUD/BINSWANGER)

1992: 'Einleitung' to Freud/Binswanger, pp. IX–XXXI (17).

2003: 'Freud als Briefschreiber [2] "Eine plötzliche Veränderung . . ." Ein Brief Freuds an seine Schwester Rosa aus dem Jahre 1885' [see also Freud 2003*l*), in *Jb. Psychoanal.*, vol. 47 (2003), pp. 195–205; letter pp. 197–202 (16).

2008*a*: 'Freud und Familie Hammerschalg – eine prägende Begegnung', in *Luzifer-Amor, Zeitschrift zur Geschichte der Psychoanalyse*, vol. 21 (2008), no. 41, pp. 63–79 (71).

2008*b*: 'Freud also Briefschreiber [10.] "Ich schreibe jetzt schon vier Wochen, schreibe, schreibe . . ." Ein Brief Freuds an Ruth Mack Brunswick aus dem Jahre 1929', in *Jb. Psychoanal.*, vol. 56 (2008), pp. 153–67; the letter 159f. [see also Freud 2008e] (257).

FICHTNER and HIRSCHMÜLLER

Gerhard Fichtner, Albrecht Hirschmüller, 'Freuds "Katharina" – Hintergrund, Entstehungsgeschichte und Bedeutung einer frühen psychoanalytischen Krankheitsgeschichte', in *Psyche*, vol. 39 (1985), pp. 220–40 (74).

FISCHER, Eugenia

'Leben und Werk von Nikolaj Jegrafowitsch Ossipov', in *Luzifer-Amor: Zeitschrift für Geschichte der Psychoanalyse*, vol. 8 (1995), no. 16, pp. 77–86 (199).

FISCHER, Isidor (ed.)
1932/33: *Biographisches Lexikon der hervorragenden Ärzte der letzten fünfzig Jahre*, 2 vols (Berlin and Vienna: Urban & Schwarzenberg (1932/33) (6, 33, 74, 106, 127).
1962: *Biographisches Lexikon der hervorragenden Ärzte der letzten fünfzig Jahre: zugleich Fortsetzung des Biographischen Lexikons der hervorragenden Ärzte aller Zeiten und Völker*, 2nd and 3rd unrevised editions (Berlin: Urban & Schwarzenberg, 1962) (144, 156).
2002: *Biographisches Lexikon der hervorragenden Ärzte der letzten fünfzig Jahre*, vols III and IV, revisions and additions by Peter Voswinckel (Hildesheim, Zurich, New York: Olms, 2002) (71).
FLOERICKE, Kurt
'Umschau über die Naturschutzbewegung', in *Kosmos – Handweiser für Naturfreunde*, vol. 12 (1909), printed in *Nationalpark Berchtesgaden* (n.d. [after 1979]), pp. 28–34 (257).
FREUD, Martin
Glory Reflected: Sigmund Freud – Man and Father by his Eldest Son (London: Angus & Robertson, 1957) (Introduction, 1, 2, 3, 4, 5, 11, 14, 16, 33, 37, 47, 91, 102, 104, 122, 149, 162, 199, 244, 295, 297).
FREUD, Sophie
My Three Mothers and Other Passions (New York: New York University Press, 1988) (104, 159, text after 295).
FREUD, W. Ernst
1987: 'Die Freuds und die Burlinghams in der Berggasse: persönliche Erinnerungen', in *Freud-Vorlesungen*, pp. 200–14 (Introduction, 54, 146, 208, 211, 212, 218, 244, 256, 271, 277, 298).
1988: 'Persönliche Erinnerungen an den Anschluss 1938', in *Sigmund Freud House Bulletin*, vol. 12, no. 2 (winter 1988), pp. 13–18 (146, text after 295).
FREUD-BERNAYS, Anna
Christfried Tögel (ed.), *Eine Wienerin in New York* (Berlin: Aufbau-Verlag, 1988) (36, 58, 67, 98, 99, 115, 119, 128, 149).
FREUD-VORLESUNGEN
Harald Leupold-Löwenthal, Inge Scholz-Strasser (eds), *Die Sigmund Freud-Vorlesungen* (Vienna and Cologne: Böhlau, 1990) (146).
FREUDIANA
Reuben Klingsberg (ed.), *Freudiana*, exh. cat. (Jerusalem: Jewish National and University Library, 1973) (60, 107).
FREYTAG-BERNDT
Touristen-Wanderkarte, sheet 19, 1: 100000, no. 493-58 (n.d.) (95).
GARDINER, Muriel
'Personal tribute to Anna Freud', in *The Bulletin of the Hampstead Clinic*, vol. 6 (1983), Part 1, Anna Freud Memorial Issue, pp. 63–5 (Introduction, 295).
GAST, Lilli
Joan Riviere: ausgewählte Schriften (Tübingen: edition diskord, 1996) (157).
GAY, Peter
A Life For Our Time (London and Melbourne: Dent, 1988) (Introduction, 5, 6, 50, 72, 90, 96, 128, 154, 156, 182, 187, 197, text after 295, 296).
GICKLHORN
Josef and Renée Gicklhorn, *Sigmund Freuds akademische Laufbahn im Lichte der Dokumente* (Vienna and Innsbruck: Urban & Schwarzenberg, 1960) (19, 27, 71, 99, 153).

Glover, Edward
'Obituary: Walter Schmideberg', in *IJ*, vol. 36 (1955), pp. 213–15 (161).
Gödde, Günter
1990: 'Freuds Adoleszenz im Lichte seiner Briefe an Eduard Silberstein', in *Luzifer-Amor, Zeitschrift für Geschichte der Psychoanalyse*, vol. 3 (1990), vol. 6, pp. 7–26 (246).
1999: *Traditionslinien des 'Unbewussten': Schopenhauer, Nietzsche, Freud* (Tübingen: edition diskord, 1999) (100).
2003: *Mathilde Freud: die älteste Tochter Sigmund Freuds in Briefen und Selbstzeugnissen* (Giessen: Psychosozial-Verlag, 2003) (Introduction, 5, 10, 11, 12, 17, text after 18, 19, 26, 98, 101, 127, 138, 146, 163, 257, 298).
Goldschmidt, Georges-Arthur
Quand Freud voit la mer: Freud et la langue allemande (Paris: Éditions Buchet/Chastel, 1988), available in German as *Als Freud das Meer sah: Freud und die deutsche Sprache*, translated by Brigitte Grosse (Zurich: Ammann, 1999) (43).
Grosskurth, Phyllis
The Secret Ring: Freud's Inner Circle and the Politics of Psychoanalysis (Toronto: MacFarlane, Walter & Ross, 1991) (174).
Grotjahn, Martin
'Franz Alexander 1891–1964: the Western mind in transition', in Franz Alexander et al. (eds), *Psychoanalytic Pioneers* (New York and London: Basic Books, 1966), pp. 384–98 (163).
Grubrich-Simitis, Ilse
(See also *Freud Bibliography*)
1978: 'Lebenschronologie Sigmund Freud', in *Werksausgabe in zwei Bänden*, vol. 2 (Frankfurt: S. Fischer, 1978), pp. 7–48 (99).
1981: 'Siegfried Bernfeld: Historiker der Freud Biographik und Freud-Biograph', in Siegfried Bernfeld and Suzanne Cassirer-Bernfeld, *Bausteine der Freud-Biographik*, edited, translated and with an introduction by Ilse Grubrich Simitis (Frankfurt: Suhrkamp, 1981), pp. 7–48 (99).
1985: 'Metapsychologie und Metabiologie: zu Sigmund Freuds Entwurf einer "Übersicht der Übertragungsneurosen"', in Sigmund Freud, *Übersicht der Übertragungsneurosen: ein bisher unbekanntes Manuskript*, edited with an essay by Ilse Grubrich-Simitis (Frankfurt: S. Fischer, 1985), pp. 83–119 (54).
1986: 'Six letters of Sigmund Freud and Sándor Ferenczi on the interrelationship of psychoanalytic theory and technique', in *International Review of Psycho-Analysis*, vol. 13 (1986), pp. 259–77 (Introduction).
1993: *Zurück zu Freuds Texten: stumme Dokumente sprechen machen* (Frankfurt: S. Fischer, 1993); available in English as *Back to Freud's Texts – Making Silent Documents Speak*, translated by Philip Storkin (New Haven, CT, and London: Yale University Press, 1996) (95, 107, 112, 142, 157, 163, 175, 251, 298).
1994: '"Kein grossartigerer, reicherer, geheimnisvollerer Stoff [. . .] als das Seelenleben"; ein früher Briefaustausch zwischen Freud und Einstein', in *Neue Rundschau*, vol. 105 (1994), no. 1, pp. 107–18 (210).
1995*a*: 'Eben mit Anna hier angekommen: über eine Ansichtskarte Sigmund Freuds – aus Anlass des 100. Geburtstags von Anna Freud', in *Frankfurter Rundschau*, no. 287, 9 December 1995 (text after 201, Appendix 1, note 10).
1995*b*: '*Urbuch der Psychoanalyse*; *hundert Jahre Studien über Hysterie* von Josef Breuer und Sigmund Freud' (essays accompanying a reprint of the first edition of *Studien über Hysterie*, 1895) (Frankfurt: S. Fischer, 1995) (Introduction).

2004: *Michelangelos Moses und Freuds 'Wagstück': eine Collage* (Frankfurt: S. Fischer, 2004) (Appendix 1, note 16).
2005: '"Wie sieht es mit der Beziehungs- und Beleuchtungsfrage bei Ihnen aus, Herr Professor?"', in *Psyche*, vol. 59 (2005), pp. 266–90 (Introduction, 154).
GÜNTHER, Henning
Sigmund Freud: eine Bildbiographie (Cologne: Benedikt Taschen, 1987) (163).
HAJOS and ZAHN
E. M. Hajos, L. Zahn, *Berliner Architektur der Nachkriegszeit* (Berlin: Albertus-Verlag, 1928) (164).
HALBAN, Dési[rée] (ed.)
(with Ursula Ebbers), *Selma Kurz: die Sängerin und ihre Zeit* (Stuttgart and Zurich: Belser, 1983) (149).
HALL, Murray G.
Österreichsche Verlagsgeschichte 1918–1938, 2 vols. (Vienna, Cologne, Graz: Böhlaus Nachf., 1985 (126).
HARMAT, Paul
Freud, Ferenczi und die ungarische Psychoanalyse (Tübingen: edition diskord, 1988) (98, 133, 163).
HAYNAL, André
'Einleitende Bemerkungen' to *Sigmund Freud/Sándor Ferenczi – Briefwechsel*, vol. 1/I (Vienna, Cologne, Weimar: Böhlau, 1993), pp. 17–41 (7).
HEENEN-WOLF, Susann
'Helene Deutsch (1884–1982)', in Ernst Federn, Gerhard Wittenberger (eds), *Aus dem Kreis um Sigmund Freud: zu den Protokollen der Wiener Psychoanalytischen Vereinigung* (Frankfurt: Fischer Taschenbuch Verlag, 1992), pp. 158–61 (166).
HELLER, Peter
(See also ANNA/EVA)
'Remarks on the Background and Major Topics of the Letters', in ANNA/EVA [1992], pp. 73–107 (98, 146, 158, 208, 212, text after 255, 257, 287).
HERMANNS and SCHULTZ
(See also SCHULTZ and HERMANNS)
Ludger M. Hermanns, Ulrich Schulz, '"Und doch ware ich . . . beinahe Berliner geworden": Sigmund Freud im Sanatorium Schloss Tegel', in *Zeitschrift für psychoanalytische Theorie und Praxis*, vol. V (1990), pp. 78–88 (text after 255).
HINTERBRANDNER, Joseph sen.
Von der alten Ruderschiffahrt am Königssee: Erinnerungen eines ehemaligen Ruderers und Stegwarts (Schönau am Königssee: Plenk, 1996) (102).
HINTERSEER and KRISCH
Gastein und seine Geschichte, 5th edition (Bad Gastein: F. u. Ch. Feichter, 1996) (75).
HIRSCHMÜLLER, Albrecht
(See also FICHTNER and HIRSCHMÜLLER; FREUD/BERNAYS)
1978: *Physiologie und Psychoanalyse in Leben und Werk Josef Breuers* (Bern: Hans Huber, 1978) (74, 126).
1989: 'Freuds "Mathilde": Ein weiterer Tagesrest zum Irma-Traum', in *Jb. Psychoanal.*, vol. 24 (1989), pp. 128–59 (71).
HISTORISCHES LEXIKON
Historisches Lexikon der Schweiz (Basel: Schwabe, since 1998) (157).
HITSCHMANN, Eduard
'Zehn Jahre Wiener Psychoanalytisches Ambulatorium (1922–1932)', in *IZ*, vol. 18 (1932), pp. 265–71 (151).

HOLZNER, Rudolf
Aus dem alten Gastein: die Geschichte einer Familie [Straubinger], (Salzburg and Stuttgart: Verlag 'Das Berglandbuch', 1957) (75).
HORNEY, Karen
'Deutsche Psychoanalytische Gesellschaft, Bericht über die Tätigkeiten im I. und II. Quartal 1930', in *IZ*, vol. 16 (1930), pp. 534–7 (277).
HOSP, Inga
Ritten: Land und Leute am Berg (Merano: Tappeiner, 1984) (14).
HUBER, Nicholas
Die Sagen vom Untersberg, 2nd edition (Salzburg: Heinrich Dieter, 1901) (95).
HUGHES, Athol
'Letters from Sigmund Freud to Joan Riviere (1921–1939)', in *International Review of Psycho-Analysis*, vol. 19 (1992), pp. 265–84 (157).
HUNNIUS, Curt
Hunnius Pharmazeutisches Wörterbuch, 8th edition (Berlin and New York: Walter de Gruyter, 1998) (83).
HUPPKE, Andrea
'Zur Geschichte des Internationalen Psychoanalytischen Verlages', in *Luzifer-Amor, Zeitschrift für Geschichte der Psychoanalyse*, vol. 9 (1996), no. 17/18, pp. 7–33 (89).
JELGERSMA, Gerbrandus
Unbewusstes Geistesleben, supplement to *IZ* (1914) (99).
JELLIFFE, Smith Ely
1925: 'Freud, Anna: the relation of beating phantasies to a day dream', in *The Psychoanalytic Review*, vol. 12 (1925), pp. 117–19 (236, 238).
1927: 'Freud, Anna: beating phantasies and day dreams', in *Journal of Nervous and Mental Diseases*, vol. 65 (Jan–Jun 1927), no. 4 (April), 442–4 (236, 238).
1983: *Jelliffe: American Psychoanalyst and Physician*, part I (by John C. Burnham); *Jelliffe's Correspondence with Sigmund Freud and C. G. Jung* (William McGuire, ed.) (Chicago, IL, London: University of Chicago Press, 1983) (113, 236).
JOAS, Götz-Armin
'Böhmische Bäder – ein Mythos im Wandel: die planerischen und konservatorischen Probleme von Karlsbad, Marienbad und Franzensbad', in *Süddeutsche Zeitung*, no. 209, 10 September 1993, p. 14 (14).
JONES I–III
Sigmund Freud: Life and Works, 3 vols (London: Hogarth Press, 1955).
Vol. I (reprinted 1972) (Introduction, 1, 4, 7, 16, 34, 39, 41, 61, 71, 98, 101, 105, 122).
Vol. II (reprinted 1967) (2, 8, 14–18, text after 18, 19, 20, 32, 33, 34, 41, 43, 46, 47, 54, 60, 67, 72, 76, 80, 87, 89, 90, 98, 99, 101, 107, 126, 133, 156, 160, 174, 175, 181, text after 201, 238, 257, Appendix 1, notes 2, 32).
Vol. III (reprinted 1957) (Introduction, 6, 20, 41, 76, 89, 92, 95, 96, 98–101, 105–10, 112, 117, 123, text after 123, 125, 126, 133, 151, 153, 156, 157, 160, 162, 174, 175, 181, 189, 196–8, 200, text after 201, 203, 204, 206, 209, 210, 212, 213, 223, 238, 244, 251, text after 255, 257, 259, 270, 271, 273, 277, 287, 288, 294, text after 295, 296–8).
JONES, Ernest
(See also JONES I–III; FREUD/JONES)
1915: 'Professor Janet on psycho-analysis: a rejoinder', in *Journal of Abnormal Psychology*, vol. 9 (1915), pp. 400–10, translated by Anna Freud as "Professor Janet über Psychoanalyse: eine Erwiderung', in *IZ*, vol. 4 (1916/17), pp. 34–43 (60, 69, 74).

1918: 'Anal-erotic character traits', in *Journal of Abnormal Psychology*, vol. 13 (1918), pp. 261–84, translated by Anna Freud as 'Über anal-erotische Charakterzüge', in *IZ*, vol. 9 (1919), pp. 69–92 (96).
1920*a*: *Treatment of Neuroses* (New York: Wm. Wood; London: Baillère, Tindall & Cox, 1920), translated by Anna Freud as *Therapie der Neurosen* (Leipzig, Vienna, Zurich: Internationaler Psychoanalytischer Verlag, 1921) (49).
1920*b*: 'Dr. James Jackson Putnam [obituary], in *IJ*, vol. 1 (1920), pp. 6–16 (49).
1922*a*: 'Preface' to translation of Freud, 1920*g* (157).
1922*b*: 'Some problems of adolescence', in *British Journal of Psychology*, vol. 13 (1922), pp. 31–47, translated by Anna Freud as 'Einige Probleme des jugendlichen Alters', in *Imago*, vol. 9 (1923), pp. 145–68 (96).
1992*c*: 'Preface' to translation of Freud 1916–1917*a* (163).
1924: Jones et al., *Glossary for the Use of Translators of Psycho-Analytical Works*, supplement to *IJ*, vol. 5 (1924), pp. 1–16 (157).
1926: 'Karl Abraham 1877–1925' [obituary], in *IZ*, vol. 12 (1926), pp. 155–83 (20).
1929: 'Freud, Sigmund', in *Encyclopaedia Britannica*, 14th edition, vol. 9, pp. 836ff. (126).
1959: *Free Associations: Memories of a Psychoanalyst* (New Brunswick, NJ, and London: Transaction Publishers, 1990) (41, 42, 45, 126).
JUNG, Carl Gustav
(See also FREUD/JUNG)
1938: 'Presidential address: Views held in common by the different schools of psychotherapy represented at the Congress, July 1938', summary in *Journal of Mental Science*, vol. 84 (1938), p. 1055 (297).
1962: *Erinnerungen, Träume, Gedanken von C. G. Jung*, recorded and edited by Aniel Jaffé (Zurich, Stuttgart: Rascher, 1962); available in English as *Memories, Dreams, Reflections*, translated by Richard and Clara Winston (London: Collins and Routledge & Kegan Paul, 1963) (17).
1975: *Über Grundlagen der analytischen Psychologie: die Tavistock Lectures 1935* (Frankfurt: Fischer Taschenbuch Verlag, 1975) (297).
KAGE, Ulrich
Die Entwicklung psychoanalytischer Polikliniken und ihr Einfluss auf die Medikalisierung der Psychoanalyse (Hamburg: 1986, diss., University of Hamburg) (151).
KARDINER, Abram
My Analysis with Freud – Reminiscences (New York: Norton, 1977) (128, 157).
KARELL
Viktor Karell et al., *Das Egerland und seine Weltbäder: Franzensbad, Karlsbad, Marienbad* (Frankfurt: Das Viergespann, 1966) (14, 57).
KATALOG
Internationaler Psychoanalytischer Verlag 1919–1938, cat. published by the Sigmund Freud Museum, Vienna (1995) (89, 194).
KAUT, Joseph
Die Salzburger Festspiele 1920–1981 (Salzburg and Vienna: Residenz, 1982) (122).
KIND, Friedrich
Gedichte (Leipzig, 1808) (298).
KIPLING, Rudyard
1894/5: *The Jungle Book* (New York: The Century Co., 1894) and *The Second Jungle Book* (New York: Century, 1895) (17, 101).
1899: *Soldier Stories* (New York: Doubleday & McClure, 1899) (17).

KIRCHER, Athanasius
Magie des Wissens – Athanasius Kircher (1602–1680): Universalgelehrter, Sammler, Visionär, exh. cat. (Würzburg: Martin von Wagner Museum, 2002) (Appendix 1, notes 45, 70).
KLEINDEL, Walter
Österreich: Daten zur Geschichte und Kultur, 4th edition revised and edited by Isabella Ackerl and Günter K. Kodek (Vienna: Ueberreuter, 1995) (5, 16, 50, 52, 65, 74, 122, 130, 132, 179).
KLEINE HISTORISCHE STÄDTE
Kleine Historische Städte in Österreich (ed.), *Kleine Historische Städte in Österreich* (Steyr, n.d. [c. 2002], Bad Ischl) (12).
KNOEPFMACHER, Hugo
'Zwei Beiträge zur Biographie Sigmund Freuds', in *Jb. Psychoanal.*, vol. 11 (1979), pp. 51–72 (61).
KNÖPFMACHER, Wilhelm
Entstehungsgeschichte und Chronik der Vereinigung 'WIEN' B'nai B'rith in Wien 1895–1935 (Vienna, 1935) (61).
KÖHLER, Helmut A.
Alpenpark und Nationalpark Berchtesgaden (Freilassung: Pannonia-Verlag, 1975, 2nd edition 1980) (101, 257).
KÖNIGSSEE
75 Jahre Motorschiffahrt auf dem Königssee, festschrift (Leonberg: Liss-Verlag, n.d. [1984]) (68, 102).
KOLA, Richard
Rückblick ins Gestrige: Erlebtes und Erfundenes (Vienna, Leipzig, Munich: Rikola, 1922) (126).
KOS, Wolfgang
Über den Semmering: Kulturgeschichte einer künstlichen Landschaft (Vienna: Edition Tusch, 1984) (5).
KOS, Wolfgang (ed.)
Die Eroberung der Landschaft: Semmering – Rax – Schneeberg, exh. cat. (Vienna: Falter, 1992) (Introduction, 5).
KRÄFTNER, Johann
'Das Bad im Klassizismus und im Biedermeier: Berarchitektur in Wien und Baden in der ersten Hälfte des 19. Jahrhunderts', in *Das Bad: Körperkultur und Hygiene im 19. Und 20. Jahrhundert*, exh. cat. (Eigenverlag der Museen der Stadt Wien, 1992), pp. 111–25 (213).
KRAUS, Andreas
Geschichte Bayerns: von den Anfängen bis zur Gegenwart, 2nd edition (Munich: C. H. Beck, 1988) (185).
KRIS, Ernst
'Introduction' in *The Origins of Psychoanalysis: Letters to Wilhelm Fliess, Drafts and Notes: 1887–1902*, authorized translation by Eric Mosbacher and James Strachey (London: Imago Publishing Co., 1954), pp. 1–47 (34).
KRISCH, Laurenz
(See also HINTERSEER and KRISCH)
2002: 'Bad Gastein: die Rolle des Antisemitismus in einer Fremdenverkehrsgemeinde während der Zwischenkriegszeit', in Robert Kriechbaum (ed.), *Der Geschmack der Vergänglichkeit: jüdische Sommerfrische in Salzburg* (Vienna, Cologne, Weimar: Böhlau, 2002), pp. 175–225 (93).

2003: *Zersprengt die Dollfussketten: die Entwicklung des Nationalsozialismus in Bad Gastein bis 1938* (Vienna, Cologne, Weimar: Böhlau, 2003) (93).

KRÜLL, Marianne

Freud und sein Vater, revised edition (Frankfurt: Fischer Taschenbuch Verlag, 1992); available in English as *Freud and His Father*, translated by Arnold J. Pomerans (London: Hutchinson, 1986) (16, 24, 42, 77, 138).

KURZWEIL, Edith

The Freudians – A Comparative Perspective (New Haven, CT: Yale University Press, 1989).

LADWIG-WINTERS, Simone

Wertheim – ein Warenhausunternehmen und seine Eigentümer. Ein Beispiel der Entwicklung der Berliner Warenhäuser bis zur "Arisierung" (Münster: LIT, 1997); also diss., FU Berlin, 1996 (127, 132, 135).

LAIER, Michael

'Das Frankfurter Psychanalytische Institut (1929–1933); Anfänge der Psychoanalyse in Frankfurt am Main', diss., material from the Sigmund Freud Institut Frankfurt, vol. 9 (Frankfurt: Sigmund Freud Institut (1989) (257).

LAMPL, Hans

'Über einen neuen Typus von Dysenteriebazillen (Bact. Dysenteriae Schmitz)', in *Wiener klinische Wochenschrift*, vol. 30 (1918), pp. 835–7 (45).

LAMPL and LANDSTEINER

See also LANDSTEINER and LAMPL

Hans Lampl, Karl Landsteiner, 'Quantitative Untersuchungen über die Einwirkung von Komplement auf Präzipitate', in *Zschr. Immunitätsf. Orig.*, vol. 26 (1917), pp. 193–8 (45).

LAMPL-DE GROOT, Jeanne

'Personal tribute to Anna Freud', in *The Bulletin of the Hampstead Clinic*, vol. 6 (1983), Part 1, Anna Freud Memorial Issue, pp. 55–60 (163).

LANDAUER, Karl

Hans-Joachim Rothe (ed.), *Theorie der Affekte und andere Schriften zur Ich-Organisation* (Frankfurt: Fischer Taschenbuch Verlag, 1991) (257).

LANDSTEINER, Karl and LAMPL, Hans

(See also LAMPL and LANDSTEINER)

1915: 'Untersuchung der Spezifität von Serumreaktionen durch Einführung verschiedenartiger Gruppen in Eiweiss', in *Centr. Physiol.*, vol. 30 (1915), p. 329f. (45).

1917*a*: 'Über die Einwirkung von Formaldehyd auf Eiweissantigen', in *Zschr. Immunitätsf. Orig.*, vol. 26 (1917), pp. 133–41 (45).

1917*b*: 'Über Antigen emit verschiedenartigen Acylgruppen', in *Biochem. Zschr*, vol. 86 (1917), pp. 343–94 (45).

LANG and SCHNEIDER

Johannes Lang, Max Schneider, *Auf der Gmain. Chronik der Gemeinden Bayerisch Gmain und Grossgmain* (Bayerisch Gmain and Grossgmain: Gemeindeverwaltungen, 1995) (98).

LEGNER, Johann

'Die Bauernbefreiung unter Kaiser Joseph II und der mährische Pflug', in *Wischauer Heimatbote*, vol. 5, no. 6 (Nov/Dec 1990), p. 9f. (77).

LEISCHING

Robert A. Kann, Peter Leisching (eds), *Ein Leben für Kunst und Volksbildung: Eduard Leisching 1858–1938. Erinnerungen* (Vienna: Verlag der Österreichischen Akademie der Wissenschaften, 1978) (125).

LENDVAI, Paul
Die Ungarn: ein Jahrtausen Sieger in Niederlagen (Munich: C. Bertelsmann, 1999); available in English as *The Hungarians: A Thousand Years of Victory in Defeat*, translated by Ann Major (London: Hurst & Company, 2003) (102).
LEONHARDT, Henrike
'Es geschah in Bad Reichenhall: Geschichte, wie Heinrich Heines Schreibtisch nach Jerusalem kam', in Gabriele Förg (ed.), *Es geschah in* . . . (Munich: Buchendorfer, 2002), pp. 209–32 (95).
LEUPOLD-LÖWENTHAL, Harald
(See also FREUD, W. E. [1987]; *FREUD-VORLESUNGEN*; *SIGMUND FREUD MUSEUM*)
1981 [1980]: 'Nachwort' to *Protokolle IV*, pp. 325–54 (246).
1984: 'Zur Geschichte der "Frage der Laienanalyse"', in *Psyche*, vol. 38 (1984), no. 2, pp. 97–120 (251, 288).
1988: 'Die Vertreibung der Familie Freud 1938', in *Sigmund Freud House Bulletin*, vol. 12, no. 2 (winter 1988), pp. 1–11 ['Richtigstellung' in vol. 13/1 (summer 1989, 46]; also in *Psyche*, vol. 43 (1989), no. 10, pp. 918–28 (12, 297, 298).
LÉVY, Kata
'Dernières vacances des Freud avant la fin du monde', in *Le Coq-Héron*, no. 117 (1990), pp. 39–44; based on the unpublished typescript in German 'Erinnerungen an den Sommer von 1918' (18 p.), kindly made available to me by Peter Lambda, Tibberton (80–5, 87, 88, 90).
LEWIS, Nolan D. C.
'Smith Ely Jelliffe 1866–1945; Psychosomatic medicine in America', in Franz Alexander et al. (eds), *Psychoanalytic Pioneers* (New York and London: Basic Books, 1966), pp. 224–33 (236).
LIEBERMAN, E. James
Acts of Will: The Life and Work of Otto Rank (New York: The Free Press, 1985) (43, 74, 100, 287).
LINDEMANN, Mary
1981: *140 Jahre Israelitisches Krankenhaus in Hamburg: Vorgeschichte und Entwicklung* (Hamburg, 1981) (144).
1997: Mary Lindemann et al., *150 Jahre Israelitisches Krankenhaus in Hamburg* (Hamburg, 1997) (144).
LIST, Eveline
'Otto Rank, Verleger', in *KATALOG* (1995), pp. 30–47 (43, 98, 155).
LOCKOT, Regine
Erinnern und Durcharbeiten – Zur Geschichte der Psychoanalyse und Psychotherapie im Nationalsozialismus (Frankfurt: Fischer Taschenbuch Verlag, 1985) (120, 131).
LOEWENSTEIN, Rudolph
'In memoriam Marie Bonaparte 1882–1962', in *Journal of the American Psychoanalytic Association*, vol. 11 (1963), no. 4, pp. 861–3 (214).
LORAND, Sandor
'Leonard Blumgart 1881–1959, obituary', in *IJ*, vol. 41 (1960), p. 640f. (154/2).
MAETZE, Gerhard
'Psychoanalyse in Berlin von 1950–1970', in H. Abraham et al., *Psychoanalyse in Berlin – Beiträge zur Geschichte, Theorie und Praxis* (Meisenheim: Anton Hain, 1971), pp. 50–75 (131).

MARÍN, Juan
Paralelo 53° Sur, retitled *Inferno azul y blanco* (Santiago de Chile, 1936, 3rd edition 1955) (277).
MARINELLI, Lydia
'Zur [sic] der Geschichte des Internationalen Psychoanalytischen Verlags', in *KATALOG* (1995), pp. 9–29 (89, 98, 114, 138, 155, 298).
MARTIN, L.[ouis] C.[harles]
'A note on Hazlitt', in *IJ*, vol. 1 (1920), pp. 414–49 (45).
MCGUIRE, William
'Introduction' to FREUD/JUNG [1974], pp. xiii–xxxvii (17).
MERESHKOVSKY, DMITRY SERGEYEVICH
The Romance of Leonardo da Vinci, translated by Bernard Guilbert Guerney (Norwalk, CT: Easton Press, 1998) (213).
MERIAN POSTER ROME
'Stadtposter', supplement in *Merian – Das Monatsheft der Städte und Landschaften*, no. 11, Nov 1991: 'Rom' (Hamburg: Hoffmann und Campe, 1991) (Appendix 1, notes 27, 41).
MEYER, Monroe A.
'In Memoriam Dr. A. Polon', in *IZ*, vol. 12 (1926), p. 574 (163).
MICHAUD, Stéphane
Lou Andreas-Salomé – l'alliée de la vie (Paris: Éd. du Seuil, 2000) (153).
MINUTES
Minutes of the Vienna Psychoanalytic Society, 5 vols (New York: International Universities Press) (See *PROTOKOLLE*).
MODENA, Emilio
'Hommage à W. R. – Psychoanalyse und Politik vor der Jahrtausendwende', in Fallend and Nitzschke, *Der 'Fall' Wilhelm Reich: Beiträge zum Verhältnis von Psychoanalyse und Politik* (Frankfurt: Suhrkamp, 1997), pp. 316–47 (209).
MODICK, Klaus
'Römische Brandung', in *Marian – Das Monatsheft der Städte und Landschaften*, Nov 1991, no. 11: 'Rom' (Hamburg: Hoffmann und Campe, 1991), p. 94f. (Appendix 1, note 53).
MOLISCH, Hans
'Julius von Wiesner [obituary]', in *Berichte der Deutschen Botanischen Gesellschaft*, vol. 34 (1916), pp. 71–99 (157).
MOLNAR, Michael
1992: *The Diary of Sigmund Freud 1929–1939* (London: Hogarth Press, 1992) (Introduction, 19, 74, 82, 110, 114, 119, 126, 146, 147, 159, 163, 204, 208, 210, 228, 238, text after 255, 257, 270, 273, 277, 287, 295, text after 295, 296–8).
2002: Essay on Freud (2002*c*) in Freud (2002*b*), pp. 256–9 (Berlin: Aufbau-Verlag, 2002) (4).
2005: 'Alien Enemy: Porträt eines Mädchens', in *Luzifer-Amor, Zeitschrift für Geschichte der Psychoanalyse*, vol. 18 (2005), no. 35, pp. 152–67 (Introduction, 47).
MONELLI, Paolo
'Vandalen ante portas', in *Marian – Das Monatsheft der Städte und Landschaften*, Nov 1991, no. 11: 'Rom' (Hamburg: Hoffmann und Campe, 1991), pp. 87–9 (Appendix 1, note 32).
MORICHAU-BEAUCHANT, R.
1911: 'Le rapport "affectif" dans la cure des psychonévroses', in *Gazette des hôpitaux*, vol. 84 (1911), pp. 1845–9 (43).

1912: 'Homosexualität und Paranoia' (translated by Otto Rank), in *Zentralblatt für Psychoanalyse, Medizinische Monatsschrift für Seelenkunde*, vol. 2 (1912), pp. 174–6 (43).

MÜHLLEITNER, Elke

Biographisches Lexikon der Psychoanalyse: Die Mitglieder der Psychologischen Mittwoch-Gesellschaft und der Wiener Psychoanalytischen Vereinigung 1902–1938, assisted by Johannes Reichmayr (Tübingen: edition discord, 1992) (3, 6, 20, 43, 54, 71, 74, 76, 93, 96, 99–101, 104, 109, 114, 125, 133, 144, 151, 153, 155, 161–3, 166, 170, 175, 187, 198, 209, 212, 215, 219, 228, 277, 287).

MÜLLER, Dorothee

'Rettung mit ungewissen Ausgang: Josef Hoffmanns Sanatorium Purkersdorf nach der Restaurierung der Fassade', in *Süddeutsche Zeitung*, 26 Jan 1996 (161).

MÜLLER, Karl

[= Carl Müller-Braunschweig] 'Psychoanalyse und Moral', in *Geschl. und Gesell.*, vol. 7 (1920), pp. 217–27 (131).

MURKEN, Barbara

1982: *Tom Siedmann-Freud (1892–1930) – Eine Ausstellung zu Leben und Werk*, exh. cat. (Munich, 1982) (107, 131).

1984: almost identical catalogue to 1982 but with other illustrations for the same exhibition in Frankfurt.

2004: '". . . die Welt is so uneben . . ." Tom Seidmann-Freud (1892–1930): Leben und Werk einer grossen Bilderbuch-Künstlerin', in *Luzifer-Amor, Zeitschrift für Geschichte der Psychoanalyse*, vol. 17 (2004), no. 33, pp. 74–103 (131, 134).

NARJANI, A.-E.

[Pseudonym for Marie Bonaparte] 'Considérations sur les causes anatomiques de la frigidité chez la femme', in *Bruxelles-Médical*, vol. 27 (Apr 1924), p. 11 (238).

NATIONALPARK BERCHTESGADEN

n.d. [1981]: Nationalparkverwaltung Berchtesgaden, Nationalpark Berchtesgaden – Geschichte eines Schutzgebietes, edited by Hubert Zierl on behalf of the Bavarian State Ministry for Regional Development and the Environment (Berchtesgaden: Anton Plenk, n.d. [1981]) (257).

1990: Nationalparkverwaltung Berchtesgaden, *Nationalpark Berchtesgaden – Ein Schutzgebiet in den Alpen mit Tradition und neuen Auftaben*, published on behalf of the Bavarian State Ministry for Regional Development and the Environment (257).

1991: Nationalparkverwaltung Berchtesgaden, *Nationalpark Berchtesgaden – Verleihung des Europadiploms an den Nationalpark Berchtesgaden*, published on behalf of the Bavarian State Ministry for Regional Development and the Environment (257).

NEISER, Emil Michael Johann

'Max Eitingon – Leben und Werk', diss., Psychiatr. Klinik Johannes Gutenberg University of Mainz, 1978 (120).

NEUFELD, Jolan

Dostojewski – Skizze zu seiner Psychoanalyse (Leipzig, Vienna, Zurich: Internationaler Psychoanalytischer Verlag, 1923) (199).

OBERNDORF, Clarence P.

A History of Psychoanalysis in America (New York: Grune & Stratton, 1953), particularly ch. 'Recollections of Psychoanalysis in Vienna, 1921–1922' (128, 156).

OSSIPOV, Nikolai

1923*a* [1922]: 'Über Tolstois Seelenleiden', lecture (17 Jun 1922) to the

Tschechische Medizinische Gesellschaft in Prague, in *Imago*, vol. 9 (1923), pp. 495–8 (199).
1923*b*: *Tolstois Kindheitserinnerungen – Ein Beitrag zu Freuds Libidotheorie* (Leipzig, Vienna, Zurich: Internationaler Psychoanalytischer Verlag, 1923) (199).
OSTWALD, Wilhelm
'Bekenntnis zum Optimismus – Die Zukunft der Menschheit', in *Neue Freie Presse*, Vienna, no. 22482, 17 Apr 1927, morning edition, pp. 2–4 (238).
PARIS, Bernard J.
Karen Horney – A Psychoanalyist's Search for Self-Understanding (New Haven, CT: Yale University Press, 1994) (277).
PERFAHL
Anton Perfahl's Führer von Bad Aussee, Grundlsee und angrenzenden Gebieten (Bad Aussee: Fitzing, n.d. [*c.* 1935]) (19, 110).
PETERICH, Eckart
1957: 'Roma Aeterna', in *Marian – Das Monatsheft der Städte und Landschaften*, vol. 10 (1957), no. 4: 'Rom' (Hamburg: Hoffmann und Campe, 1991), pp. 4–12 (Appendix 1, note 41).
1963: *Italien – Ein Führer*, vol. 3: *Apulien – Kalabrien – Sizilien – Sardinien – Malta* (Munich: Prestel, 1963) (13).
PETERS, Uwe Henrik
Anna Freud – Ein Leben für das Kind (Frankfurt: Fischer Taschenbuch Verlag, 1984); available in English as *Anna Freud – A Life Dedicated To Children* (London: Weidenfeld & Nicolson, 1985) (Introduction, 5, 6, 13, 14, 19, 20, 22, 25, 26, 48, 53, 84, 86, 101, 168, 174, 216).
PFEIFFER, Ernst
'Notes', in FREUD/ANDREAS-SALOMÉ, pp. 211–40 (156).
PICHLER, Hans
'Case History of Prof. Sigmund Freud', in JONES III, pp. 499–521 (197, 287, 297).
PIERCE Clark L[eon], see Clark, L[eon] Pierce.
PIWITT, Hermann P.
'Von allen Engeln verlassen – Die Campagne', in *Marian – Das Monatsheft der Städte und Landschaften*, Nov 1991, no. 11: 'Rom' (Hamburg: Hoffmann und Campe, 1991), pp. 118–28 (Appendix 1, notes 46, 48).
PLÄNKERS and FEDERN
Tomas Plänkers, Ernst Federn, *Vertreibung und Rückkehr – Interview zur Geschichte Ernst Federns und der Psychoanalyse* (Tübingen: edition discord, 1994) (76, 187, 246, 291).
PLOETZ, Karl Julius
1940: *Auszug aus der Geschichte* (Berlin, Leipzig: Ploetz, 1940) (52, 65, 66).
1980: *Der Grosse Ploetz – Auszug aus der Geschichte* (Freiburg and Würzburg: Ploetz, 1980) (46, 50, 52, 75, 102, 132, 185, 296).
PROTOKOLLE
(See also *MINUTES*)
Hermann Nunberg †, Ernst Federn (eds), *Protokolle der Wiener Psychoanalytischen Vereinigung* (Frankfurt: S. Fischer).
Vol. I, 1906–1908 (1976) (41, 76, 93, 109, 144, 187, 228).
Vol. II, 1908–1910 (1977) (6, 16, 20, 96, 142, 228).
Vol. III, 1910–1911 (1979) (33, 114, 142, 215, 228).
Vol. IV, 1912–1918 (1981) (76, 80, 82, 99, 105, 125, 131, 153, 161, 228, 296, 298).

Purkersdorf
Hoffmann-Bau Purkersdorf bei Wien, Denkschrift zur Rettung und Wiederherstellung des Sanatoriumbaus Purkersdorf, published by Klaus KG, Purkersdorf [1995] (161).
Putnam, James Jackson
1910: 'On the etiology and treatment of psychoneuroses', in *Boston Medical and Surgical Journal*, vol. 136 (1910), p. 75 [Translation by Freud, see 1911*j*] (49).
1903: 'On certain of the broader issues of the psychoanalytical movement', in *Transactions of the Association of American Physicians*, vol. 28 (1913), pp. 513–29; translated by Anna Freud as 'Allgemeine Gesichtspunkte zur psychoanalytischen Bewegung', in *IZ*, vol. 4 (1916/17), pp. 1–20 (49, 60, 69, 74).
Raffalt, Reinhard
'Mit der Kutsche durch zwei Jahrtausende', in *Marian – Das Monatsheft der Städte und Landschaften*, vol. 10 (1957), no. 4: 'Rom' (Hamburg: Hoffmann und Campe, 1991), pp. 20–26 (Appendix 1, note 12).
Raknes, Ola
Wilhelm Reich and Orgonomy (Princeton, NJ: American College of Orgonomy Press, 2004) (209).
Rank, Otto
1910/11: 'Bericht über die II. private psychoanalytische Vereinigung in Nürnberg am 30. und 31. März 1910', in *Jb*, vol. II/2 (1910/11), 731–42 (8).
1911: 'Bericht über die II. private psychoanalytische Vereinigung in Nürnberg am 30. und 31. März 1910', in *Zentralblatt für Psychoanalyse – Medizinische Monatsschrift für Seelenkunde*, vol. 1 (1911), pp. 129–31 (8).
Reader's Encyclopedia
William Rose Benét (ed.), *The Reader's Encyclopedia* (New York: Thomas Y. Crowell Company, 1948, 1955, 6th edition 1958) (95).
Régis and Hesnard
1913: Emmanuel Régis, Angelo-Louis-Marie Hesnard, 'La doctrine de Freud et de son école', in *L'Encéphale*, vol. 8 (1913), pp. 356–78, 446–81, 537–64 (43).
1914: Emmanuel Régis, Angelo-Louis-Marie Hesnard, *La psychoanalyse* [sic] *des névroses et des psychoses – ses applications médicales et extra-médicales* (Paris: F. Alcan, 1914) (43).
Reich, Wilhelm
1927*a*: 'Zur Technik der Deutung und der Widerstandsanalyse – über die gesetzmässige Entwicklung der Übertragungsneurose', in *IZ*, vol. 13 (1927), pp. 141–59 (209).
1927*b*: 'Bericht über das "Seminar für psychoanalytische Therapie" am Psychoanalytischen Ambulatorium in Wien (1925/26)', in *IZ*, vol. 13 (1927), pp. 241–4 (209).
1927*c*: *Die Funktion des Orgasmus – Zur Psychopathologie und zur Soziologie des Geschlechtslebens* (Leipzig, Vienna, Zurich: Internationaler Psychoanalytischer Verlag, 1927); integrated in *Die Entdeckung des Orgons I: Die Funktion des Orgasmus – Sexualökonomische Grundprobleme der biologischen Energie* (Frankfurt: Fischer Taschenbuch Verlag, 1981); available in English as *The Function of the Orgasm – Sex-Economic Problems of Biological Energy*, translated by Vincent R. Carfagno (New York: Farrar, Straus & Giroux, 1973) (209).
Reik, Theodor
Dreissig Jahre mit Sigmund Freud (Munich: Kindler, 1976); available in English as *From Thirty Years With Freud*, translated from the German [unnamed translator] (London: Hogarth Press, 1942) (114, 133).

REININGER, Elisabeth
'Marienbad – Das Weltbad des Stiftes Tepl', in Viktor Karell et al., *Das Egerland und seine Weltbäder: Franzensbad, Karlsbad, Marienbad* (Frankfurt: Das Viergespann, 1966), pp. 201–13 (128).
REINL, Max
'Franzensbad – Sein Werden und seine berühmtesten Kurgäste aus der deutschen Geisteswelt', in Viktor Karell et al., *Das Egerland und seine Weltbäder: Franzensbad, Karlsbad, Marienbad* (Frankfurt: Das Viergespann, 1966), pp. 215–41 (128).
RICHTER, Werner
Bismarck – Eine Biographie (Frankfurt: Fischer Taschenbuch Verlag, 1971); available in English as *Bismarck*, translated by Brian Battershaw (New York: Putnam, 1965) (257).
RITTEN
Tourismusverein Ritten (ed.), *Grüss Göttingen am Ritten – Zeit und Raum*, brochure, responsible for the content: Peter Righi (Ritten, South Tyrol, n.d.); [a revised, updated and enlarged edition published in 2000 also contains a chapter about the visit of the Freud family to Ritten in 1911] (14, 15).
ROAZEN, Paul
1975: *Freud and His Followers* (New York: Knopf, 1975) (156, 198, 228, 296, 297).
1992: *Helen Deutsch: A Psychoanalyst's Life* (New Brunswick, NJ: Transaction Publishers, 1992) (166).
1993: *Meeting Freud's Family* (Amherst, MA: University of Massachusetts Press, 1993) (74, 198, 228).
1995: *How Freud Worked – First-Hand Accounts of Patients* (Northvale, NJ: Aronson, 1995) (198, 228).
ROMM, May E.
'Abraham Arden Brill 1874–1948; first American translator of Freud', in Franz Alexander et al. (eds), *Psychoanalytic Pioneers* (New York, London: Basic Books, 1966), pp. 210–23 (238).
ROMMEL, Otto
'Entstehung und Aufbau des "Buches der Gedichte"', in Anton Wildgans, *Sämtliche Werke*, vol. 1 (1949), *Gedichte*, pp. 380–402 (99).
ROSS, Victor
'Eva Marie Rosenfeld (1892–1977): A Woman of Valor. A Personal Memoir (with illustrations)', in ANNA/EVA [1992], pp. 23–60 (82, 208, 212, text after 255, Appendix 3).
ROTHE, Hans-Joachim
(See also LANDAUER)
1991: 'Einleitung' to Landauer, pp. 7–23 (257).
2004: 'Karl Launders Exil in Amsterdam im Spiegel seines Briefwechsels mit Max Horkheimer', in *Jb. Psychoanal.*, vol. 48 (2004), pp. 135–49 (257).
ROUDINESCO, Elisabeth
La bataille de cent ans: histoire de la psychanalyse en France, vol. 1: 1885–1939; vol. 2: 1925–1985 (Paris: Seuil, 1986).
RUBINS, Jack L.
Karen Horney – Gentle Rebel of Psychoanalysis (New York: Dial Press, 1978) (277).
RUNDBRIEFE
Gerhard Wittenberger, Christfried Tögel (eds.), *Die Rundbriefe des 'Geheimen Komitees'* (Tübingen: edition discord).

Rundbriefe 1, 1913–1920 (1999) (89, 100, 107, 116, 126, 128, 137, 156, 158, 160).
Rundbriefe 2, 1921 (2001) (95, 107, 125, 126, 133, 153, 155, 157, 159, 199).
Rundbriefe 3, 1922 (2003) (89, 155–7, 165, 181).
[For non-published *Rundbriefe* after 1923 – where not indicated – see the list of Unpublished Materials] (Introduction, 126, 156, 199, text after 201, 253, 256).

SABLIK, Karl
1983: *Julius Tandler – Mediziner und Sozialreformer* (Vienna: A. Schendl, 1983) (110).
1985: 'Sigmund Freud und Julius Tandler: eine rätselhafte Beziehung', in *Sigmund Freud House Bulletin*, vol. 9, no. 2 (winter 1985), pp. 12–19 (110).

SACHS, Hanns
Freud: Master and Friend (London: Imago Publishing, 1945; reprint, originally published 1944) (27, 54, 123, 126, 151).

SAYERS, Janet
Mothers of Psychoanalysis: Helen Deutsch, Karen Horney, Anna Freud, Melanie Klein (New York: Norton, 1991).

SCHAUER, Rainer
'Eine zweite Heimat' (Altaussee im steirischen Salzkammergut), *Die Zeit*, no. 37, 4 September 1991, p. 63f. (2, 122).

SCHEIDHAUER, Marcel
Le rêve freudien en France – avancées et resistances: 1900–1926 (Paris: Navarin, 1985) (43).

SCHILLER, Friedrich v.
Schillers Werke (Berlin, Leipzig, Vienna, Stuttgart: Deutsches Verlagshaus Bong & Co., n.d. [1907]) (76).

SCHLEUSSINGER, August
Klein Roland, Der sterbende Roland, Der getreue Eckart, auf Quarta erklärt, programme (Ansbach: Brügel, 1876) (129).

SCHNELL, Hugo
Bad Reichenhall – St. Zeno, Kunstführer Nr. 157 (Regensburg: Schnell & Steiner, 1936, 2nd completely revised edition, 1995) (95).

SCHNITZLER, Arthur
1981: Therese Nickl, Heinrich Schnitzler (eds), *Briefe 1875–1912* (Frankfurt: S. Fischer, 1981) (72, 95, 127).
1984: Therese Nickl, Heinrich Schnitzler (eds), *Briefe 1913–1931* (Frankfurt: S. Fischer, 1984) (154/2).
1985: Therese Nickl, Heinrich Schnitzler (eds), *Jugend in Wien – Eine Autobiographie* (Frankfurt: S. Fischer, 1985); available in English as *My Youth in Vienna*, translated by Catherine Hutter (New York, Chicago, San Francisco: Holt, Rinehart & Winston, 1970) (72, 116, 198).

SCHOLZ-STRASSER, Inge
(See also ENGELMAN; *FREUD-VORLESUNGEN*; *SIGMUND FREUD MUSEUM*)
'Adolf Josef Stofer: Journalist, Redakteur, Direktor des Internationalen Psychoanalytischen Verlags 1925–1932', in *KATALOG* (1995), pp. 56–74 (162).

SCHRÖTER, Michael
(See also FREUD/EITINGON)
1996: 'Zur Frühgeschichte der Laienanalyse: Struktur eines Kernkonflikts der FreudSchule', in *Psyche*, vol. 50 (1996), pp. 1127–75 (108, 138, 251).
2002: 'Max Eitingon and the struggle to establish an international standard for psychoanalytic training (1925–1929)', in *IJ*, vol. 83 (2002), pp. 875–93 (251).
2004: 'Der Steuermann: Max Eitingon und seine Rolle in der Geschichte der

Psychoanalyse', editor's introduction and appendixes, in *Sigmund Freud/Max Eitingon: Briefwechsel 1906–1939* (Tübingen: edition diskord, 2004), pp. 1–33, 933ff. (76, 100, 120, 174, 296).
SCHULTZ and HERMANNS
(See also HERMANNS and SCHULTZ)
U.[lrich] Schultz, L.[udger] M. Hermanns, 'Das Sanatorium Schloss Tegel Ernst Simmels – Zur Geschichte und Konzeption der ersten Psychoanalytischen Klinik', in *Psychotherapie · Psychosomatik · Medizinische Psychologie*, vol. 37, no. 2 (19987), pp. 58–67 (100, text after 255).
SCHUR, Max
Freud: Living and Dying (London: Hogarth Press, 1972) (16, 82, 144, 197, text after 201, 212, 223, text after 255, 277, 287, 294, text after 295, 296–8).
SEIBT, Gustav
'Neue Spiele im alten Rom', in *Die Zeit*, no. 16, 11 April 2001, p. 39 (Appendix 1, notes 3, 9, 11).
SIEBENKIRCHEN, Hans
'Im Schatten der Cestius-Pyramide', in *Merian: Das Monatsheft der Städte und Landschaften*, vol. 10 (1957), no. 4 'Rom', (Hamburg: Hoffmann und Campe, 1957), p. 54 (Appendix 1, note 25).
SIGMUND FREUD-HAUS
Sigmund Freud-Gesellschaft, Vienna, Berggasse 19 (ed.), *Katalog* (Vienna: Löcker & Wögenstein, 1975) (6, 163).
SIGMUND FREUD MUSEUM
Vienna IX, Berggasse 19, Harald Leupold-Löwenthal et al. (ed.), *Katalog* (Vienna: Christian Brandstätter, n.d.) (126).
SIMMEL, Ernst
1919: 'Psychoanalyse der Massen', in *Vossische Zeitung*, 24 August 1919 (100).
1927: 'Eröffnung einer psychoanalytischen Klinik in Berlin' (circular to doctors), in *IZ*, vol. 13 (1927), p. 245f. (text after 255).
SNYDER, Carl
1907: *Das Weltbild der modernen Naturwissenschaft nach den Ergebnissen der neusten Forschungen*, auth. trans. By Hans Kleinpeter, 2nd revised edition (Leipzig: Barth, 1907) (149).
1917: *Die Endlichkeit des Weltalls* und *Die Fortschritte auf dem Wege zur Erklärung der Elektrizität*, two essays (Leipzig: Barth, 1917) (149).
SPANJAARD, Jacob
'August Stärcke 1880–1954: the source of castration anxiety', in Franz Alexander et al. (eds), *Psychoanalytic Pioneers* (New York and London: Basic Books, 1966), pp. 321–32 (142).
SPECKER, E.
'Paul Bernays zum 70. Geburtstag', in *Neue Zürcher Zeitung*, 17 October 1958 (168).
SPEIER, Hermine
'Auf dem Weg zur Sixtina: die Vatikanischen Sammlungen', in *Merian: Das Monatsheft der Städte und Landschaften*, vol. 10 (1957), no. 4 'Rom' (Hamburg: Hoffmann und Campe, 1957), pp. 45–50 (Appendix 1, note 15).
SPEISER und SMEKAL
Paul Speiser, Ferdinand G. Smekal, *Karl Landsteiner: Entdecker der Blutgruppen und Pionier der Immunologie*, 3rd unrevised edition (Berlin: Blackwell Ueberreuter, 1990) (45).

SPITTELER, Carl
Imago, novel (Jena: Diederichs, 1906 [also Frankfurt: Suhrkamp, 1979] (27).
STÄRCKE, August
Psychoanalyse und Psychiatrie (supplement 4 of *IZ*) (Leipzig, Vienna, Zurich: Internationaler Psychoanalytischer Verlag, 1921) (142).
STAMMBAUM LANGE
Hanns-Walter Lange, *Genealogical Tree of the Freud Family* [consisting of 'Genealogical Tree' and 19-page 'Table' incl. 'Addenda 1989'], A Genealogical Study of the Bernays Family [consisting of 'Genealogical Tree I' and 35-age 'Table I', 'Genealogical Tree II' and pp. 36–74 'Table IIa', 'Genealogical Tree IIb', and pp. 75–99 'Table IIb'] (London, 1987) (1, 3, 4, 6, 11, 12, 16, 20, 36, 42, 49, 54, 98, 99, 104, 115, 119, 120, 127, 131, 150, 162, 167, 168, 175, 192, 208).
STANGL, Thomas
Personalbibliographien von Professoren und Dozenten der Inneren Medizin an der Medizinischen Fakultät Wien im ungefähren Zeitraum von 1890–1950, thesis, Medical Faculty of the University of Erlangen-Nuremberg, 1972 (126).
STEINLECHNER, Gerhard
'"... und ware glücklich gewesen, fliehen zu können ..." August Aichhorn im nationalsozialistischen Wien', in K. Fallend et al. (eds), *Der Einmarsch in die Psyche* (Vienna: Junius, 1989), pp. 79–90 (170).
STEPHAN, Rainer
'Die Altausseer Vergangenheit oder Wie die Provinz zur Welt und wie die Welt zur Provinz wurde', *Süddeutsche Zeitung*, no. 246, 23/24 October 1993, p. 17 (2, 122).
STERBA, Richard F.
Erinnerungen eines Wiener Psychoanalytiker (Frankfurt: Fischer Taschenbuch Verlag, 1985) (6).
STRACHEY, James
1955: 'Editor's Note to the English translation of Freud 1941*d*', in *S. E,*, vol. 18 (1955), pp. 175f. (142).
1966: 'General Preface', in *S.E.*, vol. 1 (1966), pp. xiii–xxii (156).
SWALES, Peter J.
'Freud, his teacher and the birth of psychoanalysis', in Paul E. Stepansky (ed.), *Freud: Appraisals and Reappraisals – Contributions to Freud Studies*, vol. 1 (Hillsdale, NJ: The Analytic Press, 1986), pp. 2–82 (74).
TACOU-RUMNEY, Laurence
Peggy Guggenheim: A Collector's Album (Paris and New York: Flammarion, 1996) (178).
TAFT, Jessie
Otto Rank: A Biographical Study (New York: Julian Press, 1958) (43, 287).
THONKE, Christian
'8. Schmidgasse 14: "Einverlaibt"', in *Kurier*, 18 February 2001, p. 3 (71).
TÖGEL, Christfeld
(See also Freud 1992*i*; FREUD-BERNAYS, A.; MOLNAR [1996]; *RUNDBRIEFE*; TÖGEL and POUH)
1989: *Berggasse – Pompeji und zurück – Sigmund Freuds Reisen in die Vergangenheit* (Tübigen: edition diskord, 1989) (1, 2, 5, 45, 67, 78, 101).
1990: 'Bahnstation Treblinka: Zum Schicksal von Sigmund Freuds Schwester Rosa Graf', in *Psyche*, vol. 44 (1990), pp. 1019–24 (11, 16).
1994: '... *und gedenke die Wisssenschaft auszubeuten: Sigmund Freuds Weg zur Psychoanalyse* (Tübigen: edition diskord, 1994) (1, 74).

2002: Comments and notes in Freud 2002*b* (2, 4, 8, 13, 34, 36, 201, Appendix 1, note 42).
2004*a*: Comments and notes in Freud-Bernays, A. (36, 150).
2004*b*: 'Freuds Berliner Schwester Maria (Mitzi) und ihre Familie', in *Luzifer Amor: Zeitschrift für Geschichte der Psychoanalyse*, vol. 17 (2004), no. 33, pp. 33–50 (11, 16, 134, 298).
TÖGEL and POUH
Christfeld Tögel, Liselotte Pouh, 'Sigmund Freud, Felix Salten und Karl Lueger', in *Luzifer Amor: Zeitschrift für Geschichte der Psychoanalyse*, vol. 8 (1995), no. 15, pp. 143–8 (223).
TWENTIETH CENTURY AUTHORS
Stanley J. Kunitz, Howard Haycraft (eds), *Twentieth Century Authors, A Biographical Dictionary of Modern Literature* (New York: H. W. Wilson Companay, 1942) (96).
UHLAND, Johann Ludwig
Hans Rüdiger Schwab (ed.), *Werke*, (2 vols), vol. 1 *Gedichte, Dramen, Versepik und Prosa* (Frankfurt: Insel, 1983) (129).
ULLRICH, Volker
Otto von Bismark (Reinbek bei Hamburg: Rowohlt, 2003) (257).
URBAN, Rudolf v.
Myself Not Least: A Confessional Autobiography of a Psychoanalyst and Some Explanatory History Cases (London and New York: Jarrolds, 1958) (76).
VARENDONCK, Julian
1908: 'Les ideals d'enfants', in *Archives de Psychologie*, vol. 7 (1908), pp. 365–82 (142).
1921*a*: *L'évolution des faculties conscientes*, diss., Faculté des lettres de Paris, 1920–1 (Paris: Alcan, and Gent: Vanderpoorten, 1921) (142).
1921*b*: *The Psychology of Day-Dreams* (London: Allen & Unwin, and New York: Macmillan, 1921) with an introduction by Sigmund Freud, authorized translation by Anna Freud entitled *Über das vorbewusste phantasierende Denken* (Leipzig, Vienna, Zurich: Internationaler Psychoanalytischer Verlag, 1922) (142, 161).
VENTURINI, E.
Rom und der Vatikan (Rome: Editrice Lozzi, n.d. [1991]) (Appendix 1, note 15).
VEREIN REGIONALENTWICKLUNG
Verein Regionalentwicklung Inneres Salzkammergut (REGIS), leaflet *Salzkammergut – Der historische Soleweg* (n.p. [Bad Ischl], 1997) (55).
WEINKE, Wilfried
Verdrängt, vertrieben aber nicht vergessen – die Fotografen Emil Bieber, Max Halberstadt, Erich Kastan, Kurt Schallenberg (Weingarten: Kunstverlag Weingarten, 2003) (19, 23, 127, 129, 162).
WEISSENSTEINER, Friedrich
Der ungeliebte Staat – Österreich zwischen 1918 und 1938 (Vienna: Österreichischer Bundesverlag, 1990) (12, 110, 122, 130, 132, 161, 179, 246).
WILDGANS, Anton
Lilly Wildgans (ed.) with the collaboration of Dr. Otto Rommel, *Sämtliche Werke* (8 vols), vol. 1 *Gedichte* (1949) (99).
WINNICOTT, Donald W.
'Ernest Jones' (obituary), in *IJ*, vol. 39 (1958), pp. 298–304 (41).
WINTER, J.[osephine]
Fünfzig Jahre eines Wiener Hauses (Vienna and Leipzig: Braumüller, 1927) (74, 116, 122).

WINTERSTEIN, Alfred
'Neuerscheinungen der psychoanalytischen Literatur', in *Neue Freie Presse*, Vienna, no. 22475, 10 April 1927, morning edition, p. 31ff. (216).
WITTELS, Franz
1924: *Sigmund Freud – Der Mann, die Lehre, die Schule* (Leipzig, Vienna, Zurich: E. P. Tal & Co., 1924) (228).
1927: *Die Befreiung des Kindes* (Stuttgart: Hippokrates, und Bern: Hans Huber, 1927) (228).
WITTENBERGER, Gerhard
(See also HEINEN-WOLF; *RUNDBRIEFE*)
1992: 'Die Rundbriefe des "Geheimen Komitees"', in Ernst Federn, Gerhard Wittenberger (eds), *Aus dem Kreis um Sigmund Freud: Zu den Protokollen der Wiener Psychoanalytischen Vereinigung* (Frankfurt: Fischer Taschenbuch Verlag, 1992), pp. 46–68 (126, 174).
1995: *Das 'Geheime Komitee' Sigmund Freuds – Institutionalisierungsprozesse in der 'Psychoanalytischen Bewegung' zwischen 1912 und 1927* (Tübingen: edition diskord, 1992) (126, 174).
WOLF, Siegmund A.
Jiddisches Wörterbuch (Mannheim: Bibliographisches Institut, Allgemeiner Verlag, n.d. [1962]) (169).
WOLFGANGSEE
Wolfgangsee Tourismus Gesellschaft mbH, Event- und WerbegesmbH Bad Ischl (eds), *Wolfgangsee – Quelle der Lebensfreude / Bad Ischl*, information brochure (March 2002) (53).
WORBS, Michael
Nervenkunst – Literatur und Psychoanalyse im Wien der Jahrhundertwende (Frankfurt: Europäische Verlagsanstalt, 1983) (20).
WUTTE, Martin
Kärntens Freiheitskampf 1918–1920, first published 1922, revised 2nd edition of 1943 (Klagenfurt: Verlag des Geschichtsvereines für Kärnten, 1985) (132).
YOUNG-BRUEHL, Elisabeth
Anna Freud: A Biography (New Haven and London: Yale University Press, 2nd edition 2008, originally published 1998) (Introduction, 5–7, 13, 14, 16, 17, 19, 20, 22, 23, 26, 28, 31, 34, 40–2, 45, 47–9, 53, 58, 60, 62, 71, 79, 82, 86, 96, 98, 99, 101, 103, 107, 108, 114, 119, 120, 129, 130, 142, 146, 151, 168, 174, 192, 196, 198, 208, 212, 259, 263, 269, 287, 197).
ZERFASS and HUPPKE
Urban Zerfass, Andrea Huppke, *Internationaler Psychoanalytischer Verlag 1919–1938* (Berlin: Antiquariat Zerfass & Linke, n.d. [1995]) (89, 138).
ZIERL, Hubert
'Der Weg zum Nationalpark', in *Nationalpark Berchtesgaden* (n.d. [1981]), pp. 7–17 (257).
ZIMBURG, Heinrich v.
'350 jahre Wirte Straubinger in Bad Gastein', in *Bad Gasteiner Badeblatt*, no. 32, 23 August 1953, pp. 359–62 (75).
ZÖRKENDÖRFER, Walter
'Karlsbad, Marienbad und Franzensbad als Heilbäder', in Karell et al., *Das Egerland und seine Weltbäder: Franzensbad, Karlsbad, Marienbad* (Frankfurt: Das Viergespann, 1966), pp. 148–64.

ZOHLEN, Gerwin
'Das Haus am See', in *Die Zeit*, no. 14, 1 April 1994, 80 ('Modernes Leben') (115, 164).
ZOTTL, Anton
Otto Rank – Das Lebenswerk eines Dissidenten der Psychoanalyse (Munich: Kindler, 1982) (43, 287).
ZOUZELKA, Christine
Alfred Francis Pribram (1839–1942) – Leben und Werk als Historiker, thesis, University of Vienna, 1968 (75, 126).
ZSCHIETZSCHMANN, Willy
'Von der Wölfin zum Pantheon', in *Merian: Das Monatsheft der Städte und Landschaften*, November 1991, vol. 11: 'Rom' (Hamburg: Hoffmann und Campe, 1957), pp. 13–19 (Appendix 1, note 50).

Unpublished Material

This list contains unpublished letters and documents cited in the footnotes, with their location where applicable. The numbers in brackets after each entry indicate the letters or annexes in which the documents are mentioned.

ANNA to EITINGON
Anna Freud's letters to Max Eitingon: LoC AF, Cont. 24 (Introduction, 19, 96, 125, 127, 168, 174, 183, 208, 209, 253, 254, 257, 289, 291, 298).
ANNA to ERNST
Anna Freud's letters to (brother) Ernst Freud: FM London (71, 86, 103, 127, 129, 141, 163, 287).
ANNA to FREUD
Postcripts to 'Martha to Freud', 12 September 1913, 13 July 1922: LoC SF, Cont. 10 (14, 176).
ANNA to KATA
Anna Freud's letters to Kata Lévy: originals given to me by Peter Lambda for quotations; now owned by Archiv zur Geschichte der Psychoanalyse e.V., Berlin (26, 47, 81, 82, 84, 86, 95, 100, 101, 103, 108, 124, 125, 287).
FERENCZI to V. FREUND
Ferenczi's letters to Anton v. Freund: translated from Hungarian by Peter Lambda, made available to me, now owned by Archiv zur Geschichte der Psychoanalyse e.V., Berlin (80).
FICHTNER, Gerhard
'"Lieblingsspeise Bücher", Freuds Bibliothek und ihre Bedeutung für sein Leben und Werk', manuscript of a talk, 2003, publication in preparation (Introduction, 60).
FREUD to ALEXANDER
Sigmund Freud's letters to Alexander Freud: LoC SF, Cont. 1 (Introduction, 60, 117, 271, 297).
FREUD to FAMILY
Sigmund Freud's letters to family members: FM London, Box 12, and LoC SF, Cont. 10 (parts of letters not contained in Freud 2003*e*) (16, text after 18, 19, 71, 127, 285).
FREUD to ERNST
Sigmund Freud's letters to (son) Ernst Freud: LoC SF, Cont. 3 (71, 106, 133, 153, 257, 271).

FREUD to JEANNE
Freud's letters to Jeanne Lampl-De Groot: LoC SF, Cont. 36 (296, 297).
FREUD to KATA
Freud's letters to Kata Lévy: LoC SF, Cont. 36, transcribed by Peter Lambda and made available to me (81, 82, 107, 109, 159, 163).
FREUD to MARTHA
Freud's letters to Martha Freud: LoC SF, Cont. 10 (14, 15).
FREUD to MARTIN
Freud's letters to Martin Freud: LoC SF, Cont. 10 and 11 (67, 82, 106, 107, 256, 257, 270, 277).
FREUD to MAX
Freud's letters to Max Halberstadt: LoC SF, Cont. 11 and 12 (105, 133, 137, 138, 146, 147, 150, 153, 158, 172, 174, 179, 188, 196).
FREUD to RUTH
Freud's letters to Ruth Mack-Brunswick: LoC SF, Cont. 20 (212, 256, 257, 261, text after 295, 296, 297).
FREUD to SOPHIE
Freud's letters to Sophie Freud: LoC SF, Cont. 11 and 12 (14, 25, 32).
FREUD to SOPHIE and MAX
Freud's letters to Sophie Freud/Max Halberstadt: LoC SF, Cont. 11 and 12 (41, 47, 59).
FREUD to WILLI
Freud's letters to Willi Lévy: LoC SF, Cont. 36 (80).
FREUD and MINNA to ERNST
Letters from Freud and Minna Bernays to Ernst Freud: LoC SF, Cont. 3 (92, 94, 95).
KALENDER
Freud's entries in *Prochaskas Familienkalender*, with narrations, anecdotes, jokes and lessons; with numerous artistically executed illustrations and a four-page information calendar (Vienna – Teschen: Verlagsbuchhandlung Karl Prochaska, k. u. k. Hofbuchdruckerei, vols 29, 30, 31 (1916, 1917, 1918): LoC SF, Cont. 48 (71, 72, 74, 75, 77–80, 87).
KATA to FREUD
Handwritten draft letter from Kata Lévy to Freud, photocopy in 'Freud to Kata' collection (96).
KURSIDEM, Franz
'Kaiserlicher Rat Professor Alexander Freud (1866–1943)', Ms: LoC SF, Cont. 1 (12, 117, 297).
LAMBDA, Peter
'Erinnerungen an Freud', Ms: made available to me by Peter Lambda, now owned by Archiv zur Geschichte der Psychoanalyse e.V., Berlin (80).
MARTHA to FREUD
Martha Freud's letters to Sigmund Freud: LoC SF, Cont. 10 and 11 (33, 34, 36, 174, 176, 177, 185, 187).
RUNDBRIEFE
The as yet unpublished *Rundbriefe* from 1928 and 1929 are indicated (253, 256). Those from 1923 and 1925 are quoted from the microfilms of the Otto Rank Collection (ORC) at the Library of Columbia University, New York (Introduction, 126, 156, 199, text after 201).
WINTERSTEIN, Alfred
'Meine Erinnerungen an Sigmund Freud': LoC SF, Cont. 113 (11).

List of Illustrations and Facsimiles with Cross-references

Ill. 16	Marie Bonaparte with chow-chow Topsy	214 SF and note 4
Ill. 17	Anna, *c.* 1931	Introduction, p. 10
Ill. 18	Anna, Sigmund, Martha and Ernst, at Marie Bonaparte's, Paris 1938	Text after 295 SF

Sigmund Freud Copyrights, London holds the rights to ills. 1, 5, 7, 10, 11, 12, 14, 16, 17 and 18; the Freud Museum London holds the rights to ills. 2, 3, 4, 6, 9 and 13. Mosche Wolff, Israel, granted us the right to print ill. 8; Dorothee Pfeiffer, Göttingen, the right to print ill. 15. I should like to thank all donors for their cooperation, particularly also Michael Molnar (London), Tom Roberts (Wivenhoe), Wilfried Weinke (Hamburg) and Kunstverlag Weingarten for their assistance in obtaining licences and print copy.

Facsimiles		*Source*
p. 31	Anna's letter of 13 July 1910	LoC SF, Cont. 2
p. 76 + 77	Name and dedication in Rilke's *Buch der Bilder*	FM London
p. 199	Hague Congress 1920 (exchange of notes)	LoC SF, Cont. 2
p. 315	Freud's letter of 21 July 1923	LoC SF, Cont. 2
p. 320 + 321	'Travel Diary', Rome	LoC AF, Cont. 162
p. 340	Drawing in Anna's letter of 12 April 1927	LoC SF, Cont. 2
p. 344	Drawing in Anna's letter of 15 April 1927	LoC SF, Cont. 2
p. 349	Anna's letter of 18 April 1927	LoC SF, Cont. 2
p. 425	Voucher for Dorothy Burlingham	LoC SF, Cont. 2

Index